# EXPRESSWAYS
## FOR WRITING SCENARIOS
### FROM PARAGRAPH TO ESSAY

## KATHLEEN T. McWHORTER
### Niagara County Community College

PEARSON
Longman

New York   San Francisco   Boston
London   Toronto   Sydney   Tokyo   Singapore   Madrid
Mexico City   Munich   Paris   Cape Town   Hong Kong   Montreal

Acquisitions Editor: Melanie Craig
Development Editor: Gillian Cook
Senior Supplements Editor: Donna Campion
Media Supplements Editor: Jenna Egan
Marketing Manager: Thomas DeMarco
Production Manager: Bob Ginsberg
Project Coordination, Text Design, and Electronic Page Makeup:
    Thompson Steele, Inc.
Senior Cover Design Manager and Cover Designer: Nancy Danahy
Cover Image: Getty Images, Inc./Comstock
Photo Researcher: Julie Tesser
Manufacturing Buyer: Lucy Hebard
Printer and Binder: Webcrafters, Inc.
Cover Printer: The Lehigh Press

Visit us at www.ablongman.com

ISBN 0-321-35537-7 (student text)
ISBN 0-321-36565-8 (annotated instructor's edition)

12345678910—WC—09 08 07 06

# Brief Contents

# Detailed Contents

## Part II ▪ Paragraph Writing Strategies    55

## Part IV ■ Strategies for Writing Essays    359

### CHAPTER 15    Sharpening Your Essay-Writing Skills    360

### CHAPTER 16    Summarizing and Synthesizing Sources    396

# Rhetorical Contents

## Narration

## Description

## Process

## Example

## Classification

## Definition

## Comparison and Contrast

## Cause and Effect

## Argument

## Expository

# Thematic Contents

Note: Asterisks (*) designate paired readings.

## Communication and Interpersonal Relationships

## Current Issues

## Diversity and World Culture

## Education

## Environment and Nature

## Family Issues and Relationships

## Gender

## Music and the Arts

## Politics/Government

## Sports and Hobbies

## Technology and Science

## Workplace and Business

# Preface

To succeed in college and in the workplace, today's students must be able to express their ideas clearly and correctly in written form, read a wide variety of texts, and interpret, react to, and critically think about what they have read. Over 30 years of experience with developmental students has convinced me that these essential skills—writing, reading, and critical thinking—are most effectively taught when integrated. Many students flourish when given the opportunity to learn and practice these skills within a stimulating, nonthreatening framework. My goal in writing *Expressways* is to help students build a solid foundation of writing, reading, and critical thinking skills—a repertoire that will prepare them for freshman composition, as well as for everyday, academic, and workplace writing.

## Overview of the Text

*Expressways* features an integrated writing-reading approach, step-by-step instruction, and a supportive tone. It teaches students the fundamentals of paragraph and essay writing through structured, sequential instruction; varied exercises that build upon each other; numerous examples of student writing; and the use of high-interest, issue-oriented or workplace-related readings.

The text also emphasizes both paragraph- and essay-writing skills. Each chapter offers both paragraph- and essay-level writing assignment options, allowing instructors to move from paragraph to essay writing whenever their students are ready. The important skills of annotating, paraphrasing, summarizing, and synthesizing are covered in Chapter 16. The text also contains a brief, introductory look at locating, synthesizing, and using appropriate sources. Sentence-level concerns are presented as integral to the clear expression of ideas; a handbook with exercises appears at the end of the text; and near the end of each chapter in Parts II–IV, a "Skill Refresher" related to sentence structure, grammar, or punctuation ties in with the handbook instruction.

The text emphasizes academic writing; most chapters contain student essays that are annotated to guide students in examining the aspects of writing taught in the chapter. For each essay the writer and the writing task are described and questions follow the reading to help students react to and evaluate it.

Writing in the workplace is also emphasized. Many students are working and are attending college to get a better job or prepare for a new career. The text demonstrates the importance of strong writing skills in the workplace and introduces students to different forms of workplace writing. The workplace scenarios motivate students to improve their writing skills, not only to do well in college but also to succeed in their careers.

## Features

The following features further distinguish *Expressways* from other developmental writing texts and make its approach unique:

■ *Visual Approach to Writing* Many students are visual learners; that is, they process information visually rather than verbally or through auditory means. Because many students are visual learners, they respond well to diagrams, charts, and maps. In each chapter, students learn to draw idea maps—visual representations of the content and organization of a paragraph or essay—in order to examine ideas. Students learn to draw revision maps of their own writing as a means of evaluating the effectiveness of the content and organization and to help them make necessary changes. Sections that feature idea or revision maps are labeled "Visualize It!"

■ *Emphasis on Reading Skills* Chapter 2 focuses on strategies for active reading including previewing, accessing prior knowledge, reading to learn, using idea maps to understand a reading, approaching difficult readings, and expanding vocabulary. It also instructs students in how to improve their writing by reading professional essays, and how to learn from sample student essays. Reading skills are emphasized throughout the text using professional readings in each chapter that include literal and critical comprehension questions and vocabulary review.

■ *Emphasis on Grammar and Correctness* Each chapter contains a Skill Refresher which reviews a common grammar problem. Part VI, "Reviewing the Basics," is a handbook written with the needs of ESL students in mind. It provides a simple, clear presentation of the forms and rules of English usage and is plentifully illustrated with examples, and includes ample exercises for skills. It is designed to help both ESL and developmental writers grasp the fundamentals of grammar, punctuation, and mechanics.

■ *Interconnected Writing in Progress Exercises* These exercises build on each other throughout the course of each chapter, and walk students through the different steps of the writing process from prewriting through drafting, writing using different modes, and revising.

■ *Emphasis on Student Success* The book begins with a lively introduction, "Writing Success Starts Here!" that focuses on the skills students need to be successful in their writing classes and in college. The first section, "Tabs: Take Charge of Your Learning," identifies five behaviors that lead to success and offers concrete strategies for implementing them using sticky tabs (see below). In the second section, "Use the Help Features in This Book," students are shown how they can benefit from various features found throughout the book, including how to examine sample student essays and how to learn from reading professional essays. The third section, "Writing Success Tips," offers practical suggestions on how to organize a time and place to write, build concentration, use computers to improve writing skills, keep a writing journal, and learn from peer review.

■ *Reusable Sticky Tabs* The tabs in the introduction are linked to key success strategies and demonstrate how students can implement each strategy. Tabs are included for keeping track of assignments ("Assignment Due" tab), marking important material to review ("Important: Review

This" tab), checking with classmates and instructors ("Follow Up With" tab), connecting and applying skills ("Useful For" tab), and strengthening vocabulary ("Vocabulary" tab). These tabs encourage students to take responsibility for their own learning and become active learners.

■ ***Emphasis on Student Writing: Academic Scenarios*** Each chapter in Parts II through IV contains an Academic Scenario that includes an annotated student essay with writing assignments to encourage students to think and write about what they have read. These student essays provide realistic models of the writing process and set realistic, attainable expectations for students.

■ ***Emphasis on Workplace Writing: Workplace Scenarios*** Titled "Workplace Scenarios," an example of writing in the workplace appears in each chapter, in Parts II through IV. These samples are intended to demonstrate the importance of chapter content in workplace writing as well as to provide models of effective writing.

■ ***High-Interest, Engaging Readings*** Beginning with Chapter 2, each chapter includes an engaging professional reading around which prewriting, critical thinking, and writing assignments are structured. Readings touch on topics within the students' realm of interest and experience, such as family relationships, sports, technology, gender differences in communication, and body language. Each reading offers students a model for the writing skills taught in the particular chapter, as well as a source of ideas and a base for discussion and collaborative learning activities.

## Organization of the Text

The text opens with an introduction, "Writing Success Starts Here!" that orients students to the textbook's features, shows students how to take charge of their own learning using sticky tabs, and offers them valuable writing success tips.

The text is organized into six parts. Part I, "Getting Started," opens with a chapter that establishes the importance of effective writing and provides an overview of the writing process, with an emphasis on prewriting techniques. This chapter also shows how a sample student paper develops through several stages from a first draft to the final version. Chapter 2, "The Active Reading Process," discusses previewing, reading to learn, idea maps, critical reading, and vocabulary.

Part II, "Paragraph Writing Strategies," covers paragraph structure and topic sentences (Chapter 3), developing a paragraph with details (Chapter 4), and the revision process (Chapter 5). Chapter 5 also introduces the "Revision Checklist" feature, which is further developed in each of the remaining chapters of the book.

In Part III, "Methods of Development," each chapter describes one of the rhetorical modes, gives examples, and provides practical advice for organizing, developing, and writing paragraphs and/or essays using that mode. The chapters cover narration, description, process, example, classification, definition, comparison and contrast, cause and effect, and argument. As in the previous sections, writing assignments build sequentially.

Students generate ideas about a topic, prepare a first draft, and revise using the "Revision Checklist" and the "Proofreading Checklist."

Part IV, "Strategies for Writing Essays," concentrates on the short essay. Chapter 15, "Sharpening Your Essay-Writing Skills," emphasizes writing effective thesis statements, supporting them with evidence, and crafting strong introductions and conclusions. Chapter 16, "Summarizing and Synthesizing Sources," presents these basic academic skills, as well as annotating and paraphrasing, in an introductory way; it also provides simple guidelines for finding and using appropriate sources. A pair of carefully selected readings appears at the end of this chapter to facilitate the teaching of these essay-related skills. Chapter 17 covers essay exams and competency tests.

Part V, "A Multicultural Reader," contains nine selections on a range of stimulating topics that represent a diverse group of authors. These readings offer instructors flexibility in choosing and assigning readings and further represent the rhetorical modes. Selections are accompanied by the same apparatus as in-chapter professional readings, thereby allowing instructors to substitute those from the Multicultural Reader for in-chapter readings where appropriate.

Part VI, "Reviewing the Basics," is a brief handbook with exercises. It reviews the principles of grammar, sentence structure, mechanics, and spelling and concludes with a set of error correction exercises.

## Chapter Format

- *Write About It!* Each chapters opens with a photograph or other image that is intended to capture the student's attention, generate interest, and connect the topic of the chapter to the student's experience. This feature engages the student and gets the student writing immediately about chapter related content.

- *Everyday, Academic, and Workplace Scenarios* Examples of everyday, academic, and workplace writing demonstrate the importance and relevance of a chapter's content to students' lives within and beyond the college environment.

- *Direct Skill Instruction* The content of each chapter is presented in simple, direct style, in short sections interspersed with opportunities to practice each skill.

- *Visualize It!* Each chapter in Part III contains an idea map that shows how paragraphs and essays in a particular mode are organized. The professional reading also contains a partially completed idea map for students to finish.

- *Academic Writing Scenarios* Each chapter in Parts II through IV features an example of academic writing used as a model of a particular writing strategy. The academic writer and the writing task are introduced and each student essay is annotated. Evaluation questions and academic writing assignments follow each essay.

- *Workplace Writing Scenarios* Each chapter features an example of workplace writing. The student writer and the writing task are introduced and evaluation questions and workplace writing assignments follow each selection of workplace writing.

- *Revision Checklist* A "Revision Checklist" appears at the end of each chapter, starting with Chapter 5. This feature provides a review of writing strategies learned in the chapter as well as a cumulative review of strategies learned in previous chapters.

- *Writing About a Reading* Each chapter contains a professional reading to serve as a stimulus for writing.

- *Thinking About the Reading* precedes each reading. It directs the student to preview the reading and contains several questions designed to activate the student's own knowledge and experience about the subject of the reading.

- *Marginal annotations* for each selection provide definitions of difficult or unusual terminology that is likely to be outside of the student's realm of knowledge or experience.

- *Getting Ready to Write* consists of five activities that prepare the student to write about the reading:

  - *Reviewing the Reading* checks the student's literal comprehension of the reading.

  - *Examining the Reading* encourages the student to analyze the content and organization of the reading by drawing or completing idea maps.

  - *Thinking Critically* encourages the student to analyze and evaluate the reading. A specific critical thinking skill is addressed in each chapter, including making inferences, understanding connotative language, and analyzing tone.

  - *Strengthening Your Vocabulary* reviews important words in the reading and reinforces the use of word mapping.

  - *Reacting to Ideas: Discussion and Journal Writing* offers the student a range of thought-provoking questions on which class discussions or collaborative learning activities may be built.

- *Writing About the Reading* provides assignments that involve the student with ideas expressed in the reading and encourages the student to write about personal experiences related to the topic of the reading. Both paragraph-level and essay-level writing assignments are provided.

- *Chapter Review and Practice* This section contains three activities designed to provide students with additional practice and help them evaluate their mastery of chapter content.

- *Chapter Review* Using a question-and-answer format, this activity allows students to test their recall of important chapter content.

- *Skill Refresher* Every chapter in Parts II through IV offers a review of a topic related to sentence structure, grammar, or punctuation. The "Skill Refresher" begins with a brief section of instruction, followed by a ten-item, self-assessment quiz. Students are directed to record their score on the "Skill Refresher Score Chart" at the back of the book. Students who miss more than two questions on the self-assessment quiz are directed to specific questions in Part VI, "Reviewing the Basics," that present a more detailed explanation of the topic.

- *Internet Activities* Students are directed to Internet sites and the book's Companion Website for additional practice and reinforcement of skills taught in the chapter.

## Ancillary Materials

- **The Instructor's Manual/Test Bank (ISBN 0-321-41194-3)** This supplement is full of useful teaching suggestions and includes an introduction to the textbook, activities to engage students' interest, advice to new instructors, and additional writing assignments. The manual also offers suggestions for handling the professional readings, sample syllabi, overhead transparencies, and a full bank of test questions.

- **The Book's Website** The Companion Website that accompanies *Expressways* offers comprehension quizzes for all professional readings in the text, additional activities, and downloadable Idea Map templates. It also provides additional practice for each Skill Refresher in the text and Skills Check exercises designed especially for ESL students.

- **The Longman Developmental English Package** Longman is pleased to offer a variety of support materials to help make teaching developmental English easier on teachers and to help students excel in their coursework. Many of our student supplements are available at no additonal cost or at a greatly reduced price when packaged with *Expressways*. Contact your local Longman sales representative for more information on pricing and how to create a package.

### Additional Support Materials for Writing Instructors:

- **Printed Test Bank for Developmental Writing (Instructor / ISBN 0-321-08486-1)**
  Features more than 5,000 questions in all areas of writing, from grammar to paragraphing through essay writing, research, and documentation.

- **Electronic Test Bank for Developmental Writing (Instructor / CD ISBN 0-321-08117-X)**
  Features more than 5,000 questions in all areas of writing, from grammar to paragraphing through essay writing, research, and documentation. Instructors simply choose questions from the electronic test bank, then print out the completed test for distribution or offer the test online.

- **Diagnostic and Editing Tests, Ninth Edition (Instructor / Print ISBN 0-321-41524-8 / CD ISBN 0-321-43323-8)**
  This collection of diagnostic tests helps instructors assess students' competence in standard written English to determine placement or to gauge progress.

- **The Longman Guide to Classroom Management (Instructor / ISBN 0-321-09246-5)**
  This guide is designed as a helpful resource for instructors who have classroom management problems. It includes helpful strategies for dealing with disruptive students in the classroom and the "do's and don'ts" of discipline.

- **The Longman Guide to Community Service-Learning in the English Classroom and Beyond (Instructor / ISBN 0-321-12749-8)**
  Written by Elizabeth Rodriguez Kessler of California State University–Northridge, this monograph provides a definition and history of service-learning, as well as an overview of how service-learning can be integrated effectively into the college classroom.

- **The Longman Instructor's Planner (Instructor / ISBN 0-321-09247-3)**
  This planner includes weekly and monthly calendars, student attendance and grading rosters, space for contact information, Web references, an almanac, and blank pages for notes.

## For Writing Students

- **The Longman Writer's Portfolio and Student Planner (ISBN 0-321-29609-5)**
  This unique supplement provides students with a space to plan, think about, and present their work. In addition to the yearly planner, it includes an assessing/organizing area (including grammar diagnostic test, spelling quiz, and project-planning worksheets), a before- and during-writing area (including peer review sheets, editing checklists, writing self-evaluations, and personal editing profile), and an after-writing area (including progress chart, final table of contents, and final assessment), as well as a student daily planner including daily, weekly, and monthly calendars.

- **Longman English Tutor Center Access Card (VP ISBN 0-201-71049-8 or Stand-Alone ISBN 0-201-72170-8)**
  Unique service offering students access to an in-house writing tutor via phone and/or e-mail. Tutor available 5 p.m.–12 a.m., Sunday– Thursday.

- **The Longman Writer's Journal, by Mimi Markus (Student / ISBN 0-321-08639-2)**
  Provides students with their own personal space for writing and contains helpful journal writing strategies, sample journal entries by other students, and many writing prompts and topics to get students writing.

- **ESL Worksheets, Third Edition (Student / ISBN 0-321-07765-2)**
  These worksheets provide ESL students with extra practice in areas they find the most troublesome. Diagnostic tests, suggested writing topics, and an answer key are included.

- **Peer Evaluation Manual, Seventh Edition (Student / ISBN 0-321-01948-2)**
  Offers students forms for peer critiques, general guidelines, and specific forms for different stages in the writing process and for various types of papers.

- **Learning Together (Student / ISBN 0-673-46848-8)**
  This brief guide to the fundamentals of collaborative learning teaches students how to work effectively in groups.

- **Longman Editing Exercises (Student / ISBN 0-205-31792-8)**
  Fifty-four pages of paragraph editing exercises give students extra practice using grammar skills in the context of longer passages.

- **100 Things to Write About (Student / ISBN 0-673-98239-4)**
  This brief book contains over 100 individual writing assignments, on a variety of topics and in a wide range of formats, from expressive to analytical writing.

- **Penguin Discount Novel Program**
  In cooperation with Penguin Putnam, Inc., Longman is proud to offer a variety of Penguin paperbacks at a significant discount when packaged with any Longman title. Excellent additions to any English course, Penguin titles give students the opportunity to explore contemporary and classical fiction and drama. The available titles include works by authors as diverse as Toni Morrison, Julia Alvarez, Mary Shelley, and Shakespeare. To review the complete list of titles available, visit the Longman-Penguin-Putnam Web site: http://www.awl.com/penguin.

- ***The New American Webster Handy College Dictionary* (Student / ISBN 0-451-18166-2)**
  A paperback reference text with more than 100,000 entries.

- ***Oxford American College Dictionary* (Student / ISBN 0-399-14415-3)**
  Drawing on Oxford's unparalleled language resources, including a 200-million-word database, this college dictionary contains more than 175,000 entries and more than 1000 illustrations, including line drawings, photographs, and maps. *Available at a significant discount when packaged with a Longman textbook.*

- ***The Oxford Essential Thesaurus* (ISBN 0-425-16421-7)**
  From Oxford University Press, renowned for quality educational and reference works, comes this concise, easy-to-use thesaurus—the essential tool for finding just the right word for every occasion. The 528-page book includes 175,000 synonyms in a simple A-to-Z format, more than 10,000 entries, extensive word choices, example sentences and phrases, and guidance on usage, punctuation, and more in exclusive "Writers Toolkit."

## MyWritingLab (www.mywritinglab.com)

This complete, online learning system is the first that will truly help students become successful writers—and therefore, successful in college and beyond.

- **Recall, Apply, and Write Exercises:** The heart of MyWritingLab is this progression of exercises within each module of the learning path. In completing the *Recall*, *Apply,* and *Write* exercises, students move from literal (*Recall*) to critical comprehension (*Apply*) to demonstrating concepts in their own writing (*Write*). This progressive learning process, not available in any other online resource, enables students to truly master the skills and concepts they need to be successful writers.

- **A Comprehensive Writing Program:** MyWritingLab includes over 9,000 exercises in grammar, writing process, paragraph development, essay development, and research.

- **A Customized Learning Path:** Based on the text in use, students are automatically provided with a customized learning path that complements their textbook's table of contents and extends textbook learning.

- **Diagnostic Testing**: MyWritingLab includes a comprehensive diagnostic test that thoroughly assesses students' skills in grammar. Based on the diagnostic test results, the students' learning path will reflect the areas in which they need help the most and those areas that they have mastered.

- **Progress Tracker**: All student work in MyWritingLab is captured in the site's Progress Tracker. Students can track their own progress and instructors can track the progress of their entire class in this flexible and easy-to-use tool.

- Other resources for students in MyWritingLab: access to an interactive **Study Skills Web site**, access to **Research Navigator,** and a complimentary subscription to our **English Tutor Center**, which is staffed by college instructors.

For more information and to view a demo, go to www.mywritinglab.com!

## State Specific Supplements

### *For Florida Adopters*

- **Thinking Through the Test: A Study Guide for the Florida College Basic Skills Exit Test, by D. J. Henry (ISBN 0-321-27660-4)**
  FOR FLORIDA ADOPTIONS ONLY. This workbook helps students strengthen their reading skills in preparation for the Florida College Basic Skills Exit Test. It features both diagnostic tests to help assess areas that may need improvement and exit tests to help test skill mastery. Detailed explanatory answers have been provided for almost all of the questions. *Package item only—not available for sale.*
  Available Versions:
  - Thinking Through the Test—A Study Guide for the Florida College Basic Skills Exit Tests: Reading and Writing, Second Edition, ISBN 0-321-27660-4
  - Thinking Through the Test—A Study Guide for the Florida College Basic Skills Exit Tests: Reading and Writing, with Answers, Second Edition, ISBN 0-321-27756-2
  - Thinking Through the Test—A Study Guide for the Florida College Basic Skills Exit Tests: Writing, with Answers, ISBN 0-321-27755-4

- Thinking Through the Test—A Study Guide for the Florida College Basic Skills Exit Tests: Writing, ISBN 0-321-27745-7

- **Writing Skills Summary for the Florida State Exit Exam, by D. J. Henry (Student / ISBN 0-321-08477-2)**
  FOR FLORIDA ADOPTIONS ONLY. An excellent study tool for students preparing to take Florida College Basic Skills Exit Test for Writing, this laminated writing grid summarizes all the skills tested on the Exit Exam.
  *Package item only—not available for sale.*

- **CLAST Test Package, Fourth Edition (Instructor / Print ISBN 0-321-01950-4)**
  These two, 40-item objective tests evaluate students' readiness for the Florida CLAST exams. Strategies for teaching CLAST preparedness are included.

### *For Texas Adopters*

- **The Longman THEA Study Guide, by Jeannette Harris (Student/ ISBN 0-321-27240-0)**
  Created specifically for students in Texas, this study guide includes straightforward explanations and numerous practice exercises to help students prepare for the reading and writing sections of THEA Test.
  *Package item only—not available for sale.*

- **TASP Test Package, Third Edition (Instructor / Print ISBN 0-321-01959-8)**
  These 12 practice pre-tests and post-tests assess the same reading and writing skills covered in the Texas TASP examination.

### *For New York/CUNY Adopters*

- **Preparing for the CUNY-ACT Reading and Writing Test, edited by Patricia Licklider (Student / ISBN 0-321-19608-2)**
  This booklet, prepared by reading and writing faculty from across the CUNY system, is designed to help students prepare for the CUNY-ACT exit test. It includes test-taking tips, reading passages, typical exam questions, and sample writing prompts to help students become familiar with each portion of the test.

## Acknowledgments

I appreciate the excellent ideas, suggestions, and advice of my colleagues who served as reviewers:

Charley Boyd, Genesee College; Cindy Catherwood, Metro Community College; Sarah Chitwood, Virginia Western Community College; David Clay, Cañada College; Kim Keeline, Southwestern College; Leanne Maunu, Palomar College; Iddah Otieno, Lexington Community College; Cathy Peppers, Idaho State University; Hollis Pruitt, Thomas Nelson Community College; Elaine Rush, College of the Sequoias; Curtis Vick,

Rockingham Community College; Carmen Wong, John Tyler Community College.

The entire editorial staff with whom I have worked deserves praise and credit for their assistance throughout the writing and revision of this text. In particular, I wish to thank Susan Kunchandy and Melanie Craig, Senior Sponsoring Editors, for their enthusiastic support throughout the project and Gillian Cook, Development Editor, whose knowledge of the field, creative energy, and organizational abilities kept me on target throughout the revision. I appreciate the efforts of Sally Steele and Bill Latimer of Thompson Steele, Inc. Their skill and expertise in designing and producing this book have proved invaluable. I also appreciate the willingness of the student and workplace writers who provided quotations and donated samples of their writing for the Writing Success Tips and Academic and Workplace Scenarios: Ebtisam Abusamak, Robert Badillo, Gentry Carlson, Veronica Evans-Johnson, Nakashia Flowers-Miller, Rachel Goodman, Dan Kerstettler, Melinda Lawson, Michaela Lozkova, Anna Majerczyk, Doug Mello, Stephanie Moore, Corinne Roberts, Ted Sawchuck, Loi To, Frank Trapasso, Dawn Trippie, and Ryan Vidaurri. I wish to thank Nela Navarro, ESL specialist, for her review of the manuscript and helpful suggestions.

Finally, I thank my students, who continue to make teaching a challenging and rewarding profession.

KATHLEEN T. MCWHORTER

# Tab Your Way to Success

Use these tabs to mark important sections and pages
of the book that you need to pay special attention to.

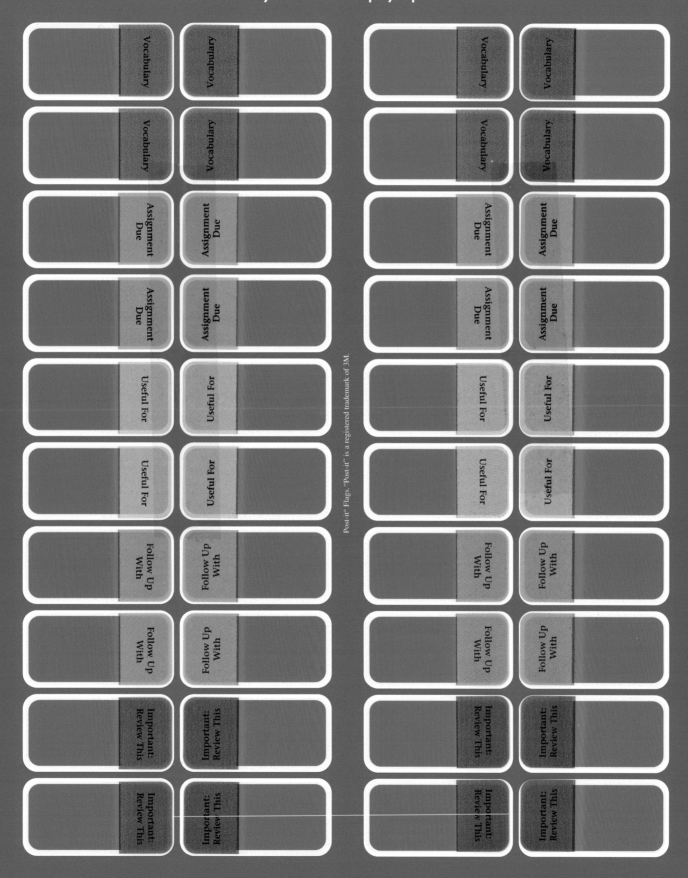

Vocabulary

Vocabulary

Vocabulary

Vocabulary

Vocabulary

Vocabulary

Vocabulary

Vocabulary

Assignment Due

Assignment Due

Assignment Due

Assignment Due

Assignment Due

Assignment Due

Assignment Due

Assignment Due

Useful For

Useful For

Useful For

Useful For

Useful For

Useful For

Useful For

Useful For

Follow Up With

Follow Up With

Follow Up With

Follow Up With

Follow Up With

Follow Up With

Follow Up With

Follow Up With

Important: Review This

Important: Review This

Important: Review This

Important: Review This

Important: Review This

Important: Review This

Important: Review This

Important: Review This

# TAKE CHARGE OF YOUR LEARNING

These tabs offer you five ways to be successful in your writing course by taking charge of your own learning. Be sure to read "Writing Success Starts Here!" for additional information.

### Important: Review This

Use this tab to identify the most important and useful materials for you in each chapter and refer to them often throughout the course. These may include strategies, rules, samples, examples, steps, tables, checklists, and idea maps.

### Follow Up With

Your instructor is here to help you. When you find things you want to talk with your instructor about, use this tab. Write your instructor's name in the blank, and mark material you have questions about. Tabs can be placed on print copies of your essays, class notes, or instructor handouts, as well as on textbook pages. Your classmates are also valuable resources and you can use this tab to mark material you want to check with one of them.

### Useful For

Use this tab when you find something useful that will apply to topics or assignments in other chapters. Also use it to mark sections that will help you in your other college courses.

### Assignment Due

Assignments, including reading assignments, writing exercises, and paragraph and essay assignments, are learning tools. Mark each assignment given with the "Assignment Due" tab and fill in the date

### Vocabulary

When you meet a word you do not know, or one that you know but do not use in your own writing, tab it using this "Vocabulary" tab. If you can get a hint about the word's meaning from the words around it, keep reading and check its meaning later. If you need the word's meaning in order to understand the sentence in which it appears, stop reading, and look it up in a dictionary right away. When you find the word's meaning, record it in the margin of the page the word appears in, and later transfer the definition to a vocabulary log.

*A Note about the Tabs:* You may run out of tabs before you finish the course. However, by then you will have built the habit of using them and can switch over to using Post-it notes for the same purpose.

# Writing Success Starts Here!

Regardless of your curriculum or major, writing is an important part of your everyday life, your college career, and your workplace. Knowing how to write well and being comfortable expressing yourself in writing in each of these areas can add a whole new dimension to your life and increase your potential for success. In this introduction you will learn numerous success strategies for becoming a better writer.

## TABS: TAKE CHARGE OF YOUR LEARNING

Success in a writing course, or any college course for that matter, involves accepting responsibility for your own learning. Your writing instructor is your guide, but you are in charge. It is not enough to attend class and do what you are asked. You have to decide what to learn and how to learn it. This section offers five strategies for taking charge of your own learning. For each strategy, sticky tabs are provided that give you a convenient way to carry it out.

### Decide What Is Important to Learn
### TAB: Important: Review This

As you work through this book, you will find a wide range of strategies, rules, samples, examples, steps, tables, checklists, and idea maps. Not everyone learns in the same way. For some students examples may be very useful, while for others a list of steps to follow may be more helpful. You should identify the most important and useful materials for you in each chapter and refer to them often throughout the course. Use the sticky tabs "Important: Review This" to mark these sections. For example, one student realized that the proofreading suggestions on p. 117 would help her, so she marked that page with a tab. Then, every time she proofread an essay, she used the tab to locate the suggestions quickly.

**xxxiii**

Here is a partial list of items that students have found useful to tab:

■ Idea maps—diagrams of how an essay is organized

■ Revision checklists

■ Annotated student essays

■ Ideas for topics to write about

■ Need to Know boxes

■ Writing Success Tips

■ ESL Tips

Important:
Review This

392    Chapter 15 ■ Sharpening Your Essay-Writing Skills

### Revision Checklist

1. Is your essay appropriate for your audience? Does it give them the background information they need? Will it interest them?

2. Will your essay accomplish your purpose?

3. Have you narrowed your topic so that you can cover your subject thoroughly in your essay?

4. Is your main point clearly expressed in a thesis statement in the introductory paragraph? Does the introductory paragraph cap- the essay?

Follow Up With

## Learn from Classmates and Instructors
## TAB: Follow Up With

You are never alone in a writing class. Your instructor is your most valuable resource. Work closely with your instructor by discussing topics, talking about writing problems, and seeking help with assignments. Do not be afraid to ask questions. When you find things you want to discuss with your instructor, use the "Follow Up With" tab. Write your instructor's name in the blank space, and use this tab to mark material you have a question about, so you can locate it easily and remember to speak with your instructor about it. Tabs can be placed on print copies of your essays, class notes, or instructor handouts, as well as on textbook pages.

Your classmates are also valuable resources. They can offer support and friendly feedback. Get together with them informally to discuss assignments, compare notes, and react to one another's papers. Mark material you want to check with other students about using the "Follow Up With" tab.

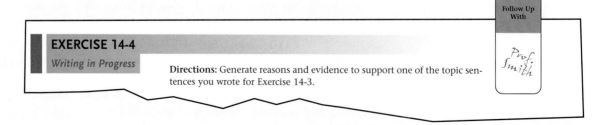

Follow Up With

**EXERCISE 14-4**
*Writing in Progress*

**Directions:** Generate reasons and evidence to support one of the topic sentences you wrote for Exercise 14-3.

Prof.
Smith

## Connect and Apply Your Skills
## TAB: Useful For

Your writing will improve when you consciously and deliberately connect skills to one another. This means that you have to use skills learned in one chapter as you complete assignments for a subsequent chapter. For example, you will need to use the topic sentence writing skills you learn in Chapter 3 when you write paragraphs in Chapter 4 on developing and arranging details. Your writing will improve more quickly if you use the skills you learn regularly and frequently. Try to apply what you learned last week to what you are writing this week. Also be sure to apply what you are learning in your writing class to the writing you may do in your other classes, in everyday writing, and in any writing you do at work. When you find information that will be useful for writing in other chapters or in other courses or situations, use the "Useful For" tab to mark it for future reference. For example, one student was taking a criminal justice course and was asked to read and summarize a news article on current police issues each week. He found the suggestions for summary writing useful, so he tabbed the page.

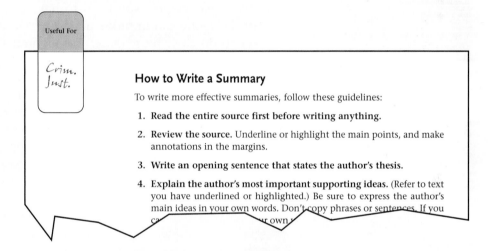

**How to Write a Summary**

To write more effective summaries, follow these guidelines:

1. **Read the entire source first before writing anything.**

2. **Review the source.** Underline or highlight the main points, and make annotations in the margins.

3. **Write an opening sentence that states the author's thesis.**

4. **Explain the author's most important supporting ideas.** (Refer to text you have underlined or highlighted.) Be sure to express the author's main ideas in your own words. Don't copy phrases or sentences. If you c̲a̲n̲... r own

## Learn from Your Assignments
## TAB: Assignment Due

Assignments, including reading assignments, writing exercises, and paragraph and essay assignments, are learning tools. Every assignment that your instructor gives is intended to teach you something. Make sure you complete all assignments carefully and completely. Mark each assignment given with the "Assignment Due" tab and fill in the date. Don't do any assignment just to get it done. Pay attention to what you are supposed to be learning. For reading assignments, highlight what is important and use the other tabs described above. For written assignments, be sure to submit neat, easy-to-read, well-labeled, and well-organized work. Keep copies of all the essays you write and be sure to keep returned, graded assignments as well. Study your instructor's comments to identify areas in which you can improve.

**Assignment Due**

10/6/06

126    Chapter 5 ■ Strategies for Revising

### Workplace Writing Assignments

1. Imagine that you have created the world's best _____ (fill in the blank with a product of your choice: can opener, ball point pen, pair of sneakers, etc.). Write a letter to a potential customer urging him or her to consider purchasing the product.

2. Assume you are Louise Wilson. Write a letter in reply to Mary Cortez. You might have further questions and you may try to negotiate for a better discount, for example.

Vocabulary

## Strengthen Your Vocabulary
## TAB: Vocabulary

Words are the building blocks of language. To write clear sentences and effective paragraphs, you need to have a solid vocabulary with which to start. Everyone can improve his or her vocabulary, and one of the easiest ways to do so is by reading. Throughout the book you will be reading numerous student and professional essays. When you encounter a word you do not know, or one that you know but do not use in your own writing, tab it using the "Vocabulary" tab. If you can get a hint about the word's meaning from the context of the words around it, keep reading and check its meaning later. If you need the word's meaning in order to understand the sentence in which it appears, stop reading and look it up in a dictionary right away. When you find the word's meaning, record it in the margin of the page the word appears on, and later transfer the definition to a vocabulary log.

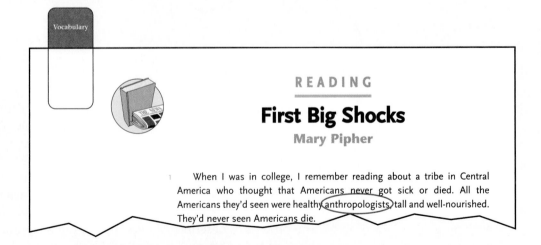

Vocabulary

### READING

# First Big Shocks
**Mary Pipher**

1    When I was in college, I remember reading about a tribe in Central America who thought that Americans never got sick or died. All the Americans they'd seen were healthy anthropologists, tall and well-nourished. They'd never seen Americans die.

**A Note About the Tabs** You may run out of tabs before you finish the course. However, by then you will have built the habit of using them and can switch over to using Post-it® notes for the same purpose.

# USE THE HELP FEATURES IN THIS BOOK

Although your instructor and your classmates are your most important sources for learning how to write well, this book also contains numerous features to help you become a successful writer.

## Chapter Objectives

> ### Chapter Objectives
>
> *In this chapter you will learn to:*
>
> **1**  Use examples to develop paragraphs and essays.
>
> **2**  Write effective topic sentences for example paragraphs.
>
> **3**  Choose appropriate and sufficient examples.
>
> **4**  Arrange your examples in a logical sequence.
>
> **5**  Use transitions to connect your ideas.

These lists of topics tell you what you should expect to learn in each chapter. If you know what you are supposed to learn before you begin, you will find that learning is easier and that you will remember more of what you read.

> ### Write About It!
>
> Write a sentence that states what behavior this photo illustrates. Then think of and describe several other instances that illustrate this behavior.
>
> The sentences you write could form the basis of an example paragraph. An **example paragraph** uses specific instances to illustrate or explain a general idea. In this chapter you will learn to use examples in writing both paragraphs and essays. You will have many occasions to use examples in your everyday, academic, and workplace writing.

## Write About It!

Each chapter opens with a photograph or other visual image that is intended to capture your attention, generate interest, and connect the topic of the chapter to your own experience. This "Write About It!" feature also starts you writing immediately about chapter-related content using an accessible topic.

## Idea Maps

Idea maps, labeled "Visualize It!" are diagrams that show the content and organization of a piece of writing. You can use these maps in several ways:

■  **To organize and guide your own writing.** Think of them as models you can follow.

■  **To help you analyze a paragraph or essay you have written.** Drawing a map of your writing will help you identify problems in organization or spot ideas that do not belong in a paragraph or essay.

■  **As an aid to understanding a professional reading that you have been assigned.** By filling in an idea map, you can assure yourself that you have understood the reading, and the process of drawing the map will help you to remember what you read. You will find extra blank idea maps on the book's Web site at www.ablongman.com/mcwhorterexpressways1e.

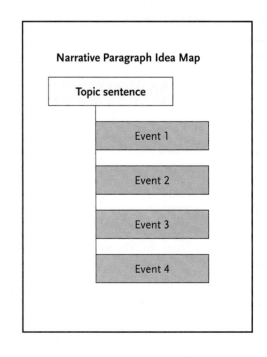

**Narrative Paragraph Idea Map**

Topic sentence

Event 1

Event 2

Event 3

Event 4

## Student Writing Samples

Sentences, paragraphs, and essays written by students appear throughout this book. These pieces of student writing are included to illustrate particular writing techniques. The chapter on writing using adjectives and adverbs, for example, includes a student paragraph that demonstrates how to use them to add interest and detail to sentences. Study each of these samples to see how each writing technique works. Use your tabs to mark those samples you want to refer to again as you write.

> ...ered, the waiter told me there would be a 15-minute delay. I tried to con-
> ...e myself it would be worth the wait. After waiting 25 minutes, I called the
> ...er; he apologized and said the kitchen was short-handed and that it would
> ...only another ten minutes. As I waited, I began to ask myself why would I
> ...t to eat the stomach of a cow, anyway? Would I hate it? Would I be able to
> ...it? Finally, my long-awaited tripe arrived. After I tasted it, I realized my fears
> ...e silly; it was delicious and well worth the long wait. I wonder what new
> ...d I should try next?
>
> ...e are some frequently used transitional words and phrases that con-
> ...ents in a sequence:

## Academic Scenarios

Most chapters include a sample student essay. These essays were written by real college students who were writing in response to classroom writing assignments. The essays are realistic models of good writing, but they are not perfect. They show you how the writer applied the techniques taught in the chapter to produce a good essay. An essay is included for each of the methods of organization presented in Chapters 6 through 14, as well; these will help you see how each method works and show you how to use it in your own writing. Before each essay, the writer and his or her writing task are described. The essays are annotated to call your attention to particular writing features or techniques. Questions follow the essay to help you further examine the writer's techniques, and academic writing assignments are suggested.

Here are some suggestions for reading and learning from student writing:

■ **Read the piece of writing more than once.** Read it once to understand the writer's message. Read it again to examine the writing technique it illustrates.

■ **Read the piece to answer this question:** What does this writer do that I can use in my own writing?

■ **Highlight as you read.** Use an "Important: Review This" tab to mark words, sentences, or paragraphs that you want to study further or that you feel work particularly well.

### AN ACADEMIC SCENARIO
### A STUDENT ESSAY
### The Academic Writer and the Writing Task

Ted Sawchuck is a student at Harrisburg Area Community College, majoring in mass communication. For his school paper, *The Fourth Estate,* he wrote an essay describing his experience as a campaign aid for Howard Dean in the summer of 2004, prior to the 2004 presidential election. Howard Dean, one of the Democratic candidates for the presidency, ran in the primaries but was defeated by John Kerry,

who became the Democratic Party's nominee. As you read the essay, note how Ted Sawchuck introduces, presents, and concludes his narrative sequence of events. This essay has been annotated; be sure to study the annotations after you have read the essay once. The thesis statement is highlighted in blue, and topic sentences are highlighted in yellow. The transitions are highlighted in green.

### Frostbite, Reporting, and The Scream: A College Journalist Inside the Last Days of Howard Dean's Iowa Campaign
#### Ted Sawchuck

Background information about Dean and campaign

Active first-person point of view used throughout

1  The mass media summed up Howard Dean's Iowa campaign as a screeching yell and a third-place finish, but I saw something different in my two weeks working for and covering it. I heard the sneers of voters who had already picked another candidate and the breathless shrieks of orange-hatted volunteers when Dean took the stage at rallies. I even talked to a cou-

## Workplace Scenarios

A variety of materials that you will write or read while on the job are included in this section. They show you how what you are learning in the chapter applies to writing in a variety of workplace situations. The chapter on writing topic sentences, for example, shows a sample job-application letter and demonstrates how topic sentences are useful to help employers locate information easily and quickly in the letter.

> ## A WORKPLACE SCENARIO
> ### A CASE REPORT
> **The Workplace Writer and the Writing Task**
>
> Maria Sanchez is a visiting nurse who checks on patients who have recently been discharged from the hospital. After each visit, she must write case notes that report the patient's condition, describe treatment, and identify future needs. Here is an excerpt from the case notes Sanchez wrote for an elderly patient. Notice that the notes are written in a chronologically arranged narrative.
>
> Mrs. Weatherly had fallen in her kitchen that morning and needed immediate first aid. Her left lower leg had a 3-inch cut and was still bleeding. I dressed the wound, and then did an examination to check for other injuries, but found none. Next, I checked her vital signs, changed her surgical dressing, and gave her a sponge bath. She was reluctant to do her breathing exercises and leg lifts, but with encouragement we got through them. I recommend that the family consider installing handrails in her home and also consider a lifeline monitor for her in case of future accidents.

A description of the writer and the writing task comes before each workplace writing sample; questions that guide you in analyzing the writing and several workplace writing assignments follow each sample. Use the suggestions listed above for Academic Scenarios for reading Workplace Scenarios as well.

## Professional Essays

The professional essays in this book were written by expert writers and have been published in books, news magazines, and journals. A professional essay appears at the end of most chapters. By studying the writing of professional writers, you can improve your own writing. As with the student writing, plan on reading each essay several times. Be sure to look for techniques that the writer uses that you can use in your own writing. Both before and after each reading, you will find questions and activities intended to guide you in reading, examining, and writing about the reading. You should complete these, even if they are not assigned by your instructor, because doing so will help you be better prepared to discuss and write about the reading.

> READING
>
> # The Charwoman
> ### Gordon Parks
>
> 1   I have one formidable, overwhelming and justifiable hatred, and that is for racists. Thorn-wielding is their occupation and I can attest to their proficiency. Throughout my childhood they kept their eyes glued to my tenderest parts, striking me, impaling me, leaving me bloodied and confused—without

## Need to Know Boxes

In many chapters you will find boxes titled "Need to Know." Pay particular attention to these boxes because they present or summarize important information. They are a quick, speedy way to review information, so refer to them often. You may want to use your "Important: Review This" tab to mark boxes that you find particularly valuable.

---

**NEED TO KNOW**

**Sensory Details**

Sensory details appeal to the five senses. Use the following questions to help you uncover sensory details about your subject.

**Touch:** What does it feel like? What is its texture? What is its weight? What is its temperature?

**Smell:** Is it pleasant or unpleasant? Is it mild or strong? Of what other smells does it remind you?

**Taste:** Is it pleasant or unpleasant? Is it sweet, sour, salty, or bitter? Of what favorite flavors does it remind you?

**Sight:** What is the color? Is there a pattern? What size is it? What shape is it?

**Sound:** Is it loud or soft? Is it high or low? Is it pleasant or unpleasant? What other sounds does it remind you of?

---

## ESL Tips

ESL (English As a Second Language) boxes appear throughout the book. They are intended to help ESL students learn and apply chapter content by pointing out special concerns, differences among languages, and typical grammatical errors. Even if you are not an ESL student, many of these boxes will emphasize or clarify important points.

---

**ELS TIP ▶ Verb Placement**

Remember in English the subject comes before the verb. All complete sentences have a subject and a verb.

subject    verb
Patricia studied for her History exam.

---

## Chapter Review and Practice

Appearing at the end of every chapter, this section offers you some, or all, of the following ways to review what you learned in a particular chapter:

■ The "Chapter Review" section provides a factual review of the skills taught in the chapter. Use this to help you remember skills you want to apply in your own writing.

■ The "Skill Refresher" section gives you an opportunity to learn to identify and correct many of the most common grammatical errors. Specifically, you will learn useful rules for identifying and avoiding these common errors and you will practice correcting them in sample sentences.

■ The "Internet Activities" section directs you to Web sites, including the Web site for this book, for additional instruction and/or practice of the skills taught in the chapter. Use this section to extend and vary your use of the skills you learn in a chapter.

---

**CHAPTER REVIEW AND PRACTICE**

**Chapter Review**

| | |
|---|---|
| WHAT IS A DOMINANT IMPRESSION? | A dominant impression is the overall attitude or feeling expressed about a topic. |
| WHERE SHOULD THIS IMPRESSION BE EXPRESSED? | It should be expressed in the topic sentence or thesis statement. |
| HOW SHOULD THE DOMINANT IMPRESSION BE SUPPORTED? | It should be supported with relevant details. |
| WHY SHOULD YOU ARRANGE THE DETAILS LOGICALLY? | A logical arrangement of details helps the reader follow the ideas. |
| HOW SHOULD DETAILS BE CONNECTED? | Transitional words and phrases should be used to connect details. |
| WHAT IS DESCRIPTIVE LANGUAGE? | Descriptive language uses exact and vivid words that appeal to the senses and provide a vivid impression of what is being described. |

# WRITING SUCCESS TIPS

Here are five practical tips that will lead you to successful writing, both in this course and in your other college classes:

## Tip #1: Organize a Place and Time to Write

Time and quiet—few people these days have much of either one. However, when it comes to writing, it is worthwhile to *create* them for yourself.

**Robert Badillo**
**Middlesex County College,**
**Edison, New Jersey**
Robert is a junior at Middlesex County College and is working toward a bachelor's degree in graphic arts.

Advice on Time Management: "Don't overwork yourself. Not everyone's a superhero. I was working full-time and taking a full course load. It was too difficult and I was beginning to mess up. I couldn't get the work done and my grades were suffering. I decided to take fewer classes. It used to be stressful but now it's a lot easier. I schedule a day at work so I just have work, and I have all my classes together on the same days. When it comes down to it you've got to decide the best way it has to be for you."

### Organizing a Place to Write

1. **Find a quiet area or an uncrowded portion of a computer lab, if possible.** If you are not using a computer, avoid areas used for other purposes, such as the dining room or kitchen table, because you'll have to move or reorganize your materials frequently. If you live in a dorm, your desk is an ideal place to write, unless the dorm is too noisy. If it is, find a quiet place elsewhere on campus, such as the library, or invest in earplugs or headphones specially designed to reduce noise.

2. **Work at a table or desk.** Don't try to write on an arm of a comfortable chair. Choose a space where you can spread out your materials and work easily.

3. **Eliminate distractions from your writing area.** Photos or stacks of unpaid bills will take your mind off your writing.

4. **Collect and organize supplies:** diskettes, stapler, pens, pencils, paper, and so on.

5. **Keep papers, quizzes, and class handouts in separate folders or sections in binders.**

6. **Keep a good college dictionary nearby** (the *Merriam-Webster's Collegiate Dictionary* or the *New American Handy Dictionaries*, for example). Also have other reference materials recommended by your instructor nearby (a thesaurus or a one-volume encyclopedia, for instance).

### Organizing a Time to Write

1.  **Reserve a block of time each day for reading this book and working on writing exercises and assignments.**

2.  **Work at the same time each day if possible.** You will end up with a schedule that is easy to follow.

3.  **Choose a time during the day when you are at the peak of your concentration.** Do not try to write when you are likely to be interrupted or are very tired or hungry. Be realistic in setting your schedule. If you plan your study time in advance, you can build in time for other activities (your favorite soap opera or Monday-night football, for example).

4.  **Begin assignments well ahead of their due dates.** This allows you enough time to plan, organize, write a first draft, ask questions, revise, and proofread. It's best to leave at least a day between finishing your draft and beginning to revise it so that you can look critically at what you've written.

5.  **If you get stuck and cannot think or write clearly, take a break.** Walk around, get a snack, or study a different subject for a time. Discuss your ideas about your assignment with a classmate. In addition to clearing your mind, taking a break will enable you to discover new ideas or clarify old ones. To get started again, reread what you've written. If you are still stuck, try one of the prewriting techniques—freewriting, brainstorming, branching, and questioning—described in Chapter 1, "The Writing Process: An Overview."

## Tip #2: Build Your Concentration

Use these suggestions to improve your ability to stick with a writing task.

**Rachel Goodman**
**Westchester University**
**West Chester, Pennsylvania**
Rachel successfully completed her associate's degree at Middlesex County College in May 2005, and has transferred to Westchester University in Pennsylvania where she is enrolled in the Elementary Education program. She plans to become an elementary school English teacher.

Advice on Concentration: "When I have a break between classes I either go to the library or sit with a friend in her car and do homework and review for class. Using the library is easier than working at home because there's nothing distracting around like the kitchen or TV. I read the (relevant) chapter before a class so I know what it's going to be about."

### Eliminate Distractions

1.  **Identify distractions.** As you are studying, make a list of what bothers you. When you have finished studying, review your list and try to find a solution for each problem.

2.  **Write down bothersome details.** When you think of an errand you have to do or a call you need to make, jot it down on a separate pad on your desk. That

way you can stop thinking about it until you have finished studying and can take the time to deal with it.

3. **Enlist the cooperation of family or roommates.** Make sure they know when and where you plan to write and understand that you need as few distractions as possible while you are working.

## Build Your Motivation and Interest

No one has trouble concentrating on tasks he or she wants to do. You can motivate yourself and stay interested in your writing task if you do the following:

1. **Choose a topic that genuinely interests you.** Although it might seem easier to use the first topic that pops into your head, take the time to discover a topic that you truly feel like writing about.

2. **Give yourself deadlines.** It is tempting to procrastinate or to work on another course assignment instead of writing. When you have a paper due, make a list of deadlines for yourself. For example, plan that you will complete a first draft by Tuesday, complete revisions by Thursday, and do a careful proofreading on Friday.

3. **Use psychological rewards.** After you complete a writing task, reward yourself by doing something enjoyable, like calling a friend or taking a walk.

## Tip #3: Use a Computer to Improve Your Writing

The computer is a valuable tool for writing. Using a computer can help you organize and outline your ideas, make revisions easily, compare several drafts of a paper, check your spelling and grammar, design tables and graphs, and produce neat, readable printouts (hard copy). Most college campuses have computer labs or centers, staffed by friendly, helpful "computer people" who love working with computers and enjoy helping others learn to use them.

**Nakashia Flowers-Miller**
**Armstrong Atlantic State University**
**Savannah, Georgia**
Nakashia graduated from Armstrong Atlantic State University in May 2004 with a bachelor's degree in music. She is currently working as a sixth-grade math and science teacher while she is working toward a master's degree in education.

Advice on Using a Computer: "I always use Word. The best thing for me about using a computer to write is the automatic spelling and grammar checks. They are number one. The second thing I find very useful is the cut and paste feature. Say I've written several paragraphs and they flow nicely, but when I reread them I realize that the second paragraph should be the third. I can just cut and paste it into place. Another thing I like about writing on the computer is that it's easy to insert tables and diagrams. You have all these tools—like the ruler that lets you set page margins, and page setup for portrait or landscape—which let you do things you would have to do manually if you were writing longhand or using a typewriter."

## Advantages

When you use a computer to write and revise an essay, you will discover it has numerous helpful features:

1.  **You can insert, revise, and correct without rewriting.**

2.  **You can search for and replace a specific word or phrase.**

3.  **Spell checkers can identify some of the misspelled words in your paper and provide the correct spelling.** Be aware, however, that they do not catch all errors. If in doubt, check a dictionary to be sure that the word you have used means what you want it to and is spelled correctly.

4.  **Word processing helps you to format your paper.**

5.  **Word processing enables you to experiment with your essay and compare different drafts or review revisions.** For example, you can rewrite a paragraph in two or three different ways by copying the paragraph, making changes in each copy, printing them, and putting them side by side for comparison. Most word processing programs have a split screen function, which allows you to see both versions onscreen at once without printing.

## Availability

Most colleges have labs with computers and word processing software available for your use. Usually, an assistant is present who can help you with problems that might arise. Some colleges offer workshops on how to use specific programs. Most public libraries also have computers available for your use.

## Tip #4: Keep a Writing Journal

A journal can be a fun, exciting, and meaningful way to improve your writing, keep track of your thoughts and ideas, and develop ideas to write about. Writing in your journal daily will change how you think about events in your life. Writing regularly will also make you a more confident writer.

**Ryan Vidaurri**
**Sam Houston State University**
**Huntsville, Texas**

Ryan is currently a junior at Sam Houston State University in Huntsville, Texas. He is pursuing a bachelor's degree in history and, as an active member of the ROTC, plans on a career in the military after graduation.

Advice on Using a Journal: "I was in an English class, Composition and Rhetoric, and we were graded just on personal journals. We had to write two pages a day. It was very informal, just expressing yourself, your feelings and thoughts. I really didn't like it at first, but once I got over the mental road-block—I never enjoyed writing in high school—getting over that speed bump really helped me. I found out I was pretty gifted. Everybody wants to express themselves in some way, and no one in our class realized this until it was part of an assignment. Our generation has kind of lost writing as a way of communicating."

### How It Works

1. **Create a computer file or buy an 8-1/2-by-11-inch spiral-bound notebook and use it exclusively for journal writing.** If you are using the college computer lab, save your file on a diskette or CD.

2. **Take ten to fifteen minutes a day to write in your journal.** You can do this during "down time"—waiting for a bus or for class to begin, for example. Some students prefer to write at the end of each day.

3. **Record your ideas, feelings, and impressions of the day.** Don't just record events; analyze what they mean to you.

4. **To get started, ask yourself thought-provoking questions such as:**

   • *What new ideas did I encounter today?* Perhaps you started thinking about world hunger or the value of religion. Describe your thoughts.

   • *What interesting conversations did I have?* Jot down some of the dialogue.

   • *What am I worrying about?* Describe the problem and brainstorm possible solutions.

   • *What are my interests?* Sometimes you may want to write about an event, a person, or a subject that interests you. You might write about a movie you have seen or a book you have read.

   • *What was a particularly pleasurable experience?* Maybe it was smelling a chocolate cake baking or feeling your dog's wet nose nudging you to wake up.

   • *What was the best/worst/most unusual thing that happened today?* Describe how you feel about it.

   • *What interesting person did I meet?* Think about what type of relationship might develop between you and this individual.

### Sample Journal Entries

#### Sample 1

Today in my biology class we talked about animal-organ transplants. I was surprised that research is going on about this. My instructor told us that scientists have experimented with putting pigs' hearts into baboons. It didn't work because the baboons' immune systems rejected the hearts. The reason for doing this is the shortage of human organs. I wonder why more people don't donate . . .

#### Sample 2

Today Dad and I took his boat out and went fishing in the river. It's been three years since I've gone fishing with him. I guess the last time was before I moved out of the house. We had a chance to talk like we used to when I saw more of him. He told me some stuff about my sisters and problems they were having with Mom. He seemed depressed and was glad to talk about it. I probably should spend more time with him, but . . .

### Why It Works

An obvious benefit of keeping a journal—whether on disk or as a notebook—is that it gives you practice in writing and the more you write, the better your writing becomes. However, a journal has many other benefits as well.

1. **Journal writing allows you to write for yourself.** Class assignments and papers are written for someone else to read. By keeping a journal you will begin to see writing as a means of personal expression. Writing in your journal can release pent-up feelings about your problems and make you feel better.

2. **Journal writing gives you experience in using writing to think about ideas, react to problems, and discover solutions.** You'll learn to use writing to discover and evaluate ideas, adding a new dimension to the way you think.

3. **Your journal will become a valuable source of ideas.** When you are asked to write a paragraph or an essay on a topic of your choice, you will be able to refer to your journal for topics you are interested in.

4. **Many students find that they enjoy journal writing and continue it long after they complete their writing courses.** A journal provides a valuable record of your ideas and experiences. Rereading a journal you wrote several years ago is like looking at old photographs—it brings back memories and helps you preserve your past.

## Tip #5: Use Peer Review

Many students have found that their peers—classmates or friends—offer valuable suggestions for revision. Peer review is an excellent way to find out what is good and what needs to be improved in your draft. Often your classmates will see things you don't because you are too involved with the topic. Here are some tips on using peer review.

**Stephanie Moore**
**Houston Community College**
**Houston, Texas**
Stephanie is currently a sophomore at Houston Community College in Houston, Texas, working toward a bachelor of science degree. Next year she plans to transfer to the Baylor School of Medicine, or the University of Houston, and specialize in histology.

Advice on Using Peer Review: "In my last English class, English 1301, we wrote lots of essays and we would have a time when we exchanged papers with each other. We would write first drafts and give them to the instructor. Then for our third drafts we would give our papers to other students. They would look at everything, including grammar and the overall flow of the paper. They would see things I would miss, like run-on sentences. They would write comments all over it. It was really helpful. I would definitely use this technique again."

### How to Find a Reviewer

A good source of reviewers is other members of your writing class. These students are working on the same skills as you are. Friends who have already taken a writing course can also make good reviewers. It is useful to get the opinion of more than one reviewer, if possible.

### What to Ask Your Reviewer

1. **Give your reviewer a copy of your draft that is easy to read, one that he or she also can write on.** Ask him or her to mark any parts that are unclear or confusing.

2. **Ask your reviewer to define your audience and your purpose for writing.** If their answers do not match what you intended, revise your draft so that your audience and purpose are clearer.

3. **Give the reviewer a copy of the revision questions found in later chapters of this book.** Ask the reviewer to focus on these questions as they read your draft.

4. **Don't automatically accept everything your reviewers say.** Weigh their comments carefully, taking into account what you want to convey in your paper, and how you want to say it.

5. **If you are uncertain about advice you've been given, talk with your instructor.**

### How to Be a Good Reviewer

If a friend or classmate asks you to review their writing, use these suggestions to guide you as you read and comment on their work:

1. **Read the draft through completely at least once before making any judgments.**

2. **Offer positive comments first.** Tell the writer what is good about the paper.

3. **Avoid general comments.** Don't just say that the topic sentence is unclear. Explain how it could be improved or what it lacks.

4. **Offer specific revision suggestions.** For instance, if you feel a paragraph needs further development, tell the writer what type of information to include.

# PART I

# Getting Started

# 1

# The Writing Process: An Overview

## Think About It!

Study the photograph above. A man and a woman are outside looking at a road map. Most likely they followed a process—a series of steps taken in a particular order—before they left to plan their route, select stopover cities, and find out about special attractions and events along the way. In much the same way as the couple planned their trip, writers must also follow a series of steps when writing a paragraph or an essay.

This chapter will explain what good writing is, show you five steps for writing well, and discuss two important factors you should consider when writing anything—your audience and your purpose. Approaching writing as a process is important in everyday life, in the classroom, and in the workplace:

EVERYDAY SCENARIOS

- Planning, writing, and revising a complaint letter to the manager of an auto repair shop
- Planning, writing, and revising a summary of an auto accident on a insurance claim

ACADEMIC SCENARIOS

- Planning, writing, and revising a plot summary of an assigned short story in American Literature
- Planning, writing, and revising a lab report in biology

WORKPLACE SCENARIOS

- Planning, writing, and revising a trip report required for reimbursement of expenses
- Planning, writing, and revising your yearly self-evaluation letter

# WRITING

## What Is Good Writing?

Once you know what is expected of you in a writing course, you will find it easier to produce quality writing. To the question "What is good writing?" many students answer, "Correct grammar, spelling, and punctuation—no errors." Actually, good writing involves much more than not making errors. Think about pieces of writing that you have enjoyed reading or found helpful. What made them satisfying?

- **Good writing requires thinking.** Good writing is a thinking process. As you read this book, you'll see that writers do a great deal of work before they actually begin writing. They think about their audience and topic, develop ideas and supporting material, and plan how best to say what they want to say. Once they have written a draft, they reevaluate their ideas to see if there is a better way to express them.

- **Good writing involves revision.** Finding the best way to express your ideas involves experimentation and change. This process is called *revision*. When you revise, you rethink ideas and improve what you have said and how you have said it. All good writers revise, sometimes many times.

- **Good writing expresses ideas clearly.** The primary focus of this text is to help you express ideas clearly. Good writers communicate with their readers in a direct and understandable way, making their main points clearly and supporting these points with details, facts, reasons, and examples. Good writers also arrange their main points logically. This book contains a variety of techniques to help you arrange ideas logically.

- **Good writing is directed toward an audience.** Suppose you were going to an interview for a part-time job. Would you wear the same clothes you wear to stop by a friend's apartment? Of course not; you modify your appearance in keeping with the situation and the people you will be seeing. Similarly, when you write, you must consider your audience. Ask yourself: Who will be reading what I write? How should I express myself so that my readers will understand what I write? Considering your audience is essential to good writing. You will learn more about considering your audience later in the chapter.

- **Good writing achieves a purpose.** In written communication, you write for a specific reason or purpose. Sometimes, in college, you write for yourself: to record an assignment, take notes in class, or to help yourself learn or remember information for an exam. Many other times, you write to communicate information, ideas, or feelings to a specific audience. You will learn more about writing with a purpose later in the chapter.

- **Good writing requires practice.** To improve your writing, you need to practice using the three basic building blocks of written language: the sentence, the paragraph, and the essay. A **sentence** expresses one or more complete thoughts. A **paragraph** expresses one main idea and is usually made up of several sentences that explain or support that idea. An *essay* consists of multiple paragraphs that explain related ideas, all of which support a larger, broader idea. This text focuses on writing paragraphs and essays. However, the "Skill Refreshers" in each chapter and in Part VI, "Reviewing the Basics," will help you write more effective sentences by answering your questions about grammar, mechanics, and punctuation. The chart below shows how the parts of paragraphs are very much like the parts of an essay.

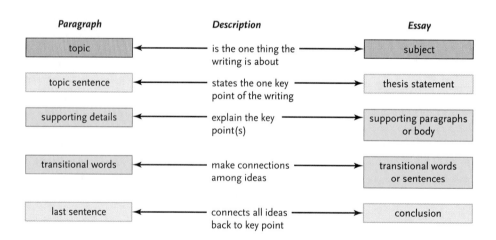

## The Five Steps in the Writing Process

Alfredo was given his first writing assignment by his sociology instructor. This was the assignment:

Visit the local zoo and spend at least one hour in the monkey house. Write a description of what you see and explain how it relates to our introductory unit on group behavior.

This assignment did not make much sense to Alfredo, but on Sunday afternoon he and a friend went to the monkey house and he found that he actually had fun watching the monkeys' antics. Because the assignment was due Tuesday, he decided that he would begin writing later that day. He sat down at the computer and said to himself, "Well, I might as well get started," and started his assignment with the following sentence:

I visited the monkey house over the weekend and saw many interesting things.

At that point Alfredo was in trouble; he didn't know what to say next. He stared at the blank paper for a while. Realizing that he *had* to write something, he tried to describe some of what three individual monkeys did while he was there. When he finished writing a page or so of description, Alfredo printed out what he'd done, put it in his notebook, and handed it in on Tuesday. The next week, when the professor returned the papers, Alfredo was angry and disappointed when he saw his grade. The instructor's note said, "I know you tried. Next time, though, plan out your essay, write a draft, and then revise it." Alfredo thought, "I really tried. This is really disappointing. I need to learn a different way to go about writing!"

Where did Alfredo go wrong? Actually, he made several mistakes, but they all stem from a larger problem. He was viewing writing as a single-step activity instead of a multi-step process. A **process** is a series of steps you follow in a specific order. Writing is a series of steps in which you **generate ideas** on what to say, **plan** how you will organize your ideas, and then **write**, **revise**, and **proofread** what you have written. The following box summarizes the steps in the writing process. You will get plenty of help with each step in this section and throughout the entire book.

Alfredo neither thought nor planned before he began writing; consequently, he had trouble knowing what to say. Then, in desperation, he resorted to simply reporting events, without placing his observations into a unifying framework. Once he finished writing, he put the assignment away and did not look at it again. When he handed in his assignment, he hadn't reread it even once to see how he could improve it, nor had he proofread for errors. In this chapter, you will learn to approach writing as a process and avoid making Alfredo's mistakes. Don't be concerned if this process is not entirely clear by the end of this chapter; the rest of the book will go into more detail on each step. You'll understand more and more as you work through each chapter and apply each step to your own writing.

Table 1-1    **The Five Steps in the Writing Process**

| Step | What It Involves |
| --- | --- |
| Generate ideas | Coming up with ideas that explain and support your topic |
| Plan and organize your ideas | Deciding what ideas to include and in what order to place them |
| Write a first draft | Putting your ideas in sentence, paragraph, and essay form |
| Revise | Rewriting, rearranging your ideas; deleting some ideas, adding others |
| Proofread | Looking for errors in typing, spelling, grammar, and punctuation |

In the course of writing, people frequently find that some of these steps overlap or that some circling back to earlier steps is necessary. For example, you may continue to organize your ideas while writing your first draft, or you may need to generate more ideas while revising. This circling back is fine; the writing process does not always go in a straight line.

If you use each of these steps, however, and are aware of their general progression, you will find that writing will be easier and more successful for you than it was for Alfredo. You will not find yourself frustrated, staring at a blank sheet of paper, or writing something that doesn't seem to hang together or say much. Instead, you will feel as if you are developing and focusing your ideas, shaping them into words, and making a point that will hold and interest your reader. You will be well on your way to producing a good paper.

## Generating Ideas

Before you begin to write a paper, the first step is to generate ideas about your topic. Although Alfredo spent time in the monkey house, he did not spend time thinking about what he saw or how it related to what he had learned in his course. He did not develop any ideas to write about.

Four good techniques you can use to generate ideas are:

- freewriting,

- brainstorming,

- branching, and

- questioning.

These techniques can help you overcome the feeling that you have nothing to say. They can unlock ideas you already have and help you discover new ones.

Since each of these four techniques provides a different way to generate ideas, feel free to choose from among them. At times, you may use several at different points in your writing process, or you may need to use only one of them for a particular writing assignment. Experiment to see what works best for you.

### Freewriting

Freewriting is writing nonstop for a limited period, usually around five or ten minutes. Write whatever comes into your mind, whether it is about the topic or not. If nothing comes to mind, you can just write, "I'm not thinking of anything."

As you write, don't be concerned with grammar, punctuation, or spelling, or with writing in complete sentences. Words and phrases are fine. Focus on recording your thoughts as they come to you. The most important thing is to keep writing without stopping. Write fast; don't think about whether what you are writing is worthwhile or makes sense. After you finish, reread what you have written. Start to think about what your main point could be, a point that would unify various details and observations and fit them into an interesting framework. Highlight everything that you might be able to use in your paper.

Alfredo discussed his sociology assignment with his writing instructor, who explained how to use freewriting to generate ideas. He suggested that Alfredo redo the assignment to see how freewriting works.

### Alfredo's Freewriting

The monkeys are behind bars like prisoners. They leap and jump and play but seem to know they can't get out. They eat with their hands—they look like impolite humans. There's an old monkey who has been there forever and he's crabby and nasty to the others. People like to go there during feeding time. Monkeys eat bananas. I can't think of anything. I can't think. It smells in the monkey house. The monkeys seemed to enjoy being watched by us. They seemed to be showing off for us. The monkey house is located next to the reptile house. I hate going there. Some monkeys threw things at us and at other monkeys and they looked angry. One monkey stole another's food but the monkey whose food was stolen didn't fight back. Most people go to the zoo during the summer. Sometimes I wonder if the zoo is really humane. Monkeys were grooming each other by picking through each other's hair. Monkeys in the zoo don't act like they would in the wild though either. I felt sorry for some of them they looked so confused. Sometimes they seemed to compete with each other to see who could do the most antics.

Alfredo reviewed what he had written and highlighted all the points having to do with his topic, group behavior—how the monkeys interacted with each other and with zoo visitors. The other topics in his freewriting—zoos as depressing places, how zoos differ from the wild, the eating habits of monkeys—did not relate to group behavior.

Freewriting is a creative way to begin translating ideas and feelings into words without being concerned about their value or worrying about correctness. You will often be pleasantly surprised, as Alfredo was, by the number of usable ideas this technique uncovers. Some ideas may be too broad or too personal or may stray from the topic. Still, once you have some ideas down on paper, you can begin to shape your material and select what you need. You can also do additional freewriting—or use another technique for generating ideas—once your topic or direction has become clear.

## EXERCISE 1-1

**Directions:** Choose three of the following topics and then, using a clock or timer, freewrite for at least five minutes on each. Be sure to write without stopping. After you finish each freewriting, reread carefully. Underline ideas that have a common thread, as you look for a group of usable ideas that would be a good focus for a paper.

1. Today's heroes

2. Rap music—its influence on attitudes and behavior, if any

3. Changes you would make where you work

4. A friend's annoying or bad habit that you wish you could break

5. The physical environment of your campus—what it is like, how it makes you feel

## Brainstorming

Brainstorming is a way of developing ideas by making a list of everything you can think of about a topic. You might list feelings, ideas, facts, examples, or problems. There is no need to write in sentences; instead, list words and phrases. Don't try to organize your ideas; just list them as you think of them. Give yourself a time limit. You'll find ideas come faster that way.

You can brainstorm alone or with friends. With your friends, you will discover a lot more ideas, because their ideas will trigger more of your own. When you've finished, read your list and mark usable ideas. One group of students came up with the following list on the topic of sports fans.

| | |
|---|---|
| sit in bleachers | baseball card collections |
| stadiums and ballparks | beer |
| have tailgate parties | betting |
| do the "wave" | cost of tickets |
| excitement and shouting | parking |
| disappointment | traffic jams in and out |
| restrooms, long lines | dress funny |
| food costs | chanting |
| bored | cold and snow |
| fanatical | hotseats |
| radio sports talk show | |

The topic of sports fans is too broad for a paragraph or short essay, but there are several groups of usable ideas here: the behavior and attitude of fans at games, the high cost of being a fan, tailgate parties, and radio sports talk shows. A student could develop a good paper on any one of these ideas, doing more brainstorming as necessary.

## EXERCISE 1-2

**Directions:** For two of the following topics, brainstorm for about five minutes each. When you finish, review your list and mark ideas that seem closely connected enough to use in writing a paragraph.

1. What makes a good commercial?

2. Why is talking to strangers sometimes fun (or not fun)?

3. Why are cellular phones so popular?

4. Why are some people always late—and what consequences does this have?

5. What is road rage?

## Branching

Branching is a visual way of generating ideas. To begin, write your topic in the middle of a whole sheet of paper and draw a circle around it. Next, think of related ideas and write them near the circle. Connect each to the circle with a line. These ideas are called the primary branches. Your topic is like a tree trunk, and your ideas are like primary limbs that branch out from it. Shown below is an example of a branching diagram that one student did for the topic "shopping at convenience stores." You can connect other related ideas to the primary branches with smaller, or secondary, branches. In the following example, the student looked at his first branching diagram, labeled Branching: Step 1, and decided to focus on the limited selection at convenience stores.

**Branching: Step 1**

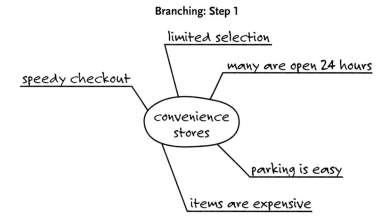

Now, the student used "limited selection" as the trunk and created three primary branches: poor-quality fruit, limited vegetables, and limited brand selection, as shown in the diagram, Branching: Step 2.

**Branching: Step 2**

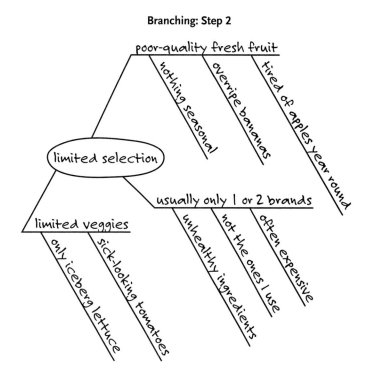

He drew secondary branches onto each of these primary ones and could have kept going.

If you use this technique, you can branch from your branches almost indefinitely. If you run out of room, you can attach extra sheets of paper. On the other hand, you don't have to develop branches for every main branch. It is often fine to choose one branch and ignore all the others.

When you have finished branching, use a highlighter or colored pencil to mark those branches that seem like good possibilities to write about.

## EXERCISE 1-3

**Directions:** Draw branching diagrams for two of the following topics. Then highlight those branches that could be the basis of a paragraph or essay.

1.  The lives of professional athletes (choose one sport to focus on)

2.  Homeless people's rights

3.  Tourists (sightseers) who litter or display a lack of respect for the site they are visiting

4.  Outdoor wedding receptions

5.  Waiting in hospital emergency rooms (or a location of your choice)

## Questioning

Another way to generate ideas about a given topic is to write down questions about it. As with freewriting and brainstorming, write any question that comes to mind. Don't worry if it seems silly, and don't stop to evaluate if it is related to the topic. If you can think of answers, include them as well, but don't limit yourself to questions for which you know the answers.

The key words *Who? What? When? Where? Why?* and *How?* can help you get started in your questioning of a topic. When you have finished, read your questions carefully. Underline those questions or answers that bring out interesting angles on a topic and which you might be able to use for writing a paragraph or an essay. Here are the questions one student wrote on the topic of dreams:

| | |
|---|---|
| Why do we dream? | Do I remember all of my dreams? |
| Do dreams have meaning in our everyday life? | Are dreams predictions? |
| How do you interpret a dream? | |
| Why are they so frightening when they hardly make sense? | Are dreams warnings? |
| | What are the most common dreams? |
| Do we dream all night? | How are dreams studied? |
| Can we control our dreams? | Do men and women have different dreams? |
| How long do dreams last? | Do children have different dreams? |

What do our bodies do while
we are dreaming?

Why do people sleepwalk?
Do they remember it?

What scary dreams can I
remember?

## EXERCISE 1-4

**Directions:** Use questioning to generate ideas on two of the following topics. Afterward, underline the questions or answers that could form the basis of an interesting paragraph or essay.

1. Giving candy for Valentine's Day

2. The best job you ever had

3. An incident of sexual harassment you have experienced, observed, or heard about

4. Drinking on campus

5. The importance of music in your life

## When to Use Which Technique

Now that you have tried freewriting, brainstorming, branching, and questioning, you are probably wondering when to use each technique. In general, there are no rules to follow. The best advice is to give them all a good chance and use the technique, or techniques, with which you are most comfortable.

You may also find that for certain topics, one technique works better than the others. For example, suppose you decide to write a paragraph about your mother's sense of humor. While it might be difficult to think of questions, freewriting might help you remember humorous events from your life with her. Suppose, however, that you are studying types of discrimination in your sociology class. Your instructor has assigned a paper that requires you to explain the effects of one type of discrimination. Asking questions about the specific topic is likely to produce useful ideas to include in your paper.

**Table 1-2    Techniques for Generating Ideas**

| Technique | How to Do It |
|---|---|
| *Freewriting* | 1. Write nonstop about your topic. <br> 2. Write whatever comes to mind without concern for correctness. <br> 3. Give yourself a time limit; then stop, review, and repeat as necessary. |
| *Brainstorming* | 1. List all ideas about your topic that come to mind. <br> 2. List words and phrases, observations, and thoughts without attention to correctness. <br> 3. Give yourself a time limit; then stop, review, and repeat as necessary. |
| *Branching* | 1. Write and circle your topic in the middle of your page. <br> 2. As you think of related ideas, write them down around the circle. Connect with lines. <br> 3. Draw additional branches as you think of additional ideas. |
| *Questioning* | 1. Ask *Who? What? When? Where? Why? How?* questions about your topic. <br> 2. Ask any other questions that come to mind. <br> 3. Include answers, if you know them. |

## Sorting Usable Ideas

Remember that freewriting, brainstorming, branching, and questioning each produce a wide range of usable ideas. You will need to sort through them to decide which ones you can put together and expand upon to produce a paper that is unified and interesting to your reader. You will read more about this process in the upcoming section "Organizing Your Ideas," and more on narrowing topics in Chapter 3, "Writing Topic Sentences."

## Choosing Your Own Topic

When your instructor assigns a topic or provides a choice of topics, part of your paper, in a sense, has been done for you. You may not like the topic(s), or you may need to narrow the topic down to make it more manageable, but at least you have a point from which to start. If your instructor directs you to choose a topic, you have greater freedom, but sometimes your first reaction may be "I don't know what to write about!"

Don't be tempted to grab just any topic in order to get on with writing. Remember that the most important element in clear writing is clear *thinking*. Invest your time in thinking about what you want to write. Use one—or several—of the four techniques you just learned for generating topics—freewriting, brainstorming, branching, or questioning. You can also generate ideas by reacting to the world around you. Here are some questions to get you involved in your world:

1. **Think of an interesting topic that was discussed in one of your classes or a topic that relates to your major.** Nursing students might, for example, think of genetic counseling for prospective parents, and accounting students of new computer software.

2. **Think of activities you have participated in over the past week.** Going to work or to church, playing softball, taking your child to the playground, shopping at a mall, or seeing a horror film could produce the following topics: communication patterns among co-workers; why attendance at church is rising (or falling); the problem with pitchers; how toddlers develop language skills; the mall as adult playground; the redeeming value of horror films.

3. **Look around you or out the window.** What do you see? Perhaps it is the television, a dog lying at your feet, traffic, or children playing tag. Possible topics are the influence of television on what we buy, pets as companions, cars as noise polluters (or entertainment), and play as a form of learning.

4. **Think of the time of year.** Think about what you do on holidays or vacation, what is happening around you in the environment, or what this season's sports or upcoming events might mean to you.

5. **Use a writing journal.** A writing journal is a notebook or computer file in which you record your thoughts and ideas on a regular basis. Many students try to write daily and find that a journal is a useful way to spur their thinking and become a more effective writer. Refer to "Writing Success Starts Here!" on pp. xxxiii–xlvi for more detailed suggestions on keeping a writing journal.

6. **Think of a controversial topic you have read about, heard about on radio or television, or argued over with a friend.** A political candidate up for reelection, a terminally ill patient's right to euthanasia, and reforms in public education are examples.

7. **As you read, listen to the news, or go about your daily life, be alert for possible topics and write them down.** Keep the list and refer to it when your next paper is assigned.

If you choose a topic that interests you, one that you know something about or are willing to read about, you will feel more like writing. You will also find that you have more to say and that what you write will be more engaging and memorable for your reader.

## EXERCISE 1-5

**Directions:** Select one of the topics listed below. Try all four techniques—freewriting, brainstorming, branching, and questioning—on the same topic.

**TOPICS**

1. Is violence a necessary part of sports?

2. What do you think of people who bring babies to adult-oriented concerts, and why?

3. How can we eat well without spending a lot of money?

4. What should a person do (or not do) when he or she loses a job or is laid off?

5. Why is it so difficult to save money?

When you have tried all four techniques, read the list of ideas produced by using each one. Mark the usable ideas. Then write short answers to the following questions:

**QUESTIONS**

1. Which technique produced the most usable ideas?

2. Which technique were you most comfortable using?

3. Which technique were you least comfortable using? Why?

## Organizing Your Ideas

Once you have generated ideas about your topic, the next step is to decide how to organize them. Ideas in a paragraph or essay should progress logically from one to another. Group or arrange your ideas in a way that makes them clear and understandable to your reader. Imagine someone picking up what you have written and reading it for the first time: will that person be able to follow your train of thought easily? That should be your the goal.

Assume you have been asked to write an essay about your experience in the workplace and how it has affected your life. Here is the brainstorming list that one student, Doug Mello, wrote. He worked at three places so he did some brainstorming about each.

**BURGER KING:**

inconvenient hours—holidays, weekends

rude customers—I felt unappreciated

pressured and rushed work environment

other workers not serious—I hated it there

**WAL-MART:**

large and confusing, responsibilities not clear

supervisor was too bossy—thought she was better than us

coworkers tried to cheat the company

went home with a headache most days

customers were always in a hurry, so I felt I should be, too

never wanted to make a career of this—looked for another job

**TRUCK DRIVER:**

liked working by myself making deliveries

working with equipment and machinery was fun

job responsibilities were clear

worked on scheduling and job routing which I enjoyed

eventually I learned that there was no future driving a truck

I decided to leave and go back to school

As Doug reviewed his brainstorming ideas, he realized his most positive experience had been as a truck driver and that it was the job that had the most impact on his life. He decided to write about how his experience as a truck driver changed the direction of his life. Doug reread his list of ideas and did more brainstorming to collect additional details. As he reread his additional brainstorming, he decided the best way to organize his ideas was in the order in which they happened.

## Using an Idea Map to Organize Your Ideas

One effective way to organize your ideas is to draw an idea map. An idea map is a visual diagram of how ideas relate to one another. Just as a campus map shows the relationship of various buildings on campus to one another, an idea map shows the relationship of ideas to one another. An idea map can help you organize your ideas into paragraphs and see how paragraphs fit together to form essays. You will learn more about drawing and using idea maps on p. 39. Here is an idea map that Doug drew for his essay on the workplace. He developed his ideas further as he drew the map.

## Visualize It! ▶

**Doug's Idea Map**

| There were no opportunities for advancement within the company. |
| --- |

| Worked as a dispatcher; saw inefficiency |
| --- |

| Developed a plan |
| --- |

| Made proposal to company president; president refused |
| --- |

| We planned our finances, and I enrolled in college. |
| --- |

| I worried about my decision; was underprepared; continued to study with my wife's encouragement. |
| --- |

## EXERCISE 1-6

*Writing in Progress*

**Directions:** Use a topic that you developed in any of the previous exercises. Determine which ideas are usable and interrelated, and arrange them in a logical order.

## Writing a First Draft

Suppose you are taking a weekend trip and are about to pack your suitcase. You have in mind what you'll be doing and whom you'll see. You look through your entire closet, then narrow your choices to several outfits. You mix and match the outfits, figure out how much will fit in the suitcase, and finally decide what to take.

Writing a draft of a paragraph or an essay is similar to packing for a trip. You have to try out different ideas, see how they work together, express them in different ways, and after several versions, settle upon what your paper will include. Drafting is a way of trying out ideas to see if and how they work.

A first draft expresses your ideas in sentence form. Work from your list of ideas, and don't be concerned with grammar, spelling, or punctuation at this point. Instead, focus on expressing and developing each idea fully. The following suggestions will help you write effective first drafts:

1. **After you have thought carefully about the ideas on your list, write one sentence that expresses the main point of your paragraph (working topic sentence) or essay (thesis statement).**

2. **Concentrate on explaining your topic sentence or thesis statement, using ideas from your list.** Focus first on those ideas you like best or that you think express your main point particularly well. Later in the writing process, you may find you need to add other ideas from your list.

3. **Think of a first draft as a chance to experiment with different ideas and ways of organizing them.** While you are working, if you think of a better way to organize or express your ideas, or if you think of new ideas, make changes. Be flexible. Do not worry about getting your exact wording at this point.

4. **As your draft develops, feel free to change your focus or even your topic, unless it has been assigned.** If your draft is not working out, don't hesitate to start over completely. Go back to generating ideas. It is always all right to go back and forth among the steps in the writing process. Most writers make a number of "false starts" before they produce a draft that satisfies them.

5. **Don't expect immediate success.** When you finish your first draft, you should feel that you have the *beginnings* of a paper you will be happy with. Now, ask yourself if you have a sense of the direction your paper will take. Do you have a main idea? Do you have supporting details? Is the organization logical? If you can answer "yes" to these questions, you have something on paper to work with and revise.

Doug, the student writing about his experience as a truck driver, wrote the following first draft of his paper. The highlighting indicates the main point that he developed as he wrote.

### First Draft

I came from a working-class family, so I had no choice but to go to work right after high school. One of the jobs was as a truck driver. At the age of twenty-nine, a company hired me that I thought offered a promising career future. After several years I knew that there were no opportunities for advancement within the company.

After five years with the company I was frequently asked for advice on routing schedules and was assigned the job of dispatching when the plant manager was on vacation. Being involved in the operations of the company allowed me to see the constant waste of time and money that resulted from day-to-day planning. I finally came up with a plan I thought would allow me to advance within the company and get out of my truck and off the road. I went to the president of the company with my proposal, which could have saved the company twice my wages each year in transportation costs. He said no, and that made me realize that I needed an education to have a future.

My wife and I devised a plan to organize our finances so I could return to school. In June of 2002 I gave a six-month notice to my employer and told him why I had decided to return to school. I applied to Modesto Junior College and started in January of 2003.

I didn't know how to study and was not prepared for college courses. My major was civil engineering. Almost immediately I wondered if I had made the right decision to return to school; it was much more work than driving a truck. One of the biggest problems I am faced with is what, or how, I am contributing to my family? My wife continually encourages me in my studies and assures me that I am contributing to our family's future.

## EXERCISE 1-7
*Writing in Progress*

**Directions:** Write the first draft of a paragraph (or two) using the topic you chose in Exercise 1-6 and the ideas you put in logical order in that exercise.

## Revising and Rewriting Drafts

Let's think again about the process of packing a suitcase. At first you may think you have included everything you need and are ready to go. Then, a while later, you think of other things that would be good to take. But because your suitcase is full, you have to reorganize everything. When you repack, you take everything out and rethink your selections and their relationships to each other. You might eliminate some items, add others, and switch around still others.

A similar thing often happens as you revise your first draft. When you finish a first draft, you are more or less satisfied with it. Then you reread it later and see you have more work to do. When you revise, you have to rethink your entire paper, reexamining every part and idea. Revising is more than changing a word or rearranging a few sentences, and it is not concerned with correcting punctuation, spelling errors, or grammar. Make these editing changes later when you are satisfied that you have presented your ideas in the optimal way. Revision is your chance to make significant improvements to your draft. It might mean changing, adding, deleting, or rearranging whole sections.

Here is a later draft of the essay shown on p. 16. In this draft, you will see that Doug expands his ideas, adds detail, and writes a title and a conclusion. You can see that he added a sentence (highlighted) that states the main point of his essay. After you have read the essay once, study the annotations. They will help you see the changes Doug made. Also look back to his first draft on p. 16 and compare the two versions.

*Doug Mello is a student at Modesto Junior College, Modesto, CA. He plans to transfer to a university and earn a bachelor of science degree in civil engineering.*

Title: suggests thesis

Background information on his life

## Education: The Open Road

Coming from a working-class family, the option of pursuing an education was, for me, not a choice. Going to work after high school was my only choice and also what my parents expected of me. One of the first jobs I had provided me with the opportunity to acquire a commercial driver's license, which allowed me to become a truck driver. Due to a good driving record and work history, my employment and wages always seemed to get better as I searched for the perfect truck-driving job. At the age of twenty-nine, a company hired me that I thought offered a promising career future. However, I failed to see where this particular road would take me. After several years I found that there were no opportunities for advancement within the company.

I realized, at this point in my life, that an education could offer challenges, opportunities, and a career that would last a lifetime.

There was one particular event that led to my decision to get an education. After five years with the company I was frequently asked for advice on routing schedules and was assigned the job of dispatching when the plant manager was on vacation. Being involved in the operations of the company allowed me to see the constant waste of time and money that resulted from day-to-day planning. I finally came up with a plan I thought would allow me to advance within the company and get out of my truck and off the road. I went to the president of the company with my proposal, which could have saved the company twice my wages each year in transportation costs. His response was, "our company is not large enough to have a transportation manager and you have no education." Obviously he believed that without an education driving trucks was the only job I was qualified to do. However, for me, driving trucks for thirty-five more years was not a career; it was only a job that was never finished. I realized that with an education, the open road could have a completely different meaning; education is a through road not a dead end.

After making the decision to return to school, my wife and I devised a plan to organize our finances. Returning to school is not something you "just do" when you have financial obligations and a family. Our plan consisted of using my income for the next two years to pay off our vehicles, and saving enough money to cover college tuition for four years by investing with a financial advisor. The two years before starting college really prepared us for what it would be like to live on one income.

In June of 2002 I gave a six-month notice to my employer and told him why I had decided to return to school. I explained that his comment on education and advancing within the company influenced my decision. He was quite shocked and said, "you're smarter than most of the people working here." I lost a lot of respect for him that day because he had great employees who were very smart and did an outstanding job for the company. I applied to Modesto Junior College and started in January of 2003.

Although I graduated from high school in 1981, I had no study skills and was in no way prepared for college courses. My major was civil engineering. Almost immediately I wondered if I had made the right decision to return to school; it was much more work than driving a truck. The list of classes that I needed in order to transfer to a four-year college was long due to my low scores on the college placement test. After completing an educational plan, I decided to complete four years at Modesto before transferring as a second semester junior to a university.

Now a full paragraph is devoted to the challenges of starting college

New details

There are real challenges in returning to school after working for over twenty years. One of the biggest I am faced with is what, or how, I am contributing to my family? My wife continually encourages me in my studies and assures me that I am contributing to our family's future. Furthermore, her education has allowed her to have a job as a schoolteacher that provides wages and benefits that support our family as I attend school. My parents have become very supportive as they realize the importance of an education. Also, the hard work is much more rewarding than truck driving ever was. At the end of each semester the challenge is rewarded with a completed class and a good grade.

Conclusion added: he reflects on his experience

In conclusion, though it is clear to me that work was easier than school, I believe the reward at the end of the academic road will be greater. To complete a semester and maintain a 3.9 GPA is more rewarding to me than a paycheck at the end of the week. As I travel to and from school each day I pass by the company I used to work for; occasionally I stop and visit. I miss the work, however, I don't miss the idea that there was nothing else in life. I now realize that work actually prepared me for college. I feel that older students have an advantage over young students. Professors know I am here for "me" not "my parents," and I have something to contribute to their classes. Work experience is the best foundation for many courses offered in college, and the biggest advantage to being an older student is applying that experience to my education.

## How to Know What to Revise: Peer Review

**Peer review** means asking one or more of your classmates to read and comment on your writing. It is an excellent way to find out what is good and what needs to be improved in your draft. For more information on how to find a reviewer, what to ask your reviewer, and how to be a good reviewer, see "Writing Success Starts Here!" on pp. xxxiii–xlvi.

## EXERCISE 1-8
### *Writing in Progress*

**Directions:** Pair up with a classmate for this exercise. Read and evaluate each other's paragraphs written for Exercise 1-5, p. 13.

---

### Tips for Revising

Use these suggestions to revise effectively:

1. **Reread the sentence that expresses your main point.** It must be clear, direct, and complete. Experiment with ways to improve it.

2. **Reread each of your other sentences.** Does each relate directly to your main point? If not, cross it out or rewrite it to clarify its connection to the main point. If all your sentences suggest a main point that is different from the one you've written, rewrite the topic sentence or thesis statement.

3. **Make sure your writing has a beginning and an end.** A paragraph should have a clear topic sentence and concluding statement. An essay should have introductory and concluding portions, their length depending on the length of your essay.

4. **Replace words that are vague or unclear with more specific or descriptive words.**

5. **Seek advice.** If you are unsure about how to revise, visit your instructor during office hours and ask for advice, or try peer review. Ask a classmate or friend to read your paper and mark ideas that are unclear or need further explanation.

6. **When you have finished revising, you should feel satisfied with what you have said and with the way you have said it.** You will learn additional strategies for revising in Chapter 5.

## EXERCISE 1-9

*Writing in Progress*

**Directions:** Revise the first draft you wrote for Exercise 1-7, following steps 1 through 6 above.

## Proofreading Your Final Draft

Proofreading is a final reading of your paper to check for errors. In this final polishing of your work, the focus is on correctness, so don't proofread until all your rethinking of ideas and revision is done. When you are ready to proofread your writing you should check for errors in:

- sentences (run-ons or fragments)

- grammar

- spelling

- punctuation

- capitalization

Beginning with the next chapter, you will find "Skill Refreshers" that provide a quick review of sentence basics. Part VI, "Reviewing the Basics," gives more detailed information on each topic.

The following tips will ensure that you don't miss any errors:

1. **Review your paper once for each type of error.** First, read it for run-on sentences and fragments. Take a short break, and then read it four more times, each time paying attention to one of the following: spelling, punctuation, grammar, and capitalization.

2. **To spot spelling errors, read your paper from last sentence to first sentence and from last word to first word.** Reading in this way, you will not get distracted by the flow of ideas, so you can focus on spotting errors. Also use the spelling checker on your computer, but be sure to proofread for the kinds of errors it cannot catch: missing words, errors that are themselves words (such as *of* for *or*), and homonyms (for example, using *it's* for *its*).

3. **Read each sentence aloud, slowly and deliberately.** This technique will help you catch endings that you have left off verbs or missing plurals.

4. **Check for errors one final time after you print out your paper.** Don't do this when you are tired; you might introduce new mistakes. Ask a classmate or friend to read your paper to catch any mistakes you missed.

Here is a paragraph that shows the errors that a student corrected during proofreading. Notice that errors in grammar, punctuation, and spelling were corrected.

> The Robert Burns said that the dog is mans best friend. To a large extent, this statement may be more true than we thinks. What makes dogs so special to human is they're unending loyalty and their unconditional love. Dogs have been known to cross the entire United states to return home. Never make fun of you or criticize you Or throw fits, and they are always happey to see you. Dogs never lye to you, never betray your confidences, and never stays angry with you for more than five minutes. World would be a better place if only people could be more like dogs.

Chapter 5, p. 118, shows you how to keep a proofreading error log and includes a proofreading checklist. See also the proofreading checklist printed inside this book's back cover.

## EXERCISE 1-10
*Writing in Progress*

**Directions:** Prepare and proofread the final version of the paragraph you have developed throughout this chapter.

## Benefits of the Five-Step Writing Process

Both college and workplace writers use the five-step writing process described in this chapter: generating ideas, organizing ideas, writing a draft, revising, and proofreading. An exception is e-mail, which usually is not as carefully planned ahead or as extensively revised. In-class essay exams, too, are an exception, since there is little time for revision (see Chapter 15).

Using the five-step writing process will yield positive results both in college and in the workplace. In college, your papers represent you. A poorly planned paper or a disorganized essay suggests that you did not think through your ideas or did not grasp how your ideas could fit together.

In the workplace, your writing not only represents *you*, it represents your company as well. An error-filled letter or report can be damaging. It calls into question your competency and creates a negative image of your company. Study the following two versions of a letter written by a sales associate to confirm a customer's order. What impression does each give of the writer and of the company she works for?

## Version 1

> Dear Mr. Franklyn,
>
> I recieved your order for 250 cases of drink mix. As you requested, we will ship them immediatly, we will ship them to your baltimore plant and charge your account for express service. The shipment will go by UPS. Thank you.
>
> Sincerely,
>
> *Lisa*
>
> Lisa Morton

## Version 2

> Dear Mr. Franklyn:
>
> Thank you for your order of 250 cases of Top Choice Sugar-Free Drink Mix in assorted flavors. As you requested, we will ship immediately by overnight UPS to your Baltimore plant and charge your account for express service.
>
>    If I can be of help in any other way, please let me know. We are glad to have your business.
>
> Sincerely,
>
> *Lisa Morton*
>
> Lisa Morton

## Considering Your Audience and Purpose

In an earlier section of the chapter, you saw that among the characteristics of good writing are "Good Writing Is Directed Toward an Audience" and "Good Writing Achieves a Purpose."

## Considering Your Audience

When you write, ask yourself, Who will be reading what I write? How should I express myself so that my readers will understand what I write? Considering your audience is essential to good writing.

What is appropriate for one audience may be inappropriate for another. For example, if you were writing about a car accident that you were involved in, you would write one way to a close friend and another way to your professor. Because your friend knows you well, she would be interested in all of the details. Conversely, because you and your professor don't know each other well, she would want to know less about your feelings about the accident and more about how it would affect your course work. Study the following excerpts. What differences do you notice?

### *E-mail to a Friend:*

> Jeff was driving the car. As we got to Cedar Road, the light turned red. Jeff was changing the radio station because Sue hates country music, and I guess he didn't notice. I yelled, "Stop!" but he went through the intersection and a van hit the back of the car. I was terrified and I felt sick. Fortunately, we were all OK. Jeff felt really terrible, especially because by the time we got to school, I had missed my biology exam.

### *Note to a Professor:*

> I missed the exam today because I was involved in a car accident. Although I was not injured, I didn't arrive on campus in time for class. Please allow me to make up the exam. I will stop by your office tomorrow during your office hours to talk.

While the e-mail to the friend is casual and personal, the note to the professor is businesslike and direct. The writer included details and described his feelings when telling his friend about the car accident, but focused on missing the exam in his note to his professor.

Writers make many decisions based on the audience they have in mind. As you write, consider:

- how many and what kinds of details are appropriate.

- what format is appropriate (for example, paragraph, essay, letter, or memo).

- how many and what types of examples should be used.

- how formal the writing should be.

- what kinds of words should be used (straightforward, technical, or emotional).

- what tone the writing should have; that is, how it should sound to readers (for example, friendly, distant, knowledgeable, or angry).

Audience is as important in the workplace as it is in personal and academic writing. You would write differently to a manager within your company than you would to a customer outside it, as the following two e-mail messages show.

### E-mail Message 1: Salesperson to Customer

| | |
|---|---|
| Subject: | Replacement Shipment of Norfolk Pine Trees |
| Date: | April 4, 2006 |
| From: | Jwatts@pcs.net |
| To: | TimRodney@bmy.com |

Hi, Tim,

I am sorry that you were displeased with our recent shipment of Norfolk pines. I cannot imagine how they could have become infested with aphids, since they were insect-free at point of shipment. Because we value your continued business, we are happy to ship a replacement order. The new shipment should arrive in the next 3–5 business days. If I can be of further help, please be sure to call or write.

Jim Watts

Farm Manager

Highland Tree Farms

(555) 123-7596

### E-mail Message 2: Salesperson to District Manager

| | |
|---|---|
| Subject: | Replacement Shipment to Rodney's Nursery |
| Date: | April 4, 2006 |
| From: | Jwatts@pcs.net |
| To: | Tbrown@highlandtrees.com |

Tim at Rodney's Nursery claims to have received an aphid-infested shipment of Norfolk pines, but of course we know they were infested after delivery. (The conditions are so bad there that I am amazed any plant survives more than a few weeks.) Because Tim is one of our best customers, I decided to ship a replacement order, even though he's trying to con us on this one. Hope this decision is OK with you.

Jim Watts

Farm Manager

Highland Tree Farms

(555) 123-7596

Both messages are casually written, since e-mail is a less formal method of communication than letters. Notice, however, that the information in each differs, as does the tone.

Here are four key questions that will help you address your audience appropriately in the workplace as well as in academic situations:

- Who is your audience and what is your relationship with that audience?

- How will the audience likely react to your message?

- What does the audience already know about the situation?

- What does the audience need to know about the situation?

In later chapters, you will learn more about adapting your writing to your audience and see how writers address specific audiences.

## Writing for a Purpose

When you call a friend on the phone, you have a reason for calling, even if it is just to stay in touch. When you ask a question in class, you have a purpose for asking. When you describe to a friend an incident you were involved in, you are relating the story to make a point or share an experience. These examples demonstrate that you use spoken communication to achieve specific purposes.

Good writing must also achieve your *intended purpose.* If you write a paragraph on how to change a flat tire, your reader should be able to change a flat tire after reading the paragraph. Likewise, if your purpose is to describe the sun rising over a misty mountaintop, your reader should be able to visualize the scene. If your purpose is to argue that the legal age for drinking alcohol should be twenty-five, your reader should be able to follow your reasoning, even if he or she is not won over to your view.

Purpose is important in both workplace writing and academic writing. The two e-mail messages just shown reveal two very different purposes. The first message, to the nursery, is intended to keep good relations with a customer who claims that he received infested trees. Yet, at the same time, the salesperson wants to suggest that the customer's claim is suspicious. The second e-mail, to the district manager, is intended to explain why a replacement shipment was sent, even though the claim was not legitimate.

In later chapters, you will learn more about writing to achieve your purpose. The chapter readings will also show you how other writers accomplish their purposes.

## EXERCISE 1-11

**Directions:** Think of a public event you have attended recently, such as a concert or film showing. Complete two of the following activities:

1. Write a paragraph describing the event to a friend.

2. Write a paragraph describing the event to your English instructor.

3. Write a paragraph describing the event as the movie or music critic for your local newspaper.

# CHAPTER REVIEW AND PRACTICE

## Chapter Review

| | |
|---|---|
| WHAT ARE THE STEPS IN THE WRITING PROCESS? | The five steps are<br>• generating ideas.<br>• organizing ideas.<br>• writing a first draft.<br>• revising.<br>• proofreading. |
| WHAT TECHNIQUES CAN HELP YOU GENERATE IDEAS? | The techniques are freewriting, branching, brainstorming, and questioning. |
| HOW CAN YOU ORGANIZE YOUR IDEAS? | Look for relationships among ideas, and present ideas logically, building upon another. Use idea maps to create a visual diagram of the relationship among your ideas. |
| WHEN WRITING A FIRST DRAFT, WHAT IS YOUR GOAL? | A first draft should express your ideas in sentence and paragraph form. Focus on ideas, not on grammar, spelling, and punctuation. |
| WHAT DOES REVISION INVOLVE? | Revision involves rethinking your ideas and evaluating how effectively you have expressed them. Revise your draft by adding, deleting, changing, and reorganizing your ideas. |
| WHAT IS PROOFREADING? | Proofreading is checking your paper for errors in sentence structure, grammar, spelling, punctuation, and capitalization. |
| WHAT TWO FACTORS SHOULD YOU CONSIDER REGARDLESS OF WHAT YOU WRITE? | Consider the audience to whom your writing is directed and your purpose for writing. |

## INTERNET ACTIVITIES

### 1.   Writer's Block

Sometimes it is hard to get started on a writing assignment. Read over and print out the tips at this site from Brigham Young University–Idaho for overcoming writer's block.

http://www.byui.edu/WritingCenter/webpages/Writer's%20Block.htm

Mark which ones you may have tried in the past with success. Then mark the ones you think might work for you in the years to come. Keep this list handy for future reference.

### 2.   Peer Review Suggestions

Examine the ideas for peer reviewing of student papers from Vanderbilt University at

http://www.vanderbilt.edu/cwp/PeerReview.htm#list

and the University of Hawaii at Manoa at

http://mwp01.mwp.hawaii.edu/peer_review.htm#developforms.

Compare the methods that are presented, especially the sample materials. What do you think would be the most valuable way to perform peer reviews? Explain your answer.

### 3.   The Importance of College Writing

In an online guide the writing center at the University of Maryland University College explains why there is so much emphasis on writing in college.

http://www.umuc.edu/prog/ugp/ewp_writingcenter/writinggde/chapter1/chapter1-03.shtml

Read this section over and summarize the information it presents about college writing.

### 4.   Choosing a Subject

Read through this information about getting started with a topic from the Paradigm Online Writing Assistant.

http://www.powa.org/discover/index.html

Complete the activities that the author provides.

### 5.   This Book's Web Site

Visit this book's Web site for additional practice on skills taught in this chapter.

http://www.ablongman.com/mcwhorterexpressways1e

# The Active Reading Process

## Write About It!

Study the two photographs above. Write a sentence explaining how they are different. One photograph shows sports fans actively involved with the game they are watching. The second photo shows spectators who seem less involved. The first set of fans is active and involved with the events on the field. They direct the plays, criticize the calls, encourage the players, and reprimand the coaches. They care enough to get actively engaged with the game. Just like interested fans, active readers get involved. They question, challenge, and criticize, as well as understand what they are reading. As a reader, you will be more successful if you become actively involved with what you read. This chapter will give you valuable tips on how to become an active, successful reader. Active reading is important in many aspects of your life, as shown below.

EVERYDAY SCENARIOS

- **Reading** your credit card statement for accuracy
- **Reading** the terms of your auto insurance policy before accepting it

ACADEMIC SCENARIOS

- **Reading** an assigned article in *Newsweek* on taser guns for a class discussion
- **Reading** an exam essay question to determine what to include in your answer

WORKPLACE SCENARIOS

- **Reading** your yearly performance evaluation before responding to it in writing
- **Reading** required worker safety regulations before starting a new job

# READING ACTIVELY

Active readers are involved with what they are reading. They interact with the author and his or her ideas. Table 2-1 contrasts the active strategies of

Table 2-1  **Active Versus Passive Reading**

| Active Readers . . . | Passive Readers . . . |
| --- | --- |
| Tailor their reading strategies to suit each assignment. | Read all assignments the same way. |
| Analyze the purpose of a reading assignment. | Read an assignment *because* it was assigned. |
| Adjust their reading speed to suit their purposes. | Read everything at the same speed. |
| Question ideas in the assignment. | Accept whatever is in print as true. |
| Skim the headings or introduction and conclusion to find out what an assignment is about before beginning to read. | Check the length of an assignment and then begin reading. |
| Make sure they understand what they are reading as they go along. | Read until the assignment is completed. |
| Read with pencil in hand, highlighting, jotting notes, and marking key vocabulary. | Simply read. |
| Develop personalized strategies that are particularly effective. | Follow routine, standard methods. |

successful readers with the passive ones of less successful readers. Throughout the remainder of this chapter and this book, you will discover specific strategies for becoming a more active reader and learner. Not all strategies work for everyone. Experiment to discover those that work for you.

## EXERCISE 2-1

**Directions:** Rate each of the following statements as either helpful (H) or not helpful (NH) in reading actively. Then discuss how each of the statements marked NH could be changed to be more helpful.

NH ___ 1. Beginning to write an essay without reviewing the chapter in which is it assigned

NH ___ 2. Giving yourself a maximum of one hour to write an essay

H ___ 3. Using different techniques to read different types of essays

H ___ 4. Highlighting important new words in an essay

NH ___ 5. Rereading an essay the same way as many times as necessary to understand it

## Previewing Before Reading

Previewing is a way of learning what a reading is about before you actually read it. It is like looking at a map before driving in an unfamiliar city. By reading brief, selected portions of an essay, you can discover a great deal about its content and its organization. You become familiar with its layout so that you can understand it more easily as you read. Previewing is not time consuming.

### How to Preview

You can preview a brief essay in two or three minutes by following these basic steps:

- **Read and think about the title.** What does it tell you about the subject? Does it offer any clues about how the author feels about the subject or how he or she will approach it?

- **Check out the author.** Read any biographical information about the author that is provided with the article. Is the author's name familiar? If so, what do you know about him or her?

- **Read the first paragraph.** Here the author introduces the subject. Look for a statement of the main point of the entire reading.

- **Read all bold headings.** Headings divide the reading into pieces and announce the topic of each section.

- **Read the first sentence under each heading.** This sentence often states the main point of the section.

- **Read the first sentence of each paragraph.** You will discover many of the main ideas of the article in the opening sentences of the paragraphs. If the reading consists of very short paragraphs, read the first sentence of every third or fourth paragraph.

- **Read the last paragraph.** Often this paragraph summarizes or concludes the reading.

The more you practice previewing, the more effective you will find it. You will find that an essay is easier to read if you have previewed it. You will also discover that you are able to remember more of what you read if you preview and then read. Be sure to use previewing for all of your college textbooks and assigned readings.

## Demonstration of Previewing

The following essay, taken from the book titled *Never Be Lied to Again,* has been highlighted to show you what to read while previewing. Preview it now, reading only the highlighted sections.

### Body Language: Never Be Lied to Again
### David J. Lieberman

Our fingers, hands, arms, and legs and their movements offer a fascinating insight into our true feelings. Most people aren't aware that their body speaks a language all its own; try as they will to deceive you with their words, the truth can be always silently observed.

You may already have read or heard about some of these clues, but they are only a small portion of the tactics that you will learn.

### The Language of the Eyes

No or little direct eye contact is a classic sign of deception. A person who is lying to you will do everything to avoid making eye contact. Unconsciously he feels you will be able to see through him—via his eyes. And feeling guilty, he doesn't want to face you. Instead he will glance down or his eyes may dart from side to side. Conversely, when we tell the truth or we're offended by a false accusation, we tend to give our full focus and have fixed concentration. We lock eyes with our accuser as if to say "You're not getting away until we get to the bottom of this."

### The Body Never Lies

### Lacking Animation

The hands and arms are excellent indicators of deceit because they are used to gesture with and are more easily visible than our feet and legs. But hands, arms, legs, and feet can *all* give us information if we're watching carefully. When someone is lying or keeping something in, he tends to be less expressive with his hands or arms. He may keep them on his lap if he's sitting, or at his side if he's standing; he may stuff his hands in his pockets or clench them. Fingers may be folded into the hands; full extension of the fingers is usually a gesture of openness.

Have you ever noticed that when you're passionate about what you're saying, your hands and arms wave all about, emphasizing your point and conveying your enthusiasm? And have you ever realized that when you don't believe in what you're saying, your body language echoes these feelings and becomes inexpressive?

Additionally, if you ask someone a question and her hands clench or go palm down, this is a sign of defensiveness and withdrawal. If she is genuinely confused at the accusations or the line of questioning, her hands turn palm-up as if to say "Give me more information; I do not understand," or "I have nothing to hide."

### Keeping Something In

When a person sits with his legs and arms close to his body, perhaps crossed but not outstretched, he is evincing the thought *I'm keeping something in*. His arms and legs may be crossed because he feels he must defend himself. When we feel comfortable and confident we tend to stretch out—claim our space, as it were. When we feel less secure, we take up less physical space and fold our arms and legs into our bodies, into what is almost a fetal position.

### Displaying Artificial Movements

Arm movements and gestures seem stiff and almost mechanical. This behavior can be readily observed by watching unpolished actors and politicians. They try to use gestures to convince us that they're impassioned about their beliefs, but there's no fluidity to their movements. The movements are contrived, not natural.

### The Unconscious Cover-up

If her hand goes straight to her face while she is responding to a question or when she is making a statement, this is often an indication of deceit. Her hand may cover her mouth while she is speaking, indicating that she really doesn't believe what she is saying to be true; it acts as a screen, an unconscious attempt to hide her words.

When she is listening she covers or touches her face as an unconscious manifestation of the thought *I really don't want to be listening to this.* Touching the nose is also considered to be a sign of deception, as well as scratching behind or on the ear or rubbing the eyes.

This should not be confused with posture associated with deep thought, which usually conveys concentration and attention.

### The Partial Shrug

The shrugging of one's shoulders is a gesture that usually indicates ignorance or indifference: "I don't know" or "I don't care." If a person makes this gesture he or she usually means to communicate that very message. However, if this gesture is fleeting—if you catch only a glimpse of it—it's a sign of something else. This person is trying to demonstrate the she is casual and relaxed about her answer, when in fact she really isn't. Because what she feels isn't a true emotion, she doesn't really shrug.

This situation is similar to that of someone who is embarrassed by a joke but wants to pretend that she thinks it's funny. What you see is a "lips only" smile, not a big grin encompassing her entire face.

### Summary

- The person will make little or no eye contact.
- Physical expression will be limited, with few arm and hand movements. What arm and hand movements are present will seem stiff, and mechanical. Hands, arms, and legs pull in toward the body; the individual takes up less space.
- His hand(s) may go up to his face or throat. But contact with his body is limited to these areas. He is also unlikely to touch his chest with an open hand gesture.
- If he is trying to appear casual and relaxed about his answer, he may shrug a little.

What did you learn about the essay from your preview? To find out how valuable previewing can be, try the following quiz in Exercise 2-2. You will find that you can answer many or all of the questions, indicating that you did learn a great deal by previewing.

## EXERCISE 2-2

**Directions:** Answer each question by marking T for True of F for False. When you have finished, check your answers on p. 39.

____T____    **1.** You can often spot a liar by studying his or her body language.

| | |
|---|---|
| __F__ | **2.** A liar will usually make direct eye contact. |
| __T__ | **3.** Hand and arm gestures may reveal that someone is lying. |
| __T__ | **4.** Crossed legs and folded arms suggest that a person has something to hide. |
| __F__ | **5.** Touching one's face is not usually an indicator of deceit. |

## EXERCISE 2-3

**Directions:** Match the previewing step listed in Column A with the type of information it provides in Column B. Use each item only once. Write the letter of your choice in the space provided.

COLUMN A

__b__   **1.** first paragraph

__e__   **2.** bold headings

__d__   **3.** section headings

__c__   **4.** last paragraph

__a__   **5.** title

COLUMN B

**a.** identifies the subject

**b.** provides an overview

**c.** summarizes the article

**d.** identify and separate main topics

**e.** indicate important information

## EXERCISE 2-4
### *Reading and Writing in Progress*

**Directions:** Choose a professional reading from Part V, "A Multicultural Reader." Preview the reading, using the steps listed above, and answer the following questions:

1. What is the topic of the reading?

2. What main point does the reading make about the topic?

3. What did you already know about the topic?

## Making Predictions

After previewing a reading assignment, you can make predictions about its content and organization. Specifically, you can anticipate what topics will be covered and how they will be presented. Ask the following questions to sharpen your previewing skills and strengthen your recall of what you read:

- How difficult is the material?

- How is it organized?

- What is the overall subject and how is it approached?

- What type of material is it (instructional material, a sample student essay, a model professional essay)?

- Why was this material assigned?

## EXERCISE 2-5
*Reading and Writing in Progress*

**Directions:** For the reading you chose in Exercise 2-4, answer the three questions above, under the heading "Making Predictions."

## Reading to Learn: Chapters, Student Essays, and Professional Essays

Before you begin reading a chapter or an assigned essay, it is helpful if you decide what you want to learn from it. By determining what to look for as you read, you will find that you learn and remember more than if you just read material because it is assigned.

In this book you should read the instructional material, the sample student writing, and the model professional essays differently and with different purposes.

### Reading Chapters in This Book

The instructional portion of each chapter teaches you specific writing skills. Chapter 3, for example, teaches you how to write a topic sentence—a sentence that states what a paragraph is about. Your focus when working through each of these chapters should be to understand each skill and to find out how to apply the skill in your own writing. Use the exercises in the chapter to help you test out the skill before you use it in a new piece of writing. Here are some specific suggestions:

1. **Plan on rereading.** After previewing the chapter, read it once to get a general understanding of the skills taught. Read it again with a "how-to" focus, paying attention to how to apply the skills to your own writing.

2. **Decide what it is you want and need to learn from the chapter.**

3. **As you read each chapter, read with a highlighter in hand.** Mark useful information that you can use when you write. Use the sticky note "Important: Review This" to mark sections that you will want to refer to frequently.

4. **Pay attention to examples.** The examples show you how a skill works and how it can be applied.

5. **Use the exercises to try out or test the skill before writing a paragraph or essay in which you use the skill.**

6. **Use the "Visualize It!" sections.** These sections contain idea maps and diagrams that show you how to create a mental picture of the organization of a piece of writing. Use them as a model, and draw similar maps of ideas you plan to include in your own writing.

## EXERCISE 2-6

**Directions:** Using Chapter 3 of this book, or another chapter assigned by your instructor, complete the following:

1. Preview the chapter.

2. Read the instructional portion of the chapter (everything that comes before the professional reading).

3. Identify each of the following sections:

   a. "Visualize It!"

   b. Workplace Scenario

   c. Examples

   d. Exercises

Determine what each section contributes to the chapter and how they can help you learn.

## Reading Student Sample Essays

The student essays included in the Academic Scenarios are intended to be realistic models of good writing. They are not perfect, but they are acceptable. The student essays also illustrate the writing techniques taught in the chapters in which they appear. The student essay in Chapter 3, "Writing Topic Sentences," was chosen because it demonstrates the use of effective topic sentences. Here are some suggestions for reading and learning from the sample student essays:

1. **Read the essay first to understand the writer's message.** Then, once you understand it, focus on aspects of writing. In particular, determine how it illustrates the skills taught in the chapter in which it is included.

2. **Plan on reading the essay several times, each time for a different purpose.** For example, you might read it once noticing how the paragraphs are organized and read it again later noticing the vocabulary the writer uses.

3. **Read with this question in mind: What techniques does this writer use that I can use in my own writing?**

4. **Read with a highlighter in hand.** Mark sentences, paragraphs, words, or phrases that you want to look at again, that you think are particularly effective, or that you want to use.

5. **Study the annotations.** The marginal notes are intended to call your attention to specific techniques or writing strategies.

*Doug Mello, Modesto Junior College, Modesto, California*

Author provides background on his situation

Different meaning of "road" introduced

Sentence that states what the essay will be about

Background of job

Quotation used to make situation real

Word signals contrasting ideas will follow

Here is a portion of the student essay that you read in Chapter 1. The annotations show some of the things you might notice as you study the essay. You will learn more about these features as you work through this book.

Reference to truck driving

## Excerpt from Education: The Open Road by Doug Mello

Coming from a working class family, the option of pursuing an education was, for me, not a choice. Going to work after high school was my only choice and also what my parents expected of me. One of the first jobs I had provided me with the opportunity to acquire a commercial driver's license, which allowed me to become a truck driver. Due to a good driving record and work history, my employment and wages always seemed to get better as I searched for the perfect truck-driving job. At the age of twenty-nine, a company hired me that I thought offered a promising career future. However, what I failed to see was where this particular road would take me. After several years I found that there were no opportunities for advancement within the company. I realized, at this point in my life, that an education could offer challenges, opportunities, and a career that would last a lifetime.

There was one particular event that that led to my decision to get an education. After five years with the company I was frequently asked for advice on routing schedules and was assigned the job of dispatching when the plant manager was on vacation. Being involved in the operations of the company allowed me to see the constant waste of time and money that resulted from day-to-day planning. I finally came up with a plan I thought would allow me to advance within the company and get out of my truck and off the road. I went to the president of the company with my proposal, which could have saved the company twice my wages each year in transportation costs. His response was, "our company is not large enough to have a transportation manager and you have no education." Obviously he believed that without an education driving trucks was the only job I was qualified to do. However, for me, driving trucks for thirty-five more years was not a career; it was only a job that was never finished. I realized that with an education, the open road could have a completely different meaning; education is a through road not a dead end.

## Reading Professional Essays

The professional essays at the end of each chapter are models of good writing. By studying the writing of professional writers, you can improve your own writing. You will need to read the essays several times. On the

first few readings, you should concentrate on understanding the message the writer is communicating. The section following each reading, titled "Examining the Reading," is intended to help you assess whether you grasp the writer's message. Then, once you are confident that you understand the reading, you are ready to examine the writing techniques used. Most importantly, look for techniques that the writer uses that you could use in your own writing. Here are a few specific suggestions:

1. **Read the "Thinking Before Reading" section that comes before the reading.** It is intended to help you get into the reading by telling you a little about the author and the reading itself. Answer the questions that ask you to connect the reading to your own experience. These will help you recall ideas and experiences that you can relate to the reading, in order to help you understand it better.

2. **Identify the writer's purpose.** Study how he or she achieves it.

3. **Study the title.** What does it reveal about the essay's content or purpose?

4. **Examine the essay's introduction.** It should do three things: 1) provide needed background information, 2) get you interested in the reading, and 3) state the essay's main point. Observe how the writer accomplishes these things.

5. **Examine the body of the essay.** Study how the writer supports his or her main points.

6. **Examine how paragraphs are organized.** How does the writer state and develop the main point of each paragraph? How are these main points explained or developed?

7. **Examine the sentences the writer creates.** How are the sentences similar to and different from those you write? Are there some sentence patterns you could model?

8. **Examine the writer's use of vocabulary.** What words/phrases seem particularly effective? How could you use them? Use the words listed in the "Strengthening Your Vocabulary" exercise that follows the reading as a guide.

9. **Examine the essay's conclusion.** Observe how the writer draws the essay to a close. Could you use this technique?

## EXERCISE 2-7
*Reading and Writing in Progress*

**Directions:** Read the essay you chose in Exercise 2-4 using two of the suggestions given above. List the two suggestions that you have chosen here.

1. _____

2. _____

## Using Idea Maps to Understand Readings

An idea map is a visual picture of the organization and content of an essay. It is a drawing that enables you to see what is included in an essay in a brief, outline form. Idea maps are used throughout this book for both reading and writing. For reading, you can use them to help you understand a reading—discover how it is organized and study how ideas relate to one another. For writing, an idea map can help you organize your own ideas and check to be sure that all the ideas you have included belong in the essay. (For more about using idea maps for writing, see p. 49 in this chapter.)

An idea map for the essay on p. 31 is shown below.

**Visualize It!**

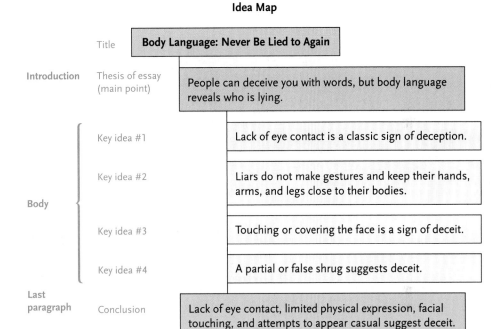

**Idea Map**

| | |
|---|---|
| Title | **Body Language: Never Be Lied to Again** |
| Introduction — Thesis of essay (main point) | People can deceive you with words, but body language reveals who is lying. |
| Body — Key idea #1 | Lack of eye contact is a classic sign of deception. |
| Key idea #2 | Liars do not make gestures and keep their hands, arms, and legs close to their bodies. |
| Key idea #3 | Touching or covering the face is a sign of deceit. |
| Key idea #4 | A partial or false shrug suggests deceit. |
| Last paragraph — Conclusion | Lack of eye contact, limited physical expression, facial touching, and attempts to appear casual suggest deceit. |

Notice how easily and quickly you can see what the essay is about and how it is organized. By filling in an idea map for a reading, you are reviewing the reading and analyzing its structure. Both of these activities will help you remember what you read. Though it takes time to draw, an idea map will save you time in the long run. You can avoid rereading, and the content of the essay will stick in your mind, preparing you for class discussions and writing about the reading. Use the model below to draw idea maps. (These models also appear on the book's Web site, at http://www.ablongman .com/mcwhorterexpressways1e.) You may need to add extra boxes or you may not need all the boxes included, depending on the number of ideas and details in the essay. The sample idea map above and the model on the next page show only the essay's main point (thesis) and the key ideas. You can draw idea maps that include details as well, if it suits your purpose.

Answers to Exercise 2-2: 1. T; 2. F; 3. T; 4. T; 5. F

# Visualize It!

**Model for Idea Map**

```
                              ┌─────────────────────────┐
                              │          Title          │
                              └─────────────────────────┘
                                          │
    Introduction          ┌───────────────────────────────┐
                          │  Thesis (main point) of essay  │
                          └───────────────────────────────┘
                                          │
                              ┌─────────────────────────┐
                           ┌  │  Topic sentence (key idea)  │
                              └─────────────────────────┘
                              ┌─────────────────────────┐
                              │  Topic sentence (key idea)  │
                              └─────────────────────────┘
    Body                                              
                              ┌─────────────────────────┐
                              │  Topic sentence (key idea)  │
                              └─────────────────────────┘
                              ┌─────────────────────────┐
                           └  │  Topic sentence (key idea)  │
                              └─────────────────────────┘
    Last                  ┌───────────────────────────────┐
    paragraph             │     Conclusion (or summary)    │
                          └───────────────────────────────┘
```

## EXERCISE 2-8
### Reading and Writing in Progress

**Directions:** Draw an idea map of the professional reading you chose in Exercise 2-4. Use the model shown above as a guide.

## Understanding Difficult Readings

The professional readings that end each chapter are intended to be challenging as well as models of good writing. Depending on your background knowledge and experience, you may encounter one or more readings that are difficult. Use the following suggestions to help you find new strategies for approaching a difficult reading.

1. **Analyze the time and place in which you are reading.** If you've been working for several hours, mental fatigue may be the source of the problem. If you are reading in a place with distractions or interruptions, you might not be able to understand what you are reading.

2. **Rephrase each paragraph in your own words.** You might need to approach complicated material sentence by sentence, expressing each in your own words.

3. **Read aloud sentences or sections that are particularly difficult.** Reading out loud sometimes makes complicated material easier to understand.

4. **Reread difficult or complicated sections.** In fact, sometimes several readings are appropriate and necessary.

5. **Slow down your reading rate.** On occasion, simply reading more slowly and carefully will provide you with the needed boost in comprehension.

6. **Write a brief outline of major points.** This will help you see the overall organization and progression of ideas.

7. **Highlight key ideas.** After you have read a section, go back and think about and highlight what is important. Highlighting forces you to sort out what is important, and this sorting process builds comprehension and recall.

## EXERCISE 2-9
### *Reading and Writing in Progress*

**Directions:** Consider the professional reading you read for Exercise 2-4. Write a paragraph that assesses and analyzes how using any of the above techniques could have improved your understanding of the reading.

## Reading Critically

Reading critically means questioning, reacting to, and evaluating what you read. Critical reading is an essential skill because most college instructors expect you not only to understand what you read, but to be able to respond to it critically. Critical thinking is also an essential workplace skill: employers hire people who can think, solve problems, and respond to issues.

Throughout this book, you will learn a variety of critical reading skills. Each end-of-the-chapter reading has a section titled "Thinking Critically." To develop the habit of thinking critically, use the following suggestions:

1. **Read an essay more than once.** Read it several times, if necessary, to understand the author's message; then read it again to analyze and evaluate the author's ideas.

2. **Read with a pen in your hand.** Highlight important passages or particularly meaningful or insightful sentences and phrases.

3. **Make marginal notes as you read.** Write marginal notes (sometimes called annotations) that record what you are thinking as you read. These notes will be helpful as you write about the reading.

4. **Look for evidence that supports the writer's ideas.** It is not enough for a writer to state an opinion; he or she should give you reasons or evidence to support his or her ideas.

5. **Ask questions as you read.** Question and challenge the author and the ideas presented. How do the ideas mesh or fit with your own knowledge, experience, beliefs, and values? If they do not fit, ask why. Do you need to adjust your thinking or do further reading or research on the topic?

## EXERCISE 2-10
*Reading and Writing in Progress*

**Directions:** Reread, annotate, and then write several critical questions you could ask about the reading you chose in Exercise 2-4.

## Building Your Vocabulary Through Reading

Your vocabulary is an important asset, both in college and in the workplace. Words are the vehicles or building blocks with which you express ideas both in speech and in writing. A strong vocabulary identifies you as a learned, educated person as well as an effective communicator.

### Figuring Out Unfamiliar Words

One of the best ways to improve your vocabulary is to read! Reading essays, by both professional and student authors, is an excellent way to build your vocabulary. As you read them, you will encounter words that you can use to expand your vocabulary. Use the "Strengthening Your Vocabulary" exercise that follows each reading to learn new words in the reading. You may also encounter other words in the reading that are unfamiliar to you or you may come upon uncommon uses for words you already know. As you find words that you want to make part of your writing vocabulary, circle or highlight them as you read, mark them with a sticky tab labeled "Vocabulary," and use the tips on page 43 to learn their meanings. Notice that the first step is not what you expect, which would be to look words up in a dictionary.

In addition to adding words to your vocabulary, you can also learn creative and interesting ways to use language. As you read, look for the following:

1. **Euphemisms** These are words that hide or disguise the importance, reality, or seriousness of something. (Ladies' room is a euphemism for toilet; "victim of friendly fire" is a euphemism for a soldier shot by his or her own troops.)

2. **Connotative meanings** Words have shades of meaning called connotations. These are the emotional associations that accompany words for some readers. The word "mother" has many connotative meanings. For some it means a warm, loving, caregiver. For others it may suggest a strict disciplinarian.

3. **Jargon** Jargon is specialized terminology used in a particular field of study. Football has its own jargon: linebackers, kick off, touchdown, etc. Academic disciplines also have their own language (psychology: drive, motivation, stressor).

## How to Figure Out Unfamiliar Words

Use the following steps to figure out a word you do not know:

1. **Pronounce the word.** Often, by "hearing" the word, you will recall its meaning.

2. **Try to figure out the word from its context—the words and sentences around the unfamiliar word.** Often there is a clue in the context that will help you figure out a meaning.

   > **Example:** During his lecture, the **ornithologist** described her research on western spotted owls as well as other species of birds.

   The context reveals that an ornithologist is a person who studies birds.

   Be sure to look for clues to meaning after the word, as well as before it.

   > **Example:** The elderly man walked with the help of a **prosthesis.** He was proud that his artificial limb enabled him to walk without assistance.

   The context reveals that a prosthesis is an artificial limb.

3. **Look for parts of the word that are familiar.** You may spot a familiar root (for example, in the word "improbability" you may see a variant spelling of the word "probable"), or you may recognize a familiar beginning (for example, in the word "unconventional," knowing that un- means "not" lets you figure out that the word means not conventional).

4. **If you still cannot figure out the word, mark it using a Vocabulary sticky tab and keep reading, unless the sentence does not make sense without knowing what the word means.** If it does not, then stop and look up the word in a print or online dictionary.

5. **When you finish reading, look up all the words you have marked.**

6. **After reading be sure to record, in a vocabulary log notebook or computer file, the words you figured out or looked up so you can review and use them frequently.**

4. **Foreign words and phrases** Many Latin, French, and Spanish words have entered our language and are used as if they are part of our language. Here are a few examples:

> Aficionado (Spanish) someone enthusiastic and knowledgeable about something
>
> Et cetera (Latin)—and so forth
>
> Faux pas (French)—embarrassing social blunder
>
> Guerilla (Spanish)—freedom fighter
>
> Status quo (Latin)—the way things are, an existing state of affairs
>
> Tête-à-tête (French)—a private conversation between two people

- **Figurative language** Figurative language consists of words and phrases that make sense creatively or imaginatively but not literally. The expression "The exam was a piece of cake" means, creatively, that the exam was easy, as eating cake is easy. But the exam did not literally resemble a cake. You will learn more about figurative language in Chapter 4, p. 102.

- **Neologisms** Neologisms are new words that have recently entered our language. As technology and society change, new words are created. Here are a few examples: blogs (Web logs or diaries), spamming (sending unwanted e-mail to someone), and egosurfing (searching online for information about yourself.)

## EXERCISE 2-11
### *Reading and Writing in Progress*

**Directions:** For the professional reading you chose in Exercise 2-4, list any words for which you did not know the meaning. For each word listed, write the meaning and indicate what method you used to figure it out (context, words parts, or dictionary).

| | WORD | MEANING | METHOD |
|---|---|---|---|
| 1. | _____ | _____ | _____ |
| 2. | _____ | _____ | _____ |
| 3. | _____ | _____ | _____ |

## Using Word Mapping

Word mapping is a visual method of expanding your vocabulary. It involves examining a word in detail by considering its meanings, synonyms (words similar in meaning), antonyms (words opposite in meaning), part(s) of speech, word parts, and usages. A word map is a form of word study. By the time you have completed the map, you will find that you have learned the word and are ready to use it in your speech and writing.

On the following page is a sample map for the word "intercepted."

# Visualize It!

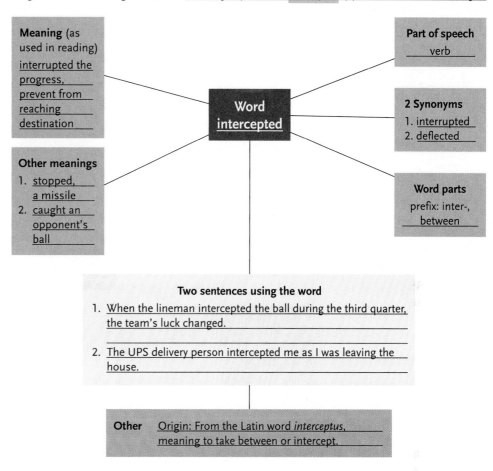

**Word Map**

**Original sentence using the word**  The drug shipment was intercepted by police at the border crossing.

**Meaning** (as used in reading) interrupted the progress, prevent from reaching destination

**Other meanings**
1. stopped, a missile
2. caught an opponent's ball

**Word intercepted**

**Part of speech** verb

**2 Synonyms**
1. interrupted
2. deflected

**Word parts** prefix: inter-, between

**Two sentences using the word**
1. When the lineman intercepted the ball during the third quarter, the team's luck changed.

2. The UPS delivery person intercepted me as I was leaving the house.

**Other**    Origin: From the Latin word *interceptus*, meaning to take between or intercept.

Use the following steps in completing a word map:

1. **When you find a word you don't know, locate the entry for the word in a dictionary.** Write the sentence in which the word appeared at the top of the map. Figure out which meaning fits the context and write it in the box labeled "Meaning (as used in reading)." Fill in the word's part of speech as used in this context.

2. **Study the dictionary entry to discover other meanings of the word.** Fill those in on the map in the box labeled "Other Meanings."

3. **Find or think of two synonyms (words similar in meaning).** You might need to use a thesaurus for this.

4. **Write two sentences using the word.**

5. **Analyze the word's parts. Identify any prefixes, roots, and suffixes.** Write the word part and its meaning in the box labeled "Word Parts."

6. **In the box labeled "Other," include any other interesting information about the word.** You might include antonyms, restrictive meanings, or the word's history or derivation).

## EXERCISE 2-12
*Reading and Writing in Progress*

**Directions:** Using a dictionary, complete the following word map for one word in the reading you chose for Exercise 2-4.

## Visualize It!

### Word Map

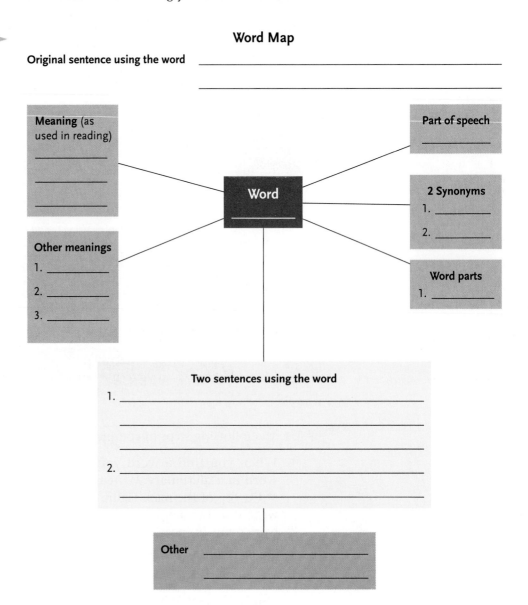

Original sentence using the word _____

_____

**Meaning** (as used in reading)

_____

_____

_____

**Other meanings**

1. _____
2. _____
3. _____

**Word**

_____

**Part of speech**

_____

**2 Synonyms**

1. _____
2. _____

**Word parts**

1. _____

**Two sentences using the word**

1. _____

_____

_____

2. _____

_____

**Other** _____

_____

## WRITING ABOUT A READING

### Thinking Before Reading

This essay first appeared in *Newsweek* magazine in August 2004. It is a good example of the kind of professional essays you will be asked to read in this book.

1. Preview the reading.

2. Connect the reading to your own experience by:

   a. brainstorming a list of acts of kindness you have performed, received, or observed.

   b. comparing it to a serious or life-threatening illness that you, a family member, or a friend have faced. What emotions did you experience?

### READING

# Saved by the Kindness of a Virtual Stranger

*My wife needed a kidney, but we didn't know how to ask friends for help. Turns out we didn't have to.*

### Mark Zelermyer

1   I grew up thinking that if miracles existed at all, they were larger than life, spectacular acts that suspended the laws of nature (think Cecil B. DeMille's "The Ten Commandments"). Even as an adult, whenever I read about some medical phenomenon that doctors were hard pressed to explain, like a late-stage tumor that disappeared long after a patient's treatment was discontinued, I chalked it up to the sort of inexplicable divine intervention that trumps macrobiotic diets and crystals. It was something to hope for in your darkest hour, perhaps, but not to expect. So when I learned that my wife would need a kidney transplant within two years, I focused on what modern medicine had to offer.

2   Her polycystic kidney disease had been controlled with medication for some 20 years, but in the spring of 2001 it began to worsen. The nephrologist explained that her best shot at regaining her health was to receive a living kidney, which would function better and longer than a cadaveric kidney. The challenge was to find a healthy person with the same type O blood who was will-

ing to undergo a regimen of tests and ultimately donate a kidney. Otherwise, she would have to start the time-consuming, punishing process of dialysis in order to get on the five-year waiting list for a cadaveric transplant.

3    I was quickly ruled out as a donor because my blood type didn't match my wife's. Her family produced no candidates either. In fact, her mother had died from complications of the same genetic disease, and her brother had received a cadaveric transplant the year before.

4    We desperately needed help, and yet we felt uncomfortable asking for it. After all, how do you ask another person to give up a kidney? We finally turned to our friends, and one of them, our rabbi, gave an impassioned appeal during Yom Kippur services. A number of congregants agreed to be tested, but all of them were eliminated after the first stage of screening. It looked as if we had hit a wall.

5    Then one evening I rode home on the train with Carolyn Hodges, a friend of mine from work. I was feeling particularly low that day, and I told her about our situation. The next day she stopped by my office and told me that she and her husband were type O's and longtime blood and platelet donors who were listed with the bone-marrow registry. They had talked it over and decided they were willing to be tested as potential matches. Carolyn was eliminated shortly thereafter, but John, whom we barely knew, emerged as the surgeon's donor of choice.

6    John is a scientist by training, and once he got the news he began diligently researching kidney disease and transplant surgery. By the time he met with the surgeon, he had compiled a list of incredibly detailed questions, the likes of which the doctor had never seen before. Most donors are blood relations who are more likely to beg the surgeon to take their kidney than grill him on the latest studies.

7    Despite his thorough research, John encountered a fair amount of resistance from his family members and close friends. They'd ask, "Why should someone in good health put himself on the line for a person he hardly knows?" But John strongly believed that this was a way for him to actively make the world a better place. He would simply tell them he had considered every potential danger and determined that the rewards—for my wife, her family and himself—outweighed the risks. He was even more reassured after talking with his daughter's teacher, who had donated a kidney to her brother years before, and his good friend who was a transplant counselor.

8    By the beginning of this past May, my wife's condition had deteriorated to the point that she was in danger of being too sick for the transplant operation. To make matters worse, the procedure required two operating rooms and a 20-person surgical team—and both were booked solid for nearly two months. We were scared.

9    Thankfully, one week later there was a last-minute cancellation, and we received word one afternoon to go to the hospital at once for pre-op work—the surgery would begin the following morning at 6:30. Without hesitation, John dropped everything and drove over.

10    I am happy to report that the operation was a success. "Little Johnny," as my wife calls her new kidney, is working exceptionally well. After John spent a few weeks recovering at home, he was able to ease back to work and resume his normal routine.

11    Except that life will never really be the way it was before the surgery for either of our families. A tremendous bond now joins us. We will forever be connected by John's generous, selfless gift of life.

12    I've learned that miracles come in myriad forms, including human. John and Carolyn Hodges are living proof.

## Getting Ready to Write

### Reviewing the Reading

1. Explain why Mrs. Zelermyer's medical condition necessitated a transplant.

2. Why was it so difficult to find a donor?

3. Why was John Hodges's family opposed to his decision?

4. How have the lives of the Zelermyers and John Hodges changed as a result of the transplant?

### Examining the Reading: Drawing an Idea Map

As described on p. 39, an idea map can help you grasp the content and organization of an essay. Drawing an idea map is also an excellent way to check your understanding and review the reading in preparation for discussing or writing about it.

Complete the following idea map of "Saved By the Kindness of a Virtual Stranger" by filling in the missing information. Because this essay relates events in story form, this map takes the form of a time line. Time lines are used to show the sequence of events.

Format for drawing time lines:

**Visualize It!**

**Model for Time Line**

Event 1

↓

Event 2

↓

Event 3

↓

Event 4

**Note:**  The number of boxes will vary from essay to essay.

# Visualize It!

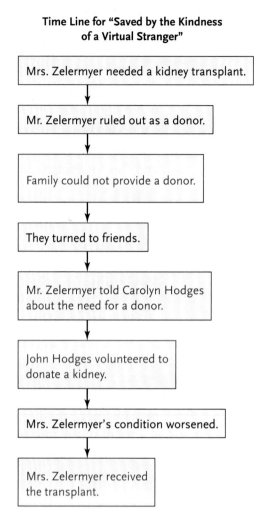

Time Line for "Saved by the Kindness
of a Virtual Stranger"

Mrs. Zelermyer needed a kidney transplant.

Mr. Zelermyer ruled out as a donor.

Family could not provide a donor.

They turned to friends.

Mr. Zelermyer told Carolyn Hodges
about the need for a donor.

John Hodges volunteered to
donate a kidney.

Mrs. Zelermyer's condition worsened.

Mrs. Zelermyer received
the transplant.

## Thinking Critically: Asking Critical Questions

An important part of thinking critically is asking questions about what you read. It is a way of expanding your thinking, as well as a way of discovering ideas to write about. Here are a few examples of critical questions you might ask about this essay. After you read and answer these, try to form a few critical questions of your own.

1. The author is writing about his wife. Do you think his perception and description of events might be colored by his emotional attachment to her? Is there evidence in the reading to suggest this?

2. What else would you like to know about John Hodges, the donor? What information might help you understand his willingness to be a donor?

3. This article was originally published in 2003. Has organ donation changed since then? That is, are people more willing to be donors, have new laws been passed to regulate organ donation, or have new cases come into the public eye?

4. Why is the author's wife, who is the donor recipient, not named?

## Strengthening Your Vocabulary

**Part A:** Using the word's context, word parts, or a dictionary, write a brief definition of each of the following words or phrases as it is used in the reading.

1. phenomenon (paragraph 1)

   _unusual occurrence_

2. inexplicable (paragraph 1)

   _difficult or impossible to explain_

3. diligently (paragraph 6)

   _making a painstaking effort_

4. deteriorated (paragraph 8)

   _grew worse_

5. congregants (paragraph 4)

   _members of a group assembled for religious worship_

**Part B:** Choose one of the above words and draw a word map of it.

## Reacting to Ideas: Discussion and Journal Writing

1. Discuss John's motivation for, and his family's reaction to, his kidney donation. Should family members have any right to prevent a relative from donating a kidney?

2. Other than through organ donations, brainstorm a list of things people could do to make the world a better place.

3. Discuss the issue of organ donation. Who should and who should not be allowed to donate? Should restrictions be placed on who can receive donated organs? Should donors be paid?

## Writing About the Reading

## Paragraph Options

1. Write a paragraph explaining whether you think miracles actually happen.

2. Write a paragraph explaining and evaluating the reasons John Hodges gave for choosing to donate his kidney.

3. Write a paragraph giving at least three reasons why you would not consider donating a kidney to a non-family member.

4. Write a paragraph describing a situation in which you helped a stranger. Describe how the act made you feel.

## Essay Options

5.  Write an essay describing a situation which might be considered as a human miracle.

6.  Write an essay describing help or assistance you received from someone unexpectedly. Discuss the possible motivations of the donor.

7.  Write an essay discussing the issue of organ sales. Give reasons why someone should or should not be allowed to sell his or her organs.

8.  Write an essay analyzing Mr. Zelermyer's attitude toward miracles and how it changed as a result of the events described in the essay.

# CHAPTER REVIEW AND PRACTICE

## Chapter Review

| | |
|---|---|
| WHAT IS ACTIVE READING? | Active reading is a method of thinking about a reading as you read it, and becoming engaged with the text. |
| WHAT IS PREVIEWING? | Previewing is a method of familiarizing yourself with the content and organization of a chapter or essay before you read it. |
| WHAT FEATURES IN THIS BOOK NEED TO BE READ IN SPECIFIC WAYS TO GET THE MOST FROM THEM? | Chapter instructional material, student essays, and professional readings each need to be read differently. |
| WHAT ARE IDEA MAPS? | Idea maps are diagrams that show the content and organization of an essay. |
| NAME TWO TECHNIQUES TO USE TO HANDLE DIFFICULT READINGS. | See numbered list under Understanding Difficult Readings heading on p. 40. |
| WHAT DOES CRITICAL READING INVOLVE? | Critical reading involves questioning and evaluating what you read. |
| HOW CAN YOU IMPROVE YOUR VOCABULARY BY READING ESSAYS? | Use context, word parts, and a dictionary to figure out words you do not know. Keep track of new words in a vocabulary log or computer file. |

## INTERNET ACTIVITIES

### 1. Academic Success and Reading

Dartmouth College offers several online handouts designed to help students read more effectively and efficiently. Two featured documents are "Six Reading Myths" and "Harvard Report on Reading." Read them over and think about how to apply these documents to your current experiences.

http://www.dartmouth.edu/~acskills/success/reading.html

### 2. How to Read an Essay

This Web site from the University of St. Thomas provides a list of questions to ask yourself when preparing to read an essay, textbook, or article. It includes a link to a useful summary sheet. Try using it on your next reading assignment.

http://www.studygs.net/reading_essays.htm

### 3. This Book's Web Site

Visit this site to find templates of idea maps and additional practice on skills taught in the chapter.

http://www.ablongman.com/mcwhorterexpressways1e

# PART II

# Paragraph Writing Strategies

# 3

# Writing Topic Sentences

## Chapter Objectives

*In this chapter you will learn to:*

1. Understand the structure of a paragraph.

2. Write effective topic sentences.

*"If you can hear me, give me a sign."*

## Write About It!

Look at the cartoon above. Write a sentence that states the main point the cartoon is making.

The sentence you have written states the main point of the cartoon—what the cartoonist intended to point out by drawing the cartoon. When you write a paragraph, you also start with the main point.

This is expressed in a sentence called the **topic sentence**. In this chapter you will learn to write effective topic sentences. You will need to be able to write effective topic sentences in a variety of situations:

---

EVERYDAY SCENARIO

- You are sending an e-mail to the technical support personnel of a computer manufacturer asking for help with a problem. Your **topic sentence** should directly state the problem.

ACADEMIC SCENARIO

- You are answering an essay exam question in sociology that asks you to briefly define and give examples of a community. Your **topic sentence** should give a brief definition of community.

WORKPLACE SCENARIO

- You are the manager of a chain restaurant and must write an incident report about a theft that occurred on premises. Your **topic sentence** should state the time, location, date, and item stolen.

---

# WRITING

## What Is a Paragraph?

The way we organize and present ideas in writing is similar to the way we present them orally. When we speak, we speak in groups of sentences. Seldom does our conversation consist of isolated statements or a series of unrelated statements. For example, you probably would *not* simply say to a friend, "I think you are making a mistake if you marry Sam." Rather, you would support your general remark by offering reasons or by giving an example of someone else who made the same kind of mistake. Similarly, in writing we group ideas into paragraphs.

A **paragraph** is a group of related sentences that develop one main thought, or idea, about a single topic. The structure of most paragraphs is not complex. There are usually two basic elements: (1) a topic sentence and (2) supporting details.

The **topic sentence** states your main point or controlling idea. The sentences that explain this main point are called **supporting details.** These details may be facts, reasons, or examples that provide further information about the topic sentence. If you were to write a paragraph based on the example above, "I think you are making a mistake if you marry Sam" would be the topic sentence and your reasons and examples would be supporting details.

Because a paragraph deals with a single idea, we say it has **unity**. A paragraph should:

- **start with the first sentence indented five letter spaces.** This spacing signals the reader that a new idea is about to begin.

- **stay focused on one idea, not switch from topic to topic.**

- **be a manageable length for your reader to digest.** Short paragraphs can seem skimpy and underdeveloped. Overly long ones can become hard for a reader to follow.

Read the following paragraph, noticing how all the details relate to one point and explain the topic sentence, which is highlighted and labeled:

Topic sentence

There is some evidence that colors affect you physiologically. For example, when subjects are exposed to red light, respiratory movements increase; exposure to blue decreases respiratory movements. Similarly, eye blinks increase in frequency when eyes are exposed to red light and decrease when exposed to blue. This seems consistent with the intuitive feelings about blue being more soothing and red being more arousing. After changing a school's walls from orange and white to blue, the blood pressure of the students decreased while their academic performance improved.

Joseph A. DeVito, *Human Communication*, p. 182

In this paragraph, look at the highlighted topic sentence. It identifies the topic as color and states that color affects you physiologically. The remaining sentences provide further information about the effects of color.

You can think about and visualize a paragraph this way:

# Visualize It!

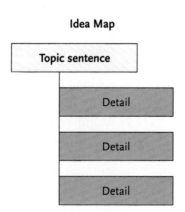

**Idea Map**

Here's how you might visualize the paragraph on color:

# Visualize It!

**Idea Map**

Colors affect people physiologically.

Respiratory movements increase in red light and decrease in blue light.

Eye blinks increase in red light and decrease in blue light.

Findings are consistent with idea that blue is soothing and red is arousing.

A change in a school's walls from orange and white to blue decreased students' blood pressure and improved academic performance.

Notice how well the topic sentence and details in the above paragraph work together to develop a main idea. The more general topic sentence is explained by the more specific details. You might ask, "How can I tell what is 'general' and what is 'specific' when I am writing?" Here are a few examples. The first three use one-word topics and details; the last two use topic sentences and detail sentences.

| | |
|---|---|
| GENERAL | emotions |
| SPECIFIC | love, fear, anger |
| GENERAL | pollution |
| SPECIFIC | air pollution, water pollution, solid waste |
| GENERAL | house building materials |
| SPECIFIC | lumber, bricks, wall board |
| GENERAL | Our insurance agent is very professional. |
| SPECIFIC | She returns calls promptly. She reviews our needs every year. She explains insurance policies in plain language. |
| GENERAL | Newspapers include a wide variety of different types of information. |
| SPECIFIC | Newspapers report world and local news events. Newspapers publish human interest stories. Newspapers advertise products and services. |

Notice that in each of these examples, the specific points explain the general by giving examples, reasons, or further information. In the same way, supporting details in your paragraph explain or support your topic sentence.

## EXERCISE 3-1

**Directions:** Complete the following sets by supplying the missing information. *Answers will vary.*

1. GENERAL    Advertisements are often misleading.

   SPECIFIC    **a.** Products often appear larger than they really are.

   **b.** _____

   **c.** _____

2. GENERAL    Television provides several types of entertainment.

   SPECIFIC    **a.** _____

   **b.** _____

   **c.** _____

3. GENERAL    _____

   SPECIFIC    **a.** Flexible work hours permit employees to work at their peak times of efficiency.

   **b.** Flexible work hours help reduce line-ups at equipment (fax machine and copier, for example).

   **c.** Flexible work hours help alleviate rush hour traffic near the office.

4. GENERAL    Many careers require specialized training.

   SPECIFIC    **a.** Nurses must learn anatomy and physiology.

   **b.** _____

   **c.** _____

5. GENERAL    _____

   SPECIFIC    **a.** Some television commercials use humor to sell their product.

   **b.** Other commercials use celebrities to convince the audience to buy the product.

   **c.** Some commercials use the message "Everyone's buying it, so why don't you?"

## Important Terms

**Paragraph:** a group of sentences that focus on a single idea

**Topic:** the one thing a paragraph is about

**Main idea:** the point the paragraph makes about a topic

**Topic sentence:** the sentence that states the paragraph's main idea

**Supporting details:** those sentences that explain the topic sentence

## Writing Effective Topic Sentences

### The Purpose of a Topic Sentence

A good topic sentence does two things:

- it makes clear what the paragraph is about—the topic.

- it expresses a view or makes a point about the topic.

In the following examples, the topic is circled and the point about the topic is underlined.

1. The first week of college is a frustrating experience.

2. Fanny's serves the best hamburgers in town.

3. State-operated lotteries are growing in popularity.

4. Time management is a vital skill in college and on the job.

## EXERCISE 3-2

**Directions:** For the following topic sentences, circle the topic and underline the view the writer takes toward the topic.

1. Sunday morning is a time for reading and relaxing.

2. My part-time job at Sears is giving me valuable sales experience.

3. Publicly funded FM radio stations need your financial support.

4. *Time,* a weekly newsmagazine, <u>presents thorough coverage of world</u> <u>events</u>.

5. Danny Everett, my favorite morning-radio personality, <u>gets my day off</u> <u>to a bright and humorous start</u>.

## EXERCISE 3-3

**Directions:** Create topic sentences by supplying a point of view about each topic. *Answers will vary. Possible answers have been provided.*

1. Shopping malls *are often appealing to teenagers.*

2. Most fast-food restaurants *are not concerned with their customers' health or nutrition.*

3. Monday morning *is a time to get organized for the week.*

4. Violence on television *may promote physical aggressiveness among young children.*

5. College professors *make sincere efforts to understand their students' needs.*

## Choosing a Manageable Topic

To write a good paragraph, you need a manageable topic, one that is the right size. Your topic must be general enough to allow you to add interesting details that will engage your reader. It must also be specific or narrow enough that you can cover it adequately in a few sentences. If your topic is too general, you'll end up with a few unrelated details that do not add up to a specific point. If your topic is too narrow, you will not have enough to say.

Suppose you have decided to write a paragraph about sports. You write the following topic sentence:

Sports are a favorite activity for many people.

This topic is much too broad to cover in one paragraph. Think of all the different aspects you could write about. Which sports would you consider? Would you write about both playing sports and watching them? Would you write about both professional and amateur sports? Would you write about the reasons people enjoy sports? The topic sentence must be more specific:

My whole family likes to watch professional football on Sunday afternoons.

Here you have limited your topic to a specific sport (football), a specific time (Sunday afternoon), and some specific fans (your family).

Here are a few other examples of sentences that are too general. Each has been revised to be more specific.

| | |
|---|---|
| TOO GENERAL | My parents have greatly influenced my life. |
| REVISED | My parents helped me make the decision to attend college. |
| TOO GENERAL | Sex education is worthwhile. |
| REVISED | Sex-education courses in high school allow students to discuss sex openly. |

If your topic is *too* specific (narrow), you will not have enough details to use in the paragraph, or you may end up including details that do not relate directly to the topic. Suppose you decide to write a paragraph about the Internet and come up with this topic sentence:

The Internet allows me to stay in touch with friends in other parts of the country.

What else would your paragraph say? You might name some specific friends and where they are, but this list wouldn't be very interesting. This topic sentence is too specific. It might work as a detail, but not as a main idea. To correct the problem, ask, "What else does the Internet allow me to do?" You might say that it allows you to stay in touch with friends by e-mail, that it makes doing research for college papers easier, and that the World Wide Web has information on careers and even specific job openings. Here is a possible revised topic sentence:

The Internet is an important part of my personal, college, and work life.

Here are a few other examples of topic sentences that are too narrow, along with revisions for each one:

| | |
|---|---|
| TOO NARROW | Only 36 percent of Americans voted in the last election. |
| REVISED | Many Americans do not exercise their right to vote. |
| TOO NARROW | Markel Carpet Company offers child-care leave to both males and females. |
| REVISED | The child-care leave policy at Markel Carpet Company is very flexible. |
| TOO NARROW | A yearly subscription to *Appalachian Voice* costs $25. |
| REVISED | *Appalachian Voice,* a magazine devoted to environmental issues, is a bargain, considering the information it provides. |

How can you tell if your topic sentence is too general or too specific? Try brainstorming or branching to generate ideas. If you find you can develop the topic in many different directions, or if you have trouble choosing details from a wide range of choices, your topic is probably too general. If you cannot think of anything to explain or support it, your topic sentence is too specific.

## EXERCISE 3-4

**Directions:** Evaluate the following topic sentences. Label each "G" for too general or "S" for too specific. Then rewrite each to create an effective topic sentence. *Corrected sentences will vary.*

_G_   1. Learning a new sport is challenging.

_____

_S_   2. Dinner for two at my favorite Italian restaurant costs $25.

_____

_S_   3. The new day care center opens earlier than most.

_____

_G_   4. Many rules of etiquette have changed over the past 25 years.

_____

_S_   5. Passive cigarette smoke makes me feel sick.

_____

## Tips for Writing Effective Topic Sentences

Use the following suggestions to write clear topic sentences:

1. **Your topic sentence should state the main point of your paragraph.** It should identify your topic and express a view toward it.

2. **Be sure to choose a manageable topic**—one that is neither too general nor too specific.

3. **Make sure your topic sentence is a complete thought.** Be sure your topic sentence is not a fragment or run-on sentence. (Refer to section C in Part VI, "Reviewing the Basics," for a review of sentence errors.)

4. **Place your topic sentence first in the paragraph.** Topic sentences often appear in other places in paragraphs, or their controlling idea is

implied, not stated. For now, it will be easier for you to put yours at the beginning. That way, as you write, you can make sure you stick to your point, and your readers will immediately be alerted to that point.

5. **Avoid announcing your topic.** Sentences that sound like announcements are usually unnecessary. Avoid such sentences as "This paragraph will discuss how to change a flat tire," or "I will explain why I object to legalized abortion." Instead, directly state your main point: "Changing a flat tire involves many steps," or "I object to abortion on religious grounds."

Not all expert or professional writers follow all of these suggestions. Sometimes, a writer may use one-sentence paragraphs or include topic sentences that are fragments to achieve a special effect. You will find these paragraphs in news and magazine articles and other sources. Although professional writers can use these variations effectively, you probably should not experiment with them too early. It is best while you are polishing your skills to use a more standard style of writing.

## EXERCISE 3-5

**Directions:** Evaluate each of the following topic sentences and mark them as follows:

E = effective                    G = too general

A = announcement                 N = not complete thought

S = too specific

_____A_____   1. This paper will discuss the life and politics of Simon Bolivar.

_____G_____   2. Japanese culture is fascinating to study because its family traditions are so different from American traditions.

_____S_____   3. The admission test for the police academy includes vocabulary questions.

_____E_____   4. The discovery of penicillin was a great step in the advancement of modern medicine.

_____A_____   5. I will talk about the reasons for the popularity of reality television shows.

_____G_____   6. Poor habits may lead to weight gain.

_____S_____   7. Each year Americans are the victims of more than one million auto thefts.

_____G_____   8. The White House has many famous rooms and an exciting history.

_____E_____    **9.** There are three factors to consider when buying a DVD player.

_____G_____    **10.** Iraq has a long and interesting history.

## EXERCISE 3-6

**Directions:** Analyze the following topic sentences. If a sentence is too general or too specific, or if it makes a direct announcement or is not a complete thought, revise it to make it more effective. *Answers will vary.*

1. World hunger is a crime.

   REVISED    _____

   _____

2. E-mail is used by a great many people.

   REVISED    _____

   _____

3. I will point out the many ways energy can be conserved in the home.

   REVISED    _____

   _____

4. Congress is very important in the United States.

   REVISED    _____

   _____

5. Drunk drivers are a serious problem.

   REVISED    _____

   _____

## EXERCISE 3-7

**Directions:** Write a topic sentence for four of the following topics, using the tips given above. Then select one of your topic sentences and use it to develop a paragraph.

1. Should suicide be legal under certain circumstances?

2. Who deserves college scholarships?

3. Why do children need parental supervision when using the Internet?

4. Why are baseball games fun to watch?

5. Is space exploration valuable or a waste of money?

6. Does the news coverage of presidential campaigns unfairly influence voters?

## EXERCISE 3-8

**Directions:** Suppose you are taking a sociology course this semester. In preparation for class discussions that will focus on issues, your instructor has assigned the following topics. Choose *one* topic and write a one-paragraph response to it.

1. Educational reform: If you could make one significant change in the public education system, what would it be?

2. Gender differences: Describe one way in which the behavior of men is different from that of women.

3. The family: What do you think is the most important function of a family? That is, why do we live in family groups? What is one key advantage? Support your answer with examples from your own experience.

4. Discrimination: Describe one instance of discrimination (sexual, racial, religious, class, or age) that you have witnessed or experienced.

# AN ACADEMIC SCENARIO
## A Student Essay
### The Academic Writer and the Writing Task

Loi To is a student at Tufts University where he is a junior majoring in political science and Russian. He writes for the campus newspaper, *The Tufts Daily,* and has contributed 26 articles. This article appeared in the March 15, 2005 issue. As you read, observe To's use and placement of topic sentences.

Title: suggests main point of the essay

# What It Means to Live in America
## Loi To

Introduction: personal details create interest

1    Every Saturday and Sunday morning since the beginning of this semester my alarm clock has shrilled at exactly seven in the morning. Rain or shine, energetic or tired, hung-over or sober, I have committed myself to getting up, putting on a shirt and tie and making the almost hour-long trek from my

house to Dorchester, Mass. In Dorchester I teach English to a group of seventeen Vietnamese immigrants all of whom have been in the United States for less than three years.

Topic sentence

2    The organization I work at, The Vietnamese American Civic Association (VACA), has a mission "to promote family self-sufficiency and well-being, and to facilitate community empowerment among the Vietnamese population of Boston and Greater Boston." It does this by providing a multitude of

Background information

services including, English to Speakers of Other Languages (ESOL) classes, citizenship and civics classes, health awareness education and outreach, youth programming, and employment services. The small role I play in contributing to VACA's mission is that of an ESOL teacher.

3    The small role I play in contributing to VACA's mission is that of an ESOL teacher. I absolutely love teaching English in the Fields Corner section of Dorchester. I'm not going to lie: the early wake-ups are almost as bad as learning that your housemates have decided that they're adopting two smelly ferrets. It's hard for me to get up sometimes, especially if I don't end up going to bed until two or three in the morning. However, I do it anyway. Why?

Thesis statement

I do it because it makes me feel good to help immigrants adjust to living in America.

Topic sentence

4    According to the curriculum I use based on the Massachusetts Department of Education frameworks, all my ESOL students should be able to answer the question, "Why did you come to America?" before leaving my intermediate level class. So as one of the components of my latest class, I asked my students to articulate the reasons they had for coming to America. The 70-year-old class clown, strikingly similar to my dad, responded by saying, "To get more freedom." The single mother with two kids said, "To get a better education for my children." The 20-year-old female assembly worker said, "To get a better life."

Topic sentence

5    I am amazed by the motivation, dedication, and hard work of all of my students, most of whom work forty hours or more a week at low paying jobs in factories, machine shops and assembly companies. But they still have enough energy to wake up early every Saturday and Sunday morning to attend six hours of English class. My sacrifice seems minuscule and almost frivolous compared to what my students are doing to pursue the "American Dream."

Topic sentence

6    I've learned many things from my students, one of which is a deeper appreciation of what it means to live in America. In this tumultuous time, when America is at war in Iraq, I think many Americans lose sight of what it means to be American. It sends chills through my spine to hear an individual say that he wants to move out of the United States because of President Bush's stance on the war in Iraq.

7    Yes, President Bush's policies were not and are not perfect, but I believe the United States is still the greatest place to live on earth. It's ironic that individuals that have been in America less than three years want to be here

more than people that have been here all their lives. I think in some ways too many people take for granted the great opportunities that come with living in America.

**Topic sentence**    8    I love living in the United States—a land where hard work and a little luck can go a long way. My family was lucky enough to come here in the late 1980s, and as a result I have had the chance to live the majority of my life in the greatest land on earth. No, things are not perfect in America. There is still homelessness, poverty and hunger. But there is also freedom, liberty and opportunity.

**Conclusion**    9    What does living in America mean to you? Being an American, in any sense of the word, does not carry just negative connotations but comes equipped with several positive meanings. Forgetting the positive aspects of life in America is as equally detrimental as ignoring the negative. When looking at what's wrong with America, don't lose sight of what's right.

## Examining Academic Writing

1. Evaluate each of To's topic sentences. Are they clear and specific?

2. Evaluate To's thesis statement. How could it be revised to be more effective?

3. Which paragraphs could be improved by adding more detail or examples?

## Academic Writing Assignments

1. Write a paragraph explaining one thing America means to you. Choose one benefit of living in America and explain its importance in your life.

2. Write a paragraph explaining one opportunity you have in America that you might not have in other countries.

3. If you have done community service, write a paragraph explaining what you learned from the experience. If you have not, write a paragraph explaining what you expect the benefits of volunteering to be.

# A WORKPLACE SCENARIO
## A JOB APPLICATION LETTER
### The Workplace Writer and the Writing Task

Topic sentences are important in letter writing, as well as in essays. One important type of letter you will write is a job application letter. It is the letter that accompanies your résumé, and it must be clear, attention-getting, and well-written. The letter that follows was written by Jason McNaught who recently graduated with an associate's degree and is applying for a job as an Internet Web site designer. As you read, notice how his well-focused topic sentences will grab his reader's attention and help him or her quickly locate needed information in the letter.

---

2344 Happy Hill Rd.
Dallas, TX 75210
April 1, 2005

Ms. Antonia Sanchez
Director of Administration
Walbank and Walbank, Inc.
599 Circle Ave.
Dallas, TX 75210

Dear Ms. Sanchez:

   I believe I possess the "proven computer skills" your ad in the March 28 issue of the Dallas Daily News requires for the position of Web Designer. A variety of successful work experiences using a wide range of computer technologies (see my résumé) taught me to use both hardware and software efficiently. I have worked with HTML, ASP, and XML languages in both Microsoft and Linux server environments. I am also a "proven" user of the software system used in your office. My past experience includes development and software support and providing training to a wide variety of clients.

   I recently completed a degree in Computer Information Systems at El Paso Community College. My coursework included work in Microsoft Word and PowerPoint, as well as courses in computer programming and maintenance. I am familiar with Flash, Fireworks, and Dreamweaver MX from Macromedia, as well as Photoshop from Adobe.

   I am particularly proud of my work during my internship as an assistant Webmaster at AMC in Dallas. As my internship evaluation (attached) demonstrates, employees found me to be knowledgeable, helpful, and informative. My experience in helping to maintain their Web site has provided an excellent foundation for the position you have available.

   I would appreciate an opportunity to demonstrate and explain my solid computer background in person. I am available for an interview any day this month. Please contact me at (555) 335-4090.

Sincerely,

*Jason McNaught*

Jason McNaught

Enclosure: Résumé

## Examining Workplace Writing

1. Explain the purpose of each paragraph as indicated by the topic sentence.

2. Which paragraphs, if any, need more detail?

3. Did you find McNaught's letter to be engaging and convincing? Explain your reasons.

## Workplace Writing Assignments

1. Assume you have just earned your college degree. Write a letter of application to an ideal employer explaining your qualifications and experience, and stating that your résumé is attached.

2. Suppose, as part of the job interview process, you are asked to write a short essay explaining your strengths and weaknesses as a potential employee. Write this essay, paying particular attention to writing clear and effective topic sentences.

3. Add a topic sentence to the following paragraph:

   A company's image is shaped by the employees that meet the consumer in person. Sloppily dressed or rude employees can lead the consumer to believe that the business itself is sloppy and inconsiderate. The company's letterhead—its format, quality, readability, and color—also creates either a positive or negative impression. The company's Web site contributes to the company's image as well. A Web site that is difficult to navigate frustrates the consumer and creates a negative image.

# WRITING ABOUT A READING

## Thinking Before Reading

The following article appeared in *Newsweek* in January 2004 and discusses the stress soldiers are experiencing during their service in the U.S. war with Iraq. As you read, notice how the writer uses clear topic sentences in each paragraph.

1. Preview the reading, using the steps discussed in Chapter 2, p. 30.

2. Connect the reading to your own experience by answering the following questions:

   a. Do you know anyone who has returned from a recent war or military conflict? If so, how willing were they to share their experiences?

   b. What stressful effects of wartime have you experienced or observed?

# Stressed Out at the Front

### Rod Nordland and T. Trent Gegax

1    Sgt. Kim Eimers understands now why her father never talked about his time as a soldier in Vietnam. When she gets back from Iraq, where she's stationed with the Fourth Infantry Division in Baqubah, she doesn't think she'll talk about her wartime experience much, either. Her own worst moment came when a mortar round hit her mess hall at the Third Brigade's base, during dinnertime. "I just lost it," she says. But so far her family still hasn't heard about the incident.

2    Capt. Glenn Palmer's worst moment came when he was giving mouth-to-mouth resuscitation to a wounded officer who had been shot by a sniper while riding in the back seat of a Humvee. Palmer, who had been driving the vehicle, kept trying to blow, even after he felt his own breath whistling out of a hole in the victim's head. "I still can't get the taste out of my mouth," says Palmer, an Army chaplain.

3    Like soldiers in every war, American men and women in Iraq have seen things they'll never be able to discuss easily. Some feel damaged in a way that can't be repaired; some will find that nightmares begin only many years later. In World War I, the condition was called shell shock, and doctors treated it in psychiatric hospitals. World War II's psychologists termed it battle fatigue, and Vietnam's shrinks coined the terms traumatic stress and posttraumatic stress disorder (PTSD). Today, the preferred term is combat stress, and the military has an official policy for dealing with it—in the field, as close as possible to the fighting.

4    Combat-stress units are deployed throughout Iraq, staffed by professionals who give soldiers counseling and advice. The military hopes that by easing soldiers' troubles in real time, and teaching them how to deal with the horrors of the job, it will reduce the wave of psychological fallout that always follows a war. Yet combat-stress teams are controversial. Some soldiers feel **stigmatized** when offered treatment in the field, and some officers believe it gives soldiers a **psychobabble** excuse for **malingering**. The Marine Corps will field its first permanent combat-stress units in the coming months.

5    War-related stress has many symptoms: irritability, frequent urination, diarrhea, tingling in extremities, sudden reaction to loud noises, insomnia, weight loss, even balding. And the basic treatment in the field is simple, best expressed as "three hots and a cot." Counselors recommend that stressed soldiers check into special "fitness centers"—with real beds, hot food and 24-hour counseling—where they are encouraged to sleep and

**stigmatized**
marked or labeled as socially undesirable

**psychobabble**
specialized term from the field of psychology used to inaccurately describe personal problems

**malingering**
pretending to be ill to avoid work

*A sergeant with a combat-stress team gets a nap.*

relax as much as they want for three days. After that, most soldiers are ready to go back to work.

6    It certainly helped in Sergeant Eimers's case. "Before it was the stress of the heat, and then it was the stress of the mortars—we've had 90 since October," she says. The one that hit near her mess hall, a structure with a fabric roof, sparked a panic as soldiers jammed into one another trying to get out the doors. She wasn't sure she could go on soldiering after that. During counseling, Eimers was relieved simply to know that she wasn't alone in feeling anxious.

7    Sometimes, stressed GIs get more than just therapy and advice. Capt. Robert Ruxin, a stress-team psychiatrist, says in about a quarter of cases antidepressants are prescribed. The drugs of choice in Iraq are Celexa and Trazodone. Army Sgt. Janice Smith, who is stationed in one of the hottest areas of the Sunni Triangle, says she takes anti-anxiety pills to help her cope. "I don't know if I will ever be able to live a normal life again," she says. "It's very hard for us not to be stressed out when soldiers are dying every day around you."

8    Some cases cannot be treated in the field. In all, a total of 538 soldiers in Iraq have been "sectioned out," or sent home for treatment of psychological problems. (The military says many of them had pre-existing mental disorders.) Still, although the Army will not divulge the overall number of GIs who have received counseling in Iraq, combat-stress treatment does seem to

help keep soldiers on duty. At the 528th Combat Stress Detachment, counselors see from two to 20 people a day. In Balad, the 113th Medical Company's fitness center typically has a caseload of four soldiers in the three-hots-and-a-cot program, plus a couple of dozen soldiers who get walk-in treatment every day. Half a dozen other combat-stress teams are deployed around Iraq.

**ethos**
attitudes and beliefs of a group

9    Some stress-reduction doctrine does have a touchy-feely aspect—talk of "identifying stressors," and therapy that includes breathing and relaxation exercises—that seems to clash with the standard military **ethos**. Capt. Robert DeCarlo, a counselor in Baqubah, says his advice to soldiers is often as simple as doing something familiar. "I like to bake a cake . . . getting a homemade cake really makes people happy." So his C-Hut looks like a Betty Crocker ad, stacked with cake mixes sent by friends and family through the military postal service. He shares his creations with his clients. The combat-stress team at Camp Warhorse actively promoted Christmas decorations as a morale booster, with a DVD player as a prize for the best-decorated **hooch**.

**hooch**
hut or quarters for troops

10    In a "normal" war, only 10 percent of the Army's forces would be in frontline combat roles—the others would have support duties and be far from harm's way. Yet in Iraq, all U.S. forces are effectively in combat roles. Typically, 25 percent of frontline soldiers will suffer from combat stress, experts say. Not all of those will go on to get full-blown posttraumatic stress disorder. But even in Gulf War I, studies put the number of PTSD victims at 5 percent to 10 percent. In Iraq, with a much longer engagement and nearly all troops potentially in harm's way, the rate could be much higher.

**déjà vu**
feeling of reliving an experience

11    Lt. Col. Daniel Lonnquist, an Army Reserve psychiatrist who works with the stress teams in Baqubah, says he feels a strong sense of **déjà vu** there. In his civilian practice, he works for the Veterans Administration, counseling Vietnam vets. At 58, he's also a Vietnam veteran himself, a rarity among troops in Iraq. "There's a lot of macho attitude here," he says. Among the Vietnam vets he sees back home, some "took 15 years to deal with their feelings about killing somebody," he says. "We have vets who for years said 'counseling is not for me' and then had to **eat humble pie**." In some respects, he thinks this war will be worse; a greater proportion of the soldiers are exposed to risk, many more are reservists and, unlike Vietnam, there's been a great deal of uncertainty about how long their tours will last. "I tell these guys, 'Talk about it with your buddies here because they'll understand . . . no one else will.'"

**eat humble pie**
to admit you have been wrong

12    Captain Palmer has memories he'll never be able to purge. "I have buried babies caught in the cross-fire and held the hand of wounded soldiers while the doctor tries to save their eyes and legs," he says. But the hardest was try-

ing to resuscitate that fellow officer, who died in the field. Palmer called on the combat-stress team for counseling, both for himself and for other soldiers involved. The initial interview is called a critical-event debrief, or CED; the idea is to get soldiers talking about what they experienced, and to leave a door open for future counseling. Within a day Captain Palmer was back in the field himself doing CEDs for other anxious soldiers.

13    Within the military, a big selling point for the combat-stress teams is that they keep soldiers fighting; in military **parlance**, frontline psychologists are a "force multiplier." The soldiers themselves sense a Catch-22 in that: getting stress relief so you can experience more stress. Lt. Marivic Fields was giving a combat-stress-prevention class for the 51st Transportation Company at Camp Anaconda recently, in a tent darkened to prevent targeting by enemy mortars. The assembled soldiers were convoy truckers; their jobs are among the most dangerous in Iraq now. "This deployment too shall pass," Fields told the group. "Like a kidney stone, it'll hurt, but it'll pass."

14    "Hey, lieutenant," called one of the soldiers in the back. "You want to get rid of our stress, send us home!"

15    "Hooah!" they all yelled.

---

**parlance**
particular way of speaking or talking

## Getting Ready to Write

### Reviewing the Reading

1. Why do many soldiers not want to talk about their wartime experiences?

2. Explain how the treatment of combat stress has changed and improved since World War I.

3. Why is stress now treated in the field—at the source of the stress?

4. Explain what the treatment called "three hots and a cot" means.

5. Why is the combat stress rate likely to be higher in the Iraq War than in other "normal" wars?

## Examining the Reading: Immediate Review and Underlining Topic Sentences

When you have read anything once, you probably can remember many of the key points and some of the supporting details, but there will be ideas you cannot recall. Also, your level of understanding may be literal—that is, you can recall facts and details, but you're not ready to interpret and react to the ideas expressed.

### Immediate Review

A quick review of the reading will improve both your comprehension and retention. The review will also help you identify portions that need to be reread; questions may also come to mind about its content.

An easy way to review the selection is to follow the same steps as for previewing (see p. 30). The best time to do this is *immediately* after you've finished reading, while the content is still fresh in your mind.

### Underlining Topic Sentences

Another valuable way to review a reading assignment is to underline the topic sentence of each paragraph. This activity forces you to decide what each paragraph is about and, at the same time, helps you remember it. You can also reread the underlined text to refresh your memory for a class discussion and to locate specific sections quickly.

Underline the topic sentence of each paragraph in "Stressed Out at the Front." *Helpful hint:* If you have difficulty identifying the topic sentence, ask yourself, "What one key, general idea do all the sentences in the paragraph discuss or explain?"

## Thinking Critically: Discovering the Author's Purpose

A writer always has a purpose for writing. A writer may write to defend an action or policy (drug testing, gun control, or flextime on the job). A writer may write to present information on a topic (the increased risk of skin cancer due to prolonged exposure to the sun). At other times, a writer may intend to entertain, express emotions, or describe an event or a person. As a reader, it is your job to recognize the author's purpose and to judge whether he or she accomplishes it effectively.

Here's how to discover the author's purpose:

1. **Ask yourself, "What is the writer trying to tell me?** What does he or she want me to do or think?"

2. **Pay close attention to the title of the piece and the source of the material because these may offer clues.** Suppose an article is titled "Twenty-six Reasons to Vote in National Elections." The title suggests that the author's purpose is to urge citizens to vote. If an essay on the lumber industry appears in *Eco-Ideas*, a magazine devoted to environmental preservation, you might predict that the author's purpose is to call for restrictions on the industry.

3. **Look for clues or statements about purpose in the beginning and concluding paragraphs of the material.** Suppose an essay concludes with a statement such as "For all these reasons, it is vitally important to have a job that is rewarding and satisfying." This statement reveals that the author's purpose is to persuade readers and win them over to a certain view.

Write a sentence stating the purpose of "Stressed Out at the Front." Explain what clues the author provided.

## Strengthening Your Vocabulary

**Part A:** Using the word's context, word parts, or a dictionary, write a brief definition of each of the following words or phrases as it is used in the reading.

1. deployed (paragraph 4) *called to military duty or action*

2. sectioned out (paragraph 8) *sent home for treatment*

3. divulge (paragraph 8) *reveal; share information*

4. clash (paragraph 9) *to be at odds with*

5. purge (paragraph 12) *to get rid of*

**Part B:** Choose one of the above words and draw a word map.

## Reacting to Ideas: Discussion and Journal Writing

1. Discuss other situations (non-military) in which on-the-scene counseling is provided.

2. For what reason(s) might the Army be unwilling to divulge the overall number of soldiers who have received stress counseling?

3. Discuss why doing something familiar relieves stress.

4. Discuss the advantages and/or disadvantages of discussing a stressful situation with others experiencing it.

5. Do you know any veterans of the Iraq War or of other wars? Are they willing to talk about their experiences? If not, what explanations, if any, do they offer for their unwillingness to talk?

## Writing About the Reading

### Paragraph Options

1. Many soldiers have a mental picture (memory) of an event that they cannot erase. Do you have a similar permanent picture in your mind of either a pleasant or unpleasant experience? Write a paragraph describing the experience. Explain why you cannot erase it from your memory.

2. Write a paragraph explaining how you know when you are under stress. What physical, emotional, or mental symptoms do you exhibit?

3. Write a paragraph explaining what activities you have found to be effective stress relievers.

### Essay Options

4. Lt. Col. Lonnquist advises soldiers to talk about their stressful experiences with their buddies. Write an essay explaining how talking about a stressful situation with others did or did not help you relieve stress.

5. The reading discusses battlefield stress. What stressful situations do you face? Write an essay identifying one stressful situation in your life and explaining its causes. Explain what you do to manage or overcome the stress.

6. A close friend is planning to start college next year, but has confided that she will find it stressful. What advice could you offer this friend about avoiding and controlling stress while attending college? Write an essay for this friend offering specific advice on how to deal with the situation.

# CHAPTER REVIEW AND PRACTICE

## Chapter Review

| | |
|---|---|
| WHAT IS A PARAGRAPH? | A paragraph is a group of related sentences that develops one main thought about a single topic. |
| WHAT IS A TOPIC SENTENCE? | A topic sentence states the main point of the paragraph. |
| WHAT ARE THE TWO PURPOSES OF A TOPIC SENTENCE? | A topic sentence has two purposes:<br>• to identify the topic<br>• to express a view or make a point about the topic |
| WHAT IS A MANAGEABLE TOPIC? | A manageable topic is one that is specific enough that you can cover it adequately in a single paragraph, but general enough to allow you to add interesting details that explain it. |
| LIST THREE TIPS FOR WRITING AN EFFECTIVE TOPIC SENTENCE. | 1. The topic sentence must be a complete thought.<br><br>2. The topic sentence should usually appear first in the paragraph.<br><br>3. The topic sentence should avoid announcing the topic. |

## Skill Refresher: Sentence Fragments

A sentence fragment is a group of words that (1) lacks a subject, (2) lacks a verb, or (3) is a dependent (subordinate) clause unattached to a complete sentence. It therefore fails to express a complete thought.

Note: A **subject** is the noun or pronoun that performs the action of the sentence. A **verb** is a word that conveys the action or state of being of the subject. A **dependent clause** is a group of words beginning with a subordinating conjunction like *although, because, if, since, unless, wherever,* or *while* or with a relative pronoun like *which, that, what, who,* or *whoever.*

In the examples below, the fragments are underlined.

My friend Anita called me last night. <u>Calls me every night</u>.
[The second group of words lacks a subject.]

<u>Anita, someone I have known all my life, and excellent at math</u>. She asked if I had finished doing my taxes.
[The first group of words lacks a verb.]

I planned to fill out the tax forms that evening. <u>Because the deadline was approaching.</u>
[The second group of words is a dependent clause unattached to a complete sentence.]

## How to Spot Fragments

A fragment begins with a capital letter and ends with a period, like a complete sentence, but it is not complete. To identify fragments in your writing, ask the following questions of each sentence:

1. **Is there a subject?** To find the subject, ask who or what is performing the action of the sentence.

    FRAGMENT    Asked Professor Gomez how long he had been teaching at Ohio State. [Who asked Professor Gomez?]

    CORRECT     Gail asked Professor Gomez how long he had been teaching at Ohio State.

2. **Is there a verb?** To find the verb, look for a word that conveys what is happening, what has happened, or what will happen. Do not confuse a verb with verbals (*-ing, -ed,* or infinitive *"to"* forms of verbs that are used as nouns or modifiers). A true verb changes form to communicate a time change. A verbal does not.

    FRAGMENT    A nervous, pressured feeling and a headache.

    CORRECT     A nervous, pressured feeling and a headache struck me.

    FRAGMENT    The express train leaving the station at four.

    CORRECT     The express train will leave the station at four.

    FRAGMENT    To get a taxi and hurry downtown.

    CORRECT     I need to get a taxi and hurry downtown.

3. **Is the dependent clause—a group of words starting with a subordinating conjunction or relative pronoun—attached to a complete sentence?** A dependent clause cannot stand alone.

    FRAGMENT    Although we wanted to go to the softball game.

    CORRECT     Although we wanted to go to the softball game, we could not find the park.

    FRAGMENT    If we had asked directions or bought a map.

    CORRECT     We might have found the park if we had asked directions or bought a map.

## How to Correct Fragments

1. Add the missing subject or verb.

   FRAGMENT    Waiting for my paycheck to be delivered.

   REVISED     I was waiting for my paycheck to be delivered.

2. Revise by combining the fragment with an appropriate existing complete sentence.

   FRAGMENT    My sister loved her job at the jewelry store. Until she got a new boss.

   REVISED     Until she got a new boss, my sister loved her job at the jewelry store.

3. Remove the word or phrase that makes the statement incomplete.

   FRAGMENT    While I was waiting for class to begin.

   REVISED     I was waiting for class to begin.

## Rate Your Ability to Spot and Correct Fragments

Place a check mark in front of each sentence fragment and then correct it so that it is a complete sentence. Place a "C" for "Complete" in front of sentences which are complete. *Corrected sentences will vary.*

_____C_____    1. Leaving the room, she turned and smiled.

_____C_____    2. Until the exam was over, the professor paced in the front of the room.

_____√_____    3. I remembered her birthday. Because we're good friends.

_____√_____    4. I realized I had forgotten my book. After I left the classroom.

_____√_____    5. Jason asked a question about centrifugal force. Before the professor moved on to the next topic.

_____√_____    6. Until the phone rang and the answering machine answered.

_____√_____    7. Hoping I would do well at the interview.

_____√_____    8. Scheduling a conference with her art history professor to discuss the topic for her final paper.

_____√_____    9. I got a B on the quiz. Because I reread my notes.

_____√_____    10. Marcus was interested in the course. Focused on the rise of communism.

Score_____

Check your answers, using the Answer Key on p. 639. If you missed more than two, you need additional review and practice in recognizing and correcting fragments. Refer to section C.1 of Part VI, "Reviewing the Basics," and to the book's Web site, http://www.ablongman.com/mcwhorterexpressways1e.

## INTERNET ACTIVITIES

### 1.   Analyzing Paragraphs

Find a newspaper or magazine article with at least five substantial paragraphs. Then use this outline from an instructor at Dakota State University.

http://www.homepages.dsu.edu/moosen/format_for_outline.htm

Identify the topic sentences in the article. Evaluate how well the author developed the paragraphs and used topic sentences.

### 2.   Reading Tips

The Writing and Reading Center at Plymouth State University has put together these reading strategies.

http://www.plymouth.edu/wrc/trouble.html

Print this page out and use it during your next reading assignment. Make note of what worked especially well for you.

### 3.   Finding a Topic

Explore some social sciences topics with this site from the writing center at California State University, Los Angeles.

http://www.calstatela.edu/centers/write_cn/sbtopgen.htm

Use the chart to develop five potential paper topics.

### 4.   This Book's Web Site

For more practice with topic sentences, refer to the book's Web site.

http://www.ablongman.com/mcwhorterexpressways1e

# 4

# Developing and Arranging Details

## Chapter Objectives

*In this chapter
you will learn to:*

1. Use details to develop your topic sentence.

2. Select relevant and sufficient details.

3. Arrange details in a paragraph.

4. Use specific words.

5. Use transitional words.

## Write About It!

What single overall feeling do you get from the photograph above? Write a sentence that expresses the emotion that is shown in the picture.

This sentence could be the topic sentence of a paragraph about the graduates shown in the picture. If you were to explain why the graduates are happy, you would be providing details that support the topic sentence. You will need to focus on details in a wide variety of situations.

EVERYDAY SCENARIO
- You are writing a claim report of an auto accident in which you were involved. Clear, accurate **details** are essential to prove you were not at fault.

ACADEMIC SCENARIO
- You are answering an essay question in psychology that asks you to explain the stages of sleep. By giving clear, accurate **details** about each stage, you will earn full credit.

WORKPLACE SCENARIO
- You are a sales rep for a mechanical supply company. Customers report a valve you sell has been malfunctioning. You must send full **details** describing the problem to the manufacturing department.

# WRITING

Supporting details are pieces of information that explain your topic sentence. If you wrote the following topic sentence, "Field hockey is the sport that taught me how to be a team player," then the supporting details that make up the remainder of your paragraph would explain why and how field hockey taught you to be a team player. Here is another example:

> If you have trouble sleeping, there are a number of things you can do to overcome the problem. First, try to develop a regular sleeping pattern. Go to bed at the same time and get up at the same time each day. Avoid sleeping late on weekends; it will throw you off schedule. Next, avoid eating or drinking caffeine in the evening. Caffeine can stay in your system for hours and keep you awake when you want to be sleeping. Also, try to read or watch television before falling asleep. Performing the same activity nightly will signal your body that bedtime is near.

In this paragraph, the details fulfill the promise the topic sentence makes—that the paragraph will tell you what to do to overcome sleeping problems. In this chapter you will learn how to write details that explain a topic sentence.

## Using Relevant and Sufficient Details

The details you choose to support your topic sentence must be both relevant and sufficient. **Relevant** means that the details directly explain and support your topic sentence. For example, if you were to write a paragraph for your employer explaining why you deserve a raise, it would not be relevant to mention that you plan to use the money to go to Florida next spring. A vacation has nothing to do with—is not relevant to—your job performance.

**Sufficient** means that you must provide enough information to make your topic sentence understandable and convincing. In your paragraph explaining why you deserve a raise, it would probably not be sufficient to say that you are always on time. You would need to provide more information about your job performance: for example, that you always volunteer to work holidays, that you've offered good suggestions for displaying new products, and that several customers have written letters praising your work.

## Selecting Relevant Details

Relevant details directly support your topic sentence. They help clarify and strengthen your ideas, whereas irrelevant details make your ideas unclear and confusing. Here is the first draft of a paragraph written by a student named Carlos to explain why he decided to attend college. Can you locate the detail that is not relevant?

> (1) I decided to attend college to further my education and achieve my goals in life. (2) I am attempting to build a future for myself. (3) When I get married and have kids, I want to be able to offer them the same opportunities my parents gave me. (4) I want to have a comfortable style of living and a good job. (5) As for my wife, I don't want her to work because I believe a married woman should not work. (6) I believe college is the way to begin a successful life.

Sentence 5 does not belong in the paragraph. The fact that Carlos does not want his wife to work is not a reason for attending college.

Use the following simple test to be sure each detail you include belongs in your paragraph:

1. Read your topic sentence in combination with each of the other sentences in your paragraph. For example,

   read topic sentence + last sentence.

   read topic sentence + second-to-last sentence.

   read topic sentence + third-to-last sentence.

2. For each pair of sentences, ask yourself, "Do these two ideas fit together?" If your answer is "No," then you have found a detail that is not relevant to your topic. Delete it from your paragraph.

Another student wrote the following paragraph on the subject of the legal drinking age. As you read it, cross out the details that are not relevant.

> (1) The legal drinking age should be raised to 25. (2) Anyone who drinks should be old enough to determine whether or not it is safe to drive after drinking. (3) Bartenders and others who serve drinks should also have to be 25. (4) In general, teenagers and young adults are not responsible enough to limit how much they drink. (5) The party atmosphere enjoyed by so many young people encourages crazy acts, so we should limit who can drink. (6) Younger people think drinking is a game, but it is a dangerous game that affects the lives of others.

Which sentence did you delete? Why did you delete it? The third sentence does not belong in the paragraph because the age of those who bartend or serve drinks is not relevant to the topic. Sentence 5, about partying, should also be eliminated or explained because the connection between partying and drinking is not clear.

## EXERCISE 4-1

**Directions:** Place a check mark by those statements that provide relevant supporting details.

1. Sales representatives need good interpersonal skills.

   ___√___ **a.** They need to be good listeners.

   ___√___ **b.** They should like helping people.

   _____ **c.** They should know their products well.

2. Water can exist in three forms, which vary with temperature.

   ___√___ **a.** At a high temperature, water becomes steam; it is a gas.

   _____ **b.** Drinking water often contains mineral traces.

   ___√___ **c.** At cold temperatures, water becomes ice, a solid state.

3. Outlining is one of the easiest ways to organize facts.

   _____ **a.** Formal outlines use Roman numerals and English letters and numerals to show different levels of importance.

   ___√___ **b.** Outlining emphasizes the relationships among facts.

   ___√___ **c.** Outlines make it easier to focus on important points.

## EXERCISE 4-2

*Writing in Progress*

**Directions:** Write a paragraph beginning with one of the topic sentences below. When you've finished, use the test described on p. 85 to make certain each detail is relevant.

1. Hunting is (is not) a cruel sport.

2. My hometown (city) has (has not) changed in the past five years.

3. Religion is (is not) important in my life.

4. White parents should (should not) be allowed to adopt African American children.

5. Most doctors are (are not) sensitive to their patients' feelings.

## Including Sufficient Detail

Including **sufficient detail** means that your paragraph contains an adequate amount of specific information for your readers to understand your main idea. Your supporting details must thoroughly and clearly explain why you believe your topic sentence is true. Be sure that your details are specific; do not provide summaries or unsupported statements of opinion.

Let's look at a paragraph a student wrote on the topic of billboard advertising.

> There is a national movement to oppose billboard advertising. Many people don't like billboards and are taking action to change what products are advertised on them and which companies use them. Community activists are destroying billboard advertisements at an increasing rate. As a result of their actions, numerous changes have been made.

This paragraph is filled with general statements. It does not explain who dislikes billboards or why they dislike them. It does not say what products are advertised or name the companies that make them. No detail is given about how the billboards are destroyed, and the resulting changes are not described. There is not sufficient support for the topic sentence. Here is the revised version:

> Among residents of inner-city neighborhoods, a national movement is growing to oppose billboard advertising. Residents oppose billboards that glamorize alcohol and target people of color as its consumers. Community activists have organized and are taking action. They carry paint, rollers, shovels, and brooms to an offending billboard. Within a few minutes the billboard is painted over, covering the damaging advertisement. Results have been dramatic. Many liquor companies have reduced their inner-city billboard advertising. In place of these ads, some billboard companies have placed public-service announcements and ads to improve community health.

If you have trouble thinking of enough details to include in a paragraph, try brainstorming or one of the other prewriting techniques described in Chapter 1, "The Writing Process: An Overview." Write your topic sentence at the top of a sheet of paper. Then list everything that comes to mind about that topic. Include examples, events, incidents, facts, and reasons. You will be surprised at how many useful details you think of.

When you finish, read over your list and cross out details that are not relevant. (If you still don't have enough, your topic may be too specific. See p. 63.) The next section will help you decide in what order you will write about the details on your list.

## EXERCISE 4-3

*Writing in Progress*

**Directions:** Reread the paragraph you wrote for Exercise 4-2 to see if it includes sufficient detail. If necessary, revise your paragraph to include more detail, always making sure the details you add are relevant. Use a prewriting technique, if necessary, to generate additional details.

## NEED TO KNOW

### Important Terms

**Relevant details:** Details that directly explain the topic sentence.

**Sufficient details:** Details that provide adequate support of the topic sentence.

**Time sequence:** Arranging ideas in the order in which they happen.

**Spatial arrangement:** Arranging ideas according to their position in space.

**Least/Most Arrangement:** Presenting ideas from least to most or most to least according to some quality or characteristic.

**Specific words:** Words that provide a great deal of information.

**Transitional words and phrases:** Words that lead the reader from one detail to another.

## Types of Supporting Details

There are many types of details that you can use to explain or support a topic sentence. The most common types of supporting details are (1) examples, (2) facts or statistics, (3) reasons, (4) descriptions, and (5) steps or procedures.

### Examples

One way a writer may support an idea is by using examples. **Examples** are specific instances or situations that illustrate an idea. Examples make ideas and concepts real and understandable. You might explain aggressive behavior by giving an example of one child pulling another child's hair.

### Facts and Statistics

Another way a writer supports an idea is by including facts and/or statistics. A **fact** is a piece of information that can be verified as correct. A **statistic** is a fact that involves numbers. The facts and statistics may provide evidence that the main idea is correct. Or the facts may further explain the main idea. For example, to prove that the divorce rate is high, the author may give statistics about the rate of divorce per 100,000 marriages and the percentage of the population that is divorced.

Be sure to give the source of any fact or statistic you take from any print or Internet source (see p. 396 for more information).

## Reasons

A writer may support an idea by giving reasons *why* a main idea is correct. **Reasons** are explanations of why something happened. You might explain *why* nuclear power is dangerous or give reasons *why* a new speed limit law should be passed by Congress.

## Descriptions

When the topic of a paragraph is a person, object, or place the writer may develop the paragraph by describing it. **Descriptions** are details that help you create a mental picture for your reader of the person, object, or place and they appeal to one of the five senses—touch, taste, smell, sight, and hearing. For example, you might describe a motorcycle by describing the sounds the engine makes and by describing its shape, parts, and color.

## Steps or Procedures

When you write a paragraph explaining how to do something or how something works, you often list steps or procedures. **Steps** are events that you complete in a specific order. For example, if you write a paragraph about how to prepare an outline for a speech, the details would list or explain the steps to take in preparing an outline.

## EXERCISE 4-4

**Directions:** For each topic sentence, write at least three different types of details that could be used to support it. Label each detail as example, fact/statistic, reason, description, or steps/procedures.

1. People make inferences about you based on the way you dress.

2. Many retailers with traditional stores have decided to market their products through Web sites as well.

3. Many Americans are obsessed with losing weight.

4. Historical and cultural attractions can be found in a variety of shapes, sizes, and locations throughout the world.

5. Using a search engine is an effective, though not perfect, method of searching the Internet.

## Methods of Arranging Details

Nan had an assignment to write a paragraph about travel. She drafted the paragraph and then revised it. As you read each version, pay particular attention to the order in which she arranged the details.

FIRST DRAFT

This summer I had the opportunity to travel extensively. Over Labor Day weekend I backpacked with a group of friends in the Allegheny Mountains. When spring semester was over, I visited my seven cousins in Florida. My friends and I went to New York City over the Fourth of July to see fireworks and explore the city. During June I worked as a wildlife-preservation volunteer in a Colorado state park. On July 15 I celebrated my twenty-fifth birthday by visiting my parents in Syracuse.

REVISION

This summer I had the opportunity to travel extensively in the United States. When the spring semester ended, I went to my cousins' home in Florida to relax. When I returned, I worked during the month of June as a wildlife-preservation volunteer in a Colorado state park. Then my friends and I went to New York City to see fireworks and look around the city over the Fourth of July weekend. On July 15th, I celebrated my twenty-fifth birthday by visiting my parents in Syracuse. Finally, over Labor Day weekend, my friends and I backpacked in the Allegheny Mountains.

Did you find Nan's revision easier to read? In the first draft, Nan recorded details as she thought of them. There is no logical arrangement to them. In the second version, she arranged the details in the order in which they happened. Nan chose this arrangement because it fit her details logically. The three common methods for arranging details are as follows:

1. Time sequence

2. Spatial arrangement

3. Least/most arrangement

We will discuss each of these methods. Then, in Part III of this book, "Methods of Development," you will learn additional methods of arranging ideas.

## Time Sequence

Time sequence means the order in which something happens. For example, if you were to write about a particularly bad day, you could describe the day in the order in which everything went wrong. You might begin with waking up in the morning and end with going to bed that night. If you were describing a busy or an exciting weekend, you might begin with what you did on Friday night and end with the last activity on Sunday. (You will learn more about this method of arrangement in Chapter 6, "Narration.")

## Spatial Arrangement

Suppose you are asked to describe the room in which you are sitting. You want your reader, who has never been in the room, to visualize it. You need to describe, in an orderly way, where items are positioned. You could describe the room from left to right, from ceiling to floor, or from door to window. In other situations, your choices might include front to back, inside to outside, near to far, east to west, and so on. This method of presentation is called spatial arrangement. How are the details arranged in the following paragraph?

> Keith's antique car was gloriously decorated for the Fourth of July parade. Red, white, and blue streamers hung in front from the headlights and bumper. The hood was covered with small American flags. The windshield had gold stars pasted on it, arranged to form an outline of our state. On the sides, the doors displayed red plastic-tape stripes. The convertible top was down, and Mary sat on the trunk dressed up like the Statue of Liberty. In the rear, a neon sign blinked "God Bless America." His car was not only a show-stopper but the highlight of the parade.

## Visualize It!

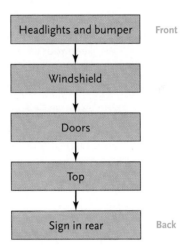

The topic you are writing about will often determine the arrangement you choose. In writing about a town, you might choose to begin with the center and then move to each surrounding area. In describing a building, you might go from bottom to top.

## EXERCISE 4-5

**Directions:** Indicate which spatial arrangement you would use to describe the following topics. Then write a paragraph on one of the topics.

1. A local market or favorite store

2. A photograph you value

3. A prized possession

4. A building in which you work

5. Your campus cafeteria, bookstore, or lounge

### The Least/Most Arrangement

Another method of arranging details is to present them in order from least to most or most to least, according to some quality or characteristic. For example, you might arrange details from least to most *expensive,* least to most *serious,* or least to most *important.*

The writer of the following paragraph uses a least-to-most arrangement:

> The entry level job in many industries today is administrative assistant. Just because it's a lower level job, don't think it's an easy job. A good administrative assistant must have good computer skills. If you aren't proficient on a computer, you won't be able to handle your supervisor's correspondence and other paper work. Even more important, an administrative assistant must be well organized. Every little problem—from answering the phone to setting up meetings to making travel arrangements—lands on the administrative assistant's desk. If you can't juggle lots of loose ends, this is not the job for you. Most important of all, though, an administrative assistant needs a sense of humor. On the busiest days, when the office is in total chaos, the only way to keep your sanity—and your temper—is to take a deep breath, smile, and say "When all this is over, I'm going to have a well-earned nervous breakdown!"

## Visualize It!

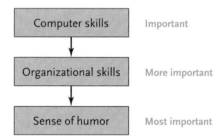

Notice that this writer wrote about a basic requirement for the job—computer skills—and then worked up to the most important requirement.

You can also arrange details from most to least. This structure allows you to present your strongest point first. Many writers use this method to construct a case or an argument. For example, if you were writing a business letter requesting a refund for damaged mail-order merchandise, you would want to begin with the most serious damage and put the minor complaints at the end, as follows:

> I am returning this merchandise because it is damaged. The white sneakers have dark streaks across both toes. One of the shoes has a red mark on the heel. The laces also have some specks of dirt on them. I trust you will refund my money promptly.

## EXERCISE 4-6

**Directions:** Write a paragraph supporting one of the following topics. Organize your details, using the most-to-least or least-to-most arrangement.

1. Reasons why you enjoy a particular sport or hobby

2. Five special items in your closet

3. Three favorite musicians or musical groups

4. Things to remember when renting an apartment

5. Why you like city (or small-town or country) living

## Using Specific Words

When you are writing a paragraph, use specific words to give your reader as much information as possible. You can think of words the way an artist thinks of colors on a palette. Vague words are brown and muddy; specific words are brightly colored and lively. Try to paint pictures for your reader with specific, vivid words. Here are a few examples of vague words along with more specific words or phrases for the same idea:

| | |
|---|---|
| VAGUE | fun |
| SPECIFIC | thrilling, relaxing, enjoyable, pleasurable |
| VAGUE | dark |
| SPECIFIC | hidden in gray-green shadows |
| VAGUE | experienced |
| SPECIFIC | five years in the job |
| VAGUE | tree |
| SPECIFIC | red maple |

The following suggestions will help you develop your details.

1. **Use specific verbs.** Choose verbs (action words) that help your reader picture the action.

   | | |
   |---|---|
   | VAGUE | The woman left the restaurant. |
   | SPECIFIC | The woman stormed out of the restaurant. |

2. **Give exact names.** Include the names of people, places, objects, and brands.

   | | |
   |---|---|
   | VAGUE | A man was eating outside. |
   | SPECIFIC | Anthony Hargeaves lounged on the deck of his yacht *Penelope*, spearing Heinz dill pickles out of a jar. |

3. **Use adjectives before nouns to convey details.**

   | | |
   |---|---|
   | VAGUE | Mary had a dog on a leash. |
   | SPECIFIC | A short, bushy-tailed dog strained at the end of the leash in Mary's hand. |

4. **Use words that appeal to the senses.** Choose words that suggest touch, taste, smell, sound, and sight.

VAGUE    The florist shop was lovely.

SPECIFIC    Brilliant red, pink, and yellow roses filled the florist shop with their heady fragrance.

To summarize, use words that help your readers create mental pictures.

VAGUE    Al was handsome.

SPECIFIC    Al had a slim frame, curly brown hair, deep brown almond-shaped eyes, and perfectly straight, glittering white teeth.

## EXERCISE 4-7

**Directions:** Rewrite these vague sentences, using specific words. *Answers will vary.*

1. The hair stylist used a gel on my hair.

   _____

2. Dress properly for an interview.

   _____

3. I found an interesting Web site on the Internet.

   _____

4. The job fair was well attended.

   _____

5. I'm going to barbecue something for dinner.

   _____

## EXERCISE 4-8

*Writing in Progress*

**Directions:** Reread the paragraph you wrote and revised in Exercises 4-2 and 4-3. As you read, underline any vague or general words. Then replace the underlined words with more specific ones.

Table 4-1  **Frequently Used Transitions**

| Arrangement | Transition |
| --- | --- |
| Time Sequence | first, next, during, eventually, finally, later, meanwhile, soon, when, then, suddenly, currently, after, afterward, before, now, until |
| Spatial | above, below, behind, in front of, beside, next to, inside, outside, to the west (north, etc.) of, beneath, nearby, on the other side of |
| Least/Most | most, above all, especially, even more |

## Using Transitional Words

Transitional words allow readers to move easily from one detail to another. They show how details relate to one another. You might think of them as words that guide and signal. They guide the reader through the paragraph and signal what is to follow. As you read the following paragraph, notice the transitional words and phrases (highlighted in green) that this student used.

> I have so many things to do when I get home today. First, I have to take my dog, Othello, for a walk. Next, I should do my homework for history and study the chapter on franchises for business. After that I should do some laundry, since my sock drawer is empty. Then my brother is coming over to fix the tailpipe on my car. Afterward, we will probably order a pizza for a speedy dinner.

Table 4-1 shows some commonly used transitional words and phrases for each method of arranging details discussed on pp. 89–92.

To understand how these transitional words and phrases work, review the sample paragraphs for each of these arrangements (pp. 91–92). Underline each transitional word or phrase.

## EXERCISE 4-9
### Writing in Progress

**Directions:** Review the paragraphs you wrote for Exercises 4-4 and 4-5. Underline any transitions you used. Revise each paragraph by adding transitional words or phrases to clarify your details.

# AN ACADEMIC SCENARIO
## A STUDENT ESSAY
### The Academic Writer and the Writing Task

Dan Kerstettler is a community college student who is taking a writing class. His instructor gave the class the following assignment:

Design a time capsule that will be opened at least 100 years from now. In it you will place objects that reveal what life in America was like at the present time. Write an essay explaining what you will place in your time capsule. Include details that describe each object.

# A Look into the Past

## Dan Kerstettler

Title: interest catching, suggests purpose of the capsule

Introduction: analysis of the time capsule task

Thesis statement

Physical details about the capsule

Note details about photo selection process

Inclusion of questions adds detail and interest

Detailed explanation of what to include and why

Specific titles add detail and interest

1    A time capsule tells a story of a particular time period through a collection of unrelated objects. The trick is not only to find objects that will hold up for the amount of time needed, but ones that can give an accurate picture of what my world was like in 2005. I think the job might have been easier with words.

2    My time capsule wouldn't be very large, that's for sure. It needs to be no larger than a breadbox, with good seals, and enclosed in a larger plastic bag. It will be buried in Memorial Park in Lemoyne, Pennsylvania, and it is to be opened when the city celebrates its bicentennial in 2105.

3    I'd need some form of removable media, like a USB or Firewire hard drive, to store the years of photos and writing I've got stored up, as well as some music and other multimedia. Also stored on the hard drive will be photos, of everything and nothing, 20 of my choosing, the top 5 chosen by friends, and the ten most-searched-for images on Google Images. That way, my impression of what's important, and the opinion of others about what is worth looking at will all be contained in one capsule.

4    The time capsule would include computer files, backed up at time of burial onto the removable drive. Users have the ability to upload pictures and to read a set of five questions. The following questions are meant to be a little bit insightful, a little bit serious, and a little bit crazy. Anyone trying to understand the present day needs to get a picture of what is going on in our minds.

   1. What is the meaning of life?
   2. Explain your politics. Be specific, and give examples.
   3. Is freedom of speech important to you? Why?
   4. What makes you laugh harder than anything else?
   5. What did you want to be when you grew up? What are you now?

5    When this capsule is opened in 2105, the print newspapers will be either completely dead or changed and dying. So, I want to include the issue of the *New York Times* from my date of birth, and its 9/11 issue. (Because the September 11, 2001 terrorist attacks have drastically changed our lives, we should at least try to explain them.) For nostalgia's sake, I will put in copies of the two college newspapers I've worked for—the "Cliff Sentinel" and the "The Daily Collegian."

6    I'd also include some good examples of the printed word, works that have deeply influenced me and helped me understand life. My top choices are:

   1. *Lord of the Flies* by William Golding. It is shocking, but it does describe human nature in paperback form.
   2. *Stranger in a Strange Land* by Robert Heinlein. This book got me through 9/11, the end of an engagement, and whenever I'm feeling as if I need to look to a book for advice, I open it.

3. "Calvin and Hobbes." I include it because Bill Watterson, the comic's creator, manages to hide a grown-up comic in a strip starring a kid and his tiger. "Calvin and Hobbes" is brilliant in a way "Dilbert," my second choice, can never be. "Dilbert" will be funny occasionally, but it won't serve as a basis for serious thought.

On a completely different tack, my time capsule would contain complete diagrams, drawings, and technical information for the most advanced internal combustion automobile engine currently in mass production. Why? It would be fascinating for the capsule opener to compare today's technology with that of 2105. It wasn't so long ago that cars ran on steam; future innovations may be just as big.

8    I need to explain a little about our modern lifestyle, so I will show how much we depend on coffee and caffeine. Maybe I will include a packet of instant coffee and a can of Pepsi. Caffeine is already a multimillion dollar industry, and I want my capsule to show the various means we use to feel more alert, stay focused, and make our brains work. Maybe I should just include a Starbuck's ad?

9    A current set of high school and college freshman textbooks should be included as well. The way we teach our youth explains a lot about us. With the increasing use of Internet-based learning and long-distance classwork, more people have access to more of an education than they would have ten years before now. I'd love to see how schooling works when the capsule is opened.

10    A tape recorder, ideally a Sony Pressman should also be included, with backups of the tape on the removable hard drive. The tape will be filled with whatever people say when you walk up to someone, say "Tell the future something," and stick a running tape recorder in his or her face. Hopefully, no one will take offense and insult me, because we wouldn't want the capsule opener to think poorly of this generation.

11    When faced with a broad subject like the contents of a time capsule, it's important to narrow and smile. You should narrow your focus until it's manageable for the size you'll need, and smile as you play with the possibilities. Who says time capsules have to be round, made of metal, or even buried? Why couldn't we have a time capsule that is completely online or a time capsule that's on display in a museum? The importance isn't in the items or its location. The meaning comes from the way the creator chose to show the present day. In the end, a time capsule does reflect the past, but I think it does a much better job of reflecting me—its creator.

*Specific objects mentioned*

*Gives reasons*

*Quotation adds detail*

*Conclusion—writer reflects on his task*

## Examining Academic Writing

1. Evaluate Kerstettler's use of detail. Which paragraphs have sufficient detail. Which paragraphs could use more detail?

2. Evaluate Kerstettler's use of transitions. How does he lead you from one object to another in his capsule?

3. Look at Kerstettler's conclusion. What new information does it contain?

## Academic Writing Assignments

1. Write a paragraph evaluating the contents of Dan Kerstettler's capsule. What do you agree should be included? What would you delete? Why?

2. Write a paragraph explaining what choices you would include as good examples of the "printed word."

3. Write an essay describing what the contents of your own time capsule would be.

# A WORKPLACE SCENARIO
## A RÉSUMÉ
### The Workplace Writer and the Writing Task

Michael Herrera is a recent college graduate who is applying for a job as a special events coordinator for a major hotel chain where he will organize events such as conferences, weddings, business meetings, and sports team visits. He prepared a résumé which is shown below. A **résumé** is a brief record of your education and work experiences that qualify you for a job. Think if it as a list of details about yourself. It includes contact information, education, work experience, and special skills and aptitudes (computer training, languages spoken, for example). As you read the résumé, pay special attention to the details Michael included in each category.

---

Michael J. Herrera
179 Spring Street, Apt. 6
Williamsville, NY 14221
(716) 555-5555
*mherr@pfgp.com*

| | |
|---|---|
| *Objective* | Special Events Coordinator for a Major Hotel/Motel Chain |
| *Education* | Erie Community College<br>Buffalo, NY<br>Associate's Degree, May 2005 |
| *Work Experience* | **Events Planner**<br>Sherbrook Hotel, Buffalo, NY<br>November, 2003–present<br>• Meet with new clients<br>• Plan and organize events with clients<br>• Supervise administrative, clerical, and technical support staff<br>• Interview potential employees<br>• Coordinate catering<br>• Initiate and update Web site |

**Associate Events Planner**
Valley Inn, Ellicottville, NY
Sept. 2001–October, 2003
• Assist with scheduling and event planning
• Supervise support staff
• Maintain client lists

**Assistant Meeting Planner**
Valley Inn, Ellicottville, NY
Summer 2000 and 2001
Part-time, September, 2000–June, 2001
• Provide data input
• Computer support
• Facilities planning

*Computer Skills*    Microsoft Excel, Word, and PowerPoint

*Languages*    Spanish

*References available upon request*

## Examining Workplace Writing

1. Highlight the sections into which the résumé is divided.

2. How is the résumé organized within each section?

3. Why is it easy to read the résumé and locate information in it?

## Workplace Writing Assignments

1. Prepare a résumé that includes your work experiences, education, and special skills up to the present. Be sure to include details as Herrera does.

2. Review the résumé you have written in #1 above. What career do you seem to be heading toward? Write a paragraph explaining a career you are considering or have chosen. Include details that explain why you are considering or have chosen it.

3. Add relevant details to the following student paragraph so that it offers sufficient support for the topic sentence:

   E-mail is a very useful communication tool, but it is not as private as people may think. Companies monitor the e-mail of their employees. There are a number of rules employees should follow when using company e-mail to make sure they do not embarrass themselves or find themselves out of a job.

## WRITING ABOUT A READING

### Thinking Before Reading

The following article, "The Most Hateful Words," taken from Amy Tan's book *The Opposite of Fate,* describes a daughter's relationship with her mother. As you read, notice how the author uses various types of detail to convey the main ideas of the essay.

1. Preview the reading, using the steps listed on p. 30.

2. Discover what you already know about family relationships by answering the questions below.

   a. In what situations have you heard "hateful words" being used?

   b. Have you ever regretted things that you have said?

### READING

# The Most Hateful Words

#### Amy Tan

1    The most hateful words I have ever said to another human being were to my mother. I was sixteen at the time. They rose from the storm in my chest and I let them fall in a fury of hailstones: "I hate you. I wish I were dead. . . ."

2    I waited for her to collapse, stricken by what I had just said. She was still standing upright, her chin tilted, her lips stretched in a crazy smile. "Okay, maybe I die too," she said between huffs. "Then I no longer be your mother!" We had many similar exchanges. Sometimes she actually tried to kill herself by running into the street, holding a knife to her throat. She too had storms in her chest. And what she aimed at me was as fast and deadly as a lightning bolt.

3    For days after our arguments, she would not speak to me. She tormented me, acted as if she had no feelings for me whatsoever. I was lost to her. And because of that, I lost, battle after battle, all of them: the times she criticized me, humiliated me in front of others, forbade me to do this or that without even listening to one good reason why it should be the other way. I swore to myself I would never forget these injustices. I would store them, harden my heart, make myself as impenetrable as she was.

4    I remember this now, because I am also remembering another time, just a few years ago. I was forty-seven, had become a different person by then,

had become a fiction writer, someone who uses memory and imagination. In fact, I was writing a story about a girl and her mother, when the phone rang.

5   It was my mother, and this surprised me. Had someone helped her make the call? For a few years now, she had been losing her mind through Alzheimer's disease. Early on, she forgot to lock her door. Then she forgot where she lived. She forgot who many people were and what they had meant to her. Lately, she could no longer remember many of her worries and sorrows.

6   "Amy-ah," she said, and she began to speak quickly in Chinese. "Something is wrong with my mind. I think I'm going crazy."

7   I caught my breath. Usually she could barely speak more than two words at a time. "Don't worry," I started to say.

8   "It's true," she went on. "I feel like I can't remember many things. I can't remember what I did yesterday. I can't remember what happened a long time ago, what I did to you. . . ." She spoke as a drowning person might if she had bobbed to the surface with the force of will to live, only to see how far she had already drifted, how impossibly far she was from the shore.

9   She spoke frantically: "I know I did something to hurt you."

10  "You didn't." I said. "Don't worry."

11  "I did terrible things. But now I can't remember what. . . . And I just want to tell you . . . I hope you can forget, just as I've forgotten."

12  I tried to laugh so she would not notice the cracks in my voice. "Really, don't worry."

13  "Okay, I just wanted you to know."

14  After we hung up, I cried, both happy and sad. I was again that sixteen-year-old, but the storm in my chest was gone.

My mother died six months later. By then she had **bequeathed** to me her most healing words, as open and eternal as a clear blue sky. Together we knew in our hearts what we should remember, what we can forget.

**bequeathed**
handed down, passed on

---

## Getting Ready to Write

### Reviewing the Reading

1. How did Tan's mother react to Amy's "most hateful words"?

2. How did these arguments affect their relationship?

3. What mental problems did Tan's mother face later in life?

4. What healing words did Tan's mother offer?

## Examining the Reading: Recognizing Types of Supporting Details

Before you can write about an author's ideas, you must understand how that author supports and explains his or her main points. Tan uses a variety of details. Specifically, she uses anecdotes (stories) and dialogue (conversation) to support her ideas. She also uses lively verbs and descriptive words and phrases to make her writing interesting.

Analyze Tan's use of supporting detail by indicating in which paragraphs and sentences she uses:

1. anecdotes. _1–3, 6–14_

2. dialogue. _1, 2, 6–13_

3. specific verbs. _3 (tormented), 8 (bobbed), 8 (drifted)_

4. adjectives to add detail. _chin tilted (1), lips stretched (2), spoke frantically (9)_

## Thinking Critically: Understanding Figurative Language

**Figurative language** refers to words or expressions that make sense on a creative or imaginative level, but do not make sense literally. Here are a few everyday figurative expressions:

The exam was a piece of cake.

George eats like a starved animal.

She's as skinny as a pencil.

The meaning of each of these is clear, but you can see that they are not factually or literally true.

Figurative language is a creative way of expressing ideas. It appeals to your imagination, senses, or emotions. It usually involves a comparison between two unlike things that share at least one common characteristic. The expression "George eats like a starved animal" takes two dissimilar things (George and a starved animal) and says they are similar in one way (how they eat). The expression creates a mental image and suggests more than it says about George's eating habits. When you visualize a person eating like a starved animal, what do you see?

The essay "The Most Hateful Words" contains numerous figurative expressions. For example, in describing the healing words her mother spoke (paragraph 15), Tan says they were "as open and eternal as a clear blue sky." This is a figurative expression: she compares her mother's words with the sky. We know that the words do not literally look like the clear blue sky; however, the words and the sky do share common characteristics—both are open and eternal.

Figurative expressions that compare two unlike things are called *similes* when they use the words *like* or *as,* and they are called *metaphors* when they do not use any comparison words.

Explain the meaning of each of the following figurative expressions used in the reading:

1. "the storm in my chest" (paragraph 1)

2. "as fast and deadly as a lightning bolt" (paragraph 2)

3. "she spoke as a drowning person might" (paragraph 8)

Write a sentence stating the author's tone. Explain how she conveys this.

## Strengthening Your Vocabulary

**Part A:** Using the word's context, word parts, or a dictionary, write a brief definition of each of the following words or phrases as it is used in the reading.

1. humiliated (paragraph 3) *lose one's dignity or pride*

2. injustices (paragraph 3) *unfair treatments*

3. impenetrable (paragraph 3) *cannot be entered or pierced*

4. bobbed (paragraph 8) *bounced up and down*

5. eternal (paragraph 5) *lasting forever, with no beginning or end*

### Part B: Word Map

Draw a word map of one of the words listed in Part A.

## Reacting to Ideas: Discussion and Journal Writing

1. Why do you think parents and children often have trouble getting along?

2. Discuss how the relationships between parents and children change as they get older.

3. What pressures do young people face today that they did not in the past? What do you see as the big challenges for the youth of the future?

## Writing About the Reading

### Paragraph Options

1. Tan describes what she felt were the most hateful words she has ever spoken. Write a paragraph describing words that you regret speaking.

2. Write a paragraph describing a difficult relationship you had with someone. What factors or circumstances made it so hard? Were you able to improve the relationship?

3. Tan and her mother had communication problems when Tan was a teenager. Write an essay about a communication problem you have experienced with a family member. Give details that make the problem clear. Try to identify the causes of the problem and describe how the problem was resolved.

4. Tan says she had become another person later in her life. Write a paragraph describing how you have changed, or become a different person, since you started college.

## Essay Options

5. The author felt that her mother treated her unfairly. Write an essay about a time when you felt you were being treated unfairly. Describe the situation and explain how you dealt with it.

6. Tan's mother's healing words were a gift, but it was an intangible one—one that she could not touch or see. Write an essay about an intangible gift someone has given you.

7. Tan describes her words as being "hateful." Write an essay about the most hateful words you have heard. You might write about a personal experience or you might write about words you have seen or heard in local, national, or international events or news.

8. Tan and her mother knew what they should remember and what they should forget. Write an essay explaining what you hope people will remember about you.

9. Everyone has their faults, and it is sometimes necessary to overlook them to build or maintain a relationship. Write about characteristics you have tried to forget or overlook in a person you care about.

# CHAPTER REVIEW AND PRACTICE

## Chapter Review

| | |
|---|---|
| WHAT IS THE FUNCTION OF DETAILS IN A PARAGRAPH? | Details support and explain the topic sentence. |
| WHAT ARE RELEVANT DETAILS? | Relevant details directly explain and support the topic sentence. |
| WHAT DOES SUFFICIENT DETAIL MEAN? | Sufficient detail means that you must provide enough details to make your topic sentence clear and understandable. |
| WHAT ARE THE COMMON TYPES OF DETAILS? | Examples, facts and statistics, reasons, descriptions, and steps and procedures. |
| WHAT ARE THREE WAYS TO ARRANGE DETAILS IN A LOGICAL ORDER? DEFINE EACH. | 1. In time sequence, events are presented in the order they happen. 2. In spatial arrangement, objects or places are described by the location in relation to one another. 3. In least/most arrangement, ideas are arranged from most to least or least to most, according to some particular quality or characteristic. |
| WHAT IS THE FUNCTION OF TRANSITIONAL WORDS AND PHRASES? | Transitional words and phrases connect details to one another and guide the reader through a paragraph. |

## Skill Refresher: Run-On Sentences

A run-on sentence (also known as a fused sentence) consists of two complete thoughts within the same sentence, without any punctuation to separate them. Each thought could stand alone as a separate sentence.

RUN-ON   Political science is a difficult course I am thinking of dropping it and taking it next semester.

RUN-ON   My younger sister will visit next weekend I probably will not have much time to study.

## How to Spot Run-Ons

You can often spot run-ons by reading them aloud. Listen for a break or change in your voice midway through the sentence. Read the two examples above to see if you can hear the break.

## How to Correct Run-Ons

Simply adding a comma to correct a run-on sentence does *not* work. Doing so leads to an error known as a comma splice. There are four basic ways to correct a run-on sentence.

1. Create two separate sentences. End the first thought with a period and begin the next with a capital letter.

   > My younger sister will visit next weekend. I probably will not have much time to study.

2. Connect the two thoughts by using a semicolon.

   > My younger sister will visit next weekend; I probably will not have much time to study.

3. Join the two thoughts by using a comma and a coordinating conjunction (*and, or, but, for, nor, so,* or *yet*).

   > My younger sister will visit next weekend, so I probably will not have much time to study.

4. Subordinate one thought to the other. To do this, make one thought into a dependent clause (a subordinate clause) by adding a subordinating conjunction (such as *although, because, since,* or *unless*) or a relative pronoun (such as *which, that, what, who,* or *whoever*). Then connect the dependent clause to an independent clause (a group of words with a subject and a verb that expresses a complete thought and that can stand alone as a complete sentence).

   > Since my younger sister will visit next weekend, I probably will not have much time to study.

## Rate Your Ability to Spot and Correct Run-Ons

Read the following sentences and place a "C" in front of the ones that are correct. Then correct each run-on, using one of the methods described above. *Corrected sentences will vary.*

_____ 1. The Civil War ended in 1865 the period of Reconstruction followed.

_____ 2. Although light and sound both emit waves they do so in very different ways.

_____ *C*     3. The Constitution forms the basis of our federal system of government and divides the government into the executive, legislative, and judicial branches.

_____     4. Archaeologists study the physical remains of cultures anthropologists study the cultures themselves.

_____     5. The body's nervous system carries electrical and chemical messages these messages tell parts of the body how to react and what to do.

_____     6. Neil Armstrong was the first human to walk on the moon this event occurred in 1969.

_____     7. Robert Frost is a well-known American poet one of his most famous poems is "The Road Not Taken."

_____     8. Algebra and geometry are two branches of mathematics calculus and trigonometry are other branches.

_____ *C*     9. There are two parts of the British parliamentary system, the House of Lords and the House of Commons; the American Congress also has two parts, the Senate and the House of Representatives.

_____    10. It is easy to become distracted by other thoughts and responsibilities while studying it helps to make a list of these distractions.

Score _____

Check your answers, using the Answer Key on p. 639. If you missed more than two, you need additional review and practice in recognizing and correcting run-on sentences. Refer to section C.2 of Part VI, "Reviewing the Basics."

## INTERNET ACTIVITIES

### 1. Details, Details

Explore the online collections of photographs from the George Eastman House.

http://www.geh.org/

Choose five photographs to evaluate. Discuss the types of details that the museum provides for each photograph. Then create a list of details that more fully describes each picture.

## 2.   Create an Essay Full of Details

Read through this lesson from the World Campus, Penn State University.

http://www.worldcampus.psu.edu/il/courses/syl/ENGL_0004l.html

Pick a part of the assignment to complete. Evaluate the usefulness of this type of assignment. Would you use any of these techniques when writing an essay?

## 3.   This Book's Web Site

Learn more about supporting details by visiting the book's Web site.

http://www.ablongman.com/mcwhorterexpressways1e

# 5

# Strategies for Revising

## Chapter Objectives

*In this chapter
you will learn to:*

1. Use idea maps to revise.

2. Consider your audience and purpose.

3. Evaluate your language.

4. Edit to correct your errors.

## Write About It!

Study the two photographs shown above. Write a sentence describing how the situation changed between the two photos.

A similar situation occurs in writing. Planning and organizing are useful and important steps, but they do not produce a finished product right away. Often you need to rework, rethink, and rewrite to produce an effective essay.

This chapter suggests strategies to help you with this process.

EVERYDAY SCENARIOS

- You are revising a list of household chores you wrote for your kids by putting the tasks in the order in which they need to be done throughout the week.

- You are revising a letter of complaint to the company that sold you defective software; your friend has told you that you should explain more about how the problem has inconvenienced you and ask the company for specific compensation.

ACADEMIC SCENARIOS

- After reading a classmate's paper for your history class, you realize you need to revise your paper to include more details.

- You are revising an outline for a speech because you realize the speech needs to appeal more directly to your audience.

WORKPLACE SCENARIOS

- You are revising your résumé after a career counselor suggested that you emphasize that you are fluent in Spanish and have traveled extensively.

- You are revising a written request for a salary increase after your co-worker told you that it needed to be more convincing.

# WHAT IS REVISION?

Revising involves looking again at every idea and sentence you have written and often making major changes to them. Editing is a part of the revision process that involves adding or deleting words and sentences, as well as correcting your grammar, spelling, and punctuation. As you saw in the overview of the writing process in Chapter 1 (p. 2), revision is essential.

## Examining Your Ideas

The most important part of revision is reevaluating your ideas. Think of revision as an opportunity to reassess your ideas in order to make what you are writing as effective as possible.

Often simply reading and rereading your writing does not help you to recognize what to change or improve. One of the best ways to discover what to revise is to use an idea map. An **idea map** is a visual display of the ideas you have written about in a paragraph or essay. Think of it as similar to a road map. A road map allows you to see how towns and cities connect to one another. An idea map allows you to see how ideas relate and connect to one another. An idea map can help you check two important features of your writing:

- your use of relevant and sufficient detail.

- the logical organization of your ideas.

To draw a paragraph idea map, follow these steps:

1. Write a shortened topic sentence at the top of your paper.

2. Then go through your paragraph sentence-by-sentence and list each detail that directly supports the topic sentence.

3. If you spot an example of one of the details already listed, or a further explanation of a detail, write it underneath the detail it relates to and indent it.

4. If you spot a detail that does not support or is not related to anything else, write it to the right of your list, as in the sample below.

## Visualize It!

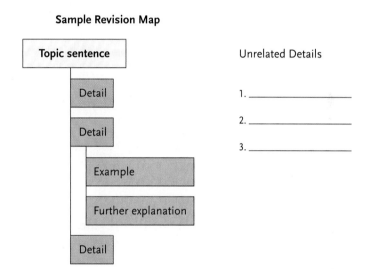

Sample Revision Map

### Relevant and Sufficient Detail

As you revise, you want to be sure you have provided enough information about your subject and that all your details directly support your topic sentence. Drawing an idea map allows you to see if you have explained each detail adequately. You will also see immediately any details that are not relevant.

Here is the first draft of a paragraph written by a student named Joe. His idea map follows.

### Draft 1

Currently, Herbalife is one of the top companies in the world for rate of growth and also for leading the industry in research and development of nutritional products. You may begin your own distributorship as I did with as little as 50 dollars. Your income potential depends on the effort you put forth. Herbalife makes health products. It is backed by a team of doctors and scientists who are the leaders in weight-loss research and maintenance on a daily basis. Herbalife will continue to be a leader because its products are of high quality and it cares about the health of the entire world. My involvement with Herbalife is just beginning, and I look forward to a profitable future.

# Visualize It!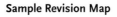

**Sample Revision Map**

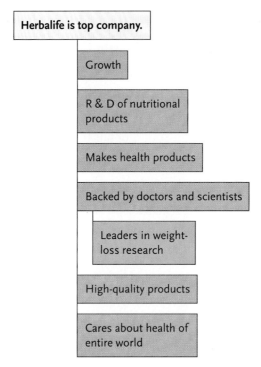

| | Unrelated Details |
|---|---|
| **Herbalife is top company.** | |
| Growth | 1. Begin distributorship— $50 |
| R & D of nutritional products | 2. Income potential depends on effort |
| Makes health products | 3. Involvement is just beginning |
| Backed by doctors and scientists | |
| Leaders in weight-loss research | |
| High-quality products | |
| Cares about health of entire world | |

Joe's map shows him how he structured his paragraph. It allows him to see whether his ideas connect and whether he has enough detail to support his main ideas. By studying this map, he can spot details that do not fit and ideas that need further development or explanation. Joe found three details (see right side of map) that did not support his original topic sentence. He realized that these details related instead to why he felt Herbalife was a good company with which to begin his own business. Joe rewrote his topic sentence to include this idea and added more explanation in his revision.

### Draft 2

Because Herbalife is one of the top companies in the world for nutrition and health, it may be a good opportunity for me to start my own business. It is a company that is not only growing rapidly but also becoming a leader in the research and development of nutritional products. Herbalife products are easy to sell because they are backed by medical doctors and scientists. The products are appealing because they are high quality and because the company demonstrates its concern for worldwide health through its advertising. You can start your own distributorship for only 50 dollars. There are no hidden costs, and you are not required to maintain a large inventory. I'm expecting my Herbalife distributorship to be the start of a business that will help me pay for college.

This second draft focuses more directly on the newly sharpened topic and includes relevant and sufficient detail. Further decisions might focus on improving sentence structure, strengthening the connection among details, and adding transitional words and phrases.

## EXERCISE 5-1

**Directions:** Read the following student paragraph and draw an idea map for it. Use your map to identify details that are not relevant to the topic and underline them.

> Employees of large companies benefit from labor unions. Labor unions protect workers' rights. Union leaders organize employees so that they can't be exploited by company management. Being a union leader is a difficult but important job. Unions are also important because they make sure that all employees are treated equally and fairly. Before unions were created, each employee had to make his or her own deal with an employer, and some workers ended up doing the same job as others but for less pay. Employers listen to unions because unions can organize strikes and contact federal agencies about violations. Sometimes strikes fail and people are out of work for long periods. Many times this is on the news. Labor unions also make sure that work sites are safe and that there are no health hazards.

## EXERCISE 5-2

*Writing in Progress*

**Directions:** Assume that you are taking a course in computer basics and that your instructor has given you a choice of the following topics as your first assignment. Choose a topic and write a first draft. Then draw an idea map that will help you evaluate whether you have relevant and sufficient detail.

1. Describe one important convenience or service you would miss if computers did not exist, and imagine life without it.

2. Give three reasons the Internet is useful.

3. Make a list of everyday products, activities, or services that do not require a computer in any way. Write a paragraph summarizing your findings.

4. How can computers and the personal information stored in them jeopardize our right to privacy? Give your views.

5. A computer-controlled robot has been developed to perform specialized types of surgery. Discuss the advantages and disadvantages of this innovation.

## Logical Organization of Ideas

Another major issue to consider as you revise is whether you have arranged your ideas in a way your readers can follow. As we saw in Chapter 4, "Developing and Arranging Details," even if you have plenty of detail, the wrong organization can throw your readers off track. In addition, you need to make sure you use transitional words and phrases to help readers follow your thoughts.

Revision maps are also useful for checking your organization. By listing the ideas in the order in which they appear in your paragraph, you can see if they are arranged logically. Study the following student paragraph and then its revision map.

## Draft 1

The women's movement has produced important changes in women's lifestyles. Women started the movement with rallies and marches. The Nineteenth Amendment to the Constitution gave women the vote. A lot of men were not happy about that. Women never used to be able to vote and they were not supposed to drink or swear or wear pants. That was ridiculous.

Women now have more rights and freedoms. But women still don't get paid as much as men. Many women have jobs in addition to taking care of their families. Women do a lot more than men. Women now have a choice about what they want to do for a career but are not rewarded as much as men.

**Visualize It!**

**Revision Map**

Women's movement produced changes in women's lifestyles.

19th amendment—voting

Couldn't vote, hold certain jobs, wear pants

Women now have more freedoms

But not as much pay

Jobs and families now

Do more than men

Have choice, but less reward

Unrelated Details

1. Started with marches
2. Men not happy
3. Ridiculous

The map shows that the details are not arranged in any specific order. Since most of them relate to changes in women's rights, these details could be arranged from past to present. The writer arranged the details in chronological order in her second draft.

## Draft 2

The women's movement has produced important changes in women's lifestyles. Before 1900, women could not vote, hold certain jobs, or wear pants. They were oppressed. The Nineteenth Amendment to the Constitution, passed in 1920, allowed women to vote. Other rights have come gradually over the years. Now women have a wide variety of job possibilities, and they certainly are not forbidden to wear pants. Women have more freedom now, but they still do not earn as much as men. Today women have more choices, but they are still short on rewards.

Notice the added transitional words and phrases in Draft 2. The writer added the phrase "Before 1900" to signal the reader that she was going to review the early status of women.

Idea maps are also useful for identifying several other common writing problems.

- If you strayed from your topic, you will see it happening on your idea map.

- If your paragraph is repetitious, you will realize as you study your idea map that you are saying the same thing more than once.

- If your paragraph is unbalanced because you have emphasized some ideas and not others that are equally important, your idea map will show it.

## EXERCISE 5-3

*Writing in Progress*

**Directions:** Study the idea map of the paragraph you wrote for Exercise 5-2. Evaluate your arrangement of details. If they are not arranged logically, number them on your map and revise your paragraph. After you have examined your ideas, you should make sure that you have expressed them effectively and appropriately. That is, you should determine whether the language you have chosen is specific and vivid, whether it is suited to your audience, and whether it achieves your purpose for writing.

## Consider Your Purpose and Audience

As we mentioned in Chapter 1, "The Writing Process: An Overview," good writing should achieve your purpose and be directed toward a specific audience. When you are ready to revise, read your draft through once or twice to get an overall impression of it. Then decide if the paragraph accomplishes what you want it to. If it doesn't, try to identify what went wrong, using the Revision Checklist on p. 116. If it is difficult to identify the reasons a draft doesn't achieve its purpose, ask a friend or classmate to read your writing and summarize what it does accomplish. This information will often give you clues about how to improve the piece.

To evaluate whether your writing is suited to your audience, read it from the audience's viewpoint. Try to anticipate what ideas your audience might find unclear, what additional information might be needed, and whether the overall reaction will be positive or negative. Imagine that someone else wrote the piece and you are reading it for the first time. Does it keep your interest and make some fresh and original points? Could you treat your subject in a more engaging way?

## EXERCISE 5-4

*Writing in Progress*

**Directions:** Evaluate whether the paragraph you wrote for Exercise 5-2 is suited to your purpose and audience. Revise your paragraph if it is not well suited.

## Examine Specific and Vivid Language

In Chapter 4, "Developing and Arranging Details," we discussed using specific and vivid words and phrases to provide accurate and interesting detail. As you revise, look for drab, nondescriptive words and phrases. Replace them with lively words that enable your reader to create a mental picture of your topic.

Here is a paragraph, with revisions, that a student wrote on the topic of aerobic dancing. Notice how she changed and replaced words to make her details more specific and vivid.

Aerobic dancing is ~~great~~ *energizing and enjoyable* exercise. It makes you ~~use a lot of~~ *stretch and exert*
muscles. *from nearly all muscle groups* It also gives your cardiovascular system a good workout because ~~it gets~~ your heart *starts* pumping and ⭕increases your rate
of breathing. You maintain the pace for ~~awhile~~ *20 or 30 minutes*, which is also
beneficial. Aerobic dancing builds endurance and stamina, which
make you *r body come alive and scream, "I'm in shape!"* ~~feel as if you are in good physical condition~~. In aero-
bics the risk of injury is slight since there is no intense strain on
any one part of the body.

---

### EXERCISE 5-5
*Writing in Progress*

**Directions:** Evaluate your use of specific and vivid language in the paragraph you wrote for Exercise 5-2. Revise the paragraph to make your language livelier and more descriptive.

## Revision Checklist

During revision, there is a lot to think about. The following Revision Checklist will help you keep in mind important questions to ask about your writing.

1. Who is your audience? How interested are they in your subject and how much do they know about it? Is your paragraph suited to your audience?

2. What is your purpose? Does your paragraph accomplish your purpose?

3. Is your main point clearly expressed in your topic sentence?

4. Is each detail relevant? Does each explain or support the topic sentence directly?

5. Have you supported your topic sentence with sufficient detail to make it understandable and believable?

6. Do you use specific and vivid words to explain each detail?

7. Do you connect your ideas with transitional words and phrases?

## What Is Editing?

Errors in grammar, spelling, and punctuation make your writing less effective. A writer who seems careless loses the reader's confidence. **Editing** is a process of making corrections. It is an important *final step* to writing a good paragraph. Of course, if you notice an error while you are drafting or revising, you should correct it. In general, however, focus on looking for errors only after you are satisfied with the content and organization of your paragraph.

### What Errors to Look For

Many students wonder how they will ever learn enough to spot all the errors in their writing. The job is easier than you think! Most students make certain types of errors. The Skill Refreshers in Chapters 3 through 17 address the most common errors students make:

- sentence fragments (p. 79)
- run-on sentences (p. 105)
- subject-verb agreement (p. 133)
- pronoun-antecedent agreement (p. 158)
- pronoun reference (p. 183)
- shifts and mixed constructions (p. 205)
- dangling modifiers (p. 228)
- misplaced modifiers (p. 250)
- verb tense (p. 270)
- coordinate sentences (p. 299)
- subordinate clauses (p. 323)
- parallelism (p. 356)
- when to use commas (p. 393)
- using colons and semicolons (p. 440)
- when to use capital letters (p. 467)

The following Proofreading Checklist will remind you to check for spelling, punctuation, and other mechanical errors. It is also reprinted inside the back cover for easy reference.

## Proofreading Checklist

1. Does each sentence end with an appropriate punctuation mark (period, question mark, exclamation point, or quotation marks)?

2. Is all punctuation within each sentence correct (commas, colons, semicolons, apostrophes, dashes, and quotation marks)?

3. Is each word spelled correctly?

4. Have you used capital letters where needed?

5. Are numbers and abbreviations used correctly?

6. Are any words omitted?

7. Have you corrected all typographical errors?

8. Are your pages in the correct order and numbered?

## Keeping an Error Log

Many students consistently make certain types of errors and not others. You can identify and learn to avoid yours by keeping a record of your mistakes. Use an error log like the sample shown below. Each time your instructor returns a paper, count how many errors you made of each type, and enter that number in the log. Soon you will see a pattern. You can then review your final drafts to locate those specific errors.

If you make frequent spelling errors, be sure to use the spelling checker on your computer. Also, keep a separate list of the words you misspell. Study them and practice writing them correctly.

## EXERCISE 5-6
### Writing in Progress

**Directions:** Check the paragraph you wrote for Exercise 5-2 for errors and correct any you find. Enter them in an error log (see sample).

**Sample Error Log**

| ASSIGNMENT | Sentences | | Grammar | Punctuation | Misspelled Words |
|---|---|---|---|---|---|
| | run-on | fragments | | | |
| 1 | one | one | subject-verb agreement<br>verb tense<br>pronoun ref. | comma | favorite<br>relies<br>knowledge |
| 2 | two | — | verb tense | comma<br>quotation | chemicals<br>majority<br>especially |
| 3 | one | — | subject-verb agreement<br>verb tense<br>pronoun ref. | comma<br>semicolon | necessary<br>hoping<br>definitely |
| 4 | | | | | |
| 5 | | | | | |
| 6 | | | | | |

# AN ACADEMIC SCENARIO:
## A STUDENT REVISION
### The Academic Writer and the Writing Task

Gentry Carlson is a student at Itasca College in Grand Rapids, MN where he is working toward two associates degrees—one in natural resources and one in geographical information systems. When he graduates he plans to transfer to Bemidji University, earn a bachelor's and a master's degree there, and develop a career in natural resources or high school or junior college teaching.

In his writing class, he was given the following assignment: Write an essay describing a difficult or challenging situation that you faced. Carlson chose to write about part of his Marine Corps training. Three ver-

sions of his essay are shown below. The first is his first draft. Carlson asked a classmate to review this draft and make suggestions. These are shown in handwriting on and at the end of the first draft. The second draft shows the changes Carlson made in the content of the essay. You will see he deleted some ideas and added others. The third draft shows the editing corrections Carlson made in sentence structure, grammar, punctuation, and spelling. Note the circled numbers that refer you to the end of the draft where each correction is explained. Study each draft carefully to learn more about how the revision process works.

## First Draft

*This is not a very strong thesis*

The Northern Training Area in Okinawa Japan is a place I hope to never visit again. The wet weather and double canopy jungle made it a very unpleasant place to be. While I was in the Marines, I had to do just that, for two straight weeks. From rain, mud, nasty insects, to fat snakes. I hope to never visit this place again.

*Topic sentence? But the paragraph is not about rain*

The worst part of this place had to have been the rain, which it did for every day for the two weeks in which I spent there. The jungle part of it was very lush and green. There was a fresh smell of vegetation which seemed, at the time, the only thing appealing about this place. TO visit this place for a day of two would have been enough for me, but, unfortunately, we had to stay for 2 weeks.

The moist conditions were not the only unpleasant part of this place, the mosquitoes, and other insects made life not so desirable here. There were spiders called banana spiders, which got there name from the color of there body. But, this was not the half of it; they had bodies about the size of a closed fist and legs about 4–6 inches in length. Imagine walking into this thing while running through the jungle with your M-16. These guys were nothing like the snakes that we hiding in the trees. The habu and the himmi habu, two of the most poisonous snakes of this area were everywhere. We were told many times not to get bit because we could not get ejected from the jungle quick enough to eget help before we died from there venom. As you can see, I have very good reasons not to return to this place.

*This paragraph needs a topic sentence*

Being in the field environment like this can also cause the Marines not to get the best of food to us. First, it rained all the time, and we did not have the best of shelter, so we constantly had a bit more of moisture in our chow than we liked. If you were a smoker, it was real difficult to do so, every time you'd light up, the rain would always put it out. Of course hygiene was almost non existent, unless you had a bar of soap and stripped down and took a shower in the rain. Now again, it was only two weeks long. Now, again, you can see why this place is not the most desirable to visit.

This place in which I speak of is a place I truly will not forget. It will always be a reminder of what it was to be a Marine. The wet, the cold, and the hungry feeling that everyone felt from day to day was something not everyone would enjoy. Unless they're crazy. But I know if I ever got the chance to visit this place again, I am sure there is some hidden beauty that I never noticed the first time I visited it.

## Peer Review Comments

Gent,

I liked your descriptions. I can really imagine being there. The stuff about the spiders and snakes is creepy! Here are a few changes you could make:

1. What point are you trying to make in the whole essay? You just keep saying you don't want to go back. Everybody knows basic training is bad news. Is there another point you can make about it all?

2. Where did you live and sleep?

3. You talk about food, but you don't mention it in your first paragraph.

4. You say you'd never go back, but in the end, you mention going back. Can you fix this somehow?

So, what happened to you after basic training?

## Second Draft—Content Revision Showing Changes in Ideas

# The Muds of Okinawa

## Gentry Carlson

The Northern Training Area in Okinawa Japan is a place I hope to never visit again. The wet weather and double canopy jungle made it a very unpleasant place to be. While I was in the Marines, I had to do just that, for

Added "good" and "living conditions" since they are part of the essay

Revised thesis statement

Added details about the rain

two straight weeks. From rain, mud, nasty insects, fat snakes, bad food, to bad living conditions to fat snakes. I hope I never visit this place again. This place gives an accurate picture of the tough training Marines go through to prepare themselves for combat under difficult conditions.

The worst part of this place had to have been the rain, which it did for every day for the two weeks in which I spent there. Mud was everywhere, at least on places where we had to walk. Because of all the rain, tThe jungle part of it was very lush and green. The creak beds in the deepest part of the jungle was always full and flowing in some certain direction. There was a fresh smell of vegetation which seemed, at the time, the only thing appealing about this place. TO visit this place for a day of two would have been enough for me, but, unfortunately, we had to stay for 2 weeks.

The moist conditions were not the only unpleasant part of this place, the mosquitoes, and other insects made life not so desirable here. There were spiders called banana spiders, which got there name from the color of there body. But, this was not the half of it; they had bodies about the size of a closed fist and legs about 4-6 inches in length. Imagine walking into this thing while running through the jungle with your M-16. These guys were nothing like the snakes that we hiding in the trees. The habu and the himmi habu, two of the most poisonous snakes of this area were everywhere. We were told many times not to get bit because we could not get ejected from the jungle quick enough to eget help before we died from there venom. As you can see, I have very good reasons not to return to this place. the jungle is unfriendly and unsafe, but now we will be used to these awful conditions in future combat situations.

Added sentence that connects this paragraph to the thesis statement
Topic sentence added

Living conditions were unbearable. Being in the field environment like this can also cause the Marines not to get the best of food to us. Because First, it rained all the time, and we did not have the best of shelter, so we constantly had a bit more of moisture in our chow than we liked. If you were a smoker, it was real difficult to do so, every time you'd light up, the rain would always put it out. Of course hygiene was almost non existent, unless you had a bar of soap and stripped down and took a shower in the rain.

New paragraph added on living/sleeping conditions

The tent we stayed in must have been left over from World War II. It leaked profusely from every seam. After about two days in this jungle, a large water puddle had formed in both of the doorways. This makes a real muddy mess. We had to stow out extra clothing underneath our cots, in hopes of keeping them dry. But, after those mud puddles filled up, most of the water had seeped under out cots and soiled any dry clothing we had. At this point, I really was ready to go home.

Sentences added that refer back to thesis statement and reveal outcome of training

This place in which I speak of is a place I truly will not forget. It will always be a reminder of what it was to be a Marine. The wet, the cold, and the hungry feeling that everyone felt from day to day was something not everyone would enjoy. Unless they're crazy. Upon leaving, I felt ready and able to face any combat situation. Actually, though, I did not get to use many of the jungle survival skills I learned because I was deployed to Saudi Arabia—in the middle of the desert!

# Draft Three—Editing and Proofreading

Gentry Carlson

The Muds of Okinawa

The Northern Training Area in Okinawa, Japan, is a place I hope to never visit again. The wet weather and double canopy jungle made it a very unpleasant place to be. While I was in the Marines, I had to do just that, for two straight weeks. ① *I survived* ~~From~~ rain, mud, nasty insects, fat snakes, bad food, ~~to~~ *and* bad living conditions. This place gives an accurate picture of the tough training Marines go through to prepare themselves for combat under difficult conditions.

The worst part of this place had to have been the rain; ② *it rained* ~~which it did for~~ every day for the two weeks ~~in which~~ I spent there. Mud was everywhere, at least on places where we had to walk. Because of all the rain, the jungle ~~part of it~~ was very lush and green. The ~~creak~~ *creek* beds in the deepest part of the jungle ~~was~~ *were* always full and flowing ③ ~~in some certain direction~~ *at a hazardous speed.* There was a fresh smell of vegetation which seemed, at the time, the only thing appealing about this place. T*o* visit this place for a day or two would have been enough for me, but, unfortunately, we had to stay for two weeks.

The moist conditions were not the only unpleasant part of this place ④ ; the mosquitoes ⑤ , and other insects made life ⑥ ~~not so desirable here.~~ *nearly unbearable.* There were spiders called banana spiders, which got their name from the color of ~~there body.~~ *their bodies.* ~~But~~ T*his* was not the half of it; they had bodies about the size of a closed fist and legs about 4–6 inches in length. Imagine ⑦ ~~walking into this thing~~ *encountering these* while running through the jungle with your M-16. These guys were nothing compared to the snakes that we saw hiding in the trees. The habu and the himmi habu, two of the most poisonous snakes of this area ⑧ , were everywhere. We were told many times not to get ~~bit~~ *bitten* because we could not get ~~ejected~~ *air lifted* from the jungle quick enough to ~~t~~get help before we died from ~~there~~ *their* venom. As you can see *t*, the jungle is unfriendly and unsafe, but now we will be used to these awful conditions in future combat situations.

Living conditions were unbearable. ~~Being in~~ *T*he field environment ~~like this~~ can also cause the Marines' ⑨ *supply units* not to get the best of food to us. Because it rained all the time, and we did not have the best ~~of~~ shelter, we constantly had a bit more ~~of~~ moisture in our chow than we liked. If ~~you were a smoker,~~ ⑩ *Smoking* ~~it~~ was real difficult ~~to do so, every time you'd light up,~~ *because* the rain would always put ~~it~~ *cigarettes* out. Of course hygiene was almost nonexistent, unless you ⑪ ~~had~~ *took* a bar of soap ~~and~~ , stripped down, and took a shower in the rain.

The tent we stayed in must have been left over from World War II. It leaked profusely from every seam. After about two days in this jungle, a large puddle had formed in both of the doorways. This makes a real muddy mess. We had to stow ⑫ ~~out~~ *our* extra cloth ⑬ ~~ing~~ *es* underneath our cots, in hopes of keeping them dry. But, after those mud puddles filled up, most of the water had seeped under our cots and soiled any dry clothing we had. At this point, I really was ready to go home.

~~This place in which I speak of~~ *The Okinawa jungle* is a place I truly will not forget. It will always be a reminder of what it was *like* to be a Marine. The wet, the cold, and the hungry feeling that everyone felt from day to day was something ~~not everyone would enjoy~~ *no one enjoyed* , unless ⑭ ~~they're~~ *they were* crazy. Upon leaving, I felt ready and able to face any combat situation. Actually, though, I did not get to use many of the jungle survival skills I learned because I was deployed to Saudi Arabia—in the middle of the desert!

1. Corrected fragment
2. Fixed awkward sentence
3. "in some certain direction" is unclear. All creeks flow in a direction.
4. Corrected run-on sentence
5. Deleted unnecessary comma
6. Inserted better choice of words
7. Inserted better choice of words
8. Inserted comma to separate parenthetical information
9. Not all Marines supply food; specific unit added
10. Improved sentence structure and deleted second person reference
11. Made elements parallel
12. Corrected typographical error that spell-check did not find.
13. Pronoun-antecedent agreement error corrected
14. Corrected fragment.

## Examining Academic Writing

1. Highlight and evaluate Carlson's use of topic sentences in his third revision. Does each announce the main point of the paragraph? Do any need further revision?

2. Evaluate Carlson's use of detail. Did he provide sufficient detail? In what paragraphs could greater detail have been provided?

3. What did you learn about the revision process from Carlson's three drafts?

## Academic Writing Assignments

1. Write a paragraph explaining a situation in which prior training proved to be beneficial or even life-saving to you.

2. Write a paragraph about your experience with some type of training. It might be driver education, a computer class, or sports training. Explain how you approached it and what you learned from it.

3. Complete the same assignment that Carlson did by writing an essay about a difficult or challenging event or experience.

# A WORKPLACE SCENARIO
## A LETTER REVISION
### The Workplace Writer and the Writing Task

Mary Cortez works as an account representative for Commerce Hotel Corporation, a company that owns several hotel chains. She is writing a letter to a potential client, Louise Wilson. Cortez wrote a draft of her letter and then revised it. The first draft and her second draft showing the revisions she made are presented below. Study each revision to see why she made each change.

---

November 12, 2005

Miss Louise Wilson
Corporate Travel Department
Brother's Electric Company
2300 Trade Way
Chicago, IL 60670

Dear Miss Wilson:

I enjoyed our recent conversation regarding the FG program and am delighted to hear that the people at Brother's Electric are thinking about joining. Incidentally, we are planning a special Thanksgiving weekend rate, so keep that in mind in case you happen to be in San Francisco for the holiday.

The enclosed brochure explains the details of the FG program. Your FG ID card is enclosed. Use it whenever you make reservations with us to obtain a corporate discount. We will see to it that your executives are treated with special courtesy and that they get to use the health club free.

We also have excellent convention facilities and banquet rooms should you want to book a convention or meeting here. We hope you and your company will take advantage of these outstanding world-class amenities. Please call me if you have any questions. I will be happy to answer them.

Sincerely,

Mary Cortez
Account Representative

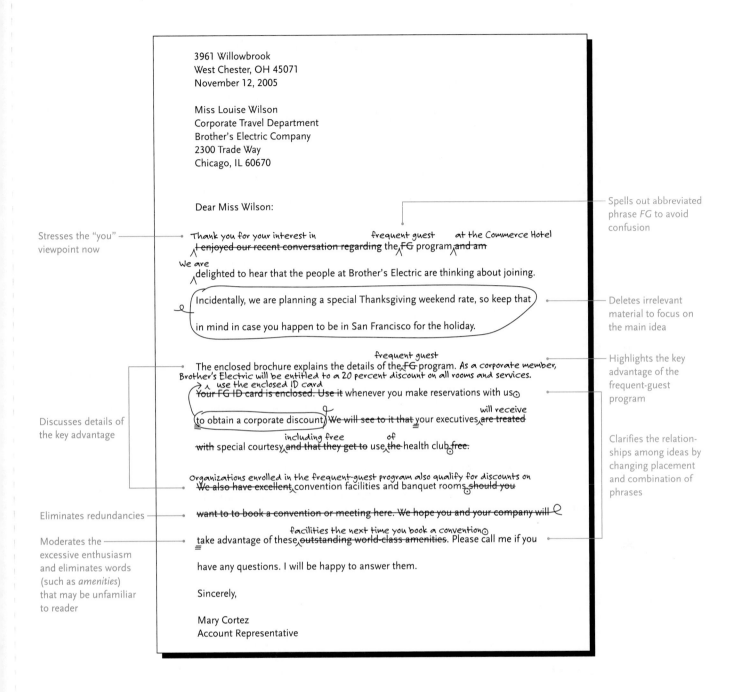

3961 Willowbrook
West Chester, OH 45071
November 12, 2005

Miss Louise Wilson
Corporate Travel Department
Brother's Electric Company
2300 Trade Way
Chicago, IL 60670

Dear Miss Wilson:

*Stresses the "you" viewpoint now*

Thank you for your interest in ~~I enjoyed our recent conversation regarding the~~ frequent guest ~~FG~~ program ~~and am~~ at the Commerce Hotel
We are delighted to hear that the people at Brother's Electric are thinking about joining.

*Spells out abbreviated phrase FG to avoid confusion*

~~Incidentally, we are planning a special Thanksgiving weekend rate, so keep that in mind in case you happen to be in San Francisco for the holiday.~~

*Deletes irrelevant material to focus on the main idea*

*Discusses details of the key advantage*

The enclosed brochure explains the details of the ~~FG~~ frequent guest program. As a corporate member, Brother's Electric will be entitled to a 20 percent discount on all rooms and services. use the enclosed ID card ~~Your FG ID card is enclosed. Use it~~ whenever you make reservations with us, to obtain a corporate discount. ~~We will see to it that~~ your executives will receive ~~are treated~~ including free with special courtesy, ~~and that they get to use~~ of the health club ~~free.~~

*Highlights the key advantage of the frequent-guest program*

*Clarifies the relationships among ideas by changing placement and combination of phrases*

*Eliminates redundancies*

Organizations enrolled in the frequent-guest program also qualify for discounts on ~~We also have excellent~~ convention facilities and banquet rooms, ~~should you want to to book a convention or meeting here. We hope you and your company will~~ facilities the next time you book a convention. take advantage of these, ~~outstanding world-class amenities.~~ Please call me if you

*Moderates the excessive enthusiasm and eliminates words (such as amenities) that may be unfamiliar to reader*

have any questions. I will be happy to answer them.

Sincerely,

Mary Cortez
Account Representative

## Examining Workplace Writing

1. What changes did Cortez make to strengthen the "sales pitch" of her letter?

2. Which changes made her letter clearer and easier to understand?

3. What further changes could Cortez make to improve her letter?

## Workplace Writing Assignments

1. Imagine that you have created the world's best _____ (fill in the blank with a product of your choice: can opener, ball point pen, pair of sneakers, etc.). Write a letter to a potential customer urging him or her to consider purchasing the product.

2. Assume you are Louise Wilson. Write a letter in reply to Mary Cortez. You might have further questions and you may try to negotiate for a better discount, for example.

# WRITING ABOUT A READING

## Thinking Before Reading

The following reading, "Your Player's Keeper," appeared in the April 2, 2004 issue of *The Chronicle of Higher Education*. The author is a college professor and an assistant football coach at Saint Olaf College. This essay addresses the problem of athletes' inappropriate behavior off the playing field. As you read, notice the author's use of detail to support each topic sentence.

1. Preview the reading, using the steps discussed in Chapter 2, p. 30.

2. Connect the reading to your own experience by answering the following questions:

    a. What role do you think a coach should have in a player's personal life?

    b. Do you know any collegiate or professional athletes who behave as if they should have special privileges?

### READING

# Your Player's Keeper

### Gordon Marino

1    For the boys who play out the athletics contests around which our civilization often seems to revolve, football coaches have special influence. They are the gatekeepers to the fields of dreams, and I can tell you from personal experience as both a player and a coach that coaches have a direct line to student athletes who might be indifferent to other authority figures.

**University of Colorado football/ sex scandal**
Several women have stated that they were raped by University of Colorado football players or recruits. The university is accused of using sex and alcohol to attract new athletes.

2     No one would think to hold a professor responsible for the criminal behavior of a student. But as the **University of Colorado football/sex scandal** makes clear, coaches are held partially accountable for the conduct of their players. Yet it is rare to hear one of them complain, "I am not my player's keeper." Just the opposite, coaches warm to the rhetoric of responsibility and the educational value of intercollegiate athletics. While every college-sports scandal elicits frenzied cries for wholesale reform, there are relatively pain- less interventions that might markedly improve the culture of elite male sports. Father figures that they most certainly are, coaches should use their attention-grabbing positions to offer the young men with whom they work, often for as long as four years, some remedial sex education.

3     Judging from my own experience as a player and from the high-school and college-age male athletes with whom I have spoken, sex education is either too abstract or too clinical to prepare young men for the specific temp- tations that they are likely to face. Although most linebackers know how to avoid getting someone pregnant and are aware of the dangers of sexually transmitted diseases, boys becoming men are seldom given an opportunity to rehearse the scenes in which they will often fumble very difficult choices.

4     Many of the sex offenses of athletes begin at parties, where some young men manage to convince themselves that the young women present are say- ing—simply by being there and drinking—that they want to sleep with a jock. Coaches need to make sure that players grasp the fact that attending a frat fest is not an indirect indication of a woman's desire to mate.

5     We lecture kids about sex and we lecture them about alcohol, but we ought to deliver at least one lecture about sex and alcohol together. I suspect that a large number of sexual-assault cases involve an intoxicated couple in which the woman does not protest one level of physical contact but then mutters "no" to another level. To make matters even murkier, she might at the same time want to continue some kind of sensuous contact. Hollywood and caveman logic have encouraged males to imagine that women shake their heads and scream "no" when they are enjoying themselves sexually, so, simple as it may seem, we need to coach young men to understand that "no" really does mean "stop." More than that, late-adolescent males need help anticipating the fact that "no" is hard to hear when you have quaffed a six- pack or three and the woman who is waving off your advances is nibbling on your ear.

6     The first teaching moment should come in August, when players report for summer practice, and those lessons and conversations should be repeated throughout the year. Before getting down to **football chalk talks**, coaches should have candid discussions with players about women's psychosexuality. When I was a football player three decades ago, there were coeds who seemed very attracted to **gridiron artists** and our animal-house parties. Football players exchanged informal notes on these women. Tough and worldly as we thought we were, most of us were exploring new psychological territory without a

**football chalk talks**
in-depth discussions of football, specific plays, and game

**gridiron artists**
football players

guide, without someone to help us understand what the women were trying to communicate to us. Someone needs to explain that young women often are ambivalent about their sexual desires and may sometimes seek to resolve that ambivalence by drinking themselves into states of mind in which they are essentially out of their minds.

7      In many sexual-assault cases, young men claim that the contact that they are being prosecuted for was consensual. It could be that no one has helped them understand that a person cannot really give consent unless she is sober. One college athlete I know is now doing hard time. He and a girl he was dating were drunk. They necked. She fell unconscious. He understood her drinking and necking to be consent, and he began having intercourse. The woman came to and understandably went first ballistic and then to the DA. The young man, who is adamant that the woman really wanted to have sexual relations, now feels like the victim of an angry woman. Coaches need to make it plain that drunken sex is as dangerous as unprotected sex. They also should let it be known that they are not going to use their often enormous political clout to defend athletes' drunken misbehavior.

8      Coaches have the authority to convince their charges of the virtue of throwing their shoulders into a 240-pound running back hurtling down the field at 25 miles per hour. Trainers in the physical arts also are well aware of the value if mentally rehearsing blocks and pass patterns, and, on the day before games, hold walk-throughs of plays. There is no reason why coaches shouldn't also help their athletes rehearse situations off the field, and utter a few well-chosen words about moral boundaries before sending their pumped-up charges out into the night after games.

**secular**
worldly

9      Men awarded for physical prowess have always been treated deferentially, and athletes no less than movie stars are **secular** America's equivalent of holy figures. People thrill just to touch the jacket or get the signature or tape from the wrist of a football player. The collegiate stars who leap across our television screens are walked through registration and assigned personal tutors. It is understandable that they would think of themselves as privileged; that sense of **entitlement** can easily devolve into the belief they have license to do what they please. When this feeling of moral **carte blanche** is mixed with the risk-taking inclinations of athletes, bad things can happen to good people. Coaches should watch for opportunities like a skipped class or an offhand remark to challenge their players' dangerous sense of false identity.

**entitlement**
right to receive something

**carte blanche**
full power, with no limitations

10     Athletes in big-ticket sports programs confront a different set of temptations from most of their classmates. Coaches know the interpersonal landscape. Rather than wag their fingers or shrug their shoulders, they need to help prepare their players for situations in life that are more complex than the intricacies of a **West Coast offense**.

**West Coast offense**
a certain coaching structure and philosophy developed by Bill Walsh and used successfully during his time with the San Francisco 49ers.

## Getting Ready to Write

### Reviewing the Reading

1. Highlight the sentence that states the main point (thesis) of the essay.

2. Why should coaches be concerned about the off-field behavior of their players?

3. What kinds of sex education do most young men get from school? What other things do they need to be told?

4. What situations does the author think college athletes are not prepared to handle?

5. Why do some college athletes feel and act privileged?

6. What actions does the author suggest coaches take to improve players' behavior off the playing field?

### Examining the Reading: Drawing Idea Maps

Earlier in this chapter, you learned to draw revision maps to check the content and organization of your own writing. Maps can also help you analyze someone else's writing. They can help you understand how the writer's ideas relate to one another and how the piece is organized. You will also find that by expressing the writer's ideas briefly in your own words, you'll remember the material you read better. Complete the idea map of "Your Player's Keeper" on the next page by filling in the missing information.

### Thinking Critically: Examining Assumptions

Assumptions are ideas a writer believes to be true but does not try to prove. A writer may take it for granted that the reader will agree with those ideas because they share a common background or set of values. Assumptions can be opinions or beliefs. Assumptions can deal with what is good or bad, right or wrong, valuable, worthwhile, or important. For example, if someone says to you, "You're not going to make that mistake again, are you?" the assumption is you have already made the mistake once. If a writer argues for restrictions to be placed on violence shown in children's television programming, he or she is assuming that showing violence is harmful.

An author may state assumptions, or they may be implied by other things he or she says. As a reader, it is your job to examine these assumptions and decide whether they are really true. Then you can evaluate whether arguments or ideas based on these assumptions make sense.

The primary assumption on which this reading is based is that football coaches can influence the behavior of their players. Do you agree with this assumption? Some people might argue that many coaches are corrupt themselves and, therefore, do not command the respect needed to influence the behavior of the athletes. Others might believe that athletes are going to behave in a certain way no matter what their coaches tell them.

# Visualize It!

**Idea Map**

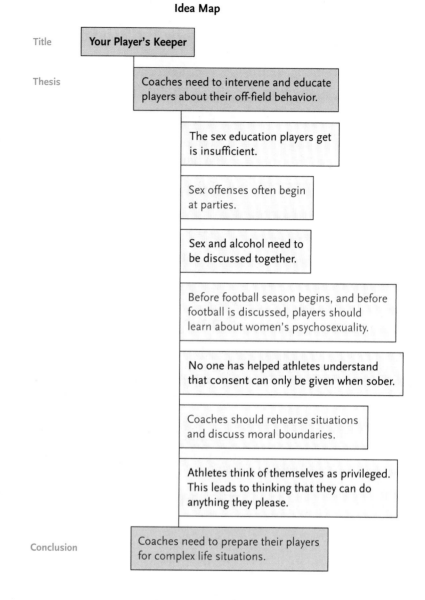

Title — **Your Player's Keeper**

Thesis — Coaches need to intervene and educate players about their off-field behavior.

The sex education players get is insufficient.

Sex offenses often begin at parties.

Sex and alcohol need to be discussed together.

Before football season begins, and before football is discussed, players should learn about women's psychosexuality.

No one has helped athletes understand that consent can only be given when sober.

Coaches should rehearse situations and discuss moral boundaries.

Athletes think of themselves as privileged. This leads to thinking that they can do anything they please.

Conclusion — Coaches need to prepare their players for complex life situations.

Here are a few more assumptions made in the reading, Choose one and write a paragraph explaining why you agree or disagree with it.

1. Women are ambivalent about their sexual desires.

2. Some men have difficulty understanding what women are trying to communicate to them.

3. Rehearsals of off-field behavior are effective in altering athletes' behavior.

## Strengthening Your Vocabulary

**Part A:** Using the word's context, word parts, or a dictionary, write a brief definition of each of the following words or phrases as it is used in the reading.

1.  gatekeepers (paragraph 1) individuals who control access to somebody

    or something

2.  rhetoric (paragraph 2) persuasive speech or writing

3.  elicits (paragraph 2) provokes a reaction

4.  ambivalent (paragraph 6) uncertain, having conflicting or mixed feelings

5.  adamant (paragraph 7) set or fixed in opinion

6.  deferentially (paragraph 9) with respect

7.  devolve (paragraph 9) transfer

**Part B:** Choose one of the above words and draw a word map of it.

## Reacting to Ideas: Discussion and Journal Writing

1.  Discuss the importance of athletics on your campus.

2.  Why are athletes held in such high regard in our society? Do some athletes command more respect than others? Why?

3.  Discuss the issue of alcohol use on your college campus. What problems are associated with student drinking? What can be done to solve these problems?

4.  Discuss the degree of influence coaches have over their players. Why does this influence exist?

5.  What is the author's attitude toward coaches? Do you think it matters that he himself is a coach?

## Writing About the Reading

## Paragraph Options

1.  Many coaches were players themselves once. Write a paragraph explaining what advantage this experience gives coaches.

2.  Write a paragraph about one well-known athlete, collegiate or professional. Evaluate his or her behavior off the playing field.

3. The author urges coaches to help players rehearse their response to moral situations off the playing field. Write a paragraph identifying and describing another situation in which practice or rehearsal is important.

## Essay Options

4. Describe the public image and behavior of a well-known athlete. Use details to help your reader visualize this person.

5. Do you think a coach should be responsible for the behavior of his players off the playing field? Write an essay explaining and giving reasons for your position.

6. The author has found that "sex education is either too abstract or too clinical . . ." Write an essay explaining why you agree or disagree with this statement. Include any suggestions that you might have for a quality sex education program.

7. Some people feel that sex education does not belong in the schools, especially elementary schools; others feel it is essential. Write an essay that explains your position on this topic. Be sure to include relevant details from your own knowledge and experiences.

# CHAPTER REVIEW AND PRACTICE

## Chapter Review

| | |
|---|---|
| WHAT IS REVISION? | Revision is examining your ideas and how you express them. |
| WHAT SHOULD YOU EXAMINE ABOUT YOUR IDEAS? | 1. Examine whether the details are relevant and sufficient. <br> 2. Evaluate the logical arrangement of your ideas. |
| WHAT WILL DRAWING AN IDEA MAP OF YOUR ESSAY SHOW? | An idea map will help you identify ideas that do not belong in the essay and it will help you evaluate your organization. |
| WHAT FEATURES OF LANGUAGE SHOULD YOU EXAMINE? | Your language should be vivid and specific and it should suit your audience and purpose. |
| WHAT IS EDITING? | Editing is making your sentences clear and grammatically correct by identifying and correcting errors in grammar, spelling, and punctuation. |
| WHAT IS AN ERROR LOG? | An error log is a record of errors you have made in essays you have written. |
| WHAT IS PROOFREADING? | Proofreading is reading your essay a final time to catch any typing errors or any grammar, punctuation, or spelling errors you may have missed during editing. |

## Skill Refresher: Subject-Verb Agreement

A verb must agree with its subject in number. A subject that refers to one person, place, or thing is called a *singular subject*. A subject that refers to more than one is called a *plural subject*.

## Guidelines

1. A singular subject must be used with a singular verb.

   The <u>dog</u> <u>wants</u> to go jogging with me.

2. A plural subject must be used with a plural verb.

The <u>dogs</u> <u>want</u> to go jogging with me.

## Mistakes to Watch For

Subject-verb agreement errors often occur in the following situations:

1. With compound subjects (two or more subjects)

   INCORRECT      <u>Yolanda</u> and <u>Lion</u> <u>wants</u> to lead the way.

   CORRECT      <u>Yolanda</u> and <u>Lion</u> <u>want</u> to lead the way.

2. When the verb comes before the subject

   INCORRECT      There <u>is</u> four gas <u>stations</u> on Main Street.

   CORRECT      There <u>are</u> four gas <u>stations</u> on Main Street.

3. When a word or phrase comes between the subject and the verb

   INCORRECT      The <u>woman</u> standing in the waves with the other swimmers <u>win</u> a prize for her endurance.

   CORRECT      The <u>woman</u> standing in the waves with the other swimmers <u>wins</u> a prize for her endurance.

4. With indefinite pronouns (pronouns like *someone* or *everybody*, which do not refer to a specific person). Some indefinite pronouns (*everyone, each, neither, such as*) take a singular verb; others (*both* or *many*) always take a plural verb. Some indefinite pronouns may take either a singular or a plural verb (*all, any, none*). Treat the pronoun as singular if it refers to something that cannot be counted. Treat the pronoun as plural if it refers to more than one of something that can be counted.

   INCORRECT      <u>Everybody</u> <u>wish</u> to become a millionaire.

   CORRECT      <u>Everybody</u> <u>wishes</u> to become a millionaire.

## Rate Your Ability to Use Subject-Verb Agreement

Circle the word or phrase that correctly completes each sentence.

1. Someone (want, wants) to revise the work schedule for next week.

2. Computers (is, are) more dependable than they were five years ago.

3. The sheriff, together with three deputies, (agree, agrees) to establish a roadblock.

4. Trisha and I (swim, swims) together every morning.

5. Neither Bo nor Jeff (know, knows) the answer.

6. Here (is, are) the technical manual.

7. Letters and memos (is, are) printed on company letterhead stationery.

8. (Candy, Candies) harms teeth because of its high sugar content.

9. (Sabrina) Sabrina and Mary) is going to the fireworks display tonight.

10. On my front lawn (was, were) two discarded soda cans.

Score _____

Check your answers, using the Answer Key on p. 640. If you missed more than two, you need additional review and practice in recognizing and correcting errors in subject-verb agreement. Refer to section C.6 of Part VI, "Reviewing the Basics." For additional practice, go to this book's Web site at  http://www.ablongman.com/mcwhorterexpressways1e.

## INTERNET ACTIVITIES

### 1.   Computer Revision

An instructor at Glendale Community College suggests that some students might benefit from the use of special computer revision techniques. Try the exercise that she created (use one of your own paragraphs for step 3).

http://www.glory.gc.maricopa.edu/~kschwalm/English101/revision.htm

Evaluate how this technique works for you.

### 2.   Commonly Misspelled Words

Check your recognition of these common words that are often spelled incorrectly. Take the quiz and make note of the words you need to study.

http://www.sentex.net/~mmcadams/spelling.html

### 3.   Editing Practice

The University of Wisconsin, Madison writing center has created this site of twelve common errors.

http://www.wisc.edu/writing/Handbook/CommonErrors.html

Examine these examples and explanations. Then choose six to work with further. Write your own sentence that needs improvement and then show how you fixed it.

### 4.   This Book's Web Site

Learn more about revision by visiting the book's Web site.

http://www.ablongman.com/mcwhorterexpressways1e

# PART III

# Methods of Development

# 6

# Narration

## Chapter Objectives

*In this chapter you will learn to:*

1. Select a topic and generate ideas.

2. Organize events in a narrative sequence.

3. Use transitions to connect your ideas.

4. Write an effective topic sentence.

## Write About It!

Study the photo above. What do you think is happening? Try to recreate the soldier's story. Why did he volunteer for the service? Where was he stationed? What did he experience there? Is he on leave or has he been discharged? What feelings is he expressing at this homecoming? Write a paragraph that answers these questions and tells this soldier's story since his enlistment.

Most likely you told the soldier's story in the order in which it happened, beginning with his enlistment and ending with his homecoming. If so, you have just written a narrative—a story that relates a sequence of events. Narration is often called for in everyday life, in academic courses, and on the job, as shown below.

EVERYDAY SCENARIOS

- Telling a friend how you spent the weekend
- Describing a frightening or humorous occurrence

ACADEMIC SCENARIOS

- Summarizing the plot of a short story
- Describing a series of historical events

WORKPLACE SCENARIOS

- Reporting on responding to a 911 call, as an EMT (emergency medical technician)
- Writing a progress report on the development of a new Web site, as the site's designer

# UNDERSTANDING NARRATIVES

Imagine that you are telling a friend about a disagreement you had with a nasty sales clerk when attempting to return a defective DVD player. Probably you would repeat the conversation in the order in which it occurred: "I said . . . , then he said . . ." and so on.

In describing your disagreement, you organize ideas in the order in which they occurred in time—that is, in time sequence. Organizing ideas by using time sequence is a common and effective writing technique. Describing events by using time sequence is called **narration.** Such writing is often referred to as **narrative.** In this chapter, you will learn more about how to write narrative paragraphs and essays to fulfill both academic and workplace assignments.

## EXERCISE 6-1

**Directions:** Working alone or with another student, brainstorm a list of times when you have recently used narration.

## Writing Narrative Paragraphs

Writing a narrative is similar to telling a story—one of the oldest, most appealing, and most enjoyable ways of communicating ideas. Throughout history, ideas have been communicated and recorded through stories, myths, fables, and legends. Stories remain popular today: movies, television shows, soap operas, and even many jokes involve a series of events organized and presented in story form.

Sometimes a narrative is a straightforward, objective recounting of events. Police reports and medical reports, for example, aim at being strictly objective, with no personal opinions. Other narratives make a point through a story. In narratives that you write for your writing class, you should be sure to make a point through the events you recount. Here is a paragraph that reports a fire that destroyed a barn. Notice that the paragraph reports objective facts, but it also makes the point that this farm is part of a caring community of friends and neighbors.

**Fire Destroys Barn on Hauser Farm**    A fire started by lightning at the Hauser dairy farm in Thompsonville Saturday night engulfed the main barn in flames by the time firefighters arrived. The fire started on the first floor and spread to the loft and roof. The fire was extinguished in two hours, but it took most of the night to excavate and bury hundreds of smoldering bales of hay. Neighbors from miles around came to help; some brought tractors, others dug by hand. At daybreak, others brought trailers and hauled the herd to a nearby farm where a temporary milking operation was set up and manned by neighboring farmers. Amy Hauser described the rescue effort: "All of my neighbors were wonderful. They kept us going when we thought all hope was lost."

## Selecting a Topic and Generating Ideas

For shorter pieces of writing, such as paragraphs and short essays, it is usually best to concentrate on a single event or experience. Otherwise, you will have too much information to cover, and you will not be able to include sufficient detail. To generate ideas for a narrative, make a list of events. Don't worry, at this point, about expressing each in sentence form or listing them in the order in which they occurred. Record in the margin any feelings you have about the events. Although you may not include them in the paragraph, they will be helpful in writing your topic sentence.

## EXERCISE 6-2

*Writing in Progress*

**Directions:** Assume you are taking an introductory psychology class this semester and your instructor has asked you to describe one of the following scenarios. Begin by making a list of the events that occurred.

1. A situation in which you observed or benefited from altruistic behavior (someone helping another person unselfishly, out of concern and compassion)

2. A vivid childhood memory

3. An experience in which you felt stress

4. A time when you were in danger and how you reacted

5. A situation in which you either rejected or gave in to peer pressure

## Writing Your Topic Sentence

A topic sentence states the main point of your paragraph. Your topic sentence should accomplish two things:

- It should identify your topic—the experience you are writing about.

- It should indicate your view or attitude toward that experience.

For example, suppose you are writing a paragraph about your first day of classes. Your view might be that the campus was confusing and frustrating or that you felt unprepared and did not know what was expected of you in your classes. Here are a few possible topic sentences that indicate a point of view:

Registration was easier that I expected because my advisor was very helpful and explained everything.

Registration was difficult because many of the classes I wanted were closed and I ended up with a very inconvenient schedule.

Sometimes you may discover your view toward the experience as you are writing about it. For example, a student drafted the following paragraph about registering for her classes:

Online registration was supposed to be simple, and it was for my friends. My registration was a nightmare. The computer in my advisor's office went down. When she tried to get back online, she learned the main system in the college had failed. We could not find out what classes were available; we could not check prerequisites; we could not even find the times my courses were being offered. We waited a while, and finally she told me to come back tomorrow. I was afraid that all the classes I wanted would be filled before I had a chance to register.

As she was writing, she realized she wished she had known more about the problems of the online registration process before she began. Then she wrote the following topic sentence:

My first registration day at college might not have been so frustrating if someone had warned me about the possibility of computer system failures at the college and told me to take a hard copy of class listings with me.

## EXERCISE 6-3
*Writing in Progress*

**Directions:** For the experience or situation you chose in Exercise 6-2, write a topic sentence that expresses your attitude toward the experience.

## Sequencing and Developing Your Ideas

The events in a narrative paragraph are usually arranged in chronological order—the order in which they happened. Sometimes, however, you may want to rearrange events to emphasize a point. If you do, make sure the sequence of events is clear enough for the reader to follow.

## Visualize It! ►

The following diagram shows you how to visualize a narrative paragraph.

**Narrative Paragraph Idea Map**

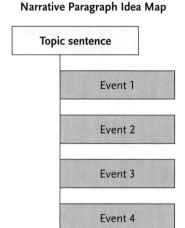

To place the events in the correct sequence, review and number your list of events.

A clear, well-written narrative should provide sufficient detail to allow your readers to understand fully the situation about which you are writing. Try to answer for your readers most of the following questions:

*When* did it happen?    *What* events occurred?

*Where* did it happen?    *Why* did they happen?

*Who* was involved?    *How* did they happen?

Be sure to include only essential and relevant details. Other details will distract readers from the events you are describing.

## EXERCISE 6-4

*Writing in Progress*

**Directions:** For the experience or situation you selected for Exercises 6-2 and 6-3, draft a paragraph describing the events in the order in which they occurred.

### Considering Your Audience and Purpose

When writing a narrative, your audience and your purpose will help you decide:

- **how much explanation and which definitions to include about each event.** An audience that is unfamiliar with the event may need more detail than readers who are familiar with it. If you are writing about a baseball game and your audience is made up of baseball fans, then you will not need to explain rules, scoring, and so forth. However, if your audience is not made up of baseball enthusiasts, you may need to explain terms such as outs, home runs, and errors.

- **how much background information to include.** If you are writing about an everyday event, such as a traffic jam most readers need little explanation about it; however, if you are writing about a holiday, such as *Cinco de Mayo,* you may need to provide your non-Hispanic readers with some background about the holiday.

## Useful Transitions

Transitions are words that connect ideas to one another. Transitions in narratives lead your readers from one event to another. They make your writing easier to follow and clearly identify important parts of your narrative. In the following paragraph, notice how each of the highlighted transitions signal that the next event is to come.

> I do not usually take risks, especially when it comes to food, but last Saturday I took a bold step and ordered tripe at Tivoli, a local Italian restaurant. When I ordered, the waiter told me there would be a 15-minute delay. I tried to convince myself it would be worth the wait. After waiting 25 minutes, I called the waiter; he apologized and said the kitchen was short-handed and that it would be only another ten minutes. As I waited, I began to ask myself why would I want to eat the stomach of a cow, anyway? Would I hate it? Would I be able to eat it? Finally, my long-awaited tripe arrived. After I tasted it, I realized my fears were silly; it was delicious and well worth the long wait. I wonder what new food I should try next?

Here are some frequently used transitional words and phrases that connect events in a sequence:

**Table 6-1   Transitions for Narrative Paragraphs**

| first | then | in the beginning | next |
|---|---|---|---|
| second(ly) | later | after | during |
| third(ly) | at last | following | after that |
| finally | | | |

## EXERCISE 6-5

**Directions:** In each blank provided, supply a transitional word or phrase that helps identify the sequence of events.

1. _____*After*_____ we left the theater, we stopped for coffee.

2. After a long drive, we _____*finally*_____ reached our destination.

3. _____*During*_____ the movie, an audience member's loudly ringing cell phone distracted everyone.

4. To evaluate the reliability of a Web site, examine its source and _____*then/next*_____ check the date of posting.

5. To preview a textbook chapter, first check the title. Secondly, read the chapter objectives. _____Thirdly_____, read the introduction.

## EXERCISE 6-6

*Writing in Progress*

**Directions:** Revise the paragraph you wrote for Exercise 6-4. Check it for transitional words and phrases and add them, as necessary, to make your ideas clearer.

## Writing Narrative Essays

Although this chapter has focused on writing narrative paragraphs, you can use many of the same skills for writing narrative essays.

### Guidelines for Narrative Essays

Here are a few guidelines to follow in writing narrative essays:

1. **Tell your story from a consistent point of view.** That is, choose one person involved in the story and tell it from his or her perspective. When explaining a complicated series of events over the course of several paragraphs, it is easy to switch from one person's perspective to another's. Before you begin writing, decide whose point of view you will use. Once you have made this decision, you are more likely to be conscious of point of view and to use it consistently.

2. **Use the same tense throughout.** Unless you have a specific reason for doing otherwise, write in one tense—past or present. That is, tell the story as it did happen (past) or as if it is happening now (present).

3. **Focus on the most important elements of your story.** Do not distract your readers by including insignificant facts, events, people, or descriptions.

4. **Use vivid language.** Help your readers visualize the action in your narrative by using descriptive detail (see p. 89) about sights, people, places, and so forth.

### Using Sequence Maps

To write a narrative essay, you must have a clear understanding of the sequence of events. A sequence map—a visual representation of key events or steps in the order in which they occur—can help you keep these in order. A sequence map looks like this:

# Visualize It!

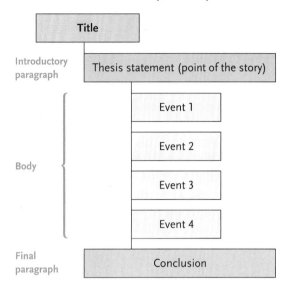

**Format for a Sequence Map**

Title

Introductory paragraph — Thesis statement (point of the story)

Body
- Event 1
- Event 2
- Event 3
- Event 4

Final paragraph — Conclusion

You'll also find sequence maps useful in understanding a variety of materials you read. Plots of novels and short stories, for example, frequently switch back and forth in time; a sequence map can help you follow events. Drawing sequence maps is also useful when studying events in history and processes and procedures in the sciences.

## EXERCISE 6-7

**Directions:** Assume you are taking a health and nutrition course. Your instructor has given you an assignment to write a one- to two-page narrative essay that illustrates one of these topics:

1. The relationship between sleep and effective functioning

2. The consequences of alcohol or drug abuse

3. The dispute between smokers and nonsmokers over a smoke-free environment

4. The appeal and health dangers of salty, fatty, or sweet snacks

5. The difficulty (or ease) of regular exercise

## AN ACADEMIC SCENARIO
### A STUDENT ESSAY
### The Academic Writer and the Writing Task

Ted Sawchuck is a student at Harrisburg Area Community College, majoring in mass communication. For his school paper, *The Fourth Estate,* he wrote an essay describing his experience as a campaign aid for Howard Dean in the summer of 2004, prior to the 2004 presidential election. Howard Dean, one of the Democratic candidates for the presidency, ran in the primaries but was defeated by John Kerry,

who became the Democratic Party's nominee. As you read the essay, note how Ted Sawchuck introduces, presents, and concludes his narrative sequence of events. This essay has been annotated; be sure to study the annotations after you have read the essay once. The thesis statement is highlighted in blue, and topic sentences are highlighted in yellow. The transitions are highlighted in green.

## Frostbite, Reporting, and The Scream: A College Journalist Inside the Last Days of Howard Dean's Iowa Campaign
### Ted Sawchuck

*Background information about Dean and campaign*

*Active first-person point of view used throughout*

1   The mass media summed up Howard Dean's Iowa campaign as a screeching yell and a third-place finish, but I saw something different in my two weeks working for and covering it. I heard the sneers of voters who had already picked another candidate and the breathless shrieks of orange-hatted volunteers when Dean took the stage at rallies. I even talked to a couple of people who didn't know who Dean was—thankfully, we had a script for that. It went something like, "Well, he's the former governor of Vermont, balanced the state's budget, signed the first bill authorizing civil unions in America . . ." and I'd keep babbling until the person either started agreeing, reached for a weapon, or showed signs of frostbite. (It's very cold in Iowa.)

*Thesis statement*

From this experience I learned that without young people who didn't need much sleep but could work long hours, campaigns would go nowhere. Here's how it went down.

*Sawchuck's trip begins*

*Topic sentence*

2   My trip started when I met the bus at the McDonald's on Eisenhower Boulevard in Harrisburg, Pennsylvania. Nineteen hours later, I unfolded myself out of a minivan, and entered the place I'd be sleeping for the next three days, a cabin at a Camp Fire girls' camp in Cedar Rapids, Iowa. I had a

mattress laid on concrete right next to the bathroom. That night, bedtime was five o'clock and wakefulness came at six thirty. It was the best hour and a half of sleep I've ever had.

*Details make trip come alive*

*Topic sentence*    3    After breakfast the next day, we piled into vans and rode forty-five minutes to the orientation meeting at Coe College where my education in the way primary politics really works began. There we had an hour of training in how to persuade people to vote for our candidate and were issued hideous orange

*Note use of detail*    hats and identification badges. Then it was back into the van and a short ride later we were pounding the pavement and knocking on doors for Dean. I met a lot of interesting people through canvassing. Three had a definite ABB (Anyone But Bush) state of mind. Some were definitely for John Kerry (the eventual nominee), John Edwards (the eventual vice-presidential nominee), Dick Gephardt (who did so badly he retired from politics) or Dean. Most were still undecided, which was somewhat surprising in a state that was getting blanketed by phone calls from both humans and machines, canvassers from out of state and in, and mailings of all types. I was grateful for the differences of opinion, though, as Iowa is an extremely cold state, and without people opening their doors, my face would never have thawed out.

*Topic sentence*    4    On the third day, Governor Dean was scheduled to speak at Jefferson High School in Cedar Rapids. Attendance was required, and we were excited. I was especially glad to finally get a chance to cover something newsworthy and give the people back in Accounts Payable a reason to sign off on my expense account. I shed my orange hat, threw on a press pass and grabbed my camera. Judith Dean, the candidate's wife, opened up with a speech that seemed to say, "Yes, I'm not a public speaker. That's why my being here is important." It worked. Dean followed with his standard stump speech, placing extra emphasis on the importance of farming and ethanol.

*Topic sentence*    5    As I listened to Dean's speeches at different events, I realized how primary politics work; candidates write one main speech and then change it slightly depending on where they go. You hear the same points often enough to be able to repeat them with the speaker, and it's fun to do so, especially when you're standing between the Associated Press and MSNBC journalists. After Cedar Rapids wrapped up, my group drove to Iowa City fast enough that I can't tell you the exact speed since there may still be a statute of limitations in effect. Dean's speech this time was again his standard, but more liberal, touching briefly on his belief in the right of women to choose to have abortions. I didn't get a crowd estimate for Cedar Rapids, but Iowa City drew at least three thousand.

*Dialogue adds interest*    6    The next morning, I woke up at six a.m. to a shirtless man in slippers shuffling by my mattress muttering, "It starts here. It starts now. It starts here. It starts now." I grumbled, wondering if this could possibly wait until

*Topic sentence*

both my eyes were open. Eventually, my eyes did open, and the campaign put me to work. That day was all phones for me. I sat down in a lawn chair with a call list, a script, and a Motorola flip-phone. The phone's battery died and I plugged it in and kept calling. Three hours later it was my time to leave. It was a good thing, too: the phone was hot enough that I was having trouble holding it.

*Topic sentence*

7    The caucus night celebration (held on the night Iowans decided who their Democratic candidate would be) was being held in Des Moines at a place called the Val-Air Ballroom. It's almost pure kitsch, and quite large. The size of the Ballroom turned out to be important, as I've seen looser-packed crowds at Fuel shows. First, Senator Tom Harkin, as he had at the past two rallies I attended, introduced Dean. Then the candidate came out in a suit, pumping his fists. He pulled off his jacket, rolled up his sleeves, and launched into his speech. Standing by the stage, I was enthralled. After all, I'd worked very hard for this man, and been rewarded with what was then viewed as a crushing defeat. Dean seemed to know that, and did his best to rally his troops. And then, the infamous screech. Interestingly enough, I didn't hear it that night. Here's why: The audio you hear on radio and TV was recorded directly from Dean's microphone. In the hall, it was incredibly loud, with at least a thousand Dean supporters cheering. The candidate yelled so they could hear him, not because of some mythical streak of anger.

*Conclusion: Sawchuck evaluates his experience*

8    It was over. Dean had been defeated. Was it worth it? Yes, working for something you believe in is always worthwhile. The ride back was 24 hours straight through. I spent most of it with a fellow volunteer, talking about the experience that would eventually become this essay.

## Examining Academic Writing

1. Draw a sequence map of Ted Sawchuck's essay.

2. Was Ted Sawchuck's essay interesting and engaging? If so, what did he do to make it so?

3. Evaluate the level and type of detail included in the essay. Was there too much or too little detail, or a sufficient amount?

4. Did Ted Sawchuck include sufficient introductory information in the essay? If not, what further information was needed?

5. What questions about Ted Sawchuck's involvement in the campaign, if any, remain unanswered? Should this information have been included in the essay?

## Academic Writing Assignments

1. Write a paragraph describing your participation or lack of participation in a recent election (national, local, or campus). Include reasons for your choice.

2. Write a narrative essay describing how you have worked or would like to work for a cause in which you believe. The cause might be a national issue (such as the war in Iraq), a local issue (such as commercial development or speed zones), or a campus issue (such as parking or minority representation on the faculty). Be sure to describe your level and type of participation in the cause, as well as its results.

3. Write a letter to Ted Sawchuck. You might commend him for political participation, ask him questions, or suggest alternative methods of political participation.

# A WORKPLACE SCENARIO
## A CASE REPORT
### The Workplace Writer and the Writing Task

Maria Sanchez is a visiting nurse who checks on patients who have recently been discharged from the hospital. After each visit, she must write case notes that report the patient's condition, describe treatment, and identify future needs. Here is an excerpt from the case notes Sanchez wrote for an elderly patient. Notice that the notes are written in a chronologically arranged narrative.

> Mrs. Weatherly had fallen in her kitchen that morning and needed immediate first aid. Her left lower leg had a 3-inch cut and was still bleeding. I dressed the wound, and then did an examination to check for other injuries, but found none. Next, I checked her vital signs, changed her surgical dressing, and gave her a sponge bath. She was reluctant to do her breathing exercises and leg lifts, but with encouragement we got through them. I recommend that the family consider installing handrails in her home and also consider a lifeline monitor for her in case of future accidents.

## Examining Workplace Writing

1. In what ways are the case notes like a narrative paragraph? How are they different?

2. What overall message is Sanchez communicating?

3. Identify transitions that Sanchez uses to link the details in her notes.

## Workplace Writing Assignments

1. Write a letter commending or complaining about an employee at a business you patronize. The business might be a restaurant, department store, grocery store, or health club, for example. Describe an event that demonstrates the main point you want to make about the employee.

2. Describe an event that occurred where you work or shop that demonstrates that the boss or an employee is either very competent or incompetent.

3. Think about a specific task that was part of a job you have held or currently hold. Perhaps it is data entry, handling travel arrangements, serving or bussing at a restaurant, or retail sales at a store. Describe the steps involved in performing that task correctly.

# WRITING ABOUT A READING

## Thinking Before Reading

The following reading, "The Charwoman," is taken from the autobiography of Gordon Parks, *Voices in the Mirror.* Parks is a famous photographer, well known for his work in *Life* magazine. In this narrative, Parks relates an experience early in his career as a photographer and describes the racial discrimination and bigotry he faced in Washington, D.C.

1. Preview the reading using the steps described in Chapter 2, page 30.

2. Connect the reading to your own experience by answering the following questions:

    a. Can photographs capture and communicate feelings?

    b. Can photographs communicate ideas?

    c. Do discrimination and racism still exist today? If so, in what forms?

### READING

# The Charwoman

### Gordon Parks

1    I have one formidable, overwhelming and justifiable hatred, and that is for racists. Thorn-wielding is their occupation and I can attest to their proficiency. Throughout my childhood they kept their eyes glued to my tenderest parts, striking me, impaling me, leaving me bloodied and confused—without

my knowing what had provoked their hostility. I came at last to think of them as beasts with cold hearts; of lost souls impassioned with hatred, slithering about in misery, their feelings severed of all humaneness and spreading over the universe like prickly cloth. Rancor seems to have been their master, and any good that befalls the targets of their grudges sets them to brooding. And though the wind sings with change they remain deaf to it; change to them is the unbearable music of imaginary monsters, which they resist. Their actions and attitudes easily identify them. Their smiles have a curl. Their voices, no matter how gentle, are bedded in loathing. At times I can only look at them in a curious silence, wondering about their feelings, and the climates that bred them. I recall having a sort of innocence about the source of their bigotry, but naïveté was no antidote for the bleeding. Washington, D.C., in 1942, bulged with racism.

2     I arrived there in January of that year with scant knowledge of the place, knowing only that beneath the gleaming monuments and gravestones lay men who had distinguished themselves. What I had learned along the way had little to do with this sprawling city where Washington and Lincoln had been empowered. Sensing this, Roy Stryker, the photographic mentor at FSA [Farm Security Administration], sent me out to get acquainted with the rituals of the nation's capital. I went in a hurry and with enthusiasm. The big blue sky was without clouds and everything seemed so pure, clean and unruffled. It appeared that the entire universe was pleasured in peace.

3     My contentment was short-lived. Within the hour the day began opening up like a bad dream; even here in this radiant, high-hearted place racism was

busy with its dirty work. Eating houses shooed me to the back door; theaters refused me a seat, and the scissoring voices of white clerks at Julius Garfinckel's prestigious department store riled me with curtness. Some clothing I had hoped to buy there went unbought. They just didn't have my size—no matter what I wanted.

4    In a very short time Washington was showing me its real character. It was a hate-drenched city, honoring my ignorance and smugly creating bad memories for me. During that afternoon my entire childhood rushed back to greet me, to remind me that the racism it poured on me had not called it quits.

5    Not only was I humiliated, I was also deeply hurt and angered to a boiling point. It suddenly seemed that all of America was finding grim pleasure in expressing its intolerance to me personally. Washington had turned ugly, and my angry past came back to speak with me as I walked along, assuring me that, even here in the nation's capital, the walls of bigotry and discrimination stood high and formidable. In all innocence, I had gone to a restaurant to eat, to a store to buy clothing and a movie theater for enjoyment. And Washington was telling me, in no uncertain terms, that I shouldn't have done it. Now I was hurrying back to Roy Stryker's office like an angry wind.

6    When I reached there he looked at me for a few moments without speaking. He didn't have to. The gloom shadowing my face told him everything. "Well," he finally asked, "tell me—how did it go?"

7    I answered him with a question. "What's to be done about this horrible place? I've never been so humiliated in my life. Mississippi couldn't be much worse."

8    "It's bad—very bad. That's why I was hesitant about taking you on here. The laboratory technicians here are all from the Deep South. You're not going to have an easy time. Their attitude about photographers is not the best. To them they are a glorified lot who roam the world while they slave away in the back rooms doing the dirty work. And slaving for a black photographer isn't going to improve that attitude. You're on your own here, and you'll have to prove yourself to them—with superior work." He rubbed his chin, thinking. "As for that city out there, well—it's been here for a long time, full of bigotry and hatred for black people. You brought a camera to town with you. If you use it intelligently, you might help turn things around. It's a powerful instrument in the right hands." He paused, thinking things through for me. "Obviously you ran into some bigots out there this afternoon. Well, it's not enough to photograph one of them and label his photograph bigot. Bigots have a way of looking like everyone else. You have to get at the source of their bigotry. And that's not easy. That's what you'll have to work at, and that's why I took you on. Read. Read a lot. Talk to other black people who have spent their lives here. They might help to give you some direction. Go through these picture files. They have a lot to say about what's happening here and

other places throughout this country. They are an education in themselves. The photographers who produced those files learned through understanding what our country's problems are. Now they are out there trying to do something about those problems. That's what you must do eventually."

9    Eventually. All well and good—but I was still burning with a need to hit back at the agony of the afternoon. I sat for an hour mulling over his advice and the humiliation I had suffered. It had grown late; the office had emptied and Stryker had left for the day. Only a black charwoman remained but she was mopping the floor in an adjoining office. "Talk to other black people who have spent their lives here," he had said. She was black, and I eased into conversation with her. Hardly an hour had gone by when we finished, but she had taken me through a lifetime of drudgery and despair in that hour. She was turning back to her mopping when I asked, "Would you allow me to photograph you?"

10    "I don't mind."

11    There was a huge American flag hanging from a standard near the wall. I asked her to stand before it, then placed the mop in one hand and the broom in the other. "Now think of what you just told me and look straight into this camera." Eagerly I began clicking the shutter. It was done and I went home to supper. Washington could now have a conversation with her portrait.

---

## Getting Ready to Write

### Reviewing the Reading

1. Why did Parks come to Washington?

2. What types of racism did he experience?

3. What advice did Stryker give Parks?

4. Why is the camera a powerful tool?

5. Why did Parks photograph the charwoman?

### Examining the Reading: Using Sequence Maps

To understand a narrative paragraph or essay, you must have a clear understanding of the sequence of events. A sequence map, shown earlier in the chapter on p. 145, can be helpful to readers as well as writers. When reading complex material, a sequence map can help you work out the order in which events occurred.

## EXERCISE 6-8

### Visualize It!

**Directions:** Complete the following sequence map for "The Charwoman" by filling in the blank boxes.

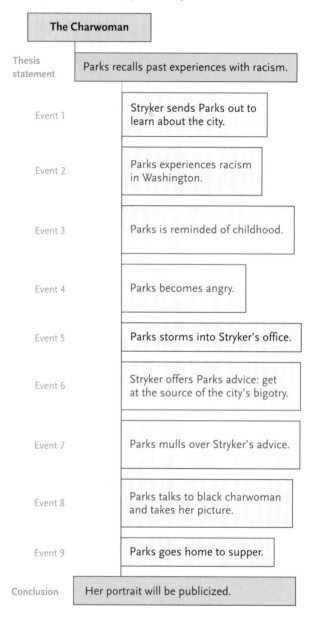

**Sequence Map**

The Charwoman

Thesis statement — Parks recalls past experiences with racism.

Event 1 — Stryker sends Parks out to learn about the city.

Event 2 — Parks experiences racism in Washington.

Event 3 — Parks is reminded of childhood.

Event 4 — Parks becomes angry.

Event 5 — Parks storms into Stryker's office.

Event 6 — Stryker offers Parks advice: get at the source of the city's bigotry.

Event 7 — Parks mulls over Stryker's advice.

Event 8 — Parks talks to black charwoman and takes her picture.

Event 9 — Parks goes home to supper.

Conclusion — Her portrait will be publicized.

## Thinking Critically: Understanding Point of View

Narratives are always told from a point of view—that is, from a particular perspective. Think of point of view as the eyes through which the story is seen. The point of view of "The Charwoman" is that of the photographer. It is his impressions, feelings, and reactions that are conveyed.

A writer's point of view is important to recognize and evaluate as you read and write about narratives (or any other type of writing that expresses attitudes and feelings). Point of view often allows you to look beyond events to see how they are perceived by the people involved. The same event, from a different person's perspective, can be described quite differently.

"The Charwoman" could be told from points of view other than that of the photographer. For example, the story could be told from the viewpoint of Roy Stryker, the author's mentor, from the charwoman's viewpoint, or even from the viewpoint of the clerks at Garfinckel's department store. Each story would, necessarily, include a different series of events and feelings. Write a paragraph telling the story from Roy Stryker's viewpoint.

## Strengthening Your Vocabulary

**Part A:** Using the word's context, word parts, or a dictionary, write a brief definition of each of the following words of phrases as it is used in the reading.

1. scant (paragraph 2) _inadequate, insufficient_

2. grim (paragraph 5) _depressing, gloomy, sternly serious_

3. agony (paragraph 9) _great pain or anguish_

4. mulling over (paragraph 9) _thinking about_

5. drudgery (paragraph 9) _exhausting, boring, unpleasant work_

**Part B:** Choose one of the above words and draw a word map of it.

## Reacting to Ideas: Discussion and Journal Writing

1. Do you think Roy Stryker knew what Parks would experience when he sent Parks out to get acquainted with the city?

2. Describe Parks's feelings as he rushed back to Stryker's office.

3. Stryker told Parks he must eventually "do something" about "our country's problems." Do you think that by taking the charwoman's photograph Parks did something?

## Writing About the Reading

### Paragraph Options

1. The narrative is told from Parks's point of view: He relates how he met, spoke with, posed, and photographed the charwoman. Write a narrative paragraph relating these same events from the point of view of the charwoman. Feel free to add details, including those that reveal how you think the charwoman felt toward Parks.

2. Stryker told Parks that he must prove himself through superior work. Write a narrative paragraph describing a situation in which you had to prove yourself.

## Essay Options

3. Write an essay explaining what Stryker meant when he said that a camera is "a powerful instrument in the right hands" and how Parks proved that statement to be correct.

4. In order to accomplish his goal, Parks followed a process in posing the charwoman. Think of a goal you have accomplished, and write an essay describing how you accomplished it and how you felt when you did.

5. Stryker told Parks he should do something about our country's problems. Choose a problem, other than racism, that our country faces today. You might choose hunger, drugs, unemployment, etc. Define the problem and describe a course of action that you could take to contribute to an understanding of, or solution to, the problem.

## Revision Checklist

1. Who is your audience? Is your paragraph or essay appropriate for them? Does it give them the background information they need? Will it interest them?

2. What is your main purpose in writing? Does your paragraph or essay accomplish this purpose?

3. Highlight your main points (topic sentences). Is each main point clearly expressed?

4. Is each topic sentence supported with relevant details? Do you have unnecessary or irrelevant details?

5. Have you supported your topic sentence with sufficient detail to make it understandable and believable?

6. Do you use specific and vivid words to explain each detail?

### For Narrative Writing

7. Have you made a point about your narrative? Have you told your readers why the process you describe is important?

8. Are the events or steps arranged in the order in which they occurred? If not, will your readers be able to follow the sequence?

9. Have you used transitional words and phrases to help readers follow the events or steps?

10. Have you written your narrative from a consistent point of view?

11. Have you proofread your narrative? (See the inside back cover of this book for a proofreading checklist.)

# CHAPTER REVIEW AND PRACTICE

## Chapter Review

### Paragraph Skills

| | |
|---|---|
| WHAT IS NARRATION? | Narration is a method of describing events by using time sequence. |
| HOW SHOULD YOU SELECT A TOPIC? | The topic should focus on a single event or experience. |
| WHAT SHOULD YOUR TOPIC SENTENCE CONTAIN? | Your topic sentence should identify your topic and express your view or attitude about it. |
| HOW SHOULD YOU ARRANGE THE DETAILS? | Arrange your details in chronological order. |
| HOW SHOULD YOU LEAD YOUR READER FROM ONE IDEA TO ANOTHER? | Use transitional words and phrases. |
| WHAT IS POINT OF VIEW? | Point of view refers to the perspective from which a story is told. A narrative should be told from a single point of view. |
| HOW SHOULD THE EVENTS BE ARRANGED? | The events should be arranged in chronological order. |
| ON WHAT SHOULD YOUR NARRATIVE FOCUS? | Focus only on important elements of the story. |
| WHAT TENSE SHOULD YOU USE IN A NARRATIVE ESSAY? | Write in only one tense, either present or past. |
| HOW CAN YOU HELP YOUR READERS VISUALIZE THE EVENTS YOU ARE DESCRIBING? | Use vivid language to help readers visualize events. |

## Skill Refresher: Pronoun-Antecedent Agreement

A pronoun (*he, she, it*) is a substitute for a noun. It must agree in number and gender (male, female) with its antecedent (the word it replaces).

noun and antecedent        pronoun

EXAMPLE        <u>Yolanda</u> left <u>her</u> handbag on the bus.

## Rules to Follow

1. If the noun is singular, the pronoun replacing it must also be singular.

   EXAMPLE        <u>Robert</u> wanted to lend me <u>his</u> class notes.

2. If the noun is plural, the pronoun substitute must be plural.

   EXAMPLE        Mark wrote <u>lyrics</u> for songs; <u>they</u> were depressing and sad.

3. Some indefinite pronouns are singular; others are plural. Use a singular pronoun to replace a singular noun and a plural pronoun to replace a plural noun.

   EXAMPLE        <u>One</u> of the team members could not find <u>his</u> keys.

   <u>Both</u> of the instructors said <u>they</u> planned to vacation in Maine.

4. Some indefinite pronouns are either singular or plural, depending on how they are used. If the pronoun refers to something that cannot be counted, use a singular pronoun to refer to it. If the pronoun refers to something that can be counted, use a plural pronoun to refer to it. ("Most of the air on an airplane" cannot be counted, so the pronoun is singular. "Most of the students in the class passed the test" can be counted, so the pronoun is plural.)

   EXAMPLE        Too much <u>ice</u> on airplane wings is dangerous, so <u>it</u> is removed before takeoff.

   Many <u>students</u> think <u>they</u> will register for an economics course.

5. Use a plural pronoun to refer to two or more nouns linked by *and*.

   EXAMPLE        <u>Sam and Mark</u> lost <u>their</u> keys.

6. If a pronoun substitutes for two or more nouns joined by *or* or *nor*, the pronoun agrees with the noun closest to it.

   EXAMPLE        Either Mrs. Marcus or her <u>sons</u> will drive <u>their</u> car.

## Rate Your Ability to Use Pronoun-Antecedent Agreement

Circle the word or phrase that correctly completes each sentence.

1. Ellen and I are going to pool (their, *our*) knowledge to write the proposal.

2. Gene or Bo brought (*his*, their) drumsticks for the practice session.

3. Each student received (*his or her*, their) transcript by mail.

4. Either the sweater or the turtleneck will be returned to the store (*it*, they) came from because I don't need both.

5. Everyone opened (*his or her*, their) book to page 50.

6. When the play was over, the audience rose from (its, *their*) seats to give a standing ovation.

7. When a speaker makes a joke, (*he or she*, they) is trying to maintain audience interest.

8. No one handed in (*his or her*, their) exam before the time was up.

9. At some point in (*their*, his or her) lives, men and women will stop to evaluate their goals and accomplishments.

10. Every sales executive must master Portuguese if (they, *he or she*) expects to succeed in Brazil.

Score _____

Check your answers, using the Answer Key on p. 640. If you missed more than two, you need additional review and practice in recognizing and correcting errors in pronoun-antecedent agreement. Refer to section C.8 of Part VI, "Reviewing the Basics." For additional practice go to this book's Web site at http://www.ablongman.com/mcwhorterexpressways1e.

## INTERNET ACTIVITIES

## 1.   Online Narratives

Visit this Web page from the Voices of Civil Rights project to read some featured stories.

http://www.voicesofcivilrights.org/voices3.html

Choose one to evaluate. Write a list of key words and phrases that you found interesting and significant.

## 2. Topics for Personal Narratives

Read over these questions that an instructor at Washington State University uses to aid her students in thinking about topics for a personal narrative.

http://www.wsu.edu/~hughesc/writing_autobiography.htm

Choose one to write about. Use some of the tips provided at the following site to help shape your essay.

http://www.wsu.edu/~hughesc/personal_narrative.htm

## 3. This Book's Web Site

Visit this site to find templates of idea maps for narration and additional practice on skills taught in the chapter.

http://www.ablongman.com/mcwhorterexpressways1e

# 7

# Description

## Chapter Objectives

*In this chapter
you will learn to:*

1. Create a dominant
   impression in your
   descriptive writing.

2. Choose details that support
   your dominant impression.

3. Choose details that vividly
   describe your topic.

4. Organize details to convey
   your topic clearly.

5. Write an effective topic
   sentence.

## Write About It!

Study the photograph above. What emotions or feelings are being expressed by the two men? Write a sentence that answers this question.

The sentence you have written could serve as a topic sentence for a paragraph describing the photograph. The remainder of the paragraph would then give details supporting your impression. In this chapter you will learn to write descriptive paragraphs and essays. Descriptive paragraphs and essays offer and explain a single impression, much like the sentence you wrote that conveys a single impression of the photograph. You will use descriptive writing in a variety of everyday, academic, and workplace situations, as shown below.

EVERYDAY SCENARIOS

- Describing a wedding to friends unable to attend
- Describing your sick child's symptoms to a doctor

ACADEMIC SCENARIOS

- Describing the results of a biology lab experiment
- Reporting what you observed when you visited an art gallery exhibit

WORKPLACE SCENARIOS

- Describing the development of an indoor air filtration system, as an environmental engineer
- Writing a job description for a job opening, as a personnel director

# UNDERSTANDING DESCRIPTION

## What Is Descriptive Writing?

Descriptive writing creates an impression. It helps the reader visualize the subject. Now suppose summer is over and you just spent a week at a lakeside cottage. You might write the following paragraph describing it.

> The rented cottage was charming because it was old-fashioned and modern at the same time. The bedrooms had colorful green and blue patchwork quilts on the beds and faded antique pictures on the walls, but the mattresses were brand new and extremely comfortable. The kitchen has the same efficient, shiny new appliances that I have at home, except for the antique wood-burning stove that makes the entire room smell pungent with smoke. Every time I entered the living room, my immediate desire was to fling myself onto the huge pillowlike sofa. An old-fashioned radio, hooked rugs, and a handmade checkerboard combined with the wood-burning fireplace to create a rustic atmosphere. From the modern redwood deck I had a peaceful view of the quiet, secluded lake. The cottage took me back in time in the best ways.

Your paragraph begins with a topic sentence that identifies your topic (the cottage) and indicates how you feel about it. This feeling or attitude toward the topic is called the **dominant impression.** The remainder of the paragraph offers details that help the reader visualize the cottage and help explain the dominant impression. Each sentence contains vivid and descriptive words and phrases. These details are called **sensory details** because they appeal to the reader's senses—touch, sight, smell, taste, and hearing. You can visualize a descriptive paragraph as follows:

# Visualize It!

**Descriptive Paragraph Idea Map**

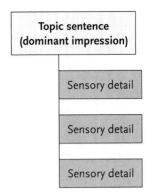

The above paragraph describing a cottage can be visualized as follows:

# Visualize It!

**Idea Map**

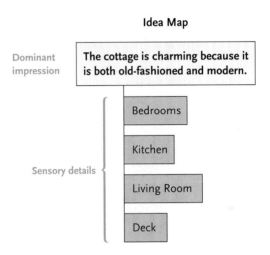

---

## EXERCISE 7-1

**Directions:** Working alone or with another student, brainstorm a list of the times in your own life when description played an important role.

## Creating a Dominant Impression

The dominant impression of a descriptive paragraph is the overall sense you want to convey about your topic or main idea. It is expressed in your topic sentence, usually at the beginning of the paragraph. Suppose you are the music critic for your college newspaper and you are writing about a recent concert. If you felt the audience was appreciative, you might write the following topic sentence:

> The audience at the recent Laura Love concert appreciated and responded well to both the old and the new songs that Love and her band performed.

Different dominant impressions of the audience are created, however, by the following topic sentences:

> The antics and immature behavior of the audience at the Laura Love concert ruined the event for me.

> Because many in the audience at the recent Laura Love concert were international students, I realized that her music has broad appeal.

The dominant impression often reflects your first reaction to a topic. Let's say you are writing about your bedroom. Think of a word or two that sums up how you feel about it. Is it comfortable? Messy? Organized? Your own territory? A place to escape? Any one of these could be developed into a paragraph. For example, your topic sentence might be:

> My bedroom is an orderly place where I am surrounded by things that are of personal value.

The details that follow would then describe objects on which you place personal value. If you have difficulty deciding on or thinking of a dominant impression for a topic, brainstorm a list of words to sum up your observations and reactions. For example, for the topic of your college health office, you might write things such as "friendly," "helpful," "smells like a doctor's office," or "antiseptic and clean." This brainstorming eventually could lead you to write about the health office as a place of impersonal, sterile sights and sounds that houses a warm and caring staff.

## EXERCISE 7-2

**Directions:** For two of the following topics, write three topic sentences that express a different dominant impression.

1. Professional athletes

   a. _____

   b. _____

   c. _____

2. A favorite food

   a. _____

   b. _____

   c. _____

3. A recent film or television show you have seen

   a. _____

   b. _____

   c. _____

## EXERCISE 7-3

**Directions:** Suppose you are taking a business course and are currently studying advertising. Your instructor has asked you to write a paragraph on one of the following topics. For the topic you select, use prewriting techniques to generate ideas and details. Then write a topic sentence that establishes a dominant impression.

1. Find an ad in a newspaper or magazine that contains a detailed scene. Describe the ad and explain whether or not it is effective. Make note of what props have been placed in the scene, what the models are wearing, and whatever else supports your answer.

2. Choose an ad you think is effective. Write a paragraph describing the person you imagine is likely to buy the product. Explain how the ad would appeal to him or her.

3. Suppose you have developed a new product (frozen gourmet pizza or a long-lasting, multicolored highlighter, for example). Write a paragraph describing the product to a company that is interested in distributing it. Be sure to describe your product in a positive, appealing way.

## Developing and Selecting Sensory Details

All the details in a descriptive paragraph must be relevant to creating your dominant impression. Begin by brainstorming a list of all the details you can think of that describe your topic or support your dominant impression. Try to visualize the person, place, or experience and write down what you see. Your details should enable your reader to paint his or her own mental picture of the topic. Here's a list of details a student produced about working at movie theaters:

| | |
|---|---|
| rude people | crowded concession stands |
| fold-up seats | greasy smell of popcorn |
| big screen | kids running up the aisle |
| headaches | squishy seats you sink into |
| people whispering | people annoying others |
| trash on floor | quieting people down |
| ticket stubs | lines at the box office |
| sticky floors | always crowded |
| dim lights | hurrying, pressure |

If you have not formed a dominant impression, review your list, looking for a pattern to your details. What feeling or impression do many of them suggest? In the above list, many of the details convey the feeling of annoyance or dislike.

After you have decided upon an impression, eliminate those details that do not support that impression. For example, the details about the screen, ticket stubs, seats, and lighting should be eliminated because they do not support the impression of annoyance.

Now read the following student paragraph on the topic of working in movie theaters. Notice how the student developed ideas from the above list. The paragraph still contains some details that do not directly support the dominant impression. Watch for them as you read.

> Movie theaters are crowded, annoying places to work. I know, I have worked part-time in three different theaters over the past four years. I often leave work with a pounding headache and jangled nerves. There is always time pressure; shows must start on time. Customers are always in a rush. They arrive minutes before a show is about to begin, yet demand to be waited on instantly at the concession stand. One regular and particularly annoying guy wearing baggy sweats and a ball cap once shouted: "Hey, over here! Get me a jumbo popcorn and a large Pepsi, and do it fast before I miss my show!" There was no "please," no "thank you," and no consideration of people standing in line ahead of him. This is just the kind of patron who carelessly spreads handfuls of these yellow kernels all over the theater floor and creates a sticky patch of spilled soda that someone has to clean up at the end of the evening. I do not enjoy assisting pushy people who are rude to others, either. Some customers talk loudly, complain about those in front of them, make obscene gestures, and generally make a nuisances of themselves during the show. It is my job to quiet them down. I'd rather throw them out. There would be no "ifs," no "ands," and no "buts," just "You're out of here." Although you do get to see some free movies, working at a movie theater is far from the ideal job.

The detail about wanting to throw annoying people out should be deleted because it does not explain why a theater is a difficult place to work.

## NEED TO KNOW

### Sensory Details

Sensory details appeal to the five senses. Use the following questions to help you uncover sensory details about your subject.

**Touch:** What does it feel like? What is its texture? What is its weight? What is its temperature?

**Smell:** Is it pleasant or unpleasant? Is it mild or strong? Of what other smells does it remind you?

**Taste:** Is it pleasant or unpleasant? Is it sweet, sour, salty, or bitter? Of what favorite flavors does it remind you?

**Sight:** What is the color? Is there a pattern? What size is it? What shape is it?

**Sound:** Is it loud or soft? Is it high or low? Is it pleasant or unpleasant? What other sounds does it remind you of?

## EXERCISE 7-4

**Directions:** For the following topic sentences, circle the letters of the details that are not relevant to the dominant impression.

1. You don't need a lot of equipment to enjoy fishing.

   a. The only necessary items are a rod and reel.

   **b.** There are many different types of rods.

   c. A net is helpful if you're fishing from a boat.

   **d.** Take a picnic lunch if you're fishing from a boat.

2. Gambling is addictive and can lead to financial disaster.

   a. Some people are unable to stop because they want to win just one more time.

   **b.** Money is exchanged for gambling chips at casinos.

   **c.** Las Vegas is a place where many people go to gamble.

   d. I know a gambler who often bets his entire paycheck on one horse race.

3. Officials at sporting events must be knowledgeable and skillful and have strong personalities.

   a. Officials must be able to withstand crowd reactions to unpopular calls.

   b. Officials must know the technicalities of the game.

   c. Officials must exert authority and win the respect of the players.

   **d.** The pay that officials receive is not commensurate with their responsibilities.

4. Starting a travel agency is a high-risk venture.

   **a.** The manager must have at least two years' experience.

   b. In most areas, there are many competing agencies.

   c. Profit margins are low, so a great many clients are needed.

   d. Total start-up costs are high, ranging up to $60,000.

## EXERCISE 7-5

*Writing in Progress*

**Directions:** Select one of the topic sentences you wrote for Exercise 7-2 or 7-3, and develop a descriptive paragraph for it, revising it if necessary.

## Using Descriptive Language

Descriptive language is exact, colorful, and appealing. It enables the reader to envision what the writer has seen. Here are two sentences about a day at the beach. The first presents lifeless, factual information; the second describes what the writer saw and felt.

> I went to the beach today, lay on the sand, and read a book.

> At Rexham beach this morning, I spread my soft plaid blanket on the white sand, got out the latest John Grisham novel, and settled down to enjoy the sun's warming rays.

You might think of descriptive language as the way the reader sees the world through the eyes of the writer. A section of Chapter 4, "Developing and Arranging Details," discusses the use of descriptive language on p. 89. Review that section before continuing with this chapter.

One of the best ways to help your reader see, as you'll remember from Chapter 4, is to use specific words that draw on your reader's five senses—sight, hearing, smell, touch, and taste. The student whose paragraph appeared on p. 166 used details like the baggy sweats and ball cap and the sticky patches of spilled soda to help you visualize the situation.

Use vivid verbs, adjectives, and adverbs to help your readers see what you are describing. When you can, use exact names of people, places, and objects ("a red Toyota," not "a car").

## EXERCISE 7-6

**Directions:** For each of the following items, write a sentence that provides a vivid description. The first one is done for you.

1. An old coat

   Mr. Busby wore a tattered, faded, stained-around-the-neck, deep burgundy leather coat.

2. A fast-food meal

   _____

3. A bride (or groom)

   _____

4. A sidewalk

   _____

5. The dog behind a sign that warns "Guard Dog on Premises"

   _____

## EXERCISE 7-7

*Writing in Progress*

**Directions:** Revise the paragraph you wrote for Exercise 7-5, adding descriptive words and phrases.

## Organizing Details and Using Transitions

The arrangement of details in a description is determined by your topic and by the dominant impression you want to convey. You want to emphasize the most important details, making sure your readers can follow your description.

One of the most common arrangements is spatial organization (which we discussed in Chapter 4, pp. 90–91). If you were describing your college campus, for example, you might start at one end and work toward the other. You might describe a stage set from left to right or a building from bottom to top.

Transitional words and phrases help your reader follow a spatial arrangement and see how details relate to each other. Some common transitional words for such an organization are shown in Table 7-1, below.

If you were describing a person, you might work from head to toe. But you might prefer to follow another common organization: from least to most important. If the dominant impression you want to convey about the person's appearance is messiness, you might start with some characteristics that are only slightly messy (an untied shoe, perhaps) and work toward the most messy (a blue-jean jacket missing one sleeve, stained with paint, and covered with burrs).

Again, transitional words and phrases will help your reader see how details relate to each other and where you are going. Common transitional words and phrases for a least-to-most-important organization are listed in Table 7-1.

**Table 7-1    Transitions for Descriptive Paragraphs**

| | |
|---|---|
| Spatial arrangement | Above, below, behind, in front of, beside, next to, outside, to the west (north, etc.) beneath, nearby, on the other side. |
| Least to most arrangement or most to least | Most, above all, especially, particularly, even more, more important, even more important, of lesser importance, of greater importance |

## EXERCISE 7-8

*Writing in Progress*

**Directions:** Evaluate the arrangement of details in the paragraph you wrote for Exercise 7-7. Does it support your dominant impression? Revise it and add transitional words and phrases, if needed.

## Applying Your Skills to Essay Writing: Description

Both descriptive paragraphs and descriptive essays share a similar purpose: to convey an impression. Consequently, the skills that you have learned for writing paragraphs will help you write effective essays. An essay also offers the opportunity to expand your ideas and provide greater detail. Use the following guidelines in writing descriptive essays:

1. **Your thesis statement should express your dominant impression.** Be sure it is specific and well focused.

2. **Consider your purpose for writing.** If your purpose is to present information, then offer plenty of factual detail. If you are writing to create a feeling or emotional response, choose details that evoke those responses.

3. **Organize your essay logically.** Divide your topic into parts and devote one paragraph to each part. For example, if you are describing the claustrophobic experience of being trapped in a crowded elevator, devote one paragraph to background details (how, when, where), another to sights, another to smells, another to thoughts that run through your mind, and a final one to the resolution of the situation.

4. **Use vivid language.** In an essay, you have the opportunity to paint detailed, exact descriptions. As one step in the revision process, focus on improving your use of descriptive language.

## EXERCISE 7-9

**Directions:** Choose one of the following assignments:

1. Go outside for approximately ten minutes and carefully observe and take notes on what you see. Write an essay that describes the scene to someone who has never been to this place. Create a dominant impression by organizing your details into a vivid word picture.

2. Select one of the topics listed in Exercise 7-3 (p. 165) that you have not written on, and write an essay on it. Note the way that the essay format gives you more room for development of ideas and details than a paragraph does.

3. Suppose you have an important job interview next week. You want to appear studious, serious, and trustworthy. Write a paragraph describing how you would dress and what you would do or say during the interview to create that impression.

4. A student group on your campus has decided to publish a directory of college courses that will describe what each course is about, how it is taught, and what is required of students. The directory is intended to be a guide that will help students select courses and instructors, so the group is asking students to submit descriptions of courses they have taken. Choose one of your courses and write a description of it that could be included in the guide.

# AN ACADEMIC SCENARIO
## A STUDENT ESSAY
### The Academic Writer and the Writing Task

Anna Majerczyk is a first-year student at Triton College in River Grove, Illinois where she is studying to be a dental hygienist. She was born in Poland and moved to Chicago two years ago to live with her mother and sister. She has taken developmental classes in reading and writing. In her writing class, her writing instructor gave the following assignment: Write

a descriptive essay about a photograph that is meaningful or important to you. Describe what is going on in the photograph and the memories it recalls. Include sufficient detail so that your readers can visualize the photograph.

Title: identifies content of the photograph

# A Photograph of Skiing with My Father
### Anna Majerczyk

Thesis statement: dominant impression

The memory of the day I took my father skiing is as clear in my mind as the high peaks of the Tatra Mountains are in this photograph. It was a day of fun and laughter; the kind of day my father and I shared when I was a child. This was the kind of day we had not had for many years.

Topic sentence

Background information: describes the physical setting

Story adds interest

Everything about that day was perfect. The sun shone brightly on my hometown of Zakopane. From the bottom of Gubalowka Hill, where this picture was taken, you could see the sharp peaks of the Tatra pushing through the clouds into the sky. Within view was Giewont, the mountain we Poles call the "sleeping knight." According to legend, the mountain is shaped like an ancient warrior, waiting for the day when his country will need him to wake up from his nap and save it from danger. On this day, with its brilliant sunshine and mild temperature, danger seemed far away and Giewont slept peacefully on.

Topic sentence

From where we stood on the lower station of the funicular, my father and I could see the rickety old cable car hauling skiers and snowboarders up Gubalowka Hill. We waited eagerly for our turn, anxious to enjoy the "white madness," as we locals call skiing. Thousands of tourists from all over the world flock to Zakopane every year. Many of them are amateurs who have chosen our lovely town as the place to try skiing for the first time. Not only is Zakopane beautiful, it's almost always really lively.

Topic sentence

This day was no exception. Sounds were everywhere; people were talking and laughing as they bustled from place to place. They sampled yummy

Sensory details

Polish treats in the restaurants, oohed and ahhed over the scenery, and clicked away madly on their cameras. In the shops tourists bargained for carved wooden boxes, little statues, and funny toys. These "must-haves" are just some of Zakopane's popular souvenirs, along with delicately painted glass ornaments, delicious cheeses, and thick, warm sweaters made from the rough wool of local sheep. Along with voices, we could hear the scrapes and snaps of boots being jammed onto or yanked off of skis. Cheerful polka music blared from radios and as my father and I walked, we found ourselves walking along to the rhythm.

*Topic sentence*

Near the entrance to the ski area, I spotted three girls dressed like friendly elves in funny yellow hats and brown jumpsuits. On their backs were packs bulging with samples of the coffee they were handing out as part of a promotion. One handed me a steaming cup of free coffee, and I recognized her as an old friend from elementary school. I did not stop to talk, however, but followed my father toward the lift where, surprisingly, the lines were short. There was no wait for tickets and soon my father and I were being carried through the cool, clean air to the summit.

*Topic sentence*

*Additional background information*

It had taken a lot of convincing to get my father to the slopes that day. He had taught me to ski when I was little. He had been a patient teacher and I had grown to love the sport. As the years went by, I began to prefer the company of my friends. I stopped spending time with my father, and ran off at every opportunity to ski with my pals. So, he put his skis away. On this day, however, none of my friends were available and I had managed to persuade my father to join me.

*Topic sentence*

*Details help us visualize her father*

Looking at him, it was hard to believe he had ever been a professional skier. He had on an outdated green jacket that was nothing like the stylish parkas I and most of the other skiers wore. On his head was an incredibly ugly purple hat decorated with orange and green zigzags, stripes, and dots. Beads of sweat stood out on his forehead and he held his twenty-year-old skis in rough hands.

*Topic sentence*

The minute he put on those ridiculously long skis, though, his awkward appearance ceased to matter. Suddenly he became the graceful pro he once had been. Together we sailed down the mountain through the crisp, clean air. The famous Zakopane scenery flew by in a blur. All I saw was my father's face, happy to be skiing again.

*Conclusion: author discusses the meaning of the photograph*

Now, when I look at this picture, it is not the rocky Tatra I see, nor the outlined face of the sleeping knight. It is the glorious sun and the blinding white snow and my father's smiling eyes. The photograph may yellow and crack with age, but my memories of that day will stay fresh forever.

## Examining Academic Writing

1. Did Majerczyk fulfill the assignment? Can you visualize the photograph?

2. Highlight five examples of particularly effective sensory details.

3. Did Majerczyk use details related to all five senses? Circle examples of each sense that you find represented.

4. How did Majerczyk arrange her details? Highlight transitions or introductory phrases that suggest the pattern of organization she used.

## Academic Writing Assignments

1. You are studying aging in your psychology class. Your instructor asks each student to choose an elderly person and write a description of that person. The description should focus on mental capabilities or weaknesses, and not be concerned with physical appearance. Write a paragraph describing the person you chose.

2. You are taking a speech communication class and have been asked to give a 2–3 minute speech on your favorite place to relax. Write a paragraph summarizing the information you would include in your speech.

3. You are taking a business class and your instructor gives the following assignment:

   > Write a paragraph describing a business establishment that has "comfort appeal." In a paragraph explain how the business is appealing and makes customers want to be there.

# A WORKPLACE SCENARIO
## A BUSINESS LETTER
### The Workplace Writer and the Writing Task

Sandra Tucillo is applying for a small business loan from First Regional Bank of Monrovia. The loan officer requested details on the product she wants to manufacture and the workshop renovation for which she needs the loan. As you read the letter below, notice Tucillo's use of descriptive details of the product and of the proposed workshop.

1765 Osprey Drive
Monrovia, CA 12340
June 23, 2005

Mr. Arnold Woodworth
First Regional Bank of Monrovia
123 Main Street
Monrovia, CA 12340

Dear Mr. Woodworth:

In response to your request for more information regarding my loan application, I am pleased to provide details of my product and proposed workshop renovation.

As you know, I intend to begin constructing and marketing my unique Hot-Water Socks. A combination of hot-water bottle and sport sock, my socks are made with waterproof channels that can be easily filled with hot tap water for instant warmth and comfort. After a long, frigid day, all you would have to do is grab a pair, add the tap water, and slip them on. Right away, your numb toes would begin to thaw and your aching ankles would be surrounded by cushiony warmth.

But before I can warm the feet, I have to make the socks. And for that I need a well-lit, well-ventilated workspace. That is where the loan comes in.

I would like to convert the dark, dilapidated garage on my grandfather's property into a safe and efficient shop. To do that, I need to make the following improvements:

1. Remove the rusted shell of a 1948 Ford truck and clean up stagnant pools of oil from the concrete floor
2. Pay landfill fees for the disposal of 27 dried-out paint cans and 43 other containers of unidentifiable but potentially toxic materials
3. Install ten 4' x 8' Thermopane windows and two 2' x 6' skylights
4. Remove rotted wood and patch gaping holes in roof
5. Bring wiring up to code and add 220 line
6. Frame and install loading doors and exterior ramp
7. Replace single dangling bulb with energy-efficient fluorescent light fixtures
8. Insulate and sheetrock 16' x 30' walls and cathedral ceiling
9. Paint interior and exterior
10. Purchase and install woodstove, plus all necessary tile, pipes, and ducts required by building code

In addition, I will need to purchase equipment including four 8' worktables; stools for myself and my assistants; 3000 pairs of Smart Wool mid-calf socks; and 1762 thick-gauge, plush-lined water bottles.

Finally, I will need to purchase additional tools, as demand for my product is already so high I will be hiring extra workers immediately. The biggest expense will be for three industrial sewing machines. I believe I can find used machines in good working order, which should save several hundred dollars each.

One day I expect to see police officers, forest rangers, mail carriers, emergency road crews—anyone who has to be outside when most of us would rather be curled up in front of a fire—finding welcome relief in a pair of my Hot-Water Socks. With your financial assistance, I know I can make that happen.

Sincerely,

*Sandra Tucillo*

Sandra Tucillo

## Examining Workplace Writing

1. What dominant impression does Tucillo convey about Hot-Water Socks?

2. What dominant impression of the existing workshop area does Tucillo convey?

3. Highlight five descriptive details that are particularly effective.

4. Is the numbered list included in the letter effective? Why is it better than a paragraph containing the same information?

5. Do you think the descriptive details helped Woodworth visualize Tucillo's product and renovation needs? Do you think they helped Tucillo make a convincing case for approval of the loan?

## Workplace Writing Assignments

1. Choose a small mechanical device (knife sharpener, can opener) or other household item (lamp, dog bed) in your home. Assume you are a technical writer and have been asked to write a description of the object so that your readers can visualize it. Write a one-paragraph description.

2. Write a memorandum describing a Web site you have found that could serve as a model for a Web site you are proposing for your company. Assume you work for a company that manufactures athletic shoes (or a product of your choice).

3. You are the purchasing agent for a public school district, and part of your job is to write specifications (often called "specs") that describe standards of construction, performance, safety, and quality for products the district intends to purchase. Your specs will be sent to companies that submit bids (prices and dates by which they will supply the items); the lowest bid must be accepted. The specs must be sufficiently detailed to guarantee that the products will be the type your teachers want and need. Write a set of specs for one of the following products:

   a. A computer printer for a school library

   b. A classroom bulletin board

   c. A microwave oven for staff use

   d. Lockers for student use

   e. An item of your choice that a school district might purchase

# WRITING ABOUT A READING

## Thinking Before Reading

The following reading, "Obåchan" by Gail Y. Miyasaki, is a good example of a descriptive essay that uses vivid, sensory detail to capture the reader's interest. The author describes her Japanese family heritage as revealed through the life of her grandmother. As you read, pay particular attention to the author's descriptive details.

1. Preview the reading, using the steps described in Chapter 2 on p. 30.

2. Connect the reading to your own experience:

   a. Brainstorm a list of details that describe your grandmother, grandfather, or other close relative. Next, review your list. What feelings does the list reveal?

   b. Do older members of your family have different ideas and values than younger members? If so, think of and describe several situations that demonstrate these differences.

### READING

# Obåchan

#### Gail Y. Miyasaki

**canefields**
sugar cane fields

1    Her hands are now rough and gnarled from working in the **canefields**. But they are still quick and lively as she sews the "futon" cover. And she would sit like that for hours Japanese-style with legs under her, on the floor steadily sewing.

2    She came to Hawaii as a "picture bride." In one of her rare self-reflecting moments, she told me in her broken English-Japanese that her mother had told her that the streets of Honolulu in Hawaii were paved with gold coins, and so encouraged her to go to Hawaii to marry a strange man she had never seen. Shaking her head slowly in amazement, she smiled as she recalled her shocked reaction on seeing "Ojitchan's" (grandfather's) ill-kept room with only **lauhala** mats as bedding. She grew silent after that, and her eyes had a faraway look.

**lauhala**
tropical palmlike tree

3    She took her place, along with the other picture brides from Japan, beside her husband on the plantation's canefields along the Hamakua coast on the island of Hawaii. The Hawaiian sun had tanned her deep brown. But the sun had been cruel too. It helped age her. Deep wrinkles lined her face

and made her skin look tough, dry, and leathery. Her bright eyes peered out from narrow slits, as if she were constantly squinting into the sun. Her brown arms, though, were strong and firm, like those of a much younger woman, and so different from the soft, white, and plump-dangling arms of so many old teachers I had had. And those arms of hers were always moving—scrubbing clothes on a wooden washboard with neat even strokes, cutting vegetables with the big knife I was never supposed to touch, or pulling the minute weeds of her garden.

pauhana
Hawaiian for "off-work"

4    I remember her best in her working days, coming home from the cane-fields at "**pauhana**" time. She wore a pair of faded blue jeans and an equally faded navy-blue and white checked work shirt. A Japanese towel was wrapped carefully around her head, and a large straw "papale" or hat covered that. Her sickle and other tools, and her "bento-bako" or lunchbox, were carried in a khaki bag she had made on her back.

5    I would be sitting, waiting for her, on the back steps of her plantation-owned home, with my elbows on my knees. Upon seeing me, she would smile and say, "Tadaima" (I come home). And I would smile and say in return, "Okaeri" (welcome home). Somehow I always felt as if she waited for that. Then I would watch her in silent fascination as she scraped the thick red dirt off her heavy black rubber boots. Once, when no one was around, I had put those boots on, and deliberately flopped around in a mud puddle, just so I could scrape off the mud on the back steps too.

6    Having retired from the plantation, she now wore only dresses. She called them "makule-men doresu," Hawaiian for old person's dress. They were always gray or navy blue with buttons down the front and a belt at the waistline. Her hair, which once must have been long and black like mine, was now streaked with gray and cut short and permanent-waved.

kimono
traditional Japanese robe

**Bon**
the Lantern Festival, the Buddhist
All Souls' Day

7    The only time she wore a **kimono** was for the "**Bon**" dance. She looked so much older in a kimono and almost foreign. It seemed as if she were going somewhere, all dressed up. I often felt very far away from her when we all walked together to the Bon dance, even if I too was wearing a kimono. She seemed almost a stranger to me, with her bent figure and her short pigeon-toed steps. She appeared so distantly Japanese. All of a sudden, I would notice her age; there seemed something so old in being Japanese.

8    She once surprised me by sending a beautiful "yūkata" or summer kimono for me to wear to represent the Japanese in our school's annual May Day festival. My mother had taken pictures of me that day to send to her. I have often wondered, whenever I look at that kimono, whether she had ever worn it when she was a young girl. I have wondered too what she was thinking when she looked at those pictures of me.

Obāchan
grandmother

9    My mother was the oldest daughter and the second child of the six children **Obāchan** bore, two boys and four girls. One of her daughters, given the name of Mary by one of her school teachers, had been disowned by her for marrying a "haole" or Caucasian. Mary was different from the others, my

mother once told me, much more rebellious and independent. She had refused to attend Honokaa and Hilo High Schools on the Big Island of Hawaii, but chose instead to go to Honolulu to attend McKinley High School. She smoked cigarettes and drove a car, shocking her sisters with such unheard of behavior. And then, after graduation, instead of returning home, Mary took a job in Honolulu. Then she met a haole sailor. Mary wrote home, telling of her love for this man. She was met with harsh admonishings from her mother.

10    "You go with haole, you no come home!" was her mother's ultimatum.

11    Then Mary wrote back, saying that the sailor had gone home to America, and would send her money to join him, and get married. Mary said she was going to go.

12    "Soon he leave you alone. He no care," she told her independent daughter. Her other daughters, hearing her say this, turned against her, accusing her of narrow-minded, prejudiced thinking. She could not understand the words that her children had learned in the American schools; all she knew was what she felt. She must have been so terribly alone then.

13    So Mary left, leaving a silent, unwavering old woman behind. Who could tell if her old heart was broken? It certainly was enough of a shock that Honolulu did not have gold-paved streets. Then, as now, the emotionless face bore no sign of the grief she must have felt.

14    But the haole man did not leave Mary. They got married and had three children. Mary often sends pictures of them to her. Watching her study the picture of Mary's daughter, her other daughters know she sees the likeness to Mary. The years and the pictures have softened the emotionless face. She was wrong about this man. She was wrong. But how can she tell herself so, when in her heart, she only feels what is right?

15    "I was one of the first to condemn her for her treatment of Mary," my mother told me, "I was one of the first to question how she could be so prejudiced and narrow-minded." My mother looked at me sadly and turned away.

16    "But now, being a mother myself, and being a Japanese mother above all, I *know* how she must have felt. I just don't know how to say I'm sorry for those things I said to her."

17    Whenever I see an old Oriental woman bent with age and walking with short steps, whenever I hear a child being talked to in broken English-Japanese, I think of her. She is my grandmother. I call her "Obåchan."

## Getting Ready to Write

### Reviewing the Reading

1. Explain Obåchan's marriage arrangements.

2. Describe the life that Obåchan led in her early years in Hawaii.

3. Why did Obåchan object to Mary's marriage?

4. How did the author's mother respond to Obåchon's treatment of Mary?

### Examining the Reading: Marking Revealing Actions, Descriptions, and Statements

Writers often reveal how they feel and what they think through description rather than through direct statements. For example, Miyasaki never directly states her feelings for Obåchan, but the details demonstrate that she loved and respected her.

As you read descriptive writing, it is helpful to highlight words, phrases, or bits of conversation that are particularly revealing about the writer's attitudes toward the subject. For example, in paragraph 7 the following passages reveal Miyasaki's attitude toward her grandmother dressed in a kimono: "She seemed almost a stranger to me. . . . She appeared so distantly Japanese. . . . there seemed something so old in being Japanese."

Actions, too, may reveal an author's feelings. In paragraph 5, the author describes wearing her grandmother's boots. This action suggests Miyasaki admired Obåchan and wanted to be like her.

To enhance your understanding of descriptive writing, review the reading and underline particularly revealing actions, descriptions, and statements.

### Thinking Critically: Understanding Connotative Language

Many words have two levels of meanings—denotative and connotative. A word's denotative meaning is its precise dictionary meaning. For example, the denotative meaning of the word *mother* is "female parent." A word's connotative meaning is the collection of feelings and attitudes that come along with that word. These are sometimes called emotional colorings or shades of meaning. The common connotation of *mother* is a warm, caring person. Connotative meanings vary, of course, among individuals.

Think of the word *rock*. The dictionary defines it as "a large mass of stone." But doesn't *rock* also suggest hardness, inability to penetrate, and permanence? Now think of the words *bony* and *skinny*. Their connotations are somewhat negative. The word *slender,* although similar in denotative meaning, has a more positive connotative meaning.

Here are several groups of words. Decide how each word differs from the others in the group.

1. fake, synthetic, artificial (they all mean "not real," but how are they different?)

2. difficult, challenging, tough

3. inspect, examine, study

4. expose, reveal, show, display

Look at these words and phrases from the reading and explain their connotative meanings:

1. paved with gold coins (paragraph 2)

2. haole (paragraph 9, 10)

3. independent daughter (paragraph 12)

4. silent, unwavering old woman (paragraph 13)

## Strengthening Your Vocabulary

**Part A:** Using the word's context, word parts, or a dictionary, write a brief definition of each of the following words as it is used in the reading.

1. fascination (paragraph 5) _having a strong attraction to or interest in_
   _something_

2. disowned (paragraph 9) _refused to acknowledge a family connection_

3. admonishings (paragraph 9) _scoldings_

4. ultimatum (paragraph 10) _forceful final statement_

5. unwavering (paragraph 11) _firm and steadfast, unable to be swayed_

**Part B:** For one of the above words, or for another word from the reading, draw a word map.

## Reacting to Ideas: Discussion and Journal Writing

1. Why does the author's mother regret accusing Obåchan of prejudice and narrow-mindedness?

2. Do you think Obåchan's own marriage experience shaped her reaction to Mary's marriage?

3. Why did the author muddy Obåchan's boots and then scrape them clean?

4. Explain the statement "there seemed something so old in being Japanese."

5. Mary was rejected by Obåchan for marrying a Causcasian. Discuss what other behaviors might cause a family to reject a family member.

## Writing About the Reading

### Paragraph Options

1. Are there habits, attitudes, customs, or behaviors that make your family seem old to you? Choose one and write a paragraph describing it and your reaction to it.

2. When Obåchan wore her kimono she seemed strange to the author. Write a paragraph explaining how someone's dress or personal appearance changed or shaped your attitude toward him or her. Be sure to include descriptive details about the dress or appearance.

3. Mary's behavior shocked her mother. Write a paragraph describing someone's behavior that shocked you or how your behavior shocked someone else. Be sure to give descriptive details about the behavior.

### Essay Options

4. Write an essay describing how Obåchan's attitudes changed as she got older. Support your essay with details from the reading.

5. Write a paragraph describing your grandmother, grandfather, or other close family relative. Reveal your attitude toward him or her through your choice of detail and connotative language.

6. Rewrite the essay, changing one or more of its outcomes. Perhaps Obåchan forgave Mary, or perhaps Mary's husband left her.

7. Write an essay describing a belief, custom, or attitude within your family that has changed from one generation to another.

## Revision Checklist

1. Is your paragraph or essay appropriate for your audience? Does it give them the background information they need? Will it interest them?

2. Will your paragraph or essay accomplish your purpose?

3. Is your main point clearly expressed in a topic sentence or thesis statement?

4. Is each detail relevant? Does each explain or support your main point?

5. Have you supported your topic sentence or thesis statement with sufficient details to make it understandable and believable?

### For Descriptive Writing

6. Have you created a dominant impression in your description? Do your details support this impression?

7. Have you used vivid and specific language to convey your details?

8. Is your organization appropriate to your topic and the dominant impression you want to create? Have you used transitional words and phrases to help your reader follow your description?

9. Have you proofread? (See the inside back cover of this book for a proofreading checklist.)

## CHAPTER REVIEW AND PRACTICE

## Chapter Review

| | |
|---|---|
| WHAT IS A DOMINANT IMPRESSION? | A dominant impression is the overall attitude or feeling expressed about a topic. |
| WHERE SHOULD THIS IMPRESSION BE EXPRESSED? | It should be expressed in the topic sentence or thesis statement. |
| HOW SHOULD THE DOMINANT IMPRESSION BE SUPPORTED? | It should be supported with relevant details. |
| WHY SHOULD YOU ARRANGE THE DETAILS LOGICALLY? | A logical arrangement of details helps the reader follow the ideas. |
| HOW SHOULD DETAILS BE CONNECTED? | Transitional words and phrases should be used to connect details. |
| WHAT IS DESCRIPTIVE LANGUAGE? | Descriptive language uses exact and vivid words that appeal to the senses and provide a vivid impression of what is being described. |

## Skill Refresher: Pronoun Reference

A pronoun refers to a specific noun and is used to replace that noun. It must always be clear to which noun a pronoun refers.

                                    noun        pronoun

EXAMPLE                 George left his backpack in the classroom.

## Rules to Follow

1.  A pronoun must refer to a specific word or words. Avoid vague or unclear references.

    INCORRECT        They said on the evening news that the president would visit France. [Who said this?]

    CORRECT          The evening news commentator reported that the president would visit France.

2.  If more than one noun is present, it must be clear to which noun the pronoun refers.

    INCORRECT        Jackie told Amber that she passed the exam. [Did Jackie pass, or did Amber pass?]

    CORRECT          Jackie told Amber, "You passed the exam."

3.  Use the relative pronouns *who, whom, which,* and *that* with the appropriate antecedent.

    INCORRECT        Sam, whom is the captain of the team, accepted the award.

    CORRECT          Sam, who is the captain of the team, accepted the award. [Sam is the subject, so the correct pronoun is who.]

## Rate Your Ability to Use Pronouns Correctly

Evaluate each of the following sentences. If there is an error in pronoun reference, revise the sentence so that each pronoun is used correctly. If the sentence is correct, mark "C" in the blank provided. *Corrected sentences will vary.*

_____  1.  Marissa told Kristin that her business proposal was accepted.

_____  2.  Brian found a briefcase in the car his manager owned.

_____  3.  Naomi put the cake on the table, and Roberta moved it to the counter after she noticed it was still hot.

_____  4.  The professor asked the student about a book he wanted to borrow.

_____  5.  Our waiter, which was named Burt, described the restaurant's specials.

_____ 6. Aaron's sister was injured in a car accident, but it would heal.

__C__ 7. In the professor's lecture, he described the process of photosynthesis.

_____ 8. Another car hit mine, which was swerving crazily.

_____ 9. In hockey games, they frequently injure each other in fights.

_____ 10. The hunting lodge had lots of deer and moose antlers hanging on its walls, and Ryan said he had killed some of them.

Score _____

Check your answers, using the Answer Key on p. 640. If you missed more than two, you need additional review and practice in using correct pronoun references. Refer to section C.9 of Part VI, "Reviewing the Basics." For additional practice, go to this book's Web site at http://www.ablongman.com/mcwhorterexpressways1e.

## INTERNET ACTIVITIES

### 1. Sensory Details

You can add depth to your descriptions with sensory details. This Web page from St. Cloud State University compares general and specific sentences.

http://www.leo.stcloudstate.edu/acadwrite/sensorydetails.html

For each type of detail listed, write your own set of general and specific sentences.

### 2. Verb Connotations

The Writing Center at Temple University compiled this list of verbs that in some way mean "says" or "states."

http://www.temple.edu/writingctr/student_resources/verbs_for_sources.htm

Print out this list and be sure to use these words in your speech and writing. Highlight the ones you feel may be most difficult to incorporate.

### 3. This Book's Web Site

Visit this site to find templates of ideas maps for description and additional practice on skills taught in the chapter.

http://www.ablongman.com/mcwhorterexpressways1e

# 8

# Process

## Chapter Objectives

*In this chapter
you will learn to:*

1. Explain processes and
   procedures.

2. Write "how-to" paragraphs
   and essays.

3. Write "how-it-works"
   paragraphs and essays.

4. Use transitions to guide
   your readers.

5. Write an effective topic
   sentence.

## Write About It!

Write a paragraph explaining how to complete the task shown in
the above photo. Organize your paragraph so someone who is unfamiliar with video stores and video rentals could complete the task easily.

The paragraph you have just written is a process paragraph—a paragraph that explains how to do something. In this chapter you will learn
more about how to write process paragraphs and essays to fulfill both
everyday, academic, and workplace tasks.

EVERYDAY SCENARIOS

- Giving directions to a shopping mall
- Explaining how to file a health insurance claim

ACADEMIC SCENARIOS

- Explaining how to do an experiment
- Explaining how to solve a math problem

WORKPLACE SCENARIOS

- Explaining how to operate a drill press
- Explaining a diet plan to a new diabetes patient

# UNDERSTANDING PROCESS WRITING

## What Is Process Writing?

A **process** is a series of steps or actions one follows in a particular order to accomplish something. When you assemble a toy, bake a cake, rebuild an engine, or put up a tent, you do things in a specific order. A **process paragraph** explains the steps to follow in completing a process. The steps are given in the order in which they are done. You can visualize a process as follows:

## Visualize It!

**Process Paragraph Idea Map**

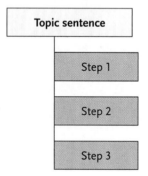

Topic sentence

Step 1

Step 2

Step 3

**Note:** The number of steps will vary.

There are two types of process paragraphs—a "how-to paragraph" and a "how-it-works" paragraph.

- **"How-to" paragraphs explain how something is done.** For example, they may explain how to change a flat tire, aid a choking victim, or locate a reference source in the library.

- **"How-it-works" paragraphs explain how something operates or happens.** For example, they may explain the operation of a pump, how the human body regulates temperature, or how children acquire speech.

Here are examples of both types of paragraphs. The first explains how to wash your hands in a medical environment. The second describes how hibernation works. Be sure to study the idea map for each.

### *"How-to" Paragraph*

Washing your hands may seem a simple task, but in a medical environment it is your first defense against the spread of disease and infection, and must be done properly. Begin by removing all jewelry. Turn on the water using a paper towel, thus avoiding contact with contaminated faucets. Next, wet your hands under running water and squirt a dollop of liquid soap in the palm of your hand. Lather the soap, and work it over your hands for two minutes. Use a circular motion, since it creates friction that removes dirt and organisms. Keep your hands pointed downward, so water will not run onto your arms, creating further contamination. Use a brush to clean under your fingernails. Then rinse your hands, reapply soap, scrub for one minute, and rinse again thoroughly. Dry your hands using a paper towel. Finally, use a new dry paper towel to turn off the faucet, protecting your hands from contamination.

## Visualize It! ➤

**Idea Map**

> **Washing hands must be done properly to control disease and infection.**
>
> Remove jewelry.
>
> Use towel to turn on faucet.
>
> Squirt dollop of soap, lather, and scrub.
>
> Use brush for fingernails.
>
> Rinse, reapply soap, scrub, and rinse again.
>
> Dry hands with paper towel.
>
> Use new paper towel to shut off faucet.

### *"How-It-Works" Paragraph*

Hibernation is a biological process that occurs most frequently in small animals. The process enables animals to adjust to a diminishing food supply. When the outdoor temperature drops, the animal's internal thermostat senses the change. Then bodily changes begin to occur. First, the animal's heartbeat slows, and oxygen intake is reduced by slowed breathing. Metabolism is then reduced. Food intake becomes minimal. Finally, the animal falls into a sleeplike state during which it relies on stored body fat to support life functions.

# Visualize It!

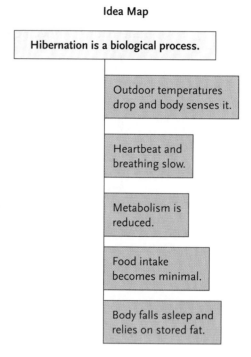

Idea Map

Hibernation is a biological process.

Outdoor temperatures drop and body senses it.

Heartbeat and breathing slow.

Metabolism is reduced.

Food intake becomes minimal.

Body falls asleep and relies on stored fat.

## Selecting a Topic and Generating Ideas

Before you can describe a process, you must be very familiar with it. You should have done it often or have a complete understanding of how it works. Both "how-to" and "how-it-works" paragraphs describe steps that occur *only* in a specified order. Begin developing your paragraph by listing these steps in the order in which they must occur. It is helpful to visualize the process.

For "how-to" paragraphs, imagine yourself actually performing the task. For complicated "how-it-works" descriptions, draw diagrams and use them as guides in identifying the steps and putting them in the proper order.

## EXERCISE 8-1

*Writing in Progress*

**Directions:** Think of a process or procedure you are familiar with, or select one from the following list, and make a list of the steps involved:

1. How to find a worthwhile part-time job.

2. How to waste time.

3. How to learn to like _____.

4. How the NFL football draft works.

5. How to win at _____.

6. How to make a marriage or relationship work.

7. How to protect your right to privacy.

8. How to improve your skill at _____.

9. How to make your boss want to promote you.

## Writing Your Topic Sentence

For a process paragraph, your topic sentence should accomplish two things:

- **It should identify the process or procedure.**

- **It should explain to your reader why familiarity with the process is useful or important (*why* he or she should learn about the process).** Your topic sentence should state a goal, offer a reason, or indicate what can be accomplished by using the process.

Here are a few examples of topic sentences that contain both of these important elements.

> Reading maps, a vital skill if you are taking vacations by car, is a simple process, except for the final refolding.

> Because leisure reading encourages a positive attitude toward reading in general, every parent should know how to select worthwhile children's books.

> To locate books in the library, you must know how to use the computerized catalog.

## EXERCISE 8-2

**Directions:** Revise these topic sentences to make clear why the reader should learn the process.

1. Making pizza at home involves five steps.

2. Making a sales presentation requires good listening and speaking skills.

3. Bloodhounds that can locate criminals are remarkable creatures.

4. The dental hygienist shows patients how to use dental floss.

5. Here's how to use a search engine.

## EXERCISE 8-3

*Writing in Progress*

**Directions:** Write a topic sentence for the process you selected in Exercise 8-1.

## Including Helpful Information

Because your readers may be unfamiliar with your topic, try to include helpful information that will enable them to understand (for how-it-works paragraphs) and follow or complete the process (for how-to paragraphs). Consider including the following:

- **Definitions** Explain terms that may be unfamiliar. For example, explain the term "bindings" when writing about skiing.

- **Needed equipment** For how-to paragraphs, tell your readers what tools or supplies they will need to complete the process. For a how-to paragraph on making chili, list the ingredients, for example.

- **Pitfalls and problems** Alert your reader about potential problems and places where confusion or error may occur. Warn your chili-making readers to add chili peppers gradually and to taste along the

## Sequencing and Developing Your Ideas

Use the following tips to develop an effective process paragraph:

1. **Place your topic sentence first.** This position provides your reader with a purpose for reading.

2. **Present the steps in a process in the order in which they happen.**

3. **Include only essential, necessary steps.** Avoid comments, opinions, or unnecessary information because it may confuse your reader.

4. **Assume that your reader is unfamiliar with your topic** (unless you know otherwise). Be sure to define unfamiliar terms and describe clearly any technical or specialized tools, procedures, or objects.

5. **Use a consistent point of view.** Use either the first person ("I") or the second person ("you") throughout. Don't switch between them. To learn more about this, see the Skill Refresher at the end of this chapter, p. 205.

## EXERCISE 8-4

*Writing in Progress*

**Directions:** Draft a paragraph for the process you chose in Exercise 8-1.

## Useful Transitions

Transitions are particularly important in process paragraphs because they lead your reader from one step to the next. Specifically, they signal to your reader that the next step is about to begin. In the following paragraph, notice how each of the highlighted transitions signal that a new step is to follow.

Do you want to teach your children something about their background, help develop their language skills, *and* have fun at the same time? Make a family album together! First, gather the necessary supplies: family photos, sheets of colored construction paper, yarn and glue. Next, fold four sheets of paper in half; this will give you an eight-page album. Unfold the pages and lay them flat, one on top of the other. After you've evened them up, punch holes at the top and bottom of the fold, making sure you get through all four sheets. Next, thread the yarn through the holes. Now tie the yarn securely and crease the paper along the fold. Finally, glue a photo to each page. After the glue has dried, have your child write the names of the people in the pictures on each page and decorate the cover. Remember to talk to your children about the people you are including in your album. Not only will they learn about their extended family, they will have great memories of doing this creative project with you.

Table 8-1 lists commonly used transitional words and phrases that are useful in process paragraphs.

Table 8-1    **Transitions for Process Paragraphs**

| | | |
|---|---|---|
| after | first | second |
| after that | following | then |
| afterwards | later | third |
| before | next | while |
| finally | | |

---

**EXERCISE 8-5**

*Writing in Progress*

**Directions:** Revise the draft you wrote for Exercise 8-4. Check transitional words and phrases and add them, as necessary, to make your ideas clearer.

## Applying Your Skills to Essay Writing: Process

Although this chapter has focused on writing process paragraphs, you can use many of the same skills for writing process essays.

### Guidelines for Writing Process Essays

Use the following guidelines for writing process essays:

1. **Before writing, list or outline the steps.** Decide how to arrange the steps and how to group them logically into paragraphs. For example, if you were writing about how to plan a wedding, you might group your steps into things to do many months ahead, things to do several weeks ahead, and things to do several days ahead.

2. **Give an overview.** If the process is long, complicated, or unfamiliar to your audience, describe that process in general terms before describing specific steps.

3. **For a difficult process, devote one paragraph to each step.** Help your reader by giving a thorough, detailed explanation of each step. By separating them into individual paragraphs, you will also help your reader distinguish one step from another.

4. **For a difficult or unfamiliar process, offer examples and make comparisons to a simpler or more familiar process.** For example, if you are writing about rugby, you might compare it to the similar and more familiar sport of football.

5. **Use the same verb tense throughout your essay.** Generally, processes are described in the present tense. There may be times, however, when you want to use the past tense; for instance, you may want to use the past tense to describe how you fixed your car this morning before leaving for school. For more about how to avoid shifts in verb tense, see the Skill Refresher at the end of this chapter, p. 000.

## EXERCISE 8-6

**Directions:** Write an essay describing one of the following processes:

1. You have inherited a large sum of money, but are required to award $5,000 to each of five homeless people. Explain how you would go about choosing those five people.

2. Suppose you learn you have a serious disease, but one that with the proper treatment is completely curable. Without proper treatment, it could be fatal. Write an essay describing the process of finding the right doctor to treat you.

3. Suppose you are shopping for a used car. You find two cars in the same price range with almost the same mileage on them. How would you decide which one to buy? Write an essay describing your decision-making process.

# AN ACADEMIC SCENARIO
## A STUDENT ESSAY
### The Academic Writer and the Writing Task

Dawn Trippie is a student at Niagara County Community College where she is studying horticulture and floral design. In the course Introduction to Horticulture, her instructor assigned a paper on composting—the process of using decayed plant matter to enrich the soil. Trippie decided to explain how to create a compost pile. Her audience is the home gardener. As you read her essay, pay attention to the sequence of events and the transitions she uses to guide her reader.

# Home Composting
## Dawn Trippie

*Title: suggests the audience for which the essay is intended*

*Introduction: addresses misconceptions*

*Definition of the term*

*Explanation of why the process is worth knowing about*

When you hear that someone is composting, the first thing that jumps in your mind is that he or she must be some weird organic gardener. Or you may think of someone who piles up junk and garbage and tosses it into the garden. Actually, composting is the scientific process of combining plant materials so that the original raw ingredients are turned into new soil. Composting is beneficial to home gardeners because plants grow much better in a garden to which compost has been added. It can also help reduce environmental waste since more than one-half of a household's waste is actually compostable. Using compost can also reduce the amount of commercial fertilizers used in your yard. Making and using compost is a long-term and worthwhile investment to your garden because it contains almost all the nutrients needed for plants to grow and thrive.

*Topic sentence identifies Step 1*

Begin by deciding what size pile you want to have. A compost pile should be at least 3 feet by 3 feet by 3 feet (3 feet square). This will allow the pile to heat up to the correct temperature so you can regulate the speed of decomposition. A pile smaller than 3 feet square may not heat up sufficiently. A pile larger than 3 feet square will need to be turned frequently to provide proper aeration during the composting process. Factors to consider in deciding the size of your pile include available space for the compost pile and the amount of household and garden material available to put in the pile.

*Helpful information*

*Topic sentence identifies Step 2*

Once you know the size, you are ready to purchase a compost container. You may build your own composting bin out of wood and wire or purchase a bin from a local garden store or municipality. A container is desirable because it keeps small animals out of the compost area.

*Step 3*

*Examples used to explain unfamiliar terms*

Now you are ready to start creating your compost pile by stockpiling ingredients. You will need both carbon based and nitrogen based materials. Carbon based materials include dried leaves, straw, and sawdust. Nitrogen based materials are things that are green and/or moist. This includes plants, weeds, vegetables, and table scraps. You can also add egg shells, nutshells, coffee grounds, fruit peels, and corn cobs.

*Step 4*

*Warning about potential problem*

Then, when they have enough leaves, grass clippings and other matter saved up, you are ready build your pile. Start with a layer of dried leaves, and alternate with layers of green matter. You will want to make sure that the ingredients that you are adding to the pile are wet, but not to the point of being soggy. While building your pile, you will want to have about thirty times as much nitrogen-based as carbon-based material. If you have too much nitrogen in your pile, your will notice a sharp, foul smell.

*Step 5*

Once the pile is built, you will need to keep track of its temperature. Your pile will start to heat up a few days after it is built. You may use a compost thermometer to measure the temperature inside the pile. You need to reach a temperature of at least 120–130 degrees for the material to begin to decompose. When the pile starts to cool down, it will need to be turned so that the outer layer is moved to the inside of the pile. The pile will start to heat again after several days. Your compost is complete when, after turning, the pile fails to heat up anymore. This composting process can take from three months to six months or more depending on weather conditions and the season of the year. Many people keep two piles, one that is actively working and one that is ready for garden use.

Finally, you have compost, so now what? Different people have different uses for their compost. It can be worked into your soil as an amendment, used as a top dressing on your gardens, or used as a mulch to help with water retention and weed suppression. Only you can decide what use is right for you. But be certain, everyone can benefit in some way from composting.

## Examining Academic Writing

1. Trippie wrote a "how-to" process essay. How could this essay be revised to become a "how-it-works" essay?

2. In what ways does Trippie reveal that she is writing for a home gardener, rather than a professional in her field?

3. Highlight the transitions she uses to make it clear she is moving from one step to another.

4. Did she provide sufficient explanation and detail when writing about a technical process? Highlight places where she was particularly effective in helping you understand the composting process.

## Academic Writing Assignments

1. Write a paragraph explaining one of the following processes:

    a. How to use the electronic card catalog in your campus library.

    b. How to obtain a campus ID card.

    c. How to apply for a student loan.

    d. How to get a tutor for a course in which you are having difficulty.

2. Write a paragraph explaining to a high school senior planning to attend college how to take notes in a college class or how to study for an exam in a specific subject.

3. Draw a map showing how to get to a particular place on campus from your writing classroom. Write a paragraph that explains this process. Test out the effectiveness of your paragraph by giving your paragraph to a classmate and asking him or her to reconstruct your map without seeing it.

4. Write a paragraph explaining how to use a software package with which you are familiar.

5. You are taking a first aid class and your instructor has asked you to write a brief essay on the rescue procedures for one of the following emergency situations. (You may need to use the Internet or print sources in your library to obtain basic information.)

   **a.** Choking

   **b.** Breathing stopped

   **c.** Poisoning

   **d.** External bleeding

# A WORKPLACE SCENARIO
## A HIRING POLICIES DOCUMENT
### The Workplace Writer and the Writing Task

The following example of workplace writing explains the hiring process for new teachers in the Leverett Elementary School in Leverett, MA, part of the Erving Union 28 Superintendency. As you read, notice that the process is detailed along with the responsibilities of the screening committee, the principal, and the superintendent of schools.

---

**LEVERETT SCHOOL COMMITTEE**

**HIRING POLICY**

A Screening Committee composed ordinarily of one School Committee member, two teachers, two parents, and the Principal will be formed by the Principal for the purpose of assisting in the selection of all teachers. The responsibility of the Screening Committee will be to review applications, select applicants to be interviewed, and interview as many candidates as necessary to ensure, whenever possible, that three final candidates may be selected.

The Principal will serve as Chairperson of the Screening Committee and will be authorized to interview prospective candidates in order to assist in the decision about which candidates are to be interviewed by the Committee. The Committee will decide which candidates to interview, except that the Committee will interview any candidate recommended to it by the Principal.

Selection of three final candidates for interview by the Superintendent will be the responsibility of the Screening Committee, except that the Principal may select additional final candidates. For positions which are exclusively housed in the Leverett Elementary School, the Principal will be responsible for the appointment of a candidate, subject to approval by the Superintendent. The Superintendent of Schools will inform the School Committee about any appointment.

It is understood that the hiring process be open until the Principal's appointment is approved by the Superintendent of Schools.

## Examining Workplace Writing

1. Draw a process map showing how teachers are hired in the Leverett School District.

2. If you were a member of the Screening Committee, what further information would you ask about the hiring process?

3. Who is the intended audience for this document?

4. By whom do you think this policy was written?

## Workplace Writing Assignments

1. Assume you are the superintendent of a school district. What process would you use to select new teachers? Write a paragraph describing the process.

2. Write a paragraph describing a process you are or were responsible for at a place where you worked. (Or, write a paragraph describing a process you have observed others performing at a local business.)

3. Based on your experience in the workplace, write a short process essay explaining how to get and keep a job.

# WRITING ABOUT A READING

## Thinking Before Reading

The following reading, "How Tattoos Work," appears on this Web site:

http://www.howstuffworks.com

This is an example of a "how-to" process essay. As you read, notice how the author details the steps in the process and uses illustrations to make certain processes clear.

1. Preview the reading, using the steps discussed in Chapter 2, p. 30.

2. Connect the reading to your own experience by answering the following questions:

   a. Do you have a tattoo or would you like to get one? Why?

   b. What risks or dangers are involved in tattooing?

### READING

# How Tattoos Work

1    It's virtually impossible to walk through a mall without spotting people of all ages with tattoos. Tattoos come in all shapes and sizes, and they can appear almost anywhere on someone's body. Permanent cosmetic studios also tattoo on eyebrows, eyeliner, and lip liner for those who want their make-up to be permanent. In these cases, you may not even know that you are looking at a tattoo! Tattoos have steadily gained popularity in the last decade—a trend that shows little sign of slowing down. In this article, we'll look at several aspects of tattooing and focus on how the tattooing process works.

## Origins

2    Believe it or not, some scientists say that certain marks on the skin of the *Iceman,* a **mummified** human body dating from about 3300 B.C., are tattoos. If that's true, these markings represent the earliest known evidence of the practice. Tattooing was rediscovered by Europeans when exploration brought them into contact with **Polynesians** and American Indians. The word tattoo comes from the **Tahitian** word tattau, which means "to mark," and was first mentioned in explorer James Cook's records from his 1769 expedition to the South Pacific.

## Meaning

3    The practice of tattooing means different things in different cultures. In early practice, decoration appears to have been the most common motive for tattooing, and that still holds true today. In some cultures, tattoos served as identification of the wearer's rank or status in a group. For example, the early Romans tattooed slaves and criminals. Tahitian tattoos served as **rites of passage**, telling the history of the wearer's life. Boys reaching manhood received one tattoo to mark the occasion, while men had another style done when they married. Sailors traveling to exotic foreign lands began to collect tattoos as souvenirs of their journeys (a dragon showed that the seaman had served on a China station), and tattoo parlors sprang up in port cities around the globe.

## Modern Tattooing

4    Today, tattoos are created by injecting ink into the skin. Injection is done by a needle attached to a hand-held tool. The tool moves the needle up and down at a rate of several hundred vibrations per minute and penetrates the skin by about one millimeter. What you see when you look at a tattoo is the ink that's left in the skin after the tattooing. The ink is not in the **epidermis**, which is the layer of skin that we see and the skin that gets replaced constantly, but instead intermingles with *cells* in the **dermis** and shows through

**mummified**
prepared for burial, like a mummy; shriveled and dried up

**Polynesians**
people living in a widely scattered group of islands in the Pacific that together form Polynesia

**Tahitian**
someone from Tahiti, one of the Polynesian islands

**rites of passage**
events or acts that mark an important transition in a person's life (from child to adult, or unmarried to married, for instance)

**epidermis**
the outmost layer of skin

**dermis**
the layer of skin just below the epidermis

the epidermis. The cells of the dermis are remarkably stable, so the tattoo's ink will last, with minor fading and dispersion, for your entire life!

### The Tattoo Machine

5    The basic idea of the electrically powered tattoo machine is that a needle moves up and down like in a sewing machine, carrying ink into your skin in the process. Today, a tattoo machine is an electrically powered, vertically vibrating steel instrument that resembles a dentist's drill (and sounds a little like it, too). It is fitted with solid needles that puncture the skin at the rate of 50 to 3,000 times a minute. The sterilized needles are installed in the

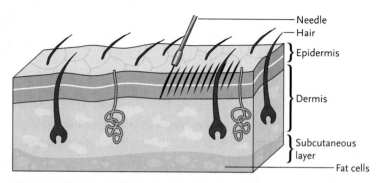

The tattoo needle inserts ink into the skin's dermal layer.

**subcutaneous (diagram)**
located, living, or made under the skin

machine and dipped in ink, which is sucked up through the machine's tube system. Then, powered by a foot switch much like that on a sewing machine, the tattoo machine uses an up-and-down motion to puncture the top layer of the skin and drive insoluble, micrometer-sized particles of ink into the second (dermal) layer of skin, about one-eighth inch deep.

### Sterilization

6    Much of the tattoo application process focuses on safety, since any puncture wound—and that's what a tattoo machine is doing to your skin— holds the potential for infection and disease transfer. The only acceptable method of sterilization for killing every living microorganism is an autoclave, a heat/steam/pressure unit (used in hospitals) that achieves and maintains 250 degrees Fahrenheit (121 C) under 10 pounds of pressure for 30 minutes or up to 270 F (132 C) under 15 pounds of pressure for 15 minutes. (Most units run a 55-minute cycle from a cold start.)

7    Most tattoo materials—inks, ink cups, gloves, and needles—are used only once to eliminate the possibility of contamination of materials. All reusable materials, such as the needle bar and the tube, must be completely clean, put into special pouches, and sterilized in the autoclave. Indicator strips on the packages change color when processing has occurred. Other equipment includes razors (for shaving the skin, since hair clogs up the tubes and hinders application) and plastic barriers (bags) that are used on spray bottles, tattoo machines, and clip cords to prevent cross-contamination.

### Prep Work

8    The tattoo artist, who has washed and inspected hands for cuts or abrasions and disinfected the work area with an EPA-approved viricidal, dons fresh gloves and generally follows this procedure:

- Places plastic bags on spray bottles
- Explains the sterilization process to client
- Opens up single-service, autoclave sterilized equipment in front of client
- Shaves and disinfects (with a mixture of water and antiseptic green soap) the area to be tattooed

8    With the outline (stencil) of the tattoo in place—or the outline of a custom tattoo drawn by hand onto the skin—the actual tattooing begins.

### Making the Outline

9    Using one single-tipped needle, the artist starts at the bottom of the right-hand side and works up (lefties generally start on the left side), so the stencil won't be lost when the artist cleans a permanent line. For single-needle work, a thinner black ink than that used for shading is used, because thinner ink can be easily wiped away from the skin without smearing.

10    As this happens, the tattoo machine is buzzing and smooth clear lines should be emerging as the needle pierces the skin, applies the ink, and gradually lifts out of the skin in a steady motion. (Experts say this is where the professionals show their mettle: In order to create clear lines and proper depth, the tattoo artist must understand how deep the needles actually need to go to produce a permanent line. Not going deep enough will create scratchy lines after healing, and going too deep will cause excessive pain and bleeding.)

### Shading

11    Once the outline is complete, the area is thoroughly cleaned with antiseptic soap and water. Then, the outline is thickened and shading is added. The tattoo artist will use a combination of needles. If this isn't done correctly, shadowed lines, excessive pain, and delayed healing will result. Again, everything must be autoclaved before use.

12    Using a thicker, blacker ink, the artist goes over the outline creating an even, solid line. Shading creates special effects. Each tattoo artist works differently, depending upon his or her training and preference.

### Color

13    After the shading is done, the tattoo is cleaned again and is now ready for color. When applying color, the artist overlaps each line of color to ensure solid, even hues with no "holidays"—uneven areas where color has either lifted out during healing or where the tattoo artist simply missed a section of skin. The tattoo is again sprayed and cleaned and pressure is applied

using a disposable towel to remove any blood and plasma excreted during the tattooing process. According to medical experts, some bleeding always occurs in tattooing, but under normal conditions (no alcohol or illegal drugs in the system, no fatigue, no tattooing over scar tissue), most stops within a few minutes after the tattoo is completed. (Reputable tattoo artists won't tattoo those who are sick, drunk, high or pregnant, and they won't apply pornographic, racist, or gang tattoos.)

### Identifying a Safe Tattoo Parlor

14    Other than the use of Universal Procedures and laws requiring that minors be tattooed only with parental permission, there are few regulations covering tattooing. Tattoo parlors must be licensed; this happens when artists qualify by completing a health department course on infectious disease transmission and passing an exam, but businesses aren't regularly inspected. (Legalization allows anyone to acquire a machine, get a license, and start tattooing whether they have any artistic ability or not—a situation that tattoo artists object to.) Here are some basic steps you can take to help ensure that you're choosing a safe tattoo parlor:

- Look around to see if the studio is clean and professional. That says a lot!
- Ask questions: Is there an autoclave? Are the needles and other materials single-use? Are EPA-approved disinfectants used? Are gloves being worn? (Professional tattoo artists won't mind the questions.)
- Play watchdog with the tattoo artist to be sure safety measures are being followed in the application of your tattoo.
- Make sure all needles are opened in front of you.
- Membership in professional organizations is not required, bur artists who participate are probably better informed about trends, innovations, and safety issues.

### Other Considerations

15    After you've explored the tattoo process and learned about all the health/safety considerations, here are several more points to consider:

- Think long and hard about the fact that a tattoo is permanent. What's cool at 18 might not be very appealing on a 40-year-old you!
- *Tattoo removal* is considerably more painful and expensive than tattooing. The process usually takes several sessions and offers varying results. Doctors say tattoos can be lightened but not always completely removed.
- Consider your career interests and plans—will sporting a highly visible tattoo hinder your success or effectiveness later on?
- Consider the ramifications. For example, you won't be able to donate blood—the American Red Cross will not accept blood donations from someone who has been tattooed in the past year.

## Getting Ready to Write

### Reviewing the Reading

1. Early cultures used tattoos for different reasons. What were three of these reasons?

2. The writer compares the tattoo machine to which two other machines?

3. In order to prevent infections and the spread of disease, what must a tattoo artist do?

4. In tattooing, what is meant by a "holiday"? Is a holiday a good thing or a negative thing?

5. Why should anyone think long and hard before getting a tattoo?

### Examining the Reading: Using Sequence Maps

To understand a narrative or process paragraph or essay, you must have a clear understanding of the sequence of events. A sequence map—a visual representation of key events or steps in the order in which they occur—can help you keep these straight.

Complete the sequence map on the following page for "How Tattoos Work" by filling in the blank boxes.

### Thinking Critically: Analyzing Tone

You can usually tell from a speaker's tone of voice how he or she feels. For example, you may be able to tell whether he or she is angry, serious, sincere, concerned, hostile, amused, or sympathetic. Although you cannot hear a writer's voice, you can sense how a writer feels about his or her subject. In other words, you can detect a *tone*. Tone is the writer's attitude toward the subject. Recognizing an author's tone is an important part of understanding, interpreting, and evaluating a piece of writing. Tone reveals feelings, attitudes, or viewpoints not directly expressed by the author. Can you sense the tone in each of the following statements?

- Anyone who throws litter out a car window should be severely punished. Not just a fine, but community service, jail time, *and* suspension of his or her driver's license.

- That poor woman's car broke down, right in the middle of the intersection. And it's so hot!

- After years of looking, I finally found the perfect job. It was a long search, but definitely worth the wait.

# Visualize It!

**Idea Map**

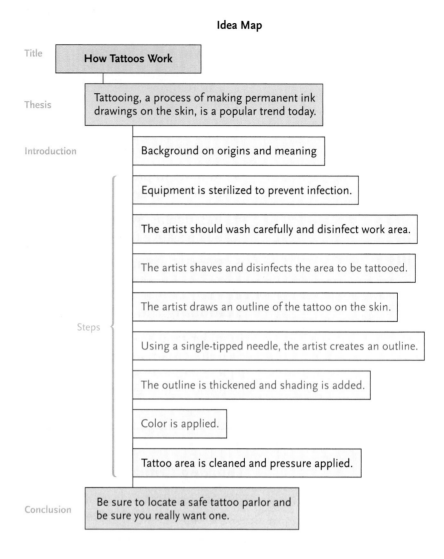

Title — **How Tattoos Work**

Thesis — Tattooing, a process of making permanent ink drawings on the skin, is a popular trend today.

Introduction — Background on origins and meaning

Steps —
- Equipment is sterilized to prevent infection.
- The artist should wash carefully and disinfect work area.
- The artist shaves and disinfects the area to be tattooed.
- The artist draws an outline of the tattoo on the skin.
- Using a single-tipped needle, the artist creates an outline.
- The outline is thickened and shading is added.
- Color is applied.
- Tattoo area is cleaned and pressure applied.

Conclusion — Be sure to locate a safe tattoo parlor and be sure you really want one.

Do you sense the first author to be angry and judgmental, the second to be sympathetic and concerned, and the third to be relieved and happy? Tone is not always as obvious as in the above statements. But you often can detect tone by studying how the author approaches his or her topic. In particular, look at the language he or she uses to describe the subject.

Complete the following activity by selecting, from the list of terms below used to describe tone, two that describe the tone of "How Tattoos Work." For each term you selected, highlight several words, phrases, or sentences in the reading where this tone is obvious.

| | | | |
|---|---|---|---|
| abstract | grim | persuasive | optimistic |
| instructive | righteous | sympathetic | distressed |
| bitter | cautionary | outraged | worried |

## Strengthening Your Vocabulary

**Part A:** Using the word's context, word parts, or a dictionary, write a brief definition of each of the following words as it is used in the reading.

1. insoluble (paragraph 5) incapable of being dissolved in liquid

2. viricidal (paragraph 8) a drug or other agent that neutralizes or destroys a virus

3. mettle (paragraph 10) strength of character; determination

4. autoclaved (paragraph 11) made sterile in an autoclave machine

5. legalization (paragraph 14) making something legal by changing a law that prohibits it

6. innovations (paragraph 14) new inventions or ways of doing something

7. ramifications (paragraph 15) consequences or outgrowths of a decision, act or judgment that may make a situation worse

**Part B:** Draw a word map for one of the words above.

## Reacting to Ideas: Discussion and Journal Writing

1. Discuss the author's purpose for writing this article. Does the author indicate any attitude for or against tattooing?

2. Discuss why a tattoo that someone got when he or she was 16 could become something he or she is ashamed of or embarrassed about 30 years later.

3. Young people consider many things to be acceptable that adults know are potentially dangerous. Besides getting a tattoo, what might a teenager think is cool that his or her parents would find legitimately frightening?

## Writing About the Reading

## Paragraph Options

1. Write a paragraph about why you or someone you know might want to get a tattoo. Explain why a tattoo is desirable.

2. If you decided to get a tattoo, write a paragraph about what you would look for in a tattoo parlor. What would make you choose one parlor over another?

3. Think of a celebrity who is known for his or her tattoos. Write a paragraph about this person's style; what image he or she is trying to project, how you feel about it, and what kind of media attention it gets him or her. Do you think all of that would be different if their tattoos were removed—even if no other changes (haircut, clothes, makeup, etc.) were made?

## Essay Options

4. Think of a rite of passage that you or someone you know has experienced. Write an essay explaining what the process involved. What age was the person when it occurred? Was it a ritual important to one particular culture or an event many people celebrate? Was it private or were there guests present?

5. Imagine you live in a society where tattoos are required for identification. Describe the tattoo you might create. In your essay, relate the design of your tattoo to your family background, culture, job or career, education, or any other feature of your life that is important in explaining who you are.

6. Currently, there are few regulations covering tattooing. Write an essay about your opinion on this issue. Is it good or bad that the rules are so loose? Would stricter laws make a difference to someone thinking of becoming a tattoo artist? What rules would you put in place if you were in charge of licensing tattoo parlors?

## Revision Checklist

1. Is your paragraph or essay appropriate for your audience? Does it give them the background information they need? Will it interest them?

2. Will your paragraph or essay accomplish your purpose?

3. Is your main point clearly expressed in a topic sentence?

4. Is each detail relevant? In other words, does each detail directly explain or support the topic sentence?

5. Have you supported your topic sentence with sufficient detail to make it understandable and believable?

6. Do you use specific and vivid words to explain each detail?

### For Process Writing

7. Does your topic sentence or thesis statement identify the process and explain its importance?

8. Are the steps arranged in the order in which they occurred? If not, will your reader be able to follow the sequence?

9. Have you used transitional words and phrases to help the reader follow the steps?

10. Have you used a consistent verb tense throughout your paragraph or essay?

# CHAPTER REVIEW AND PRACTICE

## Chapter Review

| | |
|---|---|
| WHAT IS A PROCESS PARAGRAPH OR ESSAY? | A process paragraph or essay describes how something is done or how something works. |
| TO WRITE AN EFFECTIVE PROCESS PARAGRAPH, WHAT KIND OF TOPIC SHOULD YOU CHOOSE? | You should choose a topic that is familiar. |
| WHAT SHOULD THE TOPIC SENTENCE OF A PROCESS PARAGRAPH ACCOMPLISH? | It should (1) identify the process or procedure you are writing about and (2) suggest its value or importance. |
| IN A PARAGRAPH OR ESSAY ABOUT A PROCESS, HOW SHOULD DETAILS BE ARRANGED? | Details should be arranged in the order in which they occur. |
| WHAT ARE THE GUIDELINES FOR WRITING PROCESS ESSAYS? | 1. Give an overview of the process, if needed. 2. Organize steps into paragraphs. 3. Give examples or make comparisons, if needed. 4. Use a consistent verb tense. |

## Skill Refresher: Avoiding Shift Errors

A **shift** is an unexpected change of the grammatical elements within a sentence or from one sentence to another within a piece of writing. Two common shifts are shifts in person and shifts in verb tense.

### Shifts in Person

Person refers to who is "talking" in a sentence. First person (I, me, myself) refers to the person who is talking. Second person refers to the person spoken to (you, your, yourself). Third person refers to the person or object being talked about (he, a person, people, she, it, they). Always use a consistent person throughout a piece of writing. Here are a few examples of common errors:

| | |
|---|---|
| SHIFT IN PERSON | If a <u>person</u> is thrifty, <u>you</u> can live on a poverty-level income. |
| CORRECT | If <u>you</u> are thrifty, <u>you</u> can live on a poverty-level income. (second person) |
| CORRECT | If a <u>person</u> is thrifty, <u>he or she</u> can live on a poverty-level income. (third person) |
| SHIFT IN PERSON | <u>I</u> realized that <u>you</u> can purchase fresh spices and herbs on the Internet. |
| CORRECT | <u>I</u> realized that <u>I</u> can purchase fresh spices and herbs on the Internet. |

## Shifts in Verb Tense

Verb tense refers to the changes made to a verb in order for it to express time. The three most common tenses are present (walks, runs), past (walked, ran), and future ( will walk, will run). Always use the same tense throughout a piece of writing, unless a change is required to indicate change. Here is an example of when a change is required:

Louise will travel to Utah 20 years after her parents visited there. (Her travel is in the future; her parents travel is in the past.)

In most situations, however, the same tense should be used throughout. Here are a few examples of common errors:

| | |
|---|---|
| SHIFT IN VERB TENSE | The computer virus <u>spread</u> so quickly that it <u>incapacitates</u> entire corporations within hours. |
| CORRECT | The computer virus <u>spread</u> so quickly that it <u>incapacitated</u> entire corporations within hours. |
| SHIFT IN VERB TENSE | The child's grades <u>continue</u> to drop; her parents <u>argued</u> about what action to take. |
| CORRECT | The child's grades <u>continued</u> to drop; her parents <u>argued</u> about what action to take. |

## Rate Your Ability to Avoid Shift Errors

Correct each of the following shift errors. If the sentence contains no errors, then write "C" for correct in the space provided. *Corrected sentences will vary.*

_____ 1. Renee stopped for coffee, bought gas, and then drives to campus for an early class.

_____  2. An electrician will repair circuits, but they won't install new electrical equipment.

_____  3. When someone deposits an out of state check in their checking account, they should expect to wait for the check to clear.

_____  4. If one forgets to sign a check, the person can expect to have the check returned to him or her.

_____  5. If a student does not write his course and section number on their exam, there is danger that it could be lost.

_____  6. When a service representative places you on hold for ten minutes, a person wonders if they are on a coffee break.

___C___  7. As we climbed the mountain, we noticed that the vegetation changed from desert plants to lush forests.

_____  8. Slang terms are popular in everyday speech; they appeared most often among teenagers and special interest groups.

_____  9. Advertisers often has used the language of sports to attract consumer interest; for example, it will use terms such as "game plan" and "winning team."

_____  10. The campaign to reduce violence on television began in the 1990s as concerned parents try to protect their children.

Score _____

Check your answers, using the Answer Key on p. 641. If you missed more than two, you need additional review and practice in recognizing shift errors. Refer to Part VI, "Reviewing the Basics," and under section D, see "Shifts in Person, Number, and Verb Tense." For additional practice, go to this book's Web site at http://www.ablongman.com/mcwhorterexpressways1e.

## INTERNET ACTIVITIES

### 1. Processes Explained

Explore the How Stuff Works Web site for science topics.

http://www.science.howstuffworks.com/

Write the steps that explain one concept described there.

## 2. Using a Flowchart

Examine this flowchart about the writing process from an instructor at Southern Illinois University, Edwardsville. Use it as a guide for making your own flowchart to describe a process you go through everyday.

http://www.siue.edu/~smoiles/wp-recur.html

## 3. This Book's Web Site

Visit this site to find templates of process idea maps and for additional practice on skills taught in the chapter.

http://www.ablongman.com/mcwhorterexpressways1e

# 9

# Example

## Chapter Objectives

*In this chapter
you will learn to:*

1. Use examples to develop paragraphs and essays.

2. Write effective topic sentences for example paragraphs.

3. Choose appropriate and sufficient examples.

4. Arrange your examples in a logical sequence.

5. Use transitions to connect your ideas.

## Write About It!

Write a sentence that states what behavior this photo illustrates. Then think of and describe several other instances that illustrate this behavior.

The sentences you write could form the basis of an example paragraph. An **example paragraph** uses specific instances to illustrate or explain a general idea. In this chapter you will learn to use examples in writing both paragraphs and essays. You will have many occasions to use examples in your everyday, academic, and workplace writing.

EVERYDAY SCENARIOS

- Explaining to a friend in an e-mail that a restaurant is pricey by telling her the costs of specific menu items—fried shrimp and Caesar salad
- Explaining that you are often mistaken for a well-known celebrity and giving several situations in which this has occurred

ACADEMIC SCENARIOS

- Answering an essay question for psychology on the causes of stress by including examples of different stressors
- Including examples in a speech on mistakes to avoid when buying a used car

WORKPLACE SCENARIOS

- Explaining to a supervisor that you deserve a raise by giving several examples of your excellent work
- Writing advertising copy for your company's product and including examples of quotations from satisfied customers

## UNDERSTANDING EXAMPLES

### What Is Example Writing?

Examples are specific instances or situations that explain a general idea or statement. Peaches and plums are examples of fruit. President's Day and Veteran's Day are examples of national holidays. Here are a few sample general statements along with specific examples that illustrate them.

| GENERAL STATEMENT | EXAMPLES |
|---|---|
| I had an exhausting day. | 1. I had two exams. |
| | 2. I worked four hours. |
| | 3. I swam 20 laps in the pool. |
| | 4. I did three loads of laundry. |

| GENERAL STATEMENT | EXAMPLES |
|---|---|
| Research studies demonstrate that reading aloud to children improves their reading skills. | 1. Whitehurst (2005) found that reading picture books to children improved their vocabulary. |
| | 2. Crain-Thompson and Dale (2003) reported that reading aloud to language-delayed children improved their reading ability. |

| GENERAL STATEMENT | EXAMPLES |
|---|---|
| You can improve your efficiency at work by working smarter, not harder. | 1. An efficient day begins the night before: Get a good night's sleep. |
| | 2. Every morning, make a list of your priorities for the day and stick to it. |
| | 3. Handle each piece of mail once; either respond to it, forward it to your assistant to handle, or throw it away. |

In each case, the examples make the general statement clear, understandable, and believable by giving specific illustrations or supporting details.

## EXERCISE 9-1

**Directions:** Working alone or with another student, brainstorm a list of examples to illustrate one of the following statements:

1. Effective teaching involves caring about students.

2. Dogs (or cats) make good companions.

3. Volunteerism has many benefits.

## Writing Your Topic Sentence

You must create a topic sentence before you can generate examples to support it. Consider what you want to say about your topic and what your main point or fresh insight is. From this main idea, compose a first draft of a topic sentence. Be sure it states your topic and your view toward it. (See Chapter 3, p. 61, if necessary, for a review of developing a viewpoint.) You will probably want to revise your topic sentence once you've written the paragraph, but for now, use it as the basis for gathering examples.

## EXERCISE 9-2

*Writing in Progress*

**Directions:** Select one of the topics listed below, write a topic sentence for it, and develop a paragraph on it, using examples.

1. Slang language

2. Daily hassles or aggravations

3. The needs of infants or young children

4. Over-commercialization of holidays

5. Irresponsible behavior of crowds or individuals at public events

## Selecting Appropriate and Sufficient Examples

The examples you select must illustrate your topic sentence. You can visualize an example paragraph as follows:

**Visualize It!**

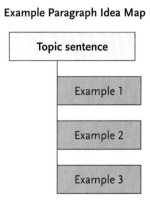

Example Paragraph Idea Map

Use brainstorming to create a list of as many examples as you can think of to support your topic sentence. Suppose your topic is dog training. Your tentative topic sentence is, "You must be firm and consistent when training dogs; otherwise, they will not respond to your commands." You might produce the following list of examples:

- My sister's dog jumps on people; sometimes she disciplines him and sometimes she doesn't.

- Every time I want my dog to heel, I give the same command and use a firm tone of voice.

- If my dog does not obey the command to sit, I repeat it, this time saying it firmly while pushing down on his back.

- The dog trainer at obedience class used a set of hand signals to give commands to his dogs.

Now review your list and select between two and four examples to support your topic sentence. The resulting paragraph is shown below:

When training dogs, you must be firm and consistent; otherwise, they will not respond to your commands. The dog trainer at my obedience class has a perfectly trained dog. She uses a set of hand signals to give commands to her dog, Belle. The same signal always means the same thing, it is always enforced, and Belle has learned to obey each command. On the other hand, my sister's dog is a good example of what not to do. Her dog Maggie jumps on people; sometimes she disciplines Maggie and sometimes she doesn't. When she asks Maggie to sit, sometimes she insists Maggie obey; other times she gets discouraged and gives up. Consequently, the dog has not learned to stop jumping on people or to obey the command to sit.

# Visualize It!

**Idea Map**

In the above paragraph, you noticed that some of the brainstormed examples were used; others were not. New examples were also added. Use the following guidelines in selecting details to include:

1. **Each example should illustrate the idea stated in your topic sentence.** Sometimes you may find that your examples do not clarify your main point or that each example you think of seems to illustrate something slightly different. If your topic is too broad, narrow your topic, using the suggestions in Chapter 3, p. 63.

2. **Each example should be as specific and vivid as possible, accurately describing an incident or situation.** Suppose your topic sentence is, "Celebrities are not reliable sources of information about a product because they are getting paid to praise it." For your first example you write: "Many sports stars are paid to appear in TV commercials." "Many sports stars" is too general. To be convincing, your example has to name specific athletes and products or sponsors: "Pete Sampras, champion tennis player, is paid to endorse Dannon yogurt; Tiger Woods, champion golfer, endorses Nike products."

3. **Choose a sufficient number of examples to make your point understandable.** The number you need depends on the complexity of the topic and your reader's familiarity with it. One example is sufficient only if it is well developed. The more difficult and unfamiliar the topic, the more examples you will need. For instance, if you are writing about how poor service at a restaurant can be viewed as an exercise in patience, two examples may be sufficient. Your paragraph could describe your long wait and your rude waiter, and make its point quite powerfully. However, if you are writing about test anxiety as a symptom of poor study habits, you probably would need more than two examples. In this case, you might discuss the need to organize one's time, set realistic goals, practice relaxation techniques, and work on self-esteem.

4. **Draw the connection for your reader between your example and your main point.** The following is a presentation by a social worker during a closed staff meeting at Carroll County Mental Health Services:

   We are continuing to see the aftereffects of last spring's tornado on our clients. In some cases, we have had to make referrals to meet our clients' needs. Several children have suffered PTSS (post traumatic stress syndrome). Natoya Johns, for example, has nightmares and panic attacks.

Natoya and the other children have been referred to Dr. Browntree at the Children's Clinic. We are also seeing increased occurrences of domestic violence that seem to be due to economic problems caused by the tornado. The worst case was Betsy Coster, who came to her counseling session with broken ribs, a black eye, and bruises. Betsy was referred to Safe Harbor, where she will receive legal and medical assistance while in protected housing. Several cases of substance abuse appeared to be aggravated by the stress of the situation. We put four clients in touch with AA, and Ken Lacoutez was referred to City Hospital for the inpatient program.

(*Note:* Names have been changed to protect client privacy.)

## EXERCISE 9-3

*Writing in Progress*

**Directions:** Brainstorm a list of examples that illustrate the topic sentence you chose in Exercise 9-2.

### NEED TO KNOW

#### Choosing Appropriate Examples

Use the following guidelines in choosing examples:

1. **Make sure your example illustrates your topic sentence clearly.** Do not choose an example that is complicated or has too many parts; your readers may not be able to see the connection to your topic sentence clearly.

2. **Choose examples that your readers are familiar with and understand.** If you choose an example that is out of the realm of your readers' experience, the example will not help them understand your main point.

3. **Choose interesting, original examples.** Your readers are more likely to pay attention to them.

4. **Vary your examples.** If you are giving several examples, choose a wide range from different times, places, people, etc.

5. **Choose typical examples.** Avoid outrageous or exaggerated examples that do not accurately represent the situation.

## Arranging Your Details

Once you have selected examples to include, arrange your ideas in a logical sequence. Here are a few possibilities:

- **Arrange the examples chronologically.** If some examples are old and others more recent, you might begin with the older examples and then move to the more current ones.

- **Arrange the examples from most to least familiar.** If some examples are more detailed or technical, and therefore likely to be unfamiliar to your reader, place them after more familiar examples.

- **Arrange the examples from least to most important.** You may want to begin with less convincing examples and finish with the strongest, most convincing example, thereby leaving your reader with a strong final impression.

- **Arrange the examples in the order suggested by the topic sentence.** In the above sample paragraph about dog training, being firm and consistent is mentioned first in the topic sentence, so an example of firm and consistent training is given first.

## Useful Transitions

Transitional words and phrases are needed in example paragraphs both to signal to your reader that you are offering an example and that you are moving from one example to another. Notice in the following paragraph how the transitions connect the examples and make them easy to follow:

> Electricity is all around us, often in the form of static electricity. For example, when we walk on a nylon rug and then touch something or someone we receive a mild electrical shock. This shock occurs because accumulated electrical energy is being discharged. Similarly, when we rub a balloon on a sweater and make the balloon stick to the wall or ceiling, energy is again discharged. Another instance of electrical discharge occurs when clothes cling together after removal from a dryer.

Table 9-1   **Transitions for Example Paragraphs**

| for example | for instance | such as | in particular |
|---|---|---|---|
| to illustrate | an example is | also | when |

## Applying Your Skills to Essay Writing: Examples

This chapter has focused on using examples to develop paragraphs. Since giving examples is one of the best ways to explain an unfamiliar or difficult topic, you will often use examples in essay writing. Use the following guidelines in writing essays that use examples:

- **Develop one example at a time.** Fully explain one example before moving to the next. In essays, you may decide to devote a paragraph to each example.

- **Make sure each topic sentence is clear.** Your topic sentence should make it clear what the examples used in the paragraph will illustrate.

- **Make each example sufficiently detailed.** Unlike when you are writing a single paragraph, you have the opportunity to use multiple paragraphs in an essay to fully explain each example. Include details and use descriptive language.

- **Use examples along with other means of development.** Sometimes an essay can be developed using only examples, but more often, you will use examples in combination with another method of development. For example, you might use examples from your personal experience as the primary means of development for an essay that discusses how attending preschool contributes to a child's intellectual and social development. In an essay on avoiding identity theft, however, you might use process as your primary means of development, but use examples to explain specific steps you can take to keep your personal information secure.

## AN ACADEMIC SCENARIO
### A Student Essay
### The Academic Writer and the Writing Task

Ebtisam Abusamak is attending Central Piedmont Community College in Charlotte, North Carolina, where she is majoring in business administration. For her Social Problems class she was asked to identify a domestic social problem and explore Ameri-

can society's attitudes toward it. Abusamak chose to write about public assistance. As you read, notice how she uses three examples to support her thesis.

Title: announces subject; suggests thesis

# The Truth About Welfare in America
### Ebtisam Abusamak

Introduction: background information that establishes the need for the welfare system

The United States Constitution says: "We hold these truths to be self-evident, that all men are created equal . . . endowed . . . with certain unalienable Rights . . . among these are Life, Liberty and the pursuit of Happiness." It was the intent of its authors to create a society in which people would be not only free, but happy as well. It is the responsibility of the U.S. government to make sure that all of its citizens are guaranteed a minimum income, enough for food, shelter, and basic necessities. This was the original purpose of welfare.

Thesis statement

Many people have a misconception about welfare; too many people think of people on welfare as lazy, stupid, or greedy, but that is not accurate. The truth is that the majority of recipients do not stay on the welfare rolls very long. Most turn to welfare because of some sort of life crisis such as unemployment, illness, or the death of a spouse. They get out of the program as soon as they are back on their feet again. Most recipients do not become permanently dependent on government aid.

*Topic sentence*

My neighbor Rachel is a good example of someone forced to turn to welfare. After her stepfather suffered a serious mental illness, her mother was hard-pressed to find extra hours at her already full-time job. She was having trouble paying bills and buying food for Rachel and her brother Nick. "We were six and thirteen at the time, and even at that young age, we knew there was something very wrong with our family," said Rachel. Finally Rachel's mother broke down and went to the county welfare office for assistance. After

*Example 1*

a couple of years, her stepfather's illness broke the family apart. Rachel and her mother stayed where they were, while her brother and stepfather moved to a state with better health care facilities. The family struggled, but Rachel's mother insisted that they only rely on the state if necessary. She was ashamed of having to use food stamps in the grocery store and every time she cashed that little government check, she turned red in the face. She'd always been a proud and resourceful woman and eventually she found a well-paying position in a large company and began working her way up from there.

Many people feel the same way Rachel's mother did. They worry constantly about how society views them, and asking for government assistance puts a huge strain on them emotionally. Unfortunately, many people are ignorant of the world of struggle around them and look down on those who are aided by the welfare system. Many people think the poor are largely responsible for their own troubles and that the wealthy deserve their privileges.

*Topic sentence*

My friend Dan W. is a good example of a person who is not responsible for his own misfortune. Dan was raised in an affluent New York family. He got into college, but quit after two years. Not knowing what he wanted to do, Dan took a construction job. A few months in, he fell from a scaffold and severely injured his back. Told he might never walk again, Dan realized he had to go back to school and finish his degree. Unfortunately, his family had cut him off when he quit school the first time, and now he had no contact with them. Dan was determined to make it on his own and applied for wel-

*Example 2*

fare. After months of painful therapy, he was finally well enough to begin classes at his local university. Dan remained on welfare for 16 months, then found a corporate sponsor that supported him while he finished school. He is now a Certified Public Accountant, living with his wife in a suburb not far from where he grew up. Asked about his time on welfare, Dan is unembarrassed. "If it hadn't been for assistance, I don't think I could have gotten through recovery. If there's anything I'm ashamed of, it is my family's attitude toward people in need. Bad things can happen to anyone and it's important to have a safety net."

*Topic sentence*

Another example of the benefits of welfare to society is my own. I grew up in a lower-middle class neighborhood. My father worked over 40 hours a

Example 3

week and was the sole provider for our family of nine. Though he had graduated with a master's degree in electrical engineering, he had come to America not knowing how to speak English. Unable to establish himself as an engineer, he became a driver for a variety of transportation services in order for us to eat. My dad worked hard, long hours just like millions of other citizens do everyday, yet he did not make nearly enough to support the needs of seven children. My family had to have some government assistance, not to live on forever, but enough to stay alive on until my father could find work in his profession. In fact, I have a brother with epilepsy who would *not* be alive today if it weren't for the health care assistance. And, without financial aid, no one in my family would have been able to go to college and become the professionals we are today.

Conclusion: ties the three examples together and provides a positive ending

People have put their attitudes and prejudices before the needs of others. Many believe that the poor do not deserve the same rights because they are not educated enough, working hard enough, or smart enough to survive. This is not true of Rachel, Dan or me—all former welfare recipients who are now giving back to society far more than we ever received.

## Examining Academic Writing

1. Evaluate the introduction. In what other ways could Abusamak introduce the topic?

2. Do you think three examples are sufficient evidence for this essay?

3. Evaluate the title. How does it support Abusamak's thesis?

4. Other than examples, what other kinds of evidence could Abusamak have used to support her thesis?

## Academic Writing Assignments

1. You are earning a degree in travel and tourism. For an introductory course you are taking, you have been asked to write a convincing letter urging a client to visit a particular travel destination. Choose a travel destination; it might be one you have visited, one you hope to visit, or even your hometown. Write a letter that uses examples to point out the highlights and features of the destination.

2. You are taking a sociology class that focuses on marriage and the family. Your instructor has asked you to choose one factor that holds a marriage or family together and write an essay about it. Choose a factor and write an essay using examples to explain how that factor holds a family together. (Hint: Factors you might choose include religion, cultural ties, common interests, or shared activities.)

3. You are taking a course in health and fitness and your instructor has assigned you to make a three-minute speech on a health-related topic. Choose one of the following and use examples to support your ideas. Write out your speech as practice.

   **a.** fad diets

   **b.** alcohol abuse

   **c.** drug abuse

# A WORKPLACE SCENARIO
## ADVERTISING COPY
### The Workplace Writer and the Writing Task

Sid Fernandes owns Warranty World, a company that sells extended automobile insurance. Warranty World has a good record of standing behind each of its contracts, but many people still have a bad impression of after-market insurance companies. Fernandes has to fight that reputation and win new business by letting people know why Warranty World is different.

Fernandes gives his advertising department the job of developing a direct mail piece to be sent to all Auto Club members. Below is the copy for that piece. As you read, notice how Warranty World uses examples to support its claim that after-market insurance is necessary and that it is the best company to provide it.

---

WHAT'S *WORSE* THAN A BREAKDOWN? AUTO REPAIRS THAT BREAK THE BANK!

When it comes to the high cost of auto repairs, you have two choices: Safe. And sorry.

Take it from these two drivers:

Driver A played it safe and bought Warranty World Extended Coverage. When his car broke down on a business trip, he didn't have to pay the repair shop a thing. Not one penny. He also didn't have to negotiate with the mechanic, fill out any paperwork, or write a check. Warranty World did it all for him.

Warranty World also paid for his rental car *and* the hotel room he had to rent while his car was being fixed.

Driver B did not buy Warranty World Extended Coverage. When *his* car broke down he had to put his trust in a mechanic he'd never met and pay more than his weekly salary for a repair he wasn't sure he needed. Person B is very sorry.

It's a fact: Most people are keeping their cars longer. It's also a fact that today's cars contain more than 5,000 high-tech components—any one of which could break at any time.

Play it safe like Person A. Call Warranty World. **We're the only extended warranty provider offered by your Auto Club!**

Warranty World gives you benefits you won't get from any manufacturer or dealer, like coverage for tire damage due to road hazards.

Still not convinced? Listen to what these longtime customers say about Warranty World:

> "I never filed a claim. So when my contract was up, Warranty World refunded my entire premium payment!"
>
> —Rose S., Wayne, NJ

> "When I went to sell my car, I got more money for it because the Warranty World Coverage was transferable to the new owner. The buyer just felt more confident about my car than the others he'd looked at. Thanks Warranty World!"
>
> —Hillary J., Tampa FL

> "I wouldn't think of having surgery without major medical coverage. And I wouldn't drive a car that's not covered by Warranty World. I can't afford it!"
>
> —Lucy S., Salinas CA

> "We checked with the Better Business Bureau. They gave Warranty World the highest rating in the industry."
>
> —James B., Springfield, IL

Do what these and thousands of other smart drivers have done: Call Warranty World. When it comes to protecting your wallet, we make the difference between safe and sorry.

## Examining Workplace Writing

1. The writer conveys nearly all the information about Warranty World through examples. Why is this effective? Is this typical of advertising you have seen or heard?

2. Evaluate the quotation boxes at the end of the ad. What do they contribute to the ad?

3. Why is this advertisement convincing? To what needs, values, or interests does this advertisement appeal?

## Workplace Writing Assignments

1. Choose a product that is sold on the Internet. Suppose you are designing a Web site for a company that sells this product. Write a piece of advertising copy for this product. Be sure to include examples from satisfied customers.

2. The company where you work has appointed you to a team that is evaluating flextime—the option for employees to choose their own hours to work. The team will recommend that the company adopt a limited flextime policy and is writing a report supporting the recommendation. You have been asked to provide three examples that illustrate the advantages of flextime for employees.

3. For the career for which you are preparing, write an essay explaining why you feel you are well-suited for the job. Support your ideas with examples of the tasks involved in the job and why you are qualified to perform those tasks.

## WRITING ABOUT A READING

### Thinking Before Reading

The following reading, "First Big Shocks," is taken from a book by Mary Pipher, titled *The Middle of Everywhere: Helping Refugees Enter the American Community*. The author presents the personal stories of people who have fled their homelands to start new lives in the United States. As you read, notice how the author uses examples to emphasize her points.

1. Preview the reading, using the steps discussed in Chapter 2, p. 30.

2. Connect the reading to your own experience by answering the following questions:

   a. Do you know anyone who has moved to America as a refugee? What is their situation?

   b. When have you been in a strange, foreign, or unfamiliar place or situation? How did you react?

R E A D I N G

# First Big Shocks

### Mary Pipher

1   When I was in college, I remember reading about a tribe in Central America who thought that Americans never got sick or died. All the Americans they'd seen were healthy anthropologists, tall and well-nourished. They'd never seen Americans die.

2   Modern refugees often come here equally naïve about us. Some have Nebraska and Alaska confused and expect mountains, ice, and grizzlies. Some think of Nebraska as a western state with cowboys, and they are ill-prepared for our factories, suburbs, and shopping malls. Many newcomers have never seen stairs, let alone escalators or elevators. Inventions such as duct tape, clothes hangers, aluminum foil, or microwaves often befuddle new arrivals.

3   Someone once said, "Every day in a foreign country is like final exam week." It's a good metaphor. Everything is a test, whether of one's knowledge of the language, the culture, or of the layout of the city. Politics, laws, and personal boundaries are different. Relations between parents and children, the genders, and the social classes are structured differently here. The simplest task—buying a bottle of orange juice or finding medicine for a headache—can take hours and require every conceivable skill.

*Dallas*

a television show about Texas millionaires that ran from 1978–1991

**Azerbaijani**

someone from the country of Azerbaijan which is in Southeastern Europe, north of Iran and bordering the Caspian Sea

**Allah**

God, in Islam

**pickle card**

a lottery game in Nebraska

**Lincoln**

the capital city of Nebraska

4    Some refugees believe they will be given a new car and a house when they arrive. Some people ask government workers "Where is my color TV? My free computer?" Others have seen *Dallas* or *Who Wants to Marry a Millionaire?* and think they will soon get rich.

5    This belief that it's easy to get rich in America is exploited by con artists. An **Azerbaijani** man received a Reader's Digest Sweepstakes notice informing him he was a millionaire. He fell to his knees and thanked **Allah** for his riches. A Vietnamese family called relatives in Ho Chi Minh City to tell them the great news that they had won the Publisher's Clearinghouse sweepstakes. A Siberian couple laughed and danced around their kitchen, already spending their expected **pickle card** winnings on a new car, a dishwasher, and a swimming pool for the kids. Later, when it became clear they hadn't won, they weren't so happy.

6    Some newcomers don't know the number of weeks in a year or what the seasons are. Others are well-educated but have gaps. Once when I was talking to a well-educated Croatian woman about our history, I brought up the sixties. I said, "It was a hard time with war and so many assassinations, those of John and Bobby Kennedy and Martin Luther King." She asked in amazement, "You mean Martin Luther King is dead?" When I said yes, she began to cry.

7    Our casual ways of dealing with the opposite sex are without precedent in some cultures. Our relaxed interactions between men and women can be alarming to some people from the Middle East. Some traditional women are suspicious of American women; it seems to them as if the American women are trying to steal their husbands because they speak to them at work or in stores.

8    An Iraqi high school student told of arriving in this country on a summer day. As she and her father drove through **Lincoln**, there were many women on the streets in shorts and tank tops. Her father kept saying to her, "Cover your eyes; cover your eyes." Neither of them had ever seen women in public without head covering.

9    There are two common refugee beliefs about America—one is that it is sin city; the other is that it its paradise. I met a Cuban mother whose sixteen-year-old daughter got pregnant in Nebraska. She blamed herself for bringing the girl to our sinful town, weeping as she told me the story. And she showed me a picture of the daughter, all dressed in white. A Mexican father told me that his oldest son was now in a gang. He talked about American movies and the violent television, music, and video games. He said, "My son wears a black T-shirt he bought at a concert. It has dripping red letters that read, 'More Fucking Blood.' " He looked at me quizzically. "America is the best country in the world, the richest and the freest. Why do you make things like this for children?"

10    On the other hand, some refugees idealize our country. They talk endlessly of the mountains of food in buffets, the endless supply of clean water, the shining cars, and the electricity. Flying into a city such as New York or Seattle, many refugees experience their first vision of America and are overwhelmed by the shining stars of light on the ground, more light than they have ever seen. One refugee from Romania captured both ideas when he said, "America is the beauty and the beast."

11    When I ask refugees what America means to them, many say, "Freedom." This may mean many things. To the Kurdish sisters it is the freedom to wear stylish American clothes and walk about freely. It's the freedom to go swimming and shopping and make a living. To many of the poor and disenfranchised, it is the radical message that everyone has rights, even though at first many refugees do not know what their rights are.

12    America means a system of laws, a house, a job, and a school for every child. In America people can strive for happiness, not even a concept in some parts of the world. They are free to become whomever they want to become. Refugees learn they can speak their minds, write, and travel. They shed the constraints of more traditional cultures. As one Bulgarian woman put it to me, "In America, the wives do not have to get up and make the husbands' breakfasts."

13    People from all over the world want to come here. They want a chance at the American Dream. They come because they want to survive and be safe and anywhere is better than where they were. However, the process of adjusting is incredibly traumatic. The Kurdish sisters were in culture shock for about six months. After a year, they are still deeply in debt, lonely, haunted by the past, and struggling to master our language and our culture. They are overwhelmed every time their bills arrive. Nasreen and Zeenat still dream nightly of their homeland.

14    It is difficult to describe or even imagine the challenges of getting started in a new country. Imagine yourself dropped in downtown Rio de Janeiro or **Khartoum** with no money, no friends, and no understanding of how that culture works. Imagine you have six months to learn the language and everything you need to know to support your family. Of course, that isn't a fair comparison because you know that the earth is round, what a bank is, and how to drive a car. And you have most likely not been tortured or seen family members killed within the last few months.

15    Picture yourself dropped in the Sudanese grasslands with no tools or knowledge about how to survive and no ways to communicate with the locals or ask for advice. Imagine yourself wondering where the clean water is, where and what food is, and what you should do about the bites on your feet, and your sunburn, and the lion stalking you. Unless a kind and generous Sudanese takes you in and helps you adjust, you would be a goner.

**Khartoum**
the capital city of Sudan

## Getting Ready to Write

### Reviewing the Reading

1. What two preconceived ideas do some refugees have about the United States?

2. What "freedoms" are available in the United States that are important to many refugees?

3. Give five examples of things that refugees in America find unfamiliar.

4. Explain the meaning of the quotation "America is the beauty and the beast."

### Examining the Reading: Using Idea Mapping to Organize an Example Essay

In an example essay, writers use examples to support their main ideas. Often these examples have accompanying details that create a vivid picture for the reader. Sometimes an author will even try to connect the examples with the experiences of the reader in order to create a personal connection that affects the reader on a deep level.

An idea map of the entire reading would be quite lengthy due to the numerous examples Pipher includes. Fill in the missing parts of the partial idea map on the next page that organizes the examples presented in the paragraphs.

### Thinking Critically: Examining Comparisons

The purpose of the reading is to make you aware of the problems that refugees face when they arrive in the United States. Both at the beginning and at the end of the essay, Pipher uses comparisons to help her readers understand the refugee experience. In paragraph 3, she compares the refugee experience to final exam week. In the last two paragraphs she asks readers to imagine being dropped in a foreign country, to highlight the similarities between that experience and that of refugees. Apply your knowledge of comparisons by answering the following questions:

1. In what ways is the refugee experience similar to final exam week in college?

2. What are the similarities between being dropped in the Sudanese grasslands and being a refugee in America?

3. How did the comparisons Pipher includes help you to understand the plight of refugees in America?

# Visualize It!

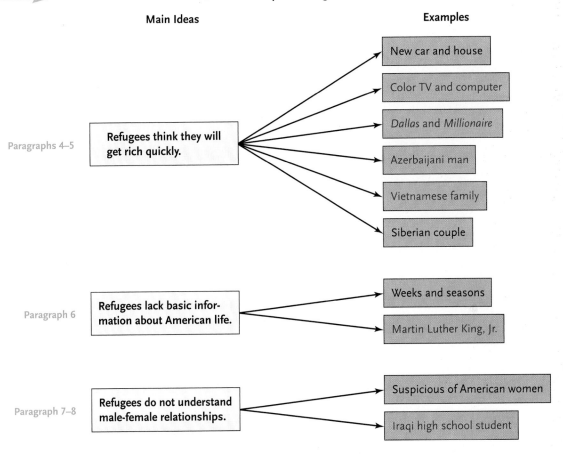

**Partial Idea Map: "First Big Shocks"**

Main Ideas                                    Examples

Paragraphs 4–5 — Refugees think they will get rich quickly.
- New car and house
- Color TV and computer
- *Dallas* and *Millionaire*
- Azerbaijani man
- Vietnamese family
- Siberian couple

Paragraph 6 — Refugees lack basic information about American life.
- Weeks and seasons
- Martin Luther King, Jr.

Paragraph 7–8 — Refugees do not understand male-female relationships.
- Suspicious of American women
- Iraqi high school student

## Strengthening Your Vocabulary

**Part A:** Using the word's context, word parts, or a dictionary, write a brief definition of each of the following words or phrases as it is used in the reading.

1. befuddle (paragraph 2) _confuse_ _____

   _____

2. exploited (paragraph 5) _made use of for one's own gain_ _____

   _____

3. precedent (paragraph 7) _something that serves as an example_ _____

   _____

4. quizzically (paragraph 9) _with disbelief_ _____

   _____

5. disenfranchised (paragraph 11) _denied a privilege or right_ _____

   _____

**Part B:** Draw a word map for one of the above words.

## Reacting to Ideas: Discussion and Journal Writing

1. Discuss possible reasons that people flee their homelands for America.

2. How difficult would it be for you to leave your native country? What would you leave behind? What would you miss most?

3. What challenges does the average American face in a foreign country?

# Writing About the Reading

## Paragraph Options

1. Choose a foreign country you have never visited. Write a paragraph giving examples of problems you would expect to face if you went there.

2. Many refugees have experienced violence and tragedy. Write a paragraph that explains how a violent or tragic event affected your life or the life of someone you know.

3. Many refugees have misperceptions about the American lifestyle. Write a paragraph describing a misperception you once held and explain how you became aware of the truth.

## Essay Options

4. Refugees may be taken advantage of by misleading advertising. Write an essay examining the practice of false or misleading advertising. Support your essay with examples of false or misleading advertising that you have seen or heard.

5. Suppose a refugee visited only your town or city, and had not seen or heard much else about America. What misperceptions about American life in general would he or she hold? Write an essay explaining these misperceptions. Give examples from the geography, society, workplace, culture, etc. of your town or city to support your ideas.

6. Relationships between American men and women are considered casual and relaxed by many refugees. Using examples, write a letter to someone planning to relocate to America explaining what to expect in male-female relationships.

7. Some of the refugees in the essay thought they would get rich quick in America. Write an essay about the American dream of going from "rags to riches." Do you think it is possible? What resources—skills, attitudes, contacts, etc.—are necessary?

## Revision Checklist

1.  Is your paragraph or essay appropriate for your audience? Does it give them the background information they need? Will it interest them?

2.  Will your paragraph or essay accomplish your purpose?

3.  Is your main point clearly expressed?

4.  Is each detail relevant? Does each explain or support your main point?

5.  Have you supported your main point with sufficient detail to make it understandable and believable?

6.  Did you use specific words to explain each detail?

### For Example Writing

7.  Does the topic sentence or thesis statement express a specific viewpoint toward the topic?

8.  Is each example understandable by itself?

9.  Are there sufficient examples to explain your main point to the intended audience?

10.  Are the examples arranged in a logical order?

11.  Are ideas connected with transitional words and phrases?

12.  Have you proofread? (See the inside back cover of this book for a proofreading checklist.)

# CHAPTER REVIEW AND PRACTICE

## Chapter Review

| | |
|---|---|
| WHAT ARE EXAMPLES? | Examples are specific instances or situations that explain a general idea or statement. |
| WHAT IS THE RELATIONSHIP BETWEEN THE TOPIC SENTENCE AND EXAMPLES? | Examples should clearly illustrate the idea stated in the topic sentence. |
| WHAT DETERMINES HOW MANY EXAMPLES ARE NEEDED TO EXPLAIN A TOPIC? | The number of examples depends on the complexity of the topic and the reader's familiarity with it. |
| WHAT POSSIBLE WAYS CAN EXAMPLES BE ARRANGED IN A PARAGRAPH OR ESSAY? | Possible arrangements are chronological, most-to-least, least-to-most, and order according to topic sentence. |
| WHAT DO TRANSITIONAL WORDS OR PHRASES DO IN EXAMPLE PARAGRAPHS? | Transitional words and phrases are needed in example paragraphs to signal to the reader that you are moving from one example to another. |
| WHAT ARE THE GUIDELINES FOR WRITING EXAMPLE ESSAYS? | Guidelines include: <br> • Develop one example at a time. <br> • Write clear topic sentences. <br> • Make examples detailed. <br> • Use examples along with other methods of development. |

## Skill Refresher: Dangling Modifiers

A modifier is a word or group of words that describes another word, or qualifies or limits the meaning of another word. When a modifier appears at the beginning of the sentence, it must be followed immediately by the word it describes. Dangling modifiers are *not* followed by the word they describe. Dangling modifiers either modify nothing or do not clearly refer to the correct word or word group.

DANGLING    <u>After getting off the bus</u>, the driver pulled away.

CORRECT    <u>After I got off the bus</u>, the driver pulled away.

## How to Correct Dangling Modifiers

There are two ways to correct dangling modifiers:

1. Add a word or words so that the modifier describes the word or words it is intended to describe. Place the new word(s) just after the modifier.

   DANGLING    <u>While sitting under the maple tree,</u> ants started to attack.

   CORRECT    While sitting under the maple tree, <u>I was attacked by ants.</u>

2. Change the modifier to a dependent clause. (You may need to change the verb in the modifier.)

   DANGLING    <u>After giving the dog a flea bath</u>, the dog hid under the bed.

   CORRECT    <u>After I gave the dog a flea bath</u>, she hid under the bed.

## Rate Your Ability to Spot and Correct Dangling Modifiers

Correct any dangling modifiers used in the following sentences. If the sentence is correct, mark "C" in front of the sentence. *Corrected sentences will vary.*

_____    1. While standing on the ladder with tarpaper, Harvey patched the roof.

_____    2. Being nervous, the test seemed more difficult than it was.

_____    3. Waiting to drop a class at the Records Office, the line seemed to go on forever.

___C___    4. After many years, Joan received her degree in engineering.

_____    5. Moving the couch, the elevator was, of course, out of order.

_____    6. Watching the evening news, the power went out.

_____    7. After deciding to mow the lawn, it began to rain.

_____    8. Being very tired, the long wait was unbearable.

_____    9. Skiing downhill, the wind picked up.

_____    10. At the age of eighteen, the phone company hired me.

Score  _____

Check your answers, using the Answer Key on p. 641. If you missed more than two, you need additional review and practice in recognizing and correcting dangling modifiers. Refer to Part VI, "Reviewing the Basics," and under section D, see "Misplaced and Dangling Modifiers." For additional practice go to this book's Web site, http://www.ablongman.com/mcwhorterexpressways1e.

## INTERNET ACTIVITIES

### 1. Writing an Example Essay

Review these writing tips from the Academic Resource Center at Wheeling Jesuit University.

http://www4.wju.edu/arc/handouts/examp_illustr.htm

Prepare a tip sheet based on information you find on this Web site for students who are learning about the illustration/example essay.

### 2. Example Essay Guidelines

Some definitions and guidelines for writing an example essay from an instructor at San Antonio College are found on this Web site.

http://www.accd.edu/sac/english/Mgarcia/writfils/Modexemp.htm

Pay particular attention to point number six. Answer the questions and develop your own outline for an example essay.

### 3. This Book's Web Site

Visit this site to find templates of idea maps for examples and additional practice on skills taught in the chapter.

http://www.ablongman.com/mcwhorterexpressways1e

# 10

# Classification

## Chapter Objectives

*In this chapter
you will learn to:*

1. Explain a topic using classification.

2. Choose a basis of classification.

3. Choose and explain subgroups.

4. Use transitional words and phrases to connect your ideas.

## Write About It!

Study the photograph above and write a sentence that explains how the information on the screens is organized.

The sentence you wrote explaining that flights are organized or grouped by whether they are arriving or departing could be the topic sentence for a paragraph using the method of classification. **Classification** is a way of explaining a topic, or presenting information about the topic, by organizing its parts into categories. Classification is often used in our everyday lives, in academic courses, and in the workplace. In this chapter you will learn to use classification in writing both paragraphs and essays.

231

# UNDERSTANDING CLASSIFICATION

## What Is Classification Writing?

Classification, the identification of types or categories within a group, is a useful way to explain information. You can visualize the method of classification as follows:

**Visualize It!**

**Classification Paragraph Idea Map**

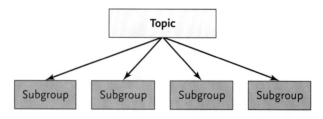

**Note:** The number of subgroups will vary.

For instance, a good way to discuss reptiles is to arrange them into categories: crocodiles, alligators, snakes, turtles, tortoises, and lizards. If you wanted to explain who makes up an orchestra, you could classify the musicians by the type of instrument they play (or, alternatively, by age, level of skill, or some other factor). You can visualize the process of classification of an orchestra as follows:

# Visualize It!

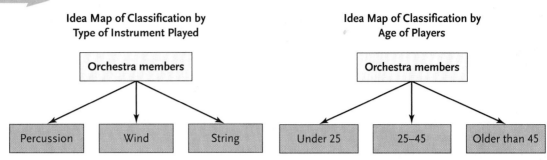

Note that subgroups in a classification system must be at the same level of detail and similar in terms of type. In other words, subgroups need to be distinct, but also comparable and matching. For example, when classifying reptiles, you would not include garter snakes as a subgroup in a series with crocodiles and alligators. Garter snakes belong to a more specific and detailed category than the other subgroups.

## EXERCISE 10-1

**Directions:** Working alone or with another student, brainstorm a list of recent times in your own life when you used classification.

## Deciding on What Basis to Classify Information

To write a paragraph using classification, you must first decide on a basis for breaking your topic down into subgroups. As the two charts for the orchestra above show, subjects can be organized in any number of ways, depending on what you want to emphasize. Suppose you are given an assignment to write about some aspect of community life. You decide to classify the recreational facilities in your town into groups. You could classify them by cost, location, or type of facility, depending on what you wanted the focus of your writing to be and what would highlight specific community issues most effectively.

The best way to lay the groundwork for your classification paragraph is to find a good general topic and then brainstorm different ways to break it into subgroups or categories. As we have seen, a subject can be classified or organized into subgroups in any number of ways, depending on what factor you want to emphasize. In considering the topic "my friends," for example, one student realized she could sort or classify them by:

| | |
|---|---|
| age | personality type |
| length of friendship | occupation |
| closeness of friendship | marital status |
| gender | status as parent |

Each of these factors could be used to classify friends into subgroups and therefore be the subject of a paper.

## EXERCISE 10-2

**Directions:** Choose one of the following topics: jobs, mail, relatives, or exercise.

Fill in the blank: "I could classify this topic by _____."

## EXERCISE 10-3

**Directions:** For each of the following topics, brainstorm to discover different ways you might classify them.

1. Topic: criminals

   Ways to classify:

   _____

   _____

2. Topic: college courses

   Ways to classify:

   _____

   _____

3. Topic: medical doctors

   Ways to classify:

   _____

   _____

Once you have brainstormed possible ways of classifying a topic, select the one that best represents or describes the topic and fulfills your purpose for writing. Assume your topic is college professors. You could classify them according to personality, teaching style, style of dress, or age. Teaching style would be a good choice because it focuses on their job responsibilities. Age, however, would not be particularly useful, unless your purpose is to explore some connection between age and the teaching profession. Style of dress would be useful if you were concerned with image and appearance.

Once you decide how you will classify, the next step is to divide your topic into subgroups. If you've decided to classify college professors according to teaching style, you could use the following subgroups:

## Visualize It!

**Idea Map of Classification of Professors**

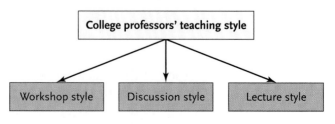

## NEED TO KNOW

### Choosing a Basis of Classification

Most topics can be classified in a number of different ways. Dogs can be classified by breed, temperament, size, or trainability, for example. Use the following tips for choosing an appropriate basis of classification:

1. **Consider your audience.** Choose a basis of classification that will interest them. Classifying dogs by size may not be as interesting as classifying them by temperament, for example.

2. **Choose a basis that is uncomplicated.** If you choose a basis that is complicated or lengthy, your topic may be difficult to write about. Categorizing dogs by breed may be unwieldy, since there are hundreds of recognized breeds.

3. **Choose a basis that you are familiar with.** While it would be possible to classify dogs by trainability, you may have to do some research or learn more about trainability in order to write about it.

## EXERCISE 10-4

*Writing in Progress*

**Directions:** For each of the following topics, brainstorm to discover ways of classifying them. Then choose one way, underline it, and list the subgroups into which you could classify the topic.

1. Topic: machines for communication

   Ways of classifying:

   _____

   Subgroups:

   _____

   _____

2. Topic: environmental pollutants

   Ways of classifying:

   _____

   Subgroups:

   _____

   _____

**3.** Topic: books

Ways of classifying:

_____

Subgroups:

_____

_____

## Writing Your Topic Sentence

Once you have chosen a way to classify a topic and have identified the subgroups you will use, you are ready to write a topic sentence. Your topic sentence should accomplish two things:

- It should identify your topic.

- It should indicate how you will classify items within your topic.

The topic sentence may also mention the number of subgroups you will use. Here are a few examples:

> An automobile exhaust system has four main sections.

> Clocks come in many sizes, from watches and alarm clocks to grandfather clocks and huge outdoor digital displays.

> Three common types of advertising media are radio, television, and newspaper.

> Since working at Denny's, I've discovered that there are three main types of customers.

### EXERCISE 10-5
*Writing in Progress*

**Directions:** For the topic you chose in Exercise 10-4, write a topic sentence that identifies your topic and explains your method of classification.

### Explaining Each Subgroup

The details in your paragraph should explain and provide further information about each subgroup. Depending on your topic and/or your audience, it may be necessary to define each subgroup. For instance, suppose you are given an essay-exam question that asks you to discuss how psychologists classify behavior. In your answer, you would want to thoroughly explain the terms *normal, neurotic,* and *psychotic*. It is often helpful to include examples as well as definitions of terms. Examples of normal, neurotic, and psychotic behavior would demonstrate your grasp of these concepts and improve your answer.

If possible, provide an equal amount of detail for each subgroup. If you define or offer an example for one subgroup, you should do the same for each of the others, as one student did in the following paragraph.

Parents discipline their children in different ways. Some use physical punishment, but this can hurt the child and make for an angry, resentful child. Others yell constantly, yet this approach does not work well because the children get used to it and pay no attention to it, or it can destroy their feelings of self-esteem. Other parents make their children feel guilty if the children do something bad. This works, but it is not direct and the child can suffer from guilt and confusion for his or her entire life. Some parents talk to their children, explain how to act, and ask for the child's ideas. When the child misbehaves, the parents explain why the action is wrong and talk about it with the child. This seems to work pretty well because the children grow up to understand right from wrong and to feel involved with solving problems.

You can visualize the above paragraph as follows:

## Visualize It! ➤

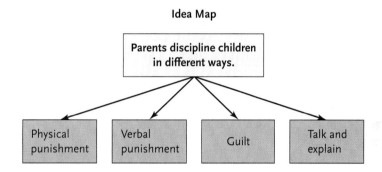

Idea Map

**Parents discipline children in different ways.**

| Physical punishment | Verbal punishment | Guilt | Talk and explain |

## EXERCISE 10-6

*Writing in Progress*

**Directions:** For the sentence you wrote in Exercise 10-5, write a paragraph classifying it into the subgroups you identified.

## Testing the Effectiveness of Your Classification

In order to test the effectiveness of your groups or categories, try to think of exceptions—items or situations that don't fit into any one of your established categories. In the example mentioned earlier—orchestras—you could consider possible exceptions. Hammered dulcimers, for example, are both string *and* percussive instruments; electronic synthesizers are neither string, percussion, nor wind instruments. If you discover many exceptions, you might need to redefine your groups or expand their number to accommodate the exceptions. You could also revise your topic sentence to indicate that you will discuss only several large or common categories, or you can restrict your topic by adding a limiting word like *most* or *common*. Here are two examples:

Most childhood temper tantrums stem from one of the following . . .

Several common varieties of flowering shrubs are . . .

## EXERCISE 10-7

*Writing in Progress*

**Directions:** Test the effectiveness of the classification system you developed for Exercise 10-6. Revise your paragraph, if needed.

## Useful Transitions

Transitions are useful in classification paragraphs to signal to your reader that you are about to begin explaining a new category. They make it easy for your reader to identify the categories and move from one to another. Notice how the highlighted transitions work in the following paragraph:

> Horticulture, the study and cultivation of garden plantings, consists of four major fields of study. First, there is pomology, the science and practice of growing and handling fruit. Then there is olericulture, which is concerned with growing and storing vegetables. A third field, floriculture, is the science of growing, storing, and cultivating flowering plants. The last category, ornamental and landscape horticulture, is concerned with using grasses, annual and perennial plants, and shrubs in landscaping.

Table 10-1 lists some frequently used transitional words and phrases used in classification paragraphs.

**Table 10-1    Transitions for Classification Paragraphs**

| First | second | third |
|-------|--------|-------|
| One | another | also |
| In addition | then | last |

## EXERCISE 10-8

*Writing in Progress*

**Directions:** Revise the paragraph you wrote for Exercise 10-6. Check transitional words and phrases and add more, as necessary, to make your ideas clearer.

## Applying Your Skills to Essay Writing: Classification

Many of the same skills you learned for writing classification paragraphs will apply to writing classification essays. Use the following guidelines.

1. **Explain your basis of classification in your introduction.** It will be helpful to your readers to understand how you have divided your topic into subgroups.

2. **Use paragraphs to separate subgroups.** Devote at least one paragraph to each type or subgroup.

3. **Maintain a balance among subgroups.** Unless you have a specific reason for doing otherwise, provide similar amounts of explanation, detail, and examples for each subgroup.

4. **Emphasize differences.** Make it clear how each subgroup differs from all the others. Use examples and definitions to help you make these distinctions.

5. **Consider your audience.** The type and amount of detail you provide throughout should depend on how much your reader knows about your topic.

# AN ACADEMIC SCENARIO
## A STUDENT ESSAY
### The Academic Writer and the Writing Task

Corrine Roberts is a student at Modesto Junior College in Modesto, California. For her introductory education class, she was asked to write an essay on the behavior of young children. She decided

to write a classification essay. As you read, notice how Roberts classifies the behavior of preschool children.

## Label the Behavior—Not the Child
### Corrine Roberts

*Background information on unfair labeling—establishes purpose for the essay*

In a day and age when children's behavior is a topic as common as the cold, adults tend to lump children into categories. This is completely unfair to the child, even though it makes life easier for adults. By placing a child in a category, parents, teachers or day care workers assume they have a child all figured out. This is wrong. Children, and I mean all children, go through different stages in their lives. What is labeled "bad" behavior might be completely natural for the age group. Let's take preschoolers, for example. From birth to around six, a child is growing more quickly than at any other time. Physical changes occur quickly. The behavior that goes along with these changes can be broken down into three broad categories: The Good, the Bad, and the Ugly.

*Thesis statement*

*Category 1*

The first category is "good." We think of a "good" child as one who is polite, helpful, kind, and always does what he or she is asked. He or she does extra work with ease, is always willing to help by setting the table or cleaning his or her room without being asked. This child is a pleasure to work with because he or she seems to know what is needed and simply does the work. But how many toddlers do you know who actually fit this description? Toddlers are *supposed* to be pushing the limits; that's how they learn. Frequently they don't like what they learn, as when they discover that Mom is a separate person and is walking out of the room and leaving them with another person for what, to the child, seems like forever! Fear of being left is completely normal, but the behavior that can go with it—clinging, screaming fits, refusing to play with other kids—can be downright awful.

*Distinguishing characteristics*

Category 2

Distinguishing characteristics

Take a peek into any day care center or pre-school and you're bound to see plenty of "bad" kids. Ages 3–6 are a time of discovery. Children have better communication skills, but still have trouble making their points without resorting to physical actions. They lack the ability to say, "Excuse me, I was playing with that first, may I have it back, please?" A four-year-old will just grab. A six-year-old may not have gotten enough sleep the night before and is now so tired she breaks into tears at the slightest annoyance. Grabbing, pushing, refusing to cooperate, and crying are all signs of a bad kid, right? Absolutely not. These are all perfectly normal behaviors for the age group. Remember, that child standing on the toilet seat may be trying to see something on the ceiling! Not every "bad" thing a child does at this age is intended to be bad.

Category 3

Distinguishing characteristics

Now let's consider two-year-olds; they belong in the "ugly" group. Most people have heard of the "Terrible Twos," a time that can last until the child is almost four. There is no getting around it; this can be a tough time. Anyone who's ever seen a three-year-old throw herself to the floor in the middle of the mall and throw a screaming fit understands. Imagine for a moment that you are two. You've just discovered that you are a separate individual. You're learning an amazing amount of things, but you don't have the words for most of it. You have absolutely no control over anything. You're picked up, buckled in, put to bed, fed at certain hours, and no one ever asks *you* if you're ready to go, sleepy or hungry! All those times your wishes are ignored, all the things you want that people keep telling you you can't have can . . . really . . . make . . . you . . . hold-your-breath-and-turn-blue-in-the-face mad. If you don't want to be put in the car, go stiff as a board. If you don't like those mashed potatoes, throw them at the dog. Unfortunately, this behavior is frequently met with negative responses. The behavior may be awful, but the child is absolutely normal and right on track.

Conclusion: reinforces purpose of the essay

Beneath it all, parents, teachers and day care workers need to remember that categories are often placed on children unfairly. It's up to us as adults to understand what they're going through at each particular stage and help them through it. So don't label the child. Learn all you can about the different ages and stages from birth to kindergarten, appreciate the huge progress your child is making, and separate the behavior from the child.

## Examining Academic Writing

1. What is Roberts's purpose for writing the essay?

2. Highlight the distinguishing characteristics of each category.

3. Circle the transitions that Roberts uses to move from one category to another.

4. Evaluate Roberts's introduction and conclusion. Are they too similar? Suggest possible revisions.

## Academic Writing Assignments

1. In preparation for a series of lectures on theft, your criminal justice instructor has asked you to write a paragraph classifying and briefly defining different types of thefts. (Hint: consider identity theft, cyber theft, and auto theft.)

2. For an Introduction to Education class, your instructor has asked you to write a paragraph classifying and briefly defining types of classroom organization. (Hint: consider discussion, online classes, etc.)

3. The essay above categorizes children. Write an essay in which you create your own categories of children or of their behavior.

# A WORKPLACE SCENARIO
## A WORK MEMO
### The Workplace Writer and the Writing Task

C. Z. Shleviek is the office manager at Trico Instruments. In the memo below he humorously suggests that employees can get better organized by using a Task Master Basket. As you read, notice how he relies on classification throughout the memo.

---

TO:      All staff
FROM:  C. Z. Shleviek, Office Manager
DATE:    August 15, 2006

MEMO: Paperwork Organization!

It has come to my attention that there is too much paperwork cluttering desks in every department. This makes a bad impression on visitors to the office and leads to company-wide disorganization.

Therefore, I am making a gift of a personalized Task Master Basket to all employees. I hope that you will each take a few minutes to sort your papers into nice, neat categories and deposit each pile into one of the Task Master's compartments. Here are some category suggestions for each department:

1. Parts Department: I know that orders come in thick and fast and occasionally the computers freeze. This is why we require each order to be printed out onto hard copy. You might want to label each of your baskets according to where the order stands: "Part Ordered but Not In," "Part Unavailable," or "Part Here." Then, when the computer goes down, you can still tell your customers the status of their order and keep them happy.

2. Customer Service: Believe it or not, I really do respond personally to all complaints—if I hear about them, that is. Please develop a system that makes it easy for me to follow up with unhappy consumers. You could label your baskets "Not Urgent; Follow Up Next Week," "Easy to Fix Now," or "Problem Child, HWC." You can take care of the first two, but I should probably deal right away with the customer who needs to be Handled With Care.

3. IT Team: I love how dedicated you all are and it's great that you're willing to stay all night to get the computers back up to speed. But the way you leave the kitchen is gross!!! You've got to remember that other people work here too, which is why I've put your Task Master Baskets in the fridge and labeled them for you: "Eat Today," "Save For Tomorrow," and "THROW OUT NOW!" PLEASE put your food in the appropriate basket and discard the stuff that's too old to eat.

You'll notice I have put my own Task Master on a table outside my office. I've labeled my basket's compartments "Suggestions," "Complaints," and "I Quit!" Say whatever you like, but put each memo in the appropriate basket.

Thank you!

## Examining Workplace Writing

1. What does Shleviek classify?

2. For each of the three departments for which Shleviek suggests a use of the Task Master Basket, identify the basis of classification.

3. Evaluate the subgroups of each classification. Are they detailed and specific?

4. Do you think Shleviek's humor will help employees receive the message more positively?

## Workplace Writing Assignments

1. Write a paragraph classifying the types of part-time jobs available to college students in your town or city or on your campus.

2. The company where you work has appointed you to a team assigned to evaluate and revise the company's sexual harassment policy. The team leader has asked each member to classify the types of behaviors he or she considers to be harassment. Write a paragraph briefly identifying and describing the types of behavior you would include.

3. Choose a business that you work for, have worked for, or with which you are familiar. Write an essay classifying one of the following: employees, areas within the physical place of operation, products, or customers.

# WRITING ABOUT A READING

## Thinking Before Reading

The following reading, "The Wild Cards: Liars," comes from a book by Jo-Ellan Dimitrius and Mark Mazzarella called *Reading People: How to Understand People and Predict their Behavior—Anytime, Anyplace*. In this excerpt, the authors present the most common types of liars. As you read, pay attention to the organization of the essay and to the characteristics of each category of liar.

1. Preview the reading, using the steps discussed in Chapter 2, p. 30.

2. Discover what you already know about lying by doing the following:

   a. Brainstorm a list of all the ways to deceive people that you can think of.

   b. Think about those times when you have lied to avoid hurting other people's feelings. What were the circumstances?

R E A D I N G

# The Wild Cards: Liars

## Jo-Ellan Dimitrius and Mark Mazzarella

1  If people were all honest with one another, reading them would be a lot easier. The problem is that people lie. I'm not talking about those who are wrong but sincerely believe they are correct, or about the delusional few who genuinely can't tell fact from fantasy. Rather, I'm referring to the one characteristic that is probably the most important in any relationship: truthfulness. And if we assume it's there when it's not—watch out!

**directly from the horse's mouth**
right from the source; this idiom has its origins in horseracing

2  Much of the information we gather about someone comes **directly from the horse's mouth**. If he is lying, the information is wrong, and we're likely to misjudge him. That's why it's so crucial to identify liars as soon as possible, and, if you have reason to doubt a person's honesty, to continue to test it until you're entirely at ease with your conclusion.

3  I have found that most liars fall into one of four basic categories: the occasional liar, the frequent liar, the habitual liar, and the professional liar.

### The Occasional Liar

4  The occasional liar, like most of us, will lie now and then to avoid an unpleasant situation or because he doesn't want to admit doing something wrong or embarrassing. Also like most of us, he does not like to lie and feels very uncomfortable when he does. Because he's uncomfortable, he'll usually reveal his lie through his appearance, body language, and voice. The stress lying causes him will leak out through such things as poor eye contact, fidgeting, or a change in the tone, volume, or patterns of his speech.

5  The occasional liar often gives his lie some thought, so it may be logical and consistent with the rest of his story. Because it's well thought out, you probably won't be able to spot the lie by its content or context, or by information from third-party sources. In fact, the occasional liar will seldom lie

about something that could be easily verified. Consequently, when dealing with an occasional liar, you need to focus on the various visual and oral clues he exhibits.

## The Frequent Liar

6    The frequent liar recognizes what she's doing but doesn't mind it as much as the occasional liar does, so she lies more regularly. Practice makes perfect: the frequent liar is much less likely to reveal her lie through her appearance, body language, and voice. Also, since it doesn't bother her as much to lie, the typical stress-related symptoms won't be as obvious. Any clues in her appearance, voice, and body language might be rather subtle. Often a better way to detect a frequent liar is to focus on the internal consistency and logic of her statements. Since the frequent liar lies more often, and tends to think her lies through less carefully than the occasional liar, she can get sloppy.

## The Habitual Liar

7    The habitual liar lies so frequently that he has lost sight of what he is doing much of the time. In most cases, if he actually thought about it, he would realize he was lying. But he doesn't much care whether what he's saying is true or false. He simply says whatever comes to mind. Because he doesn't care that he's lying, the habitual liar will give very few, if any, physical or vocal clues that he's being dishonest. But because he gives so little thought to his lies and they come so thick and fast, the habitual liar doesn't bother to keep track of them. As a result they are often inconsistent and obvious. So while it's hard to detect the physical and vocal clues in a habitual liar, it's easier to spot his inconsistencies. Listen carefully and ask yourself whether the liar is contradicting himself and whether what he's saying makes sense. Asking a third party about the liar's stories will also help you confirm your suspicions.

8    The habitual liar is fairly uncommon, so most of us are temporarily taken in when we encounter one. An acquaintance of mine told me she worked with a woman for several months before her suspicions that the co-worker was a habitual liar were confirmed by an obvious and quite ridiculous lie. The liar, a brown-eyed brunette, came to work one day sporting blue contact lenses of an almost alien hue. When my friend commented on her lenses, the liar said, "These aren't contacts. They're my real eye color. It's just that I've always worn brown contact lenses before."

9    More than once, a client has told me that his adversary lies all the time and will undoubtedly lie on the witness stand. I **counsel** my client not to worry: the habitual liar is the easiest target in a lawsuit. In real life, she can run from one person to another, from one situation to the next, lying as she goes, and no one compares notes. There are no court reporters or transcripts

**counsel**
give professional legal advice

of testimony; no one reveals what every witness has said to every other witness, and nobody pores over everything the liar has written on the subject to see whether it's all consistent. But in **litigation**, that is exactly what happens—and suddenly the habitual liar is exposed. It's very rewarding to see.

**litigation**
a legal dispute

### The Professional Liar

10    The professional liar is the hardest to identify. He doesn't lie indiscriminately, like the habitual liar. He lies for a purpose. For example, a mechanic who routinely cons motorists about their "faulty" transmissions will have his diagnosis carefully prepared. A real estate salesman who doesn't want to acknowledge a leaky roof will respond quickly to an inquiry about the stains on the ceiling with a rehearsed, very spontaneous sounding statement: "That was old damage from a water leak in the attic. All it needs is a little touch-up paint."

11    The professional liar has thought the lie through and knows exactly what he's going to say, how it will fly, and whether the customer can easily verify it. Such a well-practiced lie will not be revealed by the liar's voice, body language, or appearance. The lie will be consistent, both internally and logically. The only sure way to detect it is to check the liar's statements against entirely independent sources. Have the roof inspected. Get a second opinion from another mechanic. Take nothing for granted.

12    Before you make a definitive call about someone who is truly important to you, always ask yourself whether the information you have about him is reliable. Is he being truthful? If your goal is to accurately evaluate someone, you can't afford to skip this step.

## Getting Ready to Write

### Reviewing the Reading

1. Highlight the essay's thesis statement.

2. Why is it useful to be able to identify liars?

3. Name the four types of liars described in the reading.

4. Why is the occasional liar difficult to spot?

5. How can you detect a "frequent liar?"

6. What is the most difficult type of liar to detect and why?

## Examining the Reading: Using Idea Mapping to Review and Organize Ideas

Your knowledge of classification provides you with a useful way to organize the information that you read. By summarizing a reading's main points in chart form, you will find the material easier to remember and review. Complete the following map for "The Wild Cards: Liars."

## Visualize It!

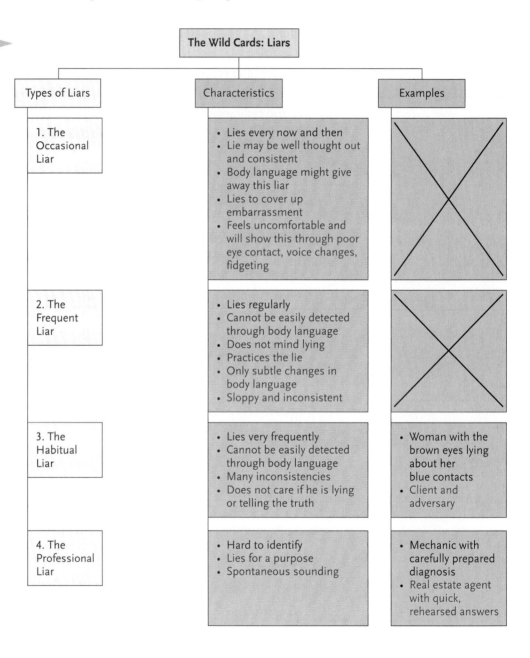

The Wild Cards: Liars

**Types of Liars**

1. The Occasional Liar

2. The Frequent Liar

3. The Habitual Liar

4. The Professional Liar

**Characteristics**

- Lies every now and then
- Lie may be well thought out and consistent
- Body language might give away this liar
- Lies to cover up embarrassment
- Feels uncomfortable and will show this through poor eye contact, voice changes, fidgeting

- Lies regularly
- Cannot be easily detected through body language
- Does not mind lying
- Practices the lie
- Only subtle changes in body language
- Sloppy and inconsistent

- Lies very frequently
- Cannot be easily detected through body language
- Many inconsistencies
- Does not care if he is lying or telling the truth

- Hard to identify
- Lies for a purpose
- Spontaneous sounding

**Examples**

- Woman with the brown eyes lying about her blue contacts
- Client and adversary

- Mechanic with carefully prepared diagnosis
- Real estate agent with quick, rehearsed answers

## Thinking Critically: Evaluating an Author's Credentials

The authors of this essay encourage readers to verify statements and get second opinions if they suspect a person of lying. You should also verify that the sources you use are written by people qualified to write on the subject. One way to do this is to research the author's credentials online or in the library.

Obtain more information about Jo-Ellan Dimitrius by going to http://www.google.com or a search engine of your choice and entering her name in the Search box. Write a paragraph summarizing her credentials. Conclude with a statement indicating whether you consider her qualified to write the book from which this reading selection was taken.

## Strengthening Your Vocabulary

**Part A:** Using the word's context, word parts, or a dictionary, write a brief definition of each of the following words or phrases as it is used in the reading.

1. delusional (paragraph 1) *having a psychosis involving false beliefs about oneself or others*

2. consistent (paragraph 5) *regulated, not varying, having no conflict*

3. adversary (paragraph 9) *one that is in opposition*

4. pores (paragraph 9) *studies with great attention*

5. spontaneous (paragraph 10) *not apparently contrived, without thought, impulsively*

**Part B:** Choose one of the above words and draw a word map of it.

## Reacting to Ideas: Discussion and Journal Writing

1. What types of liars do you come across most often?

2. Which type of liar do you think is the most destructive? Why?

3. Can the world ever be free of liars? Why or why not?

4. Are liars ever justified in not telling the truth? Why or why not?

5. What lies have you told that you have later come to regret telling?

## Writing About the Reading

## Paragraph Options

1. Write a paragraph classifying the situations the occasional liar might lie about.

2. The "Occasional Liar" lies to get out of an uncomfortable situation. Write a paragraph about a time when you witnessed this type of liar in action.

3. In the reading, the authors refer to body language (gestures, facial expressions, posture) as an important part of a liar's behavior. Write a paragraph about one type of body language that you have found useful to focus on when interacting with other people.

## Essay Options

4. Write an essay classifying the reasons why people lie.

5. Academic dishonesty is a problem on many campuses. Choose one form of academic dishonesty and write a paragraph explaining in what way it involves deception.

6. Write an essay describing a situation in which you were lied to. Identify the type of liar and explain how you detected and responded to the lie.

7. The author does not give examples of occasional and frequent liars. Choose one of these categories of liar, occasional or frequent, and write a paragraph that defines the type of liar and gives several examples of this liar.

## Revision Checklist

1. Is your paragraph or essay appropriate for your audience? Does it give them the background information they need? Will it interest them?

2. Will your paragraph or essay accomplish your purpose?

3. Is your main point clearly expressed?

4. Is each detail relevant? Does each explain or support your main point?

5. Have you supported your main point with sufficient detail to make it understandable and believable?

6. Did you use specific words to explain each detail?

### For Classification Writing

7. Does the topic sentence or thesis statement identify the topic and method of classification?

8. Is each subgroup adequately explained?

9. Is equal detail provided for each subgroup?

10. Are the subgroups presented in a logical order?

11. Are ideas connected with transitional words and phrases?

12. Have you proofread? (See the inside back cover of this book for a proofreading checklist.)

# CHAPTER REVIEW AND PRACTICE

## Chapter Review

| | |
|---|---|
| WHAT IS CLASSIFICATION? | Classification is a method of explaining a topic by organizing its parts into categories. |
| WHAT IS A BASIS OF CLASSIFICATION? | A basis of classification is the factor you use to break your topic into categories. |
| WHAT SHOULD THE TOPIC SENTENCE OF A CLASSIFICATION PARAGRAPH DO? | The topic sentence should (1) identify the topic, and (2) explain how you will classify items within your topic. |
| WHAT DETAILS SHOULD A CLASSIFICATION PARAGRAPH CONTAIN? | A classification paragraph should provide details about each subgroup in your classification system. |
| HOW CAN YOU TEST THE EFFECTIVENESS OF YOUR CLASSIFICATION? | Try to think of exceptions that do not fit the categories you have created. |
| WHAT ARE THE FUNCTIONS OF TRANSITIONS? | Transitions help identify each category and lead the reader from one category to the next. |
| WHAT ARE THE GUIDELINES FOR WRITING CLASSIFICATION ESSAYS? | • Explain your basis of classification in your introduction.<br>• Use paragraphing to separate subgroups.<br>• Provide similar amounts of detail about each subgroup.<br>• Make sure it is clear how categories differ.<br>• Provide detail appropriate and sufficient for your audience. |

## Skill Refresher: Misplaced Modifiers

Misplaced modifiers are words or phrases that do not modify or explain other words the way the writer intended.

| | |
|---|---|
| MISPLACED | <u>Crisp and spicy</u>, the waitress served our table the chicken wings. [Was the waitress crisp and spicy, or were the wings?] |
| CORRECT | The waitress served our table the <u>crisp, spicy</u> chicken wings. |
| MISPLACED | I saw a dress <u>in a magazine</u> that cost $1200. [Did the magazine or the dress cost $1200?] |
| CORRECT | <u>In a magazine</u>, I saw a dress that cost $1200. |
| MISPLACED | <u>Already late for class</u>, the red light delayed Joe even longer. [Was the light or Joe late for class?] |
| CORRECT | The red light delayed Joe, <u>already late for class</u>, even longer. |

### How to Avoid Misplaced Modifiers

To avoid misplaced modifiers, place the modifier immediately before or after the word or words it modifies.

### Rate Your Ability to Spot and Correct Misplaced Modifiers

Correct the sentences containing misplaced modifiers. Mark "C" in front of correct sentences. *Corrected sentences will vary.*

_____ 1. Studiously, the report was previewed by Marietta before she began answering the questions from the sales staff.

_____ 2. The book was checked out by a student that Mark had returned late.

___C___ 3. Julia Oliva proudly turned in her proposal for flextime that had taken two months to complete.

_____ 4. Shocked, the article about donations that political candidates receive from interest groups caused Lily to reconsider how she viewed campaign promises.

_____ 5. The student-loan check was cashed by Bryant that was desperately needed.

_____ 6. Angry with the delay, the referee finally arrived and the crowd booed.

    *c*       **7.** Called Aboriginals, the native people of Australia have a culture rich with hunting skills and legends.

          **8.** Young, unhappy, and lovelorn, the poetry of Emily Dickinson reveals a particular kind of misery and pain.

          **9.** A national problem, the governors of all the states met to discuss homelessness.

          **10.** When the AIDS epidemic began, concerned about the risk of contagion, many AIDS patients were refused treatment by health care workers.

Score _____

Check your answers using the Answer Key on p. 642. If you missed more than two, you need additional review and practice in recognizing and correcting misplaced modifiers. Refer to Part VI, "Reviewing the Basics," and under section D, see "Misplaced and Dangling Modifiers." For additional practice go to this book's Web site, http://www.ablongman.com/ mcwhorter expressways1e.

# INTERNET ACTIVITIES

## 1. Research Guides

Many libraries create research guides to help students locate a variety of useful sources. Look over this guide to film resources from Cornell University.

http://www.library.cornell.edu/olinuris/ref/filmbib.html

How are these resources arranged on this page? How are they arranged in the library? What advantages are there to posting such a guide on the library's Web site?

## 2. Guide to Snowflakes

Scientists use classification to put their subjects into categories. On this site, a physics professor from CalTech explains the different types of snowflakes.

http://www.its.caltech.edu/~atomic/snowcrystals/class/class.htm

Review the site and then create a poster summarizing the different types of snowflakes.

## 3. This Book's Web Site

Visit this site to find templates of idea maps for classification and additional practice on skills taught in the chapter.

http://www.ablongman.com/mcwhorterexpressways1e

# 11

# Definition

## Chapter Objectives

*In this chapter you will learn to:*

1. Explain a topic by using definition.

2. Identify the group and distinguishing characteristics of a definition.

3. Write an effective topic sentence.

4. Support your definition using details.

5. Use transitions to guide your reader.

## Write About It!

Study the photo above. The women may be instant messaging or taking a picture of themselves using a photo phone. Write a paragraph defining one of these popular uses of technology that represents a certain fad.

The paragraph you have just written is a definition paragraph. A **definition paragraph** explains a topic by defining what it is and often uses examples or other details to explain it further. You will have numerous opportunities to use definition in everyday, academic, and workplace situations. In this chapter you will learn to use definition in both paragraphs and essays.

EVERYDAY SCENARIOS

- Defining a slang term that a parent has asked about
- Explaining to a child what an antibiotic medicine is and why he or she must take it

ACADEMIC EXAMPLES

- Writing an essay-exam answer defining photosynthesis
- Reading a section of a psychology textbook defining schizophrenia

WORKPLACE EXAMPLES

- Explaining, as a veterinary technician, the meaning of the term *laryngeal trauma* to a dog owner
- An environmental engineer giving a community group the technical definitions of soil erosion and sediment control

# UNDERSTANDING DEFINITION

All of us have had to explain the meaning of a term or concept at one time or another. You may have been asked to explain an unfamiliar term used in conversation. If you say, "I just found out that Martha is suffering from anorexia nervosa," you may need to define the illness to those who are unfamiliar with it. Relative terms (those that imply a comparison with something else) also require definition. For example, you might say a coat is expensive and a car is expensive. Your listener would know that the two items do not have the same dollar value, but would want to know what "expensive" means for each item. Clear, crisp definitions are important to making your ideas clear and understandable.

## EXERCISE 11-1

**Directions:** Working alone or with another student, brainstorm a list of recent times in your own life when you needed to define something.

## What Is Definition?

A definition is an explanation of what something is. It has three essential parts:

- The term being defined or the topic being described
- The group, or category, to which the term or topic belongs
- Its distinguishing characteristics

Suppose you had to define a *lemur*—that is the term being defined. If you said it was an animal, then you would be stating the group to which it belongs. **Group** means the general category something is part of. If you said a lemur lives in Madagascar and has a long, slim muzzle, you would be describing some of its distinguishing characteristics. Distinguishing characteristics are those details that allow you to tell the item apart from others in its same group. The details about the long, slim muzzle, enable one to distinguish it from other animals in Madagascar. Here are a few more examples:

| Term | Group | Distinguishing Characteristics |
| --- | --- | --- |
| daisy | flower | white petals, yellow center, long stem |
| ring | jewelry | worn on a finger or toe, round band |
| anger | emotion | occurs when a person's feelings are hurt or plans do not happen as anticipated |

## EXERCISE 11-2

**Directions:** For each term or topic listed below, describe the group it belongs to and at least two of its distinguishing characteristics.

| Term | Group | Distinguishing Characteristic |
| --- | --- | --- |
| 1. football | _____ | _____ |
| 2. a hero | _____ | _____ |
| 3. instant messaging | _____ | _____ |
| 4. terrorism | _____ | _____ |
| 5. body language | _____ | _____ |

## Writing Your Topic Sentence

The topic sentence of a definition paragraph should identify the term or topic you are explaining. It should also place the topic in a general group or category to which it belongs. It may also provide one or more distinguishing characteristics.

In the topic sentence below, the term being defined is *mythomaniac,* the general group or category is "person," and the distinguishing feature is "an abnormal tendency to exaggerate."

A *mythomaniac* is a person who has an abnormal tendency to exaggerate.

Here is another example:

term    group    distinguishing characteristic

A *kuchen* is a German coffeecake that is made with yeast dough and often contains raisins.

distinguishing characteristic

You can distinguish a kuchen from other coffeecakes by the fact that it contains yeast and raisins.

Be sure you do not use the term you are defining, or a variation of it, as part of your definition. Do not define memorization by writing that it is the process of memorizing information.

You can visualize a definition paragraph as follows:

## Visualize It! ➤

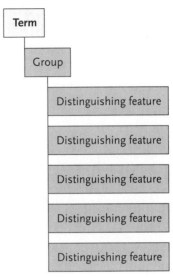

**Definition Paragraph Idea Map**

Here is an example of a definition paragraph, along with an idea map showing its organization:

> Ragtime music, with its distinct piano style, was developed at the turn of the twentieth century. Ragtime music usually has four themes. The themes are divided into four musical sections of equal length. When playing ragtime music, the left hand plays the chords and the right hand plays the melody. There is an uneven accenting between the two hands.

## Visualize It! ➤

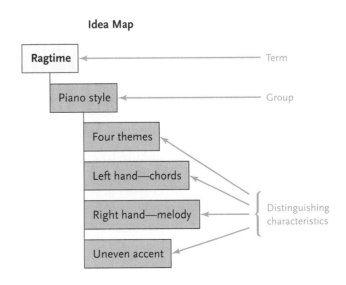

**Idea Map**

In writing about any term or topic, especially an unfamiliar one, it is helpful to do some research. If possible, talk to others about their understanding of a particular term. Check the meaning of the term in a dictionary or glossary. Don't copy what you find. Instead, express its meaning using your own words.

## EXERCISE 11-3
*Writing in Progress*

**Directions:** Write a topic sentence that includes a group and a distinguishing characteristic for each of the following terms or topics.

1. comedian  _____

2. horror film  _____

3. sex appeal  _____

4. age discrimination  _____

5. gay rights  _____

## NEED TO KNOW
### Defining Unfamiliar Topics

If it is likely that your readers are unfamiliar with the topic you are defining, or it is out of the realm of their experience, you may need to give them more help in order for them to understand it. For example, if you are a surfer, but you know most of your audience are not surfers, and you are writing about a term used only by surfers, then you may need to take extra care in explaining it. Use the following suggestions:

1. **Compare an unfamiliar topic to one that is familiar to your readers.** If you are writing about rugby, you might compare it to football, a more familiar sport to a U.S. audience. Be sure to make the connection obvious to your readers by pointing out characteristics that the two sports share.

2. **Explain how a topic is different from things similar to it.** If you are describing the golden retriever breed of dog, for example, you might explain that golden retrievers differ from Labrador retrievers in coloration, length of fur, and thickness of coat.

3. **Be sure to explain unfamiliar terms you may use.** For example, in defining a *wipeout* in surfing, you might use other related terms such as *take out* (catch a wave and begin to ride) or *barrel* (the inside of a hollow wave). Be sure to define any unfamiliar terms as well.

## Developing Your Paragraph

Usually your topic sentence will *not* be sufficient to give your reader a complete understanding of the term or topic you are defining. For instance, when asked to define the term *discrimination,* one student wrote the following topic sentence:

> Discrimination is the unfair treatment of people because they belong to a particular group.

This sentence is not enough to explain the term completely to your reader. Discrimination can be explained further in the following ways:

1. **Give examples.** Examples can make a definition more vivid and interesting to your reader. (To learn more about using examples, see Chapter 9)

   Discrimination is the unfair treatment of people because they belong to a particular group. When my parents didn't talk to a new family in the neighborhood because they were of a different religion, it was discrimination. When my cousin Joan interviewed for a job and it went to a man, even though she had more experience, it was discrimination.

2. **Break the term into subcategories.** Breaking your subject down into subcategories helps to organize your definition. For example, you might explain the term *discrimination* by listing some of its types: racial, gender, and age. (To learn more about subcategories, see Chapter 10.)

   Discrimination is the unfair treatment of people because they belong to a particular group. One kind of discrimination is racial. When a person is treated differently because of his or her sex, it is gender discrimination. A third kind of discrimination is age discrimination. That occurs when people are treated differently because of how old or young they are.

3. **Explain what the term is not.** To bring the meaning of a term into focus for your reader, it is sometimes helpful to give counter examples, or to discuss ways the term means something different from what one might expect.

   Discrimination is the unfair treatment of people because they belong to a particular group. Discrimination is not rare in America, even though America is committed to equal opportunity for all. Most people experience discrimination in some form at some time in their lives. People are discriminated against because of their race, age, religion, handicap, gender, appearance, national origin, family background, or other factors that have nothing to do with a person's qualifications or abilities.

4. **Trace the term's meaning over time.** If the term has changed or expanded in meaning over time, it may be useful to trace this development as a way of explaining the term's current meaning.

> Discrimination is the unfair treatment of people because they belong to a particular group. In the past, discrimination meant the ability to tell the difference between things. People were said to have discriminating taste in food or fashion. The ability to discriminate was considered a positive trait. More recently, discrimination has come to have a negative meaning. The term now refers to prejudice against certain people. At first, it was used to mean only racial discrimination. Then it was used to describe prejudice towards women and homosexuals. Now we have age discrimination, too, when some businesses and organizations discriminate against teenagers and senior citizens because of their age.

## EXERCISE 11-4
*Writing in Progress*

**Directions:** Select one of the topic sentences you wrote for Exercise 11-3. Develop a paragraph defining that topic

## Useful Transitions

When you use definition to explain your topic, use strong transitional words and phrases to help your reader follow your presentation of ideas. The table below offers useful transitional words and phrases for this method of organization. Here is an example of a definition paragraph that uses transitions to guide the reader from one distinguishing characteristic to the next:

> The Small Business Administration (SBA) is an agency of the United States federal government. It was created by Congress as part of the Small Business Act of 1853. One purpose is to assist people attempting to start a small business by guiding them in establishing a business plan and procuring necessary financing. A second purpose is to help small businesses become profitable by offering management and marketing advice, for example. The agency also helps small companies identify funding sources, federal assistance funds, and government contracts.

Table 11-1  **Transitions for Definition Paragraphs**

| Can be defined as | | means | is |
|---|---|---|---|
| One | a second | another | also |

## EXERCISE 11-5
*Writing in Progress*

**Directions:** Revise the paragraph you wrote for Exercise 11-4. In particular, consider your organization, use of examples, and the clarity of your explanation.

## Applying Your Skills to Essay Writing: Definition

So far, this chapter has focused on writing definition paragraphs. When your term or topic is difficult, abstract, complicated, or confusing, you may need to write an essay rather than a single paragraph in order to explain it. Many of the same skills you have learned apply to definition essays.

Here are some additional guidelines for writing definition essays:

1. **Your thesis statement should identify the term or topic being defined and the group to which it belongs.**

2. **Explain the importance of understanding the term or topic you are defining.** Give your readers a reason to read. If you are defining a slang expression, for example, explain to your readers why or in what situations they may need to know the term.

3. **Devote a paragraph to each distinguishing characteristic of your topic.** Explain each distinguishing characteristic in detail, giving examples or using description.

4. **Provide sufficient details so that your topic is understandable.** Suppose, for example, your purpose is to define the term *democracy*—an abstract, important concept with wide-ranging applications. Here are a few ways you can expand a definition to make it clearer:

   - **Explain the term's etymology (origin).** For example, explain that *democracy* comes from two Greek words: *demos* (common people) and *kratia* (strength or power).

   - **Trace the term's use or history.** For example, you might summarize the term's use throughout history.

   - **Provide realistic examples.** To make your definition clear and understandable, use examples to which your audience can relate. Choose a country and explain how democracy works in it or how it has benefited from a democratic system of government.

   - **Draw upon other methods of development.** You might also use comparison and contrast (see Chapter 12, "Comparison and Contrast"), classification (see Chapter 10, "Classification") or cause and effect (see Chapter 13, "Cause and Effect"). For example, you could describe different types of democracy, contrast a democracy and a monarchy, or explain what it is about democracy that has made it such a successful form of government in the United States.

## EXERCISE 11-6

**Directions:** Assume you are taking a course in mass media this semester and must choose to write about one of the media listed below. Choose one medium from the list, and then pick one form of the medium and write an essay defining it. For example, for the medium of television you could write about soap operas or reality shows; for radio you could choose to write about talk shows or sports commentary.

1. television
2. popular magazines
3. radio
4. film

# AN ACADEMIC SCENARIO
## A STUDENT ESSAY
### The Student Writer and the Writing Task

Ted Sawchuck is a student majoring in journalism. For his writing class, he was asked to write a definition essay about a new technology or innovation. He

chose to write about blogs. As you read, notice how he identifies the characteristics of blogs.

## Blogs: A New Frontier
### Ted Sawchuck

*Background information*

To borrow a phrase from an old musical, the Information Superhighway is alive with the sound of blogging. Once upon a time, people wrote. They wrote letters to friends, to their congressman, and to newspapers. They wrote in journals and kept diaries to create records of their lives. Today, instead, people keep "blogs." Blogs are a form of communication through online journals or "Web logs." Unlike traditional written media, a blog allows anyone anywhere to post anything about everything and have it read by everyone who finds it. It is this freedom that makes blogging so special.

*Thesis statement*

*Topic sentence (Characteristic 1)*

Blogs can focus on a specific topic—anything from underground rap to foreign policy to tornado chasing to Hollywood gossip—or just be general ideas or ranting and ravings about whatever is on the author's mind. Once something is blogged, it's instantly viewable by people all across the world, making blogging the best thing to happen to free speech since the First Amendment. All you need is Internet access and the ability to fill out a form and remember a password to join the growing ranks of bloggers.

Blogs are international. They allow people around the world to communicate and share ideas. DansData.com is a great example of the international nature of blogging. Dan reviews gadgets from his home in Australia. Without a Web presence, most Americans wouldn't know a thing about him. Also breaking ground in international blogging is an Iraqi girl who goes by the name of "River" and posts about life in Iraq after the war. Her blog isn't political, but a daily record of life in a time and place of great historical significance.

Unlike River, many bloggers are political. They may be liberals, conservatives, moderates, or people who believe that government is unnecessary. Bloggers post news as soon as it happens. They often check facts to make sure that what newspapers have printed is true. By keeping people talking about stories the major news networks have left behind, bloggers are performing a public service.

Personal blogs, while receiving a small number of hits compared to big political blogs, are still very popular. Typical personal blogs usually contain comments on the blogger's day or messages to friends. Bloggers do not worry about being correct or how they format their blog. For example, look at the following post, made by a blogger who calls herself "Nyteflame":

> "Monday, May 09, 2005
> i have one more paper to get done and three finals tomorrow AHHHH. i wanted to end up doing a lot of walking tonight but i need to study a lot. mel is going with me on the camping trip YAY!!

Some bloggers use cute, fancy names instead of their real names. This is big among the political bloggers; "Instapundit," "Atrios," "The Rude Pundit," "Billmon," and "Orcinus" are popular. Hiding one's identity is great for those who do not want to mix their blog lives with their real lives, but it's harder to judge the blog of someone who doesn't publish their real name. "Orcinus" is the name of the blog run by David Neiwert, and he is the author of two books and winner of a National Press Club award. Blogs run by people whose identities can be checked can be relied upon much more than blogs run by nobodies.

The great thing about blogs is that they allow for give and take of information and ideas. A blogger not only talks to his audience but listens to them as well. Blogs can be used to spread important information. If a post contains inaccurate information or a weak argument, readers will jump on it, posting links and criticizing the point being made. The result is not just one person speaking on an issue, but a discussion.

The rules of blogging haven't been established yet. Blogging is a new frontier. That's great because new frontiers mean new ideas and change. But it's also risky because there are no set rules or standards. Navigating the blogosphere requires caution and careful checking, and honesty on the part of bloggers and readers. Despite their problems, blogs are an amazing new source of information and discussion.

## Examining Academic Writing

1. Did Sawchuck provide sufficient information to a reader who has never heard of, read, or posted a blog? If not, what further information is needed?

2. Suggest alternate, more descriptive titles for the essay.

3. What did you learn about the author from this essay?

4. What is the author's purpose for writing?

5. Would more examples from real blogs have strengthened the essay? If so, identify places where they could have been used.

## Academic Writing Assignments

1. You are taking a psychology course and an essay question reads: "Define stress and give several examples of it sources." Write an answer for this essay question.

2. You are taking a speech communication class and have been asked to choose a team sport and a particular player in that sport. Your task is to define that player's position and his or her contribution to the team as a whole in a two-minute speech.

3. You are taking a course in business advertising and are studying various gimmicks and ploys advertisers use to convince people to buy their products. You have been asked to choose one gimmick and write a paragraph defining it and giving examples of it.

# A WORKPLACE SCENARIO
## A BUSINESS LETTER
### The Workplace Writer and the Writing Task

Paul Queeg is president of the Acme Boat Company, a small, privately owned company in Watertown, NY, on the St. Lawrence River that makes customized boats. In the letter shown below, Queeg replies to a customer request for more information on the sailboats Acme builds. As you read, notice how Queeg defines each of his products.

---

Acme Boat Building
123 Main Street
Watertown, NY 13601
October 10, 2005

1779 Plain Rd.
Savannah, GA 31415

Dear Mr. Cousteau:

In response to your inquiry of July 12, I would like to clear up some confusion regarding your request to order a sailboat.

Acme would be glad to build you a boat. However, we need you to define exactly the kind of boat you would like. Simply ordering a "sailboat" is not enough. A sailboat is any boat with a large piece of material attached to a mast that uses wind to make it move. A sailboat can be used for sport and leisure; it can be small enough for only one person or large enough for several people. A sailboat can be as simple as a board with one sail or so complex that it requires a motor in addition to sails.

If you are primarily interested in day sailing, you will need a day sailing boat. This is designed for use during the day, with no—or minimal—overnight accommodations. Day sailing boats are either **centerboard boats**, which are small, simple, and can be launched from the beach or off a ramp (like a windsurfer or a catamaran); or **keel boats**, which are larger and kept in the water most of the time. Centerboard boats are, naturally, the less expensive of the two.

If you are considering overnight sailing, you'll want a cruising sailboat. These boats have a galley for preparing meals and bunks for sleeping. They are large enough to accommodate two or more people and can usually be handled by a crew of two.

If you're interested in racing, you'll want a racing sailboat. Any sailboat can be used for racing, but there are only two forms of racing. The form you choose will determine the boat you will need. In "one-design racing," all boats are the same; the outcome depends on the experience and skill of the competitors. In "handicap racing," different kinds of boats compete against each other. It's therefore important to research which boats have proven to be the fastest and what innovations or improvements have been made on them during the past year. If you are considering racing, you should decide which type of race you will be entering before ordering your boat.

So you see, Mr. Cousteau, you don't just need a sailboat—you need your sailboat. I hope the information provided here will help you define exactly what that boat will be. Once you do, we'll build you a beauty.

Sincerely,
P. F. Queeg, President

## Examining Workplace Writing

1. Circle each term that is defined in the letter above.

2. For each term Queeg defines, highlight its distinguishing characteristics.

3. What other methods of development, in addition to definition, does Queeg use to explain the terms he defines?

4. How would you describe the tone of Queeg's letter? What attitude does he take toward the customer?

## Workplace Writing Assignments

1. You are the director of a walk-in medical treatment facility and need to explain AIDS to families who are unaware of its dangers. Write a brief definition of the disease for a brochure you are planning to distribute to all patients.

2. You are the editor of your favorite magazine. In trying to expand the magazine's market, you are writing advertising copy for a mailing to college students. Write a paragraph defining your magazine in a way that will appeal to college students.

3. The company where you work has appointed you to a team assigned to evaluate and revise the company's affirmative action policy. As a starting point for discussion and understanding, the team leader has asked each member to share his or her definition of affirmative action. Write a paragraph that you would submit to the group.

# WRITING ABOUT A READING

## Thinking Before Reading

The following article appeared on www.webroot.com. It is a good example of a professional essay that defines something. As you read, identify the distinguishing characteristics of spyware.

1. Preview the reading, using the steps discussed in Chapter 2, p. 30.

2. Connect the reading to your own experience by completing the following:

   a. Brainstorm a list of things you regularly do online. Do you think any of your online activities might make you vulnerable to spyware?

   b. When you use a computer, are you concerned that someone may be tracking your usage?

## READING

# Spyware Defined

**malware**

spyware specifically designed to destroy or harm other software or networks

**trackware**

spyware that tracks or follows everything a person does on his or her computer

**adware**

spyware that collects marketing information about the user in order for advertisers to send them specific pop-up ads

**applications**

computer programs or software designed to perform specific tasks

**EULA**

end user license agreement; a document that explains the terms and conditions of what a user may do with software he or she buys

**Trojans**

computer programs that look valid but contain hidden functions that cause damage to other programs

**browser**

a piece of computer software used to search for information on the World Wide Web

**dialers**

spyware that maliciously dials a long distance number from your dial-up modem; often associated with adult Web sites

**screenshots**

pictures the computer takes of the information showing on the monitor

**bandwidth**

the amount of information that can be communicated through a particular connection to the Internet

1    Spyware, which includes **malware**, **trackware**, and **adware**, is the categorical name for any application that may track your online and/or offline PC activity and is capable of locally saving or transmitting those findings for third parties sometimes with but more often without your knowledge or consent.

2    Anyone that uses a computer is susceptible to spyware infection. Your online actions, whether you're surfing the Internet or checking e-mail, can attract spyware files, **applications**, or programs. These programs find their way onto your system and install themselves in several possible places on your PC, including your registry, start up menu, and files and folders. Many spyware programs ensure their survival by sprinkling traces of the program throughout your system to make full removal more difficult (and sometimes nearly impossible). Once installed, spyware operates silently in the background.

3    Spyware jumps onto a PC in a number of ways. It can be installed by a hacker or someone who uses your computer, through a pop-up window or ad, via an instant messenger service, or delivered through a spam e-mail or an attachment in e-mail. File-sharing programs and swapping music, photos or other files are also well-known avenues for spyware infection. Sometimes spyware is bundled with a desired program, and is disclosed in buried text as part of the end-user-license agreement (**EULA**). These days, spyware may hop onto your system when you visit certain Web sites.

4    Spyware comes in many forms including adware, keyloggers, **Trojans**, system monitors, **browser** hijackers, and **dialers**. It ranges from benign—adware tracking cookies, which let online companies to track your activities on a Web site and tailor popup advertising messages based on your choices—to more nefarious spyware programs like Trojans, keyloggers, and system monitors, which are capable of capturing keystrokes, online **screenshots**, and personally identifiable information like your social security number, bank account numbers, logins and passwords, or credit card numbers.

5    Ultimately, your identity and private information can be compromised by these malicious programs. On a corporate level, spyware can compromise network and data security, corporate assets and trade secrets.

6    Aside from potential identity theft, many spyware programs steal from you by cluttering your computer's memory resources and eating **bandwidth** as they "talk" to the spyware's home base using your Internet connection. This could lead to your computer suffering system crashes and/or slower performance.

**firewall**
software that prevents
unauthorized access to other
system software or data

7    If you haven't thought about it already, you may want to consider a good spyware remover to protect your PC and your privacy from the prying eyes that are most likely residing on your system. Today, spyware protection is just as important as having a good anti-virus program and a **firewall**.

---

## Getting Ready to Write

### Reviewing the Reading

1. What is "spyware?" How does it differ from other software?

2. Who is vulnerable to spyware infection?

3. What problems can spyware create?

4. Why is spyware so difficult to remove?

5. What should you do to protect your computer?

### Examining the Reading: Using Idea Mapping to Review and Organize Ideas

Your knowledge of definition provides you with a useful way to organize the information that you read. By summarizing a reading's main points in chart form, you will find the material easier to remember and review.

Complete the idea map of "Spyware Defined" on the following page by filling in the missing information in the boxes.

### Thinking Critically: Examining the Author's Purpose

As you know, there are a variety of purposes for writing; writers may write to inform, entertain, or express their personal feelings, for example. Writers may also have more than one purpose. For instance, a writer who writes about credit card fraud may inform her readers about it but may also share her personal experiences as the victim of it. Writers of definition essays may also write for a variety of purposes.

Write a paragraph analyzing the author's purpose(s) in writing the article "Spyware Defined." Refer to specific sections of the reading to support your ideas.

### Strengthening Your Vocabulary

**Part A:** Using the word's context, word parts, or a dictionary, write a brief definition of each of the following words or phrases as it is used in the reading.

1. insidious (subhead) _slowly and subtly destructive_

2. susceptible (paragraph 2) _easily influenced or affected by something_

# Visualize It!

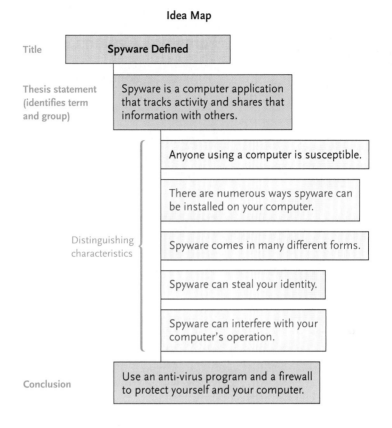

**Idea Map**

Title — **Spyware Defined**

Thesis statement (identifies term and group) — Spyware is a computer application that tracks activity and shares that information with others.

Distinguishing characteristics —
- Anyone using a computer is susceptible.
- There are numerous ways spyware can be installed on your computer.
- Spyware comes in many different forms.
- Spyware can steal your identity.
- Spyware can interfere with your computer's operation.

Conclusion — Use an anti-virus program and a firewall to protect yourself and your computer.

3. benign (paragraph 4) *harmless*

4. nefarious (paragraph 4) *immoral or evil*

5. compromised (paragraph 5) *exposed to danger; made lower in value*

6. malicious (paragraph 5) *deliberately harmful*

**Part B:** Choose one of the above words and draw a word map.

## Reacting to Ideas: Discussion and Journal Writing

1. Does the information in this article change the way you feel about opening your e-mail? What might you do differently?

2. Do you think it's fair for businesses to place cookies in your computer in order to create advertising aimed specifically at you? How are spyware cookies different from scanners in a grocery store that capture information about what you buy?

3. Identify theft is a growing national problem. Other than through computer use, how does it occur? How can you protect yourself?

## Writing About the Reading

### Paragraph Options

1. Write an e-mail to a friend warning them about spyware. Define what it is and explain its risks and dangers.

2. Think of a business that might benefit from placing spyware on your computer. Write a paragraph describing the business (real or fictitious) and explaining what information could help the company improve its business.

### Essay Options

3. Write an essay defining identity theft.

4. Write an essay describing a hacker. What kind of person might spend his or her time breaking into other people's computers? Use your imagination and plenty of details to flesh out your description.

5. Write an essay about the pros and cons of working online. How does the Internet help you do what you do better? Are there any ways in which it actually makes things more difficult for you at work or at school?

## Revision Checklist

1. Is your paragraph or essay appropriate for your audience? Does it give them the background information they need? Will it interest them?

2. Will your paragraph or essay accomplish your purpose?

3. Is your main point clearly expressed?

4. Is each detail relevant? Does each explain or support your main point?

5. Have you supported your main point with sufficient detail to make it understandable and believable?

6. Did you use specific words to explain each detail?

### For Definition Writing

7. Does the topic sentence or thesis statement identify the term or topic to be defined?

8. Do you identify the group to which the term or topic belongs and include distinguishing characteristics?

9. Does the paragraph or essay include sufficient detail (examples, classification, description, explaining what the term is not, tracing its origin) arranged in an easily understandable order?

10.  Are specific words and phrases used?

11.  Are ideas connected with transitional words and phrases?

12.  Have you proofread? (See the inside back cover of this book for a proofreading checklist.)

# CHAPTER REVIEW AND PRACTICE

## Chapter Review

| | |
|---|---|
| **WHAT ARE THE THREE PARTS OF A DEFINITION?** | The three parts are:<br>• the term or topic being defined.<br>• the group to which the term or topic belongs.<br>• the term or topic's distinguishing characteristics. |
| **WHAT SHOULD THE TOPIC SENTENCE DO?** | It should identify the term or topic being defined. It may also provide one or more of the distinguishing characteristics of the term or topic. |
| **HOW DO YOU DEVELOP A DEFINITION PARAGRAPH?** | Develop a definition paragraph by giving examples of the topic, breaking it into subcategories, explaining what the topic is not, and tracing its history over time. |
| **HOW CAN YOU HELP READERS UNDERSTAND AN UNFAMILIAR TOPIC?** | Help readers understand an unfamiliar topic by comparing it to something familiar and by explaining what distinguishes the topic from things similar to it. |
| **WHAT ARE THE GUIDELINES FOR WRITING DEFINITION ESSAYS?** | The guidelines are:<br>• Identify the topic in your thesis statement.<br>• Explain its importance.<br>• Devote a paragraph to each distinguishing characteristic.<br>• Provide sufficient detail.<br>• Explain the topic's origin.<br>• Trace the topic's history.<br>• Provide realistic examples.<br>• Use other methods of development. |

## Skill Refresher: Verb Tense

Verbs are words that express action or a state of being. There are two kinds of verbs, regular, and irregular. The **tense** of a verb expresses time—it indicates whether an action, process, or occurrence takes place in the present, past, or future. **Regular verbs** follow standard rules for forming tense, while **irregular verbs** do not. Verbs such as *move, talk,* and *walk* are examples of regular verbs. Verbs such as *run, stand,* and *write* are examples of irregular verbs. Use the following guidelines to avoid errors in regular verb tense.

1. **If an action happened in the past, the regular verb should end in –*ed*. Do not drop or omit –*ed* endings.**

   INCORRECT    Helen <u>want</u> to go to the movies last night.

   CORRECT      Helen <u>wanted</u> to go to the movies last night.

   INCORRECT    The accused murderer <u>face</u> the jury before he was sentenced.

   CORRECT      The accused murderer <u>faced</u> the jury before he was sentenced.

2. **Be sure to add –*s* or –*es* to present tense verbs that have singular subjects (singular means they refer to one person).**

   INCORRECT    Ramon <u>want</u> to become a history teacher.

   CORRECT      Ramon <u>wants</u> to become a history teacher.

3. **Use helping verbs to express time correctly.** Helping verbs are verbs that show when an action occurred. They are used with a main verb.

   INCORRECT    I <u>go</u> to the bookstore tomorrow.

   CORRECT      I <u>will go</u> to the bookstore tomorrow.

   INCORRECT    Jason <u>sit</u> at his computer for hours until he finishes his essay.

   CORRECT      Jason <u>will sit</u> at his computer for hours until he finishes his essay.

### Rate Your Ability to Use Verb Tense Correctly

Some of the following sentences contain errors in verb tense. If the sentence is correct, write "C" in the space provided. If the sentence is incorrect, correct the error. *Corrected sentences will vary.*

_____    1. Maggie called and ask Jen if she wanted a ride to the basketball game.

_____    2. Louisa wear a beautiful red dress to her sister's wedding last week.

____C____    3. Rob waited until he was introduced, and then he ran on stage.

_____  4. Marni answered an e-mail she receive from her boyfriend.

_____C_____  5. The group had ordered buffalo-style chicken wings, and they were not disappointed.

_____  6. Julie spend the afternoon stringing bead if it rains.

_____  7. We hope the package from my aunt arrive in tomorrow's mail.

_____  8. Yolanda claim to be the best cook in Erie County.

_____  9. Anthony broken his wrist again.

_____  10. My car stopped running before I ever pay off the loan for it.

Score  _____

Check your answers using the Answer Key on p. 642. If you got more than two wrong, you need additional review and practice with verb tense. Refer to Part VI, "Reviewing the Basics," and under Section C, see "Uses of Verb Tenses." For additional practice go to this book's Web site, http://www.ablongman.com/mcwhorterexpressways1e.

## INTERNET ACTIVITIES

### 1.  Official Definitions

The government creates definitions for use in policy setting. Read over the way that the Census Bureau defines poverty.

http://www.census.gov/hhes/poverty/povdef.html

Write a paragraph summarizing this definition.

### 2.  Analyze These

Read these definition essays from students in an online English group at Milwaukee Area Technical College.

http://online.matc.edu/eng-201/unit4.htm

Choose two to analyze. Create idea maps that organize the information in the essays.

### 3.  This Book's Web Site

Visit this site to find templates of idea maps for definition and additional practice on skills taught in the chapter.

http://www.ablongman.com/mcwhorterexpressways1e

# 12

# Comparison and Contrast

## Write About It!

Study the two photographs above. Write a few sentences explaining how the classes are the same and how they are different.

You have just written a comparison and contrast paragraph. **Comparison** focuses on how two or more things are the same. **Contrast** focuses on how two or more things are different. You will have numerous opportunities to use comparison and contrast in everyday, academic, and workplace situations. In this chapter you will learn to use comparison and contrast in both paragraphs and essays.

EVERYDAY SCENARIOS

- Doing some **comparison** shopping before buying a computer
- **Comparing** and **contrasting** two films you have seen recently

ACADEMIC SCENARIOS

- Writing an essay for a literature class, **comparing** and **contrasting** two poems
- **Comparing** and **contrasting** the viewpoints of experts on the issue of genetic engineering

WORKPLACE SCENARIOS

- **Comparing** and **contrasting** two building sites as part of a feasibility study for company relocation
- **Comparing** and **contrasting** educational computer games as a library media specialist

# UNDERSTANDING COMPARISON AND CONTRAST

Shopping for a used car? Imagine that you eventually narrow your choices to two cars—a Nissan and a Chevrolet. Each meets your basic requirements in terms of cost, mileage, and mechanical reliability. Which do you buy? How do you choose? Or suppose you are thinking of changing your major from accounting, but you can't decide whether to switch to marketing or business administration. Again, how do you decide? In each situation, you find similarities and differences among your options. When you consider similarities, you are comparing. When you consider differences, you are contrasting.

## What Are Comparison and Contrast?

Comparison and contrast are two ways of organizing information about two or more subjects. **Comparison** focuses on similarities; **contrast** focuses on differences. When writing paragraphs, it is often best to focus either on similarities or on differences, instead of trying to cover both in a short piece of writing. Essay-length pieces can focus on both similarities and differences, but it is often easier to concentrate on one or the other in an essay, too. Comparing and contrasting ideas can get complicated. Excellent planning and organization are required. Consequently, a major portion of this chapter is devoted to strategies for organizing your material and planning your writing.

# EXERCISE 12-1

**Directions:** Working alone or with another student, brainstorm a list of times in your own life when you used comparison and contrast.

## Identifying Similarities and Differences

If you have two items to compare or contrast, the first step is to figure out how they are similar and how they are different. Be sure to select subjects that are neither too similar nor too different. If they are, you will have either too little or too much to say. Follow this effective two-step approach:

1. **Brainstorm to produce a two-column list of characteristics.**

2. **Match up the items and identify points of comparison and contrast.**

### Brainstorming to Produce a Two-Column List

Let's say you want to write about two friends—Rhonda and Maria. Here is how to identify their similarities and differences:

1. **Brainstorm and list the characteristics of each person.**

| RHONDA | MARIA |
|---|---|
| Reserved, quiet | Age 27 |
| Age 22 | Single parent, two children |
| Private person | Outgoing |
| Friends since childhood | Loves to be center of attention |
| Married, no children | Loves sports and competition |
| Hates parties | Plays softball and tennis |
| Fun to shop with | |
| Tells me everything about her life | |

2. **When you finish your list, match up items that share the same point of comparison or contrast—age, personality type, marital status—as shown below.**

| RHONDA | MARIA |
|---|---|
| Reserved, quiet | Age 27 |
| Age 22 | Single parent, two children |
| Private person | Outgoing |
| Friends since childhood | Loves to be center of attention |
| Married, no children | |
| Hates parties | |

3. **When you have listed an item in a certain category for one person but not for the other, think of a corresponding detail that will balance the lists.** For instance, you listed "friends since childhood" for Rhonda, so you could indicate how long you have known Maria. This will give you additional points of comparison and contrast.

## EXERCISE 12-2
*Writing in Progress*

**Directions:** Make a two-column list of similarities and differences for two of the following topics:

1. Two courses you are taking

2. Two tasks (one difficult, one easy)

3. Two forms of communication

4. Two decisions you made recently

5. Two businesses

6. Two types of entertainment

## Identifying Points of Comparison and Contrast

The next step is to reorganize the lists so that the items you matched up appear next to each other. Now, in a new column to the left of your lists, write the term that describes or categorizes each set of items in the lists. These are general categories we will call "Points of Comparison/Contrast." **Points of comparison and contrast** are the characteristics you use to examine your two subjects. As you reorganize, you may find it easier to group several items together. For example, you might group some details about Rhonda and Maria together under the category of personality. Study the following list, noticing the points of comparison and contrast in the left-hand column.

| POINTS OF COMPARISON/CONTRAST | RHONDA | MARIA |
|---|---|---|
| Personality | Quiet, reserved, private person | Outgoing, loves to be center of attention |
| Marital status | Married, no children | Single parent, two children |
| Length of friendship | Friends since childhood | Met at work last year |
| Shared activities | Go shopping | Play softball together, go to parties |

## EXERCISE 12-3
*Writing in Progress*

**Directions:** For the two topics you chose in Exercise 12-2, match up the items and identify points of comparison/contrast.

This two-step process can work in reverse order as well. You can decide points of comparison/contrast first and then brainstorm characteristics for each point. For example, suppose you are comparing and contrasting two restaurants. Points of comparison/contrast might be location, price, speed of service, menu variety, and quality of food. If you are comparing or contrasting Professors Rodriguez and Meyer, you might do so using the following points:

| POINTS OF COMPARISON/CONTRAST | PROFESSOR MEYER | PROFESSOR RODRIQUEZ |
| --- | --- | --- |
| Amount of homework | | |
| Type of exams | | |
| Class organization | | |
| How easy to talk to | | |
| Grading system | | |
| Style of teaching | | |

You could then fill in columns 2 and 3 with appropriate details, as shown below.

| POINTS OF COMPARISON/CONTRAST | PROFESSOR MEYER | PROFESSOR RODRIQUEZ |
| --- | --- | --- |
| Amount of homework | Assignment due for every class | Hardly any |
| Type of exams | Essay | Multiple choice and essay |
| Class organization | Well organized | Free and easy |
| How easy to talk to | Always around, approachable | Approachable but talks a lot |
| Grading system | 50% class participation, 50% essay exams | 100% exams |
| Style of teaching | Lecture | Class discussion, questions |

Once you have completed your three-column list, the next step is to study your list and decide whether to write about similarities or differences, or both. It is usually easier to concentrate on one or the other. If you see similarities as more significant, you might need to omit or de-emphasize differences—and vice versa if you decide to write about differences.

## EXERCISE 12-4

**Directions:** List at least three points of comparison/contrast for each of the following topics. Then choose one topic and make a three-column list on a separate sheet of paper.

1. Two films you have seen recently

   Points of comparison/contrast:

   a. _____

   b. _____

   c. _____

   d. _____

   e. _____

2. Two jobs you have held

   Points of comparison/contrast:

   a. _____

   b. _____

   c. _____

   d. _____

   e. _____

3. Baseball and football players

   Points of comparison/contrast:

   a. _____

   b. _____

   c. _____

   d. _____

   e. _____

## Writing Your Topic Sentence

Your topic sentence should do two things:

• It should identify the two subjects that you will compare or contrast.

• It should state whether you will focus on similarities, differences, or both.

It may also indicate what points you will compare or contrast. Suppose you are comparing two world religions—Judaism and Hinduism. Obviously, you could not cover every aspect of these religions in a single paragraph. Instead, you could limit your comparison to their size, place of worship, or the type of divine being(s) worshipped.

Here are a few sample topic sentences that meet the above requirements:

1. Judaism is one of the smallest of the world's religions; Hinduism is one of the largest.

2. Neither Judaism nor Hinduism limits worship to a single location, although both hold services in temples.

3. Unlike Hinduism, Judaism teaches belief in only one god.

Be sure to avoid topic sentences that announce what you plan to do. Here's an example: "I'll compare network news and local news and show why I prefer local news."

### EXERCISE 12-5

*Writing in Progress*

**Directions:** For the two topics you worked with in Exercises 12-2 and 12-3, write a topic sentence for each.

## Organizing Your Paragraph

Once you have identified similarities and differences and drafted a topic sentence, you are ready to organize your paragraph. There are two ways you can organize a comparison or contrast paragraph:

• subject by subject.

• point by point.

### Subject-by-Subject Organization

In the **subject-by-subject method**, you write first about one of your subjects, covering it completely, and then about the other, covering it completely.

Ideally, you cover the same points of comparison and contrast for both, and in the same order. Let's return to the comparison between Professors Meyer and Rodriguez. With subject-by-subject organization, you first discuss Professor Meyer—his class organization, exams, and grading system; you then discuss Professor Rodriguez—her class organization, exams, and grading system. You can visualize the arrangement this way:

# Visualize It! ➤

**Subject-by-Subject Organization Map**

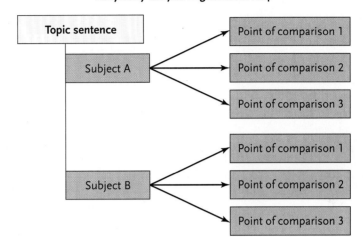

To develop each subject, focus on the same kinds of details and discuss the same points of comparison in the same order. If you are discussing only similarities or only differences, organize your points within each topic, using a most-to-least or least-to-most arrangement. If you are discussing both similarities and differences, you might discuss points of similarity first and then points of difference, or vice versa.

Here is a sample paragraph using the subject-by-subject method and a map showing its organization:

> Two excellent teachers, Professor Meyer and Professor Rodriguez, present a study in contrasting teaching styles. Professor Meyer is extremely organized. He conducts every class the same way. He reviews the assignment, lectures on the new chapter, and explains the next assignment. He gives essay exams and they are always based on important lecture topics. Because the topics are predictable, you know you are not wasting your time when you study. Professor Meyer's grading depends half on class participation and half on the essay exams. Professor Rodriguez, on the other hand, has an easy-going style. Each class is different and emphasizes whatever she thinks will help us better understand the material. Her classes are fun because you never know what to expect. Professor Rodriguez gives both multiple-choice and essay exams. These are difficult to study for because they are unpredictable. Our final grade is based entirely on the exams, so each exam requires a lot of studying beforehand. Although each professor teaches very differently, I am figuring out how to learn from each particular style.

## Visualize It!

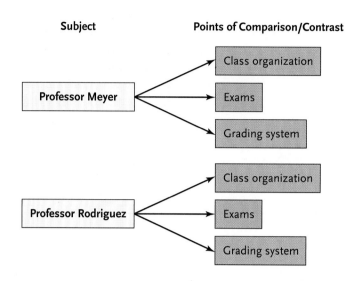

Subject                    Points of Comparison/Contrast

## EXERCISE 12-6

*Writing in Progress*

**Directions:** Using the subject-by-subject method of organization, write a comparison or contrast paragraph using one of the topic sentences you wrote for Exercise 12-5.

## Point-by-Point Organization

In the **point-by-point method of organization**, you discuss both of your subjects together for each point of comparison and contrast. You can visualize this organization as follows:

## Visualize It!

**Point-by-Point Organization Map**

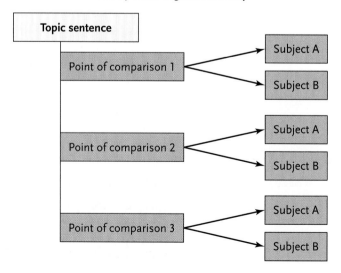

When using this organization, maintain consistency by discussing the same subject first for each point. (That is, always discuss Professor Meyer first and Professor Rodriguez second for each point.)

If your paragraph focuses only on similarities or only on differences, arrange your points in a least-to-most or most-to-least pattern.

Here is a sample paragraph using the point-by-point method and a map showing its organization:

> Professor Meyer and Professor Rodriguez demonstrate very different teaching styles in how they operate their classes, how they give exams, and how they grade us. Professor Meyer's classes are highly organized; we work through the lesson every day in the same order. Professor Rodriguez uses an opposite approach. She creates a lesson to fit the material, which enables us to learn the most. Their exams differ too. Professor Meyer gives standard, predictable essay exams that are based on his lectures. Professor Rodriguez gives both multiple-choice and essay exams, so we never know what to expect. In addition, each professor grades differently. Professor Meyer counts class participation as half of our grade, so if you talk in class and do reasonably well on the exams, you will probably pass the course. Professor Rodriguez, on the other hand, counts the exams 100 percent, so you *have* to do well on them to pass the course. Each professor has a unique, enjoyable teaching style, and I am learning a great deal from each.

## Visualize It!

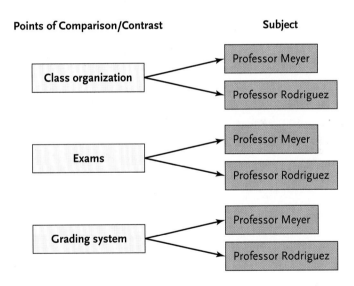

**EXERCISE 12-7**

*Writing in Progress*

**Directions:** Using the point-by-point method of organization, write a comparison and contrast paragraph on the topic you chose for Exercise 12-6.

## Developing Your Points of Comparison and Contrast

As you discuss each point, don't feel as if you must compare or contrast in every sentence. Your paragraph should not just list similarities and/or differences. For every point, provide explanation, descriptive details, and examples.

Try to maintain a balance in your treatment of each subject and each point of comparison and contrast. Give equal attention to each point and each subject. If you give an example for one subject, try to do so for the other as well.

## Useful Transitions

Transitions are particularly important in comparison and contrast writing. Because you are discussing two subjects and covering similar points for each, your readers can easily become confused. Table 12-1 lists commonly used transitional words and phrases.

**Table 12-1    Transitions for Comparison and Contrast Paragraphs**

| | |
|---|---|
| To show similarities: | likewise, similarly, in the same way, too, also |
| To show differences: | however, on the contrary, unlike, on the other hand |

Each method of organization uses different transitions in different places. If you choose a subject-by-subject organization, you'll need the strongest transition in the middle of the paragraph, when you switch from one subject to another. You will also need a transition each time you move from one point to another while still on the same subject. In the following paragraph written by a paralegal comparing recent court cases, notice the transitional sentence highlighted in green.

> *Green v. Lipscomb* and *Walker v. Walker* are the two most recent cases that deal with the custody of siblings. *Green* holds that siblings have a right to live together. It says that when a court decides custody, putting siblings together is the controlling concern. In this case, custody was given to the father because it was in the best interest of the oldest child to live with him. The other children were to live there as well because it was more important that they live together. *Walker* presents a more subjective position. *Walker* says that while the sibling relationship is an important factor in deciding custody, it alone is not controlling. The best interest of each child must be evaluated. The sibling relationship must be considered in this evaluation.

This paragraph uses a subject-by-subject organization. A strong transition emphasizes the switch from one case to another.

If you choose point-by-point organization, use transitions as you move from one subject to the other. On each point, your reader needs to know quickly whether the two subjects are similar or different. Here is an example:

> Although colds and hay fever are both annoying, their symptoms and causes differ. Hay fever causes my eyes to itch and water. I sneeze excessively, bothering those around me. Colds, on the other hand, make me feel stuffy, with a runny nose and a cough. For me, hay fever arrives in the summer, but colds linger on through late fall, winter, and early spring. Their causes differ, too. Pollens produce hay fever. I am most sensitive to pollen from wildflowers and corn tassels. Unlike hay fever, viruses, which are passed from person to person by air or body contact, cause colds.

Notice that each time the writer switched from hay fever to colds, a transition was used.

## EXERCISE 12-8

*Writing in Progress*

**Directions:** Reread the paragraphs you wrote for Exercises 12-6 and 12-7. Add transitions to make your organization clearer.

## Applying Your Skills to Essay Writing: Comparison and Contrast

When comparing or contrasting in detail, you will probably find that an essay, rather than a single paragraph, is needed. Use the following suggestions for writing comparison and contrast essays:

1. **Be sure your essay has a concise thesis statement.** Your thesis statement, like your paragraph's topic sentence, should identify your subjects, indicate whether you will focus on similarities, differences, or both, and express a viewpoint toward your subjects.

2. **Focus on your purpose for writing.** Usually, your primary purpose is not to show how one thing is similar to or different from another. Instead, your purpose is to make a point or reach a conclusion through comparison or contrast. In comparing two poems, for example, you may want to examine how two poets from different centuries and different parts of the world describe the same human dilemma.

3. **Choose meaningful points of comparison.** With many topics, there are many possible points of comparison. Be sure to choose points of comparison that will support your purpose in writing and your thesis statement. For example, if your purpose in writing is to discuss characteristics of desirable employees, when you compare two employees your points of comparison might be reliability, initiative, and trustworthiness. If, however, your purpose in writing is to discuss worker productivity, your points of comparison might be aspects of job performance, such as total number of hours worked, total number of sales, and so forth.

4. **Be sure to follow the organization you have chosen (subject-by-subject or point-by-point) consistently throughout your essay.**

5. **Use transitions to guide your reader.** Transitions are even more important in essays than in paragraphs. With longer and oftentimes more complicated comparisons or contrasts, essays must have transitions to enable readers to follow your train of thought.

## NEED TO KNOW

### Organizing Your Details

Regardless of the method of organization you choose, it is important to organize the details in each method so that your paragraph or essay is easy to follow. Use the following suggestions;

**For subject-by-subject organization:**

- Be sure to cover the same points of comparison for each subject.

- Cover the points of comparison in the same order in each half of your paragraph or essay.

- Make sure you include a strong transition that signals you are moving from one subject to another.

**For point-by-point organization:**

- As you work back and forth between your subjects, try to mention the subjects in the same order.

- Decide how to organize your points of comparison. You could move from the simplest to the most complex similarity, or from the most obvious to least obvious difference, for example.

## EXERCISE 12-9

**Directions:** Suppose you are taking a course titled "Marriage and Family" and are studying the social role of families and the customs of dating and marrying in Western culture. Your instructor has asked you to complete one of the following assignments. Choose one topic and draft an essay.

1. The functions of a family include emotional support, economic support, and socialization (the sharing of beliefs, attitudes, and values). Choose two families you know and compare and/or contrast how they function, using one or more of these points of comparison as well as any of your own choosing.

2. The functions of dating include entertainment, learning to get along with others, development of companionship and intimacy, and opportunity to choose a spouse. Think of two dates you have had and compare and/or contrast them, using some or all of these points of comparison.

3. The functions of weddings are to make a public announcement of a lifelong commitment between two people, to provide a celebration, to make a marriage legal, and to serve as a marker or milestone for the beginning of a new life. Think of two weddings you have attended and compare and/or contrast how well each fulfilled some or all of these functions.

# AN ACADEMIC SCENARIO
## A STUDENT ESSAY
### The Academic Writer and the Writing Task

Frank Trapasso is a student at the University of Massachusetts and is taking a writing class. His instructor assigned a comparison and contrast essay. Students were allowed to choose their own topic. Trapasso decided to write about customers he encounters in his summer job. As you read, be sure to observe how Trapasso organizes his essay.

## How May I Help You?
### Frank Trapasso

*Interesting, catchy title*

*Dialog captures reader's attention*

"Hello, this is Parks and Recreation Customer Support. My name is Frank. How may I help you?"

*Background on requirements of the job*

I take park reservations over the phone as my summer job. This experience has taught me that customer service reps and customers have very different goals for their time on the phone. Let's start with mine. For each and every call, I have a list of 46 things I have to ask and verify. My list contains everything from "Does the customer want to bring a pet?" to "Will there be a responsible adult over the age of 18 at each campsite?" It's my job; I don't make the rules, and I'm frequently monitored for quality control.

Now, if I don't ask at least 90% of the questions on any call my bosses are listening in on, I'll be punished. Three calls below 90% means I'm fired. The callers? They may be frustrated by my questions, but they won't lose their jobs and they will end up with a pretty nice vacation. And I can't just ask things once: I'm required to ask multiple times for certain information, to make sure I've got it right. All the callers are required to do is sit back, put their feet up, chew gum, drink coffee, and *answer the questions*.

*Thesis*

*Paragraph introduces both subjects*

*Subject 1*

*Subject 2*

There are two kinds of situations I encounter on the phone: regulars and newbies. My favorite is the regulars. These are people who go to parks every year to meet up with friends, get away from the kids . . . whatever. They call in wanting a specific site at a specific park on a specific date. Half my calls are regulars. The other half consists of "newbies," people who have no earthly idea of what they want. Each half has its own peculiarities and presents its own complications.

*Point of Comparison A*

The regulars are the people who reserve regularly. They seem to understand that I will ask the questions and their job is to supply the answers, but they get annoyed when I ask them to repeat information. I explain it's routine and that I'm required to verify all information. They ask why I don't have that information when they've been calling every year for the last two decades. I tell them—again—that I'm required to ask. If I'm lucky, they answer. If I'm not, we waste time with attitude.

Point of Comparison B

Point of Comparison C

Usually regulars know what they want, and if it is available, my job is relatively easy. They have a favorite site in mind and can give me its number or location. Also, regulars usually know to call early enough for the space to be open and, as long as it is, those calls are easy. Well, everything is easy until I start in with my list of 46 questions. I begin with the basics; name, correct spelling of the name, address, verify address again. Now, if the site they want is not open, my immediate response is to try and find a different one that fits the description of the one they wanted; in the woods, near the lake, right next to the bathrooms, or whatever it is they like about the first site. Those who have called before don't have a problem with this. Regulars understand "first come first served" and that CSR Frank can't unreserve the site they want and give it to them.

Point of Comparison D

Transitional sentence makes it clear he is switching to Subject 2

Point of Comparison A

Those who are calling for the first time, however, are a different story entirely. Newbies tend to flood us with information because they think that we need to know they want something in Gifford Pinchot State Park sometime this summer before we've even gotten their names. Since I have to do things in a specific order, I stop them and ask for their names. The callers? They snap out something helpful like "Why do you need my name? I'm just trying to make a reservation!" These people are one of the reasons I keep aspirin at my desk. These people test my ability to leave work each day with sanity and without a headache. These people are the reason I end up laid out in bed for the entire night right after my shift. The callers? They may curse at me once or twice after they hang up, but I don't think they let it ruin their evening plans.

Point of Comparison B

Point of Comparison C

Point of Comparison D

Conclusion: a final comment about the job

Newbies often don't really know what they want, and I have to take the time to explain locations, facilities, and services. They ask what seems like hundreds of questions which I try to answer politely. Worse yet, these people have no idea that sites fill up quickly, and realize too late that they should have called earlier. And, when they finally decide what they want and it is unavailable, newbies think I can magically create a site for them.

Next time you need customer service, take a moment to think about what the person you're talking to is required to accomplish during the call—and help them accomplish it. Cordiality and politeness on both ends of the phone will make the CSR's job *and* your reservation process easier. And that's a win-win situation.

## Examining Academic Writing

1. What type of organization did Trapasso use?

2. Evaluate Trapasso's thesis. How could it be improved?

3. Did Trapasso include a sufficient number of points of comparison?

4. What overall attitude toward his job does Trapasso reveal through the essay?

## Academic Writing Assignments

1. You are taking a business marketing class and are studying advertising. Your instructor has asked you to choose two advertisements in the same medium (magazine, radio, or television). Your assignment is to compare or contrast the two advertisements according to three points. (Hint: for points of comparison you might choose the purpose of the ad as well as its effectiveness, subjects, message, gimmicks, appeal, etc.)

2. In your sociology class you are studying subcultures—groups within our society that have a unique set of customs, values, or ways of doing things. Examples of subcultures are basketball players, restaurant workers, jazz musicians, and computer hackers. Your assignment is to choose two subcultures that you belong to or with which you are familiar. Write a paragraph comparing the subcultures.

3. For a course in interpersonal communication, you are studying age differences in communication. Think of ways in which two age groups communicate differently. Write a short essay explaining these differences.

# A WORKPLACE SCENARIO
## A FLYER
### The Workplace Writer and the Writing Task

Alice Witcoff is a sales representative at Mentko's—an pharmaceutical sales company. Her company always has a competition among representatives and awards a prize to the representative with the highest yearly sales. She received a letter from her district manager informing her that she had won.

The letter directed her to choose the vacation package she wanted from among three choices. Enclosed was a flyer comparing her three options. The flyer is shown below. As you read, notice how comparison and contrast are used effectively.

Congratulations! As the top-performing sales person for the past 12 months, we are pleased to inform you that you have won an **all-expenses-paid trip for two** to one of Custer Travel Agency's resort partners.

To claim your prize, simply compare the three options below and choose the package that best suits your interests.

|  | WILD WEST WEEKEND | DELUXE DISCOUNTS | RIVERSIDE RELAXATION |
|---|---|---|---|
| THEME | Grab your cowboy boots and go west to Custer's Ranch-O-Rama, the jewel of the Black Hills in historic South Dakota. Wild and woolly fun! | New Jersey is the shopping capital of the East Coast and no wonder—there's no sales tax on clothes! It's a bargain hunter's paradise and a race for the best deal. | It's the Three "R"s —Resting, Reading, and Relaxing—in the Wisconsin Dells, the waterpark capital of the country! |

| LODGING | Rustic cabin made of hand-hewn logs with bunks for four. Outdoor showers; no electricity. Gas lamps are provided and each cabin has a woodstove. | Standard AAA three-star hotel with choice of one king or two double beds. High-speed Internet; spa and fitness center on premises. | Cozy antique-filled Scandinavi-Inn Bed and Breakfast, complete with featherbed and quilts stuffed with down from the inn's own ducks. |
|---|---|---|---|
| MENU | All meals are served outdoors and cooked over a fire at Buffalo Bill's Steamin' Bar-B-Q pit. | Choose from among dozens of major chains, delis, and specialty restaurants. | Your hosts Sig and Betty Hargittsen's fine home cooking is featured. |
| WHAT TO DO | • Hiking tour of historic Deadwood Gulch<br>• Three-hour mule-back ride through Badlands National Park<br>• Sunset climb at Mount Rushmore, scene of the world's greatest mountain carving<br>• Thrill to the excitement of a rodeo, where you may get to take a turn on a bucking bronco! | Shop 'til you drop at Liz Claiborne • Anne Klein • Donna Karan • Geoffrey Beene • DKNY Jeans • Jones NY • Leather Express • Tommy Hilfiger • Kenneth Cole • Nine West and more!<br>• Spa treatment with massage for those aching feet!<br>• Dinner and show at the Secaucus Hilton | • Take a ride in an ox-drawn wagon through a working dairy farm, where you'll see how the famous Wisconsin cheese is made.<br>• Enjoy the scenery as you float down the Dells River on a Riverboat Ramble.<br>• Cast a line into Otter Springs Pond, where the walleye are always biting and everyone is guaranteed to catch something. |
| CHILDREN | Under 5 no extra charge. Children 5–12 may accompany parents for a fee of $100.00 each. | Not suitable for children. | Children over 10 only, for a fee of $100.00 each |

## Examining Workplace Writing

1. Identify the subjects and points of comparison in the flyer.

2. Which sentence in Witcoff's flyer serves the same purpose as the thesis statement of a comparison-contrast essay?

3. What are the advantages of presenting the options in a table rather than in a paragraph? What are the disadvantages?

## Workplace Writing Assignments

1. You are a youth counselor who helps unemployed high school graduates find jobs. You are preparing a pamphlet on how to conduct a job search. For the chapter on job interviews, you decide to compare employer reactions to an inappropriately dressed applicant and to an appropriately dressed applicant. Write this section using a subject-by-subject organization.

2. You work at a local, independently owned bookstore. The owner realizes that she faces stiff competition from online bookstores such as Amazon.com. She has asked you to write an article for her next monthly newsletter, comparing and contrasting shopping online with visiting a bookstore.

**3.** You work part-time in your college's admissions office as a student assistant. The director of admissions has asked you to write a letter comparing your college with another you considered attending. Your comparison will be used by the admissions staff in preparing publicity materials.

## WRITING ABOUT A READING

### Thinking Before Reading

This reading, "The Talk of the Sandbox: How Johnny and Suzy's Playground Chatter Prepares Them for Life at the Office" by Deborah Tannen was first published in *The Washington Post* in 1994. The selection examines differences between men's and women's communication at work. This reading is a good example of comparison and contrast organization, so as you read notice how Tannen organizes her ideas.

1.  Preview the reading, using the steps described in Chapter 2, p. 30.

2.  Activate your thinking by answering the following:

    **a.** Do you think men and women differ in how they communicate? If so, why?

    **b.** At work, have you observed differences in the ways men and women communicate? If so, what are they?

### READING

# The Talk of the Sandbox: How Johnny and Suzy's Playground Chatter Prepares Them for Life at the Office

Deborah Tannen

1    Bob Hoover of the *Pittsburgh Post-Gazette* was interviewing me when he remarked that after years of coaching boys' softball teams, he was now coaching girls and they were very different. I immediately whipped out my yellow pad and began interviewing him—and discovered that his observations about how girls and boys play softball parallel mine about how women and men talk at work.

**lord it over**
to act in a superior or bullying way

**in the dog house**
in disgrace

2    Hoover told me that boys' teams always had one or two stars whom the other boys treated with deference. So when he started coaching a girls' team, he began by looking for the leader. He couldn't find one. "The girls who are better athletes don't **lord it over** the others," he said. "You get the feeling that everyone's the same." When a girl got the ball, she didn't try to throw it all the way home as a strong-armed boy would; instead, she'd throw it to another team member, so they all became better catchers and throwers. He went on, "If a girl makes an error, she's not **in the doghouse** for a long time, as a boy would be."

3    "But wait," I interrupted. "I've heard that when girls make a mistake at sports, they often say 'I'm sorry,' whereas boys don't." "That's true," he said, "but then the girl forgets it—and so do her teammates. For boys, sports is a performance art. They're concerned with how they look." When they make an error, they sulk because they've let their teammates down. Girls want to win, but if they lose, they're still all in it together—so the mistake isn't as dreadful for the individual or the team. What Hoover described in these youngsters were the seeds of behavior I have observed among women and men at work.

4    The girls who are the best athletes don't "lord it over" the others—just the ethic I found among women in positions of authority. Women managers frequently told me they were good managers because they did not act in an authoritarian manner. They said they did not flaunt their power, or behave as though they were better than their subordinates. Similarly, linguist Elisabeth Kuhn found that women professors in her study informed students of course requirements as if they had magically appeared on the syllabus ("There are two papers. The first paper, ah, let's see, is due . . . It's back here [referring to the syllabus] at the beginning"), whereas the men professors made it clear that they had set the requirements ("I have two midterms and a final").

5    A woman manager might say to her secretary, "Could you do me a favor and type this letter right away?" knowing that her secretary is going to type the letter. But her male boss, on hearing this, might conclude she doesn't feel she deserves the authority she has, just as a boys' coach might think the star athlete doesn't realize how good he is if he doesn't expect his teammates to treat him with deference.

6    I was especially delighted by Hoover's observation that, although girls are more likely to say, "I'm sorry," they are actually far less sorry when they make a mistake than boys who don't say it, but are "in the doghouse" for a long time. This dramatizes the **ritual** nature of many women's apologies. How often is a woman who is "always apologizing" seen as weak and lacking in confidence? In fact, for many women, saying "I'm sorry" often doesn't mean "I apologize." It means "I'm sorry that happened."

**ritual**
an established pattern of behavior

7    Like many of the rituals common among women, it's a way of speaking that takes into account the other person's point of view. It can even be an automatic conversational smoother. For example, you left your pad in someone's office; you knock on the door and say, "Excuse me, I left my pad on your desk," and the person whose office it is might reply, "Oh, I'm sorry.

Here it is." She knows it is not her fault that you left your pad on her desk; she's just letting you know it's okay.

8    Finally, I was intrigued by Hoover's remark that boys regard sports as "a performance art" and worry about "how they look." There, perhaps, is the rub, the key to why so many women feel they don't get credit for what they do. From childhood, many boys learn something that is very adaptive to the workplace: Raises and promotions are based on "performance" evaluations and these depend, in large measure, on how you appear in other people's eyes. In other words, you have to worry not only about getting your job done but also about getting credit for what you do.

9    Getting credit often depends on the way you talk. For example, a woman told me she was given a poor evaluation because her supervisor felt she knew less than her male peers. Her boss, it turned out, reached this conclusion because the woman asked more questions: She was seeking information without regard to how her queries would make her look.

10    The same principle applies to apologizing. Whereas some women seem to be taking underserved blame by saying "I'm sorry," some men seem to evade deserved blame. I observed this when a man disconnected a conference call by accidentally elbowing the speaker-phone. When his secretary reconnected the call, I expected him to say, "I'm sorry; I knocked the phone by mistake." Instead he said, "Hey, what happened?! One minute you were there, the next minute you were gone!" Annoying as this might be, there are certainly instances in which people improve their fortunes by covering up mistakes.

11    If Hoover's observations about girls' and boys' athletic styles are fascinating, it is even more revealing to see actual **transcripts** of children at play and how they mirror the adult workplace. Amy Sheldon, a linguist at the University of Minnesota who studies children talking at play in a day care center, compared the conflicts of pre-school girls and boys. She found that boys who fought with one another tended to pursue their own goals. Girls tended to balance their own interests with those of the other girls through complex verbal negotiations.

12    Look how different the negotiations were. Two boys fought over a toy telephone: Tony had it; Charlie wanted it. Tony was sitting on a foam chair with the base of the phone in his lap and the receiver lying beside him. Charlie picked up the receiver, and Tony protested, "No, that's my phone!" He grabbed the telephone cord and tried to pull the receiver away from Charlie, saying, "No, that—uh, it's on MY couch. It's on MY couch, Charlie. It's on MY couch. It's on MY couch." It seems he had only one point to make, so he made it repeatedly as he used physical force to get the phone back. Charlie ignored Tony and held onto the receiver. Tony then got off the couch, set the phone base on the floor and tried to keep possession of it by overturning the chair on top of it. Charlie managed to push the chair off, get the telephone and win the fight.

13    This might seem like a typical kids' fight until you compare it with a fight Sheldon videotaped among girls. Here the contested objects were toy medical instruments: Elaine had them; Arlene wanted them. But she didn't just

**transcripts**
written records of conversations

grab for them; she argued her case. Elaine, in turn, balanced her own desire to keep them with Arlene's desire to get them. Elaine lost ground gradually, by compromising.

14    Arlene began not by grabbing but by asking and giving a reason: "Can I have that, that thing? I'm going to take my baby's temperature." Elaine was agreeable, but cautious: "You can use it—you can use my temperature. Just make sure you can't use anything else unless you can ask." Arlene did just that; she asked for the toy syringe: "May I?" Elaine at first resisted, but gave a reason: "No, I'm gonna need to use the shot in a couple of minutes." Arlene reached for the syringe anyway, explaining in a "beseeching" tone, "But I—I need this though."

15    Elaine capitulated, but again tried to set limits: "Okay, just use it once." She even gave Arlene permission to give "just a couple of shots." Arlene then pressed her advantage, and became possessive of her property: "Now don't touch the baby until I get back, because it IS MY BABY! I'll check her ears, okay?" (Even when being demanding, she asked for agreement: "okay?") Elaine tried to regain some rights through compromise: "Well, let's pretend it's another day, that we have to look in her ears together." Elaine also tried another approach that would give Arlene something she wanted: "I'll have to shot her after, after, after you listen—after you look in her ears," suggested Elaine. Arlene, however, was adamant: "Now don't shot her at all!"

16    What happened next will sound familiar to anyone who has ever been a little girl or overheard one. Elaine could no longer abide Arlene's selfish behavior and applied the ultimate **sanction**: "Well, then, you can't come to my birthday!" Arlene uttered the predictable retort: "I don't want to come to your birthday!"

17    The boys and girls followed different rituals for fighting. Each boy went after what he wanted; they slugged it out; one won. But the girls enacted a complex negotiation, trying to get what they wanted while taking into account what the other wanted.

18    Here is an example of how women and men at work used comparable strategies: Maureen and Harold, two managers at a medium-size company, were assigned to hire a human-resources coordinator for their division. Each favored a different candidate, and both felt strongly about their preferences. They traded arguments for some time, neither convincing the other. Then Harold said that hiring the candidate Maureen wanted would make him so uncomfortable that he would have to consider resigning. Maureen respected Harold. What's more, she liked him and considered him a friend. So she said what seemed to her the only thing she could say under the circumstances: "Well, I certainly don't want you to feel uncomfortable here. You're one of the pillars of the place." Harold's choice was hired.

19    What was crucial was not Maureen's and Harold's individual styles in isolation but how they played in concert with each other's style. Harold's threat to quit ensured his triumph—when used with someone for whom it was a

**sanction**
approve of or accept

**trump card**
a valuable resource held in reserve until needed

**trump card**. If he had been arguing with someone who regarded this threat as simply another move in the negotiation rather than a non-negotiable expression of deep feelings, the result might have been different. For example, had she said, "That's ridiculous; of course you're not going to quit!" or matched it ("Well, I'd be tempted to quit if we hired your guy"), the decision might well have gone the other way.

20  Like the girls at play, Maureen was balancing her perspective with those of her colleague and expected him to do the same. Harold was simply going for what he wanted and trusted Maureen to do likewise. This is not to say that all women and all men, or all boys and girls, behave any one way. Many factors influence our styles, including regional and ethnic backgrounds, family experience and individual personality. But gender is a key factor, and understanding its influence can help clarify what happens when we talk.

**devil's advocate**
one who argues against a position only for the sake of argument

21  Understanding the ritual nature of communication gives you the flexibility to consider different approaches if you're not happy with the reaction you're getting. Someone who tends to avoid expressing disagreement might learn to play "**devil's advocate**" without taking it as a personal attack. Someone who tends to avoid admitting fault might find it is effective to say "I'm sorry"—that the loss of face is outweighed by a gain in credibility. There is no one way of talking that will always work best. But understanding how conversational rituals work allows individuals to have more control over their own lives.

---

## Getting Ready to Write

### Reviewing the Reading

1. What do girls and boys' sports teams demonstrate about gender relationships?

2. How do men's apologies differ from those of women?

3. How do boys' and girls' negotiations differ?

4. Explain what happened in the negotiations between Maureen and Harold. Why was Harold's choice hired?

5. Why is it useful to understand differences in gender communication?

## Examining the Reading: Using the Three-Column List for Review

The three-column list that you constructed to organize your ideas before writing also may be used as an effective study and review technique. As you read other writers' comparison and contrast pieces, organize your notes on their ideas in a three-column format. A three-column list for "The Talk of the Sandbox" would be organized this way:

**Visualize It!**

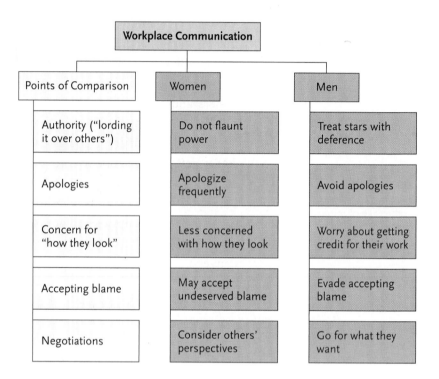

Complete the above three-column list by supplying details from the reading.

## Thinking Critically: Identifying and Examining Supporting Evidence

Most writers who express their opinions, state viewpoints, make generalizations, or offer hypotheses also provide data or evidence in support of their ideas. Your task as a critical reader is twofold: first, identify the evidence, and second, weigh and evaluate the quality of this evidence.

In assessing the adequacy of evidence, consider the type of evidence and the relevance of that evidence. The following types of evidence are commonly used:

- personal experience or observation

- statistical data

- examples, particular events, or situations that illustrate an idea

- analogies (comparisons with similar situations)

- informed opinion (the opinions of experts and authorities)

- historical documentation

- experimental evidence

- research results

By evaluating the evidence an author uses to support an idea or opinion, you determine if the statement is accurate and believable or if the opinion is well reasoned.

Ask the following questions:

1. Is the evidence relevant?

2. How does the evidence support the main statement?

3. Is there a sufficient amount of evidence?

4. Is the evidence representative? That is, is the evidence typical of the body of information that is available—or did the author find an exceptional piece of evidence to support his or her statement?

5. Is there evidence available that the author did not report and that does not support his or her statement?

Not all of these questions are easily answered. In some situations, you may have to do additional research. With most textbooks, you can be confident that the author, a scholar and expert in the discipline, has provided you with relevant, representative evidence. However, when reading other sources, approach evidence with a questioning, critical viewpoint.

Make a list of the types of evidence that Tanner uses in "The Talk of the Sandbox."

## Strengthening Your Vocabulary

**Part A:** Using the word's context, word parts, or a dictionary, write a brief definition of each of the following words or phrases as it is used in the reading.

1. deference (paragraph 2) respect

2. authoritarian (paragraph 4) strict, severe, rigid, demanding obedience

3. intrigued (paragraph 8) interested or fascinated

4. compromise (paragraph 13) settlement of a dispute in which both parties agree to accept less than they originally wanted

5. adamant (paragraph. 15) set in opinion, determined not to be influenced or to reconsider

6. credibility (paragraph 21) *believability* _____

_____

**Part B:** Draw a word map of one of the words above.

### Reacting to Ideas: Discussion and Journal Writing

Use the following questions to generate ideas about the reading:

1. Did the author use point-by-point or subject-by-subject organization?

2. With what in the reading did you particularly agree or disagree with? Explain, using evidence from your own experience.

3. Should women be raised to be more assertive in their negotiations? If your answer is yes, why do you think so?

4. Do you agree that men and women communicate differently? If so, why?

## Writing About the Reading

### Paragraph Options

1. Drawing from the information contained in the reading, write a paragraph that compares how girls and boys play. Use a point-by-point organization.

2. Write a paragraph explaining one or more differences you have observed in how girls and boys play.

3. Write a paragraph comparing men and women on some other characteristic, such as use of emotion, aggressiveness, or nurturing ability.

### Essay Options

4. Write an essay defending or disagreeing with the author's generalization that some women seem to take undeserved blame, but "some men seem to evade deserved blame." Develop your essay through examples from your personal experience.

5. Write an essay defending or disagreeing with Tannen's view of men's or women's sports.

6. Write an essay describing a person you know who exhibits some or many of the characteristics Tannen identifies for that person's gender.

## Revision Checklist

1. Is your paragraph or essay appropriate for your audience? Does it give them the background information they need? Will it interest them?

2. Will your paragraph or essay accomplish your purpose?

3. Is your main point clearly expressed?

4. Is each detail relevant? Does each explain or support your main point?

5. Have you supported your main point with sufficient detail to make it understandable and believable?

6. Do you use specific words to explain each detail?

### For Comparison and Contrast Writing

7. Does your topic sentence or thesis statement identify the two subjects that you compare or contrast?

8. Does your topic sentence or thesis statement indicate whether you will focus on similarities, differences, or both?

9. Is your comparison and contrast writing organized using a subject-by-subject or point-by-point arrangement?

10. For each point of comparison, have you provided sufficient explanation, descriptive details, and examples?

11. Have you used transitions to indicate changes in subject or point of comparison?

12. Have you proofread? (See the inside back cover of this book for a proofreading checklist.)

# CHAPTER REVIEW AND PRACTICE

## Chapter Review

| | |
|---|---|
| WHAT DOES COMPARISON FOCUS ON? WHAT DOES CONTRAST FOCUS ON? | Comparison focuses on similarities. Contrast focuses on differences. |
| WHAT IS THE BEST WAY TO BRAINSTORM IDEAS FOR COMPARISON AND CONTRAST? | Use a two-column list. |
| WHAT ARE POINTS OF COMPARISON? | Points of comparison are the characteristics or features by which the subjects are examined. |
| WHAT SHOULD THE TOPIC SENTENCE OF A COMPARISON AND CONTRAST PARAGRAPH CONTAIN? | The topic sentence should:<br>• Identify the two subjects.<br>• Indicate whether the paragraph will focus on similarities, differences, or both. |
| WHAT IS SUBJECT-BY-SUBJECT ORGANIZATION? | Subject-by-subject organization focuses on the characteristics of one subject and then examines the characteristics of the second subject. |
| WHAT IS POINT-BY-POINT ORGANIZATION? | Point-by-point organization examines one subject and then the other according to each characteristic of the comparison. |
| WHAT ARE THE GUIDELINES FOR WRITING A COMPARISON AND CONTRAST ESSAY? | Guidelines include focusing on purpose, writing a clear thesis statement, using meaningful points of comparison, carefully following the chosen method of organization, and using transitions to guide the reader. |
| WHY ARE TRANSITIONS IMPORTANT IN COMPARISON AND CONTRAST PARAGRAPHS AND ESSAYS? | Transitions are important because two subjects are being discussed and readers can become confused. |

## Skill Refresher: Coordinate Sentences

Two or more equally important ideas can be combined into one sentence. Each idea must be an independent clause, which is a group of related words that contains a subject and a predicate and that can grammatically stand alone as a sentence. This type of sentence is called a **coordinate sentence.**

### How to Combine Ideas of Equal Importance

There are three ways to combine ideas of equal importance:

1. Join the two independent clauses with a comma and a coordinating conjunction (*and, so, for, but, yet, or, nor*).

   EXAMPLE   1. Russell recommended that we try the Mexican restaurant down the street.

   2. The restaurant turned out to be excellent.

   COMBINED   Russell recommended that we try the Mexican restaurant down the street, <u>and</u> it turned out to be excellent.

2. Join the two clauses by using a semicolon.

   EXAMPLE   1. The candidates for mayor made negative comments about each other.

   2. Many people disapproved of the candidates' tactics.

   COMBINED   The candidates for mayor made negative comments about each other<u>;</u> many people disapproved of their tactics.

3. Join the clauses by using a semicolon and a conjunctive adverb (a word such as *however, therefore, thus*) followed by a comma.

   EXAMPLE   1. Professor Sullivan did not discuss the chapter on polar winds.

   2. The exam included several questions on polar winds.

   COMBINED   Professor Sullivan did not discuss the chapter on polar winds<u>; however,</u> the exam included several questions on the topic.

### Rate Your Ability to Write Coordinate Sentences

Combine each of the following pairs of sentences to form coordinate sentences.   *Answers will vary.*

1. A field study observes subjects in their natural settings. Only a small number of subjects can be studied at one time.

2. The Grand Canyon is an incredible sight. It was formed less than ten million years ago.

3. Many anthropologists believe that Native Americans migrated to North and South America from Asia. Alaska and Siberia used to be connected 25 thousand years ago.

4. Neon, argon, and helium are called inert gases. They are never found in stable chemical compounds.

5. The professor returned the tests. He did not comment on them.

6. Ponce de Leon was successful because he was the first European to "discover" Florida. He did not succeed in finding the fountain of youth he was searching for.

7. The lecture focused on the cardiopulmonary system. The students needed to draw diagrams in their notes.

8. Rudy had never read *Hamlet*. Rufus had never read *Hamlet*.

9. Presidents Lincoln and Kennedy were assassinated. President Ford escaped two assassination attempts.

10. Marguerite might write her paper about *Moll Flanders*. She might write her paper about its author, Daniel Defoe.

Score _____

Check your answers, using the Answer Key on p. 642. If you missed more than two, you need additional review and practice in working with coordinate sentences. Refer to Part VI, "Reviewing the Basics" and, under section D, see "Coordination." For additional practice go to this book's Web site, http://www.ablongman.com/mcwhorterexpressways1e.

## INTERNET ACTIVITIES

### 1. Contrast/Comparison Flyer

Print out this guide from the Dallas Baptist University Writing Center. Use it to write a short essay using the topic provided in the guide.

http://www.dbu.edu/uwc/QR_Flyers/Specific_Assignments/Comparison.PDF

### 2. Comparing Apples and Oranges

Read this analysis of the old saying about not being able to compare apples and oranges.

http://www.improb.com/airchives/paperair/volume1/v1i3/air-1-3-apples.html

Make a list of other seemingly incomparable things and include ways that you could indeed compare them.

### 3. This Book's Web Site

Visit this site to find templates of idea maps and additional practice on skills taught in the chapter.

http://www.ablongman.com/mcwhorterexpressways1e

# 13

# Cause and Effect

## Chapter Objectives

*In this chapter
you will learn to:*

1. Understand cause-and-effect relationships.

2. Write effective topic sentences.

3. Develop and organize supporting details.

4. Use transitions effectively.

5. Write cause-and-effect essays.

## Write About It!

Study the photograph above. Write an explanation of what happened that caused the environmental damage shown. Also explain what might be done to prevent such damage.

You have just written a draft of a cause-and-effect paragraph. Cause and effect is concerned with why things happen (**cause**) and the result of an action or event (**effect**). Cause and effect is a common method of organizing and presenting information and you will encounter it frequently in everyday, academic, and workplace situations. In this chapter you will learn to use cause and effect in both paragraphs and essays.

EVERYDAY SCENARIOS

- A letter to a bank explaining why a loan payment is late
- A car-accident report to your insurance company explaining how an accident occurred

ACADEMIC SCENARIOS

- Essay exam questions that begin with "Explain why" or "Discuss the causes of"
- An assignment that asks you to agree or disagree with a statement and explain your reasons

WORKPLACE SCENARIOS

- A letter to a customer explaining why you can't reimburse her for an antique quilt damaged during dry cleaning
- A letter to a loan applicant explaining why the bank won't increase his home equity line of credit

# UNDERSTANDING CAUSE AND EFFECT

## What Is Cause and Effect?

Each day we face situations that require cause-and-effect analysis. Some are daily events; others mark important life decisions. Why won't my car start? Why didn't I get my student loan check? What will happen if I skip class today? How will my family react if I decide to get married? We seek to make sense of and control our lives by understanding cause-and-effect relationships. **Causes** are explanations of why things happen. **Effects** are explanations of what happens as a result of an action or event.

## EXERCISE 13-1

**Directions:** Working alone or with another student, brainstorm a list of times in your own life when cause and effect played an important role.

## Distinguishing Between Cause and Effect

How do we distinguish between cause and effect? To determine a cause, ask:

**"Why did this happen?"**

To identify an effect, ask:

**"What happened because of this?"**

Let's consider an everyday situation: You turn the ignition key, but your car won't start because it's out of gas. This is a simple case in which one cause produces one effect. You can diagram this situation as follows:

**Visualize It!**

Here are a few other examples of one cause producing one effect:

**Visualize It!**

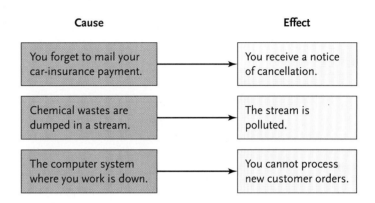

Most situations, however, are much more complicated than those shown above, and even a simple cause-and-effect sequence may contain hidden complexities. Perhaps your car was out of gas because you forgot to buy gas, and you forgot because you were making preparations for the upcoming visit of a good friend. Suppose you missed your math class because the car would not start, and an exam was scheduled for that day. Missing the exam lowered your average, and as a result, you failed the course.

You can see, then, that cause and effect often works like a chain reaction: one cause triggers an effect, which in turn becomes the cause of another effect. In a chain reaction, each event in a series influences the next, as shown in the following example:

**Visualize It!**

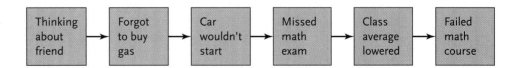

At other times, many causes may contribute to a single effect, as shown in the following diagram:

**Visualize It!**

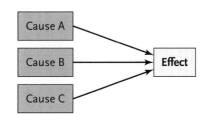

For example, there may be several reasons why you decided to major in accounting:

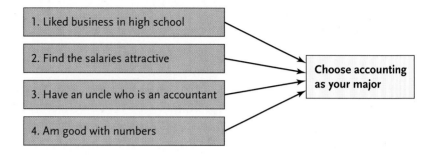

At other times, a single cause can have multiple effects, as shown below:

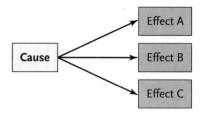

Suppose, for example, you decide to reduce your hours at your part-time job:

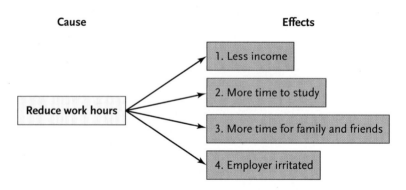

Multiple causes and multiple effects, then, are common. When analyzing a cause-and-effect situation that you plan to write about, ask yourself the following questions:

1. What are the causes? What are the effects? (To help answer these questions, draw a diagram of the situation.)

2. Which should be emphasized—cause or effect?

3. Is there a single cause or are there multiple causes? Single or multiple effects?

4. Is a chain reaction involved?

# EXERCISE 13-2

*Writing in Progress*

**Directions:** Complete each of the following diagrams by adding a cause or an effect, as needed. The first one is done for you. Answers will vary.

## Visualize It! ➤

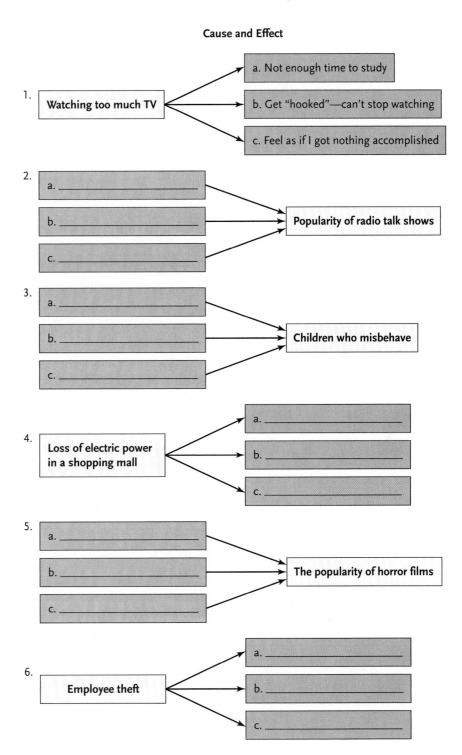

**Cause and Effect**

1. Watching too much TV
   a. Not enough time to study
   b. Get "hooked"—can't stop watching
   c. Feel as if I got nothing accomplished

2. a. _____
   b. _____
   c. _____
   → Popularity of radio talk shows

3. a. _____
   b. _____
   c. _____
   → Children who misbehave

4. Loss of electric power in a shopping mall
   a. _____
   b. _____
   c. _____

5. a. _____
   b. _____
   c. _____
   → The popularity of horror films

6. Employee theft
   a. _____
   b. _____
   c. _____

## Writing Your Topic Sentence

To write effective topic sentences for cause-and-effect paragraphs, do the following:

1. **Clarify the cause-and-effect relationship.** Before you write, carefully identify the causes and the effects. If you are uncertain, divide a sheet of paper into two columns. Label one column "Causes" and the other "Effects." Brainstorm about your topic, placing your ideas in the appropriate column.

2. **Decide whether to emphasize causes or effects.** In a single paragraph, it is best to focus on either causes or effects—not both. For example, suppose you are writing about students who drop out of college. You need to decide whether to discuss why they drop out (causes) or what happens to students who drop out (effects). Your topic sentence should indicate whether you are going to emphasize causes or effects. (In essays, you may consider both causes and effects.)

3. **Determine if the events are related or independent.** Analyze the causes or effects to discover if they occurred as part of a chain reaction or if they are not related to one another. Your topic sentence should suggest the type of relationship about which you are writing. If you are writing about a chain of events, your topic sentence should reflect this—for example, "A series of events led up to my sister's decision to drop out of college." If the causes or effects are not related to one another, then your sentence should indicate that—for example, "Students drop out of college for a number of different reasons."

Now read the following paragraph that a sales representative wrote to her regional manager to explain why she had failed to meet a monthly quota. Then study the diagram that accompanies it. Notice that the topic sentence makes it clear that she is focusing on the causes (circumstances) that led to her failure to make her sales quota for the month.

> In the past, I have always met or exceeded my monthly sales quota at Thompson's Office Furniture. This January I was $20,000 short, due to a set of unusual and uncontrollable circumstances in my territory. The month began with a severe snowstorm that closed most businesses in the area for most of the first week. Travel continued to be a problem the remainder of the week, and many purchasing agents did not report to work. Once they were back at their desks, they were not eager to meet with sales reps; instead, they wanted to catch up with their backlog of paperwork. Later that month, an ice storm resulted in power losses, again closing most plants for almost two days. Finally, some of our clients took extended weekends over the Martin Luther King holiday. Overall, my client contact days were reduced by more than 25%, yet my sales were only 15% below the quota.

# Visualize It!

Causes                                          Effect

Snowstorm closed businesses

Ice storm closed plants                          I was $20,000 short

Extended MLK holiday

## EXERCISE 13-3
*Writing in Progress*

**Directions:** Review the diagrams you made for Exercise 13-2. For each situation, write a topic sentence for a paragraph that will explain either its causes *or* effects.

## Organizing Supporting Details

Providing supporting details for cause-and-effect paragraphs requires careful thought and planning. Details must be relevant, sufficient, and effectively organized.

### Providing Relevant and Sufficient Details

Each cause or effect you describe must be relevant to the situation introduced in your topic sentence. Suppose you are writing a paragraph explaining why you are attending college. Each sentence must explain this topic. You could not include ideas, for example, about how college is different from what you expected.

If, while writing, you discover you have more ideas about how college is different from what you expected than you do about your reasons for attending college, you need to revise your topic sentence in order to refocus your paragraph.

Each cause or reason requires explanation, particularly if it is *not* obvious. For example, it is not sufficient to write, "One reason I decided to attend college was to advance my position in life." This sentence needs further explanation. For example, you could discuss the types of advancement (financial, job security, job satisfaction) you hope to attain.

Jot down a list of the causes or reasons you plan to include. This process may help you think of additional causes and will give you a chance to consider how to explain or support each one. You might decide to eliminate one or to combine several. Here is one student's list of reasons for attending college.

# Visualize It!

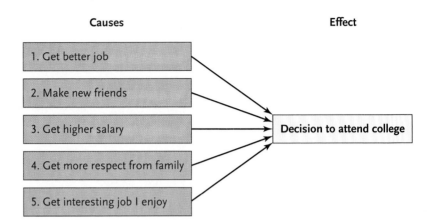

By listing his reasons, this student realized that the first one—to get a better job—was too general and was covered more specifically later in the list, so he eliminated it. He also realized that "get higher salary" and "get interesting job" could be combined. He then wrote the following paragraph:

There are three main reasons I decided to attend Ambrose Community College. First, and most important to me, I want to get a high-paying, interesting job that I will enjoy. Right now, the only jobs I can get pay minimum wage, and as a result, I'm working in a fast-food restaurant. This kind of job doesn't make me proud of myself, and I get bored with routine tasks. Second, my parents have always wanted me to have a better job than they do, and I know my father will not respect me until I do. A college degree would make them proud of me. A third reason for attending college is to make new friends. It is hard to meet people, and everyone in my neighborhood seems stuck in a rut. I want to meet other people who are interested in improving themselves like I am.

## Organizing Your Details

There are several ways to arrange the details in a cause-and-effect paragraph. The method you choose depends on your purpose in writing, as well as your topic. Suppose you are writing a paragraph about the effects of a hurricane on a coastal town. Several different arrangements of details are possible:

1. **Chronological** A chronological organization arranges your details in the order in which situations or events happened. The order in which the hurricane damage occurred becomes the order for your details. This arrangement is similar to the arrangement you learned in Chapter 6, "Narration." A chronological arrangement works for situations and events that occurred in a specific order.

2. **Order of importance** In an order-of-importance organization, the details are arranged from least to most important or from most to least important. In describing the effects of the hurricane, you could discuss the most severe damage first and then describe lesser damage. Alternatively, you could build up from the least to the most important damage for dramatic effect.

3. **Spatial** Spatial arrangement of details uses physical or geographical position as a means of organization. In describing the hurricane damage, you could start by describing damage to the beach and work toward the center of town.

4. **Categorical** This form of arrangement divides the topic into parts or categories. Using this arrangement to describe hurricane damage, you could recount what the storm did to businesses, roads, city services, and homes.

As the hurricane example shows, there are many ways to organize cause-and-effect details. Each has a different emphasis and achieves a different purpose. The organization you choose, then, depends on the point you want to make.

Once you decide on a method of organization, return to your preliminary list of effects. Study your list again, make changes, eliminate, or combine. Then rearrange or number the items on your list to indicate the order in which you will include them.

## EXERCISE 13-4

**Directions:** Choose one of the following topic sentences and develop a paragraph using it. Organize your paragraph by using one of the methods described above.

1. Exercise has several positive (or negative) effects on the body.

2. Professional athletes deserve (or do not deserve) the high salaries they are paid.

3. There are several reasons why parents should reserve time each day to spend with their children.

4. Many students work two or even three part-time jobs; the results are often disastrous.

## EXERCISE 13-5

*Writing in Progress*

**Directions:** Write a paragraph developing one of the topic sentences you wrote for Exercise 13-3. Be sure to include relevant and sufficient details. Organize your paragraph according to one of the methods described above.

## Useful Transitions

To blend your details smoothly, use the transitional words and phrases listed below.

Table 13-1  **Transitions for Cause-and-Effect Paragraphs**

| For causes | For effects |
| --- | --- |
| because, due to, one cause is . . . , another is . . . , since, for, first, second | consequently, as a result, thus, resulted in, one result is . . . , another is . . . , therefore |

The student paragraph on p. 000 is a good example of how transitional words and phrases are used. Notice how these transitions function as markers and help you to locate each separate reason.

## EXERCISE 13-6

**Directions:** In each blank provided, supply a transitional word or phrase that strengthens the connection between the two ideas.

1. Many companies have day care centers for children. _____As a result,_____ employees are able to manage child care problems easily.

2. Computers provide an easy way to store and process information quickly. _____Consequently,_____ computers have become an integral part of most businesses.

3. Animal skins are warm and very durable; _____therefore,_____ almost every culture has made use of them for clothing or shelter.

4. _____Because_____ some people refused to accept his views and beliefs, Martin Luther King, Jr., was brutally murdered.

## EXERCISE 13-7
*Writing in Progress*

**Directions:** Reread the paragraphs you wrote for Exercises 13-4 and 13-5. Add transitional words and phrases, if needed, to connect your details.

## Applying Your Skills to Essay Writing: Cause and Effect

When writing cause-and-effect essays, keep the following suggestions in mind:

1. **Write an effective thesis statement.** Be sure that your thesis statement states the cause-and-effect relationship clearly and directly. Do not leave it for your reader to figure out what the relationship is. Here is an example:

   WEAK, INDIRECT THESIS    Temperatures can be dangerous for animals. Many suffer from heat stroke or dehydration.

   CLEAR, DIRECT THESIS    High summer temperatures can be dangerous for household pets because they can cause heat stroke or dehydration.

2. **Remember your purpose for writing as you plan your essay.** There are two main purposes for writing cause-and-effect essays:

   - to inform

   - to persuade

   For example, you may be writing to explain the effects of cigarette smoking or to convince your reader that the effects of smoking are harmful. Focus your essay to suit your purpose and choose details accordingly.

3. **Focus on primary—immediate and direct—causes or effects.** Unless you are writing a lengthy paper, it is best to limit yourself to primary causes or effects. Secondary causes or effects—those that occur later or are indirectly related—may confuse and distract your reader. For example, the immediate effects of cigarette smoking would include physical effects on smokers and those around them. The secondary effects might include higher medical insurance rates due to the costs of treating smoking-related illnesses.

4. **Strengthen your essay by using supporting evidence.** In explaining causes and/or effects, you may need to define terms, offer facts and statistics, or provide examples, anecdotes, or personal observations that support your ideas.

5. **Be cautious in determining cause-and-effect relationships.** Many errors in logic can occur in regard to cause-and-effect relationships. Do not assume that because one event occurs close in time to another, it caused the other or that they are even related.

6. **Qualify or limit your statements about cause-and-effect relationships.** Unless there is clear, indisputable evidence that one event is related to another, qualify your statements by using such wording as "It appears that the cause was . . ." or "Available evidence suggests. . . ."

## NEED TO KNOW

### Avoiding Errors in Logical Reasoning

Cause-and-effect relationships are often complex and it is easy to make errors when thinking and writing about them. Here are three ways to avoid common errors:

1. **Do not overlook underlying causes.** While it may appear that one thing causes another, it is possible that what you perceive as a cause may be only a symptom. For example, if a person complains of abdominal pain and is vomiting, you may think he or she just has a stomachache. However, it is possible the person has appendicitis, the pain and vomiting are actually symptoms, and an infected appendix is the true cause of the discomfort. To avoid this type of error, be sure to look for hidden, underlying causes rather than simply accepting an obvious explanation of an event.

2. **Do not assume that things that follow one another cause one another.** Just because Event Y follows Event X, it is not necessarily true that one caused the other. For example, an advertisement shows a family eating a particular brand of breakfast cereal and then shows everyone having a successful day at school and at work. The ad suggests that eating the cereal caused everyone to have a good day. To avoid this error, be sure to look for evidence that establishes the cause-and-effect relationship.

3. **Do not make the mistake of thinking things that happen at the same time are automatically related.** Because two events happen at once does not necessarily mean that one caused the other. For example, increased sales in beach umbrellas could occur at the same time that sales of portable fans increase. It is not logical to assume that the sale of beach umbrellas caused the increased sales of fans. More likely, both were caused by a heat wave. To avoid this error, check for evidence that connects the two events.

## EXERCISE 13-8

**Directions:** Suppose you are taking a course in education and have been assigned a paper. Select one of the following topics and write a one-page paper on it.

1. Watch a television show or movie that contains violence, and consider what it might teach a young child watching it alone about what is right and wrong, and about how people behave and should behave. Summarize your findings.

2. Talk to or think of someone who has dropped out of high school. What problems facing that person seem to be related to dropping out? Summarize your findings.

3. What are the effects of the course registration system used at your school? As you answer this question, use examples to support your points.

# AN ACADEMIC SCENARIO
## A STUDENT ESSAY
### The Academic Writer and the Writing Task

Veronica Evans-Johnson is a student at Durham Technical College where she is studying criminal justice. For her writing class, Veronica was asked to write a cause-and-effect essay; she

chose to write about the causes of procrastination. As you read, notice that she devotes one paragraph to each cause of procrastination.

*Straightforward title that identifies the subject of the essay*

## Causes of Procrastination
### Veronica Evans-Johnson

*Definition of the term*

*Thesis statement*

Do you put off difficult or unpleasant tasks until tomorrow? If so, you are guilty of procrastination. Procrastination is the habit of putting off work or tasks that you are responsible for doing. It is a habit many people have and one they find it hard to break. There are a variety of reasons why people procrastinate, and whatever the cause, the results of procrastination are always the same—frustration.

*Cause 1*

Procrastination is common among students. Some students may lack the skills needed to complete an assignment and would rather put off doing the work than risk feeling "stupid." For instance, if a student does not know how to locate sources to complete a research paper, he or she, instead of facing this problem, may postpone writing the research paper until the night

*Example*

*Effect*

before it is due. By not facing his or her inability to conduct research and by not getting help from a college librarian, this student runs the risks of getting a poor grade, failing a course, or worse.

*Cause 2*

Other students put off doing homework because it's just not fun. They would rather have a good time than tackle the work in front of them. They may think they can leave their assignments until the last minute and still get them done on time, but usually the work suffers. The result may be a bad

*Effect*

grade and the frustration of knowing that they would have received a much better grade if they'd spent more time preparing.

*Cause 3*

Another common cause behind many people's tendency to put things off is poor work habits. Many students have trouble organizing, prioritizing tasks, and scheduling time. This problem is complicated by the fact that many students are so busy, working full-time or multiple jobs, caring for family, doing housework and going to school that they're exhausted and can't *make* the time to get organized.

Cause 4

There are also many emotional and psychological causes for procrastinating. Fear of failure and fear of success are opposite sides of the same coin, but equally troubling. One person may believe that no matter what he or she does, failure is inevitable. Another person may be afraid of the attention or added responsibilities that success would bring. Still someone else may feel overwhelmed by the size of a project and not know where to start. And then there are the perfectionists. These people set unrealistic goals and hold themselves to impossible standards. They feel they have no choice but to put off doing things until conditions are just right—which, if you're a perfectionist, is never.

Addresses cures for procrastination

Unfortunately, we all face doing things at some time in our lives that we dislike. It could be housework, balancing a checkbook, or writing a report. Rather than wishing away unpleasant tasks, try to identify the reason you don't want to do them. Preparation is also a good cure for procrastination. Identify the task, make a list of what needs to get done and in what order, and set priorities. If a task seems huge and overwhelming, try breaking it down into separate parts and set aside a small amount of time for each. Every time one small part is completed, the overall task becomes smaller. This can make a big project more manageable.

Conclusion: refers back to the frustration mentioned in the first paragraph

Finally, whatever your reason for procrastinating, take a good, hard look at it. If you stop putting off the things that need to be done today, you'll be taking a big step toward a life of fewer frustrations tomorrow.

## Examining Academic Writing

1. How does Evans-Johnson personally engage the reader?

2. Do you think more examples would have improved the essay?

3. Evans-Johnson presents effects for causes annotated as 1 and 2, but does not do so for 3 and 4. Should she have done so?

4. Suggest ways Evans-Johnson could make the introduction more lively and interesting.

5. Are there causes of procrastination that the author did not address?

## Academic Writing Assignments

1. You are taking a course in computer basics. Your instructor has asked the class to write a paragraph explaining why spamming—the process of sending advertisements to a large number of e-mail addresses—is a wasteful practice.

2. For a health and wellness class, you have been asked to choose an unhealthy practice or habit and to write an essay explaining why it is unhealthy. (You might choose smoking, binge drinking, or overeating, for example.)

3. In your criminal justice class you are studying white collar crimes—non-violent crimes that are carried out in one's place of employment. Write a paragraph exploring reasons why an employee might commit a crime against his or her company.

# A WORKPLACE SCENARIO
## WRITING A SPEECH
### The Workplace Writer and the Writing Task

Glen Corma is the owner of Glennie's Restaurant. As a small business owner, he was asked to give a speech at a meeting of the American Express Establishment Services convention. The text of his speech, which is shown below, explains the reasons he chose to accept the American Express credit card at his restaurant. As you read, identify and highlight each reason.

Text of the Speech:

You know the old saying "never say never"? It's true. My being here is proof that you shouldn't ever say never.

When I opened my restaurant Glennie's back in 2002, I said I would never take the American Express card. At the time, American Express rates were high and MasterCard and Visa's were low. I thought the extra expense wasn't worth it. AmEx tried to persuade me of the value of taking the card; that card holders spend more on eating out and that I'd pick up a lot more corporate business. But it would have cost me over $10,000.00 a year to accept the card and at the time I didn't think I needed it. Glennie's was constantly booked and, in fact, I joked that we didn't have room to seat American Express card holders! So I said "never" to AmEx and forgot about it.

As time went on, other restaurants opened in the area. Suddenly I had competition I'd never had before. And I noticed that some customers would leave when they found out I didn't take AmEx, choosing to eat at one of the competitors who did. Still, business was good and I figured I didn't need them.

Then, three things happened in rapid succession. First, American Express rolled back its rates. Second, one day a new customer came into the restaurant. When it came time to pay and he found out we didn't take American Express, he went ballistic. He stood there, in front of all my regulars, yelling that he couldn't believe a restaurant of this stature wouldn't take American Express. Now, I assume that if someone's got an American Express card, they've got other cards. And he did—but he wouldn't use them. All of his other cards were personal accounts and this was a business lunch. No way was he going to spend his own money and do all the paperwork to get reimbursed when he had a company AmEx card.

The third thing was the final straw. One of my regular customers ate at one of the new restaurants that had opened near me. He came into Glennie's the next day and gave his report: the food wasn't as good, the décor was boring—and he planned to go back. Why? You guessed it; they took his American Express card.

316 Chapter 13 ■ Cause and Effect

> I realized that in today's competitive environment, I couldn't afford to keep saying "Never!" to American Express. So I signed up. And six months later, I know what an important decision it was. Forty-four percent of the American Express charges coming in are from corporate clients. And they do spend more.
>
> Here's even more proof; even though we didn't do any advertising, within one week 50 percent of the charges at Glennie's went to American Express. And customers I hadn't seen in months started coming back on a regular basis.
>
> Last week, an account rep from American Express came in for lunch. He wanted to make sure there weren't any problems and he wanted to try Glennie's for himself. He asked my wife and me to join him, ordered enough food for ten people, and picked up the check.
>
> How did he pay? With his American Express card, of course!
>
> And so, ladies and gentlemen, I leave you with a promise: I will never say never again.

## Examining Workplace Writing

1. Was Glen's speech informative or persuasive (intended to get listeners to agree with him)?

2. Was Glen's speech interesting and engaging? If so, why?

3. Evaluate Glen's introduction and conclusion. Why are they effective?

4. In what ways does speech writing differ from traditional essays written to be read in print?

## Workplace Writing Assignments

1. You work for your town's summer recreation department as a life-guard at the local pool. There have been several accidents, all minor, but people were injured. Your supervisor has asked you to write a notice about pool safety to post at the entrance. Write a list of do's and don'ts (causes) that will result in pool safety and reduce accidents (effects).

2. You have a part-time job as a sales clerk in a candy shop. Customers often ask you for samples, but company policy does not allow you to give them out. Write a memo to your boss explaining the advantages (effects) of giving free samples to serious customers.

3. You own a local car wash and have received a number of customer complaints about your employees' attitude toward and treatment of them. Write a memo to your employees suggesting behaviors (causes) that will promote customer satisfaction (effects).

# WRITING ABOUT A READING

## Thinking Before Reading

The following article, "Why We Love Bad News," first appeared in *Psychology Today Magazine*. In it, the writer Hara Marano reports on the research of two scientists that explains why negative information has a stronger impact than positive information and shows how this affects our lives. As you read, identify both causes and effects.

1. Preview the reading using the steps described in Chapter 2, p. 30.

2. Activate your thinking by answering the following questions:

    **a.** When someone says, "I have good news and bad news . . . ," which do you usually ask to hear first? Why?

    **b.** Imagine you have a job that pays well, but a boss who never has anything positive to say about your work. Would you continue in that job or look elsewhere?

### READING

# Why We Love Bad News

#### Hara Marano

1   Why do insults once hurled at us stick inside our skull, sometimes for decades? Why do political smear campaigns outpull positive ones?

2   The answer is, nastiness makes a bigger impact on your brain.

3   And that, says Ohio State University psychologist John T. Cacioppo, Ph.D., is due to the brain's "negativity bias": your brain is simply built with a greater sensitivity to unpleasant news. The bias is so automatic that it can be detected at the earliest stage of the brain's information processing.

4   In studies he has done, Cacioppo showed people pictures known to arouse positive feelings (such as a Ferrari or a pizza), those certain to stir up negative feelings (like a mutilated face or dead cat) and those known to produce neutral feelings (a plate, a hair dryer). Meanwhile, he recorded electrical activity of the brain's **cerebral cortex** that reflects the magnitude of information processing taking place.

5   The brain, Cacioppo demonstrated, reacts more strongly to stimuli it deems negative. That is, there is a greater surge in electrical activity. Thus,

**cerebral cortex**

a layer of gray matter that covers the brain and coordinates sensory and motor information

our attitudes are more heavily influenced by downbeat news than good news.

6    Our capacity to weigh negative input so heavily evolved for a good reason—to keep us out of harm's way. From the dawn of human history our very survival depended on our skill at dodging danger. The brain developed systems that would make it unavoidable for us not to notice danger and thus, hopefully, respond to it.

7    All well and good. Having the built-in brain apparatus supersensitive to negativity means that the same bias also is at work in every sphere of our lives at all times.

8    So it should come as no surprise to learn that it plays an especially powerful role in our most intimate relationships. Numerous researchers have found that there is "an ecology of marriage," an ideal balance between negativity and positivity in the atmosphere between partners.

9    Psychologist John Gottman, Ph.D., at the University of Washington is one. He finds that there seems to be some kind of thermostat operating in healthy marriages that regulates the balance between positive and negative. For example, when partners get contemptuous—that is, when they fight by hurling criticism with the intent to insult the partner, which the partner rightly perceives as especially hurtful—they correct it with lots of positivity—touching, smiling, paying compliments, laughing, and other such acts. They don't correct necessarily right away, but they definitely do it sometime soon.

10    What really separates contented couples from those in deep marital misery is a healthy balance between their positive and negative feelings and actions toward each other. Even couples who are volatile and argue a lot stick together by balancing their frequent arguments with a lot of demonstrations of love and passion.

equilibrium
balance

11    Because of the disproportionate weight of the negative, balance does not mean a 50-50 **equilibrium**. Gottman, for example, as part of his research carefully charted the amount of time couples spent fighting versus interacting positively. Across the board he found that a very specific ratio exists between the amount of positivity and negativity required to make a marriage satisfying.

12    That magic ratio is 5 to 1. As long as there is five times as much positive feeling and interaction between husband and wife as there is negative, the marriage was likely to be stable over time. In contrast, those couples who were heading for divorce were doing far too little on the positive side to compensate for the growing negativity between them.

13    Other researchers have found the same thing. It is the frequency of small positive acts that matters most, in a ratio of about 5 to 1.

14    Interestingly, occasional large positive experiences—say, a big birthday bash—are nice, but they don't make the necessary impact on our brain to override the tilt to negativity. It takes frequent small positive experiences to tip the scales toward happiness.

---

## Getting Ready to Write

### Reviewing the Reading

1.  State the author's thesis in your own words.

2.  Why do candidates who run negative campaign ads get more votes than other politicians?

3.  How did Dr. Cacioppo prove his theory about the brain's reaction to positive and negative stimuli?

4.  What group of people did John Gottman study?

5.  Explain what a 5-to-1 ratio means.

### Examining the Reading: Using an Idea Map to Grasp Cause-and-Effect Relationships

"Why We Love Bad News" explores why the brain instinctively reacts to negative information and how this can affect our lives, particularly our personal relationships. Complete the map of the reading on the following page. You will notice that it first examines causes and then moves to effects:

### Thinking Critically: Evaluating Cause-and-Effect Relationships

Even though scientific research is usually accepted as sound, different influences can affect the outcome of an experiment. These influences are called "variables." For example, suppose a researcher gives a group of people a dose of vitamins and find that the group is healthier than a group of people who did not take the vitamins. What factors (variables) other than the vitamins could account for the differences? If the non-vitamin group ate a healthier diet than the vitamin-taking group, diet is a variable that could account for the differences.

Think of some variables that might have caused Dr. Cacioppo and Dr. Gottman's experiments to have different outcomes. Answer the following questions to help you analyze variables that affect cause-and-effect relationships.

1.  How could gender (using only men or only women) affect the outcome of the studies?

# Visualize It!

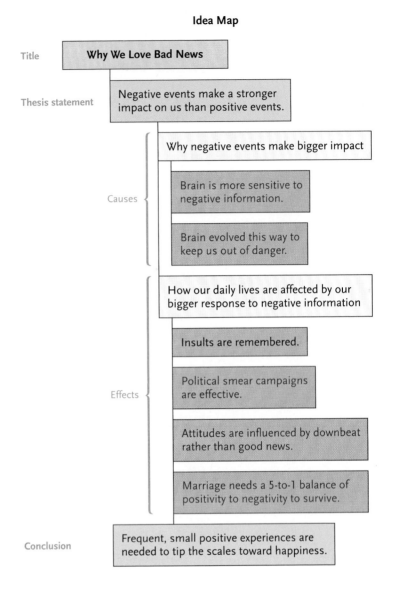

**Idea Map**

**Title** — Why We Love Bad News

**Thesis statement** — Negative events make a stronger impact on us than positive events.

**Causes**
- Why negative events make bigger impact
  - Brain is more sensitive to negative information.
  - Brain evolved this way to keep us out of danger.

**Effects**
- How our daily lives are affected by our bigger response to negative information
  - Insults are remembered.
  - Political smear campaigns are effective.
  - Attitudes are influenced by downbeat rather than good news.
  - Marriage needs a 5-to-1 balance of positivity to negativity to survive.

**Conclusion** — Frequent, small positive experiences are needed to tip the scales toward happiness.

2. How might age affect the outcome of the studies? Would children and adults have the same or different responses?

3. How might educational level affect the outcome of the studies? Would people with graduate degrees respond differently than people who did not go to college?

## Strengthening Your Vocabulary

**Part A:** Using the word's context, word parts, or a dictionary, write a brief definition of each of the following words or phrases as it is used in the reading.

1. bias (paragraph 3) *preference, prejudice*

2. stimuli (paragraph 5) plural of "stimulus," something that causes a reaction

3. input (paragraph 6) information that a person takes in

4. sphere (paragraph 7) area of interest, subject

5. volatile (paragraph 10) explosive, unstable, hot-tempered

6. disproportionate (paragraph 11) unequal, lopsided, unbalanced

7. compensate (paragraph 12) to make up for something, to make amends

**Part B:** Draw a word map of one of the words above.

## Reacting to Ideas: Discussion and Journal Writing

1. Knowing that the brain reacts more strongly to negative stimuli, can you think of places you would never want to work or jobs you would never consider taking?

2. Do you think a test could be developed to determine what kind of relationship couples will have *before* they get married? If so, would you take the test?

3. Based on the 5-to-1 ratio, what could a boss do to make a workplace better? Give some examples.

4. If a teacher corrected you in front of the whole class one day, then brought in a cake the next day, which do you think you would remember longer? Why?

## Writing About the Reading

### Paragraph Options

1. Think about something that happened in your life that seemed big at the time, but really didn't have much effect on the rest of your life. Write a paragraph that describes what happened, how you felt about it then, and how you feel about it now.

2. Imagine you are doing the same research as Dr. Cacioppo and Dr. Gottman. You have to pick three pictures to show your subjects. Describe your pictures in detail. Predict which picture will cause the most brain activity in your subjects and which the least.

3. Write a paragraph about a partner, spouse, or friend who once insulted you or did something nasty to you. How did it affect your relationship with that person?

## Essay Options

4. Choose a small experience that had a big effect on your life (see paragraph 14 of the reading). Write an essay about this experience and why you think it made such an impact.

5. Besides a 5-to-1 ratio of positive to negative input, what are some other factors that make a good relationship? List some of these factors and use examples to show how they might make a couple happy.

## Revision Checklist

1. Is your paragraph or essay appropriate for your audience? Does it give them the background information they need? Will it interest them?

2. Will your paragraph or essay accomplish your purpose?

3. Is your main point clearly expressed?

4. Is each detail relevant? Does each explain or support your main point?

5. Have you supported your main point with sufficient detail to make it understandable and believable?

6. Do you use specific and vivid words to explain each detail?

### For Cause-and-Effect Writing

7. Does your topic sentence or thesis statement indicate whether you will emphasize causes or effects?

8. Does your topic sentence or thesis statement indicate whether the events you are describing are related or independent?

9. Are your details presented in one of the following arrangements: chronological, order of importance, spatial, or categorical?

10. Have you used transitional words and phrases to blend your details smoothly?

11. Have you proofread? (See the inside back cover of this book for a proofreading checklist.)

# CHAPTER REVIEW AND PRACTICE

## Chapter Review

| | |
|---|---|
| WHAT IS CAUSE AND EFFECT? | **Cause** focuses on the reasons an event or behavior happened. **Effect** is the explanation of what happens as a result of an action or event. |
| WHAT SHOULD YOUR TOPIC SENTENCE CONTAIN? | It should identify the cause-and-effect relationship, and focus on either causes or effects. |
| HOW SHOULD THE DETAILS BE ORGANIZED? | Three common choices are chronological, order of importance, spatial, and categorical. |
| WHAT ARE THE GUIDELINES FOR WRITING CAUSE-AND-EFFECT ESSAYS? | Write a strong thesis, focus on primary causes or effects, provide adequate supporting evidence, avoid logical errors, and qualify or limit the cause-and-effect relationship. |

## Skill Refresher: Subordinate Clauses

Subordination is a way of showing that one idea is less important than another. When an idea is related to another idea, but less important, the less important idea can be expressed as a dependent clause. Dependent clauses contain a subject and a verb but do not express a complete thought and cannot stand alone as grammatically complete sentences. They are always used in combination with a complete sentence or an independent clause.

### One Way to Combine Ideas of Unequal Importance

When a less important idea is combined with one of greater importance, it is helpful to show how the ideas relate to one another. Use a word such as *after, although, before, while, when,* and *because* to begin the dependent clause and show its relationship to the more important idea. For a more complete list of these words used to join an independent and a dependent clause, see section D.4, on p. 600. In the examples that follow, the subordinating conjunctions are underlined.

After I finished the exam, I went to the coffee shop. [The word *after* indicates that the two ideas are related in time.]

Because I missed the bus, I was late for work. [The word *because* indicates that missing the bus was the reason for being late.]

I won't be able to make my tuition payment <u>unless</u> my student loan comes in soon. [The word *unless* indicates that the tuition payment depends on the student loan.]

The two clauses can appear in either order. When the dependent clause appears first, a comma follows it. (Refer to the first and second examples above.) When the independent clause comes first, a comma is usually not needed. (See the third example above.)

## Rate Your Ability to Use Subordinate Clauses

Combine each of the following pairs of sentences to form a sentence in which one idea is more important than the other. Add or delete words as necessary.

1. He was an insurance agent. Now he's a banker.

2. Grape juice is fermented. Grape juice becomes wine.

3. It is important for children to be immunized. Children who are not immunized are vulnerable to many dangerous diseases.

4. A poem should be read carefully. Next, it should be analyzed.

5. My boss is very knowledgeable. She has no sense of humor at all.

6. I was giving a speech in my communications class. At the same time, Richard Rodriguez was giving a speech on campus.

7. I started my assignment for French class. I was relieved that it was a very easy assignment.

8. Infants may seem unaware of their surroundings. They are able to recognize their mother's voice and smell from birth.

9. She loves to travel. She wants to become a travel agent.

10. The hypothalamus is a tiny part of the brain. It has many very important functions, including the regulation of hormones, body temperature, and hunger.

Score _____

Check your answers, using the Answer Key on p. 643. If you missed more than two, you need additional review and practice in working with subordinate clauses. Refer to Part VI, "Reviewing the Basics," and under section D, see "Subordination." For additional practice go to this book's Web site at http://www.ablongman.com/mcwhorterexpressways1e.

## INTERNET ACTIVITIES

### 1. Your Decisions

Use this worksheet from El Paso Community College to organize an essay about the causes and effects of a decision that you have made.

http://www.epcc.edu/Student/Tutorial/Writingcenter/Handouts/
essaytypes/Handouts/CauseandEffect.pdf

Consider actually composing the essay for practice.

### 2. Youth Homelessness

Skim this information from the City of Seattle about youth homelessness.

http://www.seattle.gov/humanservices/fys/HomelessYouth/
HomelessYMyths.htm#Underlying

Write a paragraph summarizing the causes and effects described here.

### 3. This Book's Web Site

Visit this site to find templates of idea maps for cause and effect and additional practice on skills taught in the chapter.

http://www.ablongman.com/mcwhorterexpressways1e

# 14

# Argument

## Chapter Objectives

*In this chapter you will learn to:*

1. Write argument paragraphs and essays.

2. Identify an issue.

3. Present a position on the issue.

4. Develop convincing support for the position.

5. Write effective topic sentences.

## Write About It!

Study the above photograph. What issues does the photograph address? Choose one issue. Write a paragraph that answers the following questions: What position (pro or con) does the bumper sticker take on the issue? What are the possible reasons for agreeing with this position?

The paragraph you have just written is a brief argument. An **argument** presents logical reasons and evidence to support a point of view on an issue. Many everyday, academic, and workplace situations require you to use argument. A few examples are shown below. In this chapter you will learn how to plan an argument, select convincing reasons and evidence to support it, and present them effectively.

EVERYDAY SCENARIOS

- An effort to convince your manager that you need Saturday nights off
- A plan for an evening out with friends that urges them to see a particular movie

ACADEMIC SCENARIOS

- A sociology paper defending or rejecting a new theory
- A position paper for environmental science on pollution controls for industry
- An essay on your college goals for a scholarship application

WORKPLACE SCENARIOS

- A memo defending a budget request
- A letter to support an employee's promotion
- A proposal to secure a contract with a prospective client

# UNDERSTANDING ARGUMENT

## What Is Argumentative Writing?

An **argument** is line of reasoning intended to persuade the reader or listener to agree with a particular viewpoint or take a particular action. If you turn on the television or radio, or open a magazine or newspaper, you are sure to encounter the most common form of argument—advertising. Commercials and ads are attempts to persuade you to buy a particular product or service. Here are a few examples:

1. "You've tried just about everything for your hay fever.... Now try your doctor. Your doctor has an advanced prescription medicine called Seldane that can relieve your allergy symptoms without causing drowsiness."

2. "We fit a square meal into a round bowl. (So we didn't have room for the fat.)—Healthy Choice."

## EXERCISE 14-1

**Directions:** Working alone or with another student, brainstorm a list of situations in which you have recently used argument.

## The Parts of an Argument

An argument presents reasons for accepting a belief or position or for taking a specific action. It has three essential parts:

- **An issue** This is the problem or controversy that the argument addresses. It is also the topic of an argument paragraph.

- **A position** A position is the particular point of view a writer has on an issue. There are always at least two points of view on an issue—pro and con. For example, you may be for or against gun control. You may favor or oppose lowering the legal drinking age.

- **Support** Support consists of the details that demonstrate your position is correct and should be accepted. There are three types of support: reasons, evidence, and emotional appeals.

Here are a few examples:

| ISSUE | POSITION | SUPPORT |
|-------|----------|---------|
| Welfare system | The welfare system is unjust and needs reform. | People cheat, deserving people cannot get benefits, and it costs taxpayers too much money. |
| Plus-minus grading system | The plus-minus grading system is confusing and unnecessary. | It costs instructors extra time, employers do not understand it, and it complicates the computation of GPA. |

You can visualize an argument paragraph as follows:

## Visualize It!

**Idea Map**

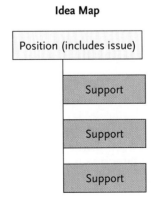

Position (includes issue)

Support

Support

Support

**Note:** Number of supporting details will vary.

Here is a sample argument paragraph:

Year-round school is advantageous to both parents and children, and more school districts should adopt a full-year calendar. Most parents work year round and find child care and supervision troublesome and expensive during the summer months when their children are not in school. Further, continuous year-round application of skills will prevent forgetting and strengthen students' academic preparation. Finally, children themselves admit they are bored in the summer and end up hanging out in malls, staying up late, and sleeping in the mornings to kill time. A well-rounded school year will produce well-rounded children and happy parents.

You can visualize this paragraph as follows:

## Visualize It!

**Idea Map**

Position
(includes issue)

Year-round school is advantageous and school districts should adopt a full-year calendar.

Parents work year-round and find supervision troublesome and expensive.

Year-round school will prevent forgetting and strengthen skills.

Children get bored with summers off.

## EXERCISE 14-2

**Directions:** For each of the following issues, write a sentence that takes a position on the issue.

1. Community service

2. Health insurance

3. Sports fan behavior

4. Air travel safety

5. Minimum wage

## Writing Your Topic Sentence

Your topic sentence should do the following:

- identify the issue

- state your position on the issue

In a lengthy argument, it may also suggest the major reasons you will offer to support your position. The following topic sentence makes it clear that the writer will argue against the use of animals for medical research:

> The use of animals in medical research should be outlawed because it is cruel, unnecessary, and disrespectful of animals' place in the chain of life.

Notice that this thesis identifies the issue and makes it clear that the writer opposes animal research. It also suggests the three major reasons she will present: (1) it is cruel, (2) it is unnecessary, and (3) it is disrespectful. You do not always have to include the major points of your argument in your topic sentence, but including them does help the reader to know what to expect. This topic sentence also makes clear what action the author thinks is appropriate: using animals in medical research should be outlawed.

Here are a few more topic sentences. Notice that they use the verbs *should, would,* and *must.*

> If we expect industries to dispose of their wastes properly, then we should provide tax breaks to cover the extra expense.

> It would be a mistake to assume racial discrimination has been eliminated or even reduced significantly over the past twenty years.

> The proportion of tenured women and minority faculty on our campus must be increased.

## EXERCISE 14-3

*Writing in Progress*

**Directions:** For three of the following issues, take a position and write a topic sentence.

1. Employee health care benefits

2. The right of insurance companies to deny medical coverage to certain individuals

3. Banning smoking in public places

4. Outlawing sport hunting of wild animals

5. Mandatory counseling for drunken drivers

6. Buying American-made products

7. Volunteer work

8. Athletes and the use of steroids

## Supporting Your Position

There are two primary types of support that can be used to explain why your position should be accepted:

- **Reasons** Reasons are general statements that back up a position. Here are a few reasons to support an argument in favor of parental Internet controls:

The Internet contains sites that are not appropriate for children.

The Internet is a place for sexual predators to find victims.

No one else polices the Internet, so parents must do so.

- **Evidence** The most common types of evidence are facts and statistics, quotations from authorities, examples, and personal experience. Each is discussed in more detail below.

## Facts and Statistics

*Facts* are statements that can be verified as correct. As in writing any other type of paragraph or essay, you must choose facts that directly support the position you express in your topic sentence. Here is an excerpt from an argument that uses facts as evidence to argue that African Americans have made significant gains in the nation's political system:

> Changes in political representation show mixed results. On the positive side, the mayors of many large U.S. cities are African American, and of 435 representatives, 39 are African American. But of 100 senators, none is African American, when we would expect about 12 based on population. Of the 495,000 elected officials in the United States, only about 9,000 are African American (*Statistical Abstract* 2001: Table 399). African Americans, who number 34.6 million, make up about 12 percent of the population, but they hold only about 2 percent of the elected offices. Yet, compared with the past, this small amount represents substantial gains in the U.S. political system.
>
> James M. Henslin, *Social Problems*

Facts expressed as numbers are called *statistics*. It is usually more effective to present more than one statistic. Suppose you are writing to persuade taxpayers that state lotteries have become profitable businesses. You might state that more than 60 percent of the adult population now buy lottery tickets regularly. This statistic would have little meaning by itself. However, if you were to state that 60 percent of adults now purchase lottery tickets, whereas five years ago only 30 percent purchased them, the first statistic would become more meaningful.

In selecting statistics to support your position, be sure to:

1. **Obtain statistics from reliable print or online sources.** These include almanacs, encyclopedias, articles in reputable journals and magazines, or other trustworthy reference material from your library. Online sources include databases, online journals, and scholarly Web sites.

2. **Use up-to-date information, preferably from the past year or two.** Dated statistics may be incorrect or misleading.

3. **Make sure you define terms and units of measurement.** For example, if you say that 60 percent of adults regularly play the lottery, you should define what "regularly" means. Does it mean daily, weekly, or monthly?

4. **Verify that the statistics you obtain from more than one source are comparable.** For example, if you compare the crime rates in New York City and Los Angeles, be sure that each crime rate was computed the same way, that each represents the same types of crimes, and that report sources were similar.

## Quotations from Authorities

You can also support your position by using expert or authoritative statements of opinion or conclusions. Experts or authorities are those who have studied your subject extensively, conducted research on it, or written widely about it. For example, if you are writing an essay calling for stricter preschool-monitoring requirements to prevent child abuse, the opinion of a psychiatrist who works extensively with abused children would provide convincing support.

## Examples

Examples are specific situations that illustrate a point. Refer to Chapter 9, "Example," for a review of how to use them as supporting details. In a persuasive essay, your examples must represent your position and should illustrate as many aspects of your position as possible. Suppose your position is that a particular movie should have been X-rated because it contains excessive violence. The evidence you choose to support this position should be clear, vivid examples of violent scenes.

The examples you choose should also, if possible, relate to your audience's experience. Familiar examples are more appealing, convincing, and understandable. Suppose you are writing to present a position on abortion. Your audience consists of career women between 30 and 40 years old. It would be most effective to use as examples women of the same age and occupational status.

## Personal Experience

If you are knowledgeable about a subject, your personal experiences can be convincing evidence. For example, if you were writing an essay supporting the position that physical separation from parents encourages a teenager or young adult to mature, you could discuss your own experiences with leaving home and assuming new responsibilities.

## EXERCISE 14-4
### Writing in Progress

**Directions:** Generate reasons and evidence to support one of the topic sentences you wrote for Exercise 14-3.

## Researching Your Topic

An argument essay must provide specific and convincing evidence that supports the topic sentence. Often it is necessary to go beyond your own knowledge and experience. You may need to research your topic. For example, if you were writing to urge the creation of an environmentally protected wetland area, you would need to find out what types of wildlife live there, which are endangered, and how successful other wetlands have been in protecting wildlife.

At other times, you may need to interview people who are experts on your topic or directly involved with it. Suppose you are writing a memo urging other employees in your department to participate in a walk-a-thon. It is being held to benefit a local shelter for homeless men and women. The director of the shelter or one of her employees could offer useful statistics, share personal experiences, and provide specific details about the clientele the shelter serves that would help you make a convincing case.

## EXERCISE 14-5
*Writing in Progress*

**Directions:** Evaluate the evidence you collected in Exercise 14-4, and research your topic further if needed. Write the first draft of the paragraph.

## Applying Your Skills to Essay Writing: Argument

The skills you learned for writing an argument paragraph apply to essay writing as well. Use the guidelines described below to write an effective argument essay.

### Guidelines for Writing Argument Essays

**1. Thesis Statement** Your thesis statement should identify the issue and state your position on the issue. It may also suggest the primary reasons for accepting the position. Place your thesis statement where it will be most effective. There are three common placements:

  **a.** Thesis statement in the beginning

**Visualize It!**

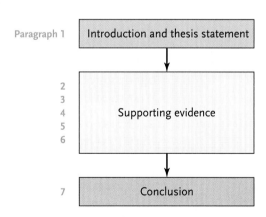

**Visualize It!**

**b.** Thesis statement after responding to objections

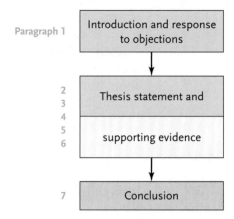

**c.** Thesis statement at the end

**Visualize It!**

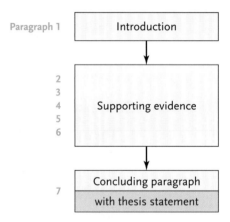

In general, placing the thesis in the beginning is best when addressing an audience in agreement with your position or one that is neutral about the topic under discussion (see Need to Know box, p. 000). For an audience that does not agree with your argument, a later placement gives you the opportunity to respond to the audience's objections before you present your thesis.

**2. Develop Convincing Support** The support you provide determines the effectiveness of your argument. Be sure to offer convincing reasons and sufficient evidence to explain each reason. Here is a sample argument written by one student. Note how she presents reasons and evidence for taking a specific action.

*Buckle Up*

As a paramedic, I am the first to arrive at the scene of many grim and tragic accidents. One horrid accident last month involved four women in one car. The front-seat passenger died instantly, another died during a mercy flight to the nearest hospital, one lost both legs, and one walked away from the accident without serious injury. Only one woman was wearing a seat belt. Guess which one? Though many people protest and offer excuses, seat belts do save lives.

Many people avoid wearing seat belts and say they'd rather be thrown free from an accident. Yet they seldom realize that the rate at which they will be thrown is the same rate at which the car is moving. Others fear being trapped inside by their seat belt in case of a fire. However, if not ejected, those without a belt are likely to be stunned or knocked unconscious on impact and will not be alert enough to escape uninjured.

Seat belts save lives by protecting passengers from impact. During a crash, a body slams against the windshield or steering wheel with tremendous force if unbelted. The seat belt secures the passenger in place and protects vital organs from injury.

Recent statistics demonstrate that a passenger is five times more likely to survive a crash if a seat belt is worn. Life is a gamble, but those are good odds. Buckle up!

This writer introduces the topic with a startling example from her personal experience. The thesis statement occurs at the end of the first paragraph. The second and third paragraphs offer evidence that supports the writer's thesis. The last paragraph concludes the essay by offering a convincing statistic and reminding the reader of the thesis "Buckle up." You can visualize this short argument as follows:

## Visualize It!

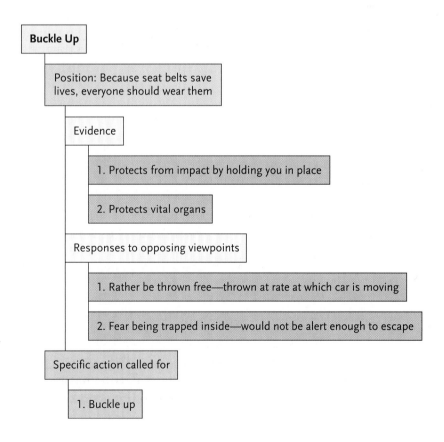

**Buckle Up**

Position: Because seat belts save lives, everyone should wear them

Evidence

1. Protects from impact by holding you in place

2. Protects vital organs

Responses to opposing viewpoints

1. Rather be thrown free—thrown at rate at which car is moving

2. Fear being trapped inside—would not be alert enough to escape

Specific action called for

1. Buckle up

## NEED TO KNOW

### Analyzing Your Audience

Analyzing your audience is a crucial step in planning a convincing argument. There are three types of audiences:

- **Audiences who agree with your position** These are the easiest to write for because they already accept most of what you will say. Audiences in agreement with you are likely to have positive feelings toward you because you think the way they do about the issue. For this audience, state your position and explain why you think it is correct.

- **Neutral audiences** These readers have not made up their minds or have not given much thought to the issue. They may have questions, they may misunderstand the issue, or they may have heard arguments supporting the opposing viewpoint. An essay written for a neutral audience should be direct and straightforward, like those written for an audience in agreement with your point of view. However, a fuller explanation of the issue is necessary to answer questions, clear up misunderstandings, and respond to opposing arguments.

- **Audiences who disagree with your position** These are the most difficult to address. Some members will have thought about the issue and taken a position that opposes yours. Others who disagree may not have examined the issue at all and are making superficial judgments or are relying on misinformation. Both types think their position is correct, so they will not be eager to change their minds. They may also distrust you, because you think differently from them. For such an audience, your biggest challenge is to build trust and confidence. Before writing, carefully analyze this audience and try to answer these questions:

  - Why does your audience disagree with your position?

  - Is their position based on real facts and sound evidence, or on personal opinion? If it is based on evidence, what type?

  - What type of arguments or reasons are most likely to appeal to your audience? For example, will they be persuaded by facts and statistics, or by statements made by authorities? Would personal anecdotes and examples work well?

Once you understand how your audience thinks, you can plan your essay more effectively.

**3. The Introduction and Conclusion** The introduction of an argument essay should interest the reader in the issue and suggest why the issue is important. The introduction may include your thesis statement, a definition of a key term, or other explanatory information.

If you delay stating your thesis until the end of your essay, make sure your conclusion contains a clear, direct thesis statement. If you state your thesis earlier, then your conclusion should summarize key points and make a final call for action. You may request that your reader take specific action, such as writing a letter to a congressional leader or joining a local environmental protection group.

**4. Opposing Viewpoints** An opposing viewpoint is the position that is the opposite of the one you took. It is effective to recognize opposing viewpoints because it builds your credibility and shows that you are open minded. For example, suppose you are arguing that gays should be allowed in the military. You could also recognize or admit that opponents believe that the presence of gays in a military unit may compromise its cohesiveness. You may also decide to refute or argue against opposing viewpoints. You could refute the notion that gays in the military compromises cohesiveness by stating that soldiers are unified against the enemy, not each other. Think of refutation as a process of finding weaknesses in the opponent's argument.

# AN ACADEMIC SCENARIO
## A STUDENT ESSAY
### The Academic Writer and the Writing Task

Ebtisam Abusamak is a student at Central Piedmont Community College. For a journalism class, she was asked to choose an issue and write a paper taking a position on the issue. For her

paper, Abusamak chose smoking in public places. As you read, study the annotations to help you evaluate her argument.

*Interest-catching title*

# Cigarettes, Anyone?
## Ebtisam Abusamak

*Background*

As a non-smoking student at Central Piedmont College, I believe my freedom is being restricted by the secondhand smoke of others. This is a violation of my constitutional rights to life—which I can only achieve if my body is healthy—liberty, and the pursuit of happiness, none of which is possible when I am surrounded by smokers. A smoking ban for all public places would protect my constitutional rights and help smokers, as well.

*Thesis statement*

*Personal experience as evidence*

When someone near me smokes, I am forced to inhale their smoke and come home smelling like an ashtray, or get up and move, even if it is completely inconvenient for me to do so. This is not just indoors. There have been countless times that I have gone outside to get fresh air and have instead been blasted with a super-sized combo of chemicals and deadly toxins with a side of rat poison. To protect my health, I must compromise my freedom of movement, which is not only completely unfair but unconstitutional as well.

*Reason 1*

Reason 2

Examples as evidence

Reason 3

Facts as evidence

Comparison

Reason 4

Recognition of opposing viewpoint

Refutation of opposing viewpoint

Conclusion
Review of primary reasons

Call for action

Secondhand smoke is known to cause thousands of deaths in the United States each year. It has been linked to an endless list of serious health problems ranging from bronchitis and asthma to lung cancer and heart disease—even Sudden Infant Death Syndrome. Many nonsmokers who are exposed to secondhand tobacco smoke suffer immediate symptoms including breathing difficulty, eye irritation, and headache, nausea, and asthma attacks.

Smoking related diseases are a preventable waste of money. If smoking was abolished, cancer levels would drop and hospitals would have much-needed extra beds. There have been many cases of non-smokers working in restaurants and bars who are diagnosed with serious illnesses due to exposure to cigarette smoke. It's ironic that, while these people are working to live, they are increasing their chances of dying due to the bad choices of the people they serve. Many smokers argue that a smoking section might help the problem. However, having a smoking section in a bar or restaurant is like having a peeing-allowed section in a public swimming pool—the stuff spreads! Would you swim there?

A ban on smoking in public places would not only improve the lives of non-smokers but would encourage smokers to quit or reduce their smoking. States such as California, where smoking in public places has been banned entirely have proven that a smoke-free environment reduces both the number of smokers in the population and the number of cigarettes they smoke.

Smokers believe that they have a right to make the choice because it's a personal decision. However, their choices not only affect them but everyone around them. People who want to smoke in public areas like to point out the examples of people living past 100 years old who have smoked their entire adult lives or the many cases of lung cancer that were not caused by smoking. There is concern for the restaurant owners whose businesses will suffer because of smoking bans. There is also a concern for tobacco farmers and the entire cigarette industry. But, when all things are considered, the inevitable loss of thousands of lives seems to greatly outweigh the challenges posed to farmers, restaurant owners, and big businesses. Would it be wrong to sacrifice the satisfaction of one customer for the life of another?

We all have the freedom to make choices regarding our own bodies, but no one has the right to willingly and knowingly put others at risk when making these choices. California and several other states have set the precedent by outlawing smoking in the work place. Other states are sure to follow, but the debate is likely to continue. Unfortunately, you will probably be affected by the effects of smoking at least once in your life, either personally or through the illness or death of a loved one. This is a life-altering issue that needs to be dealt with immediately through smoking bans in all public places. For once, I would like to take a breath of fresh air.

## Examining Academic Writing

1. For what type of audience is Abusamak writing—neutral, in agreement, or not in agreement?

2. Did you find her argument convincing? Why or why not?

3. What other reasons could she have included?

4. Abusamak did not use research to write her paper. Would facts and statistics have strengthened her essay? If so, what should she have included?

## Academic Writing Assignments

1. You are taking an ecology class. You have been asked to select a type of environmental pollution and develop an argument urging steps be taken to control it in your community.

2. You are taking a political science class and you are studying voter registration and participation. Your instructor has asked you to write an editorial for your local newspaper urging that either more citizens become registered voters or more voters use their voting privilege.

3. You are taking a zoology class and are studying the function of zoos. You are considering such questions as: Do zoos protect animals or put them on display? Do they preserve endangered species or do they sacrifice animal needs for those of humans? Write an essay that takes a position on zoos. Develop an argument that supports your position.

# A WORKPLACE SCENARIO
## A PETITION
### The Workplace Writer and the Writing Task

Juanita Garcia is a nurse at Valley Visiting Nurses Association. She is also president of the nurses bargaining unit. Because Juanita has two small children, she is interested in reducing her work hours and sharing her job responsibilities with another nurse. She has written the following petition to present to the association's board of directors:

To all nurses at VVNA: PLEASE add your signature at the bottom if you agree it's time we were allowed to job share!

PETITION

We, the undersigned employees at Valley Visiting Nurses Association, are submitting this petition in the belief that everyone at VVNA—nurses and administration alike—would benefit from instituting a job-sharing policy.

There has been a dramatic shift in the workplace over the past century. According to the Bureau of Labor Statistics, the percentage of American women in the labor force rose from 33 percent in 1950 to 60 percent by 2000, and that in 61 percent of American homes, both husband and wife work outside the home. Yet of these working couples, only 1 percent of full-time child care is provided by men.

As a small company administrator, news of a pregnancy from one of your employees may not be cause for congratulations. Who will do that person's job when it comes time for parental leave? And what if that employee decides not to return when the leave is up? For many parents, it can be a wrenching decision to leave a young child and return to work. For them and for you the solution lies in a flexible job-sharing policy.

Job sharing is just what it sounds like: two employees sharing one position. In a company like ours, it would be extremely easy to implement, as we all do essentially the same job, taking care of patients. You hired each of us because we have the appropriate education, training, and compassion. There is not one among us who could not do the job of any of the others. Job sharing would in no way have a negative effect on the company. In fact, employees who job share would have more energy and be less distracted in a four-hour day than they might in an eight-hour one, especially after a long night with a child.

Other benefits to you, the employer, would include:
- increased flexibility, with more workers trained and ready to meet an increase in demand.
- greater continuity when one worker is sick or on vacation.
- a reduction in employee absenteeism, sickness, and stress.
- an increase in employee commitment and loyalty.

As for the last point, employee loyalty is cost-effective. Lower turnover saves the company money in the long run. Think about the time and money you spend hiring and training new employees. By offering your workers the flexibility of job sharing, they will be more likely to return to work after parental leave, even if their hearts lie in being hands-on parents. You will not have to advertise for a new worker, or take time out to interview or train someone new.

Good nurses are in short supply. We believe that by having a job-sharing policy, VVNA will be able to attract and retain the best workers. After all, we are not selling pencils or shoes; we are selling care and compassion. In order to maintain the high level of service we provide, it is necessary that we feel supported by our company. For this reason, as well as the others stated above, we urge you to begin allowing job sharing.

## Examining Workplace Writing

1. What is the issue and what position does Garcia take on the issue?

2. What types of evidence does Garcia offer?

3. For what type of audience does Garcia seem to be writing?

4. Is the argument convincing? Why or why not?

5. Why does Garcia focus on benefits to the employer rather than on benefits to the nurses?

## Workplace Writing Assignments

1. You are a nurse at a residential care center for developmentally disabled children. You are organizing a holiday party for the children, but you need the staff to contribute money for gifts and food. Write a letter to the center's staff urging them to participate.

2. You are a high school science teacher, and your students do not have Internet access in the school building. Write a memo or letter to your principal explaining why Internet access is important and urging him or her to support your budget request for an Internet provider service.

3. You are a member of a health and wellness committee where you work. The committee has received numerous complaints from employees about the lack of appetizing and nutritional food in the company cafeteria. On behalf of the committee, write a letter to the cafeteria manager urging her to revise the menu. Make specific suggestions about the types of foods that should be served.

# WRITING ABOUT A READING

## Paired Readings

Both "The Captive Panther" and "Predators on the Prowl" deal with wild animals and their relationship to humans. "The Captive Panther" takes a single position on keeping animals in zoos. "Predators on the Prowl" examines two viewpoints about wild animals that hunt and kill other animals and occasionally humans. Read each to examine the arguments they present.

## Thinking Before Reading

### Reading 1: The Captive Panther

"The Captive Panther" first appeared in the book *Inhumane Society: The American Way of Exploiting Animals* by Michael W. Fox. The author presents arguments against keeping wild animals in captivity. As you read, notice how Fox builds his persuasive argument.

1. Preview the reading, using the steps discussed in Chapter 2, p. 30.

2. Connect the reading to your own experience by answering the following questions:

   a. How do you feel when you visit a zoo or aquarium?

   b. What purposes do zoos or aquariums serve?

# The Captive Panther

### Michael W. Fox

**psyche**
the mind

1    Some experiences can be so painfully intense that they are soon forgotten. Amnesia protects the **psyche**. Then again, in anticipation of vicarious suffering, we may simply tune out certain experiences altogether. Other times, perhaps for good reason, the psyche is not so protected. It is as if the soul—the observing, feeling self—is actually burned by certain experiences. The imprint is branded so indelibly that we can go back and review every detail so completely that the experience is actually relived. I had just such an experience with a panther in a zoo many years ago.

2    The first time that I ever really *saw* an animal in a cage was in a small zoo at the Jardin des Plantes, a natural history museum in Paris. I entered a large, ornate Victorian rotunda that housed a few animals in small wrought-iron cages. I now recall seeing only one animal there. At first it appeared not to see me even though I stood beside its cage for a long time.

3    Time did end that day as a part of me separated and was incorporated as part of the creature in the cage.

4    In retrospect, I was probably mesmerized by what at first appeared to be a shiny black serpent in constant motion. Its liquid form brushed across the front of the cage. After insinuating itself around some artificial rocks and a body-polished tree stump toward the back of the enclosure, it ricocheted off a ceramic-tiled wall to again caress the front of the cage. Form and motion were so unified and the pattern of movement within the confines of the cage so repetitive that at first encounter the creature was barely recognizable as a panther, or black leopard. Her movements were executed with such precision—even to the point of always touching the tree trunk with her left hip and the same ceramic tile with her right front paw—that she was more like a perpetual motion machine than a **sentient** being.

**sentient**
conscious, experiencing feeling

5    And then I saw the blood—a streak of blood down her left thigh, draining from an open sore that would never heal until the cat was freed from the hypnotic lines she traced and was so inexorably bound to execute. Each scraping turn around the tree trunk kept the sore open, like a broken heart bleeding for the loss of all that was wild and free.

6    I wondered if she felt any pain. Her yellow-green eyes were like cold glass, with neither fire nor luster. Perhaps this was a slow ritual form of suicide, gradually grinding and rubbing and shredding the body to pieces to free the wild spirit within. I saw the glint of white bone—or was it tendon—through the cat's thigh muscles winking as she turned and paced before me.

And there was no pad left on the right front paw that struck the tile wall polished ocher with the patina of dried blood and serum. Yet still the crippled creature continued her measured **minuet**.

**minuet**
a certain type of dance

7    The panther body, denied freedom of expression and fulfillment of purpose, had become a prison for the creature spirit within. Following and anticipating every movement she made, I began to breathe in rhythm with the cat. I felt part of myself entering her cage while the rotunda started to revolve faster and faster around that part of my consciousness that remained in my body outside of the cage. Then when I entered the prison of her body the other visitors strolling around the rotunda became **ephemeral** shadow-beings, as if they were part of a dream and the only thing that was real was the measured universe of the tortured panther.

**ephemeral**
short-lived

8    Confined in such limited space, how else could this boundless spirit of the jungle respond? Her rhythmic, trancelike actions were more than thwarted attempts to escape. Was her compulsive animation designed simply to help her cope with the emptiness of existing in body without any purpose for the spirit, a kind of living death?

9    The cage may be the last refuge for many endangered species, but such "protective custody" is a sad reflection indeed of how far we have desecrated nature's creation. Zoos have been as slow to address the psychological needs of the animals they keep as they have to question their own purpose. But times are changing; more and more people have begun to feel and see the world through the eyes of the animals. The cage bars are disappearing as we begin to empathize and come to realize that the fate of the animal kingdom is inextricably linked with the fate of humanity. The black panther in the cage is a mirror reflecting our own condition. And we are not helpless to do something about both.

10    But when we reach into the cage with our hearts, we may feel very differently about keeping animals in zoos or ever visiting a zoo again.

11    Do zoos educate the public adequately to political action and compassionate concern for the plight of wildlife and nature? Are they not too tame, sanitized, and beautiful? They are becoming facsimiles of how animals once were in the wild. Some zoo safari parks are run for profit and secondarily for entertainment. And zoos are also an illusion, a false assurance to the public that lions and cheetahs and tigers and elephants are plentiful and lead free and easy lives. Some amusement parks even have safari zoos purely for public entertainment. This is surely an unethical exploitation of wildlife.

12    Even the best of zoos cannot justify their existence if they do not sufficiently inform and even shock the public into compassionate concern and political action. I know of no zoo that exhibits crippled but otherwise healthy animals that have been maimed by trappers and hunters.

13    Regarding the claim that the best zoos are helping save species from extinction by breeding them in captivity, it may be best to let them become

extinct if there is no place for them in the wild. Life in captivity can never fulfill any species or individual, because the animal *is* its natural environment, and no species lives in isolation from others. Certainly the better zoos have seminatural environments—miniswamps, artificial rivers, climatrons, and mixed-species exhibits. But to what end? For exhibition. They are not conserving nature by creating high-tech facsimiles thereof. And even if such artificial environments enhance the overall welfare and reproductivity of endangered species, where are their offspring to go? To other zoo collections.

14    I believe that even the best zoos and aquaria in the world are not doing an adequate job of nature conservation. They have taken more species from the wild than they have ever put back, and until this situation is dramatically reversed, zoos cannot make any claim to effective nature conservation. Breeding endangered species in captivity is animal preservation, not conservation, and animals preserved forever in a cage or synthetic habitat are at best unreal.

15    As for zoos' often high-blown research into exotic animal diseases, nutrition, and reproduction, all of this would be unnecessary if we had just left wildlife alone and respected their rights and protected their habitats.

16    Are zoos a necessary evil? Wildlife's last refuge? Sometimes I think so. Sometimes I think not. I respect the many people who are dedicated to good zoo management, research, species preservation, and veterinary medicine. But all this dedication may be seriously misplaced if we lose sight of the fact that the problems of zoo animals and the crisis of wildlife's threatened **annihilation** are primarily man-made.

annihilation
destruction

17    Building better zoos at the expense of efforts to conserve nature is wrong. We should need no zoos and we are misguided if we do not work

toward this end, however far into the future it might be. Zoos are not so much a necessary evil as they are a tragic mirror of an evil for which we may yet atone.

18    As it is estimated that at the current rate of habitat destruction, some 500,000 to 2 million plant and animal (including insect) species will soon be extinct, obviously captive breeding in zoos is not the answer. Habitat protection is the only solution, and all nations and peoples must be prepared to make the necessary adjustments and sacrifices if the health and vitality of the Earth is to be preserved.

19    One of the best exhibits in any zoo that I have ever visited was a large mirror behind bars. The caption read: *Homo sapiens,* a dangerous, predatorial tool- and weapon-making primate. Status: endangered by its own doing.

20    There can be no communion with our animal kin when they are held captive, no matter what the justifications may be for their "protective custody." The zoo is a trick mirror that can delude us into believing that we love and respect animals and are helping to preserve them. And like the animal circus, the zoo can have a pernicious influence on children's attitudes toward wild creatures. We cannot recognize or celebrate the sanctity and dignity of nonhuman life under such conditions. There can be no communion: only amusement, curiosity, amazement, and perhaps sympathy. The deprivation of these creatures and the loss of wildness and wilderness are ours also. When we fail collectively to feel these things, and in the process come to accept and patronize the zoo as some cultural norm, we lose something of our own humanity—that intuitive wisdom and a sense of reverence for all life that are the hallmarks of a truly civilized society.

Fox, *Inhumane Society: The American Way of Exploiting Animals*

*Homo sapiens*
species of modern human beings

---

## Getting Ready to Write

### Reviewing the Reading

1. Describe the panther that Fox encountered. How did seeing this animal affect him?

2. For what purposes do zoos exist?

3. Name some fundamental faults with zoos. What needs have zoos failed to meet for their animals? How might this problem be fixed?

4. How does the author refute the argument that zoos save animals from extinction?

5. What does the author believe to be the real reason for the existence of zoos?

## Examining the Reading: Using Idea Maps to Examine Persuasive Essays

One of the best ways to understand persuasive writing is to reduce the ideas in an essay to a simple map or outline. Examining the major pieces of evidence in the essay will allow you to analyze the relationship among the ideas objectively. Use the following format to map the major steps of an argument. Fill in the missing parts of the following idea map that organizes "The Captive Panther."

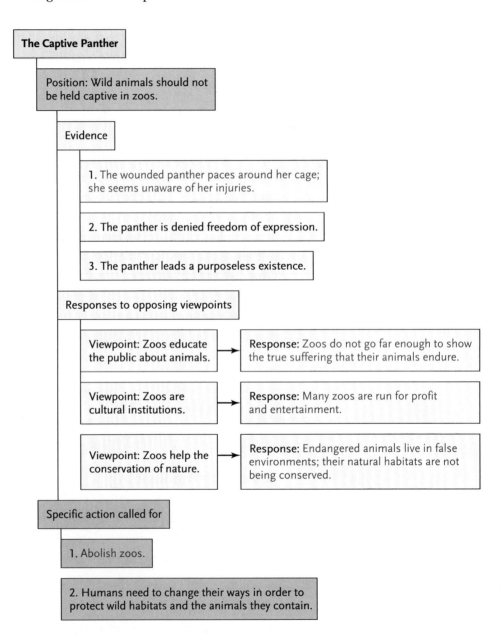

**Visualize It!**

**The Captive Panther**

Position: Wild animals should not be held captive in zoos.

Evidence

1. The wounded panther paces around her cage; she seems unaware of her injuries.

2. The panther is denied freedom of expression.

3. The panther leads a purposeless existence.

Responses to opposing viewpoints

Viewpoint: Zoos educate the public about animals. → Response: Zoos do not go far enough to show the true suffering that their animals endure.

Viewpoint: Zoos are cultural institutions. → Response: Many zoos are run for profit and entertainment.

Viewpoint: Zoos help the conservation of nature. → Response: Endangered animals live in false environments; their natural habitats are not being conserved.

Specific action called for

1. Abolish zoos.

2. Humans need to change their ways in order to protect wild habitats and the animals they contain.

## Thinking Critically: Evaluating Persuasive Writing

Persuasive writing is meant to be convincing. As you read a convincing piece, it is easy to be swept along by the writer's line of reasoning. Fox begins his essay with a graphic description that tugs at the reader's emo-

Table 14-1    **Critical Questions**

| *Facts and Statistics* |
| --- |
| Are they relevant? |
| Are they up-to-date? |
| Do they logically connect with the issue in question? |

| *Quotations from Authorities* |
| --- |
| Are the persons quoted experts? |
| Would other experts agree? |
| What do the quotations contribute to the writer's ideas? |

| *Examples* |
| --- |
| Is each example relevant to the issue? |
| Does each example illustrate something that is typical or exceptional? |
| Can you think of other examples that would confirm or disprove the writer's position? |

| *Personal Experience* |
| --- |
| Is the writer's personal experience relevant to the issue? |
| Is the writer's personal experience typical of most people's? |
| Can you think of other personal experiences that would confirm or disprove the writer's position? |

tions. Not all writers do this, but when they do, it is difficult not to accept their arguments.

The best way to read persuasive writing is with a critical, questioning attitude. As you read, ask yourself questions such as these: Why should I believe this? How do I know this is correct? Mark and annotate as you read. Place question marks next to ideas you want to question or consider further. Use the questions listed in Table 14-1 to evaluate the evidence a writer provides.

Using the questions in Table 14-1, evaluate the strength of the arguments that Fox presents. Write a paragraph on each argument explaining why you accept or reject it.

## Strengthening Your Vocabulary

**Part A:** Using the word's context, word parts, or a dictionary, write a brief definition of each of the following words or phrases as it is used in the reading.

1. vicarious (paragraph 1) *feeling something someone else feels*

   *as if you are actually feeling it yourself*

2. indelibly (paragraph 1) *permanently, unable to be removed*


3. insinuating (paragraph 4) *creeping, moving into slowly*

4. inexorably (paragraph 5) relentlessly, showing no signs of stopping

5. desecrated (paragraph 9) treated as if not sacred

6. pernicious (paragraph 20) harmful, destructive

7. reverence (paragraph 20) awe and respect

**Part B:** Choose one of the above words and draw a word map.

## Reacting to Ideas: Discussion and Journal Writing

1. Analyze the audience for whom the essay is written. Does Fox perceive his audience as agreeing, disagreeing, or neutral?

2. What is the most and least convincing evidence Fox offers?

3. Why did Fox begin the essay with the description of the panther?

4. What is the difference between animal preservation and animal conservation?

5. Do you agree that the zoo is "a trick mirror," which deludes us into believing that we love and respect animals?

## Writing About the Reading

### Paragraph Options

1. Write a paragraph describing an animal you have observed. Reveal your attitude toward the animal through your description.

2. Write a paragraph about an effort in your community to conserve nature or preserve the habitat of wildlife. How have people in your area reacted to this effort?

3. Fox mentions a sign he saw which stated that the human species is "Endangered by its own doing." Write a paragraph that explains this statement and reflects your opinion toward this statement.

### Essay Options

4. Write a persuasive essay to your state or local officials (a) urging the closing of a nearby zoo, (b) the building of a more humane zoo, or (c) the expansion of the existing zoo.

5. Write a persuasive essay arguing for or against using animals in a circus or in other animal performances such as at Sea World.

6. Write an essay for or against people wearing coats made of animal fur.

## Thinking Before Reading

### Reading 2: Predators on the Prowl

Marc Peyser wrote this article, "Predators on the Prowl" for the January 8, 1996 edition of *Newsweek*. He describes arguments for and against the hunting of mountain lions. As you read, notice the types of evidence he uses to show the various sides of this issue.

1. Preview the reading, using the steps discussed in Chapter 2, p. 30.

2. Connect the reading to your own experience by answering the following questions:

   a. Have you ever encountered a wild animal? What did you do?

   b. How do you feel about hunting for sport?

R E A D I N G

# Predators on the Prowl

### Marc Peyser

predators
animals that hunt, kill, and eat other animals

1    For Iris Kenna, Cuyamaca Rancho State Park near San Diego was like a second home. By day, she strolled its fields in search of exotic birds. At night, the 56-year-old high-school counselor sometimes slept under the stars. But one morning almost exactly a year ago, Kenna encountered something unfamiliar, and it saw her first. Without warning, a 140-pound male mountain lion pounced on her from behind. The struggle was brief. The animal dragged the dying, 5-foot-4 Kenna into dense brush to hide her from competing **predators**. Rangers found her only after two hikers spotted a pair of glasses, a backpack and a human tooth by the path she had been on. The rangers followed a trail of her clothes for 30 yards until they came to Kenna's body. The back of her scalp was ripped off; the rest of her was riddled with bites. No one had heard a scream, or even a roar.

2    Kenna is the most vivid symbol of an angry, shifting debate over how people and predators can coexist. In the high-growth Western states, many residents love living near the wild, and they are inclined to preserve it no matter what the risks. But violent deaths like Kenna's—and a string of other

mountain-lion attacks—are making a powerful case for fighting back. Californians will vote in March [1996] on opening the way to mountain-lion hunting, which has been prohibited there for more than 20 years.* But Oregon, Arizona and Colorado recently changed their hunting laws to ensure that predatory animals—including bears, wolves and coyotes—would be protected. "It's overwhelmingly popular to have these animals in our **ecosystems**," says Tom Dougherty of the National Wildlife Federation. "But if they're in your backyard, some people aren't loving it."

**ecosystems**
groups of organisms that depend on each other for survival

3    The most acute mountain-lion problem is in California. That's partly because the state's human population has doubled every 25 years this century. As more people built more houses, they usurped territory once largely inhabited by wild animals. But the mountain lion (alternately called cougar, puma and panther) has also been questionably served by environmentalists. In 1972, preservation-minded Californians banned hunting the majestic animals (except when they pose an imminent danger to people or livestock). The cougar population ballooned, from an estimated 2,400 lions to 6,000 today. Without hunters to thin the ranks, increased competition for food has sent hungry mountain lions to suburban backyards, shopping centers and elementary schools in search of nourishment—a deer or, lacking that, a collie. Even children have been mauled. "People are afraid to go on a picnic without taking a firearm," says state Sen. Tim Leslie, a prominent anticougar advocate. In the wake of Kenna's death, Gov. Pete Wilson authorized the March [1996] ballot initiative—one that could lead to controlling the cougar population.

4    But in other places, sentiment favors animals at least as much as people. A survey of Coloradans living near the Rockies found that 80 percent believe that development in mountain-lion territory should be restricted. What's more, when wildlife authorities killed the cougar that killed a woman named Barbara Schoener in California in 1994, donors raised $21,000 to care for the cougar's cub—but only $9,000 for Schoener's two children. Arizona recently outlawed trapping cougars (though hunting is legal), while Colorado and Oregon don't allow mountain-lion hunters to use bait or dogs. "There's a value shift about how people view wildlife, a high willingness to accept mountain lions on the **urban fringe**—even if they kill people," says Michael Manfredo, who conducted the survey at Colorado State University. That open-mindedness will certainly be tested as Westerners reintroduce predators—grizzly bears in Idaho, wolves in New Mexico and in Yellowstone National Park. It's a jungle out there—and it's getting more junglelike every day.

**urban fringe**
edges of a city

*The measure did not pass and the ban on mountain-lion hunting remains in California. However, during the 2005–2006 session, a state assemblyman once again proposed legislation to lift the ban. The bill was in committee as of this book's publication.

## Getting Ready to Write

### Reviewing the Reading

1.  What happened to Iris Kenna? Why is her story significant?

2.  Where is the hunting of predators illegal, according to the reading?

3.  Summarize the mountain lion problem in California.

4.  What are some other names for the mountain lion?

5.  What are some future challenges in the debate over introducing predators to the wild?

### Examining the Reading: Using Idea Maps to Examine Argument Essays

One of the best ways to understand a piece of persuasive writing is to reduce the ideas in it to a simple map or outline. Examining the major pieces of evidence in an essay will allow you to analyze the relationship among the ideas objectively. Use the following format to map the major steps of an argument. Fill in the missing parts of this idea map that organizes "Predators on the Prowl."

## Visualize It!

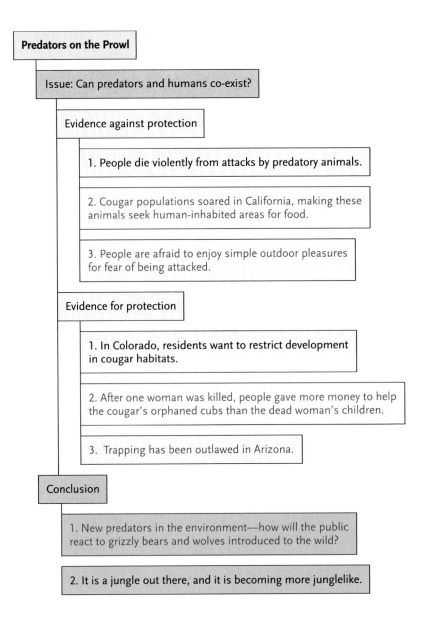

**Predators on the Prowl**

Issue: Can predators and humans co-exist?

Evidence against protection

1. People die violently from attacks by predatory animals.

2. Cougar populations soared in California, making these animals seek human-inhabited areas for food.

3. People are afraid to enjoy simple outdoor pleasures for fear of being attacked.

Evidence for protection

1. In Colorado, residents want to restrict development in cougar habitats.

2. After one woman was killed, people gave more money to help the cougar's orphaned cubs than the dead woman's children.

3. Trapping has been outlawed in Arizona.

Conclusion

1. New predators in the environment—how will the public react to grizzly bears and wolves introduced to the wild?

2. It is a jungle out there, and it is becoming more junglelike.

## Thinking Critically: Evaluating Alternative Viewpoints

Using the questions listed in Table 14-1 on p. 347, evaluate the evidence and arguments presented by Peyser. What types of evidence are offered? Which evidence is most relevant? Which arguments are most convincing? How would you find out more about this issue?

## Strengthening Your Vocabulary

**Part A:** Using the word's context, word parts, or a dictionary, write a brief definition of each of the following words or phrases as it is used in the reading.

1. riddled (paragraph 1) *pierced with holes*

2. symbol (paragraph 2) *sign or representation*

3. acute (paragraph 3) *serious, severe, intense*

4. usurped (paragraph 3) *take over wrongfully, seize without the right to*

5. imminent (paragraph 3) *about to happen, impending*

6. sentiment (paragraph 4) *feeling, attitude*

**Part B:** Choose one of the above words and draw a word map.

## Reacting to Ideas: Discussion and Journal Writing

1. Why do you think the public contributed more money to caring for the cougar's cub than to caring for Barbara Schoener's children? To which fund would you prefer to contribute?

2. What do you think those in favor of protecting predators would say to Iris Kenna's family if the state of California urged tighter restrictions on predators? What arguments might those in favor of protection raise?

3. Who do you think should have first rights to an area of land—the people who own it or the animals who live there?

## Writing About the Reading

### Paragraph Options

1. Write a paragraph about the use of public elections (votes) to decide matters such as mountain lion hunting. Should these kinds of issues be left to legislators to decide? Should the general public vote on them?

2. Write a paragraph about development in your area. Do you think builders are encroaching on too many wild areas? How does your community react to development?

3. Michael Manfredo is quoted in the article as saying, "It's a jungle out there—and it's getting more junglelike everyday." Write a paragraph that explains this quote. Describe how this notion affects your life.

## Essay Options

4. Write an essay discussing whether the author is for or against restricting wildlife predators. Refer to sections of the reading to support your points.

5. What is your position on the issue of restricting wildlife predators? If you are in favor of it, write an essay describing what laws should be enacted, restrictions imposed, or guarantees offered. If you oppose restriction, what actions should be taken to protect wildlife predators?

6. Write an essay describing what you think Iris Kenna's family would say to those who want to protect predators. Summarize the arguments they might use.

## Writing About the Readings

### "The Captive Panther"

### "Predators on the Prowl"

Both "The Captive Panther" and "Predators on the Prowl" deal with wild animals and their relationship to humans. Using these two readings as sources, write an essay discussing the problem of wild animals interacting with humans. What issues are involved? What problems arise?

## Revision Checklist

1. Is your essay appropriate for your audience? Does it give them the background information they need? Will it interest them?

2. Will your essay accomplish your purpose?

3. Have you narrowed your topic so that you can cover your subject thoroughly in your essay?

4. Is your main point clearly expressed in a thesis statement in the introductory paragraph? Does your introductory paragraph capture the reader's interest and lead into the body of the essay?

5. Does each paragraph of your essay have a topic sentence that supports your essay's main point?

6. Is each paragraph's topic sentence supported by relevant and sufficient detail?

7. Are your paragraphs arranged in a logical sequence and connected by transitional words and phrases?

8. Is the tone of your essay appropriate for your purpose and audience?

9. Does your conclusion reemphasize your thesis statement and draw the essay to a close?

10. Does your title identify the topic and interest the reader?

## For Argument Essays

11. Have you analyzed the position your audience takes on the issue about which you are writing?

12. Have you researched your topic to obtain adequate and convincing evidence?

13. Does your thesis statement identify the issue and state your position on it?

14. Does your thesis statement foreshadow your supporting points?

15. Have you provided convincing evidence?

16. Have you proofread? (See the inside back cover of this book for a proofreading checklist.)

# CHAPTER REVIEW AND PRACTICE

## Chapter Review

| | |
|---|---|
| WHAT IS AN ARGUMENT? | An argument is a line of reasoning intended to persuade the reader to accept a viewpoint or take an action. |
| DEFINE THE THREE PARTS OF AN ARGUMENT. | 1. **Issue**—The problem or controversy that the argument addresses<br>2. **Position**—The point of view on the issue<br>3. **Support**—The reasons or evidence that indicates the position should be accepted |
| WHAT SHOULD YOUR TOPIC SENTENCE CONTAIN? | It should identify the issue and state your position on the issue. |
| WHAT ARE THE TWO PRIMARY TYPES OF SUPPORT? | The two types of primary support are reasons and evidence. |
| WHAT ARE THE COMMON TYPES OF EVIDENCE? | Common evidence includes facts and statistics, quotations from authorities, examples, and personal experience. |
| WHY IS RESEARCH SOMETIMES NECESSARY? | Research is sometimes necessary to locate sufficient evidence to support your position. |
| WHAT ARE THE GUIDELINES FOR WRITING ARGUMENT ESSAYS? | 1. Choose an appropriate placement of your thesis statement.<br>2. Develop convincing support.<br>3. The introduction should interest the reader; the conclusion should present a final call to action or a review of key points. |
| WHY SHOULD YOU ANALYZE YOUR AUDIENCE? | How you write your essay and the types of evidence you offer depends on your audience. |

## Skill Refresher: Parallelism

Parallelism means that words, phrases, or clauses in a series have similar grammatical form. Making corresponding parts of a sentence parallel in structure and length makes your writing clearer and easier to read.

## What Should Be Parallel?

1. **Words in series**   When two or more nouns, verbs, or adjectives appear together in a sentence, they should be parallel in grammatical form. Verbs should be in the same tense.

INCORRECT    All day long the workers on the construction project next door were <u>banging</u>, <u>thumping</u>, and <u>pounded</u> so loudly I couldn't concentrate on my job.

CORRECT    All day long, the workers on the construction project next door <u>banged</u>, <u>thumped</u>, and <u>pounded</u> so loudly that I couldn't concentrate on my job.

2. **Phrases**

INCORRECT    My sister likes <u>wearing crazy hats</u>, <u>dressing in funky clothes</u>, and <u>to go to classic movies</u>.

CORRECT    My sister likes <u>wearing crazy hats</u>, <u>dressing in funky clothes</u>, and <u>going to classic movies</u>.

3. **Clauses**

INCORRECT    While Yolanda <u>worked</u> on her history paper, her husband <u>was watching</u> the baby.

CORRECT    While Yolanda <u>worked</u> on her history paper, her husband <u>watched</u> the baby.

## Rate Your Ability to Use Parallel Structure

Identify the sentences that lack parallelism and correct them. If the sentence is correct, write "C" in the space provided. Answers will vary.

_____  **1.** The new president drew an organizational chart on the board, passing out a handout of it, and described how the company would be reorganized.

__C___  **2.** Down syndrome is caused by the presence of an extra chromosome, a microscopic deviation from the norm that has important consequences.

_____  **3.** Working at home allows me to set my own hours, spend less on clothes, and I can work without interruption.

_____  **4.** Professor Bargo's poetry class read famous poets, analyzed their poetry, and researches their lives.

_____  **5.** The clam, oysters, and the mussel are examples of mollusks.

__C___  **6.** There are many alternative sources of energy available including solar, wind, and atomic power.

_____ 7. The United Nations was formed in 1945 to renounce war, uphold personal freedoms, and bringing about worldwide peace and well-being.

_____ 8. As a graphic artist, he does illustrations, chooses type, and to plan page layout.

_____ 9. The Eighteenth Amendment to the Constitution implemented Prohibition, but the Twenty-First Amendment, ratified 14 years later, repeals it.

___C___ 10. Black holes, pulsars, and quasars are studied by astronomers and physicists.

Score _____

Check your answers, using the Answer Key on p. 643. If you missed more than two, you need additional review and practice in using parallel structure. Refer to Part VI, "Reviewing the Basics," and under section D, see "Parallelism." For additional practice, go to this book's Web site at http://www.ablongman.com/mcwhorterexpressways1e.

## INTERNET ACTIVITIES

### 1. Web Tutorial

The University of Michigan Library has prepared a tutorial on information literacy. Go through the Web research portion of the tutorial.

http://www.lib.umich.edu/ugl/searchpath/mod5/index.html

Be sure to complete the online quiz at the end!

### 2. Advertising Analysis

Many advertisements use persuasive techniques in creative ways. Visit the online exhibit Web pages of the William F. Eisner Museum of Advertising & Design.

http://www.eisnermuseum.org/exhibits/online.shtm#

Explore all the exhibits and then choose one to evaluate. Explain how the ads try to achieve their goal.

### 3. This Book's Web Site

Visit this site to find templates of idea maps for argument and additional practice on skills taught in this chapter.

http://www.ablongman.com/mcwhorterexpressways1e

# PART IV

## Strategies for Writing Essays

# 15

# Sharpening Your Essay-Writing Skills

## Chapter Objectives

*In this chapter you will learn to:*

1. Plan your essay.

2. Write effective thesis statements.

3. Support your thesis with evidence.

4. Write more effective introductions and conclusions.

5. Use revision maps to revise.

## Write About It!

Study the photograph above. Write a sentence that states what this photograph suggests about technology.

The sentence you have written could be the thesis statement for an essay on the overuse of technology. A thesis statement specifies the main point that will be developed in an essay. In this chapter you will learn to plan, organize, and write essays. Much of the writing you do everyday, in college, and in the workplace will involve writing paragraphs and grouping them to form a connected piece of writing.

EVERYDAY SCENARIOS

- A letter requesting reconsideration of an insurance claim that was denied.
- A letter of complaint to a hotel that lost your reservation.

ACADEMIC SCENARIOS

- A report on visiting an art gallery for an art history course
- An essay exam in biology on the causes of species extinction

WORKPLACE SCENARIOS

- A trip report summarizing activities and outcomes of a recent sales trip
- A report on a market research survey in preparation for introducing a new product

# WRITING ESSAYS

We have all used a dull knife, a dull saw, or a dull pencil. It is possible, of course, to use dull tools, but the results usually are not very satisfying. Sometimes you might similarly feel, "I'm doing what I'm supposed to be doing when I write an essay—generating good ideas and organizing them as best I can—but something is missing from the end result."

This chapter is all about sharpening your essay-writing skills so that the end result—your papers—will be more interesting, more effective, and more satisfying to write and to read. Specifically, this chapter will help you polish your thesis statement; support it with substantial evidence; show connections among your ideas; write effective introductions, conclusions, and titles; and use revision maps to revise.

Depending on your topic, you may need to obtain additional information through reading or research. You may need to locate specifics—facts, statistics, or examples to support your main points.

Here is a brief essay that a student wrote for her interpersonal communications class. Her essay is based on her own observations and information found in *Manwatching,* a book by Desmond Morris.

## How to Spot a Liar

If you suspected a friend were lying to you, what would you do to confirm your suspicions? Most of us would listen more carefully to what the person says, and try to "catch" him or her saying something contradictory. Most liars are experienced—they've been practicing for a long time. They are very careful about what they say; therefore, they seldom make a slip. To spot a liar, stop paying attention to *what* is said; instead, pay attention to the person's voice, face, and body.

How a person speaks reveals more than what he or she says. While choice of words is easy to control, the voice often betrays a person's emotions. Because areas of the brain involved with emotion control the voice, the voice tends to reveal emotion. When a person lies, the voice tends to be higher pitched and the rate of speech tends to slow down.

Even more revealing than voice is a person's face. The face is the primary place we display emotions. We use different facial expressions to convey fear, anger, happiness, or guilt. Facial expressions are harder to fake than words because you can rehearse or practice what you will say, but you cannot practice how you will feel. Liars tend to make exaggerated expressions—a smile that is drawn out too long or a frown that is too severe. Eyes are especially revealing. Liars' eyes lack a genuine, warm twinkle when they smile, and they make less eye contact with the person to whom they are talking.

The body is the most revealing of all. While many liars try to control their voice and face, many do not know that their body has its own language. Posture and gestures reveal a person's feelings. Liars tend to make less enthusiastic gestures. At times, the gesture may not fit with what is being said. Liars tend to hold themselves at a greater distance from other people. They also have a less relaxed body position. You may notice, too, nervous behaviors such as twisting a ring or toying with a button.

Spotting a liar is never easy, but you will have the most success if you watch rather than listen. As we all know, actions are more important than words.

This essay is factual. The author does not include opinions about or personal experience with liars. The introductory sentence interests the reader by posing a hypothetical question. The next sentence tells us that our assumptions are frequently wrong and explains why. The last sentence in the paragraph states the author's thesis. The next three paragraphs explain how characteristics of the voice, face, and body can be interpreted to spot liars. The concluding paragraph restates the thesis in more general terms and ends with a widely accepted expression.

## Planning Your Essay

Since the purpose of an essay is always to provide information that your audience can understand and use, be certain that all of your information is clear and correct. This involves selecting an appropriate level of detail, choosing a logical method of development, obtaining complete and correct information, and deciding on an appropriate tone.

### Selecting an Appropriate Level of Detail

A student wrote the following paragraph as part of an essay for a class assignment. His audience was his classmates.

When the small, long-iron clubhead is behind the ball, it's hard to stop tension from creeping into your arms. When this happens, your takeaway becomes fast and jerky. Your backswing becomes shorter and you lose your rhythm. Even worse, this tension causes your right hand to uncock too early. One result is that the clubhead reaches its peak speed before it hits the ball. Another result is the clubhead goes outside the line of play and cuts across the ball steeply from outside to in. A slice or pull results.

Did you find the paragraph clear and easy to understand? Unless you know a lot about golf, you probably found it confusing. This writer made a serious error: he failed to analyze his audience. He assumed they knew as much about golf as he did. Readers who do not play golf would need more background information. Terms specific to golf should be defined.

Analyzing your audience is always the first step when writing any essay. It will help you assess how much and what type of detail to include. Here are some key questions to begin your analysis:

- Is my reader familiar with the topic?

- How much background or history does my reader need to understand the information?

- Do I need to define any unfamiliar terms?

- Do I need to explain any unfamiliar people, places, events, parts, or processes?

Suppose you are writing an essay on how to find an apartment to rent. As you plan your essay, you need to decide how much information to present. This decision involves analyzing both your audience and your purpose.

First, consider how much your audience already knows about the topic. If you think your readers know a lot about renting apartments, briefly review in your essay what they already know and then move to a more detailed explanation of new information.

On the other hand, if your topic is probably brand new to your readers, capture their interest without intimidating them. Try to relate the topic to their own experiences. Show them how renting an apartment resembles something they already know. For example, you might compare renting an apartment to other types of shopping for something with certain desired features and an established price range.

If you are uncertain about your audience's background, it is safer to include information they may already know rather than to assume that they know it. Readers can skim or skip over information they know, but they cannot fill in gaps in their understanding without your help.

The author of the sample essay on liars on p. 000 did not assume any knowledge by the reader about nonverbal communication. Each idea was explained completely.

Once you have made these decisions about your audience, you will want to specify your purpose. Is your purpose to give your readers an overview of a topic or do you want to give your readers specific, practical information about it? You would need much more detail for the second purpose than you would for the first. The author's purpose in writing the sample essay on liars on p. 000 was very practical. She intended to tell you exactly what to look for in order to identify when someone is lying.

## EXERCISE 15-1

*Writing in Progress*

**Directions:** For two of the following topics, define your audience and purpose and generate a list of ideas to include in an essay.

1. The lack of privacy in our society

2. The value of sports

3. Balancing job and school

4. Choosing a career

5. How to make new friends

## Obtaining Complete and Correct Information

At times, you know enough about your topic to explain it clearly and completely. At other times, however, you need additional information. For ideas on how to locate, use, and document sources, consult Chapter 16, "Summarizing and Synthesizing Sources."

## Choosing a Logical Method of Development

Analyzing your audience and purpose will also help you choose which method or methods of development to use. Essays use the same methods of development that you learned in Chapters 6 through 14—narration, description, process, example, classification, definition, comparison and contrast, cause and effect, and argument. You can select the one that suits your audience and purpose best.

The sample essay on liars uses the process method of development. However, the supporting paragraphs are arranged from least to most important. Suppose you are writing an essay on the stages of language development in children. If your audience is unfamiliar with the topic, practical, realistic examples of a child's speech at each stage may be the most effective method for helping your readers understand the topic. If your audience is more knowledgeable, examples or definitions may be unnecessary. A more direct, straightforward process explanation would be appropriate.

Your method of development depends on your purpose. Here are a few examples:

---

### Choosing a Method of Development

| IF YOUR PURPOSE IS TO . . . | USE . . . |
|---|---|
| Trace events over time | Narration (see Chapter 6) |
| Present a visual or sensory image | Description (see Chapter 7) |
| Explain how something works or perform a specific task | Process (see Chapter 8) |
| Explain a topic, using specific examples | Example (see Chapter 9) |
| Explain a topic by showing the parts into which it can be divided or the group to which it belongs | Classification (see Chapter 10) |
| Explain what something is | Definition (see Chapter 11) |
| Emphasize similarities or differences between two topics or explain something by comparing it to something already familiar | Comparison and Contrast (see Chapter 12) |
| Explain why something happened | Cause and Effect (see Chapter 13) |
| Convince your readers to accept a viewpoint or take an action | Argument (see Chapter 14) |

Suppose you are majoring in accounting and must write an essay about why you chose accounting as a major. You could explain your choice in several different ways. If your purpose is to show others that you made the right choice, you would probably trace the history of your decision. If your purpose is to encourage other students to choose accounting, you would probably describe the job of an accountant, giving vivid details about its opportunities and rewards. If your purpose is to get a job with an accounting firm, you might give examples of the types of problems accountants solve and the challenges they face. If you choose the first approach, narrative or cause and effect would be the best method for developing your essay. Description would be best for the second approach, and example would be best for the third. The chart below demonstrates how audience and purpose work together in your choice of method.

### Considering Audience and Purpose

| AUDIENCE | PURPOSE | METHOD OF DEVELOPMENT |
|---|---|---|
| Family, friends, interested others | Show that you made the right choice. | Narrative, cause and effect |
| Students | Encourage them to major in accounting. | Description |
| Potential employers | Demonstrate your understanding of the job and its challenges. | Example |

Although your essay should have a logical overall development, you can use more than one method of development within the essay. Assume you are writing an essay on family responsibility. You might choose definition for your first paragraph and define how you will use the term *responsibility*. The next three paragraphs could classify family responsibility by types, such as financial responsibility, physical-care responsibility, emotional-support responsibility, and so forth. In each of these paragraphs, you might include an example of each type. Although you chose several different methods of development, the essay follows a logical overall development.

## EXERCISE 15-2

**Directions:** For each of the following thesis statements, suggest at least one possible method of development. If appropriate, suggest several methods. Then select one thesis statement and draft an outline that demonstrates your method(s) of development.

1. Thesis statement: The steps in preparing an oral presentation parallel the steps in writing a report.

   Method of development: _____

2. Thesis statement: Soap operas allow viewers to escape into a fantasy world where they can share the characters' problems and joys.

   Method of development: _____

3. Thesis statement: A listener reveals his or her attitude toward a speaker through nonverbal signals.

   Method of development: _____

4. Thesis statement: Children inherit much from their parents, including good or bad financial habits.

   Method of development: _____

5. Thesis statement: Today, U.S. history courses include the contributions of African Americans, Native Americans, Asian Americans, and Hispanic Americans.

   Method of development: _____

## Deciding on an Appropriate Tone

Since the purpose of an essay is to present information, your tone should reflect your seriousness about the topic. **Tone** means how you sound to your readers and how you feel about your topic. An essay can have a serious, argumentative, or informative tone, for example. A humorous, sarcastic, flip, or very informal tone can detract from your essay and suggest that what you say should not be taken seriously.

As a general rule, your tone should reflect your relationship to your audience. The less familiar you are with your audience, the more formal your tone should be.

Here are a few examples of sentences in which the tone is inappropriate for most academic and career writing:

| | |
|---|---|
| INAPPROPRIATE | Making jump shots is a mean task, but I'm gonna keep tossing 'em till I'm the best there is. |
| REVISED | Learning to make jump shots is difficult, but I'm going to practice until I'm the best on the team. |
| INAPPROPRIATE | I just couldn't believe that my best friend was a druggie. |
| REVISED | I was shocked to learn that my best friend uses drugs. |
| INAPPROPRIATE | I busted a gut trying to make that sale and I got zilch. |
| REVISED | I tried very hard to make the sale but didn't succeed. |

Following these suggestions will help keep your tone appropriate:

1. Avoid slang expressions.

2. Use first person pronouns (*I, me*) sparingly.

3. Make your writing sound more formal than casual conversation or a letter to a close friend.

4. To achieve a more formal tone, avoid informal or everyday words. For example:

   Use *met* instead of *ran into.*

   Use *children* instead of *kids.*

   Use *annoying* instead of *bugging.*

## EXERCISE 15-3

**Directions:** Revise each of the following statements to give it a more formal tone.

1. I used to be a goof-off when I was in high school, but now I am trying to get with education.

2. Sam is the kind of guy every woman would like to sink her claws into.

3. Because Marco is one of those easy-going types, people think they can walk all over him.

4. In my talk to the group, I hit on why scanners are a big money-saver.

5. Emily Dickinson is a fabulous poet; some of her poems really hit me.

### Make Your Conclusion Strong

The conclusion of an essay should remind your reader of your thesis statement. Do not simply restate it. Summarize your main points and what your essay says about your thesis. Finally, your conclusion should draw the essay to a close. Ask questions that still need to be answered, or make a final statement about the topic.

## EXERCISE 15-4
*Writing in Progress*

**Directions:** For one of the topics you selected in Exercise 15-1, generate ideas to include in an essay.

## Write Strong Thesis Statements

To develop a sound essay, you must begin with a well-focused thesis statement. A thesis statement tells your reader what your essay is about and gives clues to how the essay will unfold. The thesis statement should not only identify your topic but also express the main point about your topic that you will explain or prove in your essay.

Some students think they should be able to just sit down and write a thesis statement. But a thesis statement very rarely just springs into a writer's mind: it evolves and, in fact, may change during the process of prewriting, grouping ideas, drafting, and revising. This section will show you how to draft a thesis statement and how to polish it into a focused statement.

## Group Your Ideas to Discover a Thesis Statement

The first step in developing a thesis statement is to generate ideas to write about. Use one of the four prewriting methods that we have studied: (1) freewriting, (2) brainstorming, (3) branching, and (4) questioning. (Refer to p. 11 of Chapter 1, "The Writing Process: An Overview," for a review of these strategies.) Once you have ideas to work with, the next step is to group or connect your ideas to form a thesis. Let's see how one student produced a thesis following these steps.

Ernie was majoring in education with the goal of becoming a special-education teacher. The instructor in one of his courses assigned a short (one to two pages) paper on educational reform. The instructor directed students to propose a particular educational change and write a paper explaining why the change is needed. After brainstorming on how he would like to see the public education system changed, Ernie decided to write about lengthening the school year. He then did a second brainstorming to discover good reasons for lengthening the school year. He came up with this list of ideas:

Kids get bored in the summer.

They would spend more time practicing skills.

Kids spend the day watching TV.

They don't see much of other kids unless they live nearby.

Kids who are weak in skills could catch up.

Others could accelerate.

School buildings are empty, wasting valuable space.

Many teachers who are unemployed for the summer want to work.

Day care or day camps are expensive.

Ernie's next step in essay writing was to select usable ideas and try to group or organize them logically. In the above brainstorming list, Ernie saw three main groups of ideas: behavioral or social skills, academic skills, and financial considerations. He sorted his list into categories:

### *Social*

Kids get bored in the summer.

Kids spend the day watching TV.

They don't see much of other kids unless they live nearby.

*Academic*

They would spend more time practicing skills.

Kids who are weak in skills could catch up.

Others could accelerate.

*Financial*

School buildings are empty, wasting valuable space.

Many teachers who are unemployed for the summer want to work.

Day care or day camps are expensive.

Once Ernie had grouped his ideas into these categories, he could write a thesis statement:

> Lengthening the school year is a good idea for social, academic, and financial reasons.

This thesis statement identifies his topic—lengthening the school year—and suggests three primary reasons why it is a good idea. You can see that this thesis statement grew out of his idea groupings. Furthermore, this thesis statement gives readers clues as to how the essay will be organized. A reader knows from this preview which reasons will be discussed and in what order.

How do you know which ideas to group? Look for connections and relationships among the ideas that you generate during prewriting. Here are some suggestions:

1. **Look for categories.** Try to discover ways your ideas can be classified or subdivided. Think of categories as titles or slots in which ideas can be placed. Look for a general term that is broad enough to cover several of your ideas. For example, Ernie discovered that academic achievement was a broad term that could include time for learning, practicing skills, and acceleration. Suppose you are writing a paper on where sexual discrimination occurs. You could break down the topic by location.

   SAMPLE THESIS STATEMENT    Sexual discrimination exists in the workplace, in social situations, and in politics.

2. **Try organizing your ideas chronologically.** Group your ideas according to the clock or calendar.

   SAMPLE THESIS STATEMENT    Tracing prostitution from its early beginnings in history to modern times reveals certain social and economic patterns.

3. **Look for similarities and differences.** When working with two or more topics, see if they can be approached by looking at how similar or different they are.

   SAMPLE THESIS STATEMENT    Two early biologists, Darwin and Mendel, held similar views about evolution.

4. **Separate your ideas into causes and effects or problems and solutions.** Events and issues can often be analyzed in this way.

   SAMPLE THESIS STATEMENT     Both employer and employees must work together to improve low morale in an office.

5. **Divide your ideas into advantages and disadvantages or pros and cons.** When you are evaluating a proposal, product, or service, this approach may work.

   SAMPLE THESIS STATEMENT     Playing on a college sports team has many advantages, but also several serious drawbacks.

6. **Consider several different ways to approach your topic or organize and develop your ideas.** As you consider what your thesis statement is going to be, push yourself to see your topic from a number of different angles or a fresh perspective.

   For example, Ernie could have considered what the regular school year lacks that school during the summer could provide (field trips, hands-on learning, tutoring, and so on). He could have examined his brainstorming list and decided to focus only on financial aspects of the issue, looking more deeply at salaries, taxes, and the cost of building maintenance. In other words, within every topic lie many possible thesis statements

## How to Write More Effective Thesis Statements

A thesis statement should explain what your essay is about and also give your readers clues to its organization. Think of your thesis statement as a promise; it promises your reader what your paper will deliver. Here are some guidelines to follow for writing more effective thesis statements:

1. **It should state the main point of your essay.** It should not focus on details; it should give an overview of your approach to your topic.

   TOO DETAILED     A well-written business letter has no errors in spelling.

   REVISED     To write a grammatically correct business letter, follow three simple rules.

2. **It should assert an idea about your topic.** Your thesis should express a viewpoint or state an approach to the topic.

   LACKS AN ASSERTION     Advertising contains images of both men and women.

   REVISED     In general, advertising presents men more favorably than women.

3. **It should be as specific and detailed as possible.** For this reason, it is important to review and rework your thesis *after* you have written and revised drafts.

| | |
|---|---|
| TOO GENERAL | Advertisers can influence readers' attitudes toward competing products. |
| REVISED | Athletic-shoe advertisers focus more on attitude and image than on the actual physical differences between their product and those of their competitors. |

4. **It may suggest the organization of your essay.** Mentioning key points that will be discussed in the essay is one way to do this. The order in which you mention them should be the order in which you discuss them in your essay.

| | |
|---|---|
| DOES NOT SUGGEST ORGANIZATION | Public-school budget cuts will negatively affect education. |
| REVISED | Public-school budget cuts will negatively affect academic achievement, student motivation, and the drop-out rate. |

5. **It should not be a direct announcement.** Do not begin with phrases such as "In this paper I will" or "My assignment was to discuss."

| | |
|---|---|
| DIRECT ANNOUNCEMENT | The purpose of my paper is to show that businesses lose money due to inefficiency, competition, and inflated labor costs. |
| REVISED | Businesses lose money due to inefficiency, competition, and inflated labor costs. |

6. **It should offer a fresh, interesting, and original perspective on the topic.** A thesis statement can follow the guidelines above, but if it seems dull or predictable, it needs more work.

| | |
|---|---|
| PREDICTABLE | Circus acts fall into three categories: animal, clown, and acrobatic. |
| REVISED | Of the three categories of circus acts—animal, clown, and acrobatic—each is exciting because of the risks it involves. |

## How to Revise Your Thesis Statement

The best time to evaluate and, if necessary, revise your thesis statement is after you have written a first draft. When evaluating your thesis statement, ask the following questions:

1. **Does my essay develop and explain my thesis statement?** As you write an essay, its focus and direction may change. Revise your thesis statement to reflect any changes. If you discover that you drifted away from your original thesis and want to maintain it, work on revising so that your paper delivers what your thesis promises.

2. **Is my thesis statement broad enough to cover all the points made in the essay?** As you develop your first draft, you may find that one idea leads naturally to another. Both must be covered by the thesis statement. For example, suppose your thesis statement is "Media coverage of national political events shapes public attitudes toward politicians." If, in your essay, you discuss media coverage of international events as well as national ones, then you need to broaden your thesis statement.

3. **Does my thesis statement use vague or unclear words that do not clearly focus the topic?** For example, in the thesis statement "The possibility of animal-organ transplants for humans is interesting," the word *interesting* is vague and does not suggest how your essay will approach the topic. Instead, if your paper discusses both the risks and benefits of these transplants, this approach should be reflected in your thesis: "Animal-organ transplants for humans offer both risks and potential benefits."

## EXERCISE 15-5

**Directions:** Identify what is wrong with the following thesis statements, and revise each one to make it more effective.

1. Jogging has a lot of benefits.

2. Counseling can help people with problems.

3. Getting involved in campus activities has really helped me.

4. Budgeting your time is important.

5. Commuting to college presents problems.

## EXERCISE 15-6

*Writing in Progress*

**Directions:** Using the topic you chose in Exercise 15-4, develop a preliminary thesis statement.

## Support Your Thesis with Substantial Evidence

Every essay you write should offer substantial evidence in support of your thesis statement. This evidence makes up the body of your essay. Evidence can consist of personal experience, anecdotes (stories that illustrate a point), examples, reasons, descriptions, facts, statistics, and quotations (taken from sources).

Many students have trouble locating concrete, specific evidence to support their thesis. Though prewriting yields plenty of good ideas and helps you focus your thesis, prewriting ideas may not always provide sufficient evidence. Often you need to brainstorm again for additional ideas. At other times, you may need to consult one or more sources to obtain further information on your topic (see Chapter 16, "Summarizing and Synthesizing Sources," pp. 396–441).

Ernie realized that he did not have enough ideas for his essay on lengthening the school year. The table below lists ways to explain a thesis statement and gives an example of how Ernie could use each in his essay.

Table 15-1   **Ways to Add Evidence**

| Topic: Lengthening the School Year | |
| --- | --- |
| **Explain Your Thesis by...** | **Example** |
| Telling a story (narration) | Relate a story about a student who needed extra time to practice skills. |
| Adding descriptive detail (description) | Add description that allows your reader to visualize how a child with too much unstructured time behaves. |
| Explaining how something works (process) | Explain how the length of the school year is determined. |
| Giving an example | Discuss specific instances of children who are falling behind academically. |
| Discussing types or kinds (classification) | Discuss types of accelerated programs that could be offered. |
| Giving a definition | Discuss the meaning of the terms *vacation*, *learning*, or *practice*. |
| Making comparisons | Compare unstructured activities to structured school activities. |
| Making distinctions (contrast) | Contrast the length of the school year in the United States with that of other countries. |
| Giving reasons (causes) | Explain why too much free time is not beneficial. |
| Analyzing effects | Explain how too much free time affects a child's behavior. |

The table above offers a variety of ways Ernie could add evidence to his essay. But he would not need to use all of them; instead, he should choose the ones that are most appropriate for his audience and purpose. Ernie could also use different types of evidence in combination. For example, he could *tell a story* that illustrates the *effects* that too much free time has on children.

Use the following guidelines in selecting evidence to support your thesis:

1. **Be sure your evidence is relevant.** That is, it must directly support or explain your thesis.

2. **Make your evidence as specific as possible.** Help your readers see the point you are making by offering detailed, concrete information. For example, if you are explaining the effects of right-to-privacy violations on an individual, include details that make the situation come alive: names of people and places, types of violations, and so forth.

3. **Be sure your information is accurate.** It may be necessary to check facts, verify stories you have heard, and ask questions of individuals who have provided information.

4. **Locate sources that provide evidence.** Because you may not know enough about your topic and lack personal experience, you may be unable to provide strong evidence. When this happens, locate several sources on your topic. Consult Chapter 16 for information on synthesizing and summarizing sources.

5. **Be sure to document any information that you borrow from other sources.** See Chapter 16, p. 396, for further information on crediting sources.

Now let's take a look at how Ernie developed his essay on lengthening the school year. As you read, notice, in particular, the types of evidence he uses and how his thesis statement promises what his essay delivers.

### Lengthening the School Year

If I were given eight weeks of vacation each year, I know exactly what I would do. I would visit my family in Arizona, do household chores, and catch up on projects I have not had time to do in three years. Schoolchildren do get eight weeks of vacation each year, but they haven't any idea of how to use it. In fact, they don't need it. There has been a lot of talk lately about lengthening the school year, and this talk deserves consideration. Extending the school year from 180 to 220 days is a good idea for a number of reasons: academic, social, and financial.

The most important reason for lengthening the school year is to improve our children's academic skills. Compared to children in many other countries, our children are falling behind, especially in math and science. In other countries, parents are much stricter with children than we are. News stories report increasing illiteracy and declining SAT scores as well. Increased time in school will give children more time to receive instruction and to practice. Kids who are weak in skills could catch up, while others could accelerate. Consider also that without two months of vacation each year, students are less likely to forget what they have learned.

A second reason for extending the school year has to do with social skills: how kids behave and get along with each other. With two months of vacation, kids have time on their hands; they get bored and don't know what to do. My son stays up late each night watching television and sleeps late in the mornings. He says, "There's nothing to do in the morning, so I kill time by sleeping." Other kids spend day and night in front of the television. They don't see other kids unless they live nearby. If they do play, their play is not supervised, since many parents must work during the summer. Year-round school would occupy daytime hours and offer sports and worthwhile social activities.

Finally, financial reasons indicate that year-round school would be a good idea. As it is, school buildings sit empty and teachers are unemployed or must find part-time jobs. The buildings could be put to good use and teachers who need money could work. Some teachers paint houses or work on construction during the summer. In addition, parents would save money, since now they have to pay for babysitting, daycare, or day camps to care for their children while they work.

Extending the school year has many advantages. Those opposed to lengthening the school year say it would be a struggle to get kids to give up their summers. Others say it would cost too much. What could we possibly buy that would be worth more than the education of our children?

## EXERCISE 15-7
*Writing in Progress*

**Directions:** Write a first draft of an essay for the thesis statement you wrote in Exercise 15-6. Support your thesis statement with at least three types of evidence.

## Use Transitions to Make Connections Among Your Ideas Clear

To produce a well-written essay, be sure to make it clear how your ideas relate to one another. There are several ways to do this:

1. **Use transitional words and phrases.** The transitional words and phrases that you learned for connecting ideas in Chapters 6 through 14 are helpful for making your essay flow smoothly and communicate clearly. Table 15-2 lists useful transitions for each method of organization. Notice the use of these transitional words and phrases in Ernie's essay: *most important, also, a second reason, finally,* and *in addition.*

**Table 15-2    Useful Transitional Words and Phrases**

| Method of Development | Transitional Words and Phrases |
| --- | --- |
| Most-Least/Least-Most | most important, above all, especially, particularly important |
| Spatial | above, below, behind, beside, next to, inside, outside, to the west (north, etc.), beneath, near, nearby, next to |
| Time Sequence | first, next, now, before, during, after, eventually, finally, at last, later, meanwhile, soon, then, suddenly, currently, after, afterward, after a while, as soon as, until |
| Narration/Process | first, second, then, later, in the beginning, when, after, following, next, during, again, after that, at last, finally |
| Description | see Spatial and Most-Least/Least-Most above |
| Example | for example, for instance, to illustrate, in one case |
| Classification | one, another, second, third |
| Definition | means, can be defined as, refers to, is |
| Comparison | likewise, similarly, in the same way, too, also |
| Contrast | however, on the contrary, unlike, on the other hand, although, even though, but, in contrast, yet |
| Cause and Effect | because, consequently, since, as a result, for this reason, therefore, thus |

2. **Write a transitional sentence.** This sentence is usually the first sentence in the paragraph. It might come before the topic sentence or it might *be* the topic sentence. Its purpose is to link the paragraph in which it appears with the paragraph before it. In Ernie's essay on p. 374, the first sentences of paragraphs 2, 3, and 4 function as transitional sentences.

3. **Repeat key words.** Repeating key words also enables your reader to stay on track. Key words often appear in your thesis statement, and by repeating some of them, you remind your reader of your thesis and how each new idea is connected to it.

You need not repeat the word or phrase exactly as long as the meaning stays the same. You could substitute "keep your audience on target" for "enables your reader to stay on track," for example. The following excerpt from an essay on clothing illustrates the use of key-word repetition.

### The Real Functions of Clothing

Just as a product's packaging tells us a lot about the product, so does a person's clothing reveal a lot about the person. Clothing reflects the way we choose to present ourselves and reveals how we feel about ourselves.

 Clothing reveals our emotions. We tend to dress according to how we feel. If we feel relaxed and comfortable, we tend to dress in comfortable, relaxed clothing. For instance, some people wear sweatshirts and sweatpants for a relaxed evening at home. If we feel happy and carefree, our clothing often reflects it. Think of how fans dress at a football game, for example. Their dress reflects casual comfort, and their team-supporting hats, T-shirts, etc., reveal their emotional support for the team.

 Clothing also reveals our expectations and perceptions.

## EXERCISE 15-8
### *Writing in Progress*

**Directions:** Review the draft you wrote for Exercise 15-7. Analyze how effectively you have connected your ideas. Add key words or transitional words, phrases, or sentences, as needed.

## Writing the Introduction, Conclusion, and Title

The introduction, conclusion, and title each serve a specific function. Each strengthens your essay and helps your reader understand your ideas.

### Writing the Introduction

An introductory paragraph has three main purposes:

- It presents your thesis statement.

- It interests your reader in your topic.

- It provides any necessary background information.

Although your introductory paragraph appears first in your essay, it does *not* need to be written first. In fact, it is sometimes best to write it last, after you have developed your ideas, written your thesis statement, and drafted your essay.

 We have already discussed writing thesis statements earlier in the chapter (see pp. 367–374). Here are some suggestions on how to interest your reader in your topic:

### Techniques for Writing Introductions

| TECHNIQUE | EXAMPLE |
|---|---|
| Ask a provocative or controversial question. | What would you do if you were sound asleep and woke to find a burglar in your bedroom? |
| State a startling fact or statistic. | Did you know that the federal government recently spent $687,000 on a research project that studied the influence of Valium on monkeys? |
| Begin with a story or an anecdote. | Mark Brown, a social worker, has spent several evenings riding in a police cruiser to learn about neighborhood problems. |
| Use a quotation. | Oscar Wilde once said, "Always forgive your enemies—nothing annoys them so much." |
| State a little-known fact, a myth, or a misconception. | It's hard to lose weight and even harder to keep it off. Right? Wrong! A sensible eating program will help you lose weight. |

A straightforward, dramatic thesis statement can also capture your reader's interest, as in the following example:

The dream job that I've wanted all my life turned out to be a complete disaster.

An introduction should also provide the reader with any necessary background information. Consider what information your reader needs to understand your essay. You may, for example, need to define the term *genetic engineering* for a paper on that topic. At other times, you might need to provide a brief history or give an overview of a controversial issue.

Now reread the introduction to Ernie's essay on p. 374. How does Ernie interest his readers? He raises the possibility of eight weeks of vacation, something most of us would like to have. He also provides essential background information: schoolchildren do get eight weeks of vacation, the school year now consists of 180 days, and lengthening the school year is an issue many people are discussing.

## EXERCISE 15-9
*Writing in Progress*

**Directions:** Revise your introduction to the essay you wrote for Exercise 15-7.

## Writing the Conclusion

The final paragraph of your essay has two functions. It should reemphasize your thesis statement and draw the essay to a close. It should not be a direct announcement, such as "This essay has been about" or "In this paper I hoped to show that."

It's usually best to revise your essay at least once *before* working on the conclusion. During your first or second revision, you often make numerous changes in both content and organization, which may, in turn, affect your conclusion.

Here are a few effective ways to write a conclusion. Choose one that will work for your essay.

1. **Suggest a new direction for further thought.** Raise a related issue that you did not address in your essay, or ask a series of questions. Ernie's essay uses this strategy.

2. **Look ahead.** Project into the future. Consider outcomes or effects.

3. **Return to your thesis.** If your essay is written to prove a point or convince your reader of the need for action, it may be effective to end with a sentence that recalls your main point or calls for action. If you choose this way to conclude, be sure not to merely repeat your first paragraph. Be sure to reflect on the thoughts you developed in the body of your essay.

4. **Summarize key points.** Especially for longer essays, briefly review your key supporting ideas. In shorter essays, this tends to be unnecessary. Ernie's essay might have ended with the following restatement:

   Extending the school year will have important advantages. Children will learn to handle their time in meaningful ways and become better educated.

If you have trouble writing your conclusion, it's probably a tip-off that you need to work further on your thesis or organization.

## EXERCISE 15-10

*Writing in Progress*

**Directions:** Write or revise a conclusion for the essay you wrote for Exercise 15-7.

## Selecting a Title

Although the title appears first in your essay, it is often the last thing you should write. The title should identify the topic in an interesting way, and it may also suggest the focus. To select a title, reread your final draft, paying particular attention to your thesis statement and your overall method of development. Here are a few examples of effective titles:

"Surprise in the Vegetable Bin" (for an essay on vegetables and their effects on cholesterol and cancer)

"Denim Goes High Fashion" (for an essay describing the uses of denim for clothing other than jeans)

"Babies Go to Work" (for an essay on corporate-sponsored day care centers)

To write accurate and interesting titles, try the following tips:

1. **Write a question that your essay answers.** For example: "Why Change the Minimum Wage?"

2. **Use key words that appear in your thesis statement.** If your thesis statement is "The new international trade ruling threatens the safety of the dolphin, one of our most intelligent mammals," your title could be "New Threat to Dolphins."

3. **Use brainstorming techniques to generate options.** Don't necessarily go with the first title that pops into your mind. If in doubt, try out some options on friends to see which is most effective.

---

### EXERCISE 15-11
*Writing in Progress*

**Directions:** Come up with a good title for the essay you wrote for Exercise 15-7.

## Using Revision Maps to Revise

In Chapter 5, "Strategies for Revising," p. 109, you learned to draw revision maps to evaluate paragraphs. The same strategy works well for essays, too. The revision map will help you evaluate the overall flow of ideas as well as the effectiveness of individual paragraphs.

To draw an essay revision map, work through each paragraph, recording your ideas in abbreviated form, as shown below. Then write the key words of your conclusion. If you find details that do not support the topic sentence, record those details to the left of the map.

## Visualize It!

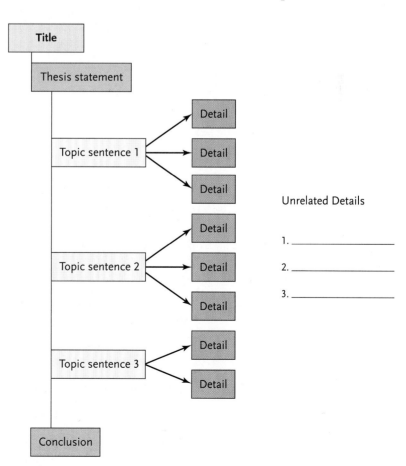

A sample revision map for the essay on p. 374 is shown below.

# Visualize It!

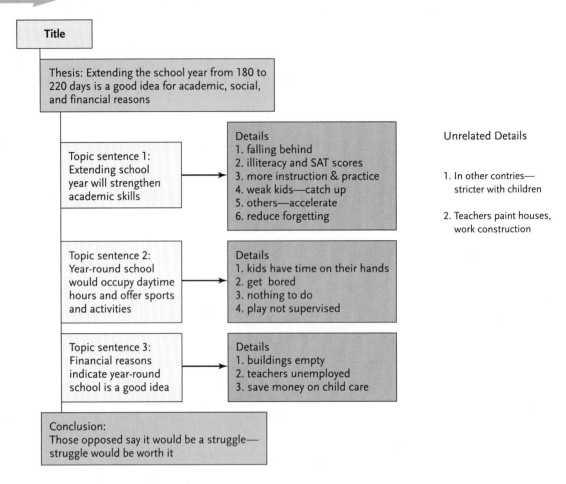

**Title**

Thesis: Extending the school year from 180 to 220 days is a good idea for academic, social, and financial reasons

Topic sentence 1: Extending school year will strengthen academic skills

Details
1. falling behind
2. illiteracy and SAT scores
3. more instruction & practice
4. weak kids—catch up
5. others—accelerate
6. reduce forgetting

Unrelated Details

1. In other contries—stricter with children

2. Teachers paint houses, work construction

Topic sentence 2: Year-round school would occupy daytime hours and offer sports and activities

Details
1. kids have time on their hands
2. get bored
3. nothing to do
4. play not supervised

Topic sentence 3: Financial reasons indicate year-round school is a good idea

Details
1. buildings empty
2. teachers unemployed
3. save money on child care

Conclusion: Those opposed say it would be a struggle—struggle would be worth it

When you've completed your revision map, conduct the following tests:

1. **Read your thesis statement along with your first topic sentence.** Does the topic sentence clearly support your thesis? If not, revise to make the relationship clearer. Repeat this step for each topic sentence.

2. **Read your topic sentences, one after the other, without corresponding details.** Is there a logical connection between them? Are they arranged in the most effective way? If not, revise to make the connection clearer or to improve your organization.

3. **Examine each individual paragraph.** Are there enough relevant, specific details to support the topic sentence?

4. **Read your introduction and then look at your topic sentences.** Does the essay deliver what the introduction promises?

5. **Read your thesis statement and then your conclusion.** Are they compatible and consistent? Does the conclusion agree with and support the thesis statement?

## EXERCISE 15-12
*Writing in Progress*

**Directions:** Draw a revision map for the essay you wrote for Exercises 15-7 through 15-11 and revise the essay accordingly.

# AN ACADEMIC SCENARIO
## A STUDENT ESSAY
### The Academic Writer and the Writing Task

Michaela Lozkova was a student at Monroe College where she was majoring in criminal justice. She also worked as a part-time deputy sheriff in her hometown. For a writing class, her instructor assigned an essay on a topic of her choice. Because Michaela had worked with Taser guns in her job as a deputy, she decided to write about their benefits.

Title: suggests thesis

# The Benefits of Tasers
## Michaela Lozkova

There is a great deal of evidence that shows that, when used properly, Tasers can minimize injuries to police officers and suspects and maximize the safety of the public. Tasers are popular among law enforcement officers because they are non-lethal. With Tasers, police have a weapon that can stop aggressive, mentally ill, or violent people without causing serious injury or death to anyone. Taser guns have many benefits that make them a valuable weapon for police to use.

Thesis statement

The Taser is a device that looks like a handgun but fires darts, rather than bullets, that send 50,000 volts of electricity into a suspect's body. This shock causes the suspect to lose muscle control and collapse. A Taser can be used from as far away as 21 feet, which means an officer can stay out of reach of a suspect while effectively stopping him or her.

Background information on Tasers

Tasers have been used successfully in the Sheriffs Department in Monroe County to control criminals. A mentally ill man, wanting to commit suicide, attacked a deputy and demanded to be shot. The officer used the Taser to subdue the man without hurting either of them. A Taser was used by another deputy who was being threatened by a man armed with a butcher knife. Police officers in a nearby county stopped an armed man who was threatening to kill a hostage. The officers said that if they hadn't had the Taser, they might have had to shoot and possibly kill the suspect, thus endangering the hostage.

Benefit 1

Examples of effective use

Tasers are not only useful for restraining criminals; they are also useful for controlling people with various forms of mental illness. For example,

Benefit 2

Example

schizophrenics sometimes have episodes of aggression or violence in which they exert super-human strength. A Taser can stop someone who is out of control and dangerous without causing serious harm to that person or anyone around him or her. A Taser may also be used to disable someone attempting suicide, for instance.

Benefit 3

Reasons

Another thing that makes Tasers safe is that fact that they can't be used secretly, without someone knowing. When fired, the device ejects confetti printed with a serial number unique to that Taser. So police officers cannot fire a Taser without being traced. Most departments check all Tasers after a shift to see if they've been fired. Therefore, an officer who uses a Taser in an inappropriate way will be caught and have to face consequences.

Discussion of objections to the use of Tasers

There is lot of proof that Tasers have saved lives; however, questions were raised when some suspects in police custody died. These questions were put to rest when medical examiners reported that the deaths, which were thought to be Taser-related, were actually caused by drug overdoses. As further proof that Tasers are safe, thousands of volunteers in the field of law enforcement have been shot with the device over the years without suffering death or serious injury. This fact was the most important in convincing me of the safety of Tasers.

Conclusion: urges public to support use of Tasers

If police across the country continue to use Tasers, more lives will be saved. I believe that the public should recognize the benefits of Tasers and support their use. After all, if they trust their police officers to carry lethal weapons, they should have no problem with those officers using this effective, non-lethal one.

## Examining Academic Writing

1. Highlight and evaluate Lozkova's thesis.

2. Did Lozkova provide sufficient background information for someone unfamiliar with Taser guns? If not, what further information is needed?

3. How could Lozkova have made her introduction more interesting and attention catching?

4. What types of details did Lozkova use to support her topic sentences?

## Academic Writing Assignments

Assume you are taking the course "Interpersonal Communication Skills." In addition to tests and quizzes, your instructor requires two papers. For your first assignment, choose a topic and use one method of prewriting to generate ideas about it. Then review your prewriting and try to group your ideas.

1.  Watch a portion of a television program with the sound turned off. If you could understand what was happening, write a paper explaining how you knew.

2.  Analyze a recent phone conversation. What feelings and emotions were expressed by you and the other person? Write a paper describing how these feelings were communicated.

3.  Suppose you are applying for a full-time job today and your potential employer asks you to describe your "people skills." Write an essay answering the employer's question.

4.  We encounter conflict in our daily lives. Write a paper describing a recent conflict you had and how you and the other person handled the situation.

5.  Describe a communication breakdown between you and another person. Why did it happen and could it possibly have been prevented? How?

6.  Describe a situation in which a person's body language (gestures, posture, facial expressions) allowed you to understand what he or she was really saying. Describe the body language and what it told you.

# A WORKPLACE SCENARIO
## A LETTER OF REFERENCE
### The Workplace Writer and the Writing Task

Nate and Marianne Fiori have responded to the help wanted ad shown below. They are required to submit an application and a letter of reference. The letter of reference, written by Nate and Marianne's current employer, Samuel Epstein, is also shown below. As you read, notice how everything in the letter supports Epstein's thesis sentence.

> HELP WANTED: Couple to manage beautifully renovated building with six rent stabilized apartments. Must be mature, responsible, and good with people. Send application and letter of reference to: abc123@apartments.com. Only qualified candidates will be contacted.

33 Gloodt St.
Chicago, IL 60607


September 1, 2005


To Whom It May Concern

   In response to your ad for responsible managers for your building, I am happy to make the following recommendation at the applicants' request.

   Nate and Marianne Fiori have been managing a building for me for the last two years. In that time, I have come to know and like them very much. They are solid, responsible, dependable workers—people you can trust with your property. They have also been more than managers to my other tenants; they have been helpful and trustworthy neighbors.

   Nate is in his final year of graduate school. He is studying to be an engineer and also holds down a job at the university bookstore. He is in all ways a serious and conscientious young man. On more than one occasion he has done minor renovations to an apartment, saving me the expense of hiring sheetrockers and painters. Whatever he did was an improvement and my property value has increased under his care.

   There are a number of elderly residents in my building. I learned from one woman that Marianne had been running errands for her since an accident forced the woman to remain in bed for several weeks. Marianne would notify this neighbor whenever she was going to the store, help her make up a shopping list, and return with everything on it. She never accepted a penny for this help, although the neighbor offered more than once, knowing that Marianne does not make much in her part-time job as a teacher's aide. Other tenants have told me that Marianne and Nate frequently help with small things, such as taking out garbage, recycling, and simple maintenance, like changing light bulbs. They do all of this without slacking off on any of their regular responsibilities, which include general maintenance, contracting repair jobs, and scheduling and supervising of outside contractors.

   The only negative thing I have to say about this couple is that they are leaving! I would love to keep them on, but I understand that they need the higher salary and larger apartment they would have for working in your building. I urge you to consider them strongly; you won't find a better couple to manage your building.


Sincerely,

   Samuel G. Epstein


## Examining Workplace Writing

1. Highlight Epstein's thesis sentence.

2. Identify the characteristics that make the Fioris good building managers.

3. Is Epstein's introductory paragraph adequate?

4. What does Epstein's final paragraph accomplish?

## Workplace Writing Assignments

1. Assume you are a language arts (reading, writing, speaking) teacher for an elementary school. Your district's school board has denied your request for classroom computers with Internet access. Write a letter to the school board explaining why computers and Internet access are important to children and are needed instructional tools.

2. Suppose you are a children's social worker. You specialize in assisting children of divorced parents. One of your clients, a 14-year-old teenager, will be allowed to choose which parent to live with. You will not try to make the decision for her, but you have told her you will offer some ideas to help her make it. Write the teenager a letter providing questions or guidelines that will help her decide.

3. You are working in merchandising for a large department-store chain. The company is running a contest for employees, asking them to submit suggestions for merchandising displays for any of the major holidays. Write a letter submitting your ideas for a creative, contest-winning display.

# WRITING ABOUT A READING

## Thinking Before Reading

This reading, "Navigating My Eerie Landscape Alone" by Jim Bobryk, first appeared in *Newsweek* magazine on March 8, 1999.

As you read, notice how the author presents and develops his thesis statement; how he organizes his essay; and how he introduces and concludes his essay.

1. Preview the reading, using the steps on p. 30 in Chapter 2.

2. Activate your thinking by answering the following:

   a. Imagine what it might be like to lose one of your senses. Would you welcome help from strangers, or prefer to be left alone? Why?

   b. Do you feel comfortable offering assistance to a disabled person? Or do you prefer to wait for them to ask for help?

# Navigating My Eerie Landscape Alone

*Unless I ask for help, strangers are so afraid of doing the wrong thing that they do nothing at all.*

### Jim Bobryk

1    Now, as I stroll down the street, my right forefinger extends five feet in front of me, feeling the ground where my feet will walk.

2    Before, my right hand would have been on a steering wheel as I went down the street. I drove to work, found shortcuts in strange cities, picked up my two daughters after school. Those were the days when I ran my finger down a phone-book page and never dialed Information. When I read novels and couldn't sleep until I had finished the last page. Those were the nights when I could point out a shooting star before it finished scraping across the dark sky. And when I could go to the movies and it didn't matter if it was a foreign film or not.

3    But all this changed about seven years ago. I was driving home for lunch on what seemed to be an increasingly foggy day, although the perky radio deejay said it was clear and sunny. After I finished my lunch, I realized that I couldn't see across the room to my front door. I had battled **glaucoma** for 20 years. Suddenly, without warning, my eyes had hemorrhaged.

**glaucoma**

an eye disorder marked by unusually high pressure within the eyeball that can lead to loss of vision

4    I will never regain any of my lost sight. I see things through a porthole covered in wax paper. I now have no vision in my left eye and only slight vision in my right. A minefield of blind spots makes people and cars suddenly appear and vanish. I have no depth perception. Objects are not closer and farther; they're larger and smaller. Steps, curbs and floors all flow on the same flat plane. My world has shapes but no features. Friends are mannequins in the fog until I recognize their voices. Printed words look like ants writhing on the pages. Doorways are unlit mine shafts. This is not a place for the fainthearted.

5    My cane is my navigator in this eerie landscape. It is a hollow fiber-glass stick with white reflector paint and a broad red band at the tip. It folds up tightly into four 15-inch sections, which can then be slipped into a black holster that attaches to my belt with Velcro.

6    Adults—unless they're preoccupied or in a hurry—will step aside without comment when they see me coming. Small children will either be scooped up apologetically or steered away by their parents. Only teenagers

sometimes try to play chicken, threatening to collide with me and then vee-ing out of the way at the last moment.

7   While I'm wielding my stick, strangers are often afraid to communicate with me. I don't take this personally—anymore. Certainly they can't be afraid that I'll lash at them with my rod. (Take *that,* you hapless sighted person! Whack!) No, they're probably more afraid *for* me. Don't startle the sword swallower. Don't tickle the baton twirler.

8   The trick for the sighted person is to balance courtesy with concern. Should he go out of his way or should he get out of the way? Will his friend-liness be misconstrued by the disabled as pity? Will an offer of help sound patronizing? These anxieties are exaggerated by not knowing the etiquette in dealing with the disabled. A sighted person will do nothing rather than take the risk of offending the blind. Still, I refuse to take a dim view of all this.

9   When I peer over my cane and ask for help, no one ever cowers in fear. In fact, I think people are waiting for me to give them the green light to help. It makes us feel good to help.

10   When I ask for a small favor, I often get more assistance than I ever expect. Clerks will find my required forms and fill them out for me. A group of people will parade me across a dangerous intersection. A salesclerk will read the price tag for me and then hunt for the item on sale. I'm no **Don Juan**, but strange (and possibly exotic) women will take my hand and walk me through dark rooms, mysterious train stations and foreign airports. Cabbies wait and make sure I make it safely into lobbies.

11   It's not like it's inconvenient for friends to help me get around. Hey, have disabled parking placard—will travel. Christmas shopping? Take me to the mall and I'll get us front-row parking. Late for the game? *No problema.* We'll be parking by the stadium entrance And if some inconsiderate interloper does park in the blue zone without a permit, he'll either be running after a fleeing tow truck or paying a big fine.

12   Worried about those age lines showing? Not with me looking. Put down that industrial-strength Oil of Olay. To me, your skin looks as clear and smooth as it was back in the days when you thought suntanning was a good idea.

13   So you see, I'm a good guy to know. I just carry a cane, that's all.

14   None of this is to make light of going blind. Being blind is dark and depressing. When you see me walking with my cane, you may think I'm lost as I **ricochet** down the street. But you'll find more things in life if you don't travel in a straight line.

**Don Juan**
a man with the reputation of being the lover of many women

**ricochet**
to bounce off of or rebound

## Getting Ready to Write

### Reviewing the Reading

1. Why is the author blind?

2. How do adults treat Bobryk when he is carrying his cane?

3. What is Bobryk's attitude toward his blindness?

4. What is Bobryk's attitude toward those who do not offer assistance?

5. Explain the meaning of the last sentence of the essay.

### Examining the Reading: Using Idea Maps to Understand a Reading

In this reading, the author discusses his loss of sight. He develops his thesis by offering vivid details of his experiences. Complete the idea map of "Navigating My Eerie Landscape Alone," using the format shown on the next page.

### Thinking Critically: Figurative Language

Figurative language refers to words or expressions that make sense on a creative or imaginative level, but do not make sense literally. Here are a few everyday figurative expressions:

> The child was like an octopus, grabbing all the toys around him.

> Samantha looked like a wet dishcloth.

The meaning of each of these is clear, but you can see that they are not factually or literally true.

Figurative language is a creative way of expressing ideas. It appeals to your imagination, senses, or emotions. It usually involves a comparison between two unlike things that share at least one common characteristic. The expression "Samantha looks like a wet dishcloth" takes two dissimilar things (Samantha and a wet dishcloth) and says they are similar in one way (how they look). The expression creates a mental image and suggests more than it says about Samantha's appearance. When you visualize a person looking like a wet dishcloth, what do you see?

The essay "Navigating My Eerie Landscape Alone" contains numerous figurative expressions. For example, in describing his diminished sight (paragraph 4), Bobryk says, "I see things through a porthole covered in wax paper." This is a metaphor: he is comparing what he is capable of seeing to looking through a small, round opening with a waxy filter over it. We know he was not literally looking through a porthole covered in wax paper; however, that vision is similar to what he sees through his blinded eyes. Figurative expressions that compare two unlike things are called *similes* when they use the words *like* or *as*, and *metaphors* when they do not use any comparison words. For example, if Bobryk had said "It was like

# Visualize It!

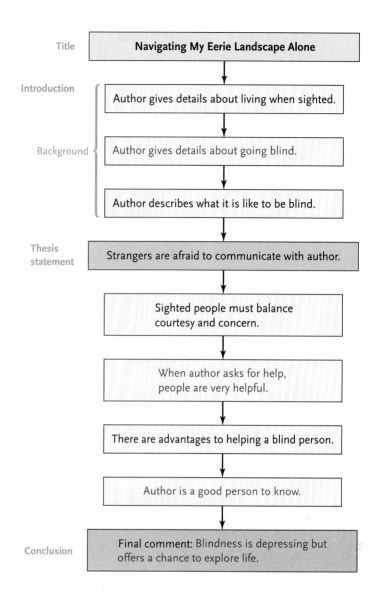

looking through a porthole covered in wax paper," that would be a simile. Explain the meaning of each of the following figurative expressions used in the reading.

1. "A minefield of blind spots" (paragraph 4)

   *dangerous areas where vision is lacking*
   _____

2. "Friends are mannequins in the fog" (paragraph 4)

   *friends appear to be unclear, stiff figures*
   _____

3. "ants writhing on the pages" (paragraph 4)

   *words seem like tiny dots moving on the page*
   _____

4. "Doorways are unlit mine shafts" (paragraph 4)

   *doorways are dark openings to unknown spaces*
   _____

## Strengthening Your Vocabulary

**Part A:** Using the word's context, word parts, or a dictionary, write a brief definition of each of the following words or phrases as it is used in the reading.

1. hemorrhage (paragraph 3) _to bleed heavily_

2. mannequin (paragraph 4) _a dummy used for displaying clothes_

3. eerie (paragraph 5) _mysterious or strange; unusual in a supernatural way_

4. misconstrued (paragraph 8) _misunderstood; analyzed or interpreted something incorrectly_

5. patronizing (paragraph 8) _treating someone as if he or she is less knowledgeable or intelligent than yourself_

6. etiquette (paragraph 8) _the rules or conventions governing proper conduct in social settings_

7. interloper (paragraph 11) _an intruder; someone who interferes in other people's affairs_

**Part B:** Choose one of the above words and draw a word map.

## Reacting To Ideas: Discussion and Journal Writing

1. Why did the author choose the title "Navigating My Eerie Landscape Alone"? What does he mean by "eerie landscape"?

2. What is the purpose of paragraph 2?

3. What does the author mean when he wrote about people not being afraid *of* him but being afraid *for* him? Find the two figurative phrases he uses to describe this phenomenon and explain what they mean.

4. Write a journal entry explaining how Bobyrk uses humor to convey his ideas.

## Writing About the Reading

### Paragraph Options

1. Write a paragraph about the things sighted people take for granted. What were some of the things the author mentioned?

2. Close your eyes tightly and walk through your room. Write a paragraph about how different the room and the things in it feel as you navigated your way through it.

3. Write a paragraph about what you would miss most if you lost your sense of smell.

### Essay Options

4. Write an essay about a time you needed help during an extraordinary situation or crisis. How did you feel about asking for that help? How did people react to your request?

5. Bobryk says it makes us feel good to help someone. Write an essay agreeing or disagreeing with this viewpoint. Use examples from your experience to support your ideas.

6. Bobryk wrote not only about how he sees the world, but how the world sees him. Write an essay about either (a) a way in which you have changed that affects your view of the world or (b) how you might change your life if you knew you were going to lose a sense or suffer a potentially fatal disease.

## Revision Checklist

1. Is your essay appropriate for your audience? Does it give them the background information they need? Will it interest them?

2. Will your essay accomplish your purpose?

3. Have you narrowed your topic so that you can cover your subject thoroughly in your essay?

4. Is your main point clearly expressed in a thesis statement in the introductory paragraph? Does your introductory paragraph capture the reader's interest and lead into the body of the essay?

5. Does each paragraph of your essay have a topic sentence that supports your main point?

6. Is each paragraph's topic sentence supported by relevant and sufficient detail?

7. Are your paragraphs arranged in a logical sequence and connected by transitional words and phrases?

8. Is the tone of your essay appropriate for your purpose and audience?

9. Does your conclusion reemphasize your thesis statement and draw the essay to a close?

10. Does your title identify the topic and interest the reader?

11. Have you proofread your paper and corrected any mechanical errors (grammar, spelling, punctuation, and so on)? (See the inside back cover of this book for a proofreading checklist.)

# CHAPTER REVIEW AND PRACTICE

## Chapter Review

| | |
|---|---|
| WHAT SHOULD YOU CONSIDER WHEN PLANNING AN ESSAY? | Be sure to select an appropriate level of detail, to obtain complete and correct information, to choose a logical method of development, and to choose an appropriate tone. |
| WHAT IS A THESIS STATEMENT? | A thesis statement expresses the main point of your essay. |
| HOW DO YOU DEVELOP A THESIS STATEMENT? | Use a prewriting technique to generate ideas. Group or arrange the ideas into meaningful categories. |
| WHAT DOES AN EFFECTIVE THESIS STATEMENT DO? | A thesis statement <ul><li>must state the main point of your essay.</li><li>should express a viewpoint about the topic.</li><li>should be specific and detailed.</li><li>may suggest the organization of the essay.</li><li>should not be a direct announcement.</li><li>should offer a fresh, interesting perspective.</li></ul> |
| HOW SHOULD YOU REVISE YOUR THESIS STATEMENT? | Use the three questions on pp. 371–372. |

| WHAT METHOD OF DEVELOPMENT AND TYPES OF DETAILS SHOULD YOU USE TO SUPPORT THE THESIS? | Develop and explain your thesis by using narration, process, description, illustration, classification, definition, comparison or contrast, cause and effect, and argument. |
|---|---|
| WHAT TYPES OF TRANSITIONS SHOULD YOU USE? | Use transitional words and phrases, transitional sentences, and repetition of key words. |
| WHAT SHOULD THE INTRODUCTION DO? | It should present your thesis, interest your reader, and provide relevant background information. |
| WHAT SHOULD THE CONCLUSION DO? | It should reemphasize the thesis statement and draw the essay to a close. |
| WHAT SHOULD THE TITLE DO? | It should identify the topic in an interesting way. |
| HOW SHOULD YOU REVISE AN ESSAY? | Use a revision idea map to revise. |

## Skill Refresher: When to Use Commas

Commas separate parts of a sentence from one another. Commas most often separate:

1. Items in a list or series.

   I need to buy jeans, socks, T-shirts, and a new tie.

2. Introductory phrases.

   After a cup of coffee, I was awake enough to read the paper.

3. Information that interrupts the sentence.

   The president of our chamber of commerce, Lucy Skarda, arranged the meeting.

4. Direct quotations.

   Barbara Walters always says, "We're in touch, so you'll be in touch."

5. Two independent clauses joined by a conjunction.

   We bill on a 60-day cycle, and we expect payment within 30 days.

6. A dependent clause from an independent clause when the dependent clause comes first in the sentence.

   Because I enjoy watching animals, I visit the zoo often.

Commas are also used in dates, addresses, numbers, and openings and closings of letters.

## Rate Your Ability to Use Commas Correctly

Punctuate each of the following sentences using commas.

1. Although I was late, my sister was still waiting for me at the restaurant.

2. They have sales offices in Minneapolis, Detroit, Cincinnati, and Pittsburgh.

3. Following the movie, we had a late lunch.

4. I bumped into a beautiful woman, Lisa's mother, on my way into the grocery store.

5. The phone rang, but I was outside.

6. My niece began to yell, "I'm Tarzan king of the jungle."

7. Ted Keith, vice president of production, is retiring next year.

8. When I entered the room, everyone was watching television.

9. I heard her call, "Wait for me."

10. Although I have visited Vancouver, I have never been to Vancouver Island.

Score _____

Check your answers, using the Answer Key on p. 644. If you missed more than two, you need additional review and practice in recognizing when to use commas. Refer to Part VI, "Reviewing the Basics," and under section E, see "Commas."

## INTERNET ACTIVITIES

### 1. Thesis Statements

Follow the steps on this Web page from Metro Community Colleges, Kansas City, Missouri.

http://www.kcmetro.cc.mo.us/maplewoods/writeplace/thesisstatement.html

Create three thesis statements for essays dealing with current events.

### 2. Introductions, Conclusions, and Titles

Use this information from the Writing Center at George Mason University to analyze the introductions, conclusions, and titles of three articles from a newspaper or magazine.

http://www.gmu.edu/departments/writingcenter/handouts/introcon.html

### 3.   Transitions

Using effective transitions is an important part of creating flow in your essays and guiding the reader through your main points. Using this handout from Purdue University, highlight transitional words and phrases in a magazine article. Evaluate the use of these transitions.

http://www.owl.english.purdue.edu/handouts/general/gl_transition.html

### 4.   This Book's Web Site

Visit this site to find templates of idea maps for essay writing and additional practice on skills taught in the chapter.

http://www.ablongman.com/mcwhorterexpressways1e

# 16

# Summarizing and Synthesizing Sources

## Chapter Objectives

*In this chapter you will learn to:*

1. Work with reference sources.

2. Write annotations, paraphrases, and summaries.

3. Use sources to support your ideas.

4. Synthesize sources.

## Write About It!

Write a sentence identifying the issue the photograph confronts. Suppose you were asked to write a paper about this issue? How would you begin? Unless you are very familiar with it, you would need to do research on the topic. You would need to locate print and Internet sources that provide further information, and use that information in your essay. You would need to summarize what you read, being sure to credit the sources you use. You would also have to put together, or synthesize, the information from a variety of sources. These are useful skills in a variety of everyday, academic, and workplace situations. In this chapter you will learn to use sources, summarize and synthesize them, and correctly credit your sources.

---

EVERYDAY SCENARIOS

- Reading performance reports for several cars you are considering purchasing and synthesizing the information
- Reading several movie reviews of a film and coming to a conclusion on whether it is worth seeing

ACADEMIC SCENARIOS

- Writing a paper for an American government class comparing the accomplishments of two presidents
- Writing a lab report for chemistry in which you summarize the findings of an experiment

WORKPLACE SCENARIOS

- Writing an executive summary of a lengthy market analysis for the president of your company
- Researching whether there is a market in a specific city for a new branch of your company

---

# USING SOURCES

In completing some of the writing assignments in this book, you may have found yourself wishing you had more detailed facts or information to support your ideas. Suppose, for example, you are writing a paper about why you think radio talk shows are popular. As you write, you realize that it would be helpful to have some statistics about which talk shows draw the largest audiences and what kinds of people make up the audience. By consulting the right books, magazine and newspaper articles, and Web sites, you can find the needed information and use it in your paper (being sure to note where you got it, of course).

Many assignments in college require you to locate and read several sources of information on a topic and then use them to support and "flesh out" your ideas. At other times, you may be asked to examine certain printed sources and come up with a new idea or thesis about them. For example, in an American government course you may be asked to read several essays or speeches by a member of Congress and to develop a thesis about his or her outlook on a particular environmental issue. Or for a political science course you may be asked to find several different newspaper or magazine accounts of an event and write about how coverage varied, depending on where the account was printed.

On the job, too, you will be called upon to use sources and pull together ideas from them. For example, a fitness specialist who manages a health club was asked by the owner to review the descriptions and specifications for five different brands of treadmills. She was asked to summarize the features of each and synthesize from these sources a recommendation of which would be best to buy.

This chapter provides practice in two ways on how to use sources in your writing—to support your ideas (summarizing sources) and to generate new ideas (synthesizing sources).

## Working with Reference Sources

Libraries are filled with sources—print, electronic, and more. They house thousands of books, journals, videos, DVDs, pamphlets, tapes, and newspapers, as well as computers that enable you to access the World Wide Web. Yet this very abundance of sources means that one of the hardest parts of doing research is locating the sources that will be the most help to you.

Many books have been written on how to do research and how to use and document print and electronic sources. Therefore, this section gives only a brief overview of the research process and offers advice on how to get started.

### Finding and Using Appropriate Sources

Suppose you are writing an essay about differences in men's and women's communication styles. Although you will find many sources on your topic, not all will be appropriate for your particular assignment.

Some sources may be too technical; others may be too sketchy. Some may be outdated, others too opinionated. Your task is to find sources that will give you good, solid, current information or points of view. Use the following tips:

1. **Keep track of all the sources you use.** There are several good reasons for doing this:

   - When you use sources in a paper, you must acknowledge them all at the end of your paper in a bibliography or "Works Cited" list. Providing your reader with information on your sources is called **documentation.**

   - You may want to refer to the source again.

   - You are more likely to avoid plagiarism if you keep accurate records of your sources. Plagiarism is using an author's words or ideas without acknowledging that you have done so. It is a serious ethical error and legal violation. In some colleges, plagiarism is sufficient cause for failing a course or even being dismissed from the college. You can easily avoid plagiarism by properly acknowledging your sources within your paper.

- Record all publication information about each print and electronic source. For print sources, record title, author(s), volume, edition, place and date of publication, publisher, and page number(s). You may want to use index cards or a small bound notebook to record source information, using a separate card or page for each source. Print the home page of Web site sources and bookmark them, in case you need to find them again. You will learn how to document sources you use later in this chapter on p. 415.

2. **Consult a reference librarian.** If you are unsure of where to begin, ask a reference librarian for advice. It is a reference librarian's job to suggest useful sources. He or she can be very helpful to you.

3. **Use a systematic approach.** Start by using general sources, either print or electronic, such as general reference books and, as needed, move to more specific sources such as periodicals and journals (scholarly magazines written for people focused on a particular area of study).

4. **Use current sources.** For many topics, such as controversial issues or scientific or medical advances, only the most up-to-date sources are useful. For other topics, such as the moral issues involved in abortion or euthanasia, older sources can be used. Before you begin, decide on a cut-off date—a date before which you feel information will be outdated and therefore not useful to you.

5. **Sample a variety of viewpoints.** Try to find sources that present differing viewpoints on the same subject rather than counting on one source to contain everything you need. Various authors take different approaches and have different opinions on the same topic, all of which can increase your understanding of the topic.

6. **Preview articles by reading abstracts or summaries.** Many sources begin with an abstract or end with a summary. Before using the source, check the abstract or summary to determine if the source is going to be helpful.

7. **Reading sources selectively.** Many students spend time needlessly reading entire books and articles thoroughly when they should be reading selectively—skimming to avoid parts that are not on the subject and to locate portions that relate directly to their topic. To read selectively,

   - use indexes and tables of contents to locate the portions of books that are useful and appropriate. In articles, use abstracts or summaries as a guide to the material's organization: the order in which ideas appear in the summary or abstract is the order in which they appear in the source itself.

   - after you have identified useful sections, preview (see p. 30) to get an overview of the material.

   - use headings to select sections to read thoroughly.

8. **Choose reliable, trustworthy sources.** The Internet contains a great deal of valuable information, but it also contains rumor, gossip, hoaxes, and misinformation. Before using a source, evaluate it by checking the author's credentials, considering the sponsor or publisher of the site, checking the date of posting, and verifying links. If you are uncertain about the information contained on a site, verify the information by cross-checking it with another source.

9. **Look for sources that lead to other sources.** Some sources include a bibliography, which provides leads to other works related to your topic. Follow links included in electronic sources.

## EXERCISE 16-1
*Writing in Progress*

**Directions:** Choose one of the broad topics below. Use a prewriting strategy to narrow the topic and develop a working thesis statement. Locate at least three reference sources that are useful and appropriate for writing a paper of two to three pages on the topic you have developed. Make a photocopy of the pages you consulted in each source. Print copies of Web sites used. Be sure to record all the bibliographic information for each source.

1. Drug testing in the workplace

2. Date rape

3. Teenage parents

4. The history of trade unions

5. The spread, control, or treatment of HIV

6. The Great Depression of the 1930s

7. Controversy over college athletic scholarships

8. Legalized gambling (or lotteries)

## Annotating a Source

In her mass-media course, L'Tanya was assigned to write a paper on how the media, such as TV, radio, and magazines, shape how people think. In a text-book, she found a report of a study on how the media portray men differently from women. It was the first information she had found on the different treatment of the sexes in the media, and the subject caught her interest.

Deciding to narrow her paper to that topic, she read the discussion carefully, highlighter in hand, thinking about ways she could develop the topic. All kinds of questions and thoughts came to mind. By highlighting, however, she was not able to record her ideas and reactions. Putting ideas on a separate sheet of paper and copying quotations from the article would not work either because she was running out of time. A friend suggested that she annotate instead.

## Why Write Annotations?

L'Tanya photocopied the article and recorded her reactions in the margins. An excerpt of the article with L'Tanya's annotations is shown below. First, read the excerpt; then study the marginal notes, called *annotations*. Then read the following sections to discover why and how to annotate.

### Excerpt

Which media? All media?

Media images of men and women also differ in other subtle ways. In any visual representation of a person—such as a photograph, drawing, or painting—you can measure the relative prominence of the face by calculating the percentage of the vertical dimension occupied by the model's head. When Dane Archer and his colleagues (1983) inspected 1,750 photographs from *Time, Newsweek,* and other magazines, they found what they called "face-ism," a bias toward greater facial prominence in pictures of men than of women. This phenomenon is so prevalent that it appeared in analyses of 3,500 photographs from different countries, classic portraits painted in the seventeenth century, and the amateur drawings of college students.

Aren't men's faces larger?

Who selects them? Were they selected randomly?

Were only portraits and drawings analyzed?

Why?
Are these stereotypes?

Why is the face more prominent in pictures of men than of women? One possible interpretation is that face-ism reflects historical conceptions of the sexes. The face and head symbolize the mind and *intellect*—which are traditionally associated with men. With respect to women, more importance is attached to the heart, emotions, or perhaps just the body. Indeed, when people evaluate models from photographs, those pictured with high facial prominence are seen as smarter and more assertive, active, and ambitious—regardless of their gender (Schwarz & Kurz, 1989). Another interpretation is that facial prominence signals power and *dominance.*

Brehm and Kassin, *Social Psychology*

Annotating allowed L'Tanya to jot down her ideas, reactions, opinions, and comments as she read. Think of annotation as scribbling down your ideas about what you are reading. It is a personal way to brainstorm and "talk back" to the author—to question, challenge, agree, disagree, or comment on what he or she is saying.

Annotations are particularly useful when you are working with a source in great detail. You can use annotations to clarify an author's meaning as well as to record your responses to what they have written. To clarify meaning, you might

- underline or highlight key ideas.

- place a star by key terms or definitions.

- number key supporting information.

- define unfamiliar words.

- paraphrase a complicated idea.

- bracket [ ] a useful example.

- mark with an asterisk (*) useful summary statements.

- draw arrows connecting ideas.

- highlight statements that reveal the author's feelings or attitudes.

In recording your responses, you might include

| | |
|---|---|
| questions | Why would . . . ? |
| challenges to the author's ideas | If this is true, wouldn't . . . ? |
| inconsistencies | But the author said earlier that . . . |
| examples | For instance . . . |
| exceptions | This wouldn't be true if . . . |
| disagreements | How could . . . ? |
| associations with other sources | This is similar to . . . |
| judgments | Good point . . . |

Overall, annotating helps clarify meaning and allows you to interact with the author's words and ideas. When you use the source in your own paper, you will be familiar with what it says and be able to go right to the part that you need.

## EXERCISE 16-2
### Writing in Progress

**Directions:** Reread one of the sources you located in Exercise 16-1 and write annotations on it.

## Writing a Paraphrase

Marcie was writing a paper on animal communication for her biology class. In a reference source, she found one passage that contained exactly the information she needed. To help herself remember both the author's main point and details, she decided to paraphrase.

A **paraphrase** is a restatement, in your own words, of a passage. In a paraphrase, you fully acknowledge who wrote the original passage and where you found it, but you condense it and recast it. It is a rewording of each sentence in the order in which each appears in the passage.

Here is an excerpt from the source, followed by Marcie's paraphrase:

### Excerpt from Source

**Communication in the Animal Kingdom**
Animal species have complex forms of communication. Ants send chemical signals secreted from glands to share information about food and enemies with other members of the colony. When honeybees discover a source of nectar, they return to the hive and communicate its location to the other worker bees through an intricate dance that signals both direction and distance. Male songbirds of various species sing in the spring to attract a female mate and also to warn other males to stay away from their territory to avoid a fight. Dolphins talk to each other at great depths of the ocean by making a combination of clicking, whistling, and barking sounds.

Kassin, *Psychology*

*Marcie's Paraphrase of "Communication in the Animal Kingdom"*

According to Kassin (252), animals have complicated ways of communicating. Ants can tell each other about food and enemies by secreting chemicals from their glands. Honeybees tell others in their hive that they have found a source of nectar by a detailed dance that indicates both where the nectar is located and how far away it is. In the spring, male songbirds sing to draw females and to warn other males to stay away so as to avoid a dispute. Using clicks, whistles, and barking sounds, dolphins communicate with each other.

## Why Write a Paraphrase?

Paraphrasing is a useful skill for many college courses. First, in combination with careful documentation of source information, it is a way to record ideas from a source for later use in a paper. It gives you complete information in a form that is easy to understand. Sometimes your paraphrase can be incorporated directly into your paper (see pp. 409–410). Remember, however, that though you have changed the wording, you are still working with someone else's ideas and not your own; therefore, it is still necessary to document the source in your paper. (Refer to the later section of this chapter, "Documenting Sources," p. 415.)

Second, you can also use paraphrasing to make an author's ideas clearer and more understandable, regardless of whether you plan to use them or not. When you paraphrase, you are forced to understand each idea fully and see how ideas relate to one another.

Finally, paraphrasing is a useful study and note-taking strategy. It allows the convenient review of difficult or complicated material. By paraphrasing a source, you think through and learn the information it contains.

## How to Paraphrase

A paraphrase involves two skills: (1) substituting synonyms and (2) rewording and rearranging sentence parts.

### Substituting Synonyms

A *synonym* is a word that has the same general meaning as another word. Take another look at Marcie's paraphrase and the original source, noticing how she substituted synonyms. For example, in the first sentence she substituted *complicated* for *complex, types* for *forms,* and so forth. When selecting synonyms, use the following guidelines:

1. **Make sure the synonym you choose fits the context (overall meaning) of the sentence.** Suppose the sentence you are paraphrasing is "The physician attempted to *neutralize* the effects of the drug overdose." All of the following words are synonyms for the word *neutralize: negate, nullify, counteract.* However, *counteract* fits the context, but *negate* and *nullify* do not. *Negate* and *nullify* suggest the ability to cancel, and a drug overdose, once taken, cannot be canceled. It can, however, be counteracted.

2. **Refer to a dictionary.** Use a print or online dictionary to check the exact meanings of words; refer to a thesaurus (a dictionary of synonyms) to get ideas for alternative or equivalent words.

3. **Do not try to replace every word in a sentence with a synonym.** Sometimes a substitute does not exist. In the sentence "Archeologists study fossils of extinct species," the term *fossils* clearly and accurately describes what archeologists study. Therefore, it does not need to be replaced.

4. **Be sure to paraphrase—that is, do not change *only* a few words.**

### Rewording and Rearranging Sentence Parts

Return to Marcie's paraphrase on p. 403. Reread her paraphrase again, noticing how the ideas within each sentence were rearranged. When rearranging sentence parts, use the following guidelines:

1. **Split lengthy, complicated sentences into two or more shorter sentences.**

2. **Be sure you understand the author's key ideas as well as related ideas.** Include both in your paraphrase. For example:

| | |
|---|---|
| ORIGINAL | Many judges hold that television cameras should not be permitted in a court of law because the defendant's right to a fair trial may be jeopardized. |
| CORRECT PARAPHRASE | Since cameras may prevent a defendant from being treated fairly, many judges feel television cameras should not be allowed in the courtroom. |
| INCORRECT PARAPHRASE | Many judges feel television cameras should not be allowed in the courtroom. |

The incorrect paraphrase does not include the reason *why* (a related idea) judges feel cameras should not be allowed.

## EXERCISE 16-3

**Directions:** Working sentence by sentence, write a paraphrase of paragraphs 3 and 4 of "Who Has the Right to Name?" at the end of this chapter. Compare your work with that of a classmate; combine both of your paraphrases to produce a revised paraphrase.

## EXERCISE 16-4
*Writing in Progress*

**Directions:** Write a paraphrase of two or three consecutive paragraphs of one of the sources you located in Exercise 16-1.

# Writing Summaries

The instructor of a speech communication class placed the book *You Just Don't Understand: Women and Men in Conversation* by Deborah Tannen on reserve in the library and assigned several sections to read. He also asked students to write a summary of a particular passage. A *summary* is a brief statement of the major points of a source. A summary is always shorter than the original.

The original passage is printed below, along with the summaries written by two students, Carlos and James. Compare the two student summaries and decide which better fits the definition.

## Original Selection

Differences in physical alignment, or body language among friends talking to each other, leap out at anyone who looks at segments of videotapes one after another. At every age, the girls and women sit closer to each other and look at each other directly. At every age, the boys and men sit at angles to each other—in one case, almost parallel—and never look directly into each other's faces. I developed the term *anchoring gaze* to describe this visual home base. The girls and women anchor their gaze on each other's faces, occasionally glancing away, while the boys and men anchor their gaze elsewhere in the room, occasionally glancing at each other.

The boys' and men's avoidance of looking directly at each other is especially important because researchers, and conventional wisdom, have emphasized that girls and women tend to be more indirect than boys and men in their speech. Actually, women and men tend to be indirect about different things. In physical alignment, and in verbally expressing personal problems, the men tend to be more indirect.

*Tannen, You Just Don't Understand: Women and Men in Conversation*

## Carlos's Summary

Although researchers and others have traditionally believed men to be more direct than women, videotapes of friends interacting show that this is an over generalization. The truth is that men and women tend to be indirect about different things. Specifically, men tend to be indirect in body language and in talking about personal problems. In each of these tapes, women sit closer to each other than men and look more directly at each other than men do.

## James's Summary

There are many differences in physical alignment as seen on videotapes of men and women. During each tape, women and girls align themselves closer (sit closer) than men and boys. Men and boys sit at angular positions—not facing each other. In fact, they never even look at each other's faces. The word *anchoring* is used to describe their visual gaze. It is said that girls and women anchor their gaze on each other's faces, but boys and men anchor their gaze everywhere else in the room except on each other's faces. They only glance at each other sometimes.

Researchers find the fact that boys and men avoid looking into each other's faces interesting because the idea that girls and women are usually more indirect than boys and men has always been universally accepted. Also researchers have advocated the idea that girls and women have a tendency to be less direct in their speech than boys and men. In reality, men and women are both indirect about different things. In the verbal expression of problems and in physical alignment, men tend to be less direct.

Did you decide that Carlos's summary was more effective? Did you notice that James repeated each idea that appeared in the original? He did not eliminate detail in order to focus only on the main points as Carlos did.

## What Is a Summary and How Is It Used?

A **summary** is a brief statement of major points. It presents only the main ideas. Usually a summary is about one-fifth of the original, or less, depending on the amount of detail needed. Summaries have four uses:

1. **A summary improves your grasp of a writer's ideas.** If you cannot summarize an article, you probably do not understand it. Writing a summary also clarifies your thinking. To write a summary you are forced to sort ideas and see how they relate.

2. **A summary records another writer's ideas, but in shortened form.** Summaries make it easier for you to keep track of a writer's important ideas and eliminate less important information.

3. **Many college instructors assign summaries.** You may be asked to submit a plot summary of a short story, a summary of a news article for economics, or a summary of your findings for a laboratory experiment in the sciences.

4. **In the workplace, you may be asked to summarize.** You might write minutes summarizing a meeting, condense a lengthy report, or briefly describe the outcomes of a sales conference you attended.

## How to Write a Summary

To write more effective summaries, follow these guidelines:

1. **Read the entire source first before writing anything.**

2. **Review the source.** Underline or highlight the main points, and make annotations in the margins.

3. **Write an opening sentence that states the author's thesis.**

4. **Explain the author's most important supporting ideas.** (Refer to text you have underlined or highlighted.) Be sure to express the author's main ideas in your own words. Don't copy phrases or sentences. If you can't express an idea in your own words, you probably don't yet understand it. Look up words, reread, talk to someone about the passage, and think about the passage to clarify its meaning.

5. **Include restated definitions of key terms, important concepts, procedures, or principles.** Do not include examples, descriptive details, quotations, or anything incidental to the main point. Do not include your opinion, even to say it was a good article.

6. **Present the ideas in the order in which they appear in the original source.**

7. **Reread your summary to determine if it contains sufficient information.** Use this test: would your summary be understandable to someone who had not read the article? If not, revise your summary to include additional information.

Be sure to note in full the bibliographic reference for each source you summarize. When you write your paper, you will need to give credit to the writer if you use information from the summary in your paper. If you don't cite your original source, you may be guilty of plagiarism, whether you intend to "copy" it or not.

## EXERCISE 16-5

**Directions:** Write a summary of "Urban Legends" at the end of this chapter on p. 427. Use the steps listed above.

## EXERCISE 16-6
### Writing in Progress

**Directions:** Write a summary of one of the sources you located for Exercise 16-1 (use a different source from the one you paraphrased).

## Using Sources to Support Your Ideas

Often when writing an essay you will find that you need additional information to support or explain your ideas. Suppose you are writing an essay on one aspect of the homeless situation in America. Your thesis states that more social programs should be funded to help homeless people regain control of their lives. In order to present a convincing paper, you need facts, statistics, and evidence to support your opinions. For example, you might need

- statistics on the numbers of homeless.

- statistics on the increase in homelessness in recent years.

- statistics on the amount of money spent on programs for the homeless.

- facts on the types of social programs currently in operation.

- facts on which programs work and which do not.

- statistics on the costs of existing programs.

To gather this information, you need to consult one or more reference sources. The following guidelines will help you use sources properly:

1. **Write a first draft of your paper.** Before consulting sources to support your ideas, work through the first three steps of the writing process: prewriting, organizing, and drafting. Get your own ideas down on paper. Once you have drafted your paper, you will be able to see what

types of supporting information are necessary. If you research first, you might get flooded with facts and with other writers' voices and viewpoints, and lose your own.

2. **Analyze your draft to identify needed information.** Study your draft and look for statements that require supporting information in order to be believable. For example, suppose you have written

> The number of homeless people is increasing in Chicago each year, and nothing is being done about the increase.

To support the first part of this statement, you need statistics on the increase in homelessness in Chicago. To support the second part, you need evidence that there has not been an increase in federal, state, or local funding for the homeless in Chicago.

The following types of statements benefit from supporting information:

• **Opinions**

| EXAMPLE | Homeless people do not know how to help themselves. |
|---|---|
| NEEDED INFORMATION | Why? What evidence supports that opinion? |

• **Broad, general ideas**

| EXAMPLE | Social programs for the homeless don't work as well as they should. |
|---|---|
| NEEDED INFORMATION | What programs are available? What evidence suggests they don't work? |

• **Cause-and-effect statements**

| EXAMPLE | Most homeless people are on the street because they lost their jobs. |
|---|---|
| NEEDED INFORMATION | How many are homeless because they lost their jobs? How many are homeless for other reasons? |

• **Statements that assert what should be done**

| EXAMPLE | The homeless should be given more assistance in locating jobs. |
|---|---|
| NEEDED INFORMATION | How much are they given now? How many are helped? For how many is assistance not available? |

3. **Write questions.** Read your draft looking for unsupported statements, underlining them as you find them. Then make a list of needed information, and form questions that need to be answered. Some students find it effective to write each question on a separate index card.

4. **Record information and note sources.** As you locate needed information, make a decision about the best way to record it. Should you photocopy or make a printout from the source and annotate it? Should you paraphrase? Should you write a summary? Your answer will depend on the type of information you are using, as well as the requirements of your assignment. Always include complete bibliographic information for each source (see pp. 417–422).

   As you consult sources, you will probably discover new ideas and perhaps even a new approach to your topic. For example, you may learn that the homeless are not all the same: some are well educated and employable, some are down on their luck, and others are burdened with problems that would make holding a job difficult. Record each of these new ideas on a separate index card along with its source.

5. **Revise your paper.** Begin by adding or incorporating new supporting information. (The next section of this chapter discusses how to add and document information from other sources.) Then reevaluate your draft, eliminating statements for which you could not locate supporting information, statements that you found to be inaccurate, and statements for which you found contradictory evidence.

## EXERCISE 16-7
*Writing in Progress*

**Directions:** Write a first draft of a paper on the topic you chose in Exercise 16-1. To support your ideas, use the three sources you located. If any of these sources are dated or not focused enough for your thesis, you may need to locate additional ones.

## Adding Information from Sources

You can incorporate researched information into your paper in one of two ways: (1) summarize or paraphrase the information or (2) quote directly from it. In both cases, you must give credit to the authors from whom you borrowed the material. This is called *citing* a source.

### Summarized or Paraphrased Information

When you paraphrase information from a source, you need to give the author credit. Do this by using an in-text citation: a brief note that refers to a source fully described in what is called the Works Cited list. This list appears at the end of your paper and provides all your sources in alphabetical order.

Follow these guidelines to write correct in-text citations:

1. **If the source is introduced by a phrase that names the author, the citation need only include the page number.**

   Masson and McCarthy argue that animals do have emotions and feelings, though humans may not know what those feelings are (1).

2. **If the author is not named in the sentence, then include both the author's name and the page number in the citation.**

> Researchers often disregard evidence of emotion if the animal is captive or treated as a pet (Masson and McCarthy 5).

Entries in the Works Cited list must follow a specific format. That is, title, author's name, publisher, place of publication, and date must be in a specific order and punctuated in a specific way in each entry. There are numerous systems used by various academic disciplines to cite information. One of the most common is the Modern Language Association (MLA) documentation system.

### Sample Entry from a Works Cited List

Masson, Jeffrey Moussaieff, and Susan McCarthy. *When Elephants Weep.* New York: Delacourt, 1995.

## Direct Quotations

At times, you may want to use an author's exact words to support one of your ideas. Do this only when a direct quotation is necessary; too many quotations make your paper seem choppy and may suggest that you rely too heavily on the thoughts and words of others.

To use a direct quotation, copy the author's words exactly and put them in quotation marks. If the quotation is lengthy (five sentences or longer), set it apart from the rest of your paper by indenting the entire quotation one inch from the left margin, double space the lines, and do not use quotation marks. You do not always have to quote full sentences; you can borrow phrases or clauses as long as they fit into your sentence, both logically and grammatically.

### Direct Quotation

Masson and McCarthy observe that "social animals who live in groups often behave in a friendly way toward other members of the group, even when they are not relatives" (78).

### Lengthy Quotation

In discussing how to judge animal emotions, Masson and McCarthy note,

> Knowing what we feel is one way to judge whether an animal feels something similar, but may not be the only, or even the best way. Are animals' similarities [to] and differences from humans the only, or even the most important, issue? Surely we can train ourselves to an empathic imaginative sympathy for other species. Taught what to look for in facial features, gestures, postures, behavior, we could learn to be more open and sensitive. (xxi).

### Partial Sentence Quotation

Masson and McCarthy observe that we all have seen "gorillas sitting motionless, seemingly in despair, or perhaps having abandoned all hope of ever being free" (xvii).

When you include a quotation in your paper, you should signal your reader that one is to follow. For example, use such introductory phrases as the following:

According to Masson and McCarthy, "[quotation]."

As Masson and McCarthy note, "[quotation]."

In the words of Masson and McCarthy, "[quotation]."

## EXERCISE 16-8

*Writing in Progress*

**Directions:** For the paper you drafted in Exercise 16-7, write in-text citations and entries for your Works Cited list. Then add two direct quotations to your paper and write entries for your Works Cited list if the source for either is not included in the list.

## Synthesizing Sources

In daily life, we often consult several sources before drawing a conclusion or making a decision. For example, you might talk with several students who have taken the course American Labor History before deciding if you want to register for it. You might talk to several friends who own pickup trucks before buying one. Suppose you're debating whether or not to see a particular film. You talk with three friends who have seen it. Each liked the movie and described different scenes. However, from their various descriptions, you may conclude that the film contains too much violence and that you don't want to see it.

In each case, you draw together several sources of information and come to your own conclusion: the course is good, the Ford pickup is best, the film is too violent for you. In these situations you are synthesizing information. *Synthesis* is a process of using information from two or more sources in order to develop new ideas about a topic or to draw conclusions about it.

Many college assignments require you to synthesize material—that is, to locate and read several sources on a topic and use them to produce a paper. Synthesizing in the college setting, then, is a process of putting ideas together to create new ideas or insights based on what you have learned from the sources you consulted. For example, in a sociology course, you may be asked to consult several sources on the topic of organized crime and then write a paper describing the relationship between organized crime and illegal drug sales. In a marketing class, your instructor may direct you to consult several sources on advertising strategies and on the gullibility of young children, and write a paper weighing the effects of television commercials on young children. Both of these assignments involve synthesizing ideas from sources.

Did you notice that, in each of the above examples, you were asked to come up with a new idea, one that did not appear in any of the sources but was *based* on all three sources? Creating something new from what you read is one of the most basic, important, and satisfying skills you will learn in college.

Synthesis is also often required in the workplace:

- As sales executive for an Internet service provider company, you may be asked to synthesize what you have learned about customer hardware problems.

- As a medical office assistant, you have extensive problems with a new computer system. The office manager asks you to write a memo to the company that installed the system, categorizing the types of problems you have experienced.

- As an environmental engineer, you must synthesize years of research in order to make a proposal for local river and stream cleanup.

## How to Compare Sources to Synthesize

Comparing sources is part of synthesizing. Comparing involves placing them side by side and examining how they are the same and how they are different. However, before you begin to compare two or more sources, be sure you understand each fully. Depending on how detailed and difficult each source is, use one or more of the techniques in this chapter (annotating, paraphrasing, and summarizing) or underline, outline, or draw idea maps to make sure that you have a good grasp of your source material.

Let's assume you are taking a speech course in which you are studying nonverbal communication, or body language. You have chosen to study one aspect of body language: eye contact. Among your sources are the following excerpts:

### Source A

Eye contact, or *gaze*, is also a common form of nonverbal communication. Eyes have been called the "windows of the soul." In many cultures, people tend to assume that someone who avoids eye contact is evasive, cold, fearful, shy, or indifferent; that frequent gazing signals intimacy, sincerity, self-confidence, and respect; and that the person who stares is tense, angry, and unfriendly. Typically, however, eye contact is interpreted in light of a pre-existing relationship. If a relationship is friendly, frequent eye contact elicits a positive impression. If a relationship is not friendly, eye contact is seen in negative terms. It has been said that if two people lock eyes for more than a few seconds, they are either going to make love or kill each other (Kleinke, 1986; Patterson, 1983).

Brehm and Kassin, *Social Psychology*

### Source B

Eye contact often indicates the nature of the relationship between two people. One research study showed that eye contact is moderate when one is addressing a very high-status person, maximized when addressing a moderately high-status person, and only minimal when talking to a low-status person. There are also predictable differences in eye contact when one person likes another or when there may be rewards involved.

Increased eye contact is also associated with increased liking between the people who are communicating. In an interview, for example, you are likely to make judgments about the interviewer's friendliness according to the amount of eye contact shown. The less eye contact, the less friendliness. In a courtship relationship, more eye contact can be observed among those seeking to develop a more intimate relationship. One research study (Saperston, 2003) suggests that the intimacy is a function of the amount of eye gazing, physical proximity, intimacy of topic, and amount of smiling. This model best relates to established relationships.

Weaver, *Understanding Interpersonal Communication*

To compare these sources, ask the following questions:

1. **On what do the sources agree?** Sources A and B recognize eye contact as an important communication tool. Both agree that there is a connection between eye contact and the relationship between the people involved. Both also agree that more frequent eye contact occurs among people who are friendly or intimate.

2. **On what do the sources disagree?** Sources A and B do not disagree, though they do present different information about eye contact (see the next paragraph).

3. **How do they differ?** Sources A and B differ on the information they present. Source A states that in some cultures the frequency of eye contact suggests certain personality traits (someone who avoids eye contact is considered to be cold, for example), but Source B does not discuss cultural interpretations. Source B discusses how eye contact is related to status—the level of importance of the person being addressed—while Source A does not.

4. **Are the viewpoints toward the subject similar or different?** Both Sources A and B take a serious approach to the subject of eye contact.

5. **Does each source provide supporting evidence for major points?** Source A cites two references. Source B cites a research study.

After comparing your sources, the next step is to form your own ideas based on what you have discovered.

## How to Develop Ideas About Sources: The Thesis Statement

Developing your own ideas is a process of drawing conclusions. Your goal is to decide what both sources, taken together, suggest. Together, Sources A and B recognize that eye contact is an important part of body language. However, they focus on different aspects of how eye contact can be interpreted. You can conclude that studying eye contact can be useful in understanding the relationship between two individuals: you can judge the relative status, the degree of friendship, and the level of intimacy between the people.

Once you decide what major idea to work with, you are ready to develop a paper. Use your newly discovered idea as your thesis statement. Then use details, documented properly, from each source to develop and support your thesis statement.

## EXERCISE 16-9

**Directions:** Read each of the following excerpts from sources on the topic of lost and endangered species. Synthesize these two sources, using the steps listed above, and develop a thesis statement about the causes of the decline and loss of plant and animal species.

### Source A

Habitat loss threatens the greatest number of species, but other factors are also important. Overhunting has eliminated many species and continues to threaten others. Whales, for example, have been hunted to near extinction, and a few countries continue to kill these huge mammals despite a nearly worldwide ban on whaling. Many animals and plants have also succumbed to competition from foreign species that humans have introduced. In East Africa, hundreds of species of tropical fishes in Lake Victoria are currently threatened by the Nile perch, a large species (up to 200 lbs.) that was introduced as a sport and food fish.

Often, as for the key deer, a combination of killing and habitat destruction has driven a species over the edge. In the past century, for instance, the Hawaiian Islands have lost half their bird species, mainly to overhunting, deforestation, and diseases carried by foreign bird species introduced into the islands. In Africa, elephants and rhinoceroses are being pushed toward extinction by habitat loss and by poachers catering to a black market for ivory and horns.

*Biology* by Campbell, Mitchell, and Reece

### Source B

The driving force behind today's alarming decline in species is the destruction, degradation and fragmentation of habitat due to our increasing human population and wasteful consumption of resources. Human populations virtually all around the globe are on the rise. . . . Because Americans consume so much more energy, food and raw material than our counterparts in other developed countries, our impact on our environment is proportionally much greater. As a result, wildlife and wild places in the United States are being pushed to the brink of extinction.

While the United States does not currently face as significant an increase in population as other countries, the movement of our population to new areas and the ensuing development has resulted in the destruction of species and their habitat. Thus, not surprisingly, there is a high correlation between human population and economic development trends in the United States and species decline and ecosystem destruction.

*http://www.sierraclub.org/habitat/habitatloss.asp* (Aug. 16, 1999)

## Documenting Sources

Whenever you use the words or ideas of other people, you must *document* the source. You must give credit to the person or place from which you borrowed the material and include full information about it in a list of references so your reader can locate it easily. Failure to provide documentation of a source is called **plagiarism**. It means using an author's words or ideas without acknowledging that you have done so.

Plagiarism is a serious ethical error and legal violation. In many colleges, students who plagiarize may fail the course in which the plagiarized paper was submitted or be dismissed from the college.

## Avoiding Plagiarism and Cyberplagiarism

When you write essays for college classes, you will probably use print and electronic sources to locate the information you need. As you read and take notes, and later, as you write the essay, you need to know the rules for indicating that you have taken information or ideas from the work of other people. You identify your sources in order to help readers find a source if they want to look into the ideas of that author further, as well as to give credit to the person who originally wrote the material or thought of the idea. **Plagiarism** means borrowing someone else's ideas or exact wording without giving that person credit. If you take information on Frank Lloyd Wright's architecture from a reference source, but do not indicate where you found it, you have plagiarized. If you take the six-word phrase "Martinez, the vengeful, despicable drug czar" from an online news article on the war on drugs without putting quotation marks around it and noting the source, you have plagiarized. Plagiarism is intellectually dishonest because you are taking someone else's ideas or wording and passing them off as your own. There are academic penalties for plagiarism. You may receive a failing grade on your paper or you may fail the entire course. At some institutions you can even be expelled.

**Cyberplagiarism** is a special type of plagiarism; it involves borrowing information from the Internet without giving credit to the source posting the information. It is also called **cut and paste plagiarism**, which refers to the ease with which a person can copy something from an Internet document and paste it into his or her own paper. Numerous Web sites offer student papers for sale on the Internet. The term *cyberplagiarism* also refers to using these papers and submitting them as one's own.

### What Constitutes Plagiarism

Plagiarism can be intentional (planned) or unintentional (done by accident or oversight). Either way it carries the same academic penalty. If you buy a paper from an Internet site or deliberately copy and paste a section of an article from a Web site into your paper, your plagiarism is intentional. If you take notes from a source and copy exact wording, forget to enclose the wording in quotation marks, and later use that exact wording in your paper, your plagiarism is unintentional, but it is still dishonest. Here are some guidelines that will help you understand exactly what is considered plagiarism:

- Plagiarism is the use of another person's words without giving credit to that person.

- Plagiarism uses another person's theory, opinion, or idea without listing where the information was taken from.

- Plagiarism results when another person's exact words are not placed inside quotation marks. Both the quotation marks and a citation (reference) to the original source are needed.

- Paraphrasing (rewording) another person's words without giving credit to that person is plagiarism.

- Using facts, data, graphs, charts, and so on without stating where you obtained them is plagiarism.

- Using commonly known facts or information is not plagiarism and you need not give a source for your information. For example, the fact that Neil Armstrong set foot on the moon in 1969 is widely known and so does not require documentation.

## How to Avoid Plagiarism and Cyberplagiarism

Use the following suggestions to avoid unintentional plagiarism:

- If you copy exact words from any source, put them in quotation marks in your notes, along with the publication information: the author, title, publisher, date of publication, and page number of the source, or, for Web sites, the author, name of the site or page, date of publication, and URL. Be sure to consult a style manual for details on how to indicate in your paper which material is borrowed and how to set up a list of the works you used in your paper.

- List sources for all the information you include in your notes regardless of whether it takes the form of direct quotations, paraphrases, or summaries of someone else's ideas.

- Never copy and paste directly from a Web site into your paper without enclosing the copied material in quotation marks and listing the source.

- List the source for any information, facts, ideas, opinions, theories, or data you use from a Web site.

- When paraphrasing someone else's words, do not use the author's wording and try not to follow the exact same organization. You still must credit the source of the information.

- Write paraphrases without looking at the original text so you will rephrase it in your own words.

## EXERCISE 16-10

**Directions:** Read the following passage from *Sociology for the Twenty-First Century* by Tim Curry, Robert Jiobu, and Kent Schwirian. Place a check mark next to each statement that is an example of plagiarism.

**Mexican Americans.** Currently, *Mexican Americans* are the second-largest racial or ethnic minority in the United States, but by early in the next century they will be the largest group. Their numbers will swell as a result of continual immigration from Mexico and the relatively high Mexican birth rate. Mexican Americans are one of the oldest racial-ethnic groups in the United States. Under the terms of the treaty ending the Mexican-American War in 1848, Mexicans living in territories acquired by the United States could remain there and were to be treated as American citizens. Those that did stay became known as "Californios," "Tejanos," or "Hispanos."

_____ **a.** Mexican Americans are the second-largest minority in the United States. Their numbers grow as more people immigrate from Mexico.

_____ **b.** After the Mexican-American War, those Mexicans living in territories owned by the United States became American citizens and were called "Californios," "Tejanos," and "Hispanos" (Curry, Jiobu, and Schwirian, 207).

_____ **c.** "Mexican Americans are one of the oldest racial-ethnic groups in the United States."

_____ **d.** The Mexican-American War ended in 1848.

## Documentation

There are a number of different documentation formats (these are often called *styles*) that are used by scholars and researchers. Members of a particular academic discipline usually use the same format. For example, biologists follow a format described in *Scientific Style and Format: A Manual for Authors, Editors, and Publishers,* and social scientists follow guidelines given in the *Publication Manual of the American Psychological Association.* Style manuals exist for other disciplines as well, including mathematics, medicine, and chemistry.

The most widely used documentation style is that of the Modern Language Association. The MLA style, as it is called, is used in English language studies and the humanities. In this section, this style is discussed briefly. For a comprehensive review of the MLA style, consult the following:

Gibaldi, Joseph. <u>MLA Handbook for Writers of Research Papers</u>. 6th ed. New York: MLA, 2003.

## An Overview of the MLA Style

### MLA In-Paper (In-Text) Citations

In your paper, if you refer to, summarize, paraphrase, quote, or in any other way use another author's words or ideas, you must indicate the source from which you took them. You do this by inserting a reference called an *in-text citation*. It refers your reader to your source list, which you include at the end of your paper. This list of sources is called "Works Cited." An in-text citation identifies the name and page number of your source and looks like this:

> The culture of poverty is not understood: "The United States is not quite sure about the causes of poverty, and is therefore uncertain about solutions." (Shipler 5).

The in-text citation "(Shipler 5)" refers the reader to the entry in the Works Cited list that gives full information about Shipler's book:

Shipler, David K. The Working Poor. New York: Knopf, 2004.

Here are the answers to a few common questions about preparing in-text citations:

1. **Where should I place the citation?** Place your citation at the end of the sentence in which you refer to, summarize, paraphrase, or quote a source. It should follow a quotation mark, but come before punctuation that ends the sentence. If a question mark ends the sentence, place the question mark before the citation and a period after the citation.

   EXAMPLE     Truss emphasizes the importance of commas by repunctu-ating ordinary expressions (81).

2. **What information should the citation contain?** If you have not mentioned the author's name in your sentence, the citation should include both the author's name and the page number of the quotation. If you did name the author when you introduced the quotation or material to be acknowledged, you do not need to repeat it in the citation. Simply give the page number.

   EXAMPLE     Writers should use common sense when using commas (Truss 96).

3. **What if I use two or more works by the same author?** If you have used two or more works by the same author, either include the relevant title in your sentence or include an abbreviated title in your citation.

   In The Working Poor, Shipler concludes . . . (68).

   Or

   Shipler concludes . . . (Working 67).

4. **What if my source has more than one author?** If there are two or three authors, include the last names of all of them. If there are four or more, include only the first author's last name and follow it with *et al.,* which means "and others."

McCleary, West, and Rodriguez (2005) argue that . . . .

Thompson et al. (2003) conclude that . . . .

## MLA Works Cited

Your list of works cited should include all the sources you referred to, summarized, paraphrased, or quoted in your paper. The list appears on a separate page at the end of your paper and is titled "Works Cited." Arrange these entries alphabetically by each author's last name. If an author is not named (as in an editorial), then alphabetize the item by title. Double-space between and within entries, and indent any continuing lines one-half inch.

1. **What format is used for books?** The basic format for a book can be illustrated as follows:

<pre>
          AUTHOR              TITLE         PLACE OF
                                         PUBLICATION  PUBLISHER  DATE
</pre>

Shipler David K. <u>The Working Poor</u>. New York: Knopf, 2004.

Special cases are handled as follows:

a. **Two or more authors**   If there are two or three authors, include all their names in the order in which they appear in the source. If there are four or more, give the first author's name only and follow it with "et al."

Brennan, Scott and Jay Withgott. <u>Environment: The Science Behind the Stories</u>. San Francisco: Cummings, 2005.

b. **Two or more works by the same author**   If your list contains two or more works by the same author, list the author's name only once. For additional entries, substitute three hyphens in place of the name.

Shipler, David K. <u>The Working Poor</u>. New York: Knopf, 2004.

---. <u>A Country of Strangers: Blacks and Whites in America</u>. New York: Random, 1998.

c. **Editor**   If the book has an editor instead of an author, list the editor's name at the beginning of the entry and follow it with "ed."

Ruttenberg, Francis, ed. <u>Perceptions of History</u>. New York: Harper, 1995.

d. **Edition**   If the book has an edition number, include it after the title.

DeVito, Joseph A . <u>Human Communication: The Basic Course</u>. 10th ed. Boston: Allyn and Bacon, 2005.

e. **Publisher**   The entire name of the publisher is not used. For example, Houghton Mifflin Company is listed as "Houghton."

2. What format is used for articles? The basic format for a periodical can be illustrated as follows:

Special cases are handled as follows:

a. **Newspaper articles**   Include the author, article title, name of the newspaper, date, section letter or number, and page(s).

Okun, Janice. "The Puck Stops Here." <u>Buffalo News</u> 8 June 2005, sec. C: 1.

b. **An article in a weekly magazine**   List the author, article title, name of the magazine, date, and page(s). Abbreviate all months except May, June, and July, and place the day before the month.

Thomas, Cathy Booth. "Finding the Way Home." <u>Time</u> 6 June 2005: 26.

## Internet Sources

Information on the Internet comes from a wide variety of sources. For example, there are journals that are online versions of print publications, but there are also journals that are only published online. There are online books, articles from online databases, government publications, government Web sites and more. Therefore, it is not sufficient merely to state that you got something from the Web and provide its URL (uniform resource locator). Citations for Internet resources must adequately reflect the exact type of document or publication that was used.

Include enough information to allow your reader to locate your sources. Since some of these electronic sources might not be stable, your citation requires more elements. It should consist of both traditional publication details such as author, title, and date, as well as special access details such as the URL and date of retrieval (the date the Web site was accessed.) Readers can then attempt to access the source using the information from the citation, but if that source has moved its virtual location, then the reader can use the traditional publication details to do a search for that source.

For some Internet sources it may not be possible to locate all the required information; provide the information that is available. Include the author's name (if available) with last name first, the full title of the document, the names of editors, compilers, or translators, if appropriate, and the title of the Web site. Include the date the document was published electronically (day, month, year) as well as the date you accessed the information. If the source was originally published in print, give the original source. Provide the page, paragraph, or section number of the print source if available. In general, give the network address or URL at the end of the citation, enclosed in angle brackets (< >). Here are a few examples of Internet and electronic citations:

**Web Site**—You consulted an entire Web site or many parts of it:

> Hiroshima Peace Site. Hiroshima Peace Memorial Museum. 2005. 6 Aug. 2005 <http://www.pcf.city.hiroshima.jp/index_e2.html>.

**Online book**—You consulted an entire online book:

> Woolf, Virginia. Monday or Tuesday. 1921. Bartleby.com Great Books Online. Ed. Steven van Leeuwen. 2005. 6 Aug. 2005 <http://www.bartleby.com/85/>.

**Online book**—You consulted part of an online book:

> Ferdowsi. "The Return of Kai Khosrau." The Epic of Kings. 1010. The Internet Classics Archive. Ed. Daniel C. Stevenson. 2000. 6 Aug. 2005 <http://www.classics.mit.edu/Ferdowsi/ kings.10.returnkaikhosrau.html>.

**Article from an online periodical**—You accessed the article *directly* from an online journal, magazine, or newspaper:

> Lynch, Wendy, and Bill Bravman. "Modern Warfare: An Overview for World History Teachers." World History Connected. 2.2 (2005): 54 pars. 6 Aug. 2005 <http://www.worldhistory connected.press.uiuc.edu/2.2/bravman.html>.

**Article from an online database**—You accessed an article using an online database:

> Escobar-Chaves, et al. "Impact of the Media on Adolescent Sexual Attitudes and Behaviors." Pediatrics 2 116.1 (2005): 303-327. Health Source–Consumer Edition. EBSCOhost. Seattle Pacific University Library. 6 Aug. 2005 <http://www.epnet.com/>.

**Online government publication**—You consulted a document published by a government entity:

> United States. Public Health Service. Office of the Surgeon General. The Health Consequences of Smoking: A Report of the Surgeon General. 2004. 6 Aug. 2005 <http://www.cdc.gov/tobacco/sgr/sgr_2004/chapters.htm>.

## Other Electronic Sources

### CD-ROM

The Bend in the Road: An Invitation to the World and Work of
L.M. Montgomery. CD-ROM. Charlottetown, P.E.I., Canada:
L.M. Montgomery Institute, 2000.

### Interview from a radio Web site

Doughty, Mike. Interview. Variety Mix. KEXP. 17 May 2005. 6
Aug. 2005. http://www.kexp.org/. Path: Live Performances;
Artists J-R; Mike Doughty: 5/17/2005. In-studio performance.

### Political advertisement viewed on the Internet

"Repudiate Robertson." Advertisement. MoveOn.org 2005. 6 Aug.
2005 <https://www.political.moveon.org/donate/
robertson.html>.

### Photograph viewed on the Internet

Hine, Lewis. Children Cotton Pickers. 1912. George Eastman
House Still Photograph Archive. 6 Aug. 2005 <http://
www.geh.org/ar/letchild/m197701830037_ful.html>.

# AN ACADEMIC SCENARIO
## A STUDENT ESSAY
### The Academic Writer and the Writing Task

Melinda Lawson was a student at Niagara County Community College when she wrote this paper for her writing class. Her assignment was to choose an issue and examine its pros and cons.

Title—direct focus on thesis

# Some Pros and Cons of Legalizing Drugs
## Melinda Lawson

Thesis statement

The question of whether or not to legalize drugs has become a major issue in the United States within the past decade. Since either approach to the resolution of the drug problem has both advantages and disadvantages, it is important to understand the consequences of each alternative in order to take a position on the issue.

*Topic sentence*

Those arguing for drug legalization believe that making illegal drugs legally available to the public will solve many drug-related problems. One of these problems is burglary, for it is a fact that some people who use certain illegal drugs become chemically addicted to such drugs and then have to support their drug habit by stealing money (or property to be sold for money) from others. This leads to a rise in burglary. However, if drugs were legalized, burglary would no longer be necessary because drugs would be sold at cost. This means that drug users, especially addicts, would not need to commit crimes in order to support their drug use. Legal drugs could be sold cheaply and profits could be used to reduce and control drug use.

*Source*

Christopher Farrell points out that the money from taxes levied on legalized drugs plus the savings from the huge amounts of money spent on the war on drugs could be used not only for drug treatment and education, but also for the war on terror and programs for our aging population (par. 6).

*Topic sentence*

Others who support legalization argue that the current policy of prohibiting drugs is not working. Our jails are filling up with nonviolent offenders who were incarcerated on drug charges (many quite minor), costing taxpayers billions of dollars per year.

*Source*

Abramsky quotes one retired judge as saying, "legalization and regulation are the only answer. It's not a perfect solution, but it's a hell of a lot better that what we're doing now" (25). Pro-legalization experts argue that if we cannot make prohibition work, then legalization seems like a worthwhile alternative.

*Transition*

*Topic sentence*

On the other side of the issue, there are people who believe that decriminalizing drugs will not only not solve the drug problem but make it worse. It is logical to assume that if drugs were to become legally available, there would be an increase in the number of drug users.

*Source*

DuPont reports that marijuana already leads young people to harder drugs and to the emergency room. There are over 100,000 marijuana-related visits to American ER's each year. Making this drug legal would only increase these problems (par. 5). Meanwhile, the drug industry ravages the developing nations where these substances are produced. If these substances were legalized in the United States, the demand would increase, causing even more misery in the drug producing nations. Our nation has attempted to pressure other governments into ending their drug trades.

*Source*

However, the *New York Times* reported that production in Peru is increasing, that Afghanistan is "on the verge of becoming a narcotics state," and that Columbia provides "over 90 percent of the cocaine and 50 percent of the heroin entering the U.S." (Brinkley A.4).

*Topic sentence*

*Source*

If addictions increase, so will health problems and, consequently, health costs. As Alsobrooks points out, illegal drugs are harmful. People are hurt or hurt others under the influence of drugs. Their hospital visits cost billions of dollars per year. During the 1990's, these costs increased at a rate of 5.9% per year (87). Possible health risks include low birth weight and birth defects of infants born to users, as well as increased health problems of the drug users themselves.

Example

Conclusion

Presents summary of
main points

Public safety is the basis for another argument against the legalization of drugs. People who drive buses, fly airplanes, fight fires, and work in hospitals all would have easy access to drugs and might use them on the job. Drunk drivers would become drugged drivers, increasing the risk of accidents. Random drug testing would be necessary, and costs and regulations would multiply.

In summary, there does not seem to be any easy solution to the drug problem in the United States. Legalizing drugs might result in a decreased crime rate, but it would also result in increased national health and safety problems. Not legalizing drugs might continue to force drug users to commit crimes to support their drug habits. Perhaps a compromise is needed. Controlled or government-regulated drug availability, rather than an open drug market, is an option worth exploring.

## Works Cited

Abramsky, Sasha. "The Drug War Goes Up in Smoke." Nation 15 Aug. 2003: 25-28.

Alsobrooks, Dan P. "Waging a Battle Against Myths." Corrections Today Dec. 2002: 86-89.

Brinkley, Joel. "Stopping Illicit Drugs Is Still Uphill Battle, Report Shows." New York Times 5 Mar. 2005: A4.

Farrell, Christopher. "A New Kind of Drug War." Business Week Online 28 Feb. 2005. Retrieved 19 March 2005. par. 6 <http://www.businessweek.com/bwdaily/dnflash/feb2005/nf20050228_1996_db013.htm>.

DuPont, Richard L. "Should Marijuana Laws Be Relaxed? No." The CQ Researcher Online 11 Feb. 2005. par. 5. 20 March 2005 <http://www.library.cqpress.com.deborah.spu.edu:80/cqresearcher/cqresrre2005021100> Document ID: cqresrre2005021100.

## Examining Academic Writing

1. How is the essay organized?

2. Examine Lawson's use of sources. What does each reference to a source contribute to the essay?

3. Suggest ways the introduction could be more interesting.

4. For what audience does Lawson seem to be writing?

## Academic Writing Assignments

1. For an education class, write an essay examining the trend toward online college courses. Do research to discover what is offered at your college and other nearby colleges. Summarize your findings in a short essay.

2. For a health class, you are asked to write an essay comparing two popular diets. Choose two diets, such as the South Beach Diet and the Zone diet, research what is involved in each, and report your findings in an essay.

3. For a business management class, your instructor has given the following assignment. Choose two local business franchises that sell the same products. You might choose two fast food restaurants, two shoe stores, or two drugstores, for example. Visit both businesses and research each on the Internet. Write an essay comparing the two businesses. Indicate which you feel is likely to be more profitable over the course of the next year.

# A WORKPLACE SCENARIO
## A COVER LETTER
### The Workplace Writer and the Writing Task

Marguerite Morger is the marketing manager for KI-D-TV. She received a business plan from a local company, Read-2-Me. The owners wish to sell the company. After studying the plan, she decided to endorse it and submit it to the vice president of Marketing and Development. To interest the VP in the proposal and because the VP was unlikely to take time to read the entire plan, Morger summarized the proposal's benefits in the following cover memo.

---

TO: Lucas Thompson, KI-D-TV, Vice-President, Marketing and Development
FROM: Marguerite J. Morger, Marketing Manager
DATE: July 2, 2005
RE: Read-2-Me Business Plan

I have read the business plan submitted by Cindy and George Schoen of Read-2-Me children's books and tapes and have come to the following conclusion:

We cannot afford to pass up the chance to buy this imaginative, financially sound company. Based on the quality of its products, customer loyalty, and willingness of the founders to continue on with us in an advisory capacity, it is a perfect fit for KI-D-TV Entertainment.

Here is a brief summary of the report:
 1. The company has been in business for three years. The financial records included in the report show a profit in its third year of operation.

---

2. The Schoens have agreed to continue on in a creative advisory capacity, contributing a minimum of ten new story ideas each year for the first three years of our ownership. This gives us plenty of time to add to the creative staff and make a smooth transition.

3. Rather than try to appeal to a broad market, the Schoens chose to narrowly target the under-five age group. They recognize that we do not offer products for children under six and suggest that their company would plug an important gap in our line.

4. The shelf appeal is strong; book and tape sets are easily recognizable by the trademarked images of animal parents reading to their animal toddlers on the covers. I personally observed kids dragging their parents over to the Read-2-Me shelf at two local bookstores. Kids want them and parents like them.

5. The Schoens present some direct research in the form of questionnaires to 1,000 customers on their mailing list, asking them to rate the different aspects of the books, including text and design, and the production values of the tapes. Using a 1-5, worst-to-best, rating system, customer satisfaction was a healthy 4.2.

6. The Schoens are interested in maintaining a relationship with us, with the idea of developing new lines targeted to different age groups. Given the success of the Read-2-Me line, this is an exciting proposition for KI-D-TV.

I offer a strong "Buy" recommendation for Read-2-Me. I think it has great potential and should not be allowed to fall into the hands of our competitors. Please contact me if you have questions or need further information.

## Examining Workplace Writing

1. Highlight the sentence that announces the purpose of the memo.

2. Do you think the numbered list is an effective means of summary for business writing?

3. What part of the memo is similar to the title of an essay?

4. Highlight parts that are similar to the introduction and conclusion in an essay.

## Workplace Writing Assignments

1. You are working as a writer for a regional magazine, *Northern Colorado Parenting,* and the managing editor has asked you to locate relevant articles to reprint in the magazine on choosing and evaluating day care centers. Use the Internet and a search engine to locate three possible articles. Print each article.

2. From the three articles you located for item 1, select the one you feel is most appropriate and write a summary for your managing editor.

3. After reviewing all three articles you found, your editor rejects all of them. Instead, she asks you to use the information you found to write your own article, titled "Making the Right Choice for Your Child." Write this article by synthesizing and documenting information from the other three.

## WRITING ABOUT A READING

### Paired Readings

### Thinking Before Reading

The following two readings deal with the same topic: urban legends. James M. Henslin's "Urban Legends" offers a compact discussion that relates urban legends to various themes. "How Urban Legends Work" by Tom Harris provides an extended explanation of these tales.

1. Preview the readings, using the steps discussed in Chapter 2, p. 30.

2. Connect the reading to your own experience by answering the following questions:

   a. What urban legends have you heard?

   b. How do urban legends affect our daily behavior?

### READING

# Urban Legends

### James M. Henslin

1   Did you hear about Katie and Paul? They were parked at Echo Bay, listening to the radio, when the music was interrupted by an announcement that a rapist-killer had escaped from prison. Instead of a right hand, he had a hook. Katie said they should leave, but Paul laughed and said there wasn't any reason to go. When they heard a strange noise, Paul agreed to take her home. When Katie opened the door, she heard something clink. It was a hook hanging on the door handle!

2   For decades, some version of "The Hook" story has circulated among Americans. It has appeared as a "genuine" letter in "**Dear Abby**," and some of my students heard it in grade school. **Urban legends** are stories with an ironic twist that sound realistic but are false. Although untrue, they usually are told by people who believe that they happened.

3   Another urban legend that has made the rounds is the "Kentucky Fried Rat."

4   One night, a woman didn't have anything ready for supper, so she and her husband went to the drive-through at Kentucky Fried Chicken. While they were eating in their car, the wife said "My chicken tastes funny."

**Dear Abby**
the name of a newspaper advice column

5    Her husband said, "You're always complaining about something." When she insisted that the chicken didn't taste right, he put on the light. She was holding fried rat—crispy style. The woman went into shock and was rushed to the hospital.

6    A lawyer from the company offered them $100,000 if they would sign a **release** and not tell anyone. This was the second time this happened.

7    Folklorist Jan Brunvand (1981, 1984, 1986) reported that urban legends are passed on by people who think that the event happened just one or two people down the line of transmission, often to a "friend of a friend." The story has strong appeal and gains credibility from naming specific people or local places. Brunvand views urban legends as "modern **morality stories**"; each one teaches a moral lesson about life.

8    If we apply Brunvand's analysis to these two urban legends, three major points emerge. First, these morals serve as warnings. "The Hook" warns young people that they should be careful about where they go, with whom they go, and what they do. The world is an unsafe place, and "messing around" is risky. "The Kentucky Fried Rat" contains a different moral: Do you *really* know what you are eating when you buy food from a fast-food outlet? Maybe you should eat at home, where you know what you are getting.

9    Second, each story is related to social change: "The Hook" to changing sexual morality, the "Kentucky Fried Rat" to changing male-female relationships, especially to changing sex roles at home. Third, each is calculated to instill guilt and fear: guilt—the wife failed in her traditional role of cooking supper, and she was punished; and fear—we should all be afraid of the dangerous unknown, whether it lurks in the dark countryside or inside our bucket of chicken. The ultimate moral of these stories is that we should not abandon traditional roles or the safety of the home.

10   These principles can be applied to an urban legend that made the rounds in the late 1980s. I heard several versions of this one; each narrator swore that it had just happened to a friend of a friend.

11   Jerry (or whoever) went to a nightclub last weekend. He met a good-looking woman, and they hit it off. They spent the night in a motel. When he got up the next morning, the woman was gone. When he went into the bathroom, he saw a message scrawled on the mirror in lipstick: "Welcome to the wonderful world of AIDS."

12   What moral and aspects of social change does this legend illustrate?

**release**
a document that frees someone from an obligation or claim

**morality stories**
stories that are intended to teach a lesson

## Getting Ready to Write

### Reviewing the Reading

1. Summarize one of the urban legends retold in this reading.

2. What is special about the way in which an urban legend is told?

3. What are some of the moral lessons that urban legends could teach?

4. Why does the belief that the story happened to a friend of a friend help to make urban legends more believable?

### Examining the Readings: Using Idea Maps to Compare Sources

Drawing idea maps is a useful way to grasp and organize ideas in an article, essay, or chapter as well as to revise your own essays (see Chapter 15, "Sharpening Your Essay-Writing Skills," p. 360). Idea mapping is also helpful in comparing sources.

Complete the map on p. 437 for the two readings in this chapter and add points of comparison if needed. Do this after you have completed the second reading.

### Thinking Critically: Examining Your Sources

When you have found a source that deals with your topic, be sure it is reliable. That is, your source must be accurate and complete. Here are some questions to ask when choosing sources:

1. **Is the source objective or biased?** Objective sources present an impartial view of the topic. Biased sources are one-sided, presenting only a particular view or opinion. Suppose you were researching how computers have changed our lives. If you consulted *Wired* or *Computer Macworld*—popular periodicals written for people who use and are involved with computers on a daily basis—you would expect to find a positive viewpoint, since a computer magazine is unlikely to report that computers negatively affect our lives. Be sure to recognize such bias and search for sources that provide alternative viewpoints.

2. **Is the source reputable?** To be sure that information you cite in your papers is accurate, use sources that are well known and established among scholars in the field. For example, an article in *Good Housekeeping* on acupuncture would not be considered a sound, scholarly source. However, an article from the *Journal of the American Medical Association* would be considered very reliable. To find out which sources are reputable, check the bibliography or reference section of your textbook, consult a research manual, or check with your reference librarian.

3. **Is the source sufficiently detailed?** Some sources, such as introductory textbooks, provide brief introductions to many topics within a general subject. Other sources research and report on a single topic in great depth. Choose a source that contains enough detail to meet your needs, but does not burden you or your reader with excess detail.

For example, if you were reading about the rights of the physically disabled, an encyclopedia entry would provide a general overview, but would not explore in detail specific issues, such as laws. On the other hand, if you consulted the periodical *Mouth: The Voice of Disability Rights,* you would find subjects explored in detail, but you probably would not find a discussion of the broad or major issues. You can assess the level of detail a source uses by going to its index, finding the listing for your topic, turning to one of the references, and quickly scanning a page or two.

Answer each of the above questions for one of the readings in this chapter.

## Strengthening Your Vocabulary

**Part A:** Using the word's context, word parts, or a dictionary, write a brief definition of each of the following words or phrases as it is used in the "Urban Legends" reading:

1. transmission (paragraph 7) _communication, messaging_

   _____

2. emerge (paragraph 8) _come forth_

   _____

3. instill (paragraph 9) _implant_

   _____

**Part B:** Choose one of the above words and draw a word map.

## Reacting to Ideas: Discussion and Journal Writing

1. Discuss an urban legend you recently heard about via the Internet.

2. Write about a true story that you heard (or experienced) that has the elements of a good urban legend?

## READING

# How Urban Legends Work
### Tom Harris

1    In 1994, the Las Vegas police reported a disturbing series of crimes along the Vegas strip. The first victim in this wave was an Ohio man in town for a sales convention. At the bar in his hotel, the man happened to strike up a conversation with an attractive young woman. According to the man, the two hit it off, sharing several drinks over the course of a couple hours. At some point, the man blacked out, and when he came to, he found himself lying in a hotel bathtub, covered in ice. There was a phone resting on the floor beside the tub, with an attached note that said, "Call 911 or you will die." He called an ambulance and was rushed to the hospital, where the doctors informed him that he had undergone massive surgery. One of his kidneys had been removed, apparently by a gang selling human organs on the black market. Following this occurrence, many similar crimes were reported, leading Las Vegas police to issue warnings to travelers visiting the city.

2    There's a good chance that you've heard this story, or some variation of it. News of the Vegas "organ harvesters" has been passed on by thousands and thousands of people over the course of 10 years. It has been relayed by word of mouth, e-mail and even printed fliers. But there is absolutely no evidence that any such thing ever occurred, in Las Vegas or anywhere else. This fictional story is a **quintessential** urban legend, an incredible tale passed from one person to another as truth.

3    In this article, we'll look at urban legends to see what they are, where they come from and why they spread so quickly. We'll also explore some ideas regarding the social significance of urban legends, as well as take a look at how the stories have changed over the years.

**quintessential**
perfect example

### What Is an Urban Legend?

4    Generally speaking, an urban legend is any modern, fictional story, told as truth, that reaches a wide audience by being passed from person to person. Urban legends are often false, but not always. A few turn out to be largely true, and a lot of them were inspired by an actual event but evolved into something different in their passage from person to person. More often than not, it isn't possible to trace an urban legend back to its original source—they seem to come from nowhere.

5    Thematically, urban legends are all over the map, but several persistent elements do show up again and again. Typically, urban legends are characterized by some combination of humor, horror, warning, embarrassment,

morality or appeal to empathy. They often have some unexpected twist that is outlandish but just plausible enough to be taken as truth.

6    In the story of the organ harvesters, you can see how some of these elements come together. The most outstanding feature of the story is its sense of horror: The image of a man waking up lying in a bathtub full of ice, with one less kidney, is a lurid one indeed. But the real hook is the cautionary element. Most people travel to unfamiliar cities from time to time, and Las Vegas is one of the most popular tourist spots in the world. The story also includes a moral lesson, in that the businessman ended up in the unpleasant predicament only after going to drink at a bar and then flirting with a mysterious woman.

7    This is what's called a cautionary tale. A variation of the cautionary tale is the contamination story, which has played out recently in the **spate** of reports about human body fluids being found in restaurant food. One of the most widespread contamination stories is the long-standing rumor of rats and mice showing up in soda bottles or other prepackaged food.

**spate**
flood, rush

8    Not all urban legends deal with such morbid, weighty issues. Many of them have no cautionary or moral element at all: They are simply amusing stories or ordinary jokes told as if they really occurred. One common "news story" reports that a man took out an insurance policy on an expensive box of cigars, smoked them all and then tried to collect a claim, saying that they had been damaged in a fire. Another tale tells of a drunk driver who is pulled over by the police. The officer asks the man to step out of the car for a sobriety test, but just as the test is about to begin, a car veers into a ditch up the road. The officer runs to help the other driver, and the drunk man takes the opportunity to flee the scene. When he gets home, he falls fast asleep on the couch. In the morning, he hears a loud knocking on his door and opens it to find the police officer from the night before. The man swears up and down he was home all night, until the officer asks to have a look in his garage. When he opens the door, he's shocked to see the officer's police cruiser parked there instead of his own car.

9    This story about the police car, in various forms, has spread all over the world. It even made it into the movie "Good Will Hunting," relayed by one of the characters as if it had happened to one of his friends. In the next section, we'll look at how urban legends like this one spread, and explore why so many people believe them.

### Friend of a Friend

10    In the last section, we saw that urban legends are unusual, funny or shocking stories, relayed from person to person as absolute truth. The most remarkable thing about urban legends is that so many people believe them and pass them on. What is it about these stories that makes people want to spread the word?

11    A lot of it has to do with the particular elements of the story. As we saw in the last section, many urban legends are about particularly heinous crimes, contaminated foods or any number of occurrences that could affect a lot of people if they were true. If you hear such a story, and you believe it, you feel compelled to warn your friends and family.

12    A person might pass on non-cautionary information simply because it is funny or interesting. When you first hear the story, you are completely amazed that such a thing has occurred. When told correctly, a good urban legend will have you on the edge of your seat. It's human nature to want to spread this feeling to others, and be the one who's got everyone waiting to hear how the story turns out. Even if you hear it as a made-up joke, you might be tempted to personalize the tale by claiming it happened to a friend. Basically, people love to tell a good story.

13    But why does an audience take this at face value, instead of recognizing it as a tall tale or unsubstantiated rumor? In most cases, it has to do with how the story is told. If a friend (let's call her Jane) tells you an urban legend, chances are she will say it happened to a friend of somebody she knows. You trust Jane to tell you the truth, and you know she trusts the person who told her the story. It seems pretty close to second-hand information, so you treat it as such. Why would Jane lie?

14    Of course, Jane isn't really lying, and her friend wasn't lying to her—both of them believe the story. They are, however, probably abbreviating the story somewhat, and you will probably abbreviate it yourself when you pass it on. In this situation, the story happened to a friend of one of your friend's friends, but to simplify things, you'll probably just say it happened to a friend of Jane's, or even to Jane herself. In this way, every person who relays the story gives the impression that he or she is only two people away from one of the characters in the story, when in reality, there are probably hundreds of people between them.

**duped**
tricked

15    Just about anybody can be **duped** into believing an urban legend because very few people distrust everything and everybody. Most of us don't investigate every single piece of information we hear—for efficiency's sake, we accept a lot of information as truth without looking into it ourselves. Psychologically, we need to trust people, just for our own sense of comfort. And if you trust somebody, you'll believe almost anything that person tells you.

16    In many cases, this trust runs so deep that a person will insist that an urban legend actually occurred, even when confronted with evidence to the contrary. Urban-legend Web sites like Snopes.com get a lot of e-mail from readers who are outraged because the site is calling their friend a liar.

17    Another reason such stories get passed on is because the details make them seem real. You may have heard stories of children being kidnapped from a specific location of a local department store, or you may have heard about various gang initiations that occurred in a specific part of your town.

Since you are familiar with the setting—you know it's a real place—the story sounds real. This level of specificity also plays into your own fears and anxieties about what could happen to you in the places you visit regularly.

18    Urban legends are spread in cultures all over the world. In these diverse regions, the familiar elements of horror, humor and caution show up again and again, though the specific themes vary. In the next section, we'll explore the significance of urban legends to find out what these persistent themes might say about the societies we live in.

### What Do Legends Mean?

19    On the Internet and in universities all over the world, you'll find a lot of people interested in the role of urban legends in modern society. Many folklorists argue that the more gruesome legends embody basic human fears, providing a cautionary note or moral lesson telling us how to protect ourselves from danger.

20    The most famous cautionary urban legend is the "Hook-hand killer" tale. In this story, a young couple on a date drive off to a remote spot to "park." Over the radio, they hear that a psychopath with a hooked hand has escaped from a local mental institution. The girl wants to leave, but her boyfriend insists there's nothing to worry about. After a while, the girl thinks she hears a scratching or tapping sound outside the car. The boyfriend assures her it's nothing, but at her insistence, they eventually drive off. When they get to the girl's house, the boyfriend goes around to the passenger side to open her door. To his horror, there is a bloody hook hanging from the door handle.

21    The warning and moral lesson of this story are clear: Don't go off by yourself, and don't engage in premarital intimacy! If you do, something horrific could happen. When the story first circulated in the 1950s, parking was a relatively new phenomenon, and parents were terrified of what might happen to their kids. Most people who tell the story today don't take it very seriously.

### Urban Legends and the Internet

22    People didn't begin talking about "urban legends" until the 1930s and 1940s, but they have existed in some form for thousands of years. Urban legends are simply the modern version of traditional folklore. In most cultures of the world, folklore has always existed alongside, or in place of, recorded history. Where history is obsessed with accurately writing down the details of events, traditional folklore is characterized by the "oral tradition," the passing of stories by word of mouth.

23    The methods of passing urban legends have also evolved over time. In the past 10 years, there has been a huge surge of urban legends on the Internet. The most common venue is forwarded e-mail. This storytelling method is unique because usually the story is not reinterpreted by each person who passes it on. A person simply clicks the "Forward" icon in their e-

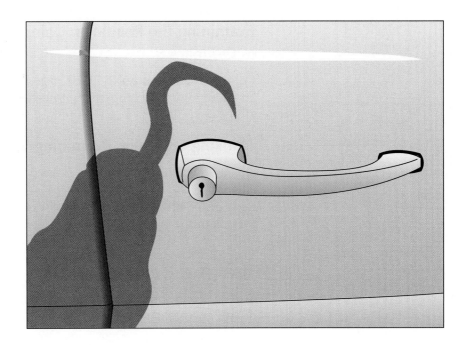

mail, and types in all his friend's e-mail addresses. Having the original story gives e-mail legends a feeling of legitimacy. You don't know the original author, but they are speaking directly to you.

24      E-mail stories demonstrate just how deep-rooted urban legends are. No matter how much "information technology" we develop, human beings will always be drawn in by the unsubstantiated rumor. In fact, information technology actually accelerates the spread of tall tales. By definition, urban legends seem to have a life of their own, creeping through a society one person at a time. And like a real life form, they adapt to changing conditions. It will always be human nature to tell bizarre stories, and there will always be an audience waiting to believe them. The urban legend is part of our make-up.

## Getting Ready to Write

### Reviewing the Reading

1. Re-tell one of the urban legends mentioned in this reading.

2. How does the author define an urban legend?

3. What are some characteristics of the urban legends presented in this reading?

4. Why do people re-tell urban legends?

5. Why do people believe urban legends?

## Examining the Readings: Using Idea Maps to Compare Sources

Complete the map on the next page for the two readings in this chapter, and add points of comparison if needed.

## Thinking Critically: Examining Your Sources

When you have found a source that deals with your topic, be sure it is reliable. That is, your source must be accurate and complete. Use the questions on p. 429–430 guide your assessment. Answer each of the questions for one of the readings in this chapter.

## Strengthening Your Vocabulary

**Part A:** Using the word's context, word parts, or a dictionary, write a brief definition of each of the following words or phrases as it is used in the reading.

1. evolved (paragraph 4) developed, unfolded

2. outlandish (paragraph 5) outrageous, strange

3. lurid (paragraph 6) shocking, gruesome

4. predicament (paragraph 6) problematic situation

5. unsubstantiated (paragraph 14) not verified by evidence

6. embody (paragraph 20) merge, blend

**Part B:** Choose one of the above words and draw a word map.

## Reacting to Ideas: Discussion and Journal Writing

1. Discuss the ways you could check a story to find out if it is true.

2. How do you feel about receiving forwarded e-mail stories, jokes, and appeals?

# Visualize It!

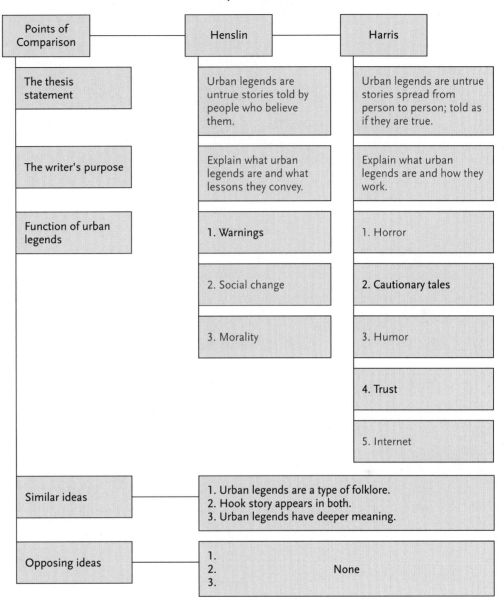

**Comparison Chart**

| Points of Comparison | Henslin | Harris |
|---|---|---|
| The thesis statement | Urban legends are untrue stories told by people who believe them. | Urban legends are untrue stories spread from person to person; told as if they are true. |
| The writer's purpose | Explain what urban legends are and what lessons they convey. | Explain what urban legends are and how they work. |
| Function of urban legends | 1. Warnings | 1. Horror |
| | 2. Social change | 2. Cautionary tales |
| | 3. Morality | 3. Humor |
| | | 4. Trust |
| | | 5. Internet |
| Similar ideas | 1. Urban legends are a type of folklore. 2. Hook story appears in both. 3. Urban legends have deeper meaning. | |
| Opposing ideas | 1. 2. None 3. | |

## Writing About the Readings

### Paragraph Options

1. Write a paragraph about the thrill of hearing a scary story. Why do we like to be frightened?

2. Write a paragraph about someone you know who always has a good story to tell.

3. Both readings mention folklore. Write a paragraph that defines and gives examples of folklore.

## Essay Options

4. Summarize the ways in which urban legends teach us a lesson.

5. Consult two or more sources on urban legends. Write an essay summarizing the new information you learned.

7. Write an essay about your thoughts on the future of the urban legend. Do you think we will just keep hearing the same stories over and over? What types of new stories might emerge? What new lessons might be taught?

## Revision Checklist

1. Is your essay appropriate for your audience? Does it give them the background information they need? Will it interest them?

2. Will your essay accomplish your purpose?

3. Have you narrowed your topic so that you can cover your subject thoroughly in your essay?

4. Is your main point clearly expressed in a thesis statement in the introductory paragraph? Does your introductory paragraph capture the reader's interest and lead into the body of the essay?

5. Does each paragraph of your essay have a topic sentence that supports your main point?

6. Is each paragraph's topic sentence supported by relevant and sufficient detail?

7. Are your paragraphs arranged in a logical sequence and connected by transitional words and phrases?

8. Is the tone of your essay appropriate for your purpose and audience?

9. Does your conclusion reemphasize your thesis statement and draw the essay to a close?

10. Does your title identify the topic and interest the reader?

11. Have you proofread your paper and corrected any errors in grammar, mechanics, and spelling? (See the inside back cover of this book for a proofreading checklist.)

# CHAPTER REVIEW AND PRACTICE

## Chapter Review

| | |
|---|---|
| HOW CAN YOU LOCATE USEFUL AND APPROPRIATE SOURCES? | Keep track of all sources, consult a librarian for help, use current and reliable sources, sample a variety of viewpoints, preview by reading abstracts or summaries, read selectively, and follow leads to additional sources. |
| WHAT IS ANNOTATING? | Annotating is a way of recording your ideas and "talking back" to the writer. |
| WHAT IS PARAPHRASING? | Paraphrasing is a way of recording ideas from a source. It is a restatement in your own words of the author's ideas. |
| WHAT IS A SUMMARY? | A summary is a condensed version of the ideas presented in a source. |
| HOW DO YOU USE SOURCES IN AN ESSAY? | Sources should be used to support and explain your own ideas. |
| WHAT TWO WAYS CAN YOU INCLUDE INFORMATION FROM SOURCES IN AN ESSAY? | You can summarize or paraphrase, or you can quote directly from the source. |
| WHAT DOES DOCUMENTING YOUR SOURCES MEAN? HOW IT IS DONE? | Documenting sources means giving credit to the author of each source you used. You do so using in-text citations and a Works Cited list. |
| WHAT IS MLA STYLE? | MLA is a documentation style used in English language studies and the humanities. It explains how to prepare in-text citations and Works Cited lists. |

## Skill Refresher: Using Colons and Semicolons

### When to Use Colons

Colons are most commonly used:

1. After an independent clause to introduce a concluding explanation.

   Use the right tool: if you want to drive a nail, use a hammer, not your shoe.

2. After an independent clause to introduce a list or series.

   The American poetry class surveyed a wide range of poets: Whitman, Dickinson, Ashbery, and Pound.

3. After an independent clause to introduce a long or formal quotation.

   Mark Twain commented on human behavior: "Man is the only animal that blushes—or needs to."

### When to Use Semicolons

Semicolons are most commonly used:

1. Between two independent clauses not connected by a coordinating conjunction (*and, but, for, nor, or, so, yet*).

   Each state has equal representation in the Senate; representation in the House of Representatives is based on population.

2. To separate items in a list when they themselves contain commas.

   The library bulletin board has a display of "Pioneers in Thought," which includes Freud, the creator of psychoanalysis; Marx, the famous communist writer; Copernicus, the father of modern astronomy; and Watson and Crick, the discoverers of DNA.

### Rate Your Ability to Use Colons and Semicolons Correctly

Place colons and semicolons where needed in the following sentences.

1. Anthropologists believe human life began in Africa skeletons that have been found there provide evidence for this.

2. The natural sciences include botany, the study of plants chemistry, the study of elements that compose matter and biology, the study of all living things.

3. The courses I am taking cover a wide range of subjects linguistics, racquetball, calculus, anatomy, and political science.

4. Time management workshops tend to be practical they do provide many useful tips.

5. The poet John Milton tells how Eve must have felt when she was created "That day I remember, when from sleep / I first awaked, and found myself reposed / under a shade on flowers, much wond'ring where / and what I was, whence thither brought, and how."

6. Engineering requires numerous math skills geometry, algebra, and Boolean logic.

7. I enjoy a variety of sports tennis, which is my favorite golf, because it is relaxing basketball, because it is a team sport and racquetball, because it is a good workout.

8. When a skull is dug up by a gravedigger, Hamlet begins what is now a famous meditation on mortality "Alas, poor Yorick!—I knew him, Horatio. . . ."

9. Knowing Spanish is a marketable skill because many clients speak it exclusively it is also useful for appreciating Latin culture.

10. My botany text has a section about coniferous trees pines, firs, cedars, and spruces.

Score _____

Check your answers, using the Answer Key on p. 644. If you missed more than two, you need additional review and practice in recognizing when to use colons and semicolons. Refer to Part VI, "Reviewing the Basics," and under section E, see "Colons and Semicolons." For additional practice go to this book's Web site at http://www.ablongman.com/mcwhorterexpressways1e.

## INTERNET ACTIVITIES

### 1.   Practice Paraphrasing

Try this exercise in paraphrasing from Purdue University.

http://www.owl.english.purdue.edu/handouts/research/r_paraphrEX1.html

Evaluate how well this technique worked for you.

### 2.   Information Cycle

The sources that you will use for your papers arise out of the information cycle. The University of Washington created an online module on this topic. Work through the tutorial and then write a summary of the information cycle.

http://www.lib.washington.edu/uwill/research101/intro00.htm

### 3.   This Book's Web Site

Visit this site to find templates of idea maps for definition and additional practice on skills taught in the chapter.

http://www.ablongman.com/mcwhorterexpressways1e

# 17

# Writing Essay Exams and Taking Competency Tests

## Chapter Objectives

*In this chapter you will learn to:*

1. Prepare for and write essay exams.

2. Take competency tests.

## Write About It!

Study the photograph above—the student is obviously stressed, perhaps because she is ill-prepared. Assume she is taking an end-of-semester essay exam. Write a paragraph offering her advice on what you have found to be effective in taking essay tests.

In this chapter you will learn to take essay exams and competency tests. Test-taking is a skill that is important throughout life, in everyday, academic, and workplace situations, as shown below.

---

EVERYDAY SCENARIOS

- You are taking a test for a driver's license.
- You are taking an exam for United States' citizenship.

ACADEMIC SCENARIOS

- You must pass an exit exam to pass your writing class.
- Your grade in your American History class will be based on three essay exams.

WORKPLACE SCENARIOS

- You have earned a degree in accounting and must pass the professional licensing exam to become a CPA (Certified Public Accountant).
- You are applying for a job in business management and must take a test to demonstrate your basic literacy skills and a psychological test to evaluate your suitability to supervise others.

---

# UNDERSTANDING EXAMS AND COMPETENCY TESTS

## What Are Essay Exams and Competency Tests?

An **essay exam** is a test that requires you to recall what you know about a given topic and write that information in the form of sentences and paragraphs. Unlike multiple choice tests, in which you only need to recognize the right answer from among the choices given, an essay test demands that you remember and organize information and express in it a clear, readable form. Because exams are usually timed, there is little opportunity for revising or proofreading.

A **competency test** is an exam in which you must demonstrate that you can perform specific skills. In a writing class, you would be asked to write an essay; in a physical education class, such as bowling, you would be asked to bowl a game.

## Preparing for Essay Exams

The best way to prepare for an essay exam is to thoroughly study and review your textbook and lecture notes. Don't simply reread. Instead, work actively with the material to identify what is important, to organize and relate ideas and concepts, and to express the ideas in your own words.

If you have been applying the getting-ready-to-write techniques suggested throughout this book to your textbooks, you'll have a head start. See Table 17-1 to review these techniques.

In addition to reviewing your textbooks and class notes, you should also review

- in-class handouts (underline and mark).

- assignments and papers (note key topics).

- previous exams and quizzes (look for patterns of error and emphasized topics).

- additional assigned readings (summarize these).

Table 17-1    **Getting-Ready-to-Write Strategies**

| Strategy | Chapter and Page Reference |
| --- | --- |
| underlining | Ch. 3, p. 76 |
| immediate review | Ch. 3, p. 76 |
| recognizing supporting details | Ch. 4, p. 84 |
| marking actions, descriptions, and statements | Ch. 7, p. 179 |
| annotating | Ch. 16, p. 400 |
| paraphrasing | Ch. 16, p. 402 |
| summarizing | Ch. 16, p. 405 |
| idea mapping | Ch. 5, p. 110 |

Using all these materials as well as your textbook, make a study sheet listing key definitions, dates, facts, principles, or events that you must commit to memory. An excerpt from a study sheet for a psychology unit on consciousness is shown below. It illustrates how information can be concisely organized for easy review.

**Study Sheet Excerpt**

<u>Sleeping and Dreaming</u>

Stages    1. Quiet sleep—4 stages        Move back
          2. REM sleep                  & forth in
                                        these stages
                                        frequently

Purpose   - not completely understood
          - part of circadian rhythm
          - rest and bodily repair
          - brain—check its circuits

Dreams    - storylike sequences of images
            and events

> - may be meaningless brain activity, but how a person recalls and organizes them is revealing
> - lucid dreaming—control own dreams
>
> Disorders  1. Insomnia—can't sleep
>            2. Hypersomnia—too much sleep
>            3. Sleepwalking
>            4. Night terrors

## Predicting Exam Questions

Once you have reviewed all of your course materials, a good way to prepare for an essay exam is to predict questions the instructor might ask. Essay-exam questions are based on broad, general topics or themes that are important to the course. To predict these questions, you need to identify the "big ideas"—important issues or concepts your instructor has emphasized. To identify the big issues, follow these guidelines:

1. **Reread your course syllabus or objectives.** These are often distributed on the first day of class, and the major headings or objectives refer to the important issues. For example, a sociology-course objective may be "Students will understand the concept of socialization and the roles of the family, peer, and reference groups." This objective identifies the key topic and suggests what you need to learn about it.

2. **Study your textbook's table of contents and the organization of individual chapters.** Identify important topics that run through several chapters. For example, in a marketing textbook, you may discover that chapters on the impact of technology, federal regulations, and consumer-protection legislation all relate to the market environment.

3. **Study your notes.** Identify lecture topics and group them into larger subjects or themes. For example, in a psychology course, individual lectures on retardation, creativity, and IQ can be grouped together under mental abilities.

4. **Evaluate previous exams to see what key ideas were emphasized.** For example, in a history course, you may find questions on the historical significance of events appearing on each exam.

5. **Listen carefully when your instructor announces, discusses, or reviews for the exam.** He or she is likely to reveal important information. Make detailed notes and study them later. For example, a biology instructor may say, "Be sure to review the structure of plants, as well as their reproduction, development, and growth cycles." This remark indicates that these topics will be on the exam.

As you'll see from Table 17-2 on p. 449, the way that essay-exam questions are worded usually suggests a method of development: narration, description, process, example, classification, definition, comparison and contrast, cause and effect, or argument. For example, the question "Trace the events that resulted in the dissolution of the Soviet Union" suggests a chronological order of development. The question "Discuss similarities in the poetic works of Frost and Sandburg" suggests a comparison-and-contrast method of development.

## EXERCISE 17-1

**Directions:** Predict and write an essay question for each of the following topics. Be sure to write the questions in complete sentences, using one of the key words shown in Table 17-2 on p. 449.

1. A mass-communications textbook chapter titled "Newspapers" with the following headings:

   The Colonial Press

   Press of the New Republic

   The People's Publishers: Pulitzer, Hearst, and Scripps

   Twentieth-Century Trends

   The Black Press

   New Latino and Native American Media

   Current Popular Journalists

   The Future of Journalism

2. "Spyware Defined," p. 265 (Chapter 11)

3. "The Talk of the Sandbox," p. 289 (Chapter 12)

## Preparation of Rough-Draft Answers

Once you have predicted possible exam questions, the next step is to draft answers. Generate ideas by locating information in your textbook and class notes that relates to the question. Organize the information, using the method of development suggested in the question, and write a rough-draft answer. This draft will be helpful in several ways:

- It forces you to analyze ideas. This is a better way to review than just rereading your notes and underlining passages in your textbook.

- You get practice in expressing important ideas in your own words.

- Your ability to retain the information will increase.

- You will save time on the exam because you will already have thought about the ideas and how to organize and express them.

To be sure that you can recall important ideas at the time of the exam, you can take one more step: reduce your draft to a brief outline or list of key topics and details.

You probably won't be able to predict all of your essay-exam questions. Some may have a different focus or require a different method of development than you predicted. However, this does *not* mean you have wasted your time. Whatever form a question may take, you will be well prepared to answer it if you've already thought about and organized your ideas on the topic.

## Taking Essay Exams

Here are a few general tips on taking essay exams. Many of these suggestions are useful for other types of exams as well.

1. **Arrive a few minutes early.** Give yourself time to get organized and collect your thoughts.

2. **Sit in the front of the room.** You'll be able to hear directions and read changes or corrections written on the chalkboard. Also, you won't be easily distracted by other students in the exam room.

3. **Read the directions carefully.** They may, for example, tell you to answer only two out of four questions.

4. **If given a choice of questions, take time to make a careful choice.** Otherwise, you may realize midway through the exam that you've picked a question you're not fully prepared to answer.

5. **Plan your time.** For example, if you have to answer two essay questions in a 50-minute class session, give yourself 20 to 25 minutes for each one. Resist the tendency to spend the most time on the first question. Keep track of time so that enough time remains to finish both questions. Allow a few minutes at the end of an in-class exam to check and proofread your answer. Allow more time for a final exam.

6. **Know how many points each question is worth.** If that information is not written on the exam, ask the instructor. Use the information to budget the time you spend on each question. Suppose you are taking an exam that has three questions with the following values:

   Question 1: 20 points

   Question 2: 30 points

   Question 3: 50 points

   Since Question 3 is worth the most points (half the total), you should spend approximately half of your time on it. Roughly divide the remaining time equally on Questions 1 and 2. Point distribution can also suggest how many ideas to include in your answer. For a 20-point question, your instructor probably expects four or five main points (4 x 5 = 20), and most instructors don't work with fractions of points. If you can think of additional ideas to include and time permits it, include them because point distribution is only an indicator, not a rule.

7. **Answer the easiest question first.** It may take less time than you budgeted, allowing you to spend additional time on harder questions. Also, you'll get off to a positive and confident start.

## EXERCISE 17-2

**Directions:** For each of the following sets of exam-question values, decide how you would budget your time.

1. Exam 1 (50-minute class)

   Question     120 points     Time: _____

   Question     220 points     Time: _____

   Question     360 points     Time: _____

2. Exam 2 (75-minute class)

   Question     117 points     Time: _____

   Question     230 points     Time: _____

   Question     320 points     Time: _____

   Question     435 points     Time: _____

3. Exam 3 (two-hour final exam)

   Question     110 points     Time: _____

   Question     230 points     Time: _____

   Question     320 points     Time: _____

   Question     440 points     Time: _____

## Analyzing Exam Questions

Exam questions often follow a recognizable format that tells you not only *what* to write but also *how* to organize it. Here is a sample exam question:

Trace the history of advertising in the United States.

This question identifies the topic—the history of advertising—and limits or narrows the topic to U.S. advertising. Notice the word *trace.* This verb suggests the method of development to use in writing the essay. *Trace* means to track something through time. Therefore, this word indicates that you should use time order for the method of development. Your answer should begin with the earliest example of advertising you know about and end with the latest. Here is another example:

Justify the United Nations' decision to authorize military action against Iraq.

This question focuses on military action against Iraq, but limits the topic to the United Nations' decision to authorize it. The verb *justify* means to explain *why* something is correct or reasonable. *Justify,* then, suggests a cause-and-effect organization, and your answer should illustrate what caused the UN to make its decision.

Table 17-2 lists verbs commonly used in essay questions, gives examples of their use, and indicates the methods of organization they suggest.

Table 17-2    **Key Words Commonly Used in Essay Questions**

| Verb | Example | Information to Include and Method of Development |
|------|---------|------------------------------------------------|
| Trace | Trace changes in water-pollution-control methods over the past 20 years. | Describe the development or progress of a particular trend, event, or process in chronological order. |
| Describe | Describe the two types of chromosomal abnormalities that can cause Down syndrome. | Tell how something looks or happened, including the answers to *who, where, why.* |
| List | List the different types of family structures and marriage relationships. | List or discuss one-by-one. Use most-to-least common or least-to-most common organization. |
| Illustrate | Illustrate, with examples from your experience, how religion shapes values. | Explain by using examples that demonstrate a point or clarify an idea. |
| Define | Define an institution and list its three primary characteristics. | Give an accurate definition of the term with enough detail to show you understand it. |
| Discuss | Discuss the antigen-antibody response in the immune system. | Consider important characteristics and main points. |
| Compare | Compare the poetry of Langston Hughes with the poetry of one of his contemporaries. | Show how items are similar as well as different; use details or examples. |
| Contrast | Contrast Marx's and Weber's theories of social stratification. | Show how the items are different; use details or examples. |
| Explain | Explain the functions of peptide and steroid hormones. | Use facts and details to make the idea or concept clear and understandable. |
| Evaluate | Evaluate the accomplishments of the gun-control movement over the past 50 years. | Assess the merits, strengths, weaknesses, advantages, or limitations of the topic. |
| Summarize | Summarize Parsons' theory of social evolution. | Cover the major points in brief form; use a sentence and paragraph form. |
| Justify | Justify the use of racial quotas in police-department hiring policies. | Give reasons that support an action, decision, or policy. |

Other key words can also provide clues about how to organize essay answers. In a question that begins "Explain three common types," the key word is *types*. The word *types* suggests classification. A question that directs you to explain effects requires you to use cause-and-effect organization.

## Answering Two-Part Questions

Some essay questions have two verbs that ask you to do two different things. Here is an example:

> Describe the characteristics of psychotic behavior, and explain how it can be treated.

This question asks you to *describe* characteristics and *explain* treatment methods. If you get a question like this, it is especially important to plan your time carefully. It is easy to get so involved in writing the first part that you don't leave enough time for the second.

Other two-part questions have only one verb, but they still require two separate discussions. Here is an example:

> Explain the effects of U.S. trade agreements on Canada and Mexico.

You would have to first discuss the effects on Canada and then discuss the effects on Mexico.

To make sure you respond to such questions accurately, underline and mark parts of the exam questions as you read them. Underline the topic and any limitations; then draw a box around the verbs that suggest which method of development you should use. Number each part of two-part questions clearly:

①        ②

Explain the effects of U.S. trade agreements on Canada and Mexico.

## EXERCISE 17-3

**Directions:** For the following essay questions, underline the topics and box the verbs that suggest the method of development (narration, process, description, definition, example, classification, comparison and contrast, or cause and effect). In the space provided, indicate the method(s) you would use to answer each question.

1. Define and illustrate the three approaches to collective behavior.

   Method of development: _____

2. Explain the function of memory cells in the human immune system and indicate how they differ from plasma cells.

   Method of development: _____

3. Discuss the advantages and disadvantages of the three basic market-survey methods.

   Method of development: _____

4. Explain the stages involved in the process of establishing prices.

   Method of development: _____

5. Trace the increasing prominence of gender-discrimination issues over the past three decades.

   Method of development: _____

## Considering Audience and Purpose

The essay-exam answer has a special audience and purpose. The audience consists of your instructor, and you know that he or she is knowledgeable about the topic. Your purpose in writing an essay answer is to demonstrate that *you* are also knowledgeable about the topic. Consequently, your answer should explain the topic thoroughly and completely. It is best to write as if your audience were *not* knowledgeable about the topic.

## Planning Your Answer

Because you are working within a time limit, you won't be able to revise. Consequently, it is even more important than usual to plan your essay carefully before you begin.

After you have read and marked each question, jot down ideas you'll include in your essay. Write them on the back of the exam or on a separate sheet of paper that you won't turn in. If the question is one that you predicted, jot down the outline of your draft essay, adjusting and adding to fit the actual question. Arrange your ideas to follow the method of development suggested in the question. Number them to indicate the order in which you'll present them in your essay. Keep in mind, too, the point value of the essay, and be sure to include sufficient ideas and explanations.

In response to this question,

Identify the stages of sleep and describe four sleep disorders.

one student made these notes:

Stages
1 Wakefulness
2 Quiet sleep
3 REM sleep (active)

Disorders
4 Hypersomnia
1 Insomnia
2 Sleepwalking
3 Night terrors

As you write your essay, other ideas may occur to you; add them to your list so they won't slip your mind.

## EXERCISE 17-4

**Directions:** Make a list of ideas to use in answering one of the following questions. Then number them to reflect how you would organize your essay.

1. The U.S. national debt has become an increasingly serious problem. One economist has suggested that each American take a 10-percent pay cut for one year. He presented statistics that demonstrated how this would drastically reduce the debt. Explain and justify your personal response to this proposal.

2. Describe the effects of the computerization of business and society on our daily lives.

3. Recently, television cameras have been allowed at several high profile trials. Discuss the pros and cons of this practice.

## Writing Your Answer

Because you will have little time to revise, it is important to write in complete sentences, supplying sufficient detail and following a logical organization. (Your instructor will not be put off by minor changes, additions, and corrections.)

Organize your essay answers as you would the other types of essays you've learned to write: begin with a thesis statement; then explain and support it.

## Writing Your Thesis Statement

Thesis statements in essay exams should be simple and straightforward. In fact, you often can simply rephrase the essay question. Here are a few examples:

| Essay Question | Thesis Statement |
| --- | --- |
| 1. Describe the psychological factors that may affect the consumer buying process. | There are five psychological factors that may affect the consumer buying process. |
| 2. Identify and give an example of the principal forms of price discrimination. | Retailers use numerous forms of price discrimination. |
| 3. Coastal areas have more moderate temperatures than inland areas at the same latitude. Explain this phenomenon. | The high specific heat of water accounts for variations between coastal and inland areas at the same latitude. |

At times, you may decide to suggest the organization or content of your answer, as in the following examples:

| Essay Question | Thesis Statement |
| --- | --- |
| 1. Describe the strategies individuals use to reinterpret a stressful event. | Individuals cope with stressful events by using reappraisal, social comparison, avoidance, or humor to reinterpret them. |
| 2. Explain the differences between primary and secondary groups. | Primary groups differ from secondary groups in their membership, purpose, level of interaction, and level of intimacy. |

In the above examples, the essay question provided a structure to which the writer added more information.

Make your thesis statement as concise and specific as possible. It should announce to your instructor that you know the answer and how you will organize it.

## EXERCISE 17-5

**Directions:** Write a thesis statement for three of the following essay questions. Answers will vary.

1. How does advertising differ from publicity?

   Thesis statement: _____

2. Explain the common types of magazines and identify the intended audience of each.

   Thesis statement: _____

3. Describe the increase in Internet shopping over the past decade.

   Thesis statement: _____

**4.** Discuss the major ways in which a group ensures that its members conform to its cultural rules.

Thesis statement: _____

**5.** Discuss several ways to test the effectiveness of an advertising campaign.

Thesis statement: _____

## Presenting Supporting Details

Write a separate paragraph for each major supporting detail. Begin each one with a topic sentence that introduces the new point. Suppose this is your thesis statement:

> There are four social factors that may affect the consumer buying process.

Your topic sentences might read as follows:

| | |
|---|---|
| Paragraph 1 | First, social role and family influence are factors that affect consumer decisions. |
| Paragraph 2 | Reference groups are a second social factor. |
| Paragraph 3 | Social class also affects the consumer's purchase decisions. |
| Paragraph 4 | Finally, cultures and subcultures affect buying decisions. |

The remainder of each paragraph should include supporting details about each factor.

## Developing Your Answers with Supporting Details

Each paragraph should provide a relevant and sufficient explanation of the topic sentence. For the above sample question on consumer buying, explain or define each psychological factor and discuss how it affects the buying decision. Here is an example of how one student developed an essay in response to the above question. Notice that he added a general explanation after his thesis statement.

> There are four social factors that may affect the consumer buying process.
> Social factors are those forces that other people exert on a buyer. First, social role and family influence affect who buys what. Everyone holds a position within a group. How you are expected to act in that position is your role. Your role, especially within your family, determines which types of purchases you are in charge of. For example, women are responsible for food and household supplies, while men buy home-repair and auto supplies.
>     Reference groups are a second social factor influencing buying decisions. A reference group is the group a person connects himself or herself with. The person accepts the attitudes and behaviors of the reference group. As a result, a person buys the same things as others in the reference group. For example,

teenagers in a particular high-school class may all purchase one expensive brand of sneakers.

Social class also affects purchasing decisions. Social class is a group of people who have similar social rank, which is determined by such things as money, education, and property. People in the same social class have common attitudes and value the same things. Because they value the same things, they purchase similar items. For example, upper-middle-class business men and women buy luxury cars, like BMWs.

Finally, cultures and subcultures influence buying decisions. Culture means everything in our surroundings made by human beings and includes values and behavior. We tend to do things the way everyone else in our culture does. Because we imitate others, we buy the same things. For example, because many women in American culture work full-time, many of them buy convenience foods. Subcultures are subdivisions within a culture—they are often created on the basis of age, geography, or ethnic background. There are even more similarities in subcultures, so the buying influence is even stronger. Thus, since consumer buying decisions are determined by numerous social forces, retailers and advertisers find predicting consumer purchases challenging and complex.

## Proofreading Your Answer

Be sure to leave enough time to proofread your answer. Check for errors in spelling, punctuation, and grammar. If time permits, make minor revisions. If you think of an important fact to add, include it. Pay attention to sentences that do not make sense, and make your changes as neatly as possible.

## If You Run Out of Time

If you run out of time before you have finished answering the last question, don't panic. Take the last minute or two to make a list or outline of the remaining points you planned to cover. Some instructors will give you partial credit for this.

## Competency Tests and Exit Exams

Some colleges require students to pass competency tests for such skills as reading, writing, and mathematics. These tests assess skills required in more advanced college courses, so think of them as readiness tests. Competency tests are designed so that you will not be placed in courses that you are inadequately prepared for or that are too difficult. Try your best, but don't be upset if you don't score at the required level. It is best to be certain you have the skills you need before tackling more difficult courses.

This section focuses on competency tests, but many suggestions here apply to other tests.

## Finding Out About the Competency Test

To feel confident and prepared for the test, find out as much about it as possible ahead of time. You'll want to know

- what kinds of questions are included. (For example, do you write an essay or correct errors in another writer's paragraphs?)

- how many questions there are.

- if there is a time limit, and if so, what it is.

- what skills the test measures.

- how the test is scored. (Do some skills count more than others?)

- if it is an essay test, are you expected to revise or recopy it?

Your instructor may be able to answer many of these questions. Also, talk with other students who have taken the test. They may be able to offer useful tips and advice.

## Preparing for Competency Tests

If you are taking the test right after finishing a writing course, you will be well prepared. Nevertheless, the suggestions on taking different types of competency tests will help you.

### Essay Tests

If your test requires that you write an essay, the following suggestions will help:

1. **Study your error log** (see Chapter 5, "Strategies for Revising," pp. 109–135). If you haven't kept one, review papers your instructor has marked to identify and make a list of your most common errors. As you revise and proofread your competency-test answers, check for each of these errors.

2. **Construct a mental revision checklist before you go into the exam.** Use revision checklists in this book as a guide. If time permits, jot your list down on scrap paper during the exam; use it to revise your essay.

3. **Reread sections of your learning journal** (see "Writing Success Starts Here!" pp. xxxiii–xlvi) in which you have written about skills you are learning and how well they work. If you have discovered, for example, that branching usually works well for generating ideas, use it during the test.

4. **Take a practice test.** Ask a classmate to make up a topic or question for you to write about. It should be the same type of question as those that will be on the test. Give yourself the time limit that will be used on the test. Then ask your classmate to evaluate your essay. Use this practice test to help yourself gauge your time during the actual test.

5. **When taking the test, if your test is timed, plan how to divide your time.** Estimate how much you will need for each step in the writing process. Wear a watch to the exam, and check periodically to see that you're on schedule.

### Error-Correction Tests

If your test requires you to edit or correct another writer's sentences or paragraphs, do the following:

1. **Review your error log or graded papers.** The errors you make when you write are likely to be those you'll have difficulty spotting on the test.

2. **Practice with a friend.** Write sample test items for each other. Pay attention to the kinds of errors you are failing to spot; you're likely to miss them on the test as well.

3. **If you are taking a state exam, practice manuals or review books may be available.** Check with your college bookstore. Take the sample tests and work through the practice exercises. Note your pattern of errors and, if necessary, get additional help from your instructor or your college's academic skills center.

4. **When taking the test, if time permits, read each sentence or paragraph several times, looking for different types of errors each time.** For example, read it once looking for spelling errors, another time to evaluate sentence structure, and so forth.

# AN ACADEMIC SCENARIO
## AN ESSAY ANSWER
## The Academic Writer and the Writing Task

Sarah Evenhardt is taking a criminal justice class. On her first exam, she found the following essay question. The essay was worth 25 points.

### Essay Question

Crime is a human act that violates criminal law. Identify the various categories of crime. Describe and provide an example of each.

### Answer

Thesis statement

Main point 1

Supporting details

Main point 2

Supporting details

There are five categories of crime. Each violates one or more aspects of criminal law. The first of these categories is index crime. Index crimes are those identified by the Federal Bureau of Investigation as serious crimes. They include criminal homicide, rape, robbery, burglary, aggravated assault, larceny, auto theft, and arson.

The second type of crime is white-collar crime. These crimes may be committed by corporations or individuals, usually within the course of daily business. The criminals are often affluent and respectable citizens. Some examples are embezzlement and income tax evasion.

*Main point 3*

*Supporting details*

*Main point 4*

*Supporting details*

*Main point 5*

*Supporting details*

A third type of crime is professional crime. Professional crimes are committed by criminals who pursue crime as a day-to-day occupation. They often use skilled techniques and are respected by other criminals. Shoplifters, safecrackers, or cargo highjackers are examples of professional criminals.

Organized crime is a fourth type of crime. Organized crime involves the sale of illegal goods and services and is conducted by criminals who organize into networks. Organized crime is often transmitted through generations and does not depend on particular individuals for its continuation. Organized crime often involves political corruption. Examples of organized crime are gambling, narcotics sales, and loan sharking.

A fifth type of crime is victimless crime. This type of crime involves willing participants; there is no victim other than the offender. Examples include drug use, prostitution, and public drunkeness.

## Examining Academic Writing

1. Taking into account the point value of the essay, do you think Evenhardt included a sufficient number of main points? Why?

2. Highlight and evaluate Evenhardt's thesis statement.

3. Evenhardt did not write a concluding sentence. Do you think it is necessary? If so, what should it have said?

4. Did Evenhardt include sufficient examples?

## Academic Writing Assignments

1. Assume your are taking an exit competency test for your writing class. Here is your assignment. The time limit is one hour.

   **Assignment:** Write an essay in response to one of the following questions:

   a. Should those living near undesirable places, such as prisons, garbage dumps, or interstate toll booths be compensated to tolerate them?

   b. Suppose you owned a home you were happy with. What events or actions in the neighborhood would make you decide to sell it, if any?

   c. Suppose a group of terrorists are threatening to kill 100 hostages unless their demands are met by midnight? Under what conditions, if any, should their demands be met? What further information might you need? Justify your answer.

2. Suppose you were given the following essay question in your writing class:

**Question:** Explain the steps in the writing process. Be sure to include techniques that you have found particularly effective for each step. Write an essay answer response.

3. Suppose you were given the following essay question in your writing class:

**Question:** Write an essay discussing how your writing has changed since you began this writing class. Explain what you do differently, what you have learned about writing, how you have improved, and what further improvements you need to make.

# A WORKPLACE SCENARIO
## A JOB APPLICATION ANSWER
### The Workplace Writer and the Writing Task

Tessa Lee was applying for work with a temporary agency—an agency that supplies workers for short-term assignments. A college student, Tessa wanted to pick up a few hours of clerical work each week without locking herself into one particular company. She knew that in order to build a reputation as a good temp worker, she would have to have more than computer and data-entry skills; she would have to demonstrate the confidence and versatility to walk into new situations and catch on quickly.

After doing well on the computer and proof-reading tests, Tessa discovered that there was a place on the application where she could demonstrate her interpersonal skills and talent for adapting to different workplaces. The question read:

> What personal qualities do you possess that make you uniquely suited for temporary work? Give as many examples as possible.

Tessa wrote the following answer:

I'm so glad to have this opportunity to tell you more about myself than you'll learn from my résumé or keyboarding test. I've been working ever since I was 8 years old. I didn't have to, no one told me I should, I just wanted to. I sold lemonade on hot days and shoveled snow in winter. I volunteered at the local animal shelter until I was old enough to be hired as a part-time employee. In high school, I worked in each of my relatives' businesses, filling in when their employees went on vacation or were out sick. I filed and answered phones in my uncle's law firm, sold shoes in my aunt's shop, and did everything from typing menus to cooking in my parents' restaurant.

During high school I volunteered at a senior center and tutored children in the elementary school I had attended. I wasn't paid for either of these activities, but got more out of them than any paycheck would have given me. I learned how important it is to simply listen. I learned how just listening to someone can make them feel respected, whether they are a supervisor or a first-grader.

This is what I feel makes me a better temp worker than someone who has only held one or two jobs in his or her life; my exposure to a wide variety of businesses, jobs, and individuals. I know that wherever you send me, I will be a respectful and hard worker.

## Examining Workplace Writing

1. Highlight Lee's thesis statement.

2. How does Lee organize her answer? Highlight the transitions she uses.

3. Evaluate Lee's conclusion? Is it effective?

4. Describe the tone of Lee's answer.

5. What personal qualities does Lee discuss?

6. How does Lee introduce her answer?

## Workplace Writing Assignments

1. Assume you have received your degree and are applying for a job in your field. Write several paragraphs summarizing your educational and work-related experiences.

2. You are applying for a position with a company in which community service is valued and expected. As part of the job application process, you are asked to write a letter describing possible contributions you could make to a specific community service organization. Write that letter, using your own volunteer interests or experiences as a base.

3. You are applying for a job as a college admissions representative. Your job would be to visit high schools and attend college/career fairs to recruit students. As part of the job application process, you are asked to write a lively one-page promotional statement emphasizing the benefits of attending the college. Base your statement on the college you are attending.

# WRITING ABOUT A READING

## Thinking Before Reading

This reading was taken from a college textbook, *Consumer Behavior*, by Michael R. Solomon. It represents the type of textbook material you might review for an essay exam.

1. Preview the reading, using the steps discussed in Chapter 2, p. 30.

2. Activate your thinking by answering the following questions:

   a. Why are advertisers interested in the Hispanic market?

   b. What television commercials have you seen that seemed to be targeted toward a specific racial or ethnic group?

### READING

# Hispanic Americans: A Growing Market Segment

## Michael R. Solomon

1   The Hispanic subculture is a sleeping giant, a segment that was until recently largely ignored by many marketers. The growth and increasing affluence of this group has now made it impossible to overlook, and Hispanic consumers are now diligently courted by many major corporations. Nike made history in 1993 by running the first Spanish-language commercial ever broadcast in prime time on a major American network. The spot, which ran during the All-Star baseball game, featured boys in tattered clothes playing ball in the **Dominican Republic**, or *La Tierra de Mediocampistas* (the Land of Shortstops). This title refers to the fact that over 70 Dominicans have played for major league ball clubs, many of whom started at the shortstop position. This ground-breaking spot also laid bare some of the issues involved in marketing to Hispanics: Many found the commercial condescending (especially the ragged look of the actors), and felt that it promoted the idea that Hispanics don't really want to assimilate into mainstream **Anglo** culture.

2   If nothing else, though, this commercial by a large corporation highlights the indisputable fact that the Hispanic American market is now being taken seriously by major marketers. Some are rushing to sign Hispanic celebrities, such as Daisy Fuentes and Rita Moreno, to endorse their products. Others are developing separate Spanish-language campaigns, often with entirely different emphases calculated to appeal to the unique characteristics of this market. For example, the California Milk Processor Board discovered that its hugely successful "got milk?" campaign was not well received by Hispanics, because biting, sarcastic humor is not part of the Hispanic culture. In addition, the notion of milk deprivation is not funny to the Hispanic homemaker, because running out of milk means she has failed her family. An alternative targeted to Hispanics features a grandmother who teaches her granddaughter how to drink milk. As she explains to her granddaughter that *"cocinado con amor y con leche"* (she cooks with love and milk), this execution reinforces cultural beliefs that old people are to be revered, a grandmother is sweet, knowledgeable and strong, and the kitchen is a magical place where food is turned into love.

### The Allure of the Hispanic Market

3   **Demographically,** two important characteristics of the Hispanic market are worth noting: First, it is a young market. The median age of Hispanic

**Dominican Republic**
A country in the West Indies on the eastern side of the island of Hispaniola

**Anglo**
Short for Anglo-American, an English-speaking, white resident of the United States

**demographically**
using the characteristics of a particular population

Americans is 23.6, compared with the U.S. average of 32. That helps to explain why General Mills developed a breakfast cereal called Buñuelitos specifically for this market. The brand name is an adaptation of *buñuelos,* a traditional Mexican pasty served on holidays.

4     Second, the Hispanic family is much larger than the rest of the population's. The average Hispanic household contains 3.5 people, compared to only 2.7 for other U.S. households. These differences obviously affect the overall allocation of income to various product categories. For example, Hispanic households spend 15 to 20 percent more of their disposable income than the national average on groceries. There are now over 19 million Hispanic consumers in the United States, and a number of factors make this market segment extremely attractive:

- Hispanics tend to be brand loyal, especially to brands from their country of origin. In one study, about 45 percent reported that they always buy their usual brand, whereas only one in five said they frequently switch brands. Another found that Hispanics who strongly identify with their ethnic origin are more likely to seek Hispanic vendors, to be loyal to brands used by family and friends, and to be influenced by Hispanic media.

- Hispanics are highly concentrated geographically by country of origin, which makes them relatively easy to reach. Over 50 percent of all Hispanics live in the Los Angeles, New York, Miami, San Antonio, San Francisco, and Chicago metropolitan areas.

- Education levels are increasing dramatically. In the period between 1984 and 1988, the number of Hispanics with four years of college increased by 51 percent. Although the absolute numbers are still low compared to the general population, the number of Hispanic men in managerial and professional jobs increased by 42 percent, and the corresponding increase of 61 percent for Hispanic women during this period was even more encouraging.

### Appealing to Hispanic Subcultures

5     The behavior profile of the Hispanic consumer includes a need for status and a strong sense of pride. A high value is placed on self-expression and familial devotion. Some campaigns have played to Hispanics' fear of rejection and apprehension about loss of control and embarrassment in social situations. Conventional wisdom recommends creating action-oriented advertising and emphasizing a problem-solving atmosphere. Assertive role models who are cast in nonthreatening situations appear to be effective.

6     As with other large subcultural groups, marketers are now beginning to discover that the Hispanic market is not homogenous. Subcultural identity is not as much with being Hispanic as it is with the particular country of origin. Mexican Americans, who make up about 62 percent of all Hispanic

**Fidel Castro**
Cuban leader who established a socialist state in Cuba in 1959

Americans, are also the fastest-growing subsegment; their population has grown by 40 percent since 1980. Cuban Americans are by far the wealthiest subsegment, but they also are the smallest Hispanic ethnic group. Many Cuban American families with high educational levels fled **Fidel Castro's** communist regime in the late 1950s and early 1960s, worked hard for many years to establish themselves, and are now firmly entrenched in the Miami political and economic establishment. Because of this affluence, businesses in South Florida now make an effort to target "YUCAs" (young, upwardly mobile Cuban Americans), especially since the *majority* of Miami residents are Hispanic American!

## Marketing Blunders

7      Many initial efforts by Americans to market to Hispanics were, to say the least, counterproductive. Companies bumbled in their efforts to translate advertising adequately or to compose copy that could capture desired nuances. These mistakes do not occur so much anymore as marketers become more sophisticated in dealing with this market and as Hispanics themselves become involved in advertising production. The following are some translation mishaps that have slipped through in the past:

- The Perdue slogan, "It takes a tough man to make a tender chicken," was translated as "It takes a sexually excited man to make a chick affectionate."
- Budweiser was promoted as the "queen of beers."
- A burrito was mistakenly called a *burrada*, which means "big mistake."
- Braniff, promoting its comfortable leather seats, used the headline, *Sentado en cuero*, which was interpreted as "Sit naked."
- Coors beer's slogan to "get loose with Coors" appeared in Spanish as "get the runs with Coors."

## Understanding Hispanic Identity

8      Native language and culture are important components of Hispanic identity and self-esteem (about three-quarters of Hispanics still speak Spanish at home), and these consumers are very sympathetic to marketing efforts that acknowledge and emphasize the Hispanic cultural heritage. More than 40 percent of Hispanic consumers say they deliberately attempt to buy products that show an interest in the Hispanic consumer, and this number jumps to over two-thirds for Cuban Americans.

9      Many Hispanic Americans are avid consumers of soap operas, called *telenovelas*. Ethnic soap operas, shown on American television, are becoming big business. Univision, the biggest Spanish-language network, airs 10 different ones each day. These shows are produced by Latin American networks, but some viewers have complained that they do not address problems of Hispanic Americans such as illegal immigration, getting a job, or speaking the language.

10      Since the beginning of the 1990s, Hispanic radio stations have been blossoming—there are now over 390 stations in the United States. This growth is partly due to the increasing size and economic clout of Hispanic consumers. It is also attributable to stations' efforts to attract younger listeners by playing more contemporary musical styles, such as *tejano, banda, ranchera,* and *nortena.* A movie about the shooting death of Selena, a popular young *tejano* singer, has fueled this interest. These new formats feature bilingual disk jockeys, who are developing a patter that some have called "Spanglish."

## Level of Acculturation

11      One important way to distinguish among members of a subculture is to consider the extent to which they retain a sense of identification with their country of origin. Acculturation refers to the process of movement and adaptation to one country's cultural environment by a person from another country.

12      This factor is especially important when considering the Hispanic market, because the degree to which these consumers are integrated into the American way of life varies widely. For instance, about 38 percent of all Hispanics live in *barrios,* or predominantly Hispanic neighborhoods, which tend to be somewhat insulated from mainstream society.

13      The acculturation of Hispanic consumers may be understood in terms of the progressive learning model. This perspective assumes that people gradually learn a new culture as they increasingly come in contact with it. Thus, we would expect the consumer behavior of Hispanic Americans to be a mixture of practices taken from their original culture and those of the new or *host culture.*

14      Research has generally obtained results that support this pattern when factors such as shopping orientation, the importance placed on various product attributes, media preference, and brand loyalty are examined. When the intensity of ethnic identification is taken into account, consumers who retained a strong ethnic identification differed from their more assimilated counterparts in the following ways:
- They had a more negative attitude toward business in general (probably caused by frustration due to relatively low income levels).
- They were higher users of Spanish-language media.
- They were more brand loyal.
- They were more likely to prefer brands with prestige labels.
- They were more likely to buy brands specifically advertised to their ethnic group.

15      Overall, the Hispanic subculture has become an important marketing segment that advertisers and media corporations cannot afford to ignore.

## Getting Ready to Write

### Reviewing the Reading

1. Why is the 1993 Nike advertisement significant?

2. What are two important characteristics of the Hispanic market?

3. What factors make the Hispanic market appealing to marketers?

4. What marketing mistakes have marketers made?

5. Define the term "acculturation" in your own words.

### Examining the Reading: Underlining and Reviewing

Reread and underline passages in the reading, as if you were preparing for an exam that includes this material. Use any other getting-ready-to-write strategy that will help you organize and recall the material. (Refer to Table 17-1, p. 444, for a list of strategies.)

### Thinking Critically: Predicting Exam Questions

Predict one essay-exam question that could be asked based on this reading.

### Strengthening Your Vocabulary

Part A: Using the word's context, word parts, or a dictionary, write a brief definition of each of the following words or phrases as it is used in the reading.

1. condescending (paragraph 1) snobby; behaving toward others in a way that shows you consider yourself superior to them

2. assimilate (paragraph 1) to integrate into a larger group, so that differences are minimized or eliminated

3. allocation (paragraph 4) the assignment or earmarking of something for a particular purpose

4. assertive (paragraph 5) acting confidently; noticeably strong

5. homogenous (paragraph 6) of the same kind

6. subsegment (paragraph 6) one part of a larger overall group

7. counterproductive (paragraph 7) making problems instead of helping to achieve a goal

8. nuances (paragraph 7) *subtle differences* _____

_____

**Part B:** Choose one of the above words and draw a word map.

## Reacting to Ideas: Discussion and Journal Writing

Compare your essay-question prediction with those of other students. Discuss ways you might respond to their questions as well as your own.

## Writing About the Reading

### Essay Options

1. Answer the essay question you predicted in the "Thinking Critically" section above.

2. Answer the following question without quoting directly from the reading:

    What does the author mean when he compares the Hispanic population in the United States to a "sleeping giant"?

3. Assume you are taking an exit exam for your writing course. Select one of the following assignments, and approach it as you would a competency exam:

    a. Write an essay about the use of language in advertising and how something written for an English-speaking consumer might not increase sales to a Hispanic consumer.

    b. The author states: "Acculturation refers to the process of movement and adaptation to one country's cultural environment by a person from another country." Write an essay that compares the ways in which groups from two different countries of origin have or have not assimilated into American culture.

    c. Write an essay about ways in which advertising has failed to reach you. Is there a specific product you would never consider using because of the way in which it is advertised?

## Revision Checklist—Essay Exams

1. Is your essay written as if it is for an audience unfamiliar with the topic?

2. Does your essay demonstrate your purpose—that you are knowledgeable about the topic?

3. Is your thesis statement concise and straightforward?

4. Is each main point developed in a separate paragraph?

5. Does each paragraph provide relevant and sufficient detail?

6. Have you made minor revisions, and have you proofread the essay?

## Revision Checklist—Competency Tests

1. Is your essay appropriate for your audience? Does it give them the background information they need? Will it interest them?

2. Will your essay accomplish your purpose?

3. Have you narrowed your topic so that you can cover your subject thoroughly in your essay?

4. Is your main point clearly expressed in a thesis statement in the introductory paragraph? Does your introductory paragraph capture the reader's interest and lead into the body of the essay?

5. Does each paragraph of your essay have a topic sentence that supports your essay's main point?

6. Is each paragraph's topic sentence supported by relevant and sufficient detail?

7. Are your paragraphs arranged in a logical sequence and connected by transitional words and phrases?

8. Is the tone of your essay appropriate for your purpose and audience?

9. Does your conclusion reemphasize your thesis statement and draw the essay to a close?

10. Have you proofread your paper and corrected any mechanical errors (grammar, spelling, punctuation, and so on)? (See the inside back cover of this book for a proofreading checklist.)

# CHAPTER REVIEW AND PRACTICE

## Chapter Review

WHAT ARE ESSAY EXAMS AND COMPETENCY TESTS?

Essay exams are tests that require you to recall what you know about a given topic and write that information in the form of sentences and paragraphs. Competency tests require you to demonstrate your ability to perform particular tasks.

| | |
|---|---|
| HOW SHOULD YOU PREPARE FOR ESSAYS EXAMS? | Use study sheets, predict possible exam questions, and draft possible answers. |
| WHAT SHOULD YOU DO WHEN TAKING AN ESSAY EXAM? | Arrive early, sit in the front, read directions carefully, make careful choices, plan your time, and pay attention to the point value of questions. |
| HOW SHOULD YOU ANALYZE EXAM QUESTIONS? | Identify the topic, and notice the verb that tells you how to organize your answer. |
| WHAT SHOULD YOUR ESSAY ANSWER INCLUDE? | It should include a thesis and supporting details. |
| WHAT SHOULD YOU DO TO PREPARE FOR A COMPETENCY TEST? | Find out what it involves, what it measures, whether there is a time limit, and how it is scored. Obtain practice or review books. |
| HOW SHOULD YOU PREPARE FOR ESSAY COMPETENCY TESTS? | Review your error log, create a mental revision checklist, review your journal, and take a practice test. |
| HOW SHOULD YOU PREPARE FOR ERROR-CORRECTION TESTS? | Review your error log, practice with a friend, and obtain practice or review books. |

## Skill Refresher: When to Use Capital Letters

Capital letters are commonly used to

1. mark the beginning of a sentence.

2. identify names of specific people, places, organizations, companies, products, titles, days, months, weeks, religions, and holidays.

3. mark the beginning of a direct quotation.

### Rate Your Ability to Use Capitalization Correctly

In each of the following sentences, capitalize wherever necessary by crossing out the lowercase letter and replacing it with a capital. If any letters are incorrectly capitalized, change them to lowercase.

1. because I spent last sunday in pittsburgh, I missed my favorite television show—*60 minutes*.

2. There are five Great Lakes—erie, michigan, ontario, huron, and superior.

3. this may, professor gilbert will give us our final exam.

4. Last week I rented my favorite movie from the video rental store on elmwood avenue.

5. One of shakespeare's most famous plays is *hamlet*.

6. I completed an internship at midcity office equipment and supply.

7. my brother will eat only rice krispies for breakfast.

8. Jean Griffith is a senator who lives in washington county.

9. I love to vacation in california because the pacific ocean is so beautiful.

10. The president of the company, Ms. Salinas, announced that sales representatives would be given american express credit cards.

Score _____

Check your answers, using the Answer Key on p. 644. If you got more than two wrong, you need additional review and practice in recognizing when to use capital letters. Refer to Part VI, "Reviewing the Basics," and under section F see "Capitalization." For additional practice go to this book's Web site at http://www.ablongman.com/mcwhorterexpressways1e.

## INTERNET ACTIVITIES

### 1.  Taking Essay Exams

Review this chart from the University of Minnesota for taking essay exams.

http://www.ucs.umn.edu/lasc/handouts/lascpdf/essayexamtool.pdf

Then write a paragraph that summarizes the process outlined here.

### 2.  Test Preparation Checklist

Complete this self-evaluation from Oakton Community College.

http://www.oakton.edu/resource/iss/testsvy.htm

Write a list of your strengths and weaknesses. Use the Web sites from Oakton to develop a plan for dealing with your weaknesses.

### 3.  This Book's Web Site

For more practice with skills taught in this chapter, refer to the book's Web site.

http://www.ablongman.com/mcwhorterexpressways1e

# PART V

# A Multicultural Reader

R E A D I N G

# Bok Lived to Tell of Capture, Slavery

Mark Melady

## WRITING ABOUT A READING

### Thinking Before Reading

The following reading, "Bok Lived to Tell of Capture, Slavery," is a news-paper account of Francis Bok's experience after being enslaved as a child in Southern Sudan. In this article, Bok describes his ordeal and his eventual escape from slavery.

1. Preview the reading using the steps described in Chapter 2, p. 30.

2. Connect the reading to your own experience by answering the follow-ing questions:

   a. What do you know about the Sudanese civil war?

   b. Does slavery still exist in some parts of the world? How do you know?

   c. Do you know anyone who has immigrated to the United States? Why did he or she leave home?

1 WORCESTER—He was 7 years old, working sunup to sundown, sleep-ing with cows, praying every night for someone to rescue him and wonder-ing why his owner did not love him.

2 "If you think slavery ended in 1865, think again," Francis Bok, 24, former slave, said at the College of the Holy Cross last night. Mr. Bok was one of tens of thousands of southern Sudanese who have been enslaved during a 20-year civil war between the largely Muslim, lighter-skinned Arabic north and the mostly Christian, black African south that has left 2 million dead. Forget political distinctions when it comes to slavery, Mr. Bok said. "It's not a matter of left or right. It's a matter of right and wrong."

3 Mr. Bok was taken captive during a slave raid on his village in Southern Sudan in 1986. His mother had allowed him to go to the market for the first time in the company of a teenage neighbor girl to sell eggs and beans raised

by the family. "I was proud that she entrusted me with her business," he said. The market, about five miles from his village, was busy and lively. He played with other children. He was so preoccupied in play that Mr. Bok did not notice the smoke coming from his village or people scattering until men arrived on horseback, firing guns.

4    "I saw men fall down and not get up," he remembered. "I saw some kids killed." A man jumped from his horse and grabbed him hard by the arm. It was the beginning of the end of his freedom. He had become the property of a Mr. Abdullah. He would never see his parents, his siblings or his home village again. Other children were taken. As the raiding party pulled away one teenage girl couldn't stop crying because she had seen her parents shot dead by the raiders. "They tried to get her to stop crying," he said. "When she couldn't, a man pulled her aside and shot her in the head. I didn't cry after that. All the other kids shut up."

5    He was brought to the Abdullah farm. He was beaten the first day and almost every day thereafter for the next 10 years. His meals were often rotting food. Some days the matriarch would not feed him. After a few months when he had learned enough Arabic to converse, he asked his owner why he was called the Arabic pejorative for black slave, why he had to sleep with the cattle and why no one loved him. "He beat me with a stick," Mr. Bok said, "and said never ask me those questions again."

6    He tried to escape but was caught, beaten and tied up. If he tried again, his owner threatened to shoot him, Mr. Bok said. "I decided I would rather die than be a slave," he said. One early morning when he was 17, after 10 years as Mr. Abdullah's chattel, he bolted. "It was four in the morning," Mr. Bok recalled, "I ran and ran through the forest."

7    When he reached the first population center, a sympathetic truck driver paid for his train fare to Khartoum, the nation's capital. There he futilely searched the refugee camps for his family. A family of 10 from the same area as his home village took him in. A few weeks later he crossed the Red Sea to Egypt and eventually made his way to Fargo, N.D., through a United Nations program. "It was cold, and I was alone," he said of Fargo. After a few months he accepted an offer from the American Anti-Slavery Group, headquartered in Boston, to work for the agency.

8    In 2001, he carried the Winter Olympic torch on its relay tour and last year attended the Sudan Peace Act signing ceremony at the White House. "I wasn't supposed to speak, just observe," he said, "but I grabbed the mike and thanked President Bush on behalf of the Sudanese people. Afterwards he held my hand and thanked me and said I had made a difference for Sudan."

## Getting Ready to Write

### Reviewing the Reading

1. What groups make up the two sides in the Sudanese civil war?

2. What was Francis Bok doing the day he was taken captive?

3. What were conditions like for Bok on the Abdullah farm?

4. How did Bok get to America?

5. Why was Bok at the White House?

### Examining the Reading

To understand a narrative, process paragraph, or essay, you must have a clear understanding of the sequence of events. A sequence map, shown earlier in Chapter 6 on p. 145, can be helpful to readers as well as writers. When reading complex material, a sequence map can help you work out the order in which events occurred. Draw a map of the reading using these guidelines.

### Thinking Critically: Supporting Evidence

Many writers provide data or evidence in support of their ideas. Critical readers must examine the evidence and evaluate its quality. The two main factors to consider when evaluating evidence are the type of evidence being presented and the relevance of that evidence. Types of evidence that are commonly used include personal experience or observation, statistical data, informed opinion, and historical documentation. Writers may also use descriptions of particular events to illustrate their ideas.

The story of Francis Bok is related through his retelling of the events to a journalist. Thus, the primary type of evidence that the writer uses is Bok's personal experience. Begin by writing a topic sentence to go with the article. Then, using the evidence provided by Bok's statements as well as the facts included by the journalist, write a paragraph that supports your topic sentence.

### Strengthening Your Vocabulary

**Part A:** Using the word's context, word parts, or a dictionary, write a brief definition of each of the following words or phrases as it is used in the reading.

1. preoccupied (paragraph 3) _absorbed in thought or activity_ _____

   _____

2. matriarch (paragraph 5) _the female head of a family or group_ _____

   _____

3. pejorative (paragraph 5) *negative or disparaging term*

_____

4. chattel (paragraph 6) *an article of personal property; a slave*

_____

5. futilely (paragraph 7) *unsuccessfully*

_____

**Part B:** Choose one of the above words and draw a word map of it.

### Reacting to Ideas: Discussion and Journal Writing

Get ready to write about the reading by discussing the following questions:

1. Explain what Bok means when he says, "It's not a matter of left or right. It's a matter of right and wrong."

2. Imagine yourself at age seven, the same age as Bok when he was captured. Contrast your own situation at that age with the circumstances into which Bok was forced.

3. How did Bok's experiences illustrate both the good and the bad in humankind?

## Writing About the Reading

### Paragraph Options

1. This narrative is told in a mostly factual tone. What does that matter-of-factness tell you about Bok? Write a paragraph describing what kind of person you think he is today, based on what you know about him from the reading.

2. After many hardships, Bok made his way to America. Put yourself in his shoes and write a paragraph describing what his first impressions of this country might have been (look in paragraph 7 for a clue). What feelings do you think he has toward his adopted country today?

3. In the last paragraph, Bok tells of President Bush's statement that he had "made a difference for Sudan." Write a paragraph explaining how Bok may have made a difference for his country.

### Essay Options

4. Throughout history, there have been many instances of slaves willing to risk death in order to obtain their freedom. Write an essay explaining what you think you might do if you were held captive. Would you, like Bok, rather die than be a slave?

5. Write an essay describing what you think Bok's captors would say to the world community about their actions. Do you think they would defend their actions or express remorse? You may choose to write from the point of view of someone in the Abdullah family or another member of the raiding party, or from your own point of view.

6. Imagine that you were given an opportunity to interview Bok. What questions would you ask him that were not answered in this reading? Write an essay detailing what you would like to know about Bok and what you would like the world to know about him. Describe your intended audience as well. You may choose to write an essay that addresses the United Nations, for example.

# Spanglish Creeps into Mainstream

## Deborah Kong

## WRITING ABOUT A READING

### Thinking Before Reading

The following reading, "Spanglish Creeps into Mainstream," was written by Deborah Kong, minority issues writer for the Associated Press. In her job, she reports on multicultural matters including the controversial blending of languages as described in this article.

1. Preview the reading using the steps described in Chapter 2, p. 30.

2. Connect the reading to your own experience by answering the following questions:

   a. What is Spanglish?

   b. Does your language contain words from other languages?

buena
good

1    In the wacky cartoon world of the "Mucha Lucha" wrestling school, Buena Girl is trying to help her friend gain weight in preparation for his match with three big "brutos." "And now for the ultimate in **buena** eats! El Masked Montana's mega torta!" she says, stuffing an enormous sandwich into his mouth. The WB network's new show is peppered with a blend of Spanish and English dialogue often called Spanglish. And TV isn't the only place you'll find it.

2    An Amherst College professor recently completed a Spanglish translation of the first chapter of "Don Quixote," and Hallmark is expanding its line of cards that mix America's most commonly spoken languages. Not everyone is happy to see Spanglish creep into the mainstream. Critics see it as a danger to Hispanic culture and advancement. But Spanglish speakers, who often move nimbly between the two languages and cultures, say it is an expression of ethnic pride. "Spanglish is proof that Latinos have a culture that is made up of two parts. It's not that you are Latino or American," said Ilan Stavans, the professor of Latin American and Latino culture who translated Miguel de Cervantes' masterpiece. "You live on the hyphen, in between. That's what Spanglish is all about, a middle ground."

3    Spanglish speakers span generations, classes and nationalities. Immigrants still learning English may turn to Spanglish out of necessity. Bilingual speakers may dip into one language, then weave in another because it's more convenient. "There are certain words or sayings that are just better in Spanish," said Danny Lopez, 28, who speaks Spanglish with friends and family, though seldom at work. "When I talk to my dad, I'll say, 'Hey Dad, I remember sitting in abuelita's cocina when we were little, and we were drinking a taza of café,'" said Lopez, describing memories of his grandmother's kitchen. His family has lived in the United States for four generations. Stavans traces Spanglish's origins back to 1848, when the treaty that ended the U.S.-Mexican War signed over much of the Southwest to the United States, abruptly transforming Spanish-speaking Mexicans into Americans.

4    But the modern phenomenon has plenty of pop culture examples, from Ricky Martin scoring a big hit with "Livin' La Vida Loca" to top-selling Mexican singer Paulina Rubio doing all of her songs in Spanglish as she opens for Enrique Iglesias. At mun2, a cable network that shows music videos, comedies, game shows, extreme sports and other programming targeted at 14- to 34-year-old Hispanics, language has evolved in the last year. When it launched, most of the programs were in Spanish. But the network, a division of NBC-owned Telemundo, will soon be mostly English and Spanglish, in response to viewer preferences, said spokeswoman Claudia Santa Cruz.

5    Stavans translated Cervantes into Spanglish this summer in response to a Spanish-language purist who asserted the linguistic mix would never be taken seriously until it produced a classic like "Don Quixote." "In un placete de La Mancha of which nombre no quiero rembrearme, vivia, not so long ago, uno de esos gentlemen who always tienen una lanza in the rack, una buckler antigua, a skinny caballo y un grayhound para el chase," his translation begins. Stavans' work signals Spanglish's move into academe: He also teaches a class on Spanglish and is working on a Spanglish dictionary, to be published next year.

6    But Antonio Garrido, of the Instituto Cervantes in New York, said a Spanglish "Don Quixote" is "a joke." "The idea is good English and good Spanish. Spanglish has no future," said Garrido, director of the institute created by the Spanish government to promote Spanish and Hispanic-American language and culture. "A person who doesn't speak English well in the United States doesn't have a future."

7    Roberto Gonzalez Echevarria, a professor of Hispanic and comparative literature at Yale University, agreed, saying Hispanics should learn to speak both English and Spanish well. He fears "we're going to end up speaking McSpanish, a sort of anglicized Spanish. I find it offensive the United States' values and cultural mores, all of that, are transmitted through the language filter into Spanish culture." He cited one example of a Spanish pitfall: In a deli in Puerto Rico, he saw a sign that warned parking was for customers only. "Violadores" will be prosecuted, it said. The word was used because it sounds like the English word for violators, but the problem is that "violador" primarily means "rapist" in Spanish, he said.

8    Stavans, who said he speaks Spanglish with his children, doesn't advocate replacing English with Spanglish. But he says it should be recognized as a valid form of communication. "Language is not controlled by a small group of academics that decide what the words are that we should use. Language is created by people and it is the job of academics to record those changes," he said.

9    A recent survey by the Los Angeles-based Cultural Access Group found 74 percent of 250 Hispanic youths surveyed in Los Angeles spoke Spanglish, most often with friends, other young people and at home. The WB network says "Mucha Lucha"—"lucha" means wrestling—reflects that reality. The zippy cartoon doesn't pause to translate Spanish phrases, but sprinkles them throughout to spice up dialogue. "This is the way that young Latino kids speak," said Donna Friedman, the Kids WB! executive vice president.

10    Hallmark says its cards also echo how people speak. "Que beautiful it is to do nada, and then descansar despues," reads one, which translates to, "How beautiful it is to do nothing, and then rest afterward." The greeting card company is expanding its line of Spanish-language cards, which includes Spanglish ones. They're aimed at younger recipients rather than mothers, aunts or grandmothers, "who may not approve of mixing languages," according to the company.

11    In Los Angeles, Lalo Alcaraz and Esteban Zul run a Web site, pocho.com, which offers "satire, news y chat for the Spanglish generation." "We don't live neatly in two worlds. I teach my kids Spanish, yet my wife and I speak English to each other," said Alcaraz, whose new Spanglish comic strip, "La Cucaracha," will appear in newspapers next month. Spanglish is "its own unique point of view. It's more of an empowering thing to us, to say we have a legitimate culture."

# Getting Ready to Write

## Reviewing the Reading

1. Define Spanglish.

2. What literary masterpiece has been partially translated into Spanglish, and why?

3. What is wrong with using the word "violador" on a parking sign?

4. According to the Cultural Access Group's survey in Los Angeles, with whom do most Hispanic youths speak Spanglish?

5. Why is Hallmark's new line of Spanglish cards aimed at younger recipients?

6. Why do some people oppose Spanglish? Why do others favor it?

## Examining the Reading

To analyze this essay, create an idea map. You might organize it using two columns, one for the pros and one for the cons of Spanglish.

## Thinking Critically: Evaluating Alternative Viewpoints

Readers often encounter alternative viewpoints on the same topic or issue. These viewpoints may be completely opposite or there may be some points of agreement. In "Spanglish Creeps into Mainstream," the author presents a variety of examples and opinions that can be grouped into two general viewpoints: those in support of Spanglish and those against it.

Once you have identified the alternative viewpoints, you must evaluate how the viewpoints differ. What types of evidence are offered? Statistical evidence, for example, may carry more weight than personal examples, depending on the issue.

Listed below are some of the people whose opinions about Spanglish are discussed in the article. For each person listed, write a brief description of his or her viewpoint regarding Spanglish.

1. Ilan Stavans, professor of Latin American and Latino culture and translator of "Don Quixote"

2. Danny Lopez, fourth-generation Mexican American

3. Antonio Garrido, director of the Instituto Cervantes

4. Roberto Gonzalez Echevarria, professor of Hispanic and comparative literature

5. Donna Friedman, executive vice president of Kids WB!

6. Lalo Alcaraz, cartoonist and co-creator of pocho.com

## Strengthening Your Vocabulary

**Part A:** Using the word's context, word parts, or a dictionary, write a brief definition of each of the following words or phrases as it is used in the reading.

1. nimbly (paragraph 2) *quickly and easily*

2. purist (paragraph 5) *one who practices or urges strict correctness*

3. mores (paragraph 7) *the attitudes or ways of a particular group*

4. advocate (paragraph 8) *argue in favor of*

5. empowering (paragraph 11) *giving power or authority to*

6. legitimate (paragraph 11) *genuine or authentic*

**Part B:** Choose one of the above words and draw a word map of it.

## Reacting to Ideas: Discussion and Journal Writing

Get ready to write about the reading by discussing the following questions:

1. Why might older generations disapprove of mixing languages?

2. How is Spanglish "an expression of ethnic pride" (paragraph 2)?

3. What is meant by the term "McSpanish" (paragraph 7)? Does that term have a positive or negative connotation?

## Writing About the Reading

### Paragraph Options

1. How does language change? Think of a word or phrase that is fairly new to our language. It might be related to technology (e.g., spamming), popular culture (e.g., crunk), or some other aspect of modern life. Write a paragraph defining the word and explaining why it is a useful addition to our language.

2. The author refers to television programs that reflect the reality of the Hispanic population. Choose a popular television show and write a paragraph describing the ways that it does or does not reflect the reality of your own experience.

3. After reading this article, which viewpoint toward Spanglish do you find yourself supporting? Write a paragraph explaining your answer. Be sure to mention what evidence in the article was most convincing to you.

## Essay Options

4. According to Ilan Stavans, Latinos "live on the hyphen, in between" (paragraph 2). Think of an aspect of your life that might be described as being "on the hyphen." It might be related to your ethnic background or to your current circumstances as a student (for example, are you also an employee or a parent?). Do you "move nimbly" between your roles? Write an essay describing the challenges of living in two worlds or balancing two (or more) roles.

5. Many people feel strongly that immigrants to America must learn to communicate in English. Others believe that some accommodations should be made in recognition of our multilingual population. Take a stand on this issue and write an essay defending your point of view.

6. In what ways, other than through language, can cultures blend? (Think of music, art, fashion, etc.) Choose one way and write an essay describing the process and outcomes.

7. This article focuses on how cultures can blend through language. Choose another aspect of culture—for example, music, art, film, or fashion—and write an essay describing how cultures can influence each other. Use specific examples to support your thesis.

### READING

# A Day Away

## Maya Angelou

## WRITING ABOUT A READING

### Thinking About the Reading

Maya Angelou is a well-known poet, educator, civil rights activist, and author. This essay was taken from *Wouldn't Take Nothing for My Journey Now.* As you read, notice her attention to detail and her vivid use of language.

1. Preview the reading using the steps described in Chapter 2, p. 30.

2. Connect the reading to your own experience by answering the following questions:

   a. What do you do when you feel like you need to get away from everyone and everything?

   b. What is the value of having absolutely nothing planned or scheduled?

1    We often think that our affairs, great or small, must be tended continuously and in detail, or our world will disintegrate, and we will lose our places in the universe. That is not true, or if it is true, then our situations were so temporary that they would have collapsed anyway.

2    Once a year or so I give myself a day away. On the eve of my day of absence, I begin to unwrap the bonds which hold me in harness. I inform housemates, my family and close friends that I will not be reachable for twenty-four hours; then I disengage the telephone. I turn the radio dial to an all-music station, preferably one which plays the soothing golden oldies. I sit for at least an hour in a very hot tub; then I lay out my clothes in preparation for my morning escape, and knowing that nothing will disturb me, I sleep the sleep of the just.

3    On the morning I wake naturally, for I will have set no clock, nor informed my body timepiece when it should alarm. I dress in comfortable shoes and casual clothes and leave my house going no place. If I am living in a city, I wander streets, window-shop, or gaze at buildings. I enter and leave public parks, libraries, the lobbies of skyscrapers, and movie houses. I stay in no place for very long.

amnesia
loss of memory

4    On the getaway day I try for **amnesia**. I do not want to know my name, where I live, or how many dire responsibilities rest on my shoulders. I detest encountering even the closest friend, for then I am reminded of who I am, and the circumstances of my life, which I want to forget for a while.

5    Every person needs to take one day away. A day in which one consciously separates the past from the future. Jobs, lovers, family, employers, and friends can exist one day without any one of us, and if our egos permit us to confess, they could exist eternally in our absence.

6    Each person deserves a day away in which no problems are confronted, no solutions searched for. Each of us needs to withdraw from the cares which will not withdraw from us. We need hours of aimless wandering or spates of time sitting on park benches, observing the mysterious world of ants and the canopy of treetops.

7    If we step away for a time, we are not, as many may think and some will accuse, being irresponsible, but rather we are preparing ourselves to more ably perform our duties and discharge our obligations.

8    When I return home, I am always surprised to find some questions I sought to evade had been answered and some entanglements I had hoped to flee had become unraveled in my absence.

**rancor**
resentment, ill-will

9    A day away acts as a spring tonic. It can dispel **rancor**, transform indecision, and renew the spirit.

———————

## Reviewing the Reading

1. How does Angelou prepare for a day away?

2. On her day away, what does Angelou do?

3. What are the benefits for Angelou of a day away?

4. When she returns from her day away, what does Angelou discover?

5. What does Angelou mean by trying "for amnesia" on her day away?

## Examining the Reading

Draw a map of the reading using the model shown on p. 40.

## Thinking Critically: Examining an Extended Example

Angelou supports her thesis that distance from everyday routines and problems is valuable by giving an extended example of her own day away. Rather than provide numerous examples, she provides just one—herself—and explains it in detail. Examine Angelou's extended example by answering the following questions:

1. What details in the extended example are particularly memorable and effective? Highlight them.

2. Is one extended example effective or would examples of other people's days away have improved the essay?

3. What other information might Angelou have included in her extended example?

4. Other than through the extended example, what other types of evidence does Angelou provide in support of her thesis?

## Strengthening Your Vocabulary

**Part A:** Using the word's context, word parts, or a dictionary, write a brief definition of each of the following words or phrases as it is used in the reading.

1. dire (paragraph 4) *serious, severe or desperate*

2. spates (paragraph 6) *large quantities* _____

_____

3. discharge (paragraph 7) *carry out* _____

_____

4. evade (paragraph 8) *avoid* _____

_____

5. entanglements (paragraph 8) *complicated situations* _____

_____

6. dispel (paragraph 9) *get rid of* _____

_____

**Part B:** Choose one of the above words and draw a word map of it.

## Reacting to Ideas: Discussion and Journal Writing

1. Do you think Angelou is irresponsible for taking a getaway day the way she does? Why or why not?

2. Why does she believe it is important to consciously separate "the past from the future" occasionally?

3. Have you ever noticed how problems sometimes seem easier to solve when you can get away from them for a while? Why do you think this is so?

## Writing About the Reading

### Paragraph Options

1. Write a paragraph describing what you do to reduce tension and refresh yourself.

2. Angelou believes that a day away "acts as a spring tonic." Explain in one paragraph why it would be healthy for you to take a day away occasionally.

3. Write a paragraph agreeing or disagreeing with Angelou's belief that everyone needs to take one day away.

### Essay Options

4. Write an essay summarizing and evaluating Angelou's reasons for taking a day away. Provide additional justification of your own.

5. What would you do on a day away? Write an essay describing where you might go and what you might do.

# For My Indian Daughter

Lewis Sawaquat

## WRITING ABOUT A READING

### Thinking Before Reading

The following reading, "For My Indian Daughter," was written by Lewis Sawaquat. In this narrative, Sawaquat describes the prejudice that Native Americans face and his own journey to understand his Native American identity.

1. Preview the reading using the steps described in Chapter 2, page 30.

2. Connect the reading to your own experience by answering the following questions:

   a. What unfair stereotypes exist about Native Americans?

   b. What aspects of popular culture help to create stereotypes?

1    My little girl is singing herself to sleep upstairs, her voice mingling with the sounds of the birds outside in the old maple trees. She is two and I am nearly 50, and I am very taken with her. She came along late in my life, unexpected and unbidden, a startling gift.

2    Today at the beach my chubby-legged, brown-skinned daughter ran laughing into the water as fast as she could. My wife and I laughed watching her, until we heard behind us a low guttural curse and then an unpleasant voice raised in an imitation war whoop.

3    I turned to see a fat man in a bathing suit, white and soft as a grub, as he covered his mouth and prepared to make the Indian war cry again. He was middle-aged, younger than I, and had three little children lined up next to him, grinning foolishly. My wife suggested we leave the beach, and I agreed.

4    I knew the man was not unusual in his feelings against Indians. His beach behavior might have been socially unacceptable to more civilized whites, but his basic view of Indians is expressed daily in our small town, frequently on the editorial pages of the county newspaper, as white people speak out against Indian fishing rights and land rights, saying in essence, "Those Indians are taking our fish, our land." It doesn't matter to them that we were here first, that the U.S. Supreme Court has ruled in our favor. It mat-

ters to them that we have something they want, and they hate us for it. Backlash is the common explanation of the attacks on Indians, the bumper stickers that say, "Spear an Indian, Save a Fish," but I know better. The hatred of Indians goes back to the beginning when white people came to this country. For me it goes back to my childhood in Harbor Springs, Mich.

5    **Theft:** Harbor Springs is now a summer resort for the very affluent, but a hundred years ago it was the Indian village of my Ottawa ancestors. My grandmother, Anna Showanessy, and other Indians like her, had their land there taken by treaty, by fraud, by violence, by theft. They remembered how whites had burned down the village at Burt Lake in 1900 and pushed the Indians out. These were the stories in my family.

6    When I was a boy my mother told me to walk down the alleys in Harbor Springs and not to wear my orange football sweater out of the house. This way I would not stand out, not be noticed, and not be a target.

**comeuppance**
deserved fate

7    I wore my orange sweater anyway and deliberately avoided the alleys. I was the biggest person I knew and wasn't really afraid. But I met my **come-uppance** when I enlisted in the U.S. Army. One night all the men in my barracks gathered together and, gang-fashion, pulled me into the shower and scrubbed me down with rough brushes used for floors, saying, "We won't have any dirty Indians in our outfit." It is a point of **irony** that I was cleaner than any of them. Later in Korea I learned how to kill, how to bully, how to hate Koreans. I came out of the war tougher than ever and strangely, white.

**irony**
humor based on opposites

8    I went to college, got married, lived in La Porte, Ind., worked as a surveyor and raised three boys. I headed Boy Scout groups, never thinking it odd when the Scouts did imitation Indian dances, imitation Indian lore.

**powwow**
a council or meeting of Native Americans

9    One day when I was 35 or thereabouts I heard about an Indian **powwow**. My father used to attend them and so with great curiosity and a strange joy at discovering a part of my heritage, I decided the thing to do to get ready for this big event was to have my friend make me a spear in his forge. The steel was fine and blue and iridescent. The feathers on the shaft were bright and proud.

10    In a dusty state fairground in southern Indiana, I found white people dressed as Indians. I learned they were "hobbyists," that is, it was their hobby and leisure pastime to masquerade as Indians on weekends. I felt ridiculous with my spear, and I left.

11    It was years before I could tell anyone of the embarrassment of this weekend and see any humor in it. But in a way it was that weekend, for all its silliness, that was my awakening. I realized I didn't know who I was. I didn't have an Indian name. I didn't speak the Indian language. I didn't know the Indian customs. Dimly I remembered the Ottawa word for dog. But it was a baby word, *kahgee*, not the full word, *muhkahgee*, which I was later to learn. Even more hazily I remembered a naming ceremony (my own). I remembered legs dancing around me, dust. Where had that been? Who had I been? "Suwaukquat," my mother told me when I asked, "where the tree begins to grow."

12    That was 1968, and I was not the only Indian in the country who was feeling the need to remember who he or she was. There were others. They had powwows, real ones, and eventually I found them. Together we researched our past, a search that for me culminated in the Longest Walk, a march on Washington in 1978. Maybe because I now know what it means to be Indian, it surprises me that others don't. Of course there aren't very many of us left. The chances of an average person knowing an average Indian in an average lifetime are pretty slim.

13    **Circle:** Still, I was amused one day when my small, four-year-old neighbor looked at me as I was hoeing in my garden and said, "You aren't a real Indian, are you?" Scotty is little, talkative, likable. Finally I said, "I'm a real Indian." He looked at me for a moment and then said, squinting into the sun, "Then where's your horse and feathers?" The child was simply a smaller, whiter version of my own ignorant self years before. We'd both seen too much TV, that's all. He was not to be blamed. And so, in a way, the **moronic** man on the beach today is blameless. We come full circle to realize other people are like ourselves, as discomfiting as that may be sometimes.

14    As I sit in my old chair on my porch, in a light that is fading so the leaves are barely distinguishable against the sky, I can picture my girl asleep upstairs. I would like to prepare her for what's to come, take her each step of the way saying, there's a place to avoid, here's what I know about this, but much of what's before her she must go through alone. She must pass through pain and joy and solitude and community to discover her own inner self that is unlike any other and come through that passage to the place where she sees all people are one, and in so seeing may live her life in a brighter future.

**moronic**

acting like a foolish or stupid person

---

## Getting Ready to Write

### Reviewing the Reading

1.  Why was the event that happened to Sawaquat and his family at the beach disturbing?

2.  At first, what did the author know about his Native American heritage? How did the author learn about his heritage?

3.  How was the author treated when he enlisted in the U.S. Army and what did he learn?

4.  When the author went to his first powwow as an adult in southern Indiana, why was he disappointed?

5.  What does Sawaquat hope for his daughter?

6.  What was the Longest Walk?

## Examining the Reading

To understand a narrative essay, you must have a clear understanding of the sequence of events. A sequence map, shown earlier in Chapter 6 on p. 145, can be helpful to readers as well as writers. Using these guidelines, draw a map of the reading.

## Thinking Critically: Connotative Language

In contrast to a word's precise dictionary meaning (its denotative meaning), a word's *connotative* meaning is the collection of feelings and attitudes that come along with that word. Writers use connotative meanings to stir your emotions or to bring to mind positive or negative associations.

When you read, be alert for meanings suggested by the author's word choice. Connotative meanings provide clues about an author's purpose and often reveal how the author feels about his or her subject.

"For My Indian Daughter" includes many examples of connotative language. For one, the author describes the man on the beach as "white and soft as a grub" (paragraph 3). What connotations come to your mind with this description? What does it reveal about the author's attitude toward the man? Make a list of three examples of connotative language in the reading. For each word or phrase, write its connotative meaning and explain what it reveals about the author's attitude.

## Strengthening Your Vocabulary

**Part A:** Using the word's context, word parts, or a dictionary, write a brief definition of each of the following words or phrases as it is used in the reading.

1. guttural (paragraph 2) having a harsh, disagreeable sound or quality

2. backlash (paragraph 4) a strong, adverse reaction

3. affluent (paragraph 5) wealthy

4. iridescent (paragraph 9) brilliant or lustrous in appearance

5. masquerade (paragraph 10) to disguise oneself

6. culminated (paragraph 12) came to completion or reached the highest point

7. discomfiting (paragraph 13) uncomfortable or unpleasant

**Part B:** Choose one of the above words and draw a word map of it.

## Reacting to Ideas: Discussion and Journal Writing

Get ready to write about the reading by discussing the following questions:

1. The phrase "met my comeuppance" (paragraph 7) means "a deserved punishment or retribution." Why do you think the author used that phrase to describe what happened to him in the Army?

2. What does Sawaquat mean when he says that he came out of the Korean War "white" (paragraph 7)? Explain the irony that he refers to in that same paragraph.

3. According to Sawaquat, why are so many whites prejudiced against Indians?

4. Sawaquat says that in the Army he learned to hate Koreans. Does this fact belong in an essay about hate and prejudice?

## Writing About the Reading

### Paragraph Options

1. Sawaquat uses two headings in this essay: "Theft" (paragraph 5) and "Circle" (paragraph 13). Write a paragraph explaining the significance of these headings.

2. In paragraph 11, Sawaquat describes the powwow weekend as "my awakening." Write a narrative paragraph describing a situation that was a turning point, or an awakening, for you.

3. Sawaquat says the man on the beach is "blameless" (paragraph 13). Do you agree with that statement? Write a paragraph explaining why or why not.

### Essay Options

4. Read the editorial page of your local newspaper. Are prejudices revealed there, as on the pages of Sawaquat's county newspaper? Write an essay addressing a controversial issue that has been in the news. Describe your feelings about the issue and why you feel the way you do. Do you think most people agree or disagree with your views?

5. Sawaquat says that "I realized I didn't know who I was" and learned more about himself and his heritage. Write an essay explaining what you've learned about yourself through an enlightening experience.

6. Reread the final paragraph of the essay. In what ways can Sawaquat (or any parent) prepare his child for what is to come? Consider the ways in which your parents may have prepared you for the future, as well as the passages you had to go through alone. Write an essay describing your experience.

# In This Arranged Marriage, Love Came Later

Shoba Narayan

## WRITING ABOUT A READING

### Thinking Before Reading

The following narrative, "In This Arranged Marriage, Love Came Later," is by Shoba Narayan, an American-educated journalist from India. In her essay, Narayan describes her decision to agree to an arranged marriage, a tradition whereby the parents of young men and women choose whom their children will marry.

1. Preview the reading using the steps described in Chapter 2, p. 30.

2. Connect the reading to your own experience by answering the following questions:

   a. Do you think your parents could choose an appropriate spouse for you?

   b. What do you think is the best predictor of a successful relationship?

1   We sat around the dining table, my family and I, replete from yet another home-cooked South Indian dinner. It was my younger brother, Shaam, who asked the question.

2   "Shoba, why don't you stay back here for a few months? So we can try to get you married."

3   Three pairs of eyes stared at me across the expanse of the table. I sighed. Here I was, at the tail end of my vacation after graduate school. I had an airplane ticket to New York from Madras, India, in ten days. I had accepted a job at an artists' colony in Johnson, Vermont. My car, and most of my possessions, were with friends in Memphis.

4   "It's not that simple," I said. "What about my car . . . ?"

5   "We could find you someone in America," my dad replied. "You could go back to the States."

6   They had thought it all out. This was a plot. I glared at my parents accusingly.

7   Oh, another part of me rationalized, why not give this arranged-marriage thing a shot? It wasn't as if I had a lot to go back to in the States. Besides, I could always get a divorce.

**yield curve and derivatives**
technical terms from the world of finance

**Giocometti, Munch, Kandinsky**
well-known twentieth-century artists

8    Stupid and dangerous as it seems in retrospect, I went into my marriage at twenty-five without being in love. Three years later, I find myself relishing my relationship with this brilliant, prickly man who talks about the **yield curve and derivatives**, who prays when I drive, and who tries valiantly to remember names like **Giacometti, Munch, Kandinsky**.

9    My enthusiasm for arranged marriages is that of a recent convert. True, I grew up in India, where arranged marriages are common. My parents' marriage was arranged, as were those of my aunts, cousins and friends. But I always thought I was different. I blossomed as a foreign fellow in Mount Holyoke College where individualism was expected and feminism encouraged. As I experimented with being an American, I bought into the American value system.

10    I was determined to fall in love and marry someone who was not Indian. Yet, somehow, I could never manage to. Oh, falling in love was easy. Sustaining it was the hard part.

11    Arranged marriages in India begin with matching the horoscopes of the man and the woman. Astrologers look for balance . . . so that the woman's strengths balance the man's weaknesses and vice versa. Once the horoscopes match, the two families meet and decide whether they are compatible. It is assumed that they are of the same religion, **caste** and social stratum.

**caste**
a division of a society based on wealth, inherited rank, or occupation; one of four social classes in India

12    While this eliminates risk and promotes homogeneity, the rationale is that the personalities of the couple provide enough differences for a marriage to thrive. Whether or not this is true, the high statistical success rate of arranged marriages in different cultures—90 percent in Iran, 95 percent in India, and a similar high percentage among Hasidic Jews in Brooklyn, and among Turkish and Afghan Muslims—gives one pause.

13    Although our families met through a mutual friend, many Indian families meet through advertisements placed in national newspapers.

14    My parents made a formal visit to my future husband's house to see whether Ram's family would treat me well. My mother insists that "you can tell a lot about the family just from the way they serve coffee." The house had a lovely flower garden. The family liked gardening. Good.

15    Ram's mother had worked for the United Nations on women's-rights issues. She also wrote humorous columns for Indian magazines. She would be supportive. She served strong South Indian coffee in the traditional stainless steel tumblers instead of china; she would be a balancing influence on my youthful radicalism.

16    Ram's father had supported his wife's career even though he belonged to a generation of Indian men who expected their wives to stay home. Ram had a good role model. His sister was a pediatrician in Fort Myers. Perhaps that meant he was used to strong, achieving women.

17    November 20, 1992. Someone shouted, "They're here!" My cousin Sheela gently nudged me out of the bedroom into the living room.

18    "Why don't you sit down?" a voice said.

19    I looked up and saw a square face and smiling eyes anxious to put me at ease. He pointed me to a chair. Somehow I liked that. The guy was sensitive and self-confident.

20    He looked all right. Could stand to lose a few pounds. I liked the way his lips curved to meet his eyes. Curly hair, commanding voice, unrestrained laugh. To my surprise, the conversation flowed easily. We had a great deal in common, but his profession was very different from mine. He had an MBA from the University of Michigan and had worked on Wall Street before joining a financial consulting firm.

21    Two hours later, Ram said, "I'd like to get to know you better. Unfortunately, I have to be back at my job in Connecticut, but I could call you every other day. No strings attached, and both of us can decide where this goes, if anywhere."

22    I didn't dislike him.

23    He called ten days later. We talked about our goals, dreams and anxieties.

24    "What do you want out of life?" he asked me one day. "Come up with five words, maybe, of what you want to do with your life." His question intrigued me. "Courage, wisdom, change," I said, flippantly "What about you?"

25    "Curiosity, contribution, balance, family and fun," he said. In spite of myself, I was impressed.

26    One month later, he proposed and I accepted. Our extended honeymoon in Connecticut was wonderful. On weekends, we took trips to Mount Holyoke, where I showed him my old art studio and to Franconia Notch in New Hampshire, where we hiked and camped.

27    It was in Taos, New Mexico, that we had our first fight. Ram had arranged for a surprise visit to the children's summer camp where I used to work as a counselor. We visited my old colleagues with their Greenpeace T-shirts and New Age commune mentality. Ram, with his clipped accent, neatly pressed clothes and pleasant manners, was so different. What was I doing with this guy? On the car trip to the airport, I was silent. "I think, perhaps, we might have made a mistake," I said slowly. The air changed.

28    "Your friends may be idealistic, but they are escaping their lives, as are you," he said. "We are married. Accept it. Grow up!"

29    He had never spoken to me this harshly before, and it hurt. I didn't talk to him during the entire trip back to New York.

30    That fight set the pattern of our lives for the next several months. In the evening, when Ram came home, I would ignore him or blame him for bringing me to Connecticut.

31    Two years into our marriage, something happened. I was ashamed to realize that while I had treated Ram with veiled dislike, he had always tried to improve our relationship. I was admitted to the journalism program at Columbia, where, at Ram's insistence, I had applied.

32    Falling in love, for me, began with small changes. I found myself relishing a South Indian dish that I disliked, mostly because I knew how much he loved it. I realized that the first thing I wanted to do when I heard some good news was to share it with him. Somewhere along the way, the "I love you, too" that I had politely parroted in response to his endearments had become sincere.

33    My friends are appalled that I let my parents decide my life partner; yet, the older they get the more intrigued they are. I am convinced that our successful relationship has to do with two words: tolerance and trust. In a country that emphasizes individual choice, arranged marriages require a familial web for them to work. For many Americans, that web doesn't exist.

34    As my friend Karen said, "How can I get my parents to pick out my spouse when they don't even talk to each other?"

---

## Getting Ready to Write

### Reviewing the Reading

1.  According to the author, how do arranged marriages begin in India?

2.  What is the statistical success rate of arranged marriages in Iran and India?

3.  Describe Ram's educational and professional background; contrast it with that of the author.

4.  How did Ram finally win the author's love and affection?

5.  What are the two characteristics to which Narayan attributes the success of her marriage?

### Examining the Reading

To understand a narrative essay, you must have a clear understanding of the sequence of events. A sequence map, shown earlier in Chapter 6 on p. 145, can be helpful to readers as well as writers. When reading complex material, a sequence map can help you work out the order in which events occurred. Draw a map of the reading using the model shown on p. 145.

### Thinking Critically: Examining Assumptions

Assumptions are ideas a writer believes to be true but does not try to prove. A writer may take it for granted that the reader will agree with those ideas because they share a common set of values or background. Assumptions can be opinions or beliefs. The author may state them or they may be implied by other things he or she says. As a reader, it is your job to examine these assumptions and decide whether they are really true. Then you can evaluate whether ideas based on these assumptions make sense.

The author makes several assumptions in this essay. For example, she assumes at the outset that if her arranged marriage didn't work out, she could easily get a divorce. Later, she makes assumptions about Ram based on her parents' visit with his parents. In general, she seems to assume that marriage is preferable to being single. What other assumptions can you find in the reading? Decide whether you agree or disagree with three of the author's assumptions and write a brief explanation for each.

## Strengthening Your Vocabulary

**Part A:** Using the word's context, word parts, or a dictionary, write a brief definition of each of the following words or phrases as it is used in the reading.

1. replete (paragraph 1) filled to satisfaction

2. retrospect (paragraph 8) looking back

3. stratum (paragraph 11) level

4. homogeneity (paragraph 12) sameness, similarity

5. flippantly (paragraph 24) lacking seriousness; lightly

6. parroted (paragraph 32) repeated mindlessly

7. appalled (paragraph 33) shocked

**Part B:** Choose one of the above words and draw a word map of it.

## Reacting to Ideas: Discussion and Journal Writing

Get ready to write about the reading by discussing the following questions:

1. What makes the idea of an arranged marriage more acceptable to Narayan than it might be to an American?

2. Why did seeing her old friends in New Mexico cause Narayan to question the wisdom of her arranged marriage?

3. The statistical success rate of marriage in America is much lower than the success rate of arranged marriages, at least in the cultures mentioned in the essay. What factors might explain this disparity?

4. What did Narayan mean by a "familial web" (paragraph 33)? How might such a "web" be helpful or harmful to a marriage?

## Writing About the Reading

### Paragraph Options

1. The story of Narayan's marriage is told from her point of view: her decision to consider an arranged marriage, her impressions of Ram and his family, and their ensuing relationship. Write a narrative paragraph relating these same events from Ram's point of view. Describe how you think he feels about arranged marriages in general and his own specifically.

2. Narayan was encouraged after her parents met with Ram's family (paragraphs 14–16). What does this passage reveal about the qualities that Narayan and her family value in others? Write a paragraph explaining your answer.

3. Despite her initial reluctance, Narayan developed an "enthusiasm for arranged marriages" (paragraph 9). Think of an experience in which you initially rejected an idea only to become an enthusiastic convert later. Write a paragraph about your experience.

### Essay Options

4. Narayan describes her friends as both "appalled" and "intrigued" (paragraph 33) at the idea of an arranged marriage. What is your reaction? Write an essay explaining why you would or would not allow your family to arrange your marriage. Be sure to give at least three reasons to convince the reader why you feel the way you do.

5. What would you say if someone asked you to come up with five words describing what you want out of life? Write an essay in which you answer the question, giving an explanation of why each word is important to you.

6. Narayan says that falling in love is easy, but sustaining it is the hard part. Do you agree or disagree that keeping relationships alive and well takes work and effort? Write an essay about a relationship that you value. Explain what is involved in keeping that relationship healthy.

# A Letter to God
### Gregorio Lopez y Fuentes

## WRITING ABOUT A READING

### Thinking Before Reading

The following story, "A Letter to God," was written by Gregorio Lopez y Fuentes, a well-known Hispanic writer. The story was translated from Spanish by Donald A.Yates.

1. Preview the reading using the steps described in Chapter 2, page 30.

2. Connect the reading to your own experience by answering the following questions:

   a. What is your source of strength in difficult situations?

   b. Why do people who help others wish to remain anonymous?

1   The house—the only one in the entire valley—sat on the crest of a low hill. From this height one could see the river and, next to the corral, the field of ripe corn dotted with the kidney-bean flowers that always promised a good harvest.

2   The only thing the earth needed was a rainfall, or at least a shower. Throughout the morning Lencho—who knew his fields intimately—had done nothing else but scan the sky toward the northeast.

3   "Now we're really going to get some water, woman."

4   The woman, who was preparing supper, replied:

5   "Yes, God willing."

6   The oldest boys were working in the field, while the smaller ones were playing near he house, until the woman called to them all:

7   "Come for dinner . . ."

8   It was during the meal that, just as Lencho had predicted, big drops of rain began to fall. In the northeast, huge mountains of clouds could be seen approaching. The air was fresh and sweet.

9   The man went out to look for something in the corral for no other reason than to allow himself the pleasure of feeling the rain on his body, and when he returned he exclaimed:

10   "Those aren't raindrops falling from the sky, they're new coins. The big drops are **ten-centavo pieces** and the little ones are fives. . . ."

**ten-centavo pieces**
coins used in Mexico
and South America

11   With a satisfied expression he regarded the field of ripe corn with its kidney-bean flowers, draped in a curtain of rain. But suddenly a strong wind began to blow and together with the rain very large hailstones began to fall. These truly did resemble new silver coins. The boys, exposing themselves to the rain, ran out to collect the frozen pearls.

12   "It's really getting bad now," exclaimed the man, mortified. "I hope it passes quickly."

13   It did not pass quickly. For an hour the hail rained on the house, the garden, the hillside, the cornfield, on the whole valley. The field was white, as if covered with salt. Not a leaf remained on the trees. The corn was totally destroyed. The flowers were gone from the kidney-bean plants. Lencho's soul was filled with sadness. When the storm had passed, he stood in the middle of the field and said to his sons:

**plague of locusts**
epidemic of insects that devastates crops

14   "A **plague of locusts** would have left more than this. . . .The hail has left nothing: this year we will have no corn or beans. . . ."

15   That night was a sorrowful one:

16   "All our work, for nothing!"

17   "There's no one who can help us!"

18   "We'll all go hungry this year. . . ."

19   But in the hearts of all who lived in the solitary house in the middle of the valley, there was a single hope: help from God.

20   "Don't be so upset, even though this seems like a total loss. Remember, no one dies of hunger!"

21   "That's what they say: no one dies of hunger. . . ."

22   All through the night, Lencho thought only of his one hope: the help of God, whose eyes, as he had been instructed, see everything, even what is deep in one's conscience.

23   Lencho was an ox of a man, working like an animal in the fields, but still he knew how to write. The following Sunday, at daybreak, after having convinced himself that there is a protecting spirit, he began to write a letter which he himself would carry to town and place in the mail.

24   It was nothing less than a letter to God.

25   "God," he wrote, "if you don't help me, my family and I will go hungry this year. I need a hundred pesos in order to resow the field and to live until the crop comes, because the hailstorm . . ."

26   He wrote "To God" on the envelope, put the letter inside and, still troubled, went to town. At the post office he placed a stamp on the letter and dropped it into the mailbox.

27   One of the employees, who was a postman and also helped at the post office, went to his boss laughing heartily and showed him the letter to God. Never in his career as a postman had he known that address. The postmaster—a fat amiable fellow—also broke out laughing, but almost immediately he turned serious and, tapping the letter on his desk, commented:

28    "What faith! I wish I had the faith of the man who wrote this letter. To believe the way he believes. To hope with the confidence that he knows how to hope with. Starting up a correspondence with God!"

29    So in order not to disillusion that prodigy of faith, revealed by a letter that could not be delivered, the postmaster come up with an idea: answer the letter. But when he opened it, it was evident that to answer it he needed something more than good will, ink and paper. But he stuck to his resolution: he asked for money from his employee, he himself gave part of his salary, and several friends of his were obliged to give something "for an act of charity."

30    It was impossible for him to gather together the hundred pesos, so he was able to send the farmer only a little more than half. He put the bills in an envelope addressed to Lencho and with them a letter containing only a single word as a signature: GOD.

31    The following Sunday Lencho came a bit earlier than usual to ask if there was a letter for him. It was the postman himself who handed the letter to him, while the postmaster, experiencing the contentment of a man who has performed a good deed, looked on from the doorway of his office.

32    Lencho showed not the slightest surprise on seeing the bills—such was his confidence—but he became angry when he counted the money. . . . God could not have made a mistake, nor could he have denied Lencho what he had requested!

33    Immediately, Lencho went up to the window to ask for paper and ink. On the public writing table, he started in to write, with much wrinkling of his brow, caused by the effort he had to make to express his ideas. When he finished, he went to the window to buy a stamp which he licked and then affixed to the envelope with a blow of his fist.

34    The moment that the letter fell into the mailbox the postmaster went to open it. It said:

35    "God: of the money that I asked for, only seventy pesos reached me. Send me the rest, since I need it very much. But don't send it to me through the mail, because the post-office employees are a bunch of crooks. Lencho."

---

## Getting Ready to Write

### Reviewing the Reading

1. What were the crops being grown by Lencho?

2. How were the crops destroyed?

3. What did Lencho ask for in his letter to God?

4. How did the postmaster come up with money for Lencho?

5. What was Lencho's response to the money?

## Examining the Reading

To understand a narrative or process paragraph or essay, you must have a clear understanding of the sequence of events. A sequence map, shown in Chapter 6 on p. 145, can be helpful to readers as well as writers. Use the model to draw a map of the readings.

## Thinking Critically: Making Inferences

An inference is a reasoned guess about what you don't know made on the basis of what you do know. Lencho made an inference, incorrectly, that the postal employees had stolen some of his money. As you read, you often need to make inferences. You may be expected to reason out, or infer, the meaning an author intended (but did not say) on the basis of what he or she did say.

Each inference you make depends on the situation, the facts provided, and your own knowledge and experience. Consider what the author has told you about Lencho. What else can you infer about him and the other characters in the story? Write a short description of one of the characters from the story, including the facts provided by the author and your own inferences.

## Strengthening Your Vocabulary

**Part A:** Using the word's context, word parts, or a dictionary, write a brief definition of each of the following words or phrases as it is used in the reading.

1. intimately (paragraph 2) _with close familiarity_

2. mortified (paragraph 12) _ashamed, humiliated, embarrassed_

3. solitary (paragraph 19) _apart from others; secluded_

4. amiable (paragraph 27) _cheerful_

5. disillusion (paragraph 29) _to take away faith or trust_

6. prodigy (paragraph 29) _a person with exceptional talents or powers_

**Part B:** Choose one of the above words and draw a word map of it.

## Reacting to Ideas: Discussion and Journal Writing

Get ready to write about the reading by discussing the following questions:

1. Think of someone you consider to be a person of faith. How does that person rely on faith when he or she is facing difficulties?

2. What good deeds have you observed that go unrecognized or unrewarded?

3. Why did the postmaster want to spare Lencho from being disillusioned (paragraph 29)?

## Writing About the Reading

### Paragraph Options

1. The author uses descriptive language in this story; for example, he calls Lencho "an ox of a man" (paragraph 23). How does this language contribute to the tone of the story? Write a paragraph explaining your answer and including other examples of descriptive language from the story.

2. Lencho writes his letter "after having convinced himself that there is a protecting spirit" (paragraph 23). Have you ever talked yourself into trying something difficult or far-fetched? How did it turn out? Write a paragraph describing your experience.

3. The statement "Things come to those who believe" might be used to summarize the main point of the reading. Write a paragraph agreeing or disagreeing with this statement.

4. Put yourself in the postmaster's shoes after he has collected the money and is "experiencing the contentment of a man who has performed a good deed" (paragraph 31), then imagine how his feelings may have changed after reading Lencho's second letter (paragraph 36). Write a paragraph explaining why the postmaster decided to help Lencho and how you think the postmaster felt about how his efforts worked out.

### Essay Options

5. The author adds a twist by having Lencho respond to the money in an unexpectedly ironic way. Write an essay describing a situation in which your own intentions did not have quite the result you were aiming for.

6. Have you ever been involved in an anonymous "act of charity" (paragraph 29) such as the one described in this story? Write an essay about how it feels to be on the giving end—or the receiving end—of an act of generosity. Discuss whether it matters if the people involved are known or anonymous.

# Little Things Are Big
## Jesus Colon

# WRITING ABOUT A READING

## Thinking Before Reading

The following reading, "Little Things Are Big," is taken from *Puerto Rican in New York and Other Sketches,* the single published volume of essays by Jesus Colon. In this narrative, Colon describes a situation in which the potential for prejudice caused him to behave in a way that conflicted with his identity as a Puerto Rican.

1. Preview the reading using the steps described in Chapter 2, p. 30.

2. Connect the reading to your own experience by answering the following questions:

   a. Do you identify yourself as part of an ethnic group?

   b. Have you ever been discriminated against? What was the basis for that discrimination (e.g., ethnic, religious, gender, or age)?

   c. Do you think your behavior is influenced by how others see you?

**Thirty-fourth Street Pennsylvania Station**
a subway station in New York City

1   It was very late at night on the eve of Memorial Day. She came into the subway at the **Thirty-fourth Street Pennsylvania Station**. I am still trying to remember how she managed to push herself in with a baby on her right arm, a valise in her left hand, and two children, a boy and a girl about three and five years old, trailing after her. She was a nice-looking white lady in her early twenties.

2   At Nevins Street, Brooklyn, we saw her preparing to get off at the next station—Atlantic Avenue—which happened to be the place where I, too, had to get off. Just as it was a problem for her to get on, it was going to be a problem for her to get off the subway with two small children to taken care of, a baby on her right arm and a medium-sized valise in her left hand.

3   And there I was, also preparing to get off at Atlantic Avenue, with no bundles to take care of—not even the customary book under my arm without which I feel that I am not completely dressed.

4   As the train was entering the Atlantic Avenue station, some white man stood up from his seat and helped her out, placing the children on the long, deserted platform. There were only two adult persons on the long platform sometime after midnight on the eve of last Memorial Day.

5    I could perceive the steep, long concrete stairs going down to the Long Island Railroad or into the street. Should I offer my help as the American white man did at the subway door, placing the two children outside the subway car? Should I take care of the girl and the boy, take them by their hands until they reached the end of the steep long concrete stairs of the Atlantic Avenue station?

6    Courtesy is a characteristic of the Puerto Rican. And here I was—a Puerto Rican—hours past midnight, a valise, two white children and a white lady with a baby on her arm palpably needing somebody to help her at least until she descended the long concrete stairs.

7    But how could I, a Negro and a Puerto Rican, approach this white lady who very likely might have preconceived prejudices against Negroes and everybody with foreign accents, in a deserted subway station very late at night?

8    What would she say? What would be the first reaction of this white American woman, perhaps coming from a small town with a valise, two children, and a baby on her right arm? Would she say: Yes, of course, you may help me. Or would she think that I was just trying to get too familiar? Or would she think worse than that perhaps? What would I do if she let out a scream as I went toward her to offer my help?

9    Was I misjudging her? So many slanders are written every day in the daily press against the Negroes and Puerto Ricans. I hesitated for a long, long minute. The ancestral manners that the most illiterate Puerto Rican passes on from father to son were struggling inside me. Here was I, way past midnight, face-to-face with a situation that could very well explode into an outburst of prejudices and chauvinistic conditioning of the "divide and rule" policy of present-day society.

10    It was a long minute. I passed on by her as if I saw nothing. As if I was insensitive to her need. Like a rude animal walking on two legs, I just moved on, half running by the long subway platform, leaving the children and the valise and her with the baby on her arm. I took the steps of the long concrete stairs in twos until I reached the street above and the cold air slapped my warm face.

11    This is what racism and prejudice and chauvinism and official artificial divisions can do to people and to a nation!

12    Perhaps the lady was not prejudiced after all. Or not prejudiced enough to scream at the coming of a Negro toward her in a solitary subway station a few hours past midnight.

13    If you were not that prejudiced, I failed you, dear lady. I know that there is a chance in a million that you will read these lines. I am willing to take that millionth chance. If you were not that prejudiced, I failed you lady, I failed you, children. I failed myself to myself.

14　　I buried my courtesy early on Memorial Day morning. But here is a promise that I make to myself here and now: If I am ever faced with an occasion like that again, I am going to offer my help regardless of how the offer is going to be received.

15　　Then I will have my courtesy with me again.

---

## Getting Ready to Write

### Reviewing the Reading

1. Why did the family on the subway seem to need assistance?

2. Why did Colon hesitate to offer help?

3. What "characteristic of the Puerto Rican" caused Colon's inner struggle?

4. What did Colon decide to do?

5. How did Colon describe himself as he passed by the family?

### Examining the Reading

To understand a narrative or process paragraph or essay, you must have a clear understanding of the sequence of events. A sequence map, shown earlier in Chapter 6 on p. 145, can be helpful to readers as well as writers. Draw a map of the reading using these guidelines.

### Thinking Critically: Discovering the Author's Purpose

A writer always has a purpose for writing. As a reader, it is your job to recognize the author's purpose and to judge whether he or she accomplishes it effectively. In order to discover the author's purpose, ask yourself, "What is the writer trying to tell me? What does he or she want me to do or think?" Also pay close attention to the title of the piece; it may offer clues to the author's purpose.

In "Little Things Are Big," the author may have more than one purpose for writing. Think about what his choice of a title tells you about his purpose. Consider what he wants you, the reader, to do or think after reading the essay. Write a paragraph to explain Colon's purpose(s) for writing. Start your paragraph with a topic sentence that begins, "Colon wants readers of this essay to . . . ," and use details from the essay to support this topic sentence.

## Strengthening Your Vocabulary

**Part A:** Using the word's context, word parts, or a dictionary, write a brief definition of each of the following words or phrases as it is used in the reading.

1. valise (paragraph 1) small suitcase

   _____

2. perceive (paragraph 5) see, become aware of

   _____

3. palpably (paragraph 6) plainly, obviously

   _____

4. preconceived (paragraph 7) an opinion formed beforehand

   _____

5. slanders (paragraph 9) false and malicious statements

   _____

6. ancestral (paragraph 9) coming from one's ancestors

   _____

7. chauvinistic (paragraph 9) a prejudiced belief in the superiority of one's

   own gender, group, or kind

**Part B:** Choose one of the above words and draw a word map of it.

## Reacting to Ideas: Discussion and Journal Writing

Get ready to write about the reading by discussing the following questions:

1. Why are Colon's race and ethnic background important in this narrative?

2. What main point does Colon express through his narrative?

3. Discuss what Colon means when he says, "I failed myself to myself" (paragraph 13).

## Writing About the Reading

### Paragraph Options

1. Colon fears that the woman would have responded negatively toward him if he had approached her to offer assistance. Write a paragraph describing a situation in which someone did, or may have, misunderstood your good intentions.

2. Write a paragraph agreeing or disagreeing with Colon's decision to offer help next time regardless of how the offer might be received.

3.  Is there anything Colon might have done or said to make his intentions clear to the woman he wanted to assist? Write a paragraph exploring options that Colon could have followed.

## Essay Options

4.  The narrative is told from Colon's point of view: he describes seeing the woman on the subway and his own subsequent actions. Write an essay relating these same events from the woman's point of view. Imagine how she perceives Colon and if her response to him is what Colon fears it would be or if she would have welcomed his help.

5.  Colon regrets that he did not offer help to the woman and vows not to make the same mistake again. Write an essay narrating an event in which you made what you now feel was a wrong decision.

6.  Write an essay describing a situation in which you observed a person's behavior being influenced by racism, prejudice, chauvinism, or other preconceived ideas.

### READING

# What I Did for Love

### Macarena del Rocío Hernández

## WRITING ABOUT A READING

### Thinking Before Reading

The following reading, "What I Did For Love," was written by Macarena del Rocío Hernández, a staff writer for the *San Antonio Express-News*. In this narrative, Hernandez relates her experience as a young, single Mexican American whose romantic problems lead her to consider a traditional Latino remedy.

1.  Preview the reading using the steps described in Chapter 2, p. 30.

2.  Connect the reading to your own experience by answering the following questions:

    a.  Do you believe in fortune tellers and tarot card readers?

    b.  In your family, at what age is it considered appropriate for women to marry? Do you agree?

**à la Mexicana**
in the Mexican style

1    I know what I will be serving at my wedding. My mother's neighbor Doña Ester García will make carne guisada, beef stew, for the main course. My uncle has volunteered one of his steers. I'm wondering whether it should be a huge affair, **à la Mexicana**, with a guest list including the mailman and distant relatives of my second cousin's inlaws. Or a simple, more Americanized ceremony, with only those by my side who have been part of my most recent life. I have some time to work out the details since I still don't have the groom.

I'm a twenty-five-year-old Mexican American whose relationships wilt faster than orchids in the Texas sun. And that, according to my aunts and cousins, makes me an old maid.

Never mind that I've spent the last seven years living and working in major cities throughout the United States where women tend to get married in their late twenties and early thirties. Whenever I come back home to La Joya, Texas, my family is quick to remind me that time is running out. My love life, or lack of it, is especially troubling to my aunts, most of whom have children who are at least seven years younger than I and already married.

**chisme**
gossip

I know about the **chisme** that the aunts swap as they huddle over the kitchen table making tamales.

5    "She studies way too much. All that work can't be good for her head," says one as she spreads masa on a cornhusk and tops it with a spoonful of beef.

"Maybe she doesn't like men. You know, in San Francisco where she used to live, there are a lot of gay people," another **tía** adds.

**tía**
aunt, older woman

I suspect they also talk about me while they watch their favorite Spanish-language soap operas, overwrought stories that always involve a poor girl crying crocodile tears as she calls out, "Carlos Jose! No me dejes. Yo te amo." (Carlos Jose! Don't leave me. I love you.)

**telenovelas**
television soap operas

It was probably during one of those pain-filled **telenovelas** that one of my tías had an epiphany. Something, she realized, must have happened to me during my childhood, some awful trauma that has made it impossible for me to keep a man.

I'll admit I can scare men off. But I think it has more to do with growing up with four older brothers who rarely spoke to me unless they wanted a shirt ironed or dinner cooked. At an early age, I began to equate marriage with slavery. I couldn't see myself spending the rest of my life washing someone else's underwear.

10    My relatives view my attitude on the subject as a disease that seems to be getting worse.

It's no secret that my mother has been praying for years for a "good man who can take care of you." And if all that prayer hasn't helped, my Tía Nelly concluded, I must be cursed.

She knew the perfect person to help me: a curandera, a healer who can cure a person of lovelessness just as easily as colic.

"I don't believe in it," my cousin said to me, "but maybe you should go."

I thought about it for a week. If I went, I'd be admitting that I have a problem. If I didn't, I might miss out on a cure.

15    I picked a Friday afternoon. I decked myself out in a short black dress and red lipstick so the curandera couldn't blame my anemic love life on the way I dressed. Tía Nelly and I drove thirty-five minutes to Rio Grande City and the curandera's storefront office.

I hid my truck in an alley so nobody I knew would see it. The store looked like an herb shop one might find on South Street in Philadelphia, except this one inhabited an old grocery. Inside were long aisles of neatly displayed candles, religious statuettes, soaps, and good luck charms. One wall offered packages of herbs and spices.

In Latino neighborhoods curanderas are considered not only healers, but also spiritual advisers. They are like doctors, psychiatrists, and priests rolled into one.

I am told my father's grandfather, Emeterio Chasco, was a curandero. He didn't charge his clients money; in exchange for banishing a fright, bad luck, or a rash, he'd receive chickens, boxes of fruit, and personal favors.

The only curandero I'd ever met was El Papi, one of my mother's younger cousins. A dark-skinned man who never married and lived with his parents in Mexico, El Papi had big crooked teeth that you saw even when he wasn't smiling. My mother doubted his spiritual powers, but people from nearby towns and ranches consulted with him in his bedroom, which was also the family living room. Nonetheless, I expected my curandera to be an older woman, with hands as worn and soft as my grandmother's. Her touch, I imagined, would be magical enough to cure anything.

20    But this curandera greeted me wearing a tight purple shirt and black pants that hugged a killer figure—curves that the bottle-blond healer told me were the product of hours at the gym. She was a middle-aged vixen, not a grandmotherly adviser. A thoroughly modern healer who drives a white convertible and recently divorced her husband of more than twenty years.

She performed her consults in the area once designated "for employees only." For $20 she gave me a card reading that she said would give us both a better handle on mi problema. She asked me to shuffle the tarot cards and then split the deck into three stacks. She instructed me to use my left hand to place the different piles back into one. I kept my left hand on the pile. She covered it with her left hand and prayed. Then she began to deal the cards. Her long, pearl-colored acrylic nails made clicking noises every time she placed one down, face up. She spread the cards out on her desk. "Your problem," she said, "is a sentimental one."

No one could hear our conversation, so I decided to be honest. "My aunt said maybe you could help me because I can't seem to find the right guy or even keep the bad ones I date."

"This is not logical. You are very pretty," she said, looking me straight in the eye. "Men are desgraciados [ingrates]. You can give everything except your heart, because they will hurt you."

After a few more minutes of reading my life in the cards, she looked at me as if to say: "This is more serious than I thought."

25    "There was a woman about five years ago, and her name starts with the letter *M*," she said. "There was money paid to keep men away from you, and it was probably done in Mexico because they will do anything over there."

But that was all she could tell me. I would, she said, have to come back the next morning so she could start doing some work on me. She asked for $48 to buy 40 candles that she'd burn while she prayed that night in hopes that everything we needed to know about the mysterious *M* would reveal itself. I would also need to pay $20 for a barrida, a cleansing ritual.

The next day the curandera was ten minutes late—she had just finished a two-hour workout. She said she had news for me. Her overnight mediation had revealed two more letters of the mystery woman's name: *A* and *R*.

"Do you know anyone whose name starts with *M-A-R*?" she asked. Half of the Latinas I know have names that start with *M-A-R*: Maria, Martina, Marrisa, Marisela, Marielena, Marina, Marta, Margarita.

Well, she said, the woman in question now dyes her hair guerro, blond. That only disqualified half.

30    "Last night," she said, "I saw a small black-and-white photo, probably from a yearbook."

Then the curandera explained what was wrong. The evil MAR woman, she said, had loved someone I was dating and had paid a dark man from Mexico to curse me, to keep men from sticking around.

The curse, she said, could be removed for $275, and even if I opted to go somewhere else, she advised me to get help as soon as possible. I couldn't remember dating anyone within the last five years who was so special that another woman would pay to have him. But I told her she could give me a barrida.

That, she promised, would definitely make me feel better, but I still needed to have the curse removed.

For the barrida, she had me stand just outside her office, facing south, in the middle of a circle that looked as if it had been burned into the floor. She instructed me to stretch my arms over my head as if I were singing or praising the Lord at church.

35    She doused her hands with lavender-scented alcohol and touched my neck, arms, hands, and legs. She then began making the sign of the cross with a brown-shelled egg that she said had been laid by a black hen. The egg was cold. I couldn't help but wonder whether it had lost its magic while sitting in the refrigerator.

The curandera prayed, fast and in Spanish, imploring the bad spirits to leave. She then lighted a candle and walked around me, asking some invisible power to illuminate me. She put the candle down and crumbled some dried leaves around the circle and poured alcohol on them. She grabbed the candle and set the circle on fire.

Her praying was so fervent and so rapid that I could understand only a few phrases: "Give her a pure love," "send her a good man." Essentially, the same thing my mom had been asking for.

It was getting hot. The flames were inching closer to my toes and there was smoke. Just when I thought I might melt I heard her say: "Jump over the flame." I did.

For the next three days, she said, before I ate anything else I was to drink half a cup of water mixed with sugar followed by a single banana cut into slices and covered with honey. She sold me two $10 candles that I was supposed to light and pray to.

40    Then she calmly reminded me that I still had to come back to get the curse removed.

But I'd had enough. I had no intention of drinking sugar water, eating honey-coated slices of banana, or lighting candles. Maybe I was afraid to rely on some vague magic I didn't understand.

Or maybe I believed in it too much, and couldn't bear the thought that it might not work.

When you live squeezed between two cultures, two languages, you are often a walking contradiction. Sometimes there is little you can do to keep both worlds at peace.

For days after the barrida I thought about everything the curandera told me. I held on to the things I wanted to believe—that I was too pretty not to attract men, that I would eventually end up with a successful, good man. And weighed those I didn't—that unless I reversed the curse there was no hope.

I wondered why a modern woman like me should listen to a curandera, even a with-it one clad in spandex. And then I remembered the words of another curandero: El Papi.

I was in the fourth grade and we were visiting his family in Nuevo Leon.

He and I were standing in the middle of the woods and I was watching him break an egg over a pile of sticks he was about to set on fire.

"Can you make someone fall in love with someone else?" I asked.

He looked up.

50    "Yes. I can," he said. "But that wouldn't be true love. You can't force love. You just have to wait for it to happen.

## Getting Ready to Write

### Reviewing the Reading

1. What caused Hernández to equate marriage with slavery?

2. How do Hernández's relatives view her love life and her attitude about it?

3. What is a curandera?

4. According to the curandera, what caused Hernández's romantic problems?

5. What does Hernández conclude about the need to have the curse removed in order to fall in love?

### Examining the Reading

To understand a narrative essay, you must have a clear understanding of the sequence of events. Draw a sequence map, shown in Chapter 6 on p. 145, as guide.

### Thinking Critically: Cause-and-Effect Relationships

Cause-and-effect relationships establish a connection between two or more actions, events, or occurrences. The relationship may be as simple as one thing causing another, or there may be multiple causes, multiple effects, or both multiple causes and multiple effects. In "What I Did For Love," the author examines her lackluster love life and its causes. Make a list of the different factors that Hernández, her relatives, and the curandera believe are the causes.

### Strengthening Your Vocabulary

**Part A:** Using the word's context, word parts, or a dictionary, write a brief definition of each of the following words or phrases as it is used in the reading.

1. overwrought (paragraph 7) overly dramatic

2. epiphany (paragraph 8) realization or sudden understanding

3. trauma (paragraph 8) a physical or emotional injury

4. equate (paragraph 9) to regard as equal or comparable

5. anemic (paragraph 15) _weak_ _____

_____

6. vixen (paragraph 20) _a sexy woman (can also mean a woman regarded_

_as quarrelsome or bad-tempered)_

7. fervent (paragraph 37) _with intense feeling_

_____

8. contradiction (paragraph 43) _something that contains parts that do not_

_fit or are inconsistent with each other_

**Part B:** Choose one of the above words and draw a word map of it.

## Reacting to Ideas: Discussion and Journal Writing

Get ready to write about the reading by discussing the following questions:

1. The author sprinkles Spanish words and references throughout the narrative. How does this add to the flavor of the essay?

2. A potential cause-and-effect relationship is introduced in the second part of the essay: the idea of a curse and a "cure." How do you feel about the chances for a successful remedy?

3. Compare Hernández's attitude about her single status to her relatives' attitudes. In what ways are they different? How are they similar?

4. How did you expect the curandera to look? Were you surprised by the description of her appearance? What contradictions were present in that character?

## Writing About the Reading

### Paragraph Options

1. The narrative is told from Hernández's point of view. How would it be different if it were told through the eyes of someone else in the story? Choose another character, perhaps one of Hernández's aunts or the curandera, and relate the same events from that person's point of view. Feel free to add details, including those that reveal how your character regards the potential success of the curandera's "cure."

2. Hernández describes how her great-grandfather was paid for his spiritual work (paragraph 18) in contrast to her own curandera's modern fees. How else does the author convey the contrasts between the old world and the new? Write a paragraph describing those contrasts.

3. What is the significance of the author's conversation with El Papi (paragraphs 45–50)? Write a paragraph explaining why you think she included the conversation and how you interpret its meaning.

## Essay Options

4. Hernández describes herself as a "walking contradiction" (paragraph 43) because of her connection to two different cultures. Have you ever felt that way? Write an essay describing an instance or instances in which you acted in a way contradictory to your personality or your beliefs. If you, like Hernández, have experienced a conflict because you are "squeezed between two cultures," (paragraph 43), describe that as well.

5. What is your opinion of fortune tellers and psychic advisers? Write an essay explaining your views and describing any experiences you may have had with someone like the curandera.

6. Hernández experiences a conflict between her values and those of her family. Write an essay describing a situation in which your values were in conflict with those of your family.

### READING

# Last Rites for the Indian Dead
#### Suzan Shown Harjo

## WRITING ABOUT A READING

### Thinking Before Reading

The following essay, "Last Rites for the Indian Dead," was written by Suzan Shown Harjo, a Native American of Cheyenne descent. The essay, which first appeared in the *Los Angeles Times,* questions the ethics of the government's policy toward the remains of American Indians.

1. Preview the reading using the steps described in Chapter 2, p. 30.

2. Connect the reading to your own experience by answering the following questions:

   a. What does the title imply about the subject of the essay?

   b. What do you consider an artifact to be?

   c. How are graveyards and cemeteries typically regarded in America?

1   What if museums, universities, and government agencies could put your dead relatives on display or keep them in boxes to be cut up and otherwise studied? What if you believed that the spirits of the dead could not rest until their human remains were placed in a sacred area?

2    The ordinary American would say there ought to be a law—and there is, for ordinary Americans. The problem for American Indians is that there are too many laws of the kind that make us the archaeological property of he United States and too few of the kind that protect us from such insults.

3    Some of my Cheyenne relatives' skulls are in the Smithsonian Institution today, along with those of at least 4,500 other Indian people who were violated in the 1800s by the U.S. Army for an "Indian **Cranial** Study." It wasn't enough that these unarmed Cheyenne people were mowed down by the cavalry at the infamous **Sand Creek massacre**; many were decapitated and their heads shipped to Washington as freight. (The Army Medical Museum's collection is now in the Smithsonian.) Some had been exhumed only hours after being buried. Imagine the grieving families' reaction on finding their loved ones disinterred and headless.

4    Some targets of the Army's study were killed in noncombat situations and beheaded immediately. The officer's account of the decapitation of the Apache chief Mangas Coloradas in 1863 shows the pseudoscientific nature of the exercise. "I weighed the brain and measured the skull," the good doctor wrote, "and found that while the skull was smaller, the brain was larger than that of **Daniel Webster**."

5    These journal accounts exist in excruciating detail, yet missing are any records of overall comparisons, conclusions, or final reports of the Army study. Since it is unlike the Army not to leave a paper trail, one must wonder about the motive for its collection.

6    The total Indian body count in the Smithsonian collection is more than 19,000, and it is not the largest in the country. It is not inconceivable that the 1.5 million of us living today are outnumbered by our dead stored in museums, educational institutions, federal agencies, state historical societies, and private collections. The Indian people are further dehumanized by being exhibited alongside the mastodons and dinosaurs and other extinct creatures.

7    Where we have buried our dead in peace, more often than not the sites have been desecrated. For more than 200 years, relic hunting has been a popular pursuit. Lately, the market in Indian artifacts has brought this abhorrent activity to a fever pitch in some areas. And when scavengers come upon Indian burial sites, everything found becomes fair game, including sacred burial offerings, teeth, and skeletal remains.

8    One unusually well-publicized example of Indian grave desecration occurred two years ago in a western Kentucky field known as Slack Farm, the site of an Indian village five centuries ago. Ten men—one with a business card stating "Have Shovel, Will Travel"—paid the landowner $10,000 to lease digging rights between planting seasons. They dug extensively on the 40-acre farm, rummaging through an estimated 650 graves, collecting burial goods, tools, and ceremonial items. Skeletons were strewn about like litter.

9    What motivates people to do something like this? Financial gain is the first answer. Indian relic-collecting has become a multimillion-dollar indus-

**cranial**

relating to the portion of the skull enclosing the brain

**Sand Creek massacre**

a battle in 1864 in which nearly 200 Cheyenne and Arapaho Indians were slaughtered along this southeastern Colorado creek

**Daniel Webster**

American statesman well-known for his public speaking skills

try. The price tag on a bead necklace can easily top $1,000; rare pieces fetch tens of thousands.

**macabre**
focusing on the gruesome, horrible details of death

10    And it is not just collectors of the **macabre** who pay for skeletal remains. Scientists say that these deceased Indians are needed for research that someday could benefit the health and welfare of living Indians. But just how many dead Indians must they examine? Nineteen thousand?

11    There is doubt as to whether permanent curation of our dead really benefits Indians. Dr. Emery A. Johnson, former assistant surgeon general, recently observed, "I am not aware of any current medical diagnostic or treatment procedure that has been derived from research on such skeletal remains. Nor am I aware of any during the 34 years that I have been involved in American Indian . . . health care."

12    Indian remains are still being collected for racial biological studies. While the intentions may be honorable, the ethics of using human remains this way without the full consent of relatives must be questioned.

13    Some relief for Indian people has come on the state level. Almost half of the states, including California, have passed laws protecting Indian burial sites and restricting the sale of Indian bones, burial offerings, and other sacred items. Representative Charles E. Bennett (D–Fla.) and Sen. John McCain (R–Ariz.) have introduced bills that are a good start in invoking the federal government's protections. However, no legislation has attacked the problem head-on by imposing stiff penalties at the marketplace, or by changing laws that make dead Indians the nation's property.

14    Some universities–notably Stanford, Nebraska, Minnesota, and Seattle—have returned, or agreed to return, Indian human remains; it is fitting that institutions of higher education should lead the way.

**funerary**
objects related to a funeral, or the burial of the dead

15    Congress is now deciding what to do with the government's extensive collections of Indian human remains and associated **funerary** objects. The secretary of the Smithsonian, Robert McAdams, has been valiantly attempting to apply modern ethics to yesterday's excesses. This week, he announced that the Smithsonian would conduct an inventory and return all Indian skeletal remains that could be identified with specific tribes or living kin.

16    But there remains a reluctance generally among collectors of Indian remains to take action of a scope that would have quantitative impact and a healing quality. If they will not act on their own—and it is highly unlikely that they will—then Congress must act.

17    The country must recognize that the bodies of dead American Indian people are not artifacts to be bought and sold as collectors' items. It is not appropriate to store tens of thousands of our ancestors for possible future research. They are our family. They deserve to be returned to their sacred burial grounds and given a chance to rest.

18    The plunder of our people's graves has gone on too long. Let us rebury our dead and remove this shameful past from America's future.

## Getting Ready to Write

### Reviewing the Reading

1. What happened to the Cheyenne at Sand Creek in 1864?

2. What reason is given as the primary motivation of those who collect Indian relics? What other reasons does the author give for those who collect the skeletal remains of Indians?

3. What is Slack Farm and what occurred there?

4. For each of the following entities, write a brief description of the group's actions on behalf of the Indian people regarding the collection of Indian remains and sacred items.

   a. State governments

   b. Federal government

   c. Universities

   d. The Smithsonian Institution

### Examining the Reading

Draw a map of the reading. Since this reading presents an argument, use one of the maps shown on pp. 333–334 as a model.

### Thinking Critically: Persuasive Writing

"Last Rites for the Indian Dead" is an example of persuasive writing. Persuasive writing is meant to convince the reader to accept a particular viewpoint. In this essay, Harjo uses emotional language to draw readers to her view.

### Strengthening Your Vocabulary

**Part A:** Using the word's context, word parts, or a dictionary, write a brief definition of each of the following words or phrases as it is used in the reading.

1. exhumed (paragraph 3) _removed from a grave_

   _____

2. desecrated (paragraph 7) _violated the sacredness of a site or an object_

   _____

3. relic (paragraph 7) _an object of historic interest_

   _____

4. abhorrent (paragraph 7) _disgusting_

   _____

5. curation (paragraph 11) <u>placement in a collection for study or exhibit</u>

---

**Part B:** Choose one of the above words and draw a word map of it.

## Reacting to Ideas: Discussion and Journal Writing

Get ready to write about the reading by discussing the following questions:

1. What kinds of things should qualify as the "archaeological property" of the United States?

2. Why have Indian burial grounds not been treated with the same respect and reverence as other cemeteries and graveyards?

3. What is the value or importance of artifacts?

4. The author states that Robert McAdams, the secretary of the Smithsonian, has tried to "apply modern ethics to yesterday's excesses" (paragraph 15). What does she mean by this statement?

## Writing About the Reading

### Paragraph Options

1. What does the author mean when she states that the Indian people are being "dehumanized" by the display of Indian skeletal remains in museum collections (paragraph 6)? Write a paragraph explaining her statement and whether or not you agree.

2. The author says that "there remains a reluctance generally among collectors of Indian remains to take action" (paragraph 16). Why do you think collectors are reluctant to take action? Should Congress force them to? Write a paragraph explaining your answer.

### Essay Options

3. In your opinion, is there an alternative viewpoint to the one expressed by the author? Write an essay from another point of view, perhaps a researcher or an archaeologist, and explain why the study of American Indian skeletal remains should continue. You may want to choose some points on which to agree rather than taking a completely opposing stance to the author's view.

4. Why do you think the author believes that "it is fitting that institutions of higher learning should lead the way" (paragraph 14)? In what ways does or should your own college or university lead the way in addressing social or ethical issues? In what areas do you believe that your school should be doing more to lead the way? Write an essay exploring the answers to these questions.

5. Write a letter to your U.S. congressional representatives urging them to take action on the issue of the remains of Indians and the artifacts from Indian graves.

# PART VI

## Reviewing the Basics

# GUIDE TO REVIEWING THE BASICS

# OVERVIEW

Most of us know how to communicate in our language. When we talk or write, we put our thoughts into words and, by and large, we make ourselves understood. But many of us do not know the specific terms and rules of grammar. Grammar is a system that describes how language is put together. Grammar must be learned, almost as if it is a foreign language.

Why is it important to study grammar, to understand grammatical terms like *verb, participle,* and *gerund* and concepts like *agreement* and *subordination*? There are several good reasons. Knowing grammar will allow you to

- **recognize an error in your writing and correct it.** Your papers will read more smoothly and communicate more effectively when they are error free.

- **understand the comments of your teachers and peers.** People who read and critique your writing may point out a "fragment" or a "dangling modifier." You will be able to revise and correct the problems.

- **write with more impact.** Grammatically correct sentences are signs of clear thinking. Your readers will get your message without distraction or confusion.

## ESL Tip
### Learning English Grammar

Learning more English grammar will help you express yourself with more clarity. Remember, you already know something about the grammar of your native language. What you already know about your native language can sometimes help you with English grammar.

As you will see in this section, "Reviewing the Basics," the different areas of grammatical study are highly interconnected. The sections on parts of speech, sentences, punctuation, mechanics, and spelling fit together into a logical whole. To recognize and correct a run-on sentence, for example, you need to know both sentence structure *and* punctuation. To avoid errors in capitalization, you need to know parts of speech *and* mechanics. If grammar is to do you any good, your knowledge of it must be thorough. As you review the following "basics," be alert to the interconnections that make language study so interesting.

Grammatical terms and rules demand your serious attention. Mastering them will pay handsome dividends: error-free papers, clear thinking, and effective writing.

# A

# Understanding the Parts of Speech

The eight parts of speech are **nouns**, **pronouns**, **verbs**, **adjectives**, **adverbs**, **conjunctions**, **prepositions**, and **interjections.** Each word in a sentence functions as one of these parts of speech. Being able to identify the parts of speech in sentences allows you to analyze and improve your writing and to understand grammatical principles discussed later in this section.

It is important to keep in mind that *how* a word functions in a sentence determines *what* part of speech it is. Thus, the same word can be a noun, a verb, or an adjective, depending on how it is used.

NOUN

He needed some blue <u>wallpaper</u>.

VERB

He will <u>wallpaper</u> the hall.

ADJECTIVE

He went to a <u>wallpaper</u> store.

---

### ESL Tip
Functions of Words

In English it is important to know how a word functions. If you know how a word functions you will know what part of speech it is. Note the examples above. The same word, *wallpaper,* has three different functions.

## A.1 NOUNS

A **noun** names a person, place, thing, or idea.

| | |
|---|---|
| People | *woman, winner, Maria Alvarez* |
| Places | *mall, hill, Indiana* |
| Things | *lamp, ship, air* |
| Ideas | *goodness, perfection, harmony* |

The form of many nouns changes to express **number** (**singular** for one, **plural** for more than one): *one bird, two birds; one child, five children.* Most nouns can also be made **possessive** to show ownership by the addition of -*'s: city's, Norma's.*

Sometimes a noun is used to modify another noun:

NOUN MODIFYING DIPLOMA

Her goal had always been to earn a <u>college</u> diploma.

Nouns are classified as **proper**, **common**, **collective**, **concrete**, **abstract**, **count**, and **noncount**.

1. **Proper nouns** name specific people, places, or things and are always capitalized: *Martin Luther King, Jr.; East Lansing; Ford Taurus.* Days of the week and months are considered proper nouns and are capitalized.

   PROPER NOUN   PROPER NOUN          PROPER NOUN

   In <u>September</u> <u>Allen</u> will attend <u>Loyola University</u>.

2. **Common nouns** name one or more of a general class or type of person, place, thing, or idea and are not capitalized: *president, city, car, wisdom.*

   COMMON NOUN   COMMON NOUN   COMMON NOUN          COMMON NOUN

   Next <u>fall</u> the <u>students</u> will enter <u>college</u> to receive an <u>education</u>.

3. **Collective nouns** name a whole group or collection of people, places, or things: *committee, team, jury.* They are usually singular in form.

   COLLECTIVE NOUN                COLLECTIVE NOUN

   The <u>flock</u> of mallards flew over the <u>herd</u> of bison.

4. **Concrete nouns** name tangible things that can be tasted, seen, touched, smelled, or heard: *sandwich, radio, pen.*

   CONCRETE NOUN          CONCRETE NOUN

   The frozen <u>pizza</u> was stuck in the <u>freezer</u>.

5. **Abstract nouns** name ideas, qualities, beliefs, and conditions: *honesty, goodness, poverty.*

   ABSTRACT NOUNS   ABSTRACT NOUN

   Their marriage was based on <u>love</u>, <u>honor</u>, and <u>trust</u>.

6. **Count nouns** name items that can be counted. Count nouns can be made plural, usually by adding *-s* or *-es: one river, three rivers; one box, ten boxes.* Some count nouns form their plural in an irregular way: *man, men; goose, geese.*

COUNT NOUN     COUNT NOUN     COUNT NOUN

The <u>salespeople</u> put the <u>invoices</u> in their <u>files</u>.

7. **Noncount nouns** name ideas or qualities that cannot be counted. Noncount nouns almost always have no plural form: *air, knowledge, unhappiness.*

NONCOUNT NOUN                      NONCOUNT NOUN

As the <u>rain</u> pounded on the windows, she tried to find the <u>courage</u> to walk home from work.

> ## ESL Tip
> **Nouns**
>
> English does not have masculine, feminine, or neuter nouns, but English does have masculine, feminine, and neuter pronouns.

## A.2 PRONOUNS

A **pronoun** is a word that substitutes for or refers to a noun or another pronoun. The noun or pronoun to which a pronoun refers is called the pronoun's **antecedent**. A pronoun must agree with its antecedent in person, number, and gender (these terms are discussed later in this section).

> After the <u>campers</u> discovered the <u>cave</u>, <u>they</u> mapped <u>it</u> for the next <u>group</u>, <u>which</u> was arriving next week. [The pronoun *they* refers to its antecedent, *campers;* the pronoun *it* refers to its antecedent, *cave;* the pronoun *which* refers to its antecedent, *group.*]

The eight kinds of pronouns are **personal, demonstrative, reflexive, intensive, interrogative, relative, indefinite,** and **reciprocal.**

1. **Personal pronouns** take the place of nouns or pronouns that name people or things. A personal pronoun changes form to indicate **person, gender, number,** and **case.**

   **Person** is the grammatical term used to distinguish the speaker (**first person:** *I, we*); the person spoken to (**second person:** *you*); and the person or thing spoken about (**third person:** *he, she, it, they*). **Gender** is the term used to classify pronouns as **masculine** (*he, him*); **feminine** (*she, her*); or **neuter** (*it*). **Number** classifies pronouns as **singular** (one) or **plural** (more than one). Some personal pronouns also function as adjectives modifying nouns (*our house*).

|  | *Singular* | *Plural* |
|---|---|---|
| First person | I, me, my, mine | we, us, our, ours |
| Second person | you, your, yours | you, your, yours |
| Third person |  |  |
| Masculine | he, him, his | } |
| Feminine | she, her, hers | } they, them, their, theirs |
| Neuter | it, its | } |

1ST PERSON SINGULAR
1ST PERSON    (PRONOUN/                    3RD PERSON              3RD PERSON
SINGULAR      ADJECTIVE)                    SINGULAR                PLURAL

I called my manager about my new clients. She wanted to know as soon as they placed their first orders. "Your new clients are important to us," she said.

3RD PERSON          2ND PERSON                            3RD PERSON
PLURAL              SINGULAR                              SINGULAR
(PRONOUN/ADJECTIVE) (PRONOUN/ADJECTIVE)

A pronoun's **case** is determined by its function as a subject (**subjective** or **nominative case**) or an object (**objective case**) in a sentence. A pronoun that shows ownership is in the **possessive case**. (See p. 586 for a discussion of pronoun case.)

2. **Demonstrative pronouns** refer to particular people or things. The demonstrative pronouns are *this* and *that* (singular) and *these* and *those* (plural). (*This, that, these,* and *those* can also be demonstrative adjectives when they modify a noun.)

This is more thorough than that.

The red shuttle buses stop here. These go to the airport every hour.

3. **Reflexive pronouns** indicate that the subject performs actions to, for, or upon itself. Reflexive pronouns end in *-self* or *-selves*.

|  | *Singular* | *Plural* |
|---|---|---|
| First person | myself | ourselves |
| Second person | yourself | yourselves |
| Third person | himself | } |
|  | herself | } themselves |
|  | itself | } |

We excused ourselves from the table and left.

4. An **intensive pronoun** emphasizes the word that comes before it in a sentence. Like reflexive pronouns, intensive pronouns end in *-self* or *-selves*.

The filmmaker herself could not explain the ending.

They themselves repaired the copy machine.

*Note:* A reflexive or intensive pronoun should not be used as a subject of a sentence. An antecedent for the reflexive pronoun must appear in the same sentence.

INCORRECT    <u>Myself</u> create colorful sculpture.

CORRECT    I <u>myself</u> create colorful sculpture.

5. **Interrogative pronouns** are used to introduce questions: *who, whom, whoever, whomever, what, which, whose.* The correct use of *who* and *whom* depends on the role the interrogative pronoun plays in a sentence or clause. When the pronoun functions as the subject of the sentence or clause, use *who.* When the pronoun functions as an object in the sentence or clause, use *whom* (see p. 587).

<u>What</u> happened?

<u>Which</u> is your street?

<u>Who</u> wrote *Ragtime*? [*Who* is the subject of the sentence.]

<u>Whom</u> should I notify? [*Whom* is the object of the verb *notify: I should notify whom?*]

6. **Relative pronouns** relate groups of words to nouns or other pronouns and often introduce adjective clauses or noun clauses (see p. 555). The relative pronouns are *who, whom, whoever, whomever,* and *whose* (referring to people) and *that, what, whatever,* and *which* (referring to things).

In 1836 Charles Dickens met John Forster, <u>who</u> became his friend and biographer.

Don did not understand <u>what</u> the consultant recommended.

We read some articles <u>that</u> were written by former astronauts.

7. **Indefinite pronouns** are pronouns without specific antecedents. They refer to people, places, or things in general.

<u>Someone</u> has been rearranging my papers.

<u>Many</u> knew the woman, but <u>few</u> could say they knew her well.

Here are some frequently used indefinite pronouns:

| *Singular* | | *Plural* |
|---|---|---|
| another | nobody | all |
| anybody | none | both |
| anyone | no one | few |
| anything | nothing | many |
| each | one | more |
| either | other | most |
| everybody | somebody | others |
| everyone | someone | several |
| everything | something | some |
| neither | | |

8. The **reciprocal pronouns** *each other* and *one another* indicate a mutual relationship between two or more parts of a plural antecedent.

Bernie and Sharon congratulated <u>each other</u> on their high grades.

## EXERCISE 1

**Directions:** In each of the following sentences (a) circle each noun and (b) underline each pronoun.

EXAMPLE   (Mark) parked <u>his</u> (car) in the (lot) (that) is reserved for (commuters) like <u>him</u>.

1. (Shakespeare) wrote many (plays) <u>that</u> have become famous and important.

2. Everyone <u>who</u> has visited (Disneyland) wishes to return.

3. (Jonathan) <u>himself</u> wrote the (report) <u>that</u> the (president) of the (company) presented to the (press.)

4. <u>That</u> (desk) used to belong to <u>my</u> (boss.)

5. <u>My</u> (integrity) was never questioned by <u>my</u> (co-workers.)

6. The (class) always laughed at (jokes) told by the (professor,) even though <u>they</u> were usually corny.

7. When will (humankind) be able to travel to the (moon)?

8. <u>Whoever</u> wins the (lottery) this (week) will become quite wealthy.

9. As the (plane) landed at the (airport,) many of the (passengers) began to gather <u>their</u> carry-on (luggage.)

10. This (week) <u>we</u> are studying (gravity); next week <u>we</u> will study (heat.)

## A.3 VERBS

Verbs express action or state of being. A grammatically complete sentence has at least one verb in it.

There are three kinds of verbs: **action verbs**, **linking verbs**, and **helping verbs** (also known as **auxiliary verbs**).

1. **Action verbs** express physical and mental activities.

Mr. Royce <u>dashed</u> for the bus.

The incinerator <u>burns</u> garbage at high temperatures.

I <u>think</u> that seat is taken.

The programmer <u>worked</u> until 3:00 A.M.

Action verbs are either **transitive** or **intransitive**. The action of a **transitive verb** is directed toward someone or something, called the **direct object** of the verb. Direct objects receive the action of the verb. Transitive verbs require direct objects to complete the meaning of the sentence.

```
         TRANSITIVE   DIRECT
SUBJECT     VERB      OBJECT
Amalia      made      clocks.
```

An **intransitive verb** does not need a direct object to complete the meaning of the sentence.

```
              INTRANSITIVE
   SUBJECT        VERB
The   traffic   stopped.
```

Some verbs can be both transitive and intransitive, depending on their meaning and use in a sentence.

INTRANSITIVE        The traffic stopped. [No direct object.]

```
                              DIRECT OBJECT
TRANSITIVE        The driver stopped the bus at the corner.
```

2. A **linking verb** expresses a state of being or a condition. A linking verb connects a noun or pronoun to words that describe the noun or pronoun. Common linking verbs are forms of the verb *be* (*is, are, was, were, being, been*), *become, feel, grow, look, remain, seem, smell, sound, stay,* and *taste.*

   Their child grew tall.

   The office looks messy.

   Mr. Davenport is our accountant.

3. A **helping (auxiliary) verb** helps another verb, called the **main verb**, to convey when the action occurred (through verb tense) and to form questions. One or more helping verbs and the main verb together form a **verb phrase.** Some helping verbs, called **modals**, are always helping verbs:

   can, could      shall, should
   may, might      will, would
   must, ought to

   The other helping verbs can sometimes function as main verbs as well:

   am, are, be, been, being, did, do, does
   had, has, have
   is, was, were

The verb *be* is a very irregular verb, with eight forms instead of the usual five: *am, are, be, being, been, is, was, were.*

```
       HELPING MAIN
        VERB   VERB
        ┌─┐   ┌─┐
```
The store <u>will</u> <u>close</u> early on holidays.

```
    HELPING          MAIN
     VERB            VERB
     ┌─┐             ┌─┐
```
<u>Will</u> the store <u>close</u> early on New Year's Eve?

## Forms of the Verb

All verbs except *be* have five forms: the **base form** (or dictionary form), the **past tense**, the **past participle**, the **present participle**, and the **-s form**. The first three forms are called the verb's **principal parts**. The infinitive consists of "to" plus a base form: *to go, to study, to talk.* For **regular verbs**, the past tense and past participle are formed by adding *-d* or *-ed* to the base form. **Irregular verbs** follow no set pattern to form their past tense and past participle.

|  | *Regular* | *Irregular* |
|---|---|---|
| Infinitive | work | eat |
| Past tense | worked | ate |
| Past participle | worked | eaten |
| Present participle | working | eating |
| *-s* form | works | eats |

Verbs change form to agree with their subjects in person and number (see p. 578); to express the time of their action (**tense**); to express whether the action is a fact, command, or wish (**mood**); and to indicate whether the subject is the doer or the receiver of the action (**voice**).

## Principal Parts of Irregular Verbs

Consult the following list and your dictionary for the principal parts of irregular verbs.

| *Base Form* | *Past Tense* | *Past Participle* |
|---|---|---|
| be | was | been |
| become | became | become |
| begin | began | begun |
| bite | bit | bitten |
| blow | blew | blown |
| burst | burst | burst |
| catch | caught | caught |
| choose | chose | chosen |
| come | came | come |
| dive | dived, dove | dived |
| do | did | done |

| Base Form | Past Tense | Past Participle |
| --- | --- | --- |
| draw | drew | drawn |
| drive | drove | driven |
| eat | ate | eaten |
| fall | fell | fallen |
| find | found | found |
| fling | flung | flung |
| fly | flew | flown |
| get | got | gotten |
| give | gave | given |
| go | went | gone |
| grow | grew | grown |
| have | had | had |
| know | knew | known |
| lay | laid | laid |
| lead | led | led |
| leave | left | left |
| lie | lay | lain |
| lose | lost | lost |
| ride | rode | ridden |
| ring | rang | rung |
| rise | rose | risen |
| say | said | said |
| set | set | set |
| sit | sat | sat |
| speak | spoke | spoken |
| swear | swore | sworn |
| swim | swam | swum |
| tear | tore | torn |
| tell | told | told |
| throw | threw | thrown |
| wear | wore | worn |
| write | wrote | written |

## Tense

The **tenses** of a verb express time. They convey whether an action, process, or event takes place in the present, past, or future.

The three **simple tenses** are **present, past,** and **future.** The **simple present** tense is the base form of the verb (and the -s form of third-person singular subjects; see p. 569); the **simple past** tense is the past-tense form; and the **simple future** tense consists of the helping verb *will* plus the base form.

The **perfect tenses,** which indicate completed action, are **present perfect, past perfect,** and **future perfect.** They are formed by adding the helping verbs *have* (or *has*), *had,* and *will have* to the past participle.

In addition to the simple and perfect tenses, there are six progressive tenses. The **simple progressive tenses** are the **present progressive,** the

**past progressive**, and the **future progressive**. The progressive tenses are used for continuing actions or actions in progress. These progressive tenses are formed by adding the present, past, and future forms of the verb *be* to the present participle. The **perfect progressive tenses** are the **present perfect progressive**, the **past perfect progressive**, and the **future perfect progressive**. They are formed by adding the present perfect, past perfect, and future perfect forms of the verb *be* to the present participle.

The following chart shows all the tenses for a regular verb and an irregular verb in the first person. (For more on tenses, see p. 569.)

|  | *Regular* | *Irregular* |
| --- | --- | --- |
| Simple present | I talk | I go |
| Simple past | I talked | I went |
| Simple future | I will talk | I will go |
| Present perfect | I have talked | I have gone |
| Past perfect | I had talked | I had gone |
| Future perfect | I will have talked | I will have gone |
| Present progressive | I am talking | I am going |
| Past progressive | I was talking | I was going |
| Future progressive | I will be talking | I will be going |
| Present perfect progressive | I have been talking | I have been going |
| Past perfect progressive | I had been talking | I had been going |
| Future perfect progressive | I will have been talking | I will have been going |

## Mood

The mood of a verb indicates the writer's attitude toward the action. There are three moods in English: **indicative**, **imperative**, and **subjunctive**.

The **indicative mood** is used for ordinary statements of fact or questions.

The light <u>flashed</u> on and off all night.

<u>Did</u> you <u>check</u> the batteries?

The **imperative mood** is used for commands, suggestions, or directions. The subject of a verb in the imperative mood is *you*, though it is not always included.

<u>Stop</u> shouting!

<u>Come</u> to New York for a visit.

<u>Turn</u> right at the next corner.

The **subjunctive mood** is used for wishes, requirements, recommendations, and statements contrary to fact. For statements contrary to fact or for wishes, the past tense of the verb is used. For the verb *be,* only the past-tense form *were* is used.

> If I <u>had</u> a million dollars, I'd take a trip around the world.

> If my supervisor <u>were</u> promoted, I would be eligible for her job.

To express suggestions, recommendations, or requirements, the infinitive form is used for all verbs.

> I recommend that the houses <u>be</u> sold after the landscaping is done.

> The registrar required that Maureen <u>pay</u> her bill before attending class.

## Voice

Transitive verbs (those that take objects) may be in either the active voice or the passive voice (see p. 574). In an **active-voice** sentence, the subject performs the action described by the verb; that is, the subject is the actor. In a **passive-voice** sentence, the subject is the receiver of the action. The passive voice of a verb is formed by using an appropriate form of the helping verb *be* and the past participle of the main verb.

SUBJECT    ACTIVE
IS ACTOR    VOICE

Dr. Hillel <u>delivered</u> the report on global warming.

SUBJECT IS RECEIVER            PASSIVE VOICE

The report on global warming <u>was delivered</u> by Dr. Hillel.

## EXERCISE 2

**Directions:** Revise the following sentences, changing each verb from the present tense to the tense indicated.

> EXAMPLE      I <u>know</u> the right answer.

> PAST TENSE      *I knew the right answer.*

1. Allison <u>loses</u> the sales to competitors.

   SIMPLE PAST   *lost*

2. Malcolm <u>begins</u> classes at the community college.

   PAST PERFECT   *had begun*

3. The microscope <u>enlarges</u> the cell.

   PRESENT PERFECT   *has enlarged*

4. Reports <u>follow</u> a standard format.

SIMPLE FUTURE  will follow _____

5. Meg Ryan <u>receives</u> excellent evaluations.

FUTURE PERFECT  will have received _____

6. Juanita <u>writes</u> a computer program.

PRESENT PERFECT  has written _____

7. The movie <u>stars</u> Brad Pitt.

SIMPLE FUTURE  will star _____

8. Dave <u>wins</u> medals at the Special Olympics.

SIMPLE PAST  won _____

9. Many celebrities <u>donate</u> money to AIDS research.

PRESENT PERFECT  have donated _____

10. My nephew <u>travels</u> to Michigan's Upper Peninsula on business.

PAST PERFECT  had traveled _____

# A.4 ADJECTIVES

**Adjectives** modify nouns and pronouns. That is, they describe, identify, qualify, or limit the meaning of nouns and pronouns. An adjective answers the question *Which one? What kind?* or *How many?* about the word it modifies.

WHICH ONE?   The <u>twisted</u>, <u>torn</u> umbrella was of no use to its owner.

WHAT KIND?   The <u>spotted</u> owl has caused <u>heated</u> arguments in the Northwest.

HOW MANY?    <u>Many</u> customers waited for <u>four</u> days for telephone service to be restored.

In form, adjectives can be **positive** (implying no comparison), **comparative** (comparing two items), or **superlative** (comparing three or more items). (See p. 589 for more on the forms of adjectives.)

POSITIVE

The computer is <u>fast</u>.

COMPARATIVE

Your computer is <u>faster</u> than mine.

SUPERLATIVE

This is the <u>fastest</u> computer I have ever used.

There are two general categories of adjectives. **Descriptive adjectives** name a quality of the person, place, thing, or idea they describe: *mysterious man, green pond, healthy complexion*. **Limiting adjectives** narrow the scope of the person, place, or thing they describe: *my computer, this tool, second try*.

### ESL Tip
#### Adjectives

Remember: In English, adjectives do not have a gender. (They are not feminine, masculine, or neuter.)

## Descriptive Adjectives

A **regular** (or **attributive**) adjective appears next to (usually before) the word it modifies. Several adjectives can modify the same word.

The enthusiastic new hair stylist gave short, lopsided haircuts.

The wealthy dealer bought an immense blue vase.

Sometimes nouns function as adjectives modifying other nouns: *tree house, hamburger bun*.

A **predicate adjective** follows a linking verb and modifies or describes the subject of the sentence or clause (see p. 544; see p. 554 on clauses).

PREDICATE ADJECTIVE

The meeting was long. [Modifies the subject, *meeting*.]

## Limiting Adjectives

The **definite article**, *the*, and the **indefinite articles**, *a* and *an*, are classified as adjectives. *A* and *an* are used when it is not important to specify a particular noun or when the object named is not known to the reader (*A radish adds color to a salad*). *The* is used when it is important to specify one or more of a particular noun or when the object named is known to the reader or has already been mentioned (*The radishes from the garden are on the table*).

A squirrel visited the feeder that I just built. The squirrel tried to eat some bird food.

When the possessive pronouns *my, your, his, her, its, our,* and *their* are used as modifiers before nouns, they are considered **possessive adjectives** (see p. 588).

Your friend borrowed my laptop for his trip.

When the demonstrative pronouns *this, that, these,* and *those* are used as modifiers before nouns, they are called **demonstrative adjectives** (see p. 521). *This* and *these* modify nouns close to the writer; *that* and *those* modify nouns more distant from the writer.

Buy <u>these</u> formatted disks, not <u>those</u> unformatted ones.

<u>This</u> freshman course is a prerequisite for <u>those</u> advanced courses.

**Cardinal adjectives** are words used in counting: *one, two, twenty,* and so on.

I read <u>four</u> biographies of Jack Kerouac and <u>seven</u> articles about his work.

**Ordinal adjectives** note position in a series.

The <u>first</u> biography was too sketchy; whereas the <u>second</u> one was too detailed.

**Indefinite adjectives** provide nonspecific, general information about the quantities and amounts of the nouns they modify. Some common indefinite adjectives are *another, any, enough, few, less, little, many, more, much, several,* and *some.*

<u>Several</u> people asked me if I had <u>enough</u> blankets or if I wanted the thermostat turned up a <u>few</u> degrees.

The **interrogative adjectives** *what, which,* and *whose* modify nouns and pronouns used in questions.

<u>Which</u> radio station do you like? <u>Whose</u> music do you prefer?

The words *which* and *what,* along with *whichever* and *whatever,* are **relative adjectives** when they modify nouns and introduce subordinate clauses.

She couldn't decide <u>which</u> job she wanted to take.

**Proper adjectives** are adjectives derived from proper nouns: *Spain* (noun), *Spanish* (adjective); *Freud* (noun), *Freudian* (adjective); see p. 519. Most proper adjectives are capitalized.

Shakespeare lived in <u>Elizabethan</u> England.

The speaker used many <u>French</u> expressions.

## EXERCISE 3

**Directions:** Review each of the following sentences by adding at least three adjectives.

EXAMPLE      The cat slept on the pillow.

REVISED      The old yellow cat slept on the expensive pillow.

1. Before leaving on a trip, the couple packed their suitcases.

   *Before leaving on a weekend skiing trip, the excited couple packed their suitcases.*

2. The tree dropped leaves all over the lawn.

   The oak tree dropped multicolored leaves all over the front lawn.

3. While riding the train, the passengers read newspapers.

   While riding the commuter train, the passengers read their morning newspapers.

4. The antiques dealer said that the desk was more valuable than the chair.

   The persistent antiques dealer said that the oak desk was worth more than

   the cherrywood chair.

5. As the play was ending, the audience clapped their hands and tossed roses onstage.

   As the new Broadway play was ending, the enthusiastic audience clapped

   their hands and tossed roses onstage.

6. Stew is served nightly at the shelter.

   Beef stew is served nightly at the local homeless shelter.

7. The engine roared as the car stubbornly jerked into gear.

   The straining engine roared as the old car stubbornly jerked into second gear.

8. The tourists tossed pennies into the fountain.

   The tourists tossed their copper pennies into the rushing fountain.

9. Computer disks were stacked on the desk next to the monitor.

   Computer disks were stacked on the sturdy wooden desk next to the

   buzzing monitor.

10. Marina's belt and shoes were made of the same material and complemented her dress.

    Marina's belt and shoes were made of the same navy blue material

    and complemented her linen dress.

# A.5 ADVERBS

**Adverbs** modify verbs, adjectives, other adverbs, or entire sentences or clauses (see p. 554 on clauses). Like adjectives, adverbs describe, qualify, or limit the meaning of the words they modify.

An adverb answers the question *How? When? Where? How often?* or *To what extent?* about the word it modifies.

| | |
|---|---|
| HOW? | Cheryl moved <u>awkwardly</u> because of her stiff neck. |
| WHEN? | I arrived <u>yesterday</u>. |
| WHERE? | They searched <u>everywhere</u>. |
| HOW OFTEN? | He telephoned <u>repeatedly</u>. |
| TO WHAT EXTENT? | Simon was <u>rather</u> slow to answer his e-mail. |

Many adverbs end in *-ly* (*lazily, happily*), but some adverbs do not (*fast, here, much, well, rather, everywhere, never, so*), and some words that end in *-ly* are not adverbs (*lively, friendly, lonely*). Like all other parts of speech, an adverb may be best identified by examining its function within a sentence.

I <u>quickly</u> skimmed the book. [Modifies the verb *skimmed*.]

<u>Very</u> angry customers crowded the service desk. [Modifies the adjective *angry*.]

He was injured <u>quite</u> seriously. [Modifies the adverb *seriously*.]

<u>Apparently</u>, the job was bungled. [Modifies the whole sentence.]

Like adjectives, adverbs have three forms: **positive** (does not suggest any comparison), **comparative** (compares two actions or conditions), and **superlative** (compares three or more actions or conditions; see also p. 589).

POSITIVE                           POSITIVE

Andy rose <u>early</u> and crept downstairs <u>quietly</u>.

COMPARATIVE                           COMPARATIVE

Jim rose <u>earlier</u> than Andy and crept downstairs <u>more quietly</u>.

SUPERLATIVE

Bill rose <u>earliest</u> of anyone in the house and crept downstairs <u>most quietly</u>.

SUPERLATIVE

Some adverbs, called **conjunctive adverbs** (or **adverbial conjunctions**)—such as *however, therefore,* and *besides*—connect the ideas of one sentence or clause to those of a previous sentence or clause. They can appear anywhere in a sentence. (See p. 567 for how to punctuate sentences containing conjunctive adverbs.)

CONJUNCTIVE ADVERB

James did not want to go to the library on Saturday; <u>however</u>, he knew the books were overdue.

The sporting-goods store was crowded because of the sale. Leila, <u>therefore</u>, was asked to work extra hours.

CONJUNCTIVE ADVERB

Some common conjunctive adverbs are listed below, including several phrases that function as conjunctive adverbs.

| | | | |
|---|---|---|---|
| accordingly | for example | meanwhile | otherwise |
| also | further | moreover | similarly |
| anyway | furthermore | namely | still |
| as a result | hence | nevertheless | then |
| at the same time | however | next | thereafter |
| besides | incidentally | nonetheless | therefore |
| certainly | indeed | now | thus |
| consequently | instead | on the contrary | undoubtedly |
| finally | likewise | on the other hand | |

# EXERCISE 4

**Directions:** Write a sentence using each of the following comparative or superlative adverbs.

EXAMPLE    better: <u>My car runs better now than ever before.</u>

1. farther: Lani lives farther from Portsmouth than I do.

2. most: Anne's paragraph on capital punishment was the most thoughtfully written.

3. more: Three years ago, Washington Street was widened; more recently, lanes for cyclists were added.

4. best: Angelo's makes the best pizza in town.

5. least neatly: My sister's room is the least neatly organized room in our house.

**6. louder:** When Whitney Houston came onstage, the crowd cheered louder than it had all evening.

**7. worse:** In recent polls, the politician fared worse than expected.

**8. less angrily:** Julio responded less angrily than his brother when the car broke down.

**9. later:** The bus arrived in Minneapolis 40 minutes later than scheduled.

**10. earliest:** The earliest I get up is 7:30 A.M.

# A.6 CONJUNCTIONS

**Conjunctions** connect words, phrases, and clauses. There are three kinds of conjunctions: **coordinating, correlative,** and **subordinating. Coordinating** and **correlative conjunctions** connect words, phrases, or clauses of equal grammatical rank. (A **phrase** is a group of related words lacking a subject, a predicate, or both. A **clause** is a group of words containing a subject and a predicate; see pp. 541 and 542.)

The **coordinating conjunctions** are *and, but, nor, or, for, so,* and *yet.* These words must connect words or word groups of the same kind. Therefore, two nouns may be connected by *and,* but a noun and a clause cannot be. *For* and *so* can connect only independent clauses.

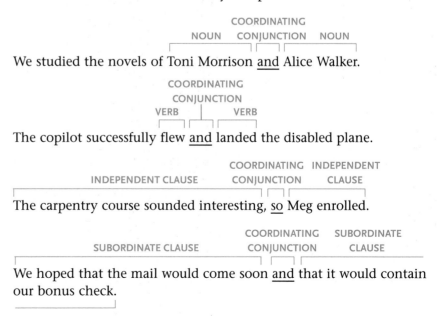

We studied the novels of Toni Morrison <u>and</u> Alice Walker.

The copilot successfully flew <u>and</u> landed the disabled plane.

The carpentry course sounded interesting, <u>so</u> Meg enrolled.

We hoped that the mail would come soon <u>and</u> that it would contain our bonus check.

**Correlative conjunctions** are pairs of words that link and relate grammatically equivalent parts of a sentence. Some common correlative conjunctions are *either/or, neither/nor, both/and, not/but, not only/but also,* and *whether/or.* Correlative conjunctions are always used in pairs.

┌──CORRELATIVE CONJUNCTIONS──┐

Either the electricity was off, or the bulb had burned out.

**Subordinating conjunctions** connect dependent, or subordinate, clauses to independent clauses (see p. 567). Some common subordinating conjunctions are *although, because, if, since, until, when, where,* and *while.*

SUBORDINATING CONJUNCTION

Although the movie got bad reviews, it drew big crowds.

SUBORDINATING CONJUNCTION

She received a lot of mail because she was a reliable correspondent.

## A.7 PREPOSITIONS

A **preposition** links and relates its **object** (a noun or a pronoun) to the rest of the sentence. Prepositions often show relationships of time, place, direction, and manner.

PREPOSITION    OBJECT OF PREPOSITION

I walked around the block.

PREPOSITION    OBJECT OF PREPOSITION

She called during our meeting.

### Common Prepositions

| | | | | |
|---|---|---|---|---|
| along | besides | from | past | up |
| among | between | in | since | upon |
| around | beyond | near | through | with |
| at | by | off | till | within |
| before | despite | on | to | without |
| behind | down | onto | toward | |
| below | during | out | under | |
| beneath | except | outside | underneath | |
| beside | for | over | until | |

Some prepositions consist of more than one word; they are called **phrasal prepositions** or **compound prepositions**.

PHRASAL PREPOSITION   OBJECT OF PREPOSITION

<u>According to</u> our <u>records</u>, you have enough credits to graduate.

PHRASAL PREPOSITION   OBJECT OF PREPOSITION

We decided to make the trip <u>in spite of</u> the <u>snowstorm</u>.

### Common Compound Prepositions

| | | |
|---|---|---|
| according to | in addition to | on account of |
| aside from | in front of | out of |
| as of | in place of | prior to |
| as well as | in regard to | with regard to |
| because of | in spite of | with respect to |
| by means of | instead of | |

The object of the preposition often has modifiers.

OBJ. OF   OBJ. OF
PREP.   MODIFIER PREP.   PREP.   MODIFIER PREP.

Not a sound came <u>from</u> the <u>child's</u> <u>room</u> <u>except</u> a <u>gentle</u> <u>snoring</u>.

Sometimes a preposition has more than one object (a **compound object**).

COMPOUND OBJECT OF PREPOSITION
PREPOSITION

The laundromat was <u>between</u> <u>campus</u> and <u>home</u>.

Usually the preposition comes before its object. In interrogative sentences, however, the preposition sometimes follows its object.

OBJECT OF PREPOSITION   PREPOSITION

<u>What</u> did your supervisor ask you <u>about</u>?

The preposition, the object or objects of the preposition, and the object's modifiers all form a **prepositional phrase**.

PREPOSITIONAL PHRASE

The scientist conducted her experiment <u>throughout the afternoon and early evening</u>.

There may be many prepositional phrases in a sentence.

PREPOSITIONAL PHRASE   PREPOSITIONAL PHRASE

The water <u>from the open hydrant</u> flowed <u>into the street</u>.

The noisy kennel was <u>underneath the beauty salon</u>, <u>despite the complaints of customers</u>.

<u>Alongside the weedy railroad tracks</u>, an old hotel <u>with faded grandeur</u> stood <u>near the abandoned brick station on the edge of town</u>.

Prepositional phrases frequently function as adjectives or adverbs. If a prepositional phrase modifies a noun or pronoun, it functions as an adjective. If it modifies a verb, adjective, or adverb, it functions as an adverb.

The auditorium <u>inside the conference center</u> has a special sound system. [Adjective modifying the noun *auditorium*.]

The doctor looked cheerfully <u>at the patient</u> and handed the lab results <u>across the desk</u>. [Adverbs modifying the verbs *looked* and *handed*.]

## EXERCISE 5

**Directions:** Expand each of the following sentences by adding a prepositional phrase in the blank.

EXAMPLE A cat hid <u>under the car</u> when the garage door opened.

1. Fish nibbled _____ as the fisherman waited.

on nearby reeds

2. The librarian explained that the books about Africa are located _____.

in the nonfiction section

3. When the bullet hit the window, shards flew _____.

in all directions

4. _____, there is a restaurant that serves alligator meat.

In Orlando

5. Polar bears are able to swim _____.

long distances

6. Heavy winds blowing _____ caused the waves to hit the house.

off the ocean

7. One student completed her exam _____.

within an hour

8. A frog jumped _____.

onto the floating lily pad

9. The bus was parked _____.

next to the stadium

10. Stacks of books were piled _____.

on the mantel

# A.8 INTERJECTIONS

**Interjections** are words that express emotion or surprise. They are followed by an exclamation point, comma, or period, depending on whether they stand alone or serve as part or all of a sentence. Interjections are used in speech more than in writing.

<u>Wow</u>! What an announcement!

<u>So</u>, was that lost letter ever found?

<u>Well</u>, I'd better be going.

# B

# Understanding the Parts of Sentences

A sentence is a group of words that expresses a complete thought about something or someone. A sentence must contain a **subject** and a **predicate**.

| *Subject* | *Predicate* |
|-----------|-------------|
| Telephones | ring. |
| Cecilia | laughed. |
| Time | will tell. |

Depending on their purpose and punctuation, sentences are **declarative**, **interrogative**, **exclamatory**, or **imperative**.

A **declarative sentence** makes a statement. It ends with a period.

SUBJECT  PREDICATE

The <u>snow</u> <u>fell</u> steadily.

An **interrogative sentence** asks a question. It ends with a question mark (?).

SUBJECT  PREDICATE

<u>Who</u> <u>called</u>?

An **exclamatory sentence** conveys strong emotion. It ends with an exclamation point (!).

SUBJECT  PREDICATE

Your <u>photograph</u> <u>is</u> in the company newsletter!

An **imperative sentence** gives an order or makes a request. It ends with either a period or an exclamation point, depending on how mild or strong the command or request is. In an imperative sentence, the subject is *you,* but this often is not included.

PREDICATE

<u>Get</u> me a fire extinguisher now! [The subject *you* is understood: (*You*) get me a fire extinguisher now!]

**ESL Tip**
Sentences

A sentence is a group of words containing both a subject and a predicate. The subject is the part of the sentence that tells you who or what the sentence is about.

The predicate is the part of the sentence that contains the main verb. It is also the part of the sentence that tells you what the subject is doing or describes the subject.

# B.1 SUBJECTS

The subject of a sentence is whom or what the sentence is about. It is who or what performs or receives the action expressed in the predicate. The subject is often a **noun**, a word that names a person, place, thing, or idea.

> Julia worked on her math homework.
>
> The rose bushes must be watered.
>
> Honesty is the best policy.

The subject of a sentence can also be a **pronoun**, a word that refers to or substitutes for a noun.

> She revised the memo three times.
>
> I will attend the sales meeting.
>
> Although the ink spilled, it did not go on my shirt.

The subject of a sentence can also be a group of words used as a noun.

> Reading e-mail from friends is my idea of a good time.

## Simple Versus Complete Subjects

The **simple subject** is the noun or pronoun that names what the sentence is about. It does not include any **modifiers**—that is, words that describe, identify, qualify, or limit the meaning of the noun or pronoun.

SIMPLE SUBJECT

The bright red concert poster caught everyone's eye.

SIMPLE SUBJECT

High-speed computers have revolutionized the banking industry.

When the subject of a sentence is a proper noun (the name of a particular person, place, or thing), the entire name is considered the simple subject.

SIMPLE SUBJECT

Martin Luther King, Jr., was a famous leader.

The simple subject of an imperative sentence is *you.*

SIMPLE SUBJECT

[You] Remember to bring the sales brochures.

The **complete subject** is the simple subject plus its modifiers.

COMPLETE SUBJECT

SIMPLE SUBJECT

The sleek, black limousine waited outside the church.

COMPLETE SUBJECT

Fondly remembered as a gifted songwriter, fiddle player, and storyteller, Quintin Lotus Dickey lived in a cabin in Paoli, Indiana.

SIMPLE SUBJECT

## Compound Subjects

Some sentences contain two or more subjects joined with a coordinating conjunction (*and, but, nor, or, for, so, yet*). Those subjects together form a **compound subject.**

COMPOUND SUBJECT

Maria and I completed the marathon.

COMPOUND SUBJECT

The computer, the printer, and the DVD player were not usable during the blackout.

## B.2 PREDICATES

The **predicate** indicates what the subject does, what happened to the subject, or what is being said about the subject. The predicate must include a **verb**, a word or group of words that expresses an action or a state of being (for example, *run, invent, build, know, will decide, become*).

Joy swam sixty laps.

The thunderstorm replenished the reservoir.

Sometimes the verb consists of only one word, as in the previous examples. Often, however, the main verb is accompanied by a **helping verb** (see p. 524).

HELPING    MAIN
VERB    VERB

By the end of the week, I <u>will have</u> <u>worked</u> twenty-five hours.

HELPING MAIN
VERB VERB

The training session <u>had</u> <u>begun.</u>

HELPING MAIN
VERB VERB

The professor <u>did</u> <u>return</u> the journal assignments.

## Simple Versus Complete Predicates

The **simple predicate** is the main verb plus its helping verbs (together known as the **verb phrase**). The simple predicate does not include any modifiers.

SIMPLE PREDICATE

The proctor hastily <u>collected</u> the blue books.

SIMPLE PREDICATE

The moderator <u>had introduced</u> the next speaker.

The **complete predicate** consists of the simple predicate, its modifiers, and any complements (words that complete the meaning of the verb; see p. 544). In general, the complete predicate includes everything in the sentence except the complete subject.

COMPLETE PREDICATE
SIMPLE PREDICATE

The music <u>sounds better from the back of the room.</u>

COMPLETE PREDICATE
SIMPLE PREDICATE

Bill <u>decided to change the name of his company to something less controversial and confusing</u>.

## Compound Predicates

Some sentences have two or more predicates joined by a coordinating conjunction (*and, but, or,* or *nor*). These predicates together form a **compound predicate.**

COMPOUND PREDICATE

Marcia <u>unlocked</u> her bicycle and <u>rode</u> away.

COMPOUND PREDICATE

The supermarket owner <u>will survey</u> his customers and <u>order</u> the specialized foods they desire.

## EXERCISE 6

**Directions:** Underline the simple subject(s) and circle the simple or compound predicate(s) in each of the following sentences.

EXAMPLE    Pamela Wong (photographed) a hummingbird.

1. A group of nurses (walked) across the lobby on their way to a staff meeting.

2. The campground for physically challenged children (is funded) and (supported) by the Rotary Club.

3. Forty doctors and lawyers (had attended) the seminar on malpractice insurance.

4. Sullivan Beach (will) not (reopen) because of pollution.

5. The police cadets (attended) classes all day and (studied) late into each evening.

6. Greenpeace (is) an environmentalist organization.

7. Talented dancers and experienced musicians (performed) and (received) much applause at the open-air show.

8. Some undergraduate students (have been using) empty classrooms for group study.

9. A police officer, with the shoplifter in handcuffs, (entered) the police station.

10. The newly elected senator (walked up) to the podium and (began) her first speech to her constituents.

# B.3 COMPLEMENTS

A **complement** is a word or group of words used to complete the meaning of a subject or object. There are four kinds of complements: **subject complements**, which follow linking verbs; **direct objects** and **indirect objects**, which follow transitive verbs (verbs that take an object); and **object complements**, which follow direct objects.

## Linking Verbs and Subject Complements

A linking verb (such as *be, become, seem, feel, taste*) links the subject to a **subject complement**, a noun or adjective that renames or describes the subject. (See p. 524 for more about linking verbs.) Nouns that function as complements are called **predicate nominatives** or **predicate nouns**. Adjectives that function as complements are called **predicate adjectives**.

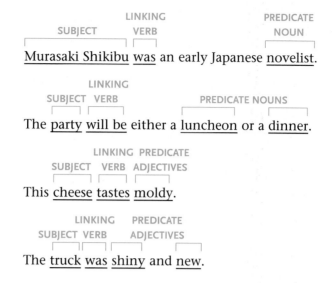

Murasaki Shikibu was an early Japanese novelist.

The party will be either a luncheon or a dinner.

This cheese tastes moldy.

The truck was shiny and new.

## Direct Objects

A **direct object** is a noun or pronoun that receives the action of a transitive verb (see p. 524). A direct object answers the question *What?* or *Whom?*

TRANSITIVE VERB    DIRECT OBJECT

The pharmacist helped us. [The pharmacist helped *whom?*]

TRANSITIVE VERB    DIRECT OBJECTS

Jillian borrowed a bicycle and a visor. [Jillian borrowed *what?*]

## Indirect Objects

An **indirect object** is a noun or pronoun that receives the action of the verb indirectly. Indirect objects name the person or thing *to whom* or *for whom* something is done.

TRANSITIVE   INDIRECT   DIRECT
VERB         OBJECT     OBJECT

The computer technician gave me the bill. [He gave the bill *to whom?*]

TRANSITIVE VERB   INDIRECT OBJECTS           DIRECT OBJECTS

Eric bought his wife and son some sandwiches and milk. [He bought food *for whom?*]

## Object Complements

An **object complement** is a noun or adjective that modifies (describes) or renames the direct object. Object complements appear with verbs like *name, find, think, elect, appoint, choose,* and *consider.*

DIRECT OBJECT      NOUN AS OBJECT COMPLEMENT

We appointed <u>Dean</u> our <u>representative</u>. [*Representative* renames the direct object, *Dean.*]

DIRECT OBJECT      ADJECTIVE AS OBJECT COMPLEMENT

The judge found the <u>defendant</u> <u>innocent</u> of the charges. [*Innocent* modifies the direct object, *defendant.*]

# B.4 BASIC SENTENCE PATTERNS

### ESL Tip
#### Sentence Patterns

It's helpful to remember these five basic sentence patterns in English. These patterns may be very different from language patterns in your native language or other languages that you have studied.

There are five basic sentence patterns in English. They are built with combinations of subjects, predicates, and complements. The order of these elements within a sentence may change, or a sentence may become long and complicated when modifiers, phrases, or clauses are added. Nonetheless, one of five basic patterns stands at the heart of every sentence.

**PATTERN 1**

| *Subject* | + | *Predicate* |
|-----------|---|-------------|
| I | | shivered. |
| Cynthia | | swam. |

**PATTERN 2**

| *Subject* | + | *Predicate* | + | *Direct Object* |
|-----------|---|-------------|---|-----------------|
| Anthony | | ordered | | a new desk. |
| We | | wanted | | freedom. |

**PATTERN 3**

| *Subject* | + | *Predicate* | + | *Subject Complement* |
|-----------|---|-------------|---|----------------------|
| The woman | | was | | a welder. |
| Our course | | is | | interesting. |

PATTERN 4

| Subject | + | Predicate | + | Indirect Object | + | Direct Object |
|---------|---|-----------|---|-----------------|---|---------------|
| My friend | | loaned | | me | | a laptop. |
| The company | | sent | | employees | | a questionnaire. |

PATTERN 5

| Subject | + | Predicate | + | Direct Object | + | Object Complement |
|---------|---|-----------|---|---------------|---|-------------------|
| I | | consider | | her singing | | exceptional. |
| Lampwick | | called | | Jiminy Cricket | | a beetle. |

## EXERCISE 7

**Directions:** Complete each sentence with a word or words that will function as the type of complement indicated.

EXAMPLE      The scientist acted _____*proud*_____ as he announced his
latest invention.                    predicate adjective

1. The delivery person handed _____*Luis*_____ the large brown
   package.                              indirect object

2. Ronald Reagan was an American _____*president*_____ .
                                        predicate noun

3. The chairperson appointed Judith our *director of public relations* .
                                        object complement

4. Protesters stood on the corner and handed out _____*flyers*_____ .
                                                    direct object

5. The secretary gave _____*Alex*_____ the messages.
                        indirect object

6. Before the storm, many clouds were _____*visible*_____ .
                                        predicate adjective

7. The beer advertisement targeted _____*young adults*_____ .
                                      direct object

8. The Super Bowl players were _____*skilled athletes*_____ .
                                  predicate noun

9. The diplomat declared the Olympics _____*a success*_____ .
                                        object complement

10. Shopping malls are _____*busy*_____ before Christmas.
                         predicate adjective

# B.5 EXPANDING THE SENTENCE WITH ADJECTIVES AND ADVERBS

A sentence may consist of just a subject and a verb.

Linda studied.

Rumors circulated.

Most sentences, however, contain additional information about the subject and the verb. Information is commonly added in three ways:

- by using adjectives and adverbs;

- by using phrases (groups of words that lack either a subject or a predicate or both);

- by using clauses (groups of words that contain both a subject and a predicate).

## Using Adjectives and Adverbs to Expand Your Sentences

**Adjectives** are words used to modify or describe nouns and pronouns (see p. 529). Adjectives answer questions about nouns and pronouns such as *Which one? What kind? How many?* Using adjectives is one way to add detail and information to sentences.

| | |
|---|---|
| WITHOUT ADJECTIVES | Dogs barked at cats. |
| WITH ADJECTIVES | <u>Our</u> <u>three</u> <u>large</u>, <u>brown</u> dogs barked at <u>the</u> <u>two</u> <u>terrified</u> <u>spotted</u> cats. |

*Note:* Sometimes nouns and participles are used as adjectives (see p. 525 on participles).

NOUN USED AS ADJECTIVE

People are rediscovering the <u>milk</u> bottle.

PRESENT PARTICIPLE          PAST PARTICIPLE
USED AS ADJECTIVE            USED AS ADJECTIVE

Mrs. Simon had a <u>swimming</u> pool with a <u>broken</u> drain.

**Adverbs** add information to sentences by modifying or describing verbs, adjectives, or other adverbs (see p. 533). An adverb usually answers the question *How? When? Where? How often?* or *To what extent?*

| | |
|---|---|
| WITHOUT ADVERBS | I will clean. |
| | The audience applauded. |
| WITH ADVERBS | I will clean <u>very</u> <u>thoroughly</u> <u>tomorrow</u>. |
| | The audience applauded <u>loudly</u> and <u>enthusiastically</u>. |

# B.6 EXPANDING THE SENTENCE WITH PHRASES

A **phrase** is a group of related words that lacks a subject, a predicate, or both. A phrase cannot stand alone as a sentence. Phrases can appear at the beginning, middle, or end of a sentence.

WITHOUT PHRASES    I noticed the stain.

Sal researched the topic.

Manuela arose.

WITH PHRASES    <u>Upon entering the room</u>, I noticed the stain <u>on the expensive carpet</u>.

<u>At the local aquarium</u>, Sal researched the topic <u>of shark attacks</u>.

<u>An amateur astronomer</u>, Manuela arose <u>in the middle of the night</u> to observe the lunar eclipse but, <u>after waiting ten minutes in the cold</u>, gave up.

There are eight kinds of phrases: **noun; verb; prepositional;** three kinds of **verbal phrases** (**participial, gerund,** and **infinitive**); **appositive;** and **absolute.**

## Noun and Verb Phrases

A noun plus its modifiers is a **noun phrase** (*red shoes, the quiet house*). A main verb plus its helping verb is a **verb phrase** (*had been exploring, is sleeping;* see p. 524 on helping verbs.)

## Prepositional Phrases

A **prepositional phrase** consists of a preposition (for example, *in, above, with, at, behind*), an object of the preposition (a noun or pronoun), and any modifiers of the object. (See p. 536 for a list of common prepositions.) A prepositional phrase functions like an adjective (modifying a noun or pronoun) or an adverb (modifying a verb, adjective, or adverb). You can use prepositional phrases to tell more about people, places, objects, or actions. A prepositional phrase usually adds information about time, place, direction, manner, or degree.

### As Adjectives

The woman <u>with the briefcase</u> is giving a presentation <u>on meditation techniques</u>.

Both <u>of the telephones</u> <u>behind the partition</u> were ringing.

## As Adverbs

The fire drill occurred <u>in the morning</u>.

I was curious <u>about the new human resources director</u>.

The conference speaker came <u>from Australia</u>.

<u>With horror</u>, the crowd watched the rhinoceros's tether stretch <u>to the breaking point</u>.

A prepositional phrase can function as part of the complete subject or as part of the complete predicate, but should not be confused with the simple subject or simple predicate.

Pat <u>ducked quickly behind the potted fern</u>.

## Verbal Phrases

A **verbal** is a verb form that cannot function as the main verb of a sentence. The three kinds of verbals are **participles, gerunds,** and **infinitives.** A **verbal phrase** consists of a verbal and its modifiers.

## Participles and Participial Phrases

All verbs have two participles: present and past. The **present participle** is formed by adding *-ing* to the infinitive form (*walking, riding, being*). The **past participle** of regular verbs is formed by adding *-d* or *-ed* to the infinitive form (*walked, baked*). The past participle of irregular verbs has no set pattern (*ridden, been*). (See p. 525 for a list of common irregular verbs and their past participles.) Both the present participle and the past participle can function as adjectives modifying nouns and pronouns.

PAST PARTICIPLE AS ADJECTIVE          PRESENT PARTICIPLE AS ADJECTIVE

<u>Irritated</u>, Martha circled the <u>confusing</u> traffic rotary once again.

A **participial phrase** consists of a participle and any of its modifiers.

We listened for Isabella <u>climbing</u> the rickety stairs.

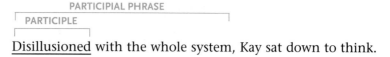

PARTICIPIAL PHRASE
PARTICIPLE

<u>Disillusioned</u> with the whole system, Kay sat down to think.

PARTICIPIAL PHRASE
PARTICIPLE

The singer, <u>having caught</u> a bad cold, canceled his performance.

## Gerunds and Gerund Phrases

A **gerund** is the present participle (the -*ing* form) of the verb used as a noun.

<u>Shoveling</u> is good exercise.

Rex enjoyed <u>gardening</u>.

A **gerund phrase** consists of a gerund and its modifiers. A gerund phrase, like a gerund, is used as a noun and can therefore function in a sentence as a subject, a direct or indirect object, an object of a preposition, a subject complement, or an appositive.

GERUND PHRASE

<u>Photocopying</u> the report took longer than Alice anticipated. [Subject]

GERUND PHRASE

The director considered <u>making</u> another monster movie. [Direct object]

GERUND PHRASE

She gave <u>running</u> three miles daily credit for her health. [Indirect object]

GERUND PHRASE

Before <u>learning</u> Greek, Omar spoke only English. [Object of the preposition]

GERUND PHRASE

Her business is <u>designing</u> collapsible furniture. [Subject complement]

GERUND PHRASE

Wayne's trick, <u>memorizing</u> license plates, has come in handy. [Appositive]

## Infinitives and Infinitive Phrases

The **infinitive** is the base form of the verb as it appears in the dictionary preceded by the word "to." An **infinitive phrase** consists of the word *to* plus the infinitive and any modifiers. An infinitive phrase can function as a noun, an adjective, or an adverb. When it is used as a noun, an infinitive phrase can be a subject, object, complement, or appositive.

INFINITIVE PHRASE

<u>To love</u> one's enemies is a noble goal. [Noun used as subject.]

INFINITIVE PHRASE

The season <u>to sell</u> bulbs is the fall. [Adjective modifying *season.*]

INFINITIVE PHRASE

The chess club met <u>to practice</u> for the state championship. [Adverb modifying *met.*]

Sometimes the *to* in an infinitive phrase is not written.

Frank helped us <u>learn</u> the new accounting procedure. [The *to* before *learn* is understood.]

*Note:* Do not confuse infinitive phrases with prepositional phrases beginning with the preposition *to.* In an infinitive phrase, *to* is followed by a verb; in a prepositional phrase, *to* is followed by a noun or pronoun.

## Appositive Phrases

An **appositive** is a noun that explains, restates, or adds new information about another noun. An **appositive phrase** consists of an appositive and its modifiers. (See p. 616 for punctuation of appositive phrases.)

APPOSITIVE

Claude Monet completed the painting <u>*Water Lilies*</u> around 1903. [Adds information about the noun *painting*]

APPOSITIVE PHRASE
APPOSITIVE

Francis, <u>my neighbor</u> with a large workshop, lent me a wrench. [Adds information about the noun *Francis*]

## Absolute Phrases

An **absolute phrase** consists of a noun or pronoun and any modifiers followed by a participle or a participial phrase (see p. 550). An absolute phrase modifies an entire sentence, not any particular word within the sentence. It can appear anywhere in a sentence and is set off from the rest of the sentence with a comma or commas. There may be more than one absolute phrase in a sentence.

ABSOLUTE PHRASE

The winter being over, the geese returned.

ABSOLUTE PHRASE

Senator Arden began his speech, his voice rising to be heard over the loud applause.

ABSOLUTE PHRASE

A vacancy having occurred, the hotel manager called the first name on the reservations waiting list.

## EXERCISE 8

**Directions:** Expand each of the following sentences by adding adjectives, adverbs, and/or phrases (prepositional, verbal, appositive, or absolute).

EXAMPLE     The professor lectured.

EXPANDED     *Being an expert on animal behavior, the professor lectured about animal-intelligence studies.*

1. Randall will graduate.     *Randall, my friend from grade school, will graduate from Camden County College this May.*

2. The race began.     *After a false start, the athletes lined up at the starting blocks and the race began.*

3. Wal-Mart is remodeling.     *Aiming for a new look, Wal-Mart is remodeling its stores.*

4. Hillary walked alone.     *Needing time to think, Hillary walked alone.*

5. Manuel repairs appliances.     *Manuel repairs appliances at his shop in Charlestown.*

6. The motorcycle was loud.     *The motorcycle was loud enough to attract the attention of pedestrians along the sidewalk.*

7. My term paper is due Tuesday.     *Now that I have an extension, my term paper is due Tuesday.*

8. I opened my umbrella.     *Hoping to stay dry, I opened my umbrella when it started to drizzle.*

9. Austin built a garage.     *Being skilled in construction, Austin built a garage at the side of his parents' house.*

10. Lucas climbs mountains.     *Lucas climbs mountains with the Appalachian Hiking Club.*

# B.7 EXPANDING THE SENTENCE WITH CLAUSES

A **clause** is a group of words that contains a subject and a predicate. A clause is either **independent** (also called **main**) or **dependent** (also called **subordinate**).

An **independent clause** can stand alone as a grammatically complete sentence.

INDEPENDENT CLAUSE    INDEPENDENT CLAUSE

SUBJECT PREDICATE   SUBJECT PREDICATE

The alarm sounded, and I awoke.

INDEPENDENT CLAUSE          INDEPENDENT CLAUSE

SUBJECT   PREDICATE       SUBJECT        PREDICATE

The scientist worried. The experiment might fail.

INDEPENDENT CLAUSE        INDEPENDENT CLAUSE

SUBJECT  PREDICATE      SUBJECT        PREDICATE

He bandaged his ankle. It had been sprained.

A **dependent clause** has a subject and a predicate, but it cannot stand alone as a grammatically complete sentence because it does not express a complete thought. Most dependent clauses begin with either a **subordinating conjunction** or a **relative pronoun**. These words connect the dependent clause to an independent clause.

### Common Subordinating Conjunctions

| | | |
|---|---|---|
| after | inasmuch as | that |
| although | in case that | though |
| as | in order that | unless |
| as if | insofar as | until |
| as far as | in that | when |
| as soon as | now that | whenever |
| as though | once | where |
| because | provided that | wherever |
| before | rather than | whether |
| even if | since | while |
| even though | so that | why |
| how | supposing that | |
| if | than | |

### Relative Pronouns

| | |
|---|---|
| that | which |
| what | who (whose, whom) |
| whatever | whoever (whomever) |

SUBORDINATING
CONJUNCTION    SUBJECT    PREDICATE

because the alarm sounded

SUBORDINATING
CONJUNCTION    SUBJECT    PREDICATE

that the experiment might fail

RELATIVE PRONOUN
(SUBJECT)    PREDICATE

which had been sprained

These clauses do not express complete thoughts and therefore cannot stand alone as sentences. When joined to independent clauses, however, dependent clauses function as adjectives, adverbs, and nouns and are known as **adjective** (or **relative**) **clauses**, **adverb clauses**, and **noun clauses**. Noun clauses can function as subjects, objects, or complements.

## Adjective Clause

DEPENDENT CLAUSE

He bandaged his ankle, <u>which had been sprained</u>. [Modifies *ankle*]

## Adverb Clause

DEPENDENT CLAUSE

<u>Because the alarm sounded</u>, I awoke. [Modifies *awoke*]

## Noun Clause

DEPENDENT CLAUSE

The scientist worried <u>that the experiment might fail</u>. [Direct object of *worried*]

Sometimes the relative pronoun or subordinating conjunction is implied or understood rather than stated. Also, a dependent clause may contain an implied predicate. When a dependent clause is missing an element that can clearly be supplied from the context of the sentence, it is called an **elliptical clause.**

ELLIPTICAL CLAUSE

The circus is more entertaining <u>than television</u> [is]. [*Is* is the understood predicate in the elliptical dependent clause.]

ELLIPTICAL CLAUSE

Canadian history is among the subjects [that] <u>the book discusses</u>. [*That* is the understood relative pronoun in the elliptical dependent clause.]

Relative pronouns are generally the subject or object in their clauses. *Who* and *whoever* change to *whom* and *whomever* when they function as objects (see p. 588).

# B.8 BASIC SENTENCE CLASSIFICATIONS

Depending on its structure, a sentence can be classified as one of four basic types: **simple**, **compound**, **complex**, or **compound-complex**.

## Simple Sentences

A **simple sentence** has one independent (main) clause and no dependent (subordinate) clauses (see p. 554). A simple sentence contains at least one subject and one predicate. It may have a compound subject, a compound predicate, and various phrases, but it has only one clause.

SUBJECT  PREDICATE

Sap rises.

SUBJECT          COMPOUND PREDICATE

In the spring the <u>sap</u> <u>rises</u> in the maple trees and <u>is boiled</u> to make a thick, delicious syrup.

## Compound Sentences

A **compound sentence** has at least two independent clauses and no dependent clauses (see p. 554). The two independent clauses are usually joined with a comma and a coordinating conjunction (*and, but, nor, or, for, so,* or *yet*). Sometimes the two clauses are joined with a semicolon and no coordinating conjunction or with a semicolon and a conjunctive adverb like *nonetheless* or *still* followed by a comma. (See p. 583 on conjunctive adverbs and p. 567 on punctuation.)

INDEPENDENT CLAUSE

Reading a novel by Henry James is not like reading a thriller, but with patience the rewards are greater.

INDEPENDENT CLAUSE

INDEPENDENT CLAUSE            INDEPENDENT CLAUSE

I set out to explore the North River near home; I ended up at
Charlie's Clam Bar.

## Complex Sentences

A **complex sentence** has one independent clause and one or more
dependent clauses (see p. 554). The clauses are joined by subordinating
conjunctions or relative pronouns (see p. 554).

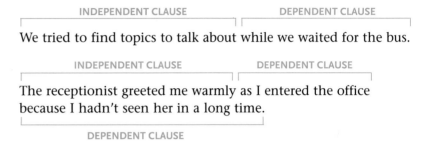

INDEPENDENT CLAUSE                    DEPENDENT CLAUSE

We tried to find topics to talk about while we waited for the bus.

INDEPENDENT CLAUSE              DEPENDENT CLAUSE

The receptionist greeted me warmly as I entered the office
because I hadn't seen her in a long time.

DEPENDENT CLAUSE

## Compound-Complex Sentences

A **compound-complex sentence** contains two or more independent
clauses and one or more dependent clauses (see p. 554).

DEPENDENT CLAUSE                    INDEPENDENT CLAUSE

If students work part-time, they must plan their studies carefully
and they must limit their social lives.

INDEPENDENT CLAUSE

INDEPENDENT CLAUSE          INDEPENDENT CLAUSE          INDEPENDENT CLAUSE

It was mid-March and the pond had begun to melt; I walked toward
it expectantly as I wondered if I could go skating one last time.

DEPENDENT CLAUSE            DEPENDENT CLAUSE

# EXERCISE 9

**Directions:** Combine each of the following pairs of sentences into a single sentence by forming independent and/or dependent clauses. You may need to add, change, or delete words.

EXAMPLE    **a.** The levee broke.

**b.** The flood waters rose rapidly.

COMBINED    *After the levee broke, the flood waters rose rapidly.*

1. **a.** Margot is a picky eater.

   **b.** Ivan, Margot's cousin, will eat anything.

   *While Margot is a picky eater, Ivan, Margot's cousin, will eat anything.*

2. **a.** Joe broke his wrist rollerblading.

   **b.** Joe started to wear protective gear.

   *After Joe broke his wrist rollerblading, he started to wear protective gear.*

3. **a.** Rick waited in line at the Department of Motor Vehicles.

   **b.** At the same time, Jean waited in line at the bank.

   *While Rick waited in line at the Department of Motor Vehicles, Jean waited in line at the bank.*

4. **a.** Beer is high in calories.

   **b.** Some beer companies now make low-calorie beer.

   *Since beer is high in calories, some beer companies now offer a low-calorie alternative.*

5. **a.** Keith says he is politically active.

   **b.** Keith is not registered to vote.

   *Although Keith says he is politically active, he not registered to vote.*

6. **a.** Miguel sprained his ankle.

   **b.** His friends drove him to the hospital.

   *When Miguel sprained his ankle, his friends drove him to the hospital.*

**7. a.** The boat sped by.

    **b.** The Coast Guard was in hot pursuit.

*The Coast Guard was in hot pursuit of the boat that sped by.*
_____

**8. a.** The weather report predicted rain.

    **b.** I brought my umbrella.

*Since the weather report predicted rain, I brought my umbrella.*
_____

**9. a.** Graffiti had been spray-painted on the subway wall.

    **b.** Maintenance workers were scrubbing it off.

*Maintenance workers were scrubbing off graffiti that had been spray-painted*

*on the subway wall.*

**10. a.** Shoppers were crowding around a display table.

    **b.** Everything on the table was reduced by 50 percent.

*Shoppers were crowding around a display table on which everything*

*was reduced by 50 percent.*

# Avoiding Sentence Errors

## C.1 SENTENCE FRAGMENTS

A complete sentence contains at least one subject and one verb and expresses a complete thought. It begins with a capital letter and ends with a period, question mark, or exclamation point (see p. 612). A **sentence fragment** is an incomplete sentence because either it lacks a subject, a verb, or both, or it is a dependent (subordinate) clause unattached to a complete sentence. In either case, it does not express a complete thought. Occasionally, a writer may knowingly use a fragment for effect or emphasis. This is known as an **intentional fragment.** However, it is best to avoid fragments in your writing; instead, use complete sentences.

| | |
|---|---|
| FRAGMENT | Walked across campus this afternoon. [This group of words lacks a subject.] |
| COMPLETE SENTENCE | Pete walked across campus this afternoon. |
| FRAGMENT | The car next to the fence. [This group of words lacks a verb.] |
| COMPLETE SENTENCE | The car next to the fence stalled. |
| FRAGMENT | Alert and ready. [This group of words lacks a subject and a verb.] |
| COMPLETE SENTENCE | Juan appeared alert and ready. |
| FRAGMENT | While I was waiting in line. [This group of words is a subordinate clause unattached to a complete sentence.] |
| COMPLETE SENTENCE | While I was waiting in line, I studied the faces of people walking by. |

## How to Spot Fragments

To find sentence fragments in your writing, use the following questions to evaluate each group of words:

1. **Does the group of words have a verb?** Be sure that the verb is a complete sentence verb and not a verbal or part of a verbal phrase (see p. 550).

COMPLETE SENTENCE     SENTENCE FRAGMENT

SENTENCE VERB     VERBAL

Doug swam laps every night. <u>To win the prize</u>.

COMPLETE SENTENCE     FRAGMENT

SENTENCE VERB     VERBAL

She felt very sleepy. <u>Wanting him to leave now</u>.

COMPLETE SENTENCE     FRAGMENT

SENTENCE VERB     VERBAL

Jason is excited. <u>Going to the interview tomorrow</u>.

COMPLETE SENTENCE     FRAGMENT

SENTENCE VERB     VERBAL

I am starting banjo lessons. <u>Beginning next week</u>.

Each of the underlined phrases needs to be either (1) rewritten as a complete sentence or (2) combined with a complete sentence.

REWRITTEN     Doug swam laps every night. He practiced to win the prize.

REWRITTEN     She felt very sleepy. She wanted him to leave now.

COMBINED     Jason is excited because he is going to the interview tomorrow.

COMBINED     Beginning next week, I am starting banjo lessons.

To distinguish between a complete sentence verb and a verbal, keep in mind the following rule: a sentence verb can change tense to show differences in time—past, present, and future. A verbal cannot demonstrate these shifts in time. You can change the sentence *I <u>have</u> a lot of homework* to *I <u>had</u> a lot of homework* or *I <u>will have</u> a lot of homework*, but the verbal phrase *<u>riding</u> a horse* cannot be changed to show differences in time.

2. **Does the group of words have a subject?** After you have found the verb, look for the subject. The subject is a noun or pronoun that performs or receives the action of the sentence (see p. 541). To find the subject, ask *who* or *what* performs or receives the action of the verb.

SUBJECT     VERB

The corner <u>bookstore</u> <u>opens</u> at noon. [*What* opens? The bookstore opens.]

Notice, however, what happens when you ask *who* or *what* about the following fragments:

> Will study math with a tutor. [*Who* will study? The question cannot be answered; no subject exists.]

> And walked away quickly. [*Who* walked away? Again, the question cannot be answered because there is no subject.]

Every sentence must have a subject. Even if one sentence has a clear subject, the sentence that follows it must also have a subject, or else it is a fragment.

SENTENCE    FRAGMENT

SUBJECT   VERB    VERB

> Peter slammed the door. And stormed out into the hall.

You know from the first sentence that it was Peter who stormed out, but the second group of words is nonetheless a fragment because it lacks a subject. Combining it with the first sentence would eliminate the problem.

> COMBINED    Peter slammed the door and stormed out into the hall.

Imperative sentences (sentences that command or suggest) have a subject that is usually not explicitly stated. They are not fragments.

> Follow me. [The subject *you* is understood: (*You*) Follow me.]

3. **Does the group of words begin with a subordinating conjunction (such as *after, although, as, because, however, since,* or *that*)?** A group of words beginning with a subordinating conjunction is a fragment unless that group of words is attached to an independent clause (see p. 554).

SUBORDINATING CONJUNCTION

> FRAGMENT    <u>While</u> I was waiting for the train.

INDEPENDENT CLAUSE

> COMPLETE SENTENCE    While I was waiting for the train, I saw Robert DeNiro.

SUBORDINATING CONJUNCTION

> FRAGMENT    <u>Although</u> the politician campaigned feverishly.

> COMPLETE SENTENCE    Although the politician campaigned feverishly, the public supported her opponent.

INDEPENDENT CLAUSE

You can also correct a fragment that is a dependent clause by omitting the subordinating conjunction and making the clause into an independent clause, a complete sentence.

> COMPLETE SENTENCE    I was waiting for the train.

> COMPLETE SENTENCE    The politician campaigned feverishly.

4. **Does the group of words begin with a relative pronoun (*that, what, whatever, which, who, whoever, whom, whomever, whose*)?** A group of words beginning with a relative pronoun is a fragment unless it forms a question with a subject and a verb or is attached to an independent clause.

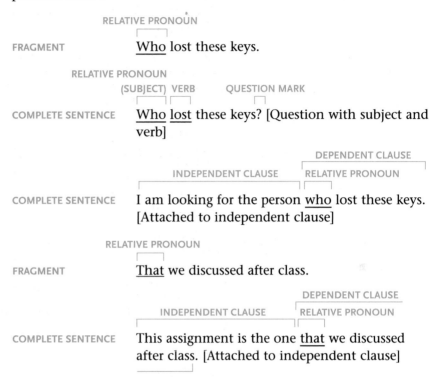

RELATIVE PRONOUN

FRAGMENT    Who lost these keys.

RELATIVE PRONOUN
(SUBJECT) VERB    QUESTION MARK

COMPLETE SENTENCE    Who lost these keys? [Question with subject and verb]

INDEPENDENT CLAUSE    DEPENDENT CLAUSE / RELATIVE PRONOUN

COMPLETE SENTENCE    I am looking for the person who lost these keys. [Attached to independent clause]

RELATIVE PRONOUN

FRAGMENT    That we discussed after class.

INDEPENDENT CLAUSE    DEPENDENT CLAUSE / RELATIVE PRONOUN

COMPLETE SENTENCE    This assignment is the one that we discussed after class. [Attached to independent clause]

Also check groups of words beginning with *how, when, where,* and *why.* If a clause beginning with one of these words neither asks a question nor is attached to an independent clause, then the word group is a fragment.

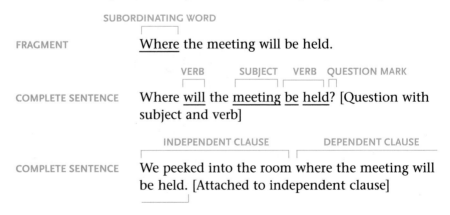

SUBORDINATING WORD

FRAGMENT    Where the meeting will be held.

VERB    SUBJECT    VERB    QUESTION MARK

COMPLETE SENTENCE    Where will the meeting be held? [Question with subject and verb]

INDEPENDENT CLAUSE    DEPENDENT CLAUSE

COMPLETE SENTENCE    We peeked into the room where the meeting will be held. [Attached to independent clause]

## How to Correct Fragments

1. **Attach the fragment to a complete sentence or an independent clause** (see p. 554).

DEPENDENT CLAUSE

FRAGMENT    While my boss was on the phone. She began to eat lunch.

| | DEPENDENT CLAUSE     INDEPENDENT CLAUSE |
|---|---|
| COMPLETE SENTENCE | While my boss was on the phone, she began to eat lunch. |

| | NO SENTENCE VERB |
|---|---|
| FRAGMENT | <u>Students who missed five classes</u>. They are ineligible for the final exam. |

| | SUBJECT                    SENTENCE VERB |
|---|---|
| COMPLETE SENTENCE | <u>Students</u> who missed five classes <u>are</u> ineligible for the final exam. |

| | NO SUBJECT |
|---|---|
| FRAGMENT | Marge sketched portraits all morning. <u>And read art history all afternoon</u>. |

| | SUBJECT          COMPOUND SENTENCE VERB |
|---|---|
| COMPLETE SENTENCE | <u>Marge</u> <u>sketched</u> portraits all morning and <u>read</u> art history all afternoon. |

2. **Remove the subordinating conjunction or relative pronoun and make sure that the remaining group of words has a subject and a sentence verb—that is, that it can stand alone as a complete sentence.**

| | |
|---|---|
| FRAGMENT | I did not finish the book. <u>Because its tedious style bored me</u>. |

| | INDEPENDENT CLAUSE |
|---|---|
| | SENTENCE VERB |
| COMPLETE SENTENCE | I did not finish the book. Its tedious style <u>bored</u> me. |
| | SUBJECT |

3. **Add the missing subject or verb or both.**

| | |
|---|---|
| FRAGMENT | The patient refused to pay her bill. <u>And then started complaining loudly</u>. |

| | SUBJECT ADDED |
|---|---|
| COMPLETE SENTENCE | The patient refused to pay her bill. Then <u>she</u> started complaining loudly. |

| | |
|---|---|
| FRAGMENT | The Winter Olympics were held in Torino. <u>Snowing every day</u>. |

| | SUBJECT ADDED |
|---|---|
| COMPLETE SENTENCE | The Winter Olympics were held in Torino. <u>It</u> <u>snowed</u> every day. |
| | SENTENCE VERB ADDED |

| | |
|---|---|
| FRAGMENT | I had to leave the car in the driveway. <u>The snow against the garage door</u>. |

COMPLETE SENTENCE    I had to leave the car in the driveway. The snow <u>had drifted</u> against the garage door.

SENTENCE VERB ADDED

## EXERCISE 10

**Directions:** Make each of the following sentence fragments a complete sentence by combining it with an independent clause, removing the subordinating conjunction or relative pronoun, or adding the missing subject or verb.

EXAMPLE    Many environmentalists are concerned about the spotted owl. Which is almost extinct.

COMPLETE SENTENCE    Many environmentalists are concerned about the spotted owl, which is almost extinct.

1. Renting a tape of the movie *Citizen Kane*. Jason learned more about the director Orson Welles by renting a tape of the movie *Citizen Kane*.

2. Spices that had been imported from India. The store stocked species that had been imported from India.

3. The police officer walked to Jerome's van. To give him a ticket. The police officer walked to Jerome's van to give him a ticket.

4. My English professor, with the cup of tea he brought to each class. My English teacher gestured with the cup of tea he brought to each class.

5. After the table was refinished. After the table was refinished, it was put on display.

6. Roberto memorized his lines. For the performance tomorrow night. Roberto memorized his lines for the performance tomorrow night.

7. A tricycle with big wheels, painted red. Athena pedaled by on a tricycle that was painted red and had big wheels.

8. On the shelf, an antique crock used for storing lard. An antique crock used for storing lard was on the shelf.

9. Because I always wanted to learn to speak Spanish. I spent a summer in Chile because I always wanted to learn to speak Spanish.

10. Looking for the lost keys. I was late for class. I was late for class because I spent so much time looking for the lost keys.

# C.2 RUN-ON SENTENCES AND COMMA SPLICES

Independent clauses contain both a subject and a predicate. When two independent clauses are joined in one sentence, they must be separated by a comma and a coordinating conjunction or by a semicolon. Failure to properly separate independent clauses creates the errors known as **run-on sentences** and **comma splices**.

A **run-on sentence** (or **fused sentence**) contains two independent clauses that are not separated by any punctuation or a coordinating conjunction (*and, but, nor, or, for, so, yet*).

A **comma splice** (or comma fault) contains two independent clauses joined only by a comma (the coordinating conjunction is missing). A comma by itself cannot join two independent clauses (see p. 554).

## How to Spot Run-on Sentences and Comma Splices

1. **You can often spot run-on sentences by reading them aloud.** Listen for a pause or a change in your voice. That may signal that you are moving from the first clause to the second. Read the following run-on sentences aloud, and see if you can hear where the two clauses in each should be separated.

   RUN-ON    We watched the football game then we ordered pizza.

   CORRECT    We watched the football game; then we ordered pizza.

   RUN-ON    My throat feels sore I hope I am not catching a cold.

   CORRECT    My throat feels sore; I hope I am not catching a cold.

2. **You can spot a comma splice by looking carefully at your use and placement of commas.** If you see a comma between two independent clauses but no coordinating conjunction after the comma, then you have probably spotted a comma splice.

   COMMA SPLICE    The average person watches 15 hours of television a week, my parents allow my brother only two hours a week.

   CORRECT    The average person watches 15 hours of television a

   COORDINATING CONJUNCTION

   week, but my parents allow my brother only two hours a week.

## How to Correct Run-on Sentences and Comma Splices

There are four ways to correct a run-on sentence or a comma splice. Not every run-on sentence or comma splice can be corrected in the same way. The method you choose will depend on the meaning of the clauses.

1. **Create two separate sentences.** End the first independent clause with a period. Begin the next with a capital letter.

   RUN-ON     We went for a walk in the woods we saw the leaves turning red and orange.

   CORRECT    We went for a walk in the woods. We saw the leaves turning red and orange.

2. **Use a semicolon.** Use a semicolon when the thoughts expressed in the independent clauses are closely related and you want to emphasize that relationship. (The word immediately following the semicolon does not begin with a capital letter unless it is a proper noun.)

   RUN-ON     It is unlikely that school taxes will increase this year citizens have expressed their opposition.

   CORRECT    It is unlikely that school taxes will increase this year; citizens have expressed their opposition.

*Note:* An independent clause containing a conjunctive adverb (such as *finally, however, meanwhile, otherwise,* or *therefore*) must be separated from another independent clause with a period or a semicolon. (See p. 534 for a list of conjunctive adverbs.) In most cases, the conjunctive adverb itself is set off with a comma or pair of commas.

   COMMA SPLICE    The road crew was repairing potholes, therefore traffic was snarled.

   CORRECT    The road crew was repairing potholes; therefore, traffic was snarled.

3. **Insert a comma and a coordinating conjunction (*and, but, for, nor, or, so, yet*).**

   RUN-ON     Americans are changing their eating habits they still eat too much red meat.

   COORDINATING CONJUNCTION

   CORRECT    Americans are changing their eating habits, <u>but</u> they still eat too much red meat.

4. **Make one clause subordinate to the other.** This method is especially effective when the idea expressed in one of the clauses is more important than the idea in the other clause. By adding a subordinating conjunction (such as *after, although, because,* or *until*), you can link a dependent clause to an independent clause. (See p. 568 for a list of subordinating conjunctions.) Be sure to use a subordinating conjunction

that explains the relationship between the dependent clause and the independent clause to which it is joined.

COMMA SPLICE    I left the store, I shut off all the lights.

DEPENDENT CLAUSE

SUBORDINATING CONJUNCTION    INDEPENDENT CLAUSE

CORRECT    <u>Before</u> I left the store, I shut off all the lights.

The subordinating conjunction *before* in the above sentence indicates the sequence in which the two actions were performed. In addition to time, subordinating conjunctions can indicate place, time, cause or effect, condition or circumstance, contrast, or manner.

| *Meaning* | *Subordinating Conjunction* | *Example* |
|---|---|---|
| place | where, wherever | I will go <u>wherever</u> you go. |
| time | after, before, when, until, once, while | <u>After</u> I left work, I went to the mall. |
| cause or effect | because, since, so that, that, as | I missed the bus <u>because</u> I overslept. |
| condition or circumstance | if, unless, as long as, in case, whenever, once, provided that | <u>If</u> I get an A on the paper, I'll be happy. |
| contrast | although, even though, even if, whereas, while | <u>Even though</u> I lost my job, I have to make my car payment. |
| manner | as, as if, as though | Marge acted <u>as if</u> she were angry. |

The dependent clause can be placed *before* or *after* the independent clause. If it is placed before the independent clause, put a comma at the end of it. Usually no comma is needed when the independent clause comes first.

COMMA SPLICE    I studied psychology, I was thinking about some of Freud's findings.

DEPENDENT CLAUSE    INDEPENDENT CLAUSE

CORRECT    When I studied psychology, I was thinking about some of Freud's findings.

INDEPENDENT CLAUSE    DEPENDENT CLAUSE

CORRECT    I was thinking about some of Freud's findings when I studied psychology.

You may add a dependent clause to a sentence that has more than one independent clause (see p. 557).

RUN-ON    We toured the hospital we met with its chief administrator she invited us to lunch.

DEPENDENT CLAUSE    INDEPENDENT CLAUSE

CORRECT    After we toured the hospital, we met with its chief administrator and she invited us to lunch.

INDEPENDENT CLAUSE

## EXERCISE 11

**Directions:** In the blank before each of the following word groups, identify if it is a run-on sentence (RO), a comma splice (CS), or a correct sentence (C). Revise the word groups that contain errors. Revisions will vary.

EXAMPLE    <u> CS </u>    The children chased the ball into the street, cars screeched to a halt.

<u> CS </u>    **1.** Inez packed for the business trip she remembered everything except her business cards.

<u> CS </u>    **2.** A limousine drove through our neighborhood, everybody wondered who was in it.

<u> RO </u>    **3.** The defendant pleaded not guilty the judge ordered him to pay the parking ticket.

<u> RO </u>    **4.** Before a big game, Louis, who is a quarterback, eats a lot of pasta and bread he says it gives him energy.

<u> CS </u>    **5.** Four of my best friends from high school have decided to go to law school, I have decided to become a paralegal.

<u> RO </u>    **6.** Felicia did not know what to buy her co-worker for his birthday, so she went to a lot of stores she finally decided to buy him a gift certificate.

<u> RO </u>    **7.** After living in a dorm room for three years, Jason found an apartment the rent was very high, so he had to get a job to pay for it.

<u> CS </u>    **8.** The cherry tree had to be cut down, it stood right where the new addition was going to be built.

<u> C </u>    **9.** Amanda worked every night for a month on the needlepoint pillow that she was making for her grandmother.

<u> CS </u>    **10.** Driving around in the dark, we finally realized we were lost, Dwight went into a convenience store to ask for directions.

# C.3 USES OF VERB TENSES

The **tense** of a verb expresses the time. It conveys whether an action, process, or occurrence takes place in the present, past, or future. There are twelve tenses in English, and each is used to express a particular time. (See p. 526 for information about how to form each tense.)

The **simple present tense** expresses actions that are occurring at the time of the writing or that occur regularly. The **simple past tense** is used for actions that have already occurred. The **simple future tense** is used for actions that will occur in the future.

| | |
|---|---|
| SIMPLE PRESENT | The chef <u>cooks</u> a huge meal. |
| SIMPLE PAST | The chef <u>cooked</u> a huge meal. |
| SIMPLE FUTURE | The chef <u>will cook</u> a huge meal. |

The **present perfect tense** is used for actions that began in the past and are still occurring in the present or are finished by the time of the writing. The **past perfect tense** expresses actions that were completed before other past actions. The **future perfect tense** is used for actions that will be completed in the future.

| | |
|---|---|
| PRESENT PERFECT | The chef <u>has cooked</u> a huge meal every night this week. |
| PAST PERFECT | The chef <u>had cooked</u> a huge meal before the guests canceled their reservation. |
| FUTURE PERFECT | The chef <u>will have cooked</u> a huge meal by the time we arrive. |

The six progressive tenses are used for continuing actions or actions in progress. The **present progressive tense** is used for actions that are in progress in the present. The **past progressive tense** expresses past continuing actions. The **future progressive tense** is used for continuing actions that will occur in the future. The **present perfect progressive, past perfect progressive**, and **future perfect progressive tenses** are used for continuing actions that are, were, or will be completed by a certain time.

| | |
|---|---|
| PRESENT PROGRESSIVE | The chef <u>is cooking</u> a huge meal this evening. |
| PAST PROGRESSIVE | The chef <u>was cooking</u> a huge meal when she ran out of butter. |
| FUTURE PROGRESSIVE | The chef <u>will be cooking</u> a huge meal all day tomorrow. |
| PRESENT PERFECT PROGRESSIVE | The chef <u>has been cooking</u> a huge meal since this morning. |
| PAST PERFECT PROGRESSIVE | The chef <u>had been cooking</u> a huge meal before the electricity went out. |
| FUTURE PERFECT PROGRESSIVE | The chef <u>will have been cooking</u> a huge meal for eight hours when the guests arrive. |

Writing all forms of a verb for all tenses and all persons (first, second, and third, singular and plural) is called **conjugating** the verb. Irregular verbs have an irregularly formed past tense and past participle (used in the past tense and the perfect tenses). (See p. 525 for a list of the forms of common irregular verbs.) Here is the complete conjugation for the regular verb *walk*.

**Conjugation of the Regular Verb *Walk***

|  | *Singular* | *Plural* |
|---|---|---|
| Simple present tense | I walk<br>you walk<br>he/she/it walks | we walk<br>you walk<br>they walk |
| Simple past tense | I walked<br>you walked<br>he/she/it walked | we walked<br>you walked<br>they walked |
| Simple future tense | I will (shall) walk<br>you will walk<br>he/she/it will walk | we will (shall) walk<br>you will walk<br>they will walk |
| Present perfect tense | I have walked<br>you have walked<br>he/she/it has walked | we have walked<br>you have walked<br>they have walked |
| Past perfect tense | I had walked<br>you had walked<br>he/she/it had walked | we had walked<br>you had walked<br>they had walked |
| Future perfect tense | I will (shall) have walked<br>you will have walked<br>he/she/it will have walked | we will (shall) have walked<br>you will have walked<br>they will have walked |
| Present progressive tense | I am walking<br>you are walking<br>he/she/it is walking | we are walking<br>you are walking<br>they are walking |
| Past progressive tense | I was walking<br>you were walking<br>he/she/it was walking | we were walking<br>you were walking<br>they were walking |
| Future progressive tense | I will be walking<br>you will be walking<br>he/she/it will be walking | we will be walking<br>you will be walking<br>they will be walking |
| Present perfect progressive tense | I have been walking<br>you have been walking<br>he/she/it has been walking | we have been walking<br>you have been walking<br>they have been walking |
| Past perfect progressive tense | I had been walking<br>you had been walking<br>he/she/it had been walking | we had been walking<br>you had been walking<br>they had been walking |
| Future perfect progressive tense | I will have been walking<br>you will have been walking<br>he/she/it will have been walking | we will have been walking<br>you will have been walking<br>they will have been walking |

Following are the simple present and simple past tenses for the irregular verbs *have, be,* and *do,* which are commonly used as helping verbs (see p. 524).

### Irregular Verbs *Have, Be,* and *Do*

|  | *Have* | *Be* | *Do* |
|---|---|---|---|
| Simple present tense | I have<br>you have<br>he/she/it has<br>we/you/they have | I am<br>you are<br>he/she/it is<br>we/you/they are | I do<br>you do<br>he/she/it does<br>we/you/they do |
| Simple past tense | I had<br>you had<br>he/she/it had<br>we/you/they had | I was<br>you were<br>he/she/it was<br>we/you/they were | I did<br>you did<br>he/she/it did<br>we/you/they did |

## Special Uses of the Simple Present Tense

Besides expressing actions that are occurring at the time of the writing, the simple present tense has several special uses.

| HABITUAL OR RECURRING ACTION | She <u>works</u> at the store every day. |
|---|---|
| GENERAL TRUTH | The sun <u>rises</u> in the east. |
| DISCUSSION OF LITERATURE | Gatsby <u>stands</u> on the dock and <u>gazes</u> in Daisy's direction. |
| THE FUTURE | He <u>leaves</u> for Rome on the 7:30 plane. |

## Emphasis, Negatives, and Questions

The simple present and the simple past tenses of the verb *do* are used with main verbs to provide emphasis, to form negative constructions with the adverb *not,* and to ask questions.

| SIMPLE PRESENT | Malcolm <u>does</u> <u>want</u> to work on Saturday. |
|---|---|
| SIMPLE PRESENT | He <u>does</u> <u>not</u> <u>want</u> to stay home alone. |
| SIMPLE PRESENT | <u>Do</u> you <u>want</u> to go with him? |
| SIMPLE PAST | Judy <u>did</u> <u>write</u> the proposal herself. |
| SIMPLE PAST | She <u>did</u> <u>not</u> <u>have</u> the money to pay professionals. |
| SIMPLE PAST | <u>Did</u> she <u>do</u> a good job? |

The modal verbs *can, could, may, might, must, shall, should, will,* and *would* are also used to add emphasis and shades of meaning to verbs. Modals are used only as helping verbs, never alone, and do not change form to indicate tense. Added to a main verb, they are used in the following situations, among others:

| | |
|---|---|
| CONDITION | We <u>can</u> play tennis if she gets here on time. |
| PERMISSION | You <u>may</u> have only one e-mail address. |
| POSSIBILITY | They <u>might</u> call us from the airport. |
| OBLIGATION | I <u>must</u> visit my mother tomorrow. |

## Common Mistakes to Avoid with Verb Tense

Check your writing carefully to make sure you have avoided these common mistakes with verb tenses.

1. **Make sure the endings *-d* and *-ed* (for past tenses) and *-s* and *-es* (for third-person singular, simple present tense) are on all verbs that require them.**

| | |
|---|---|
| INCORRECT | I <u>have walk</u> three miles since I left home. |
| CORRECT | I <u>have walked</u> three miles since I left home. |

2. **Use irregular verbs correctly** (see p. 525).

| | |
|---|---|
| INCORRECT | I will <u>lay</u> down for a nap. |
| CORRECT | I will <u>lie</u> down for a nap. |

3. **Use helping verbs where they are necessary to express the correct time.**

| | |
|---|---|
| INCORRECT | I <u>go</u> to class tomorrow. |
| CORRECT | I <u>will go</u> to class tomorrow. |

4. **Avoid colloquial language or dialect in writing.** Colloquial language is casual, everyday language often used in conversation. Dialect is the language pattern of a region or an ethnic group.

| | |
|---|---|
| INCORRECT | I didn't <u>get</u> the point of that poem. |
| CORRECT | I didn't <u>understand</u> the point of that poem. |
| INCORRECT | The train <u>be</u> gone. |
| CORRECT | The train <u>has</u> gone. |

Other common mistakes with verbs are failing to make the verb agree with the subject (see p. 578) and using inconsistent or shifting tenses (see p. 596).

### ESL Tip
**Verb Tense**

These are common mistakes for both native speakers of English and for students who speak English as a second language.

## EXERCISE 12

**Directions:** Correct any of the following sentences with an error in verb form or verb tense. If a sentence contains no errors, write "C" for correct beside it.

EXAMPLE     You ~~is~~ *are* next in line.

_____   1. Molly called and ask *ed* Jen if she wanted a ride to the basket-ball game.

_____   2. Eric went to a party last week and ~~meets~~ *met* a girl he knew in high school.

*C*   3. I cook spaghetti every Wednesday, and my family always enjoys it.

_____   4. A package c~~o~~*a*me in yesterday's mail for my office mate.

_____   5. Louisa ~~wears~~ *wore* a beautiful red dress to her sister's wedding last week.

_____   6. Marni answered a letter she receive*d* from her former employer.

_____   7. Rob waited until he was introduced, and then he r~~u~~*a*n on stage.

_____   8. The audience laughed loudly at the comedian's jokes and applaud*ed* ~~y~~ spontaneously at the funniest ones.

*C*   9. The group had ordered buffalo-style chicken wings, and it was not disappointed when the meal arrived.

_____   10. Julie spend*t*~~s~~ the afternoon answering correspondence when sales were slow.

# C.4 ACTIVE AND PASSIVE VOICES

When a verb is in the active voice, the subject performs the action of the verb. The direct object receives the action (see p. 545). The active voice expresses action in a lively, vivid, energetic way.

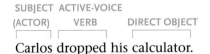

SUBJECT  ACTIVE-VOICE
(ACTOR)     VERB        DIRECT OBJECT

Carlos <u>dropped</u> his calculator.

SUBJECT   ACTIVE-VOICE
(ACTOR)        VERB   DIRECT OBJECT

The supermarket <u>gave</u> samples of prepared food.

When a verb is in the passive voice, the subject is the receiver of the action of the verb. The passive voice is formed by using an appropriate form of the verb *be* plus the past participle of the main verb. The actor is often expressed in a prepositional phrase introduced by the preposition *by*. Thus the passive voice tends to be wordier and to express action in a more indirect way than the active voice.

SUBJECT        PASSIVE-VOICE    OBJECT OF PREPOSITION
(RECEIVER)         VERB              (ACTOR)

The calculator <u>was dropped</u> by Carlos.

SUBJECT                    PASSIVE-VOICE    OBJECT OF PREPOSITION
(RECEIVER)                     VERB                (ACTOR)

Samples of prepared food <u>were given</u> by the supermarket.

Sometimes the actor is not expressed in a passive-voice sentence.

ACTIVE      I <u>did</u> not <u>remove</u> the Halloween decorations until Christmas.

PASSIVE    The Halloween decorations <u>were</u> not <u>removed</u> until Christmas.

As a general rule, you should use the active voice because it is more effective, simpler, and more direct than the passive. In two situations, however, the passive may be preferable: (1) if you do not know who performs the actions and (2) if the object of the action is more important than the actor.

PASSIVE    The handle of the dagger <u>had been wiped</u> clean of fingerprints. [It is not known who wiped the dagger.]

PASSIVE    The poem "Richard Corey" by Edwin Arlington Robinson <u>was discussed</u> in class. [The poem is more important than who discussed the poem.]

## ESL Tip
### Active Voice

In some languages students are required, as part of academic writing, to use the passive voice. In English, it is generally best to use the active voice because it is considered clearer and more effective. This is especially true if you are writing for academic or business purposes.

# EXERCISE 13

**Directions:** Revise each of the following sentences by changing the verb from passive voice to active voice.

EXAMPLE    The patient was operated on by an experienced surgeon.

REVISED    <u>An experienced surgeon operated on the patient.</u>

1. The coin collection was inherited by Roderick from his grandfather.

   Roderick inherited the coin collection from his grandfather.

2. A large stack of orders was delivered by the staff.

   The staff delivered a large stack of orders.

3. The presidential advisers were relied on by the president.

   The president relied on his advisers.

4. Ice cream was served to the children at the birthday party by one of the adults.

   One of the adults served ice cream to the children at the birthday party.

5. Tools were packed in a box by Terry.

   Terry packed tools in a box.

6. Scuba-diving equipment was handed to the students by the licensed instructor.

   The licensed instructor handed scuba-diving equipment to the students.

7. Alaska was visited by my parents last fall.

   My parents visited Alaska last fall.

8. A large order was placed by Wonderments Gift Shop.

   Wonderments Gift Shop placed a large order.

9. The shipment was delivered by United Parcel Service.

   *United Parcel Service delivered the shipment.*

10. Trash was collected and disposed of by the picnickers before they left for home.

    *The picnickers collected and disposed of trash before they left for home.*

# C.5 SUBJUNCTIVE MOOD

The **mood** of a verb conveys the writer's attitude toward the expressed thought. There are three moods in English. The **indicative mood** is used to make ordinary statements of fact and to ask questions. The **imperative mood** is used to give commands or make suggestions. The **subjunctive mood** is used to express wishes, requirements, recommendations, and statements contrary to fact (see p. 527).

INDICATIVE    Laurel <u>lies</u> in the sun every afternoon.

IMPERATIVE    <u>Lie</u> down and rest!

SUBJUNCTIVE   It is urgent that she <u>lie</u> down and rest.

The subjunctive mood requires some special attention because it uses verb tenses in unusual ways. Verbs in the subjunctive mood can be in the present, past, or perfect tense.

PRESENT    His mother recommended that he <u>apply</u> for the job.
           If truth <u>be</u> told, Jacob is luckier than he knows.

PAST       If she walked faster, she could get there on time.
           She ran as if she <u>were</u> five years old again.

PERFECT    If I <u>had known</u> his name, I would have said hello.

Here are several rules for using the subjunctive correctly:

1. **For requirements and recommendations, use the present subjunctive (the infinitive) for all verbs, including *be*.**

   Mr. Kenefick requires that his students <u>be</u> drilled in safety procedures.

   The dentist recommended that she <u>brush</u> her teeth three times a day.

2. **For present conditions contrary to fact and for present wishes, use the past subjunctive (the simple past tense) for all verbs; use *were* for the verb *be* for all subjects.**

   I wish that the workday <u>began</u> later.

   If Andrew <u>were</u> not so stubborn, he would admit that Adele is right.

3. **For past conditions contrary to fact and for past wishes, use the perfect subjunctive (*had* plus the past participle) for all verbs, including *be*.**

If Monty <u>had been</u> at home, he would have answered the phone when you called.

When Peter told me what an exciting internship he had abroad last summer, I wished I <u>had gone</u> with him.

# C.6 SUBJECT-VERB AGREEMENT

A subject and its verb must agree (be consistent) in person (first, second, third) and in number (singular, plural). (See p. 586 on the person of pronouns and p. 525 on verb forms in all persons and numbers.) The most common problems with subject-verb agreement occur with third-person present-tense verbs, which are formed for most verbs by adding *-s* or *-es* to the infinitive. (See pp. 525–526 for the present- and past-tense forms for certain irregular verbs.)

## Agreement Rules

1. **Singular subjects.** For a singular subject (one person, place, thing, or idea), use a singular form of the verb: *I dance, he dances, Sally dances, the dog dances; I am, you are, Sally is.*

2. **Plural subjects.** For a plural subject (two or more persons, places, things, or ideas), use the plural form of the verb: *we dance, they dance, the girls dance, the dogs dance; we are, they are, children are.*

## Common Mistakes to Avoid

1. **Third-person singular.** Do not omit the *-s* or *-es* for a present-tense verb used with the pronoun *he, she,* or *it* or any singular noun.

    INCORRECT    <u>She</u> <u>watch</u> the training video.

    CORRECT    <u>She</u> <u>watches</u> the training video.

    INCORRECT    <u>Professor Simmons</u> <u>pace</u> while he lectures.

    CORRECT    <u>Professor Simmons</u> <u>paces</u> while he lectures.

2. **Compound subjects.** Two or more subjects joined by the coordinating conjunction *and* require a plural verb, even if one or both of the subjects are singular.

    INCORRECT    <u>Anita</u> and <u>Mark</u> <u>plays</u> cards.

    CORRECT    <u>Anita</u> and <u>Mark</u> <u>play</u> cards.

When both of the subjects refer to the same person or thing, however, use a singular verb.

> The <u>president</u> and <u>chairman of the board</u> <u>is</u> in favor of more aggressive marketing.

When a compound subject is joined by the conjunction *or* or *nor* or the correlative conjunctions *either/or, neither/nor, both/and, not/but,* or *not only/but also,* the verb should agree in number with the subject nearer to it.

> Neither the <u>books</u> <u>nor</u> the <u>article</u> <u>was</u> helpful to my research.

> <u>Sarah</u> <u>or</u> the <u>boys</u> <u>are</u> coming tomorrow.

3. **Verbs before subjects.** When a verb comes before a subject, as in sentences beginning with *here* or *there,* it is easy to make an agreement error. Because *here* and *there* are adverbs, they are never subjects of a sentence and do not determine the correct form of the verb. Look for the subject *after* the verb, and, depending on its number, choose a singular or plural verb.

SINGULAR  SINGULAR
VERB    SUBJECT
> There <u>is</u> a <u>bone</u> in my soup.

PLURAL   PLURAL
VERB    SUBJECT
> There <u>are</u> two <u>bones</u> in my soup.

4. **Words between subject and verb.** Words, phrases, and clauses coming between the subject and verb do not change the fact that the verb must agree with the subject. To check that the verb is correct, mentally cancel everything between the subject and its verb to see if the verb agrees in number with its subject.

SINGULAR                    SINGULAR
SUBJECT                      VERB
> The new <u>list</u> of degree requirements <u>comes</u> out in the spring.

PLURAL                      PLURAL
SUBJECT                      VERB
> <u>Expenses</u> surrounding the sale of the house <u>were</u> unexpectedly low.

Phrases beginning with prepositions such as *along with, as well as,* and *in addition to* are not part of the subject and should not be considered in determining if the verb is singular or plural.

SINGULAR SUBJECT
> The <u>lamp</u>, together with some plates, glasses, and china teacups, <u>was broken</u> during the move.
SINGULAR VERB

5. **Indefinite pronouns as subjects.** Some indefinite pronouns (such as *everyone, neither, anybody, nobody, one, something,* and *each*) take a singular verb (see p. 522).

(see p. 522)

<u>Everyone</u> appreciates the hospital's volunteers.

Of the two applicants, <u>neither</u> <u>seems</u> well qualified.

The indefinite pronouns *both, many, several,* and *few* always take a plural verb. Some indefinite pronouns, such as *all, any, most, none,* and *some,* may take either a singular or plural verb. Treat the indefinite pronoun as singular if it refers to something that cannot be counted and as plural if it refers to more than one of something that can be counted.

<u>Some</u> of the ice <u>is</u> still on the road.

<u>Some</u> of the ice cubes <u>are</u> still in the tray.

<u>All</u> of the spaghetti <u>tastes</u> overcooked.

<u>All</u> of the spaghetti dishes <u>taste</u> too spicy.

6. **Collective nouns.** A collective noun refers to a group of people or things (*audience, class, flock, jury, team, family*). When the noun refers to the group as one unit, use a singular verb.

The <u>herd</u> <u>stampedes</u> toward us.

When the noun refers to the group members as separate individuals, use a plural verb.

The <u>herd</u> <u>scatter</u> in all directions.

7. **Nouns with plural forms but singular meaning.** Some words appear plural (that is, they end in *-s* or *-es*) but have a singular meaning. *Measles, hysterics, news,* and *mathematics* are examples. Use a singular verb with them.

<u>Mathematics</u> <u>is</u> a required course.

*Note:* Other nouns look plural and have singular meanings, but take a plural verb: *braces, glasses, trousers, slacks, jeans, jodhpurs,* and *pajamas.* Even though they refer to a single thing (to one pair of jeans, for example), these words take a plural verb.

His <u>pajamas</u> <u>were covered</u> with pictures of tumbling dice.

8. **Relative pronouns in adjective clauses.** The relative pronouns *who, which,* and *that* sometimes function as the subject of an adjective clause. When the relative pronoun refers to a singular noun, use a singular verb. When the pronoun refers to a plural noun, use a plural verb.

Anita is a person <u>who</u> never <u>forgets</u> faces. [*Who* refers to *person,* which is singular.]

The students <u>who</u> lost their keys <u>are</u> here. [*Who* refers to *students,* which is plural.]

## EXERCISE 14

**Directions:** Circle the verb that correctly completes each sentence.

EXAMPLE    Everybody (like, likes) doughnuts for breakfast.

1. Physics (is, are) a required course for an engineering degree.

2. Most of my courses last semester (was, were) in the morning.

3. The orchestra members who (is, are) carrying their instruments will be able to board the plane first.

4. Suzanne (sing, sings) a touching version of "America the Beautiful."

5. Here (is, are) the performers who juggle plates.

6. Kin Lee and his parents (travel, travels) to Ohio tomorrow.

7. A box of old and valuable stamps (is, are) in the safety deposit box at the bank.

8. The family (sit, sits) on different chairs arranged throughout the attorney's conference room.

9. Judith and Erin (arrive, arrives) at the train station at eleven o'clock.

10. Directions for operating the machine (is, are) posted on the wall.

## C.7 PRONOUN-ANTECEDENT AGREEMENT

A pronoun must agree with its **antecedent,** the word it refers to or replaces, in person (first, second, or third), in number (singular or plural), and in gender (masculine, feminine, or neuter).

Ronald attended the meeting, but I did not have a chance to talk with him. [The third-person, masculine, singular pronoun *him* agrees with its antecedent, *Ronald.*]

We had planned to call our sister, but her line was busy. [*Our* agrees with its antecedent, *We; her* agrees with its antecedent, *sister.*]

### Agreement Rules

1. **Use a singular pronoun to refer to or replace a singular noun.** (A singular noun names one person, place, or thing.)

Juanita filed her report promptly.

2. **Use a plural pronoun to refer to or replace a plural noun.** (A plural noun names two or more persons, places, or things.)

The <u>shirts</u> are hung on <u>their</u> hangers.

3. **Use singular pronouns to refer to indefinite pronouns that are singular in meaning.**

| | | | | |
|---|---|---|---|---|
| another | each | everything | no one | somebody |
| anybody | either | neither | nothing | someone |
| anyone | everybody | nobody | one | something |
| anything | everyone | none | other | |

SINGULAR      SINGULAR
ANTECEDENT   PRONOUN

<u>Someone</u> left <u>her</u> handbag under this table.

SINGULAR ANTECEDENT                SINGULAR COMPOUND PRONOUN

<u>Everyone</u> in the office must do <u>his or her</u> own photocopying.

*Note:* To avoid the awkwardness of *his or her,* consider rephrasing your sentence with a plural antecedent and plural pronoun.

PLURAL ANTECEDENT    PLURAL PRONOUN

Office <u>workers</u> must do <u>their</u> own photocopying.

4. **Use a plural pronoun to refer to indefinite pronouns that are plural in meaning.**

both     few     many     several

<u>Both</u> of the journalists said that <u>they</u> could see no violations of the cease-fire.

5. **The indefinite pronouns *all, any, most, none,* and *some* can be singular or plural, depending on how they are used.** If the indefinite pronoun refers to something that cannot be counted, use a singular pronoun to refer to it. If the indefinite pronoun refers to something that can be counted, use a plural pronoun to refer to it.

<u>Most</u> of the voters feel <u>they</u> can make a difference.

<u>Most</u> of the air on airplanes is recycled repeatedly, so <u>it</u> becomes stale.

6. **Use a plural pronoun to refer to a compound antecedent joined by *and,* unless both parts of the compound refer to the same person, place, or thing.**

PLURAL ANTECEDENT        PLURAL PRONOUN

<u>My girlfriend and I</u> planned <u>our</u> wedding.

SINGULAR ANTECEDENT          SINGULAR PRONOUN

<u>My neighbor and best friend</u> started <u>her</u> book bindery at the local warehouse.

7. **When antecedents are joined by** *or, nor, either/or, neither/nor,* *both/and, not/but,* **or** *not only/but also,* **the pronoun agrees in number with the nearer antecedent.**

<u>Neither his brothers nor Sam</u> has made <u>his</u> plane reservations.

<u>Neither Sam or his brothers</u> have made <u>their</u> plane reservations.

*Note:* Two or more singular antecedents joined by *or* or *nor* require a singular pronoun.

<u>Neither Larry nor Richard</u> signed <u>his</u> name legibly.

<u>Eva or Anita</u> will bring <u>her</u> saxophone.

8. **Collective nouns refer to a specific group** *(army, class, family).* When the group acts as a unit, use a singular pronoun to refer to the noun. When each member of the group acts individually, use a plural pronoun to refer to the noun.

The <u>band</u> marched <u>its</u> most intricate formation.

The <u>band</u> found <u>their</u> seats in the bleachers but could not see the game because the sun was in <u>their</u> eyes.

## EXERCISE 15

**Directions:** Revise the sentences below that contain agreement errors. If a sentence contains no errors, write a "C" for correct in the blank.

EXAMPLE     Somebody dropped ~~their~~ ring down the drain.    *his or her*

_____C_____  1. Many of the residents of the neighborhood have had their homes tested for radon.

_____  2. Each college instructor establishes ~~their~~ own grading policies.    *his or her*

_____  3. The apples fell from ~~its~~ tree.    *their*

_____  4. Anyone may submit ~~their~~ painting to the contest.    *his or her*

_____C_____  5. All the engines manufactured at the plant have their vehicle-identification numbers stamped on.

_____  6. No one requested that the clerk gift-wrap ~~their~~ package.    *his or her*

_____  7. Either Professor Judith Marcos or her assistant, Maria, graded the exams, writing ~~their~~ comments in the margins.    *her*

_____  8. James or his parents sails the boat every weekend.

_____ 9. Few classes were canceled because of the snowstorm; ~~it~~ *they* met as regularly scheduled.

_____ 10. Not only Ricky but also the Carters will take ~~his~~ *their* children to Disneyland this summer.

## C.8 PRONOUN REFERENCE

A pronoun refers to or replaces a noun or pronoun previously mentioned, called the pronoun's **antecedent.** As you write, you must always make sure that a reader knows to which noun or pronoun a pronoun refers. The antecedent of each pronoun must be clear. Sometimes you may need to reword a sentence to solve a problem of unclear antecedent.

INCORRECT   Lois walked with Pam because <u>she</u> did not know the route. [Who did not know the route? The antecedent of *she* is unclear.]

CORRECT   Lois did not know the route, so she walked with Pam.

### How to Use Pronouns Correctly

1. **A pronoun may refer to two or more nouns in a compound antecedent.**

   <u>Mark and Dennis</u> combined <u>their</u> efforts to fix the leaky faucet.

2. **Avoid using a pronoun that could refer to more than one possible antecedent.**

   INCORRECT   Rick told Garry that <u>he</u> was right.

   CORRECT   Rick told Garry, "You are right."

3. **Avoid using vague pronouns like *they* and *it* that often have no clear antecedent.**

   INCORRECT   <u>It</u> says in the paper that K-Mart is expanding the Williamsville store.

   CORRECT   <u>The article</u> in the paper says that K-Mart is expanding the Williamsville store.

   INCORRECT   <u>They</u> told me that we were required to wear surgeons' masks to view the newborns.

   CORRECT   <u>The obstetrics nurses</u> told me that we were required to wear surgeons' masks to view the newborns.

INCORRECT    On the bulletin boards, <u>it</u> says that there is a fire drill today.

CORRECT    <u>The notice</u> on the bulletin board says that there is a fire drill today.

4. **Avoid unnecessary or repetitious pronouns.**

INCORRECT    My sister <u>she</u> said that she lost her diamond ring.

CORRECT    My sister said that she lost her diamond ring.

5. **Be sure to use the relative pronouns *who, whom, which,* and *that* with the appropriate antecedent.** *Who* and *whom* refer to persons or named animals. *That* and *which* refer to unnamed animals and to things.

<u>Mary Anne</u> was the team member <u>who</u> scored the most points this year.

<u>Dublin, who</u> is a golden retriever, barked at everyone.

My sister gave me a ring <u>that</u> has three opals.

Highway 33, <u>which</u> has ten hairpin turns, is difficult to drive.

6. **Use *one* if you are not referring specifically to the reader.** Use the second-person pronoun *you* only to refer to the reader. In academic writing, avoid using *you.*

INCORRECT    Last year, <u>you</u> had to watch the news every night to keep up with world events.

CORRECT    Last year, <u>one</u> had to watch the news every night to keep up with world events.

7. **Place the pronoun close to its antecedent so that the relationship is clear.**

INCORRECT    Margaux found a <u>shell</u> on the beach <u>that</u> her sister wanted.

CORRECT    On the beach Margaux found a <u>shell</u> <u>that</u> her sister wanted.

# EXERCISE 16

**Directions:** Revise each of the following sentences to correct problems in pronoun reference. If a sentence contains no errors, write a "C" for correct in the blank. *Corrected sentences will vary.*

EXAMPLE    It said that the grades would be posted on Tuesday.

REVISED    *The professor's note said that the grades would be posted on Tuesday.*

_____    1. The puppy whom my sister brought home was quite cute.

_____    2. Laverne and Louise they pooled their money to buy a new stereo system.

_____    3. They said on the news that the naval base will be shut down.

___C___    4. The street that was recently widened is where I used to work.

_____    5. Ivan sat on the couch in the living room that he had bought yesterday.

_____    6. You should highlight in your textbooks for higher comprehension.

_____    7. Christina handed Maggie the plate she had bought at the flea market.

_____    8. Bridget found the cake mix in the aisle with the baking supplies that she needed for tonight's dessert.

_____    9. The answering machine who answered the phone beeped several times.

_____    10. It said in the letter that my payment was late.

## C.9 PRONOUN CASE

A pronoun changes **case** depending on its grammatical function in a sentence. Pronouns may be in the **subjective case**, the **objective case**, or the **possessive case**.

### PERSONAL PRONOUNS

| *Singular* | *Subjective* | *Objective* | *Possessive* |
|---|---|---|---|
| First person | I | me | my, mine |
| Second person | you | you | your, yours |
| Third person | he, she, it | him, her, it | his, her, hers, its |

| *Plural* | *Subjective* | *Objective* | *Possessive* |
|---|---|---|---|
| First person | we | us | our, ours |
| Second person | you | you | your, yours |
| Third person | they | them | their, theirs |

### RELATIVE OR INTERROGATIVE PRONOUNS

| | *Subjective* | *Objective* | *Possessive* |
|---|---|---|---|
| Singular and plural | who | whom | whose |
| | whoever | whomever | |

## Pronouns in the Subjective Case

Use the **subjective case** (also known as the **nominative case**) when the pronoun functions as the subject of a sentence or clause (see p. 541) or as a subject complement (also known as a predicate nominative; see p. 544). A predicate nominative is a noun or pronoun that follows a linking verb and identifies or renames the subject of the sentence.

SUBJECT

<u>She</u> has won recognition as a landscape architect.

Cathie volunteers at the local hospital. The most faithful volunteer is <u>she</u>.

SUBJECT COMPLEMENT

The subjective case is also used when a pronoun functions as an appositive to a subject or subject complement (see p. 544).

The only two seniors, <u>she</u> and her best friend, won the top awards.

## Pronouns in the Objective Case

Use the objective case when a pronoun functions as a direct object, indirect object, or object of a preposition (see pp. 545 and 546).

DIRECT OBJECT

George helped <u>her</u> with the assignment.

INDIRECT OBJECT

George gave <u>her</u> a book.

OBJECTS OF THE PREPOSITION

George gave the book to <u>him</u> and <u>her</u>.

The objective case is also used when the pronoun functions as the subject of an infinitive phrase or an appositive to an object.

SUBJECT OF INFINITIVE      INFINITIVE PHRASE

I wanted <u>him</u> to go straight home.

DIRECT OBJECT          APPOSITIVE TO OBJECT

The district manager chose two <u>representatives</u>, Marnie and <u>me</u>.

*Note:* When a sentence has a compound subject or compound objects, you may have trouble determining the correct pronoun case. To determine how the pronoun functions, mentally recast the sentence without the noun or other pronoun in the compound construction. Determine how the pronoun functions by itself and then decide which case is correct.

SUBJECTIVE CASE

They and Mary Jo brought the beverages. [Think: "*They* brought the beverages." *They* is the subject of the sentence, so the subjective case is correct.]

OBJECTIVE CASE

Behind you and <u>me</u>, the drapery rustled. [Think: "Behind *me*." *Me* is the object of the preposition *behind,* so the objective case is correct.]

## Pronouns in the Possessive Case

Possessive pronouns indicate to whom or to what something belongs. The possessive pronouns *mine, yours, his, hers, its, ours,* and *theirs* function just as nouns do.

SUBJECT

<u>Hers</u> is the letterhead with the bright blue lettering.

DIRECT OBJECT

I liked <u>hers</u> the best.

The possessive pronouns *my, your, his, her, its, our,* and *their* are used as adjectives to modify nouns and gerunds (see p. 530).

<u>Our</u> high-school reunion surprised everyone by <u>its</u> size.

<u>Your</u> attending that reunion will depend on <u>your</u> travel schedule.

## *Who* and *Whom* As Interrogative Pronouns

When *who, whoever, whom,* and *whomever* introduce questions, they are interrogative pronouns. How an interrogative pronoun functions in a clause determines its case. Use *who* or *whoever* (the subjective case) when the interrogative pronoun functions as a subject or subject complement (see p. 544). Use *whom* or *whomever* (the objective case) when the interrogative pronoun functions as a direct object or an object of a preposition.

SUBJECT

SUBJECTIVE CASE    <u>Who</u> is there?

OBJECT OF PREPOSITION

OBJECTIVE CASE    To <u>whom</u> did you give the letter?

## *Who* and *Whom* As Relative Pronouns

When *who, whoever, whom,* and *whomever* introduce subordinate clauses, they are relative pronouns. How a relative pronoun functions in a clause determines its case. Use *who* or *whoever* (subjective case) when a relative pronoun functions as the subject of the subordinate clause. Use *whom* or *whomever* (objective case) when a relative pronoun functions as an object in the subordinate clause.

SUBJECTIVE CASE     The lecturer, <u>who</u> is a journalist from New York, speaks with great insight and wit. [*Who* is the subject of the subordinate clause.]

OBJECTIVE CASE     The journalist, <u>whom</u> I know from college days, came to give a lecture. [*Whom* is the direct object of the verb *know* in the subordinate clause.]

# C.10 CORRECT ADJECTIVE AND ADVERB USE

Adjectives and adverbs modify, describe, explain, qualify, or restrict the words they modify (see pp. 529 and 533). **Adjectives** modify nouns and pronouns. **Adverbs** modify verbs, adjectives, and other adverbs; adverbs can also modify phrases, clauses, or whole sentences.

ADJECTIVES     <u>red</u> car; the <u>quiet</u> one

ADVERBS     <u>quickly</u> finish; <u>only</u> four reasons; <u>very</u> angrily

## Comparison of Adjectives and Adverbs

**Positive** adjectives and adverbs modify but do not involve any comparison: *green, bright, lively.*

**Comparative** adjectives and adverbs compare two persons, things, actions, or ideas.

COMPARATIVE ADJECTIVE     Michael is <u>taller</u> than Bob.

COMPARATIVE ADVERB     Antonio reacted <u>more calmly</u> than Robert.

Here is how to form comparative adjectives and adverbs. (Consult your dictionary if you are unsure of the form of a particular word.)

1. **If the adjective or adverb has one syllable, add *-er*. For certain two-syllable words, also add *-er*.**

   cold → colder      slow → slower      narrow → narrower

2. **For most words of two or more syllables, place the word *more* in front of the word.**

   reasonable → more reasonable      interestingly → more interestingly

3. **For two-syllable adjectives ending in -*y*, change the -*y* to -*i* and add -*er*.**

drowsy → drowsier      lazy → lazier

**Superlative** adjectives and adverbs compare more than two persons, things, actions, or ideas.

SUPERLATIVE ADJECTIVE      Michael is the <u>tallest</u> member of the team.

SUPERLATIVE ADVERB      She studied <u>most diligently</u> for the test.

Here is how to form superlative adjectives and adverbs:

1. **Add -*est* to one-syllable adjectives and adverbs and to certain two-syllable words.**

cold → coldest      fast → fastest      narrow → narrowest

2. **For most words of two or more syllables, place the word *most* in front of the word.**

reasonable → most reasonable      interestingly → most interestingly

3. **For two-syllable adjectives ending in -*y*, change the -*y* to -*i* and add -*est*.**

drowsy → drowsiest      lazy → laziest

## Irregular Adjectives and Adverbs

Some adjectives and adverbs form their comparative and superlative forms in irregular ways.

| *Positive* | *Comparative* | *Superlative* |
|---|---|---|
| **Adjectives** | | |
| good | better | best |
| bad | worse | worst |
| little | littler, less | littlest, least |
| **Adverbs** | | |
| well | better | best |
| badly | worse | worst |
| **Adjectives and Adverbs** | | |
| many | more | most |
| some | more | most |
| much | more | most |

## Common Mistakes to Avoid

1. **Do not use adjectives to modify verbs, other adjectives, or adverbs.**

INCORRECT      Peter and Mary take each other <u>serious</u>.

CORRECT      Peter and Mary take each other <u>seriously</u>. [Modifies the verb *take*]

2. **Do not use the adjectives *good* and *bad* when you should use the adverbs *well* and *badly*.**

   INCORRECT  Juan did <u>good</u> on the exam.

   CORRECT  Juan did <u>well</u> on the exam. [Modifies the verb *did*]

3. **Do not use the adjectives *real* and *sure* when you should use the adverbs *really* and *surely*.**

   INCORRECT  Jan scored <u>real</u> well on the exam.

   CORRECT  Jan scored <u>really</u> well on the exam. [Modifies the adverb *well*]

   INCORRECT  I <u>sure</u> was surprised to win the lottery.

   CORRECT  I <u>surely</u> was surprised to win the lottery. [Modifies the verb *was surprised*]

4. **Do not use *more* or *most* with the *-er* or *-est* form of an adjective or adverb.** Use one form or the other, according to the rules above.

   INCORRECT  That was the <u>most</u> <u>tastiest</u> dinner I've ever eaten.

   CORRECT  That was the <u>tastiest</u> dinner I've ever eaten.

5. **Avoid double negatives—that is, two negatives in the same clause.**

   INCORRECT  He did <u>not</u> want <u>nothing</u> in the refrigerator.

   CORRECT  He did <u>not</u> want <u>anything</u> in the refrigerator.

6. **When using the comparative and superlative forms of adverbs, do not create an incomplete comparison.**

   INCORRECT  The heater works <u>more efficiently</u>. [More efficiently than what?]

   CORRECT  The heater works <u>more efficiently than it did before we had it repaired</u>.

7. **Do not use the comparative form for adjectives and adverbs that have no degree.** It is incorrect to write, for example, *more square, most perfect, more equally,* or *most straight.* Do not use a comparative or superlative form for any of the following adjectives and adverbs:

   *Adjectives*

   | complete | equal | infinite | pregnant | unique |
   |----------|-------|----------|----------|--------|
   | dead | eternal | invisible | square | universal |
   | empty | favorite | matchless | supreme | vertical |
   | endless | impossible | parallel | unanimous | whole |

   *Adverbs*

   | endlessly | infinitely | uniquely |
   |-----------|------------|----------|
   | equally | invisibly | universally |
   | eternally | perpendicularly | |
   | impossibly | straight | |

## EXERCISE 17

**Directions:** Revise each of the following sentences so that all adjectives and adverbs are used correctly. If the sentence is correct, mark "C" in the blank provided. *Corrected sentences will vary.*

EXAMPLE    I answered the question polite.

_____   **1.** Michael's apartment was more expensive.

_____   **2.** When I heard the man and woman sing the duet, I decided that the woman sang best.

___*C*___   **3.** Our local movie reviewer said that the film's theme song sounded badly.

_____   **4.** The roller coaster was excitinger than the merry-go-round.

_____   **5.** *The Scarlet Letter* is more good than *War and Peace*.

_____   **6.** Susan sure gave a rousing speech.

_____   **7.** Last week's storm seemed worst than a tornado.

_____   **8.** Some women thought that the Equal Rights Amendment would guarantee that women are treated more equally.

_____   **9.** Taking the interstate is the most fast route to the outlet mall.

_____   **10.** Professor Reed had the better lecture style of all my instructors.

# D

# Writing Effective Sentences

## D.1 MISPLACED AND DANGLING MODIFIERS

A **modifier** is a word, phrase, or clause that describes, qualifies, or limits the meaning of another word.

WORD — She wore a <u>red</u> dress. [The adjective "red" describes the dress.]

PHRASE — I like the taste <u>of vanilla ice cream</u>. [The phrase "of vanilla ice cream" qualifies the word "taste."]

CLAUSE — The boy <u>who fell from the horse</u> was hospitalized. [The clause "who fell from the horse" explains which boy was hospitalized.]

Modifiers that are not correctly placed can make a sentence confusing.

### Misplaced Modifiers

**Misplaced modifiers** do not describe or explain the words the writer intended them to. A misplaced modifier often appears to modify the wrong word or can leave the reader confused as to which word it does modify.

MISPLACED — Max bought a chair at the used-furniture shop <u>that was large and dark</u>. [Was the chair or the furniture shop large and dark?]

MISPLACED    The instructor announced that the term paper was due on April 25 <u>at the beginning of class</u>. [Are the papers due at the beginning of class on the 25th, or did the instructor make the announcement at the beginning of class?]

You can easily avoid misplaced modifiers if you make sure that modifiers immediately precede or follow the words they modify.

CORRECT    Max bought a chair <u>that was large and dark</u> at the used-furniture shop.

CORRECT    Max bought a <u>large, dark</u> chair at the used-furniture shop.

CORRECT    <u>At the beginning of class</u>, the instructor announced that the term paper was due on April 25.

## Dangling Modifiers

**Dangling modifiers** do not clearly describe or explain any part of the sentence. Dangling modifiers create confusion and sometimes unintentional humor. To avoid dangling modifiers, make sure that each modifier has a clear antecedent.

DANGLING    <u>Rounding the curve</u>, a fire <u>hydrant</u> was hit by the speeding car. [The modifier suggests that the hydrant rounded the curve.]

CORRECT    <u>Rounding the curve</u>, the speeding <u>car</u> hit the fire hydrant. [Modifies *car*]

DANGLING    <u>Uncertain of what courses to take next semester</u>, the academic <u>adviser</u> listed five options. [The modifier suggests that the adviser was uncertain of what courses to take.]

CORRECT    <u>Uncertain of what courses to take next semester</u>, the <u>student</u> spoke to an academic adviser, who listed five options.

DANGLING    Flood <u>damage</u> was visible <u>crossing the river</u>. [The modifier makes it sound as though flood damage was crossing the river.]

CORRECT    Flood damage was visible <u>as we crossed the river</u>.

There are two common ways to revise dangling modifiers:

1. **Add a word or words that the modifier clearly describes.** Place the new material just after the modifier, and rearrange other parts of the sentence as necessary.

   DANGLING    <u>While watching television</u>, the <u>cake</u> burned.

   CORRECT    <u>While watching television</u>, <u>Sarah</u> burned the cake.

2. **Change the dangling modifier to a subordinate clause.** You may need to change the verb form in the modifier.

DANGLING    While watching television, the cake burned.

CORRECT    While Sarah was watching television, the cake burned.

## EXERCISE 18

**Directions:** Revise each of the following sentences to correct misplaced or dangling modifiers.

EXAMPLE    Deciding which flavor of ice cream to order, another customer cut in front of Roger.

REVISED    While Roger was deciding which flavor of ice cream to order, another customer cut in front of him.

1. Tricia saw an animal at the zoo that had black fur and long claws.

   At the zoo, Tricia saw an animal that had black fur and long claws.

2. Before answering the door, the phone rang.

   As Morgan was answering the door, the phone rang.

3. I could see large snowflakes falling from the bedroom window.

   From the bedroom window, I could see large snowflakes falling outside.

4. Honking, Felicia walked in front of the car.

   The driver was honking when Felicia walked in front of the car.

5. After leaving the classroom, the door automatically locked.

   As Kareem was leaving the classroom, the door automatically locked behind him.

6. Applauding and cheering, the band returned for an encore.

   The crowd was applauding and cheering when the band returned for an encore.

7. The waiter brought a birthday cake to our table that had 24 candles.

   The waiter brought a birthday cake that had 24 candles to our table.

8. Books lined the library shelves about every imaginable subject.

   Books about every imaginable subject lined the library shelves.

9. While sobbing, the sad movie ended and the lights came on.

   While Jesse was sobbing, the sad movie ended and the lights came on.

10. Turning the page, the book's binding cracked.

    As Jill was turning the page, the book's binding cracked.

# D.2 SHIFTS IN PERSON, NUMBER, AND VERB TENSE

The parts of a sentence should be consistent. Shifts within a sentence in person, number, or verb tense will make the sentence confusing and difficult to read.

## Shifts in Person

**Person** is the grammatical term used to distinguish the speaker or writer (**first person:** *I, we*), the person spoken to (**second person:** *you*), and the person or thing spoken about (**third person:** *he, she, it, they,* and any noun, such as *Joan* or *children*). A sentence or a paragraph should use the same person throughout.

SHIFT        If a <u>student</u> studies effectively, <u>you</u> will get good grades.

CORRECT      If <u>you</u> study effectively, <u>you</u> will get good grades.

## Shifts in Number

**Number** distinguishes between singular and plural. A pronoun must agree in number with its antecedent, the word to which it refers (see p. 581). Related nouns within a sentence also must agree in number. (Sometimes you need to change the form of the verb when you correct the inconsistent nouns or pronouns.)

SHIFT        When a <u>homeowner</u> <u>does</u> not <u>shovel</u> the snow in front of <u>their</u> <u>house</u>, <u>they</u> risk getting fined.

CORRECT      When <u>homeowners</u> <u>do</u> not <u>shovel</u> the snow in front of <u>their</u> <u>houses</u>, <u>they</u> risk getting fined.

## Shifts in Verb Tense

The same verb tense should be used throughout a sentence unless meaning requires a shift.

                                         PRESENT     FUTURE

REQUIRED SHIFT    After my cousin <u>arrives</u>, we <u>will go</u> to the movies.

                              PAST                          PRESENT

INCORRECT    After Marguerite <u>bought</u> the health foods store, she <u>seems</u> more confident.

                              PAST                          PAST

CORRECT      After Marguerite <u>bought</u> the health foods store, she <u>seemed</u> more confident.

|  | PAST |  | PRESENT |
|---|---|---|---|
| INCORRECT | Pamela <u>heard</u> the clock strike twelve, and then she <u>goes</u> for a midday walk. | | |

|  | PAST |  | PAST |
|---|---|---|---|
| CORRECT | Pamela <u>heard</u> the clock strike twelve, and then she <u>went</u> for a midday walk. | | |

## EXERCISE 19

**Directions:** Revise each of the following sentences to correct errors in shift of person, number, or tense. If a sentence contains no errors, write a "C" in the blank.

EXAMPLE    Boats along the river were tied to their dock<sub>s</sub>

_____ 1. When people receive a gift, ~~you~~ *they* should be gracious and polite.

_____ 2. When we arrived at the inn, the lights ~~are~~ *were* on and a fire ~~is~~ *was* burning in the fireplace.

_____ 3. Before Trey drove to the cabin, he pack*ed* a picnic lunch.

___C___ 4. The artist paints portraits and weaves baskets.

_____ 5. The lobsterman goes out on his boat each day and ~~will~~ check*s* his lobster traps.

___C___ 6. All the cars Honest Bob sells have a new transmission.

_____ 7. Rosa ran the 100-meter race and ~~throws~~ *threw* the discus at the track meet.

_____ 8. Public schools in Florida have an air-conditioning system*s*

_____ 9. Office workers sat on the benches downtown and ~~are~~ *were* eating their lunches outside.

_____ 10. Before a scuba diver goes underwater, ~~you~~ *he or she* must check and recheck ~~your~~ *his or her* breathing equipment.

# D.3 COORDINATION

**Coordination** is a way to give related ideas equal emphasis within a single sentence. Your readers will better understand the flow of your thoughts if you connect coordinate ideas.

## How to Combine Ideas of Equal Importance

There are three ways to combine ideas of equal importance when those ideas are expressed in independent clauses (see p. 554).

1. **Join the two independent clauses with a comma and a coordinating conjunction (*and, but, nor, or, for, so, yet*).**

   INDEPENDENT CLAUSE    INDEPENDENT CLAUSE

   I passed the ball, but Sam failed to catch it.

You should choose a coordinating conjunction that properly expresses the relationship between the ideas in the two clauses.

| *Coordinating Conjunction* | *Meaning* | *Example* |
|---|---|---|
| and | addition; one idea added to another | I went shopping, <u>and</u> I spent too much money. |
| but, yet | contrast | I wanted to grill fish, <u>but</u> Peter was a vegetarian. |
| or | alternatives or choices | Tonight I might go to the movies, <u>or</u> I might work out. |
| nor | not either | Julie was not in class, <u>nor</u> was she in the snack bar. |
| for | cause and effect | We went walking, <u>for</u> it was a beautiful evening. |
| so | result | I was early for the appointment, <u>so</u> I decided to doze for a few minutes. |

2. **Join the two independent clauses with a semicolon.**

   We decided to see the new Spike Lee film; it was playing at three local theaters.

Use this method when the relationship between the two ideas is clear and requires no explanation. Usually, the two clauses must be very closely related.

*Note:* If you join two independent clauses with only a comma and fail to use a coordinating conjunction or semicolon, you will produce a comma splice. If you join two independent clauses without using a punctuation mark and a coordinating conjunction, or a semicolon, you will produce a run-on sentence (see p. 567).

3. **Join the two independent clauses with a semicolon and a conjunctive adverb followed by a comma.** A conjunctive adverb can also be used at the beginning of a sentence to link the sentence with an earlier one.

| Conjunctive Adverb | Meaning | Example |
|---|---|---|
| therefore, consequently, thus, hence | cause and effect | I am planning to become a nurse; <u>consequently</u>, I'm taking a lot of science courses. |
| however, nevertheless, nonetheless, conversely | differences or contrast | We had planned to go bowling; <u>however</u>, we went to hear music instead. |
| furthermore, moreover, also | addition; a continuation of the same idea | To save money I am packing my lunch; <u>also</u>, I am walking to work instead of taking the bus. |
| similarly, likewise | similarity | I left class as soon as I finished the exam; <u>likewise</u>, other students also left. |
| then, subsequently, next | sequence in time | I walked home; <u>then</u> I massaged my aching feet. |

## EXERCISE 20

**Directions:** Complete each of the following sentences by adding a coordinating conjunction or a conjunctive adverb and the appropriate punctuation.

EXAMPLE    Teresa vacationed in Denver last year; <u>similarly,</u> Jan will go to Denver this year.

1. Our professor did not complete the lecture; nevertheless, _____ he did give an assignment for the next class.

2. A first-aid kit was in her backpack; therefore, _____ the hiker was able to treat her cut knee.

3. An opening act began the concert; subsequently, _____ the headline band took the stage.

4. I always put a light on when I leave the house; moreover, _____ I often turn on a radio to deter burglars.

5. Sue politely asked to borrow my car, and _____ she thanked me when she returned it.

6. My roommate went to the library; consequently, _____ I had the apartment to myself.

7. Steve and Todd will go to a baseball game, or _____ they will go to a movie instead.

8. Cheryl looks like her father, but _____ her hair is darker and curlier than his.

9. Maureen took a job at a bookstore; subsequently, _____ she was offered a job at a museum.

10. Our neighbors bought a barbecue grill; subsequently, _____ we decided to buy one.

# D.4 SUBORDINATION

Subordination is a way to show that one idea is not as important as another. When two clauses are related, but one is less important, the less important one can be expressed as a dependent (subordinate) clause (see p. 554). Dependent clauses do contain a subject and a verb, but they do not express a complete thought. They must always be added to a complete sentence or independent clause. If a dependent clause is used alone, it is a fragment and must be corrected (see p. 560).

## How to Combine Ideas of Unequal Importance

1. **Introduce the less important idea with a subordinating conjunction.** Choose a subordinating conjunction that properly shows the relationship of the less important idea to the more important one. Common subordinating conjunctions are *after, although, because, before, unless, when,* and *while.* (See p. 554 for a complete list.)

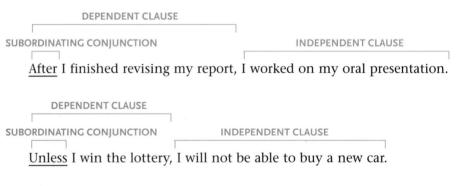

After I finished revising my report, I worked on my oral presentation.

DEPENDENT CLAUSE
SUBORDINATING CONJUNCTION    INDEPENDENT CLAUSE

Unless I win the lottery, I will not be able to buy a new car.

2. **Introduce the less important idea with a relative pronoun (such as *who, which, that,* or *what*).** A relative pronoun usually introduces a clause that functions as a noun when the clause is attached to an independent clause. (See p. 522 for more on relative pronouns.)

DEPENDENT CLAUSE
RELATIVE PRONOUN

The professor who won the award is on leave this semester.

The courses that I am taking in night school are challenging.

## EXERCISE 21

**Directions:** Combine each of the following pairs of sentences by subordinating one idea to the other with a coordinating conjunction or a relative pronoun.

EXAMPLE    **a.** One kind of opossum can glide like a bird.

        **b.** The opossum lives in Australia.

COMBINED    One kind of opossum, which lives in Australia, can glide like a bird.

1. **a.** Trina can get discount movie tickets.

   **b.** Trina's husband manages a movie theater.

Trina can get discount movie tickets because her husband

manages a theater.

2. **a.** Rob hit the ground with his tennis racket.

   **b.** Rob's tennis racket broke.

When Rob hit the ground with his tennis racket, the racket broke.

3. **a.** The car has satellite radio and a sunroof.

   **b.** I bought the car yesterday.

The car that I bought yesterday has satellite radio and a sunroof.

4. **a.** Visitors to the automobile museum can learn a lot about the mechanics of cars.

   **b.** Visitors enjoy looking at many old cars.

Visitors to the automobile museum, who enjoy looking at many old cars,

can learn a lot about the mechanics of cars.

5. **a.** The sorority will hold its fall picnic next week.

   **b.** The picnic will be held if it does not rain.

The sorority will hold its picnic next week, provided that it does not rain.

6. **a.** Vicky went to the library to work on her term paper.

   **b.** Then Vicky went to pick up her son from the day care center.

After Vicki went to the library to work on her term paper, she went to

pick up her son from the day care center.

7.  **a.** Oprah Winfrey may run for public office someday.

   **b.** Oprah Winfrey is a talk-show host.

   Oprah Winfrey is a talk-show host who may run for public office someday.

8.  **a.** I will go shopping for a rain slicker tomorrow.

   **b.** I will not go if my roommate has one that I can borrow.

   I will go shopping for a rain slicker tomorrow, unless my roommate

   has one that I can borrow.

9.  **a.** Linda and Pablo got divorced.

   **b.** They could not agree on anything.

   Linda and Pablo got divorced because they could not agree on anything.

10. **a.** The yacht sailed into the marina.

   **b.** The yacht is owned by the Kennedy family.

   The yacht that is owned by the Kennedy family sailed into the marina.

# D.5 PARALLELISM

Parallelism is a method of ensuring that words, phrases, and clauses in a series are in the same grammatical form.

## What Should Be Parallel?

1. **Words or phrases in a series.** When two or more nouns, verbs, adjectives, adverbs, or phrases appear together in a sentence connected by a coordinating conjunction (such as *and, or,* or *but*), the words or phrases should be parallel in grammatical form.

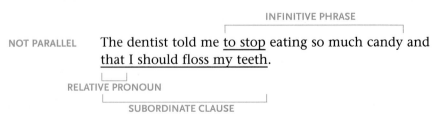

NOT PARALLEL     The dentist told me <u>to stop</u> eating so much candy and <u>that I should floss my teeth</u>.

INFINITIVE PHRASE

PARALLEL    The dentist told me <u>to stop</u> eating so much candy and <u>to floss</u> my teeth.

INFINITIVE PHRASE

NOUN    GERUND    INFINITIVE PHRASE

NOT PARALLEL    A well-rounded <u>diet</u>, <u>exercising</u>, and <u>to get enough sleep</u> are essential to good health.

NOUN    NOUN    NOUN

PARALLEL    A well-rounded <u>diet</u>, <u>exercise</u>, and enough <u>sleep</u> are essential to good health.

2. **Independent clauses joined with a coordinating conjunction.** Independent clauses within a sentence should be parallel in tense and in construction.

ACTIVE VOICE

NOT PARALLEL    The drivers <u>waited</u> patiently as the work crew cleaned up the wreck, but after an hour the horns <u>were honked</u> loudly by all the drivers.

PASSIVE VOICE

ACTIVE VOICE

PARALLEL    The drivers <u>waited</u> patiently as the work crew cleaned up the wreck, but after an hour they <u>honked</u> their horns loudly.

ACTIVE VOICE

PAST TENSE    PRESENT TENSE

NOT PARALLEL    Barry <u>wanted</u> to go to the concert, but Julia <u>wants</u> to stay home and watch a video.

PAST TENSE    PAST TENSE

PARALLEL    Barry <u>wanted</u> to go to the concert, but Julia <u>wanted</u> to stay home and watch a video.

3. **Items being compared.** When elements of a sentence are compared or contrasted, use the same grammatical form for each element.

NOUN    INFINITIVE PHRASE

INCORRECT    Mark wanted a <u>vacation</u> rather than <u>to save</u> money to buy a house.

INFINITIVE PHRASE    INFINITIVE PHRASE

CORRECT    Mark wanted <u>to take</u> a vacation rather than <u>to save</u> money to buy a house.

## EXERCISE 22

**Directions:** Revise each of the following sentences to achieve parallelism.

EXAMPLE    Rosa has decided to study nursing instead of going into accounting.

REVISED    _Rosa has decided to study nursing instead of accounting._

1. The priest baptized the baby and congratulates the new parents.

   The priest baptized the baby and congratulated the new parents.

2. We ordered a platter of fried clams, a platter of corn on the cob, and fried shrimp.

   We ordered a platter of fried clams, a platter of corn on the cob, and a platter

   fried shrimp.

3. Lucy entered the dance contest, but the dance was watched by June from the side.

   Lucy entered the dance contest, but June watched from the side.

4. Léon purchased the ratchet set at the garage sale and buying the drill bits there too.

   Léon purchased the ratchet set at the garage sale, and he bought the drill bits

   there too.

5. The exterminator told Brandon the house needed to be fumigated and spraying to eliminate the termites.

   The exterminator told Brandon the house needed to be fumigated and sprayed

   to eliminate the termites.

6. The bus swerved and hit the dump truck, which swerves and hit the station wagon, which swerved and hit the bicycle.

   The bus swerved and hit the dump truck, which swerved and hit the station

   wagon, which swerved and hit the bicycle.

7. Channel 2 covered the bank robbery, but a python that had escaped from the zoo was reported by Channel 7.

   Channel 2 covered the bank robbery, while Channel 7 reported that a python that

   had escaped from the zoo.

8. Sal was born while Bush was president, and Clinton was president when Rob was born.

   Sal was born while Bush was president, and Rob was born while Clinton was

   president.

9. The pediatrician spent the morning with sore throats, answering questions about immunizations, and treating bumps and bruises.

   *The pediatrician spent the morning treating sore throats, answering questions about immunizations, and treating bumps and bruises.*

10. Belinda prefers to study in the library, but her brother Marcus studies at home.

    *Belinda prefers to study in the library, but her brother Marcus prefers to study at home.*

# D.6 SENTENCE VARIETY

Good writers use a variety of sentence structures to avoid wordiness and monotony and to show relationships among thoughts. To achieve **sentence variety**, do not use all simple sentences or all complex or compound sentences (see pp. 556–557), and do not begin or end all sentences in the same way. Instead, vary the length, the amount of detail, and the structure of your sentences.

1. **Use sentences of varying lengths.**

2. **Avoid stringing simple sentences together with coordinating conjunctions (*and, but, or,* and so on).** Instead, use some introductory participial phrases (see p. 550).

   SIMPLE    There was a long line at the deli, <u>so</u> Chris decided to leave.

   VARIED    <u>Seeing the long line at the deli</u>, Chris decided to leave.

3. **Begin some sentences with a prepositional phrase.** A preposition shows relationships between things (*during, over, toward, before, across, within, inside, over, above*). Many prepositions suggest chronology, direction, or location (see p. 536).

   <u>During the concert</u>, the fire alarm rang.

   <u>Inside the theater</u>, the crowd waited expectantly.

4. **Begin some sentences with a present or past participle (*cooking, broken*; see p. 550).**

   <u>Barking</u> and <u>jumping</u>, the dogs greeted their master.

   <u>Still laughing</u>, two girls left the movie.

   <u>Tired</u> and <u>exhausted</u>, the mountain climbers fell asleep quickly.

5. **Begin some sentences with adverbs (see p. 533).**

   <u>Angrily</u>, the student left the room.

   <u>Patiently</u>, the math instructor explained the assignment again.

6. **Begin some sentences with infinitive phrases** (*to* plus the infinitive form: *to make, to go*; see p. 551).

<u>To get breakfast ready on time</u>, I set my alarm for 7 A.M.

7. **Begin some sentences with a dependent clause introduced by a subordinating conjunction** (see p. 554).

<u>Because</u> I ate shellfish, I developed hives.

8. **Begin some sentences with a conjunctive adverb.**

<u>Consequently</u>, we decided to have steak for dinner.

### ESL Tip
**Sentence Variety**

In English, good writing is characterized by a variety of sentence structures. Remember that one way to practice your English grammar and to add variety to your writing is to revise and edit your sentences. Also, be sure you are not using only the kinds of sentences that you are most comfortable with; experiment with using different sentence structures.

## EXERCISE 23

**Directions:** Combine each of the following pairs of simple sentences into one sentence, using the technique suggested in brackets.

EXAMPLE    **a.** The dog barked and howled.

**b.** The dog warned a stranger away.
[Use present participle (*-ing* form).]

COMBINED    <u>Barking and howling, the dog warned a stranger away.</u>

1. **a.** Professor Clark has a Civil War battlefield model.

**b.** He has it in his office.

[Use prepositional phrase.]

Professor Clark has a Civil War battlefield model on the shelf in his office.

2. **a.** Toby went to Disneyland for the first time.

**b.** He was very excited.
[Use past participle (*-ed* form).]

Excited, Toby went to Disneyland for the first time.

3. **a.** Teresa received a full scholarship.

   **b.** She does not need to worry about paying her tuition.
   [Use subordinating conjunction.]

   *Because Teresa received a full scholarship, she does not need to*

   *worry about paying her tuition.*

   _____

4. **a.** Lance answered the phone.

   **b.** He spoke with a gruff voice.
   [Use adverb.]

   *Gruffly, Lance answered the phone.*

   _____

5. **a.** The truck choked and sputtered.

   **b.** The truck pulled into the garage.
   [Use present participle (*-ing* form).]

   *Choking and sputtering, the truck pulled into the garage.*

   _____

6. **a.** Rich programmed his VCR.

   **b.** He taped his favorite sitcom.
   [Use infinitive (*to*) phrase.]

   *To tape his favorite sitcom, Rich programmed his VCR.*

   _____

7. **a.** The postal carrier placed a package outside my door.

   **b.** The package had a foreign stamp on it.
   [Use prepositional phrase.]

   *The postal carrier placed a package with a foreign stamp on it outside my door.*

   _____

8. **a.** The instructor asked the students to take their seats.

   **b.** She was annoyed.
   [Use past participle (*-ed* form).]

   *Annoyed, the instructor asked the students to take their seats.*

   _____

9. **a.** Shyla stood outside the student union.

   **b.** She waited for her boyfriend.
   [Use present participle (*-ing* form).]

   *Waiting for her boyfriend, Shyla stood outside the student union.*

   _____

10. **a.** Bo walked to the bookstore.

**b.** He was going to buy some new highlighters.
[Use infinitive (*to*) phrase.]

To buy some new highlighters, Bo walked to the store.

# D.7 REDUNDANCY AND WORDINESS

Redundancy results when a writer says the same thing twice. Wordiness results when a writer uses more words than necessary to convey a meaning. Both redundancy and wordiness detract from clear, effective sentences by distracting and confusing the reader.

## Eliminating Redundancy

A common mistake is to repeat the same idea in slightly different words.

> The <u>remaining</u> chocolate-chip cookie is the <u>only one left</u>, so I saved it for you. [*Remaining* and *only one left* mean the same thing.]

> The vase was <u>oval in shape</u>. [Oval is a shape, so *in shape* is redundant.]

To revise a redundant sentence, eliminate one of the redundant elements.

## Eliminating Wordiness

1. **Eliminate wordiness by cutting out words that do not add to the meaning of your sentence.**

   WORDY   In the final analysis, choosing the field of biology as my major resulted in my realizing that college is hard work.

   REVISED   Choosing biology as my major made me realize that college is hard work.

   WORDY   The type of imitative behavior that I notice among teenagers is a very important, helpful aspect of their learning to function in groups.

   REVISED   The imitative behavior of teenagers helps them learn to function in groups.

   Watch out in particular for empty words and phrases.

   | *Phrase* | *Substitute* |
   |---|---|
   | until such time as | until |
   | due to the fact that | because |
   | at this point in time | now |
   | in order to | to |

2. **Express your ideas simply and directly, using as few words as possible.** Often by rearranging your wording, you can eliminate two or three words.

the fleas that my dog has → my dog's fleas

workers with jobs that are low in pay → workers with low-paying jobs

3. **Use strong, active verbs that convey movement and give additional information.**

WORDY     I was in charge of two other employees and needed to watch over their work and performance.

REVISED   I supervised two employees, monitored their performance, and checked their work.

4. **Avoid sentences that begin with *"There is"* and *"There are."*** These empty phrases add no meaning, energy, or life to sentences.

WORDY     There are many children who suffer from malnutrition.

REVISED   Many children suffer from malnutrition.

## EXERCISE 24

**Directions:** Revise each of the following sentences to eliminate redundancy and wordiness. Revisions will vary.

EXAMPLE   Janice, who is impatient, usually cannot wait for class to end and packs up all of her books and notebooks in her backpack before the class is over.

REVISED   Janice is impatient and usually packs everything in her backpack before class ends.

1. My co-workers are friendly, nice, and cooperative and always willing to help me.

2. Fran and Joe are returning again to the branch office where they met.

3. Lynn changed from her regular clothes into her shorts and T-shirt in order that she could play basketball.

4. Due to the fact that Professor Reis assigned 100 pages of reading for tomorrow, I will be unable to join the group of my friends at the restaurant tonight.

5. In my mythology class, we discussed and talked about the presence of a Noah's ark–type story in most cultures.

6. Darryl offered many ideas and theories as to the reason why humans exist.

7. There are many children who have not been immunized against dangerous childhood diseases.

8. Scientists have been studying the disease AIDS for many years, but they have been unable to find a cure for the disease.

9. The brown-colored chair was my father's favorite chair.

10. The briefcase that Julio has carried belonged to his brother.

## D.8 DICTION

**Diction** is the use and choice of words. Words that you choose should be appropriate for your audience and express your meaning clearly. The following suggestions will help you improve your diction:

1. **Avoid slang expressions.** Slang refers to the informal, special expressions created and used by groups of people who want to give themselves a unique identity. Slang is an appropriate and useful way to communicate in some social situations and in some forms of creative writing. However, it is not appropriate for academic or career writing.

   SLANG      My sister seems permanently <u>out to lunch</u>.

   REVISED      My sister seems out of touch with the world.

   SLANG      We <u>pigged out</u> at the ice-cream shop.

   REVISED      We consumed enormous quantities of ice cream at the ice-cream shop.

2. **Avoid colloquial language.** Colloquial language refers to casual, everyday spoken language. It should be avoided in formal situations. Words that fall into this category are labeled *informal* or *colloquial* in your dictionary.

   colloquial      I almost <u>flunked</u> <u>bio</u> last <u>sem</u>.

   revised      I almost failed biology last semester.

   colloquial      What are <u>you all doing later</u>?

   revised      What are you doing later?

3. **Avoid nonstandard language.** Nonstandard language consists of words and grammatical forms that are used in conversation but are neither correct nor acceptable standard written English.

   | *Nonstandard* | *Standard* |
   |---|---|
   | hisself | himself |
   | knowed | known, knew |
   | hadn't ought to | should not |
   | she want | she wants |
   | he go | he goes |

4. **Avoid trite expressions.** Trite expressions are old, worn-out words and phrases that have become stale and do not convey meaning as effectively as possible. These expressions are also called *clichés*.

**Trite Expressions**

| | | |
|---|---|---|
| needle in a haystack | sadder but wiser | as old as the hills |
| hard as a rock | white as snow | pretty as a picture |
| face the music | gentle as a lamb | |

**ESL Tip**
Diction

Learning to use correct diction in English does take some practice. Remember that in your native language, or in other languages you have studied, you also have to choose your words carefully. Be sure you use academic language and not informal, slang, or colloquial language in your college writing.

## EXERCISE 25

**Directions:** Revise each of the following sentences by using correct diction.

EXAMPLE    This here building is Clemens Hall.

REVISED    <u>This building is Clemens Hall.</u>

1. Jean ~~freaked out~~ when I told her she won the lottery. *was thrilled*

2. He ~~go~~ to the library. *went*

3. The campus is ~~wider than an ocean.~~ *very large*

4. Marty sits next to me in ~~chem.~~ *chemistry class*

5. Sandy's new stereo ~~is totally cool and has an awesome sound.~~
*has incredible sound*

6. We ~~went nuts~~ when our team won the game. *cheered and ran onto the field*

7. ~~Them~~ CD players ~~sure~~ are ∧ expensive. *very*

8. I think Nathan is ~~as sharp as a tack~~ because he got every question on the exam right. *very intelligent*

9. Nino ~~blew~~ class ~~off~~ today to go rock climbing with his ~~pals.~~
        *skipped*                                                    *friends*

10. Dr. Maring's pager beeped in the middle of the meeting and she had to ~~hightail it~~ to a phone ∧.
     *get*              *quickly*

# E Using Punctuation Correctly

## E.1 END PUNCTUATION

### When to Use Periods

Use a period in the following situations:

1. **To end a sentence unless it is a question or an exclamation.**

   We washed the car even though we knew a thunderstorm was imminent.

Note: Use a period to end a sentence that states an indirect question or indirectly quotes someone's words or thoughts.

   INCORRECT    Margaret wondered if she would be on time?

   CORRECT    Margaret wondered if she would be on time.

2. **To punctuate many abbreviations.**

   M.D.     B.A.     P.M.     B.C.     Mr.     Ms.

Do not use periods in acronyms, such as *NATO* and *AIDS,* or in abbreviations for most organizations, such as *NBC* and *NAACP.*

Note: If a sentence ends with an abbreviation, the sentence has only one period, not two.

   The train was due to arrive at 7:00 P.M.

### When to Use Question Marks

Use question marks after direct questions. Place the question mark within the closed quotation marks.

   She asked the grocer, "How old is this cheese?"

Note: Use a period, not a question mark, after an indirect question.

   She asked the grocer how old the cheese was.

## When to Use Exclamation Points

Use an exclamation point at the end of a sentence that expresses particular emphasis, excitement, or urgency. Use exclamation points sparingly, however, especially in academic writing.

What a beautiful day it is!     Dial 911 right now!

### ESL Tip
#### Punctuation

Practice recognizing the punctuation marks used in English, and make sure you know what they mean and how to use them. Using punctuation incorrectly can sometimes change the meaning of your sentences. Here are two examples:

1. When your friends help, you stop working.
   When your friends help you, stop working.

2. Did she finally marry Roger?
   Did she finally marry, Roger?

# E.2 COMMAS

The comma is used to separate parts of a sentence from one another. If you omit a comma when it is needed, you risk making a clear and direct sentence confusing.

## When to Use Commas

Use a comma in the following situations:

1. **Before a coordinating conjunction that joins two independent clauses** (see p. 598).

   Terry had planned to leave work early, but he was delayed.

2. **To separate a dependent (subordinate) clause from an independent clause when the dependent clause comes first in the sentence** (see p. 600).

   After I left the library, I went to the computer lab.

3. **To separate introductory words and phrases from the rest of the sentence.**

   Unfortunately, I forgot my umbrella.

   To pass the baton, I will need to locate my teammate.

   Exuberant over their victory, the football-team members carried the quarterback on their shoulders.

4. **To separate a nonrestrictive phrase or clause from the rest of a sentence.** A **nonrestrictive** phrase or clause is added to a sentence but does not change the sentence's basic meaning.

To determine whether an element is nonrestrictive, read the sentence without the element. If the meaning of the sentence does not essentially change, then the commas are *necessary*.

My sister, who is a mail carrier, is afraid of dogs. [The essential meaning of this sentence does not change if we read the sentence without the subordinate clause: *My sister is afraid of dogs.* Therefore, commas are needed.]

Mail carriers who have been bitten by dogs are afraid of them. [If we read this sentence without the subordinate clause, its meaning changes considerably: *Mail carriers are afraid of (dogs).* It seems to say that *all* mail carriers are afraid of dogs. In this case, adding commas is not correct.]

5. **To separate three or more items in a series.**

*Note:* A comma is *not* used *after* the last item in the series.

I plan to take math, psychology, and writing next semester.

6. **To separate coordinate adjectives: two or more adjectives that are not joined by a coordinating conjunction and that equally modify the same noun or pronoun.**

The thirsty, hungry children returned from a day at the beach.

To determine if a comma is needed between two adjectives, use the following test. Insert the word *and* between the two adjectives. Also try reversing the order of the two adjectives. If the phrase makes sense in either case, a comma is needed. If the phrase does not make sense, do not use a comma.

The tired, angry child fell asleep. [*The tired and angry child* makes sense; so does *The angry, tired child.* Consequently, the comma is needed.]

Sarah is an excellent psychology student. [*Sarah is an excellent and psychology student* does not make sense, nor does *Sarah is a psychology, excellent student.* A comma is therefore not needed.]

7. **To separate parenthetical expressions from the clauses they modify.** Parenthetical expressions are added pieces of information that are not essential to the meaning of the sentence.

Most students, I imagine, can get jobs on campus.

8. **To separate a transition from the clause it modifies.**

In addition, I will revise the bylaws.

9. **To separate a quotation from the words that introduce or explain it.**

*Note:* The comma goes *inside* the closed quotation marks.

"Shopping," Barbara explained, "is a form of relaxation for me."

Barbara explained, "Shopping is a form of relaxation for me."

10. **To separate dates, place names, and long numbers.**

October 10, 1981, is my birthday.

Dayton, Ohio, was the first stop on the tour.

Participants numbered 1,777,716.

11. **To separate phrases expressing contrast.**

Sam's good nature, <u>not his wealth</u>, explains his popularity.

## EXERCISE 26

**Directions:** Revise each of the following sentences by adding commas where needed.

EXAMPLE    Until the judge entered, the courtroom was noisy.

1. "Hello," said the group of friends when Joan entered the room.

2. Robert DeNiro, the actor in the film, was very handsome.

3. My parents frequently vacation in Miami, Florida.

4. Drunk drivers, I suppose, may not realize they are not competent to drive.

5. Jeff purchased a television, couch, and dresser for his new apartment.

6. Luckily, the windstorm did not do any damage to our town.

7. Frieda has an early class, and she has to go to work afterward.

8. After taking a trip to the Galápagos Islands, Mark Twain wrote about them.

9. The old, dilapidated stadium was opened to the public on September 15, 1931.

10. Afterward, we will go out for ice cream.

# E.3 UNNECESSARY COMMAS

It is as important to know where *not* to place commas as it is to know where to place them. The following rules explain where it is incorrect to place them:

1. **Do not place a comma between a subject and its verb, between a verb and its complement, or between an adjective and the word it modifies.**

   INCORRECT    The stunning, imaginative, and intriguing, painting, became the hit of the show.

   CORRECT    The stunning, imaginative, and intriguing painting became the hit of the show.

2. **Do not place a comma between two verbs, subjects, or complements used as compounds.**

   INCORRECT    Sue called, and asked me to come by her office.

   CORRECT    Sue called and asked me to come by her office.

3. **Do not place a comma before a coordinating conjunction joining two dependent clauses** (see p. 554).

   INCORRECT    The city planner examined blueprints that the park designer had submitted, and that the budget officer had approved.

   CORRECT    The city planner examined blueprints that the park designer had submitted and that the budget officer had approved.

4. **Do not place commas around restrictive clauses, phrases, or appositives.** Restrictive clauses, phrases, and appositives are modifiers that are essential to the meaning of the sentence.

   INCORRECT    The girl, who grew up down the block, became my life-long friend.

   CORRECT    The girl who grew up down the block became my lifelong friend.

5. **Do not place a comma before the word *than* in a comparison or after the words *like* and *such as* in an introduction to a list.**

   INCORRECT    Some snails, <u>such as,</u> the Oahu tree snail, have more colorful shells, <u>than</u> other snails.

   CORRECT    Some snails, such as the Oahu tree snail, have more colorful shells than other snails.

6. **Do not place a comma next to a period, a question mark, an exclamation point, a dash, or an opening parenthesis.**

   INCORRECT    "When will you come back?," Dillon's son asked him.

   CORRECT    "When will you come back?" Dillon's son asked him.

   INCORRECT    The bachelor button, (also known as the cornflower) grows well in ordinary garden soil.

   CORRECT    The bachelor button (also known as the cornflower) grows well in ordinary garden soil.

7. **Do not place a comma between cumulative adjectives.** Cumulative adjectives, unlike coordinate adjectives (see p. 614), cannot be joined by *and* or rearranged.

   INCORRECT    The light, yellow, rose blossom was a pleasant birthday surprise. [*The light and yellow and rose blossom* does not make sense, so the commas are incorrect.]

   CORRECT    The light yellow rose blossom was a pleasant birthday surprise.

## E.4 COLONS AND SEMICOLONS

### When to Use a Colon

A colon follows an independent clause and usually signals that the clause is to be explained or elaborated on. Use a colon in the following situations:

1. **To introduce items in a series after an independent clause.** The series can consist of words, phrases, or clauses.

   I am wearing three popular colors: magenta, black, and white.

2. **To signal a list or a statement introduced by an independent clause ending with *the following* or *as follows*.**

   The directions are as follows: take Main Street to Oak Avenue and then turn left.

3. **To introduce a quotation that follows an introductory independent clause.**

My brother made his point quite clear: "Never borrow my car without asking me first!"

4. **To introduce an explanation.**

Mathematics is enjoyable: it requires a high degree of accuracy and peak concentration.

5. **To separate titles and subtitles of books.**

*Biology: A Study of Life*

*Note:* A colon must always follow an independent clause. It should not be used in the middle of a clause.

> INCORRECT    My favorite colors are: red, pink, and green.

> CORRECT    My favorite colors are red, pink, and green.

## When to Use a Semicolon

Use a semicolon in the following situations:

1. **To separate two closely related independent clauses not connected by a coordinating conjunction** (see p. 567).

Sam had a 99 average in math; he earned an A in the course.

2. **To separate two independent clauses joined by a conjunctive adverb** (see p. 533).

Margaret earned an A on her term paper; consequently, she was exempt from the final exam.

3. **To separate independent clauses joined with a coordinating conjunction if the clauses are very long or if they contain numerous commas.**

By late afternoon, having tried on every pair of black checked pants in the mall, Marsha was tired and cranky; but she still had not found what she needed to complete her outfit for the play.

4. **To separate items in a series if the items are lengthy or contain commas.**

The soap opera characters include Marianne Loundsberry, the heroine; Ellen and Sarah, her children; Barry, her ex-husband; and Louise, her best friend.

5. **To correct a comma splice or run-on sentence** (see p. 566).

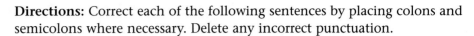

## EXERCISE 27

**Directions:** Correct each of the following sentences by placing colons and semicolons where necessary. Delete any incorrect punctuation.

EXAMPLE    <u>Samuel Clemens disliked his name; therefore, he used Mark Twain as his pen name.</u>

1. The large, modern, and airy, gallery houses works of art by important artists, however, it has not yet earned national recognition as an important gallery.

   The large, modern, and airy gallery houses works of art by important artists;

   however, it has not yet earned national recognition as an important gallery.

2. Rita suggested several herbs to add to my spaghetti sauce, oregano, basil, and thyme.

   Rita suggested several herbs to add to my spaghetti sauce: oregano, basil,

   and thyme.

3. Vic carefully proofread the paper, it was due the next day.

   Vic carefully proofread the paper; it was due the next day.

4. Furniture refinishing is a great hobby, it is satisfying to be able to make a piece of furniture look new again.

   Furniture refinishing is a great hobby; it is satisfying to be able to make a

   piece of furniture look new again.

5. The bridesmaids in my sister's wedding are as follows, Judy, her best friend Kim, our sister, Franny, our cousin, and Sue, a family friend.

   The bridesmaids in my sister's wedding are as follows: Judy, her best friend; Kim,

   our sister; Franny, our cousin; and Sue, a family friend.

6. Mac got a speeding ticket, he has to go to court next Tuesday.

   Mac got a speeding ticket; he has to go to court next Tuesday.

7. I will go for a swim when the sun comes out, it will not be so chilly then.

   I will go for a swim when the sun comes out; it will not be so chilly then.

8. Will was hungry after his hockey game, consequently, he ordered four hamburgers.

   Will was hungry after his hockey game; consequently, he ordered four hamburgers.

9. Sid went to the bookstore to purchase *Physical Anthropology Man and His Makings,* it is required for one of his courses.

   Sid went to the bookstore to purchase *Physical Anthropology: Man and His*

   *Makings;* it is required for one of his courses.

10. Here is an old expression, "The way to a man's heart is through his stomach."

    Here is an old expression: "The way to a man's heart is through his stomach."

# E.5 DASHES, PARENTHESES, HYPHENS, APOSTROPHES, QUOTATION MARKS

## Dashes (—)

The dash is used to (1) separate nonessential elements from the main part of the sentence, (2) create a stronger separation, or interruption, than commas or parentheses, and (3) emphasize an idea, create a dramatic effect, or indicate a sudden change in thought.

> My sister—the friendliest person I know—will visit me this weekend.

> My brother's most striking quality is his ability to make money—or so I thought until I heard of his bankruptcy.

Do not leave spaces between the dash and the words it separates.

## Parentheses ( )

Parentheses are used in pairs to separate extra or nonessential information that often amplifies, clarifies, or acts as an aside to the main point. Unlike dashes, parentheses de-emphasize information.

> Some large breeds of dogs (golden retrievers and Newfoundlands) are susceptible to hip deformities.

> The prize was dinner for two (maximum value, $50.00) at a restaurant of one's choice.

## Hyphens (-)

Hyphens have the following primary uses:

1. **To split a word when dividing it between two lines of writing or typing** (see p. 628).

2. **To join two or more words that function as a unit, either as a noun or as a noun modifier.**

   mother-in-law                    single-parent families
   twenty-year-old                  school-age children
   state-of-the-art sound system

## Apostrophes (')

Use apostrophes in the following situations:

1. **To show ownership or possession.** When the person, place, or thing doing the possessing is a singular noun, add -'s to the end of it, regardless of what its final letter is.

   The man's DVD player             John Keats's poetry
   Aretha's best friend

   With plural nouns that end in -s, add only an apostrophe to the end of the word.

   the twins' bedroom               postal workers' hours
   teachers' salaries

   With plural nouns that do not end in -s, add -'s.

   children's books                 men's slacks

   Do not use an apostrophe with the possessive adjective *its*.

   INCORRECT    It's frame is damaged.

   CORRECT      Its frame is damaged.

2. **To indicate omission of one or more letters in a word or number.** Contractions are used in informal writing, but usually not in formal academic writing.

   it's [it is]                     hasn't [has not]
   doesn't [does not]               '57 Ford [1957 Ford]
   you're [you are]                 class of '89 [class of 1989]

## Quotation Marks (" ")

Quotation marks separate a direct quotation from the sentence that contains it. Here are some rules to follow in using quotation marks.

1. **Quotation marks are always used in pairs.**

*Note:* A comma or period goes at the end of the quotation, inside the quotation marks.

> Marge declared, "I never expected Peter to give me a watch for Christmas."

> "I never expected Peter to give me a watch for Christmas," Marge declared.

2. **Use single quotation marks for a quotation within a quotation.**

> My literature professor said, "Byron's line 'She walks in beauty like the night' is one of his most sensual."

*Note:* When quoting long prose passages of more than four typed lines, do not use quotation marks. Instead, set off the quotation from the rest of the text by indenting each line ten spaces from the left margin. This format is called a **block quotation.**

The opening lines of the Declaration of Independence establish the purpose of the document:

> When in the Course of human events it becomes necessary for one people to dissolve the political bonds which have connected them with another, and to assume among the powers of the earth, the separate and equal station to which the Laws of Nature and of Nature's God entitle them, a decent respect to the opinions of mankind requires that they should declare the causes which impel them to the separation.

3. **Use quotation marks to indicate titles of songs, short stories, poems, reports, articles, and essays.** Books, movies, plays, operas, paintings, statues, and the names of television series are italicized (or underlined to indicate italics).

> "Rappaccini's Daughter" (short story)

> *60 Minutes* [or <u>60 Minutes</u>] (television series)

> "The Road Not Taken" (poem)

4. Colons, semicolons, exclamation points, and question marks, when not part of the quoted material, go outside of the quotation marks.

> What did George mean when he said, "People in glass houses shouldn't throw stones"?

## EXERCISE 28

**Directions:** To the following sentences, add dashes, apostrophes, parentheses, hyphens, and quotation marks where necessary.

EXAMPLE   "You are not going out dressed that way!" said Frank's roommate.

1. My daughter in law recently entered medical school.

   My daughter-in-law recently entered medical school.

2. At the bar I worked in last summer, the waitresses tips were always pooled and equally divided.

   At the bar I worked in last summer, the waitresses' tips were always pooled

   and equally divided.

3. Youre going to Paris next summer, aren't you?

   You're going to Paris next summer, aren't you?

4. The career counselor said, The computer field is not as open as it used to be.

   The career counselor said, "The computer field is not as open as it used to be."

5. My English professor read aloud Frost's poem Two Look at Two.

   My English professor read aloud Frost's poem "Two Look at Two."

6. Frank asked me if I wanted to rent a big screen television for our Super Bowl party.

   Frank asked me if I wanted to rent a big-screen television for our Super Bowl

   party.

7. Rachel the teaching assistant for my linguistics class spent last year in China.

   Rachel—the teaching assistant for my linguistics class—spent last year

   in China.

8. Macy's is having a sale on womens boots next week.

   Macy's is having a sale on women's boots next week.

9. Trina said, My one year old's newest word is Bzz, which she says whenever she sees a fly.

Trina said, "My one-year-old's newest word is 'Bzz.' which she says whenever

she sees a fly."

10. Some animals horses and donkeys can interbreed, but they produce
infertile offspring.

Some animals (horses and donkeys) can interbreed, but they produce infertile

offspring.

# F

# Managing Mechanics and Spelling

## F.1 CAPITALIZATION

In general, capital letters are used to mark the beginning of a sentence, to mark the beginning of a quotation, and to identify proper nouns. Here are some guidelines on capitalization:

| *What to Capitalize* | *Example* |
|---|---|
| 1. First word in every sentence | Prewriting is useful. |
| 2. First word in a direct quotation | Sarah commented, "That exam was difficult!" |
| 3. Names of people and animals, including the pronoun *I* | Aladdin<br>Janet Reno<br>Spot |
| 4. Names of specific places, cities, states, nations, geographic areas or regions | New Orleans<br>the Southwest<br>Lake Erie |
| 5. Government and public offices, departments, buildings | Williamsville Library<br>House of Representatives |
| 6. Names of social, political, business, sporting, cultural organizations | Boy Scouts<br>Buffalo Bills |
| 7. Names of months, days of the week, holidays | August<br>Tuesday<br>Halloween |
| 8. In titles of works: the first word following a colon, the first and last words, and all other words except articles, prepositions, and conjunctions | *Biology: A Study of Life*<br>"Once More to the Lake" |
| 9. Races, nationalities, languages | African American, Italian, English |

| | |
|---|---|
| 10. Religions, religious figures, sacred books | Hindu, Hinduism, God, Allah, the Bible |
| 11. Names of products | Tide, Buick |
| 12. Personal titles when they come right before a name | Professor Rodriguez Senator Hatch |
| 13. Major historic events | World War I |
| 14. Specific course titles | History 201, Introduction to Psychology |

## EXERCISE 29

**Directions:** Capitalize words as necessary in the following sentences. Circled letters need capitalization.

EXAMPLE    Farmers in the midwest were devastated by floods last summer.

1. My mother is preparing some special foods for our hanukkah meal; rabbi epstein will join us.

2. My american politics professor used to be a judge in the town of evans.

3. A restaurant in the galleria mall serves korean food.

4. A graduate student I know is writing a book about buddha titled *the great one: ways to enlightenment.*

5. at the concert last night, cher changed into many different outfits.

6. An employee announced over the loudspeaker, "attention, customers! we have pepsi on sale in aisle ten for a very low price!"

7. Karen's father was stationed at fort bradley during the vietnam war.

8. Last tuesday the state assembly passed governor allen's budget.

9. Boston is an exciting city; be sure to visit the museum of fine arts.

10. Dan asked if i wanted to go see the bolshoi ballet at shea's theatre in november.

# F.2 ABBREVIATIONS

An abbreviation is a shortened form of a word or phrase that is used to represent the whole word or phrase. The following is a list of common acceptable abbreviations:

| *What to Abbreviate* | *Example* |
|---|---|
| 1. Some titles before or after people's names | Mr. Ling Samuel Rosen, M.D. *but* Professor Ashe |

**2.** Names of familiar organizations, corporations, countries     CIA, IBM, VISTA, USA

**3.** Time references preceded or followed by a number     7:00 A.M.
3:00 P.M.
A.D. 1973

**4.** Latin terms when used in footnotes, references, or parentheses     i.e. [*id est,* "that is"]
et al. [*et alii,* "and others"]

Here is a list of things that are usually *not* abbreviated:

| | *Example* | |
|---|---|---|
| *What Not to Abbreviate* | *Incorrect* | *Correct* |
| **1.** Units of measurement | thirty in. | thirty inches |
| **2.** Geographic or other place names when used in sentences | N.Y.<br>Elm St. | New York<br>Elm Street |
| **3.** Parts of written works when used in sentences | Ch. 3 | Chapter 3 |
| **4.** Names of days, months, holidays | Tues. | Tuesday |
| **5.** Names of subject areas | psych. | psychology |

## EXERCISE 30

**Directions:** Correct the inappropriate use of abbreviations in the following sentences. If a sentence contains no errors, write "C" beside it.

EXAMPLE     We live thirty ~~mi.~~ outside NYC.

_We live thirty miles outside New York City._

___C___    **1.** Frank enjoys going to swim at the YMCA on Oak St.

_____

_____    **2.** Prof. Jorge asked the class to turn to ~~pg.~~ 8.

_page___

_____    **3.** Because he is seven ~~ft.~~ tall, my brother was recruited for the high school ~~b-ball~~ team.

_feet_     _basketball_

___C___    **4.** When I asked Ron why he hadn't called me, he said it was Northeast Bell's fault—i.e., his phone hadn't been working.

_____

_____    **5.** Tara is flying TWA to ~~KC~~ to visit her parents next ~~Wed.~~

_Kansas City_     _Wednesday_

_____C_____     **6.** At 11:30 P.M., we turned on NBC to watch *The Tonight Show*.

_____     **7.** Last ~~wk.~~ I missed my ~~chem.~~ lab.

        week       chemistry laboratory

_____     **8.** The exam wasn't too difficult; only ~~ques.~~ no. 15 and ~~ques.~~ no. 31 were extremely difficult.

        question       question

_____     **9.** Dr. Luc removed the mole from my ~~rt.~~ hand using a laser.

        right

_____     **10.** Mark drove out to ~~L.A.~~ to audition for a role in MGM's new movie.

        Los Angeles

# F.3 HYPHENATION AND WORD DIVISION

On occasion you must divide and hyphenate a word on one line and continue it on the next. Here are some guidelines for dividing words.

1. **Divide words only when necessary.** Frequent word divisions make a paper difficult to read.

2. **Divide words between syllables.** Consult a dictionary if you are unsure how to break a word into syllables.

   di-vi-sion            pro-tect

3. **Do not divide one-syllable words.**

4. **Do not divide a word so that a single letter is left at the end of a line.**

   INCORRECT                 a-typical

   CORRECT                   atyp-ical

5. **Do not divide a word so that fewer than three letters begin the new line.**

   INCORRECT   visu-al

   CORRECT     vi-sual

   INCORRECT   caus-al [This word cannot be divided at all.]

6. **Divide compound words only between the words.**

   some-thing            any-one

7. **Divide words that are already hyphenated only at the hyphen.**

   ex-policeman

## EXERCISE 31

**Directions:** Insert a diagonal (/) mark where each word should be divided. Mark "N" in the margin if the word should not be divided.

EXAMPLE    every/where

| | | | |
|---|---|---|---|
| _____ | **1.** en/close | _____ | **6.** dis/gusted |
| N | **2.** house | _____ | **7.** chan/delier |
| _____ | **3.** sax/ophone | _____ | **8.** head/phones |
| N | **4.** hardly | N | **9.** swings |
| _____ | **5.** well/known | N | **10.** abyss |

## F.4 NUMBERS

Numbers can be written as numerals (600) or words (six hundred). Here are some guidelines for when to use numerals and when to use words:

| *When to Use Numerals* | *Example* |
|---|---|
| 1. Numbers that are spelled with more than two words | 375 students |
| 2. Days and years | August 10, 1993 |
| 3. Decimals, percentages, fractions | 56.7<br>59 percent<br>1¾ cups |
| 4. Exact times | 9:27 A.M. |
| 5. Pages, chapters, volumes; acts and lines from plays | chapter 12<br>volume 4 |
| 6. Addresses | 122 Peach Street |
| 7. Exact amounts of money | $5.60 |
| 8. Scores and statistics | 23–6    5 of every 12 |

| *When to Use Words* | *Example* |
|---|---|
| 1. Numbers that begin sentences | Two hundred ten students attended the lecture. |
| 2. Numbers of one or two words | sixty students,<br>two hundred women |

## EXERCISE 32

**Directions:** Correct the misuse of numbers in the following sentences. If a sentence contains no errors, write "C" next to it.

EXAMPLE    The reception hall was filled with ~~500~~ guests.

*The reception hall was filled with five hundred guests.*

_C_    **1.** At 6:52 A.M. my roommate's alarm clock went off.

____    **2.** I purchased ~~9~~ turtlenecks for ~~one dollar and fifty-five cents~~ each.

*nine        $1.55*

____    **3.** ~~35~~ floats were entered in the parade, but only 4 received prizes.

*Thirty-five*

____    **4.** Act ~~three~~ of *Othello* is very exciting.

*3*

____    **5.** Almost ~~fifty~~ percent of all marriages end in divorce.

*50*

_C_    **6.** The Broncos won the game 21–7.

____    **7.** We were assigned volume ~~two~~ of *Don Quixote,* beginning on page 351.

*2*

____    **8.** The hardware store is located at ~~three forty-four~~ Elm Street, ~~2~~ doors down from my grandmother's house.

*344        two*

____    **9.** Maryanne's new car is a ~~2~~-door V-8.

*two*

____    **10.** Our anniversary is June ~~ninth, nineteen eighty-nine~~.

*9, 1989*

# F.5 SUGGESTIONS FOR IMPROVING SPELLING

Correct spelling is important to a well-written paragraph or essay. The following suggestions will help you submit papers without misspellings:

1. **Do not worry about spelling as you write your first draft.** Checking a word in a dictionary at this point will interrupt your flow of ideas. If you do not know how a word is spelled, spell it the way it sounds. Circle or underline the word so you remember to check it later.

2. **Keep a list of words you commonly misspell.** This list can be part of your error log.

3. **Every time you catch an error or find a misspelled word on a paper returned by your instructor, add it to your list.**

4. **Study your list.** Ask a friend to quiz you on the words. Eliminate words from the list after you have passed several quizzes on them.

5. **Develop a spelling awareness.** You'll find that your spelling will improve just by your being aware that spelling is important. When you encounter a new word, notice how it is spelled and practice writing it.

6. **Pronounce words you are having difficulty spelling.** Pronounce each syllable distinctly.

7. **Review basic spelling rules.** Your college library or learning lab may have manuals, workbooks, or computer programs that cover basic rules and provide guided practice.

8. **Be sure to have a dictionary readily available when you write.**

9. **Read your final draft through once, checking only for spelling errors.** Look at each word carefully, and check the spelling of those words of which you are uncertain.

# F.6 SIX USEFUL SPELLING RULES

The following six rules focus on common spelling trouble spots:

1. **Is it *ei* or *ie*?**

   ***Rule:*** Use *i* before *e*, except after *c* or when the syllable is pronounced *ay* as in the word *weigh.*

   EXAMPLE    *i* before *e:* believe, niece

   except after *c:* receive, conceive

   or when pronounced *ay:* neighbor, sleigh

|   | *Exceptions:* | either | neither | foreign | forfeit |
|---|---|---|---|---|---|
|   |   | height | leisure | weird | seize |

2. **When adding an ending, do you keep or drop the final *e*?**

*Rules:* **a.** Keep the final *e* when adding an ending that begins with a consonant. (Vowels are *a, e, i, o, u,* and sometimes *y*; all other letters are consonants.)

| hope → hopeful | aware → awareness |
|---|---|
| live → lively | force → forceful |

**b.** Drop the final *e* when adding an ending that begins with a vowel.

| hope → hoping | file → filing |
|---|---|
| note → notable | write → writing |

| *Exceptions:* | argument | truly | changeable |
|---|---|---|---|
|   | awful | manageable | courageous |
|   | judgment | noticeable | outrageous |
|   | acknowledgment |   |   |

3. **When adding an ending, do you keep the final *y*, change it to *i*, or drop it?**

*Rules:* **a.** Keep the *y* if the letter before the *y* is a vowel.

delay → delaying     buy → buying     prey → preyed

**b.** Change the *y* to *i* if the letter before the *y* is a consonant, but keep the *y* for the *-ing* ending.

| defy → defiance | marry → married |
|---|---|
| → defying | → marrying |

4. **When adding an ending to a one-syllable word, when do you double the final letter if it is a consonant?**

*Rules:* **a.** In one-syllable words, double the final consonant when a single vowel comes before it.

drop → dropped     shop → shopped     pit → pitted

**b.** In one-syllable words, *don't* double the final consonant when two vowels or a consonant comes before it.

repair → repairable     sound → sounded

real → realize

5. **When adding an ending to a word with more than one syllable, when do you double the final letter if it is a consonant?**

   *Rules:* **a.** In multisyllable words, double the final consonant when a single vowel comes before it *and* the stress falls on the last syllable. (Vowels are *a, e, i, o, u,* and sometimes *y.* All other letters are consonants.)

   begin´ → beginning            transmit´ → transmitted

   repel´ → repelling

   **b.** In multisyllable words, do *not* double the final consonant (a) when two vowels or a vowel and another consonant come before it *or* (b) when the stress is not on the last syllable.

   despair → despairing          ben´efit → benefited

   conceal → concealing

6. **To form a plural, do you add *-s* or *-es*?**

   *Rules:* **a.** For most nouns, add *-s.*

   cat → cats      house → houses

   **b.** Add *-es* to words that end in *-o* if the *-o* is preceded by a consonant.

   hero → heroes      potato → potatoes

   *Exceptions: zoos, radios, ratios,* and other words ending with two vowels.

   **c.** Add *-es* to words ending in *-ch, -sh, -ss, -x,* or *-z.*

   church → churches      fox → foxes      dish → dishes

# Error Correction Exercises

Revise each of the following paragraphs. Look for errors in sentence structure, grammar, punctuation, mechanics, and spelling. Rewrite these paragraphs with corrections.

## Paragraph 1

Jazz is a type of music, originating in new orleans in the early Twenties, and contained a mixture of African and European musical elements. There are a wide variety of types of jazz including: the blues, swing, bop and modern. Jazz includes both hard and soft music. Unlike rock music, jazz does not goes to extremes. Rock bands play so loud you can't understand half of the words. As a result, jazz is more relacking and enjoyable.

Jazz is a type of music, originating in New Orleans in the early 1920s and contains

a mixture of African and European musical elements. There is a wide variety of

types of jazz including the blues, swing, bop, and modern. Jazz includes both hard

and soft music. Unlike rock music, jazz does not go to extremes. Rock bands play

so loudly it is difficult to understand the words. As a result, jazz is more relaxing

and enjoyable.

## Paragraph 2

every one thinks vacations are great fun but that isnt allways so. Some people are to hyper to relax when their on vaccation. My sister Sally is like that. She has to be on the move at alltimes. She can never slow down and take it easy. She goes from activity to activity at a wild pace. When Sally does have a spare moment between activities, she spends her freetime thinking about work problems and her family and their problems and what she should do about them when she gets back. Consequently, when Sally gets back from a vacation she is exhausted and more tense and upset then when she left home.

Everyone thinks vacations are great fun, but that is not always the case. Some

people are too stressed to relax on their vaccation. My sister Sally is a good

example. She has to be on the move at all times. She goes from activity to

activity at a wild pace. When Sally does have a spare moment between activities,

she spends her freetime thinking about work, family problems and what she should

do about them when she gets home. Consequently, when Sally gets back from a

vacation, she is exhausted and more tense and upset than when she left home.

## Paragraph 3

Soap operas are usually serious eposdes of different people in the world of today. There about fictuous people whom are supposed to look real. But each character has their unique prblems, crazzy relationships and nonrealistical quirks and habits.In real live, it would never happen.The actors are always getting themself into wiered and unusall situation that are so of the wall that they could never be real. Its just to unreal to have 20 looney people all good frinds.

Soap operas are usually serious episodes about different people in the world of

today. They are about fictitious people who are supposed to appear real; however,

these characters have their unique problems, crazy relationships, and

unrealistical quirks and habits that in real life would never happen. It is not

possible for so many odd people to be good friends.

## Paragraph 4

Here are two forms of music, we have rock music and we have country music. First, these two sound differen. Rock music is very loud and with a high base sound, sometimes you can't even understand the words that the singer is singing. On the other hand, country music is a bit softer with a mellow but up beat sound. Although country music sometimes sounds boring, at least you can understand the lyrics when listening to it. Country singers usually have a country western accent also unlike rock singers.

Rock and country are two kinds of music that sound very different. Rock music is

very loud with a high bass sound, and sometimes you cannot even understand

the words. On the other hand, country music is softer, with a mellow but upbeat

sound. Although country music sometimes sounds boring, at least you can

understand the lyrics.

*Essay 1*

### What A Good Friend Is

I have this friend Margaret who is really not too intelligent. It took awhile before I could accept her limitations. But, I had to get to know Margaret and her feelings. We are like two hands that wash each other. I help her, she helps me. when I need her to babysit for me while I'm at work it's done. If she needs a ride to the dentist she's got it. All I need is to be given time to do them. We help each other and that is why we are friends.

Good friends; Friends that do for one another. To tell the friend the truth about something that is asked of them. And for the other to respect your views as you would theirs. A friend is there to listen if you have a problem and to suggest something to help solve the problem but, yet not telling you just what to do. Or just to be the shoulder to cry on. Good friends go places and do things together. Good Friends are always there when you need them.

_____

*A Good Friend*

I have a friend, Margaret, who is really not too intelligent. Once I got to know

Margaret and her feelings, I could accept her limitations. I help her and she helps

me. If I need her to babysit for me while I'm at work, it is done. If she needs a ride

to the dentist, I take her. We help each other and that is why we are friends.

     Good friends are people who help each other and respect each other's views.

A friend is there to listen if you have a problem and to help solve the problem,

rather than just telling you what to do. A friend will also give you a shoulder to

cry on. Good friends go places and do things together, and are always there when

you need them.

_____

_____

_____

_____

_____

_____

_____

_____

*Essay 2*

## Putting Labels on People

People tend to label someone as stupid if they are slower and takes more time in figuring out an assignment or just trying to understand directions. My friend Georgette is a good example. People make fun of her. When a person has to deal with this type of ridicule by her fellow students or friend she start to feel insecure in speaking up. She start to think she is slower mentally, she gets extremely paranoid when asked to give answer in class. She feels any answer out of her mouth will be wrong. Her self-image shoots down drastically, like a bottom less pit. that She will avoyd in answering all answers even when she's almost positive she's right. It's the possibility of being wrong that will keep her from speaking. Then when some one else gives the answer she seess she was right, she would become extremely anoid at herself for not answering the question. As a result, she start to run away from all challenges, even the slightest challenge will frighten her away. Do from the teasing of her friends, Georgette will lock herself away from trying to understand and her famous words when facing to a challenge will be I can't do it!

Therefore, when a person makes a mistake, you should think of what you say before you say it and be sure it's not going to hurt the person. You comments may help destroy that person self confidence.

---

*Putting Labels on People*

People tend to label others as "stupid" if they are slower and take more time in figuring out assignments or in understanding directions. My friend Georgette is a good example. People make fun of her, and it makes her feel insecure about speaking up. She starts to doubt herself, and she gets extremely paranoid when asked to give answers in class. She is afraid to be wrong. She will avoid answering all questions even if she is almost positive that she is right. When someone else gives the answer, and she sees that she was right, she is annoyed at herself for not answering the question. As a result, she starts to run away from all challenges. Due to her friends' teasing, Georgette locks herself away; her famous words when facing a challenge are, "I can't do it!"

Therefore, when someone makes a mistake, it is important to think before saying something that will hurt that person. Your comments may help to destroy that person's self-confidence.

# Skill Refresher Score Chart

| Skill Refresher | Score (%) | Where to Get Help in Part VI: Reviewing the Basics |
|---|---|---|
| 3 Sentence Fragments (p. 79) | _____ | C.1 (p. 560) |
| 4 Run-on Sentences (p. 105) | _____ | C.2 (p. 566) |
| 5 Subject-Verb Agreement (p. 133) | _____ | C.6 (p. 578) |
| 6 Pronoun-Antecedent Agreement (p. 158) | _____ | C.7 (p. 581) |
| 7 Pronoun Reference (p. 183) | _____ | C.8 (p. 584) |
| 8 Avoiding Shift Errors (p. 205) | _____ | D.2 (p. 596) |
| 9 Dangling Modifiers (p. 228) | _____ | D.1 (p. 593) |
| 10 Misplaced Modifiers (p. 250) | _____ | D.1 (p. 593) |
| 11 Verb Tense (p. 270) | _____ | C.3 (p. 569) |
| 12 Coordinate Sentences (p. 299) | _____ | D.3 (p. 597) |
| 13 Subordinate Clauses (p. 323) | _____ | D.4 (p. 600) |
| 14 Parallelism (p. 356) | _____ | D.5 (p. 602) |
| 15 When to Use Commas (p. 393) | _____ | E.2, E.3 (p. 613) |
| 16 Using Colons and Semicolons (p. 440) | _____ | E.4 (p. 617) |
| 17 When to Use Capital Letters (p. 467) | _____ | F.1 (p. 625) |

# Skill Refresher Answer Key

## Sentence Fragments (p. 79)

Answers may vary.

1. Correct
2. Correct
3. Because we're good friends, I remembered her birthday.
   I remembered her birthday because we're good friends.
4. After I left the classroom, I realized I had forgotten my book.
   I realized I had forgotten my book after I left the classroom.
5. Before the professor moved on to the next topic, Jason asked a question about centrifugal force.
   Jason asked a question about centrifugal force before the professor moved on to the next topic.
6. The phone rang, and the answering machine answered.
   The phone rang; the answering machine answered.
7. I was hoping I would do well at the interview.
   I researched the company, hoping I would do well at the interview.
8. Anita scheduled a conference with her art history professor to discuss the topic for her final paper.
9. I got a "B" on the quiz because I reread my notes.
   Because I reread my notes, I got a "B" on the quiz.
10. Marcus was interested in the course that focused on the rise of communism.
    Marcus was interested in the course because it focused on the rise of communism.

## Run-On Sentences (p. 105)

Answers may vary.

1. The Civil War ended in 1865; the period of Reconstruction followed.
   The Civil War ended in 1865, and the period of Reconstruction followed.
2. Although light and sound both emit waves, they do so in different ways.
3. Correct
4. Archaeologists study the physical remains of cultures; anthropologists study the cultures themselves.
   Archaeologists study the physical remains of cultures, while anthropologists study the cultures themselves.
5. The body's nervous system carries electrical and chemical messages. These messages tell parts of the body how to react and what to do.
   The body's nervous system carries electrical and chemical messages that tell parts of the body how to react and what to do.
6. Neil Armstrong was the first human to walk on the moon. This event occurred in 1969.
   Neil Armstrong was the first human to walk on the moon; this event occurred in 1969.
7. Robert Frost is a well-known American poet; one of his most famous poems is "The Road Not Taken."
   Robert Frost is a well-known American poet. One of his most famous poems is "The Road Not Taken."
8. Algebra and geometry are two branches of mathematics; calculus and trigonometry are other branches.
9. Correct

10. Since it is easy to become distracted by other thoughts and responsibilities while studying, it helps to make a list of these distractions.

    It is easy to become distracted by other thoughts and responsibilities while studying. It helps to make a list of these distractions.

## SKILL REFRESHER—CHAPTER 5

### Subject-Verb Agreement (p. 133)

1. wants
2. are
3. agrees
4. swim
5. knows
6. is
7. are
8. Candy
9. Sabrina
10. were

## SKILL REFRESHER—CHAPTER 6

### Pronoun-Antecedent Agreement (p. 158)

1. our
2. his
3. his or her
4. it
5. his or her
6. their
7. he or she
8. his or her
9. their
10. he or she

## SKILL REFRESHER—CHAPTER 7

### Pronoun Reference (p. 183)

Answers may vary.
1. Marissa told Kristin, "My business proposal was accepted."
2. In the car, Brian found a briefcase that his manager owned.
   Brian found a briefcase in his manager's car.
3. Naomi put the cake on the table, and Roberta moved it to the counter after she noticed the cake was still hot.
4. The professor asked the student to lend him a book.
   The professor asked the student, "Could I borrow that book?"
5. Our waiter, who was named Burt, described the restaurant's specials.
6. Aaron's sister was injured in a car accident, but she would heal.
7. Correct

8. Another car, which was swerving crazily, hit mine.
   The car that was swerving crazily hit mine.
9. In hockey games, the players frequently injure each other in fights.
10. The hunting lodge had lots of deer and moose antlers hanging on its walls, and Ryan said he had killed some of the deer.
    The hunting lodge had lots of deer and moose antlers hanging on its walls, and Ryan said he had killed some of these animals.

## SKILL REFRESHER—CHAPTER 8

### Avoiding Shift Errors (p. 205)

1. Renee stopped for coffee, bought gas, and then drove to campus for an early class.
2. Electricians will repair circuits, but they won't install new electrical equipment.
3. When people deposit out-of-state checks in their checking accounts, they should expect to wait for the checks to clear.
4. If you forget to sign a check, you can expect to have the check returned to you.
5. If a student does not write the course and section number on his or her exam, there is a danger that it could be lost.
6. When a service representative places you on hold for ten minutes, you wonder if he or she is on a coffee break.
7. Correct
8. Slang terms are popular in everyday speech; they appear most often among teenagers and special interest groups.
9. Advertisers often have used the language of sports to attract consumer interest; for example, they have used terms such as "game plan" and "winning team."
10. Correct

## SKILL REFRESHER—CHAPTER 9

### Dangling Modifiers (p. 228)

Answers may vary.
1. While standing on the ladder, Harvey patched the tarpaper roof.
2. Since I was nervous, the test seemed more difficult than it was.
   The test seemed more difficult than it was because I was nervous.
3. I was waiting to drop a class at the Records Office; the line seemed to go on forever.
   Everyone was waiting to drop a class at the Records Office; thus, the line seemed to go on forever.
4. Correct
5. The elevator was, of course, out of order while I was moving the couch.
   We discovered, while moving the couch, that the elevator was, of course, out of order.
6. While we were watching the evening news, the power went out.
   The power went out while Marge was watching the evening news.
7. After I decided to mow the lawn, it began to rain.
8. Since I was very tired, the long wait was unbearable.
   The long wait was unbearable because I was very tired.
9. Skiing downhill, we noticed that the wind picked up.
   While I was skiing downhill, the wind picked up.
10. The phone company hired me at the age of eighteen.

## SKILL REFRESHER—CHAPTER 10
### Misplaced Modifiers (p. 250)

Answers may vary.

1. Marietta studiously previewed the report before she began answering the questions from the sales staff.
2. The book that Mark had returned late was checked out by another student.
3. Correct
4. The shocking article about donations that political candidates receive from interest groups caused Lily to reconsider how she viewed campaign promises.
   The article about donations that political candidates receive shocked Lily, causing her to reconsider how she viewed campaign promises.
5. Bryant cashed the student loan check that he desperately needed.
6. The angry crowd booed the referee when he finally arrived.
   Angry with the delay, the crowd booed the referee when he finally arrived.
7. Correct
8. The poetry of Emily Dickinson, a young, unhappy, and lovelorn woman, reveals a particular kind of misery and pain.
   The poetry of the young, unhappy, and lovelorn Emily Dickinson reveals a particular kind of misery and pain.
9. The governors of all the states met to discuss homelessness, a national problem.
10. When the AIDS epidemic began, health-care workers were concerned about the risk of contagion and refused treatment to many AIDS patients.

## SKILL REFRESHER—CHAPTER 11
### Verb Tense (p. 270)

1. Maggie called and asked Jen if she wanted a ride to the basketball game.
2. Louisa wore a beautiful red dress to her sister's wedding last week.
3. Correct
4. Marni answered an e-mail she received from her boyfriend.
5. Correct
6. Julie will spend the afternoon stringing bead if it rains.
7. We hope the package from my aunt will arrive in tomorrow's mail.
8. Yolanda claims to be the best cook in Erie County.
9. Anthony broke his wrist again.
10. My car stopped running before I ever paid off the loan for it.

## SKILL REFRESHER—CHAPTER 12
### Coordinate Sentences (p. 299)

Answers will vary.

1. A field study observes subjects in their natural settings; therefore, only a small number of subjects can be studied at one time.
2. The Grand Canyon is an incredible sight; it was formed less than ten million years ago.
3. Alaska and Siberia used to be connected 25,000 years ago; consequently, many anthropologists believe that Native Americans migrated to North and South America from Asia.
4. Neon, argon, and helium are called inert gases, and they are never found in stable chemical compounds.
5. The professor returned the tests, but he did not comment on them.

6. Ponce de Leon was successful because he was the first European to "discover" Florida; however, he did not succeed in finding the fountain of youth he was searching for.
7. The lecture focused on the cardiopulmonary system; therefore, the students needed to draw diagrams in their notes.
8. Rudy had never read *Hamlet,* nor had Rufus ever read *Hamlet.*
9. Presidents Lincoln and Kennedy were assassinated, but President Ford escaped two assassination attempts.
10. Marguerite might write her paper about *Moll Flanders,* or she might write her paper about its author, Daniel Defoe.

## SKILL REFRESHER—CHAPTER 13

## Subordinate Clauses (p. 323)

Answers will vary.
1. Although he was an insurance agent, now he's a banker.
2. When grape juice is fermented, it becomes wine.
3. It is important for children to be immunized since children who are not immunized are vulnerable to many dangerous diseases.
4. After a poem is read carefully, it should be analyzed.
5. Although my boss is very knowledgeable, she has no sense of humor at all.
6. While I was giving a speech in my communications class, Richard Rodriguez was giving a speech on campus.
7. When I started my assignment for French class, I was relieved that it was a very easy assignment.
8. Although infants may seem unaware of their surroundings, they are able to recognize their mother's voice and smell from birth.
9. Because she loves to travel, she wants to become a travel agent.
10. Although the hypothalamus is a tiny part of the brain, it has many very important functions, including the regulation of hormones, body temperature, and hunger.

## SKILL REFRESHER—CHAPTER 14

## Parallelism (p. 356)

Answers may vary.
1. The new president drew an organizational chart on the board, passed out a handout of it, and described how the company would be reorganized.
2. Correct
3. Working at home allows me to set my own hours, spend less on clothes, and work without interruption.
4. Professor Bargo's poetry class read famous poets, analyzed their poetry, and researched their lives. Professor Bargo's poetry class reads famous poets, analyzes their poetry, and researches their lives.
5. Clams, oysters, and mussels are examples of mollusks.
   The clam, the oyster, and the mussel are examples of mollusks.
6. Correct
7. The United Nations was formed in 1945 to renounce war, uphold personal freedoms, and bring about worldwide peace and well-being.
8. As a graphic artist, he does illustrations, chooses type, and plans page layout.
9. The Eighteenth Amendment to the Constitution implemented Prohibition, but the Twenty-First Amendment, ratified fourteen years later, repealed it.
10. Correct

## SKILL REFRESHER—CHAPTER 15

### When to Use Commas (p. 393)

1. Although I was late, my sister was still waiting for me at the restaurant.
2. They have sales offices in Minneapolis, Detroit, Cincinnati, and Pittsburgh.
3. Following the movie, we had a late lunch.
4. I bumped into a beautiful woman, Lisa's mother, on my way into the grocery store.
5. The phone rang, but I was outside.
6. My niece began to yell, "I'm Tarzan, king of the jungle."
7. Ted Keith, vice president of production, is retiring next year.
8. When I entered the room, everyone was watching television.
9. I heard her call, "Wait for me."
10. Although I have visited Vancouver, I have never been to Vancouver Island.

## SKILL REFRESHER—CHAPTER 16

### Using Colons and Semicolons (p. 440)

1. Anthropologists believe human life began in Africa; skeletons that have been found there provide evidence for this.
2. The natural sciences include botany, the study of plants; chemistry, the study of elements that compose matter; and biology, the study of all living things.
3. The courses I am taking cover a wide range of subjects: linguistics, racquetball, calculus, anatomy, and political science.
4. Time management workshops tend to be practical; they do provide many useful tips.
5. The poet, John Milton, tells how Eve must have felt when she was created: "That day I remember, when from sleep / I first awaked, and found myself reposed / under a shade on flowers, much wond'ring where / and what I was, whence thither brought, and how."
6. Engineering requires numerous math skills: geometry, algebra, and Boolean logic.
7. I enjoy a variety of sports: tennis, which is my favorite; golf, because it is relaxing; basketball, because it is a team sport; and racquetball, because it is a good workout.
8. When a skull is dug up by a gravedigger, Hamlet begins what is now a famous meditation on mortality: "Alas, poor Yorick!—I knew him, Horatio. . . ."
9. Knowing Spanish is a marketable skill because many clients speak it exclusively; it is also useful for appreciating Latin culture.
10. My botany text has a section about coniferous trees: pines, firs, cedars, and spruces.

## SKILL REFRESHER—CHAPTER 17

### When to Use Capital Letters (p. 467)

1. Because I spent last Sunday in Pittsburgh, I missed my favorite television show—*60 Minutes.*
2. There are five Great Lakes—Erie, Michigan, Ontario, Huron, and Superior.
3. This May, Professor Gilbert will give us our final exam.
4. Last week I rented my favorite movie from the video rental store on Elmwood Avenue.
5. One of Shakespeare's most famous plays is *Hamlet.*
6. I completed an internship at Midcity Office Equipment and Supply.
7. My brother will eat only Rice Krispies for breakfast.
8. Jean Griffith is a senator who lives in Washington County.
9. I love to vacation in California because the Pacific Ocean is so beautiful.
10. The president of the company, Ms. Salinas, announced that sales representatives would be given American Express credit cards.

# Credits

## Photo Credits

## Text Credits

# Index

# Correction and Editing Marks

| Abbreviation | Meaning | Page |
|---|---|---|
| ab or abbr | abbreviation error | 626 |
| adj | adjective | 529, 589 |
| adv | adverb | 533, 589 |
| agr | faulty agreement | 578, 581 |
| awk | awkward | |
| ca or case | case | 586 |
| cap | capital letter | 625 |
| coord | coordination | 597 |
| cs | comma splice | 546 |
| d | diction | 610 |
| dm | dangling modifier | 594 |
| frag | fragment | 560 |
| fs | fused sentence | 566 |
| hyph | hyphenation | 628 |
| irreg | error in irregular verb | 525 |
| jar | jargon | |
| lc | use lowercase letter | 625 |
| mm | misplaced modifier | 593 |
| ms | manuscript form | |
| nonst | nonstandard usage | 610 |
| num | faulty use of numbers | 629 |
| pass | ineffective passive voice | 574 |
| ref | pronoun reference error | 584 |
| sp | misspelled word | 631 |
| sub | subordination | 600 |
| t | verb tense error | 526, 569 |
| trans | transition | 95 |
| s-v agr | subject-verb agreement | 578 |
| v or vb | verb error | 523 |
| w | wordy | 608 |
| wc | word choice error | 80 |
| ww | wrong word | |
| ?? | unclear or illegible | |
| ¶ or par | new paragraph | |
| no ¶ | no new paragraph | |
| // | parallelism | 602 |
| ⌢ | close up space | |
| # | add space | |
| ^ | insert | |
| ℓ | delete | |
| t/e/h/ | transpose | |
| x | obvious error | |